Fundamentals of Cognition

Fundamentals of Cognition

Michael W. Eysenck

Ψ Psychology Press
Taylor & Francis Group
HOVE AND NEW YORK

First published 2006
by Psychology Press
27 Church Road, Hove, East Sussex, BN3 2FA

Simultaneously published in the USA and Canada
by Psychology Press
270 Madison Ave, New York NY 10016

Psychology Press is an imprint of the Taylor & Francis Group, an informa business

© 2006 Psychology Press

Typeset in Times by Wearset Ltd, Boldon, Tyne and Wear
Printed and bound in Spain by Compass Press Ltd
Cover design by Richard Massing

The publisher makes no representation, express or implied, with regard to the accuracy of the information contained in this book and cannot accept any legal responsibility or liability for any errors or omissions that may be made.

British Library Cataloguing in Publication Data
A catalogue record for this book is available from the British Library

Library of Congress Cataloging in Publication Data
Eysenck, Michael W.
  Fundamentals of cognition / Michael W. Eysenck.
    p. cm.
  Includes bibliographical references and index.
ISBN 1-84169-373-1 (hardcover) — ISBN 1-84169-374-X (softcover)
 1. Cognition.   I. Title.
  BF311.E938 2006
  153–dc22

                                           2005036752

ISBN10: 1-84169-373-1 (hbk)
ISBN10: 1-84169-374-X (pbk)

ISBN13: 978-1-84169-373-6 (hbk)
ISBN13: 978-1-84169-374-3 (pbk)

To my daughter Fleur with love

A professor is someone who talks in other people's sleep.
(Anonymous)

Contents

About the author   x

Preface   xi

1 **Approaches to cognitive psychology**   2
   Introduction   3
   Experimental cognitive psychology   5
   Cognitive neuropsychology   6
   Computational cognitive science   9
   Cognitive neuroscience   12
   How useful is cognitive psychology?   15
   Structure of the book   18
   Evaluation and chapter summary   19
   Further reading   20

Part I
Visual perception and attention   22

2 **Visual illusions: Seeing and acting**   26
   Introduction   27
   Two visual systems: Illusions   29
   Two visual systems: General   33
   Evaluation and chapter summary   36
   Further reading   37

3 **How far away is that object?**   38
   Introduction   39
   Size perception   44
   Evaluation and chapter summary   46
   Further reading   47

4 **Perception without awareness?**   48
   Introduction   49
   Unconscious perception and
      perceptual defense   50
   Blindsight   54
   Conclusions   57
   Evaluation and chapter summary   58
   Further reading   59

5 **What is this I see before me?**   60
   Introduction   61

Perceptual organization   62
Viewpoint-dependent or
   viewpoint-invariant?   64
Disorders of object recognition   68
Evaluation and chapter summary   72
Further reading   73

6 **What's in a face?**   74
   Introduction   75
   Who are you?   78
   Theoretical approaches   83
   Evaluation and chapter summary   86
   Further reading   87

7 **Seeing with the mind's eye**   88
   Introduction   89
   Does visual imagery resemble visual
      perception?   91
   Brain systems in imagery   95
   Evaluation and chapter summary   99
   Further reading   101

8 **In sight but out of mind**   102
   Introduction   103
   When is change blindness found?   106
   What causes change blindness?   109
   Evaluation and chapter summary   113
   Further reading   113

9 **What do we attend to in vision?**   114
   Introduction   115
   Do we attend to locations or objects?   118
   Disorders of attention: Unattended
      stimuli   119
   Cross-modal effects   122
   Evaluation and chapter summary   124
   Further reading   125

10 **Multitasking**   126
   Introduction   127
   What determines dual-task
      performance?   131

Theoretical perspectives   136
Evaluation and chapter summary   140
Further reading   141

Part II
Learning and memory   142

11 The long and the short of human memory   146
Introduction   147
Short-term vs. long-term memory   149
Amnesia   153
Evaluation and chapter summary   160
Further reading   163

12 Short-term or working memory   164
Introduction   165
Baddeley's working memory model   166
Phonological loop   167
Visuospatial sketchpad   169
Central executive   170
Working memory and intelligence   173
Evaluation and chapter summary   175
Further reading   177

13 Learning without awareness?   178
Introduction   179
Complex normal learning   181
Learning in amnesics   184
Brain-imaging research   185
Evaluation and chapter summary   187
Further reading   189

14 It's slipped my mind   190
Introduction   191
Are traumatic memories repressed?   196
Memories interfere with each other   198
Encoding specificity   200
Consolidation theory   201
What about the future?   202
Evaluation and chapter summary   203
Further reading   205

15 The story of my life   206
Introduction   207
What do elderly people remember?   211
Emotional personal memories   214
Model of autobiographical memory   215
Evaluation and chapter summary   218
Further reading   219

16 Should we believe eyewitnesses?   220
Introduction   221

What influences eyewitness accuracy?   222
Eyewitness identification   225
Interviewing eyewitnesses   227
Evaluation and chapter summary   230
Further reading   231

Part III
Language   232

17 Read all about it!   236
Introduction   237
Reading aloud   238
Parsing   243
It's in the eyes   246
Evaluation and chapter summary   249
Further reading   250

18 What are you saying?   252
Introduction   253
What difference does context make?   255
TRACE model   256
Cohort model   258
Disorders of speech perception   261
Parsing   263
Understanding the message   265
Evaluation and chapter summary   266
Further reading   269

19 What does this mean?   270
Introduction   271
Schemas   275
Pragmatics   279
Construction–integration model   281
Evaluation and chapter summary   284
Further reading   287

20 Talking the talk   288
Introduction   289
Speech errors   293
Word processing: Ordered or disordered?   296
Speech disorders   300
Evaluation and chapter summary   303
Further reading   305

21 What's in a concept?   306
Introduction   307
Prototype approach   310
Exemplar approach   313
Concept learning   315
Evaluation and chapter summary   318
Further reading   321

Part IV
Thinking and reasoning   322

22 How accurate are our judgments?   326
   Introduction   327
   Our judgments are OK!   329
   Do heuristics make us smart?   332
   Kahneman and Tversky:
      More heuristics   333
   Evaluation and chapter summary   337
   Further reading   339

23 What am I going to do?   340
   Introduction   341
   Losses and gains   342
   What will people think?   348
   Complex decision making   351
   Evaluation and chapter summary   354
   Further reading   355

24 Finding the solution   356
   Introduction   357
   Does insight exist?   361
   How useful is past experience?   364
   General Problem Solver   368
   Evaluation and chapter summary   372
   Further reading   373

25 How do you become an expert?   374
   Introduction   375
   Chess-playing expertise   377
   Deliberate practice   382
   Evaluation and chapter summary   384
   Further reading   385

26 Reasoning   386
   Introduction   387
   Reasoning problems   389
   Theoretical approaches   392
   What about individual differences?   397
   How rational are we?   399
   Evaluation and chapter summary   401
   Further reading   403

Part V
Broader issues   404

27 Cognition and emotion   406
   Introduction   407
   Does affect require cognition?   407
   Emotion, learning, and memory   411
   Emotion, attention, and perception   418
   Evaluation and chapter summary   420
   Further reading   421

28 What is consciousness?   422
   Introduction   423
   In two minds?   427
   Global workspace theories   430
   Evaluation and chapter summary   433
   Further reading   435

References   437

Glossary   475

Author index   483

Subject index   495

ABOUT THE AUTHOR

Michael W. Eysenck is one of the best-known British psychologists. Since 1987, he has been Professor of Psychology at Royal Holloway University of London, which is one of the leading departments in the United Kingdom. His academic interests lie mainly in cognitive psychology, with most of his research focusing on the role of cognitive factors in anxiety in normal and clinical populations.

He is an author of many titles, and his previous textbooks published by Psychology Press include *A2 Psychology: Key Topics* (2006), *Psychology for A2 Level* (2001), *Psychology for AS Level* (2000), *Psychology: A Student's Handbook* (2000), *Cognitive Psychology: A Student's Handbook, Fifth Edition* (2005, with Mark Keane), *Simply Psychology, Second Edition* (2002), *Perspectives on Psychology* (1994), *Individual Differences: Normal and Abnormal* (1994), and *Principles of Cognitive Psychology, Second Edition* (2001). He has also written the research monographs *Anxiety and Cognition: A Unified Theory* (1997), and *Anxiety: The Cognitive Perspective* (1992), along with the popular title *Happiness: Facts and Myths* (1990). He is also a keen supporter of Crystal Palace football club.

PREFACE

Cognitive psychology is concerned with the processes that allow us to make sense of the world around us and to make (reasonably) sensible decisions about how to cope with everyday life. As such, it is of huge importance within psychology as a whole. Indeed, the advances made by cognitive psychology have permeated most of the rest of psychology—areas such as developmental psychology, social psychology, and abnormal psychology and even emotion and motivation have been transformed by the cognitive approach. As a cognitive psychologist, I may be biased but I genuinely believe that cognitive psychology is at the heart of psychology.

The Chinese have a saying, "May you live in interesting times." It has been my good fortune during my career to see cognitive psychology become increasingly interesting. An important reason stems from technological advances that permit us to observe the brain in action in considerable detail. You have probably seen some of the fruits of such research in the brightly colored pictures of the brain found within the covers of numerous magazines. In this book, there is much coverage of the exciting discoveries based on brain imaging.

I would like to express my gratitude to all those who helped in the preparation of this book, especially Bruce Bridgeman, Marc Brysbaert, Christian Olivers, and John Parkinson. I am especially grateful to Marc Brysbaert. He kindly pinpointed problems with my previous introductory textbook on cognitive psychology. More importantly, he provided several very constructive suggestions as to how to structure this book, nearly all of which I have adopted.

Finally, I want to express my profound gratitude to my family. This book is appropriately dedicated to my elder daughter Fleur even though she has a low opinion of psychology and doesn't regard it as a science!

Michael W. Eysenck
Santo Domingo, Dominican Republic

CHAPTER 1

CONTENTS

Introduction 3

Experimental cognitive psychology 5

Cognitive neuropsychology 6

Computational cognitive science 9

Cognitive neuroscience 12

How useful is cognitive psychology? 15

Structure of the book 18

Evaluation and chapter summary 19

Further reading 20

Approaches to cognitive psychology

INTRODUCTION

There is more general interest than ever in understanding the mysteries of the human brain and the mind. So far as the media are concerned, numerous television programs, films, and books have been devoted to the more dramatic and/or accessible aspects of the brain and its workings. You have undoubtedly seen pretty colored pictures of the brain in magazines, revealing which parts of the brain are most active when people are engaged in various tasks. So far as science is concerned, there has been an explosion of research on the brain by scientists from several different disciplines including cognitive psychologists, cognitive neuroscientists, biologists, and so on.

The efforts of many scientists interested in the brain fall within the compass of cognitive psychology. What *is* the subject matter of cognitive psychology? It consists of the main internal psychological processes involved in making sense of the environment and deciding what actions might be appropriate. These processes include attention, perception, learning, memory, language, problem solving, reasoning, and thinking. There is some dispute concerning how vital it is to focus on the brain itself, with some cognitive psychologists claiming that it is totally unnecessary to do so. However, most cognitive psychologists (including the author of this book) accept that we need to make use of *all* the kinds of evidence available to us if we are going to cope with the challenge of understanding human cognition. Thus, information about patterns of brain activity is of relevance to cognitive psychology (the various brain-imaging techniques are discussed later in the chapter).

At one time, most cognitive psychologists subscribed to the information-processing approach. A version of this approach popular about 35 years ago is shown in Figure 1.1. According to this version, a stimulus (an environmental event such as a problem or a task) is presented. This stimulus causes certain internal cognitive processes to occur, and these processes finally produce the desired response or answer. Processing directly affected by the stimulus input is often described as **bottom-up processing**. It was typically assumed that only *one* process occurs at any moment in time. This is known as **serial processing**, and means that the current process is completed before the next one begins.

KEY TERMS
Bottom-up processing: processing that is directly influenced by environmental stimuli.
Serial processing: processing in which one process is completed before the next process starts; see parallel processing.

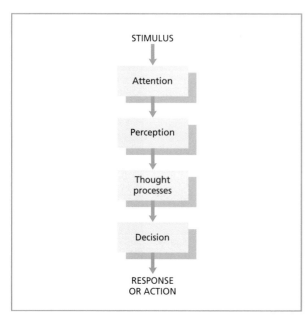

Figure 1.1 An early version of the information-processing approach.

Figure 1.2 Diagram to demonstrate top-down processing.

Alas, we now know that this entire information-processing approach represents a drastic over-simplification of a complex reality. There are numerous situations in which processing is not exclusively bottom-up, but also involves top-down processing. **Top-down processing** is processing influenced by the individual's expectations and knowledge rather than simply by the stimulus itself. Look at the triangle shown in Figure 1.2, and read what it says. Unless familiar with the trick, you probably read it as "Paris in the spring". If so, look again, and you will see that the word "the" is repeated. Your expectation that it was the well-known phrase (i.e., top-down processing) dominated the information actually available from the stimulus (i.e., bottom-up processing).

Most cognition involves a mixture of bottom-up and top-down processing. An especially clear demonstration of this comes from a study by Bruner, Postman, and Rodrigues (1951), in which participants expected to see conventional playing cards presented very briefly. When black hearts were presented, some participants claimed to have seen purple or brown hearts. There was an almost literal blending of the black color stemming from bottom-up processing and of the red color stemming from top-down processing due to the expectations that hearts will be red.

The traditional information-processing approach was also over-simplified in assuming that processing is necessarily serial. In fact, there are numerous situations in which some or all of the processes involved in a cognitive task occur at the same time—this is known as **parallel processing**. It is often difficult to know whether processing on a given task is serial or parallel. However, we are much more likely to use parallel processing when performing a task on which we are highly practiced than one we are just starting to learn (see Chapter 10). For example, someone taking their first driving lesson finds it almost impossible to change gear, to steer accurately, and to pay attention to other road users at the same time. In contrast, an experienced driver finds it easy, and can even hold a conversation as well.

FOUR MAJOR APPROACHES

One of the most dramatic changes within cognitive psychology in recent decades has been the huge increase in the number of weapons available to cognitive psychologists trying to conquer the citadel of the human brain and mind. Forty years ago, most cognitive psychologists carried out laboratory studies on normal individuals. Nowadays, in contrast, many cognitive psychologists study brain-damaged individuals, others construct elaborate computer-based models of human cognition, and still others make use of numerous brain-imaging techniques.

Four major approaches to human cognition have now been developed:

- *Experimental cognitive psychology*: This is the traditional approach and involves carrying out experiments on healthy individuals, typically under laboratory conditions.
- *Cognitive neuropsychology*: This approach (developed in the 1970s) involves studying patterns of cognitive impairment shown by brain-damaged patients to provide valuable information about normal human cognition.
- *Computational cognitive science*: This approach (developed in the 1970s and 1980s) involves developing computational models to further our understanding of human cognition.
- *Cognitive neuroscience*: This approach (which has become of major importance within the last 15 years) involves using numerous brain-imaging techniques to study aspects of brain functioning and structure relevant to human cognition. Note that the term "cognitive neuroscience" is often used in a broader sense to indicate an approach to understanding human cognition based on considering evidence about brain functioning as well as about behavior, and about how brain functioning influences behavior. What is common to both definitions is the importance attached to the use of brain-imaging techniques.

Describe the approaches that characterize cognitive psychology.

There is no need for researchers to select only one of these approaches at the expense of the other three. Indeed, cognitive psychologists increasingly use two or even three of these approaches in their research.

EXPERIMENTAL COGNITIVE PSYCHOLOGY

For many decades, nearly all research in cognitive psychology involved carrying out experiments on healthy individuals under laboratory conditions. Such experiments are typically tightly controlled and "scientific." Researchers have shown great ingenuity in designing experiments to reveal the processes involved in attention, perception, learning, memory, and so on. In consequence, the findings of experimental cognitive psychologists have played a major role in the development and subsequent testing of most theories in cognitive psychology.

Experimental cognitive psychology was for many years the engine room of progress in cognitive psychology. Indeed, all three of the newer approaches to cognitive psychology have benefited from it. For example, consider the case of cognitive neuropsychology. It was only when cognitive psychologists had developed reasonable accounts of normal human cognition that the performance of brain-damaged patients began to be understood properly. Before that, it was hard to decide which patterns of cognitive impairment were theoretically important. Cognitive neuropsychologists often carry out studies on individual patients, and use the data from such patients to test theoretical predictions coming from experimental cognitive psychology. Such single case studies would be of little interest in the absence of any relevant theory.

How have other approaches in psychology benefited from the experimental approach?

One of the greatest successes of experimental cognitive psychology has been the way its approach has influenced several other areas within psychology. For example, social, developmental, and clinical psychology have all become much more "cognitive" in recent years (an example in the clinical area is discussed later in the chapter). Many of the experimental tasks used by researchers in those areas were initially developed in the research laboratories of experimental cognitive psychologists.

What are the main limitations of experimental cognitive psychology? First, how people behave in the laboratory may differ significantly from how they behave in everyday life. Thus, laboratory research may lack **ecological validity**, which is the extent to which the findings of laboratory studies are applicable to everyday life. In the real world, people are constantly behaving so as to have an impact on the environment (e.g., turning on the television to watch a favorite program). In contrast, most research in cognitive psychology involves what Wachtel (1973) referred to as the "implacable [unyielding] experimenter." That is to say, the sequence of stimuli the experimenter presents to participants is *not* influenced by their behavior, but rather is determined by the experimenter's predetermined plan.

Second, experimental cognitive psychologists typically obtain measures of the speed and accuracy of task performance. These measures provide only *indirect* evidence about the internal processes involved in human cognition and about their relationship to each other. It would often be very useful to supplement behavioral data with information about brain processes and structures as in cognitive neuroscience and cognitive neuropsychology.

Third, it has always puzzled me that most cognitive psychologists fail to take individual differences seriously. Much of cognitive psychology (e.g., decision making, reasoning, expertise) is concerned with intelligent thinking and behavior. As a result, you might imagine that cognitive psychologists would forge links between cognitive psychology and the area of intelligence (in which the primary focus is on individual differences). This is starting to happen. In this book, individual differences in intelligence are related to various topics such as multitasking (Chapter 10), working memory (Chapter 12), and expertise (Chapter 25). In addition, there is increasing recognition that individual differences in personality influence cognition in many ways. Relevant research is discussed mainly in Chapter 15 on autobiographical memory and in Chapter 27 on cognition and emotion.

COGNITIVE NEUROPSYCHOLOGY

Cognitive neuropsychology is concerned with the cognitive performance of brain-damaged patients. It is easy to see that it is important to understand the problems faced by such patients with a view to helping them to cope with everyday life. However, the major goal of cognitive neuropsychology is to use information gained from brain-damaged patients to understand normal cognition. This goal is based on the assumption that, "Complex systems often reveal their inner workings more clearly when they are malfunctioning than when they are running smoothly" (McCloskey, 2001, p. 594). As an example, McCloskey described how he only began to understand how his laser printer worked when it started misprinting things. Thus, we may develop an understanding of cognitive processing in intact individuals by focusing on the particular problems in cognition experienced by brain-damaged patients.

Numerous fascinating conditions produced by brain damage are considered in this book. Here I will mention just two of them to give you a flavor of what cognitive neuropsychology is all about. First, there is blindsight, a puzzling condition that is discussed in Chapter 4. Patients with blindsight deny they can see objects presented to the "blind" parts of their visual field. Thus, it would seem natural to assume they have no perceptual abilities at all in these areas. However, their performance is reasonably good when they are asked to guess whether a stimulus is in one of two locations, or to guess whether a stimulus is absent or present! The study of patients with blindsight tells us that various perceptual processes can operate with some efficiency in the absence of any conscious experience of seeing.

Second, there is a condition known as prosopagnosia or face blindness (discussed in Chapter 6). Patients with this condition suffer much embarrassment because they cannot recognize faces. As a result, they are in constant danger of greeting complete strangers as long-lost friends or ignoring close friends. What is intriguing is that the perceptual impairment is not general, and so the problem is *not* simply one of poor eyesight. Prosopagnosics have reasonably good object recognition for most objects other than faces. That suggests that there is a part of the brain specialized for face recognition. However, as you will see in Chapter 6, that notion has become increasingly controversial.

What are the advantages and disadvantages of adopting a single case study design?

MAJOR ASSUMPTIONS

Coltheart (2001) identified the main theoretical assumptions of cognitive neuropsychology, and we will consider two of them here. First, the cognitive system is based on **modularity**, meaning that it consists of numerous independent processors or modules. For example, we might explain prosopagnosia by assuming there is a module that responds only to face stimuli, and that is the module damaged in patients with prosopagnosia.

Second, there is the assumption of **subtractivity**. The basic idea is that brain damage impairs one or more modules but cannot lead to the development of any new ones. As a result, the study of brain-damaged patients with damage to module *x* can provide very useful information about the role of module *x* in normal human cognition.

One way in which cognitive neuropsychologists try to understand how the cognitive system works is by searching for dissociations. A **dissociation** occurs when a patient performs at the same level as healthy individuals on one task but is severely impaired on a second task. For example, amnesic patients perform well on tasks involving short-term memory but have very poor performance on most long-term memory tasks (see Chapter 11). This suggests that short-term memory and long-term memory involve separate modules. However, it could be argued that brain damage reduces the ability to perform difficult (but not easy) tasks, and that long-term memory tasks are more difficult than short-term memory ones. Suppose, however, that we found other patients who had very poor performance on most short-term

KEY TERMS
Modularity: the assumption that the cognitive system consists of several fairly independent processors or modules.
Subtractivity: the notion that brain damage can subtract or remove aspects of brain functioning but cannot lead to the development of new ones.
Dissociation: the finding that a brain-damaged patient performs one task at a normal level but performs very poorly on a second task.

memory tasks but who had intact long-term memory. We would then have a **double dissociation**: some patients performing at the same level as healthy individuals on task X but being impaired on task Y, with others showing the opposite pattern. This double dissociation provides strong evidence that there are separate short-term and long-term memory systems.

One of the issues that cognitive neuropsychologists have had to grapple with is that of whether they focus on individuals or groups in their research. In research on intact individuals, we can have more confidence in our findings if they are based on fairly large groups of participants. However, the group-based approach is very problematical when applied to brain-damaged patients. The reason is that patients typically differ among themselves in the pattern of impairment. As a result, group data can be confusing and very difficult to interpret.

Most cognitive neuropsychologists now accept that it is generally preferable to study individual patients, hoping thereafter to replicate or repeat the findings with data from other patients. However, that approach is not without its own problems. As Shallice (1991, p. 433) pointed out, "A selective impairment found in a particular task in some patient could just reflect: the patient's idiosyncratic strategy, the greater difficulty of that task compared with the others, a premorbid lacuna [gap] in that patient, or the way a re-organized system but not the original system operates." In spite of these problems, cognitive neuropsychological studies (whether based on groups of patients or individual cases) have proved very informative about human cognition.

STRENGTHS AND LIMITATIONS

As we will see throughout this book, the cognitive neuropsychological approach has contributed much to our understanding of normal human cognition. For example, evidence based on double dissociations has provided powerful support for the distinction between separate short-term and long-term memory systems (see Chapter 11) and for the notion that there are three routes in reading (see Chapter 17).

There are various limitations with the cognitive neuropsychological approach to normal human cognition. First, the organization of the human brain is far less neat and tidy than is implied by cognitive neuropsychologists with their emphasis on modularity. As Banich (1997, p. 52) pointed out, "The brain is composed of about 50 billion *interconnected* neurons. Therefore, even complex cognitive functions for which a modular description seems apt rely on a number of interconnected brain regions or systems."

Second, cognitive neuropsychology generally seems more comfortable dealing with relatively *specific* aspects of cognitive functioning, perhaps because more general aspects do not lend themselves readily to a modular account. For example, consider the study of language, which may be regarded as the "jewel in the crown" of cognitive neuropsychology. Much of the research has been on the reading and spelling of individual words by brain-damaged patients, with little emphasis on broader issues concerned with the comprehension of texts or speech.

Third, in order for cognitive neuropsychology to make rapid progress, it would be ideal to find patients in whom brain damage had affected only *one*

KEY TERM
Double dissociation: the finding that some individuals (often brain-damaged) do well on task A and poorly on task B, whereas others show the opposite pattern.

module. In fact, however, brain damage is typically much more extensive than that. When several different processing modules or processors are damaged, it is generally difficult to interpret the findings. However, a technique used by cognitive neuroscientists known as transcranial magnetic stimulation (discussed shortly) offers hope for the future. In essence, this technique can very briefly inhibit processing in a fairly small part of the brain. As such, it may allow us to see what happens when only a single module is not functioning.

COMPUTATIONAL COGNITIVE SCIENCE

Another way of studying cognition is to construct artificial systems doing some of the same things as brains—this is computational cognitive science. We will start by distinguishing between computational modeling and artificial intelligence. **Computational modeling** involves programming computers to model or mimic some aspects of human cognitive functioning. In contrast, **artificial intelligence** involves constructing computer systems that produce intelligent outcomes, but the processes involved typically bear little resemblance to those used by humans. For example, a chess program known as Deep Blue managed to beat the then World Champion, Garry Kasparov. It did so by considering huge numbers of moves every second, and thus its approach was radically different from that adopted by human chess players. Computational modeling and artificial intelligence have both made substantial contributions. However, we will focus on computational modeling because it is of more *direct* relevance to understanding human cognition.

What unique strengths does the computational approach bring to cognitive psychology in general?

The computational cognitive science approach receives much less attention in this book than any of the other three main approaches. Why is this? One reason is because computational models tend to be complex and difficult to understand, and this book provides a simple introduction to cognitive psychology. Another reason is that (with several outstanding exceptions) the computational cognitive science approach has probably contributed rather less to our understanding of human cognition than the other approaches.

COMPUTATIONAL MODELING

In the end, scientific understanding is expressed in terms of models rather than data. Computational cognitive scientists who want to develop a computational model start by identifying as precisely as possible the processes used by humans when performing some task or tasks. This may well involve relying heavily on one or more previous theories that have been developed to understand performance on that task. What is the point in simply taking an existing theory and implementing it as a program? One important reason is that theories that are only expressed verbally often contain hidden assumptions or vague terms. This is much less likely to happen with a computer program, because *all* the details need to be spelled out.

Let's consider a concrete example of an influential model that was expressed verbally and omitted many details. Atkinson and Shiffrin (1968) proposed a model of memory in which it was assumed that rehearsal

KEY TERMS
Computational modeling: constructing computer programs that simulate or mimic some aspects of human cognitive functioning; see artificial intelligence.
Artificial intelligence: this involves developing computer programs producing intelligent outcomes in ways different from human functioning; see computational modeling.

(saying to-be-learned material to oneself) leads to the long-term storage of the information being rehearsed—the more times a word is rehearsed, the better it is remembered over time (see Chapter 11). This model was used to account for findings from studies in which a list of words was presented followed by the participants writing down as many list words as possible in any order. If we wanted to make precise predictions, we would need to know the following (at least): How long does it take to rehearse one word? How many words are rehearsed together? How rapidly does information about a rehearsed word accumulate in long-term memory? Atkinson and Shiffrin (1968) did not provide answers to most of those questions, but they would need to be answered to produce an adequate computer model.

PRODUCTION SYSTEMS AND CONNECTIONIST NETWORKS

We will briefly discuss two of the main types of computational model: production systems and connectionist networks. For a fuller account, consult either Eysenck and Keane (2005) or Anderson and Lebiere (2003). **Production systems** consist of productions, where a production is an "IF . . . THEN" rule. An everyday example is, "If the green man is lit up, then cross the road." In a typical production system model, there is a long-term memory containing numerous IF . . . THEN rules. There is also a working memory (i.e., a system holding information currently being processed). If information from the environment that "green man lights up" reaches working memory, it will match the "IF" part of the rule in long-term memory and trigger the "THEN" part of the rule (i.e., cross the road).

Many aspects of cognition can be specified as sets of IF . . . THEN rules. For example, chess knowledge can easily be represented as a set of productions based on rules such as, "If the Queen is threatened, then move the Queen to a safe square." In this way, people's basic knowledge of chess can be regarded as a collection of productions. Some production system models such as Anderson's (1993) ACT-R (Adaptive Control of Thought—Rational) are sufficiently comprehensive that they can account for a wide range of findings.

In the past 20 years, there has been considerable interest in connectionist networks, or parallel distributed processing (PDP) models as they are sometimes called. This interest was triggered by books by Rumelhart, McClelland, and the PDP Research Group (1986) and by McClelland, Rumelhart, and the PDP Research Group (1986). **Connectionist networks** make use of elementary units or nodes connected together in various structures or layers, but there is no direct connection from stimulus to response. Strictly speaking, Pavlov used connectionist models to explain how anatomical connections between sensory and motor areas mediate controlled behavior (Bruce Bridgeman, personal communication). As a result, Rumelhart et al. sometimes referred to neo-connectionist networks to distinguish them from Pavlov's very different approach. However, since the term "connectionist networks" is generally used to refer to the models produced by Rumelhart et al. and by other researchers, we will (slightly incorrectly) follow common usage.

A key feature of connectionist networks is that they show evidence of learning. For example, Sejnowski and Rosenberg (1987) produced a connectionist network called NETtalk. It was given 50,000 trials to learn the spelling–sound relationships of a set of 1000 words. After this training, NETtalk achieved 95% success in identifying the sounds of the words on which it had been trained, and it was also 77% correct on a further 20,000 words. This is reasonably impressive even though the 50,000 trials it needed indicate that NETtalk learns more slowly than the average child!

The controversial claim is often made that the structure of a connectionist network resembles the way in which the neurons in the brain are organized. However, this claim is hotly disputed. For example, Churchland and Sejnowski (1994) pointed out that each cortical neuron is connected to only about 3% of the neurons in the surrounding square millimeter of cortex. In contrast, it is assumed in most connectionist networks that the basic units are much more interconnected.

Three features of most connectionist networks are of particular importance. First, whereas most previous theories assumed that knowledge (e.g., about a word or a concept) is represented in a given location, connectionist models are typically based on the assumption that knowledge is represented in a *distributed* way throughout the network.

Second, connectionist networks differ from most previous computational models in that they can "learn" to modify their outputs to achieve various goals. Third, connectionist networks operate in a "rule-like" way but do not actually make use of any rules. This contrasts with the typical assumption (e.g., Fodor, 2000; Pinker, 1999) that human cognition depends on numerous rules.

STRENGTHS AND LIMITATIONS

Computational modeling of psychological theories provides a strong test of their adequacy. The reason is that computational modelers have to be explicit about every theoretical assumption in their computational model, unlike traditional theories expressed in verbal terms. Another advantage of computational modeling is that it supports the development of more complex theories in cognitive psychology. In many cognitive theories, theorists can rapidly reach a point where the theory's complexity makes it very difficult to say what the theory might predict. In contrast, the predictions from a computational model can be generated rapidly and easily by simply running the model with the appropriate stimuli. Finally, computational models based on production systems or connectionist principles (e.g., Anderson's Adaptive Control of Thought—Rational model or ACT-R) can provide more comprehensive accounts of cognitive functioning than more traditional theories and models.

What are the main limitations of the computational cognitive science approach? First, computational models are relatively rarely used to make *new* predictions. Computational cognitive scientists typically develop a model of performance on some task that accounts for existing human data but does not go beyond that. It is a significant achievement to develop a precise model that mimics human performance. However, it would certainly be more impressive if new predictions were made and confirmed.

Second, most computational models are limited in scope. Human cognition is typically influenced by severally potentially conflicting motivational and emotional forces, many of which may be operative at the same time. Very few computational models even try to capture these wider aspects of cognition.

Third, the greatest promise of computational cognitive science is that it will lead to the development of a general unified theory of cognition to weld the fragmentary theories of cognitive psychology together. Probably the two most successful of such unified theories are ACT-R and connectionism. However, these theories have had a fairly modest impact within cognitive psychology, and there is some skepticism concerning their fundamental potential (Cooper & Shallice, 1995).

COGNITIVE NEUROSCIENCE

If you had to examine reaction times, which cognitive neuroscience technique would you choose? Why may others be unsuitable?

Technological advances mean we now have numerous new and exciting ways of obtaining detailed information about the brain's functioning and structure. In principle, we can work out *where* and *when* in the brain specific cognitive processes occur. Such information allows us to determine the order in which different parts of the brain become active when someone is performing a task. It also allows us to find out whether two tasks involve the same parts of the brain in the same way, or whether there are important differences.

Brief information concerning some of the most important techniques for studying brain activity is contained in Table 1.1 (fuller descriptions of these

---

Table 1.1 Major techniques used to study the brain

- *Single-unit recording*: This technique involves inserting a micro-electrode one 10,000th of a millimeter in diameter into the brain to study activity in single neurons. This is a very sensitive technique.
- *Event-related potentials (ERPs)*: The same stimulus is presented repeatedly, and the pattern of electrical brain activity recorded by several scalp electrodes is averaged to produce a single waveform. This technique allows us to work out the timing of various cognitive processes.
- *Positron emission tomography (PET)*: This technique involves the detection of positrons, which are the atomic particles emitted from some radioactive substances. PET has reasonable spatial resolution but poor temporal resolution, and it only provides an indirect measure of neural activity.
- *Functional magnetic resonance imaging (fMRI)*: This technique involves the detection of magnetic changes in the brain. fMRI has superior spatial and temporal resolution to PET, but provides only an indirect measure of neural activity.
- *Magneto-encephalography (MEG)*: This technique measures the magnetic fields produced by electrical brain activity. It provides fairly detailed information at the millisecond level about the time course of cognitive processes, and its spatial resolution is reasonably good.
- *Transcranial magnetic stimulation (TMS)*: This is a technique in which a coil (or pair of coils) is placed close to the participant's head and a large, very brief pulse of current is run through it. This produces a short-lived magnetic field, inhibiting processing in the brain area affected. This technique has (jokingly!) been compared to hitting someone's brain with a hammer.

techniques can be found in Eysenck & Keane, 2005). Which of these techniques is the best? There is no simple answer. Each technique has its own strengths and limitations, and so researchers focus on matching the technique to the issue they want to address. At the most basic level, the various techniques vary in the precision with which they identify the brain areas active when a task is performed (spatial resolution), and the time course of such activation (temporal resolution). Thus, the techniques differ in their ability to provide precise information concerning *where* and *when* brain activity occurs. The spatial and temporal resolution of some of the main techniques are shown in Figure 1.3. In general terms, high spatial and temporal resolution is advantageous if a very detailed account of brain functioning is required. In contrast, low temporal resolution can be more useful if a general overview of brain activity during an entire task is needed.

In the course of this book, we will refer from time to time to specific areas within the brain. At the most general level, the cerebral cortex is divided into four main divisions or lobes (see Figure 1.4). There are four

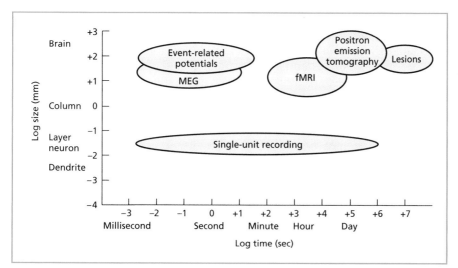

Figure 1.3 The spatial and temporal ranges of some techniques used to study brain functioning. Adapted from Churchland and Sejnowski (1991).

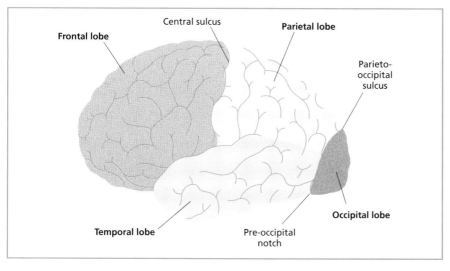

Figure 1.4 The four lobes, or divisions, of the cerebral cortex in the left hemisphere. From Gazzaniga et al. (1998). Reproduced with permission of the author.

lobes in each brain hemisphere: frontal; parietal; temporal; and occipital. The frontal lobes are divided from the parietal lobes by the central sulcus (*sulcus* means furrow or groove), and the parieto-occipital sulcus and the pre-occipital notch divide the occipital lobes from the parietal and frontal lobes.

For future reference, it is useful to know the meaning of various terms used to describe more precisely the brain area activated during the performance of some task. Some of the main terms are as follows:

dorsal: superior or on top
ventral: inferior or at the bottom
lateral: situated at the side
medial: situated in the middle.

STRENGTHS AND LIMITATIONS

Do brain-imaging techniques provide the answers to all our prayers? There are at least three reasons for doubting whether they do. First, most brain-imaging techniques indicate only that there are *associations* between patterns of brain activation and behavior (e.g., performance on a reasoning task is associated with activation of the prefrontal cortex at the front of the brain). Such associations are essentially correlational, and of limited value. As Walsh and Rushworth (1999, p. 126) pointed out, "Mapping techniques record brain activity which is correlated with some behavioral event. But the correlations do not show that an area is necessary for a particular function." For example, suppose that a given brain area *x* is activated when we solve a complex problem. We cannot be certain that important processes associated with problem solution occur in brain area *x*. For example, it is possible that anxiety associated with thoughts of possible failure on the problem causes activation of that brain area.

Second, numerous brain-imaging studies have lacked any clear theoretical basis. Far too often, researchers have merely found that some parts of the brain are activated during performance of a given task whereas others parts are not. Such findings are of no particular interest if they were not predicted on the basis of some theory and so do not lend themselves to theoretical explanation. The good news is that there is a clear trend towards more and more brain-imaging studies being theoretically based.

Third, consider the colored maps you must have seen claiming to show which areas of the brain were activated when a given task was performed. In fact, all the colored areas are those where the amount of brain activity exceeded some threshold level determined by the experimenter. The problem is that the number of brain areas identified as active during performance of a task can vary wildly depending on the threshold level that is set (Savoy, 2001). To make matters worse, there are generally no very convincing arguments as to the appropriate setting of the threshold level. The key point here was made very clearly by Savoy (2001, p. 30): "Will area A in the cortex show a change in activity (an increase or decrease) in response to task X, compared to its response to task Y? If our imaging system is powerful enough ... then the answer will almost always be Yes, for any A, X, and Y."

Much progress has been made in addressing the limitations identified above, with researchers starting to move away from purely correlational data.

For example, we can show that activity in a given area of the brain is necessary to perform a task effectively by using transcranial magnetic stimulation (TMS), which is discussed in Table 1.1. In essence, TMS involves applying pulses of current to some area of the brain, thus causing a "temporary lesion." Suppose you believed that brain area *x* was involved in performing a task. If TMS applied to that particular area of brain led to impairment of task performance, it would be reasonable to conclude that that brain area is necessary for good task performance. On the other hand, if TMS applied to that brain area had *no* effect on task performance, we would conclude that that brain area is not needed to perform the task effectively. We will shortly consider a concrete example of this approach in action.

What about the criticism that brain-imaging studies contribute nothing to our theoretical understanding? That was certainly true of much of the earlier research. However, matters have changed now that we have a reasonably clear idea of the kinds of processing associated with most areas of the brain. For example, consider the issue of the processes involved in visual imagery (see Chapter 7). According to Kosslyn and his colleagues (e.g., Kosslyn & Thompson, 2003), visual imagery typically involves many of the same processes as visual perception. In contrast, Pylyshyn (e.g., 2002, 2003) argues that visual imagery does *not* involve the same processes as visual perception, but instead depends on rather abstract forms of thinking and knowledge. We know that visual perception involves Areas 17 and 18 (early visual cortex). As a result, we can easily carry out theoretically important studies: if visual imagery tasks produce activation of early visual cortex, Kosslyn's theoretical approach receives support. To cut a long story short, visual imagery is often (but not always) associated with much activation in early visual cortex (see Kosslyn & Thompson, 2003, for a review).

The notion that visual imagery involves many of the same processes as visual perception can also be tested by using repeated transcranial magnetic stimulation (TMS). If Area 17 is necessary for visual imagery, then magnetic stimulation applied to it should impair performance on a visual imagery task. Precisely that finding was reported by Kosslyn et al. (1999).

HOW USEFUL IS COGNITIVE PSYCHOLOGY?

Some critics of cognitive psychology are skeptical about the contribution that cognitive psychology has made to providing real and lasting benefits to society. In fact, cognitive psychology has contributed substantially to society in many ways, but here I will focus on the ways in which the cognitive approach has benefited patients seeking treatment for various anxiety disorders.

COGNITIVE APPROACHES TO THERAPY

Suppose a friend of yours is suffering from very high levels of anxiety or depression. Naturally you are concerned about their welfare, and wonder what advice you should give. You might imagine that drugs designed to reduce anxiety (e.g., Valium) or depression (e.g., Prozac) would solve the problem. However, while drugs can certainly provide extremely valuable

What commonalities exist in cognitive therapies?

short-term relief, there are long-term issues with many drugs relating to possible addiction and to various side-effects.

Over the past 20 to 30 years, there has been a dramatic increase in the use of cognitive approaches to therapy in the treatment of depression and anxiety disorders, in part because such forms of therapy pose no problems of addiction or side-effects. The central assumption underlying these approaches is that patients have an interpretive bias: they *misinterpret* information about themselves and the world around them by believing it to be more threatening than is objectively the case (see Chapter 27 for a fuller discussion). Such misinterpretations are cognitive in nature, and are thought to play a major role in the development and maintenance of anxiety and depression. Below we consider two of the main anxiety disorders: panic disorder and social phobia.

Panic disorder is an anxiety disorder in which the patient has numerous very upsetting panic attacks consisting of symptoms such as pounding heart, sweating, shortness of breath, chest pain, dizziness, and fear of dying. According to several theorists (e.g., Clark, 1986), the main reason why patients with panic disorder experience panic attacks is because they have catastrophic misinterpretations of their bodily sensations. Supportive evidence comes from studies involving a biological challenge (e.g., inhalation of a mixture of carbon dioxide and oxygen) designed to produce some of the symptoms of a panic attack. Not surprisingly, patients with panic disorder are far more likely than normal individuals to experience a panic attack under biological challenge (see Eysenck, 1997, for a review). If this is due to interpretive bias, we should find that there are small or non-existent differences between panic patients and normal controls in their actual physiological activity in response to challenge. As predicted, panic patients have been found to respond comparably to healthy controls on measures of heart rate, respiratory rate, forearm muscle tension, and blood pressure (Eysenck, 1997).

Social phobia is an anxiety disorder in which the patient has a strong fear of being humiliated or embarrassed in social situations leading him or her to avoid such situations. The most important interpretive bias of social phobics is that they regard their own social behavior and performance to be significantly worse and incompetent than is actually the case. Evidence for this was reported by Rapee and Lim (1992) in a study in which social phobics and healthy controls gave a public talk. The public-speaking performance of the two groups as rated by observers did not differ significantly (see Figure 1.5). However, the social phobics differed from the controls in rating their own public-speaking performance as much worse than did observers, thus showing clear evidence of an interpretive bias.

It seems puzzling that social phobics often maintain their interpretive biases over a period of several years. You would think their experiences in numerous social situations would lead them to realize that their perception of their own social performance was inaccurate and then to change it. The answer to this puzzle was provided by Clark and Wells (1995). According to them, social phobics use various safety-seeking behaviors designed to reduce the anxiety they experience in social situations. For example, they avoid eye contact, talk very little, and avoid talking about themselves. As a result, they do not obtain much feedback from other people in social situations, and this relative lack of feedback allows the interpretive bias to remain intact.

Interpretive bias is not the only bias from which social phobics suffer. In addition, as Clark and Wells (1995) pointed out, social phobics have an attentional bias involving excessive attention to their own behavior and internal state in social situations. This was shown by Stopa and Clark (1993) in a study in which social phobics, patients with other anxiety disorders, and healthy controls spoke out loud the thoughts they had had during a previous social inter-action. The key finding was that there were sub-stantial group differences in the percentage of their thoughts devoted to negative evaluations of themselves and of their own behavior. Social phobics spent 39% of the time focusing nega-tively on themselves, whereas patients with other anxiety disorders spent 9% of their time doing the same, with the figure being 6.5% for controls.

Attentional bias causes problems for social phobics in various ways (Bögels & Mansell, 2004). They focus on their aroused internal state and mistakenly assume that other people can see how anxious they are. Excessive focus on them-selves means that social phobics are fairly oblivious to the effect their behav-ior is having on other people. This prevents them from observing positive or encouraging reactions from others, and thus helps to maintain their high level of social anxiety.

Figure 1.5 Public-speaking performance of normal controls and social phobics, based on self-ratings and observer ratings (high scores indicate poor performance). Data from Rapee and Lim (1992).

COGNITIVE THERAPY

We will illustrate the value of the cognitive approach to therapy by focusing on social phobia, which has a lifetime incidence of about 15% in several Western countries. Social phobia has often been treated by means of **expo-sure therapy**, in which patients are exposed to what they regard as threaten-ing social situations. It is assumed that social phobics have excessive fears about social situations, and they fail to realize this because of their tendency to avoid such situations. Accordingly, exposure therapy leads to a reduction in social phobics' excessive fears and reduces their subsequent avoidance of social situations.

Exposure therapy is of proven effectiveness (Wells & Clark, 1997). However, it is a limited form of treatment from the cognitive perspective. According to the cognitive approach, the main emphasis in therapy should be on removing social phobics' attentional and interpretive biases, which play a major role in the maintenance of social phobia. Exposure therapy doesn't focus directly on attentional bias, and its failure to address social phobics' safety-seeking behaviors reduces its effectiveness in eliminating interpretive bias.

In an attempt to eliminate attentional bias, Wells and Papageorgiou (1998) compared exposure therapy plus instructions emphasizing external attentional focus with exposure therapy on its own. At the end of therapy, patients rated its effectiveness on a 100-point scale. The mean rating for therapy including external attentional focus was 92.5 compared to only 37.5 for exposure therapy on its own.

We will consider two ways of reducing interpretive bias in social phobics. First, patients can be instructed to eliminate the safety-seeking behaviors that are maintaining the interpretive bias. Wells, Clark, Salkovskis, Ludgate, Hackmann, and Gelder (1995) compared exposure therapy plus instructions to avoid safety-seeking behaviors with exposure therapy on its own. The former form of therapy was significantly more effective. Second, patients in social situations can be provided with detailed feedback about their social performance. For example, social phobics can watch videotapes of themselves in social situations, and see for themselves that their social behavior is more adequate than they feared. This approach has also proved valuable in reducing interpretive bias.

Wells and Clark (1997) developed a form of cognitive therapy incorporating the ideas discussed here. This was compared against exposure therapy on its own and against exposure therapy plus Prozac (Clark, 1999). The new form of cognitive therapy was found to be significantly more effective than the other forms of therapy in reducing the symptoms of social phobia.

STRUCTURE OF THE BOOK

Cognitive psychology covers a huge (and increasing) number of topics, not all of which could possibly be covered in a book such as this. Instead, what I have tried to do is to select topics that are currently regarded as both interesting and important. Note that these topics are related to each other because virtually all cognitive processes and structures within the cognitive system are interdependent. Consider, for example, a student reading a book to prepare for an examination. The student is *learning*, but there are several other processes going on as well. *Visual perception* is involved in the intake of information from the printed page, and there is *attention* to the content of the book. In order for the student to benefit from the book, he or she must possess considerable *language skills*, and must also have *stored knowledge* relevant to the material in the book. There may be an element of *problem solving* in the student's attempts to relate what is in the book to the possibly conflicting information he or she has learned elsewhere. Furthermore, what the student learns will depend on his or her *emotional state*. Finally, the acid test of whether the learning has been effective and has produced *long-term memory* comes during the examination itself when the material contained in the book must be *recalled*.

The words italicized in the previous paragraph indicate some of the main ingredients of human cognition, and form the basis of much of the coverage of cognitive psychology in this book. As you can see from the contents page, 27 topics are covered in the chapters that follow. These topics are all separate from each other, but can nevertheless be placed into a fairly small number of categories. More specifically, the structure of this book involves five categories or parts: visual perception and attention; learning and memory; language; thinking and reasoning; and broader issues. In the interests of providing a coherent account of human cognition, I have provided a general introduction to each of the five parts of the book.

The categories used in this book are similar to those used in many other textbooks. However, these categories are somewhat arbitrary, and may convey the impression that cognitive psychology can be neatly divided up. The reality is entirely different. For example, I have used a category labeled "language." However, it would be ludicrous to argue that language is totally irrelevant to the other categories. For example, much of what we learn and remember is language-based, and language is heavily involved in most of our thinking and reasoning. It is nevertheless the case that only the topics considered in the language section focus on attempts to understand the nature of language itself.

Why are the categories ordered in the way that they are? Consider what happens when visual or auditory stimuli are presented. Initially, the individual attends to these stimuli and uses perceptual processes to identify them. After that, information about these stimuli may be learned and subsequently remembered. Next, the individual may engage in complex processes of thinking and reasoning based on information presented to him or her. Throughout all of these stages of processing, language typically plays a part. Finally, there is the category labeled "broader issues." In essence, the topics considered here (cognition and emotion; consciousness) are ones that involve most (or all) of the processes and structures discussed in the previous sections. Accordingly, it seems appropriate to finish with these topics. Finally, please note that the evaluation of the theories and research discussed is to be found at the end of each chapter in a section entitled Evaluation and Chapter Summary.

EVALUATION AND CHAPTER SUMMARY

Introduction
- There is an important distinction between processing directly triggered by the stimulus input (bottom-up processing) and top-down processing based on internal factors (e.g., knowledge; expectations).
- Processing can be serial (one process at a time) or parallel (more than one process at a time) and is mostly parallel.
- There are four major approaches to studying human cognition varying in their reliance on healthy or brain-damaged participants, use of brain-imaging techniques, and computational models.

Experimental cognitive psychology
- The experimental cognitive psychology approach involves laboratory studies of healthy participants, and underpins all of cognitive psychology.
- This approach sometimes produces findings not applicable to everyday life, and provides only indirect evidence of the internal processes involved in cognition.

Cognitive neuropsychology
- The cognitive neuropsychology approach involves laboratory studies of brain-damaged patients, and is based on various assumptions (e.g., modularity; subtractivity).

- This approach has shed much light on the structure of the human cognitive system in areas such as reading and memory.
- This approach is most effective when applied to specific aspects of cognitive functioning localized in some area of the brain and is least effective when applied to general aspects of cognition distributed across the brain.

Computational cognitive science
- The computational cognitive science approach in the form of computational modeling involves programming computers to mimic aspects of human cognitive functioning.
- This approach forces researchers to specify in detail all the assumptions of a theory, and has revealed vagueness in many previous theories.
- This approach is rarely used to make new predictions, and most computational models are limited in scope.

Congnitive neuroscience
- The cognitive neuroscience approach involves using various techniques (e.g., brain imaging) to study the brain.
- This approach provides relatively direct information about the brain and helps to clarify the meaning of indirect behavioral data.
- This approach tells us *where* in the brain processing is occurring, but sometimes fails to tell us *what* is happening.

How useful is cognitive psychology?
- Cognitive psychology has proved extremely valuable in understanding many mental disorders (e.g., anxiety disorders).
- Cognitive therapy depends in part on cognitive psychology and has proved a very effective form of treatment for anxiety disorders and for depression.

FURTHER READING

- Anderson, J.R., & Lebiere, C. (2003). The Newell Test for a theory of cognition. *Behavioral and Brain Sciences, 26*, 587–640. The authors assess the relative strengths and weaknesses of two key theories of computational modeling (the connectionist and ACT-R production system approaches) in terms of several criteria.
- Eysenck, M.W., & Keane, M.T. (2005). *Cognitive psychology: A student's handbook*. Hove, UK: Psychology Press. Most of the issues discussed in this chapter are dealt with in more detail in Chapter 1 of this textbook.
- Gazzaniga, M.S., Ivry, R.B., & Mangun, G.R. (2002). *Cognitive neuroscience: The biology of the mind* (2nd ed.). New York: Norton. This book provides a good account of the ways in which cognitive neuroscience has increased our understanding of human behavior.

- Harley, T.A. (2004). Does cognitive neuropsychology have a future? *Cognitive Neuropsychology*, *21*, 3–16. This article (and replies to it in the same issue of the journal by Caplan, McCloskey, Dell, Coltheart, Vallar, Shallice, & Lambon Ralph) provide interesting views on many key issues relating to cognitive neuropsychology, connectionism, and cognitive neuroscience. Be warned that the experts often have very different views from each other!

PART I

CONTENTS

2 Visual illusions: Seeing and acting   26

3 How far away is that object?   38

4 Perception without awareness?   48

5 What is this I see before me?   60

6 What's in a face?   74

7 Seeing with the mind's eye   88

8 In sight but out of mind   102

9 What do we attend to in vision?   114

10 Multitasking   126

Visual perception and attention

Visual perception is of enormous importance to us in our everyday lives. It allows us to move around freely, to see people with whom we are talking, to read magazines and books, to admire the wonders of nature, and to watch films and television. It is very important for visual perception to be accurate— if we misperceive how close we are to the edge of a cliff or how close cars are to us as we try to cross the road, the consequences are quite likely to be fatal. Thus, it comes as no surprise to discover that far more of the human cortex is devoted to vision than to any other sensory modality.

What do we mean by perception? According to Sekuler and Blake (2002, p. 621), it is, "the acquisition and processing of sensory information in order to see, hear, taste, or feel objects in the world; also guides an organism's actions with respect to those objects." Visual perception generally seems so simple and effortless that we are in danger of taking it for granted. In fact, it is very complex, and numerous processes are involved in transforming and interpreting sensory information. Supporting evidence comes from the efforts of researchers in artificial intelligence who have tried to program computers to "perceive" the environment. As yet, no computer can match more than a fraction of the skills of visual perception possessed by nearly every adult human.

There is a vast literature on visual perception, and we are only going to be able to consider a small number of relevant topics in this book. We make a start by considering visual illusions in Chapter 2. It seems paradoxical that our visual perception is typically very accurate, and yet psychologists have created literally hundreds of visual illusions that deceive most people. The unexpected solution to this paradox is discussed in detail in Chapter 2.

One of the fundamental aspects of visual perception concerns our ability to work out the distance from us of the various objects in our field of vision. If we make mistakes in depth perception, we may bump into objects as we walk around, and may find it very hard to pick up objects (e.g., food, cups). Many of the factors enabling us to judge distance accurately are discussed in Chapter 3.

When we think of visual perception, we almost always think in terms of our conscious perception of the world around us. Indeed, the very notion of "unconscious" perception may seem bizarre and impossible. However, consider something as simple as looking out of a window and seeing a tree (as I have just done). The conscious perception of a tree didn't come from nowhere. Instead, it depended on various perceptual processes below the level of conscious awareness. The whole issue of unconscious visual perception is discussed in Chapter 4.

The single most important function of visual perception is to allow us to identify the objects in the world around us. Just imagine if you lived in a world in which most of the objects around you were unfamiliar—it would be a very frightening and unpleasant experience. The main processes involved are discussed in Chapter 5. Within the general topic of object recognition there is face recognition. Faces are among the most important objects we see every day, and it is extremely embarrassing if we fail to recognize someone we know. It is sometimes argued that the processes involved in face recognition differ from those involved in object recognition in general. That explains why face recognition is discussed in its own separate chapter (Chapter 6).

Over the centuries it has generally been argued that there are close similarities between visual perception on the one hand and visual imagery on the other hand. Most people agree their visual images resemble visual perception, except that their images are less clear and detailed. However, the issue has proved controversial, and some experts have argued that visual imagery is very different from visual perception. In Chapter 7, we see how brain-imaging research has provided striking evidence that very similar processes are involved in visual imagery and visual perception.

There are important links between perception and attention, and that is why the two topics are both considered within this part of the book. In general terms (and with some exceptions), it can be argued that we need to attend to an object to perceive it consciously. Some of the most convincing evidence to support that argument comes in the form of a phenomenon known as "change blindness". What happens with change blindness is that people often fail to notice some fairly pronounced change in the environment. The evidence concerning change blindness (discussed in detail in Chapter 8) indicates that it is due mainly to a lack of attention to the part of the visual world that has changed. People are generally surprised when it is pointed out to them that they haven't noticed what would seem to be an obvious change in the environment. What seems to happen is that we tend to exaggerate the extent to which we have managed to pay attention to the entire visual scene in front of us – this is something that magicians take full advantage of when fooling us with their tricks!

Visual attention possesses several characteristics. However, the most obvious feature of attention is that it is *selective*. In other words, we choose to attend to certain people or objects in the environment at any given moment while ignoring everything else. At one time, it was popular to argue that visual attention is like a spotlight or zoom lens that focuses on a given area of the visual field. According to the zoom-lens metaphor, visual attention is fairly complex and sophisticated. More specifically, it was claimed in this metaphor that visual attention can be concentrated on a small part of the visual field or can expand to encompass a larger area. The strengths and weaknesses of this theoretical approach to focused visual attention are considered in some detail in Chapter 9 of this book.

Finally, in Chapter 10 we consider an issue in the field of attention that is of considerable relevance in today's 24/7 world. The issue in question is the vexed one of how we manage to cope with trying to do several different things at the same time (this is known as multitasking). Many people think that they are very good at multitasking, but sadly the research evidence generally indicates that this is not the case. In spite of the problems we typically have with multitasking, there are some circumstances in which we can cope effectively and efficiently with two tasks at the same time. Those circumstances are discussed in Chapter 10.

In sum, this part of the book is concerned with some of the key topics in the areas of perception and attention. What were the factors determining my decisions about what to include and exclude? In essence, I deliberately tried to select topics that are of real relevance and importance in everyday life. My hope is that when you have finished reading this part of the book, you will agree with me that psychologists have made excellent progress in understanding how we attend to (and perceive) the world around us.

CHAPTER 2

CONTENTS

Introduction	27
Two visual systems: Illusions	29
Two visual systems: General	33
Evaluation and chapter summary	36
Further reading	37

Visual illusions: Seeing and acting

INTRODUCTION

Vision is obviously hugely important to us in various ways, but what is its major function? As Milner and Goodale (1998, p. 2) pointed out, "Standard accounts of vision implicitly assume that the purpose of the visual system is to construct some sort of internal model of the world outside." As we will see, one of the major themes of this chapter is that this is a grossly over-simplified view.

We typically trust the evidence of our senses (including vision), and assume the "internal model of the world" that we construct is an accurate one. When we look at the world around us, we are very confident that what we can see corresponds *precisely* to what is actually there. Indeed, the human species would probably have become extinct a very long time ago if we perceived the environment inaccurately! If we thought the edge of a precipice was further away than was actually the case, or that the jump from a wall to the ground was 1 meter (3 feet) when it was actually 3 meters (10 feet), then our lives would be in danger. In spite of these apparently persuasive arguments in favor of accurate visual perception, psychologists have found that we are subject to numerous visual illusions, a few of which are discussed below.

First, there is the Müller–Lyer illusion (see Figure 2.1). Your task is to compare the lengths of the two vertical lines. Nearly everyone says that the vertical line on the left looks longer than the one on the right. In fact, however, they are the same length, as can be confirmed by using a ruler! Second, there is the Ebbinghaus illusion (see Figure 2.2). In this illusion, the central circle surrounded by smaller circles looks larger than a central circle of the same size surrounded by larger circles. In fact, the two central circles are the *same* size. Third, there is the Ponzo illusion (see Figure 2.3). In this illusion, the rectangle labeled A seems larger than the rectangle labeled B, in spite of the fact that they are actually the same length.

The existence of the Müller–Lyer, Ebbinghaus, and Ponzo illusions (plus many others) leaves us with an intriguing paradox. How is it that the human species has been so successful given that our visual perceptual processes are apparently very prone to error? Consider your answer to that question before reading on.

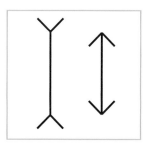

Figure 2.1 The Müller–Lyer illusion.

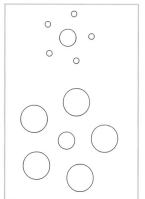

Figure 2.2 The Ebbinghaus illusion.

Why is size constancy an extremely useful perceptual illusion in the real world?

One plausible answer is that most visual illusions involve very artificial figures, are far removed from the world around us, and so can be dismissed as tricks played by psychologists with nothing better to do. There is some truth in that argument, but it doesn't account for all visual illusions. For example, you can show the Müller–Lyer illusion with real three-dimensional objects by following the lead of DeLucia and Hochberg (1991). They found evidence for the typical Müller–Lyer effect when three 2-foot-high fins were placed on the floor in an arrangement like that shown in Figure 2.4. You can confirm their findings by placing three open books in a line so that the ones on the left and the right are open to the right and the one in the middle is open to the left. The spine of the book in the middle should be the same distance from the spines of each of the other two books. In spite of this, the distance between the spine of the middle book and the spine of the book on the right should look longer.

Another visual illusion that can be demonstrated in the real world is the vertical–horizontal illusion shown in Figure 2.5. The two lines are actually the same length, but the vertical line appears longer than the horizontal one. This tendency to overestimate vertical extents relative to horizontal ones can be shown with real objects by taking a teacup, a saucer, and two spoons of the same length. Place one spoon horizontally on the saucer and the other spoon vertically in the cup. You should find that the vertical spoon looks longer.

We have seen that we can't explain away all visual illusions on the basis that they are highly artificial. A better explanation of visual illusions was suggested by Gregory (1970). He argued that we treat two-dimensional illusion figures as if they were three-dimensional, even though we know they are only two-dimensional. For example, people typically see a given object as having a constant size by taking account of its apparent distance. **Size constancy** means that an object is perceived as having the same size whether it is looked at from a short or a long distance away. This constancy contrasts with the size of the retinal image (the image on the retina inside the eye) that becomes progressively smaller as an object recedes into the distance (see Figure 2.6). According to Gregory's misapplied size-constancy theory, this kind of perceptual processing is applied wrongly to produce several illusions.

It is easiest to see what Gregory (1970) had in mind with the Ponzo illusion (see Figure 2.3). The long lines look like railway lines or the edges of a road receding into the distance. As a result, the top rectangle A can be seen as further away from us than the bottom rectangle B. If it were a three-dimensional scene, then rectangle A would be longer than rectangle B. It looks longer to us because of misapplied size constancy.

The same kind of explanation can be applied to the Müller–Lyer illusion. According to Gregory (1970), the left figure looks like the inside corners of a room, whereas the right figure is like the outside corners of a building. Thus, the vertical line in the left figure is further away from us than its fins, whereas the vertical line in

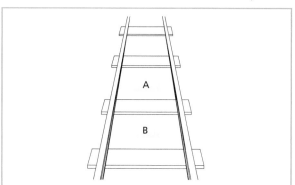

Figure 2.3 The Ponzo illusion.

the right figure is closer to us than its fins. Since the size of the retinal image is the same for both vertical lines, the principle of size constancy tells us that the line that is further away (i.e., the one in the left figure) must be longer. This is precisely the Müller–Lyer illusion.

There are real problems with Gregory's account of the Müller–Lyer illusion. According to Matlin and Foley's (1997) incorrect comparison theory, our perception of visual illusions is influenced by parts of the figure not being judged. Thus, for example, the vertical lines in the Müller–Lyer illusion may seem longer or shorter than their actual length simply because they form part of a large or small object. Evidence in line with incorrect comparison theory was reported by Coren and Girgus (1972). The size of the Müller–Lyer illusion was greatly reduced when the fins were in a different color from the vertical lines. Presumably this made it easier to ignore the fins.

It seems more difficult to apply Gregory's theory to the Ebbinghaus illusion. It is also puzzling that we allegedly treat visual illusions as *three*-dimensional objects when they seem flat and *two*-dimensional, a notion that sounds distinctly odd. According to Gregory, cues to depth are used *automatically* whether or not the figures are seen to be lying on a flat surface. As Gregory predicted, the two-dimensional Müller–Lyer figures appear three-dimensional when presented as luminous models in a darkened room.

Earlier we discussed research by DeLucia and Hochberg (1991). They found that the Müller–Lyer effect could be obtained even when it was obvious that all the fins were at the same distance from the viewer (see Figure 2.4). It is very difficult (or impossible) to explain these findings on Gregory's theory.

A much better explanation of the paradox that visual perception seems very accurate in everyday life but can be error-prone in the laboratory was proposed by Milner and Goodale (1995, 1998). According to them, we have *two* visual perceptual systems! In very crude terms, one system is used to allow us to move safely around our environment without knocking into objects or falling over precipices, whereas a different system is used to recognize objects and to perceive visual illusions. These two systems generally interact, but can operate fairly independently of each other. The model proposed by Milner and Goodale (1995, 1998) is discussed below.

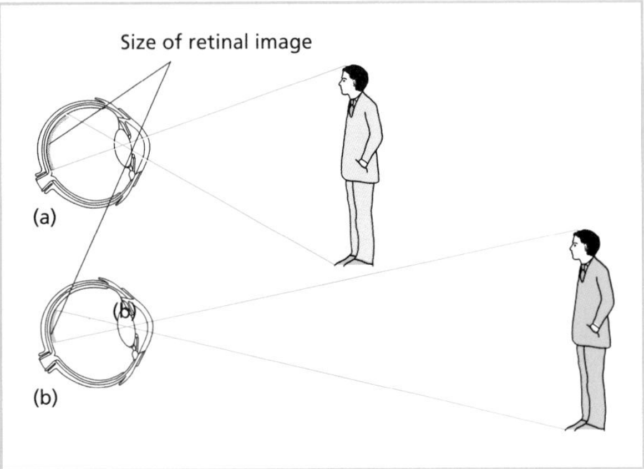

Figure 2.4 The spine of the middle book is closer to the spine of which other book? Now check your answer with a ruler.

Figure 2.5 The vertical–horizontal illusion.

TWO VISUAL SYSTEMS: ILLUSIONS

As mentioned above, Milner and Goodale (1995, 1998) put forward a perception–action model in which they argued that there is a crucial distinction between vision for perception and vision for action. The two systems make use of different information and fulfill different functions. The

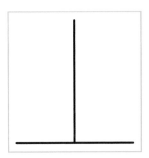

Size of retinal image

(a)

(b)

Figure 2.6 The retinal image halves in size when the distance from the eye doubles. Goldstein, *Sensations and perception*, 6th edition, 2002. Copyright Thomson.

vision-for-perception system is what we immediately think of when considering visual perception. It is the system used to decide that the animal in front of us is a cat or a buffalo, or to admire the paintings of Cézanne. More generally, this is the system allowing us to construct an "internal model of the world."

In contrast, the vision-for-action system is used for visually guided action. It is the system we use when running to return the ball when playing tennis or some other sport. Note that we aren't consciously aware that two systems are involved in visual perception and action. However, as is so often the case, our conscious experience is a fallible guide to what is actually happening.

Separate visual processing streams have been identified for the two systems identified by Milner and Goodale (see Figure 2.7). First, there is the ventral stream that starts in area V1 and projects to the inferotemporal cortex and is involved in object recognition. Second, there is the dorsal stream that also starts in area V1 but projects to the posterior parietal cortex. The dorsal stream is involved in the guidance of action.

Within the context of the perception–action model, most studies on visual illusions have involved the system concerned with vision for perception. Suppose we were to carry out additional studies on the visual illusions, but this time we set things up so participants would use the perception-for-action system. We could do this by using three-dimensional versions of the illusions, and instructing participants to reach for a key object (e.g., one of the central circles in the Ebbinghaus illusion). Milner and Goodale (1995, 1998) argued that the perception-for-action system should generally *not* be deceived by the visual illusions. If illusions present when the perception-for-vision system is used disappear when the perception-for-action system is used, this would provide reasonable support for the perception–action model.

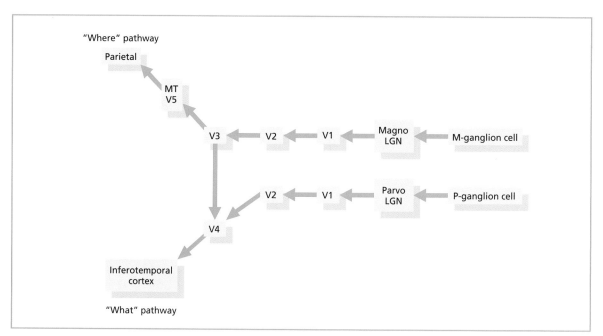

Figure 2.7 A very simplified illustration of the pathways and brain areas involved in vision. There is much more interconnectivity within the brain (VI onwards) than is shown, and there are additional unshown brain areas involved in vision. Adapted from Goldstein (1996).

The most surprising conclusion that follows from Milner and Goodale's approach was summarized neatly by Bridgeman, Gemmer, Forsman, and Huemer (2000, p. 3540): "Common sense tells us that one must accurately perceive an object's location and properties to interact effectively with it. This intuition is in error, however ... humans produce effective motor behavior despite inadequate or erroneous perceptual information. Perception is not required to visually guide an action."

ILLUSIONS REVISITED

Since the mid-1990s, there have been numerous studies in which people have reached out to grasp parts of illusory figures and objects (see Glover, 2004, for a review). The prediction that any illusory effect should be smaller when action is involved than when participants simply make visual judgments has been confirmed in most (but by no means all) studies. A few relevant studies are considered below.

Haart, Carey, and Milne (1999) used a three-dimensional version of the Müller–Lyer illusion (see Figure 2.1). There were two tasks:

1. A matching task, in which participants indicated the length of the shaft on one figure by the size of the gap between their index finger and thumb. This was designed to involve the vision-for-perception system.
2. A grasping task, in which participants rapidly grasped the target figure lengthwise using their index finger and thumb. This task was designed to involve the vision-for-action system.

What Haart et al. (1999) found is shown in Figure 2.8. There was a strong illusion effect when the matching task was used, but there was no illusory

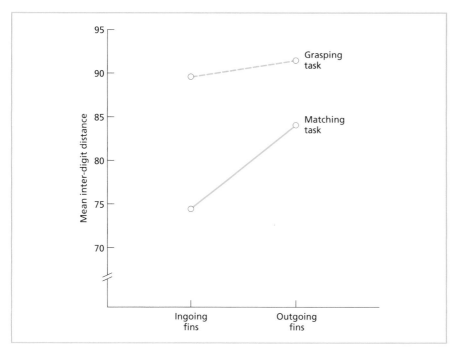

Figure 2.8 Performance on a three-dimensional version of the Müller–Lyer illusion as a function of task (grasping vs. matching) and type of stimulus (ingoing fins vs. outgoing fins). Based on data in Haart et al. (1999).

effect at all with the grasping task. These findings were as predicted by the perception–action model, leading Haart et al. (1999, p. 1442) to conclude, "These data suggest separate systems of processing involved in perception and the visual control of action."

THE PLOT THICKENS

According to the perception–action model, we are generally not deceived by visual illusions when we respond to them with our perception-for-action system. However, matters are actually more complex than that. Glover (2004) reviewed the literature on grasping and other movements towards illusory figures. He discovered that people's *initial* hand movements are very often influenced by the illusion, but their *subsequent* hand movements become progressively more accurate as they approach the figure on object in question. For example, Glover and Dixon (2002) carried out a study on the Ebbinghaus illusion (see Figure 2.2). Participants were instructed to adjust their grip so that it was appropriate for grasping the target (i.e., the circle in the center of the display). Grip aperture was influenced by the illusion when the hand was some distance from the target, but the extent of the illusory effect decreased as the hand approached the target.

Similar findings were reported by Glover and Dixon (2001). Participants saw a small bar on a background grating which caused the bar's orientation to be misperceived. Their task was to pick up the bar. The effects of the illusion on hand orientation were fairly large early in the reaching movement, but had almost disappeared when the hand approached the bar (see Figure 2.9).

What do these findings mean? A neat explanation was provided by Glover (2004). He argued in his planning–control model that *two* systems are involved in the production of human action. As you may have guessed from the name of the model, these are the planning system and the control system. Here are some of the key features of the two systems:

1. *Planning system*: This system is involved in selecting an appropriate target (e.g., pint of beer), deciding how to grasp it, and so on. It is used mainly before a hand or other movement starts, but is also used early during the movement. This system is prone to error because it is influenced by several factors (e.g., the visual context in which the object to be grasped is presented; the nature of the object).

2. *Control system*: This system is involved in ensuring that movements are accurate and in making adjustments if required. It is used *after* the planning system, and operates during the carrying out of a movement. Unlike the planning system, the control system is influenced only by physical characteristics of the target object (e.g., its size and shape).

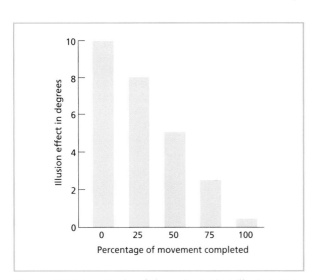

Figure 2.9 Magnitude of the orientation illusion as a function of time into the movement. Based on data in Glover and Dixon (2001).

According to the planning–control model, responses to visual illusions should often be inaccurate if they depend on the planning system (because it takes account of the surrounding visual context). In contrast, responses to visual illusions should typically be accurate if they depend on the control system (because it is influenced only by physical features of the object to be grasped). Since the planning system is used at an earlier stage than the control system, it follows that visual illusions should have more influence on hand movements early rather than late in those movements.

What can the study of visual illusions tell us about how our own visual system operates?

TWO VISUAL SYSTEMS: GENERAL

We have seen that there is good evidence from the study of visual illusions for the existence of two visual systems. In fact, there is much additional evidence supporting the two-system approach, some of which we will consider in this section.

COGNITIVE NEUROPSYCHOLOGY

Milner and Goodale's (1995, 1998) notion that there are two somewhat separate visual systems (one specialized for perception and one for action) can be investigated by studying brain-damaged patients. We would expect to find some patients (those with damage to the dorsal stream) having reasonably intact vision for perception but severely impaired vision for action. There should also be other patients (those with damage to the ventral stream) showing the opposite pattern of intact vision for action but very poor vision for perception.

If the action system is less susceptible to illusions, what are the implications for real-world visual experiences?

Patients with optic ataxia are relevant to Milner and Goodale's theory. According to Georgopoulos (1997, p. 142), patients with **optic ataxia** "do not usually have impaired vision or impaired hand or arm movements, but show a severe impairment in visually guided reaching in the absence of perceptual disturbance in estimating distance." For example, Perenin and Vighetto (1988) found that patients with optic ataxia had great difficulty in rotating their hands appropriately when reaching towards (and into) a large oriented slot in front of them. As predicted, such patients typically have damage in parts of the posterior parietal lobe forming part of the dorsal pathway (Perenin & Vighetto, 1988).

Glover (2003) has reviewed evidence indicating that most patients with optic ataxia don't actually have problems with *all* aspects of reaching for objects. Remember that he argues that reaching for objects involves successive stages of planning and control. According to Glover (2003, p. 447), "Optic ataxia can be characterized as a deficit in the visual on-line guidance of actions, with action planning remaining relatively intact." For example, Jakobson, Archibald, Carey, and Goodale (1991) studied VK, a patient with optic ataxia who had difficulty in grasping objects. However, close inspection of her grip aperture at different points in grasping indicated that her *initial* planning was essentially normal.

What about patients with deficient vision for perception but intact vision for action? Some patients with visual form agnosia fit this pattern. **Visual agnosia** is a condition involving severe problems with object recognition.

KEY TERMS
Optic ataxia: a condition in which there are problems with making visually guided movements.
Visual agnosia: a condition in which there are great problems in recognizing objects presented visually even though visual information reaches the visual cortex.

DF is the most studied patient having visual agnosia coupled with fairly good spatial perception. DF's difficulties with object recognition were shown in her inability to identify any of a series of drawings of common objects. In contrast, DF "had little difficulty in everyday activities such as opening doors, shaking hands, walking around furniture, and eating meals . . . she could accurately reach out and grasp a pencil orientated at different angles" (Milner et al., 1991).

Dijkerman, Milner, and Carey (1998) assessed DF's performance on various tasks when presented with several differently colored objects. DF showed good vision for action in that she reached out and touched the objects as accurately as healthy individuals. However, she had poor vision for perception. She was unable to copy the objects in their correct spatial positions, and she couldn't distinguish accurately between the colored objects.

According to Milner and Goodale's (1995, 1998) perception–action model, DF's brain damage should be in the ventral stream underlying object recognition rather than in the ventral stream underlying vision for action. James, Culham, Humphrey, Milner, and Goodale (2003) confirmed these predictions. DF showed no greater activation in the ventral stream when presented with drawings of objects than when presented with scrambled line drawings. However, she showed high levels of activation in the dorsal stream when grasping for objects. As James et al. (2003, p. 2473) concluded, "In contrast to the evident dysfunction in her ventral stream, DF's dorsal stream appears to be functioning remarkably well."

DUAL-PROCESS APPROACH

What are the main differences between optic ataxia and visual agnosia?

What has been said so far has indicated some of the important differences between the ventral system used in object recognition and the dorsal system used to guide behavior. However, there are several other differences that haven't been discussed so far. Norman (2002) extended Milner and Goodale's (1995, 1998) perception–action model in his dual-process model based on separate ventral and dorsal systems. Norman (2002, p. 95) agreed with Milner and Goodale concerning the primary functions of these systems: "The dorsal system deals mainly with the utilization of visual information for the guidance of behavior in one's environment. The ventral system deals mainly with the utilization of visual information for 'knowing' one's environment, that is, identifying and recognizing items previously encountered and storing new visual information for later encounters."

There are limitations with focusing so much on anatomical differences in order to identify the two visual systems (Bridgeman, personal communication). According to Bridgeman et al. (2000), the primary distinction is a *functional* one—there is a cognitive representation that drives perception (similar to the ventral system) and there is a sensori-motor representation that controls visually guided behavior and action (similar to the dorsal system).

We can understand the essence of Norman's (2002) dual-process approach if we consider the differences he identified between the two visual processing systems (see Table 2.1). As you can see, each system has its own particular strengths and limitations with the two systems together allowing us to interact very successfully with the environment. The ventral system can provide very detailed visual processing, permitting accurate object recogni-

Table 2.1 Eight main differences between the ventral and dorsal systems (based on Norman, 2002).

Factor	Ventral system	Dorsal system
1. Function	Recognition/identification	Visually guided behavior
2. Sensitivity	High spatial frequencies: details	High temporal frequencies: motion
3. Memory	Memory-based (stored representations)	Only very short-term storage
4. Speed	Relatively slow	Relatively fast
5. Consciousness	Typically high	Typically low
6. Frame of reference	Allocentric or object-centered	Egocentric or body-centered
7. Visual input	Mainly foveal or parafoveal	Across retina
8. Monocular vision	Generally reasonably small effects	Often large effects (e.g., motion parallax)

tion at the conscious level (even though it fouls up when confronted by visual illusions). However, it has the disadvantages of operating fairly slowly and being relatively insensitive to motion. In contrast, the dorsal system is very sensitive to motion and rapidly provides the basic information needed for action. However, it has the disadvantage of providing relatively imprecise visual information that is often not accessible to consciousness.

What are the limitations with the dual-process approach (and the similar perception–action model)? First, as Norman (2002, p. 96) admitted, "The proposed integrative theory and its concomitant dual-process approach are clearly an oversimplified view of what transpires in visual perception." Second, while both theories emphasize the separateness of the two visual systems, the reality is that there are numerous *interactions* between the dorsal and ventral systems. For example, Creem and Proffitt (2001) argued that perception for action sometimes involves the ventral system as well as the dorsal. According to them, we should distinguish between *effective* and *appropriate* grasping. We can grasp a toothbrush effectively by its bristles, but appropriate grasping involves picking it up by the handle. The key assumption is that appropriate grasping involves accessing stored knowledge about the object, with the consequence that appropriate grasping depends in part on the ventral stream.

What is the dual-process approach to visual perception? Is it an oversimplification?

Creem and Proffitt (2001) obtained evidence supporting the above assumption. Participants were asked to pick up various familiar objects with distinct handles (e.g., toothbrush, hammer, knife). The handle always pointed away from the participant, and the measure of interest was the percentage of occasions on which the objects were grasped appropriately. When this was the only task being performed, over 70% of the objects were grasped appropriately. However, performance was much worse when the participants found it hard to retrieve object knowledge from the ventral system because they had to perform a memory task at the same time. In this condition, only 25% of the objects were grasped appropriately. Thus, involvement of the ventral system is necessary to produce consistent appropriate grasping of objects.

EVALUATION AND CHAPTER SUMMARY

Introduction
- Visual perception is typically very accurate in everyday life and yet becomes inaccurate and distorted when we are presented with any of the well-known visual illusions.
- There are various explanations for this apparent paradox.
- One explanation is simply to dismiss findings on the visual illusions as irrelevant to ordinary visual perception because they involve highly artificial figures.
- Another possibility is to argue that the difficulty we have with visual illusions is that we treat them as three-dimensional figures even though we know they are only two-dimensional.
- A third possibility is that there are two rather separate visual perception systems. One of these systems (the vision-for-perception system) is used to make sense of the visual illusions, whereas the other system (the vision-for-action system) is used to move around the environment rapidly and safely.

Two visual systems: Illusions
- According to the perception–action model, there are separate vision-for-perception and vision-for-action systems.
- It is predicted that we will show illusory effects when using the former system but not when using the latter system.
- The available evidence provides some support for this prediction. However, our initial movement towards an object is often subject to an illusory effect, with the extent of any such effect decreasing as we approach the object.
- According to the planning–control model, visually guided movements are initially influenced by the planning system, but thereafter are influenced mainly by the control system.
- The planning system is more affected than the control system by illusory effects, which is why our movements towards target objects in illusory displays become progressively more accurate as we approach them.

Two visual systems: General
- Studies on brain-damaged patients have provided evidence supporting the notion that there are two separate visual systems.
- Patients with optic ataxia have damage to the dorsal stream and combine greatly impaired vision for action with reasonably intact visual object recognition.
- In contrast, some patients with visual agnosia have damage to the ventral stream and combine severely impaired visual object recognition with reasonable vision for action (e.g., grasping).
- According to the dual-process approach, the ventral stream typically provides detailed and accurate visual processing but operates slowly.
- In contrast, the dorsal system operates rapidly and is very sensitive to motion but it doesn't provide detailed consciously accessible visual information.

FURTHER READING

- Bruce, V., Green, P.R., & Georgeson, M.A. (2003). *Visual perception: Physiology, psychology and ecology* (4th ed.). Hove, UK: Psychology Press. Evidence on two visual systems is discussed thoroughly in this excellent textbook.
- Milner, A.D., & Goodale, M.A. (1995). *The visual brain in action*. Oxford: Oxford University Press. This important book provides an accessible and well-written introduction to some of the theoretical ideas discussed in this chapter.
- Morgan, M. (2003). *The space between our ears: How the brain represents visual space*. London: Weidenfeld & Nicolson. Some of the issues discussed in this chapter are considered in context in this entertaining book.
- Sekuler, R., & Blake, R. (2006). *Perception* (5th ed.). New York: McGraw-Hill. There is good introductory coverage of visual illusions and the two major visual processing systems in this textbook.

CHAPTER 3

CONTENTS

Introduction 39

Size perception 44

Evaluation and chapter summary 46

Further reading 47

How far away is that object?

INTRODUCTION

Most of us have no difficulty at all in perceiving the world around us as three-dimensional. This is more impressive than it might sound given that the retinal image used as the basis for visual perception is only *two*-dimensional and thus lacks depth. Of crucial importance to our *three*-dimensional experience is depth perception, which includes seeing some objects as closer to us than others. A crucial consequence of accurate depth perception is that we can reach out and pick up objects or walk around without knocking into anything (unless we have had too much to drink!).

Many psychologists have de-emphasized the importance of movement to depth perception by carrying out studies in which the observer and the objects presented are both static. In real life, in contrast, cues to depth are often provided by movement either of the observer or of objects in the visual environment. For example, **motion parallax** is a cue based on movement of an object's image over the retina due to movement of the observer's head. If you move sideways, the image of a nearby object moves further across the retina than does the image of an object at a greater distance from you. Something similar happens when you look through the windows of a moving train. The apparent speed of objects passing is faster the nearer they are to you. Rogers and Graham (1979) asked observers to look with one eye at a display containing about 2000 random dots. When there was relative motion of part of the display (motion parallax), the observers reported seeing a three-dimensional surface standing out in depth from its surroundings. Thus, motion parallax on its own can produce the perception of depth.

Gibson (1950) emphasized the information provided by our movement through the environment. One of his key ideas was the notion of **optic flow**. This consists of the changes in the pattern of light reaching an observer that is created when he or she moves or parts of the environment move. Gibson (1950) illustrated the perceptual experience produced by optic flow by considering a pilot approaching a landing strip. The point towards which the pilot is moving (the focus of expansion) appears motionless, with the rest of the visual environment apparently moving away from that point (see Figure 3.1). The further away any part of the landing strip is from that point, the greater is

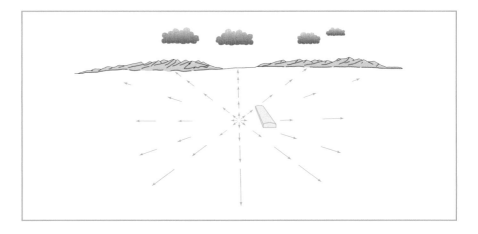

its apparent speed of movement. Thus, optic flow provides valuable information about the layout and distance of objects in the environment.

In this chapter, the major focus will be on depth cues available even if the observer and the objects in the environment are all static. These depth cues can conveniently be divided into monocular, binocular, and oculomotor cues. **Monocular cues** are those requiring only the use of one eye, although they can be used readily when someone has both eyes open. **Binocular cues** are those involving both eyes being used together. Finally, **oculomotor cues** are kinesthetic, depending on sensations of muscular contractions of the muscles around the eye.

Do you think that depth perception depends more on monocular cues or binocular ones? In some ways, it seems natural to argue that binocular vision is crucial to our perception of the world as three-dimensional, and so binocular cues are more important than monocular ones. As we will see, the truth is more complex. Binocular cues are only really effective when looking at objects very close to us. In contrast, numerous monocular cues are effective when viewing objects either close to us or far away.

MONOCULAR CUES

There are several monocular cues to depth. They are often called *pictorial cues*, because painters over the centuries have used them to create the impression of three-dimensional scenes when painting on two-dimensional canvases. One of the main pictorial cues is *linear perspective*—parallel lines pointing directly away from us seem progressively closer together as they recede into the distance (e.g., train tracks or the edges of a freeway). This convergence of lines creates a powerful impression of depth in a two-dimensional drawing.

Another monocular cue used by painters is *aerial perspective*. Light is scattered as it travels through the atmosphere, and this is especially so if the atmosphere is dusty. As a result, more distant objects lose contrast and seem somewhat hazy. O'Shea, Blackburn, and Ono (1994) mimicked the effects of aerial perspective. Reducing the contrast of features within a picture led those features to appear more distant. Thus, reduced contrast from aerial perspective is an effective cue to distance.

Another monocular cue related to perspective is *texture*. Many objects (e.g., cobble-stoned roads, carpets) possess texture, and textured objects slanting away from us have what Gibson (1979) described as a **texture gradient**. This is a gradient (rate of change) of texture density as you look from the front to the back of a slanting object (see Figure 3.2). If you were unwise enough to stand between the rails of a train track and look along it, you would see that the details would become less clear as you looked into the distance.

Evidence that texture is an important cue to distance was reported by Sinai, Ooi, and He (1998). Observers were good at judging the distance of objects within 7 meters (23 feet) of them when the ground in between had a uniform texture. However, distances were systematically overestimated when there was a gap (e.g., a ditch) in the texture pattern. Distance judgments were also prone to error when the ground between the observer and the object was divided into two regions having very different textures (e.g., concrete, grass).

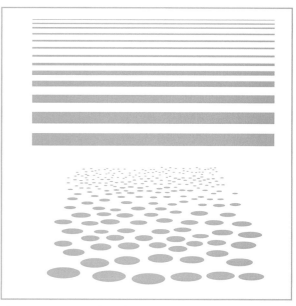

Figure 3.2 Examples of texture gradients creating an impression of depth. Bruce et al. (2003).

Another important monocular cue is *interposition*, in which a nearer object hides part of a more distant object from view. You can see how powerful interposition can be by looking at Kanizsa's (1976) illusory square (see Figure 3.3). There is a strong impression of a square in front of four blue circles in spite of the fact that most of the contours of the square are missing. In other words, the visual system makes sense of the four sectored black disks by perceiving an illusory interposed white square.

Shadows can provide surprisingly powerful depth cues. Kersten, Mamassian, and Knill (1997) presented observers with a gray ball and a dark ellipse (shadow) moving together in a box. In one condition, the shadow remained in contact with the bottom of the object, whereas in a second condition there was an *increasing* gap between the ball and its shadow followed by a *decreasing* gap. In the first condition, the ball seemed to slide backwards and forwards across the box, whereas it seemed to rise and fall in the second condition.

Not surprisingly, our knowledge of the familiar size of objects often influences our depth perception. For example, there is a sculptor whose sculptures include an enormous realistic-looking chair that is actually about 10 meters (33 feet) high. If you look at a photograph of this chair, it looks as if it is a normal-sized chair close to the camera, whereas in reality it is actually a long way away.

Think about a typical landscape painting. What cues can the artist employ to suggest depth exists on a flat canvas?

KEY TERM
Texture gradient: the rate of change of texture density from front to back of a slanting object.

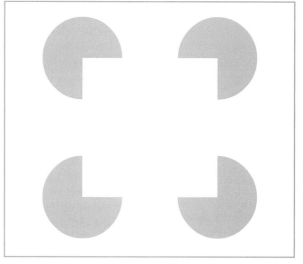

Figure 3.3 Kanizsa's (1976) illusory square.

Ittelson (1951) investigated the effects of *familiarity* in a study in which observers looked at playing cards through a peephole. This peephole ensured that the observers relied on monocular vision and couldn't make use of most cues to depth. There were three playing cards (normal size, half size, and double size) presented one at a time at a distance of 2.28 meters from the observer. On the basis of familiar size, the judged distance of the normal card should have been 2.28 meters, that of the half-size card 4.56 meters, and that of the double-size card 1.14 meters. The actual judged distances were 2.28 meters, 4.56 meters, and 1.38 meters, indicating that familiar size can be a powerful determinant of distance judgments.

A final monocular cue we will consider is *image blur*, which resembles aerial perspective. As Mather (1997, p. 1147) pointed out, "If one image region contains sharply focused texture, and another contains blurred texture, then the two regions may be perceived at different depths, even in the absence of other depth cues." He discussed his own findings on ambiguous stimuli consisting of two regions of texture (one sharp and one blurred) separated by a wavy boundary. When the boundary was sharp, the sharp texture was seen as nearer. However, the opposite was the case when the boundary was blurred. Thus, the boundary is seen as part of the nearer region.

In sum, there are many monocular cues we can use to ensure accurate depth perception. Most of the evidence we have discussed so far involves manipulating only *one* depth cue and observing its effects on depth perception. In the real world, of course, we are typically presented with several depth cues all at the same time, and it is a matter of importance to work out what happens in such circumstances. This issue is discussed a little later in the chapter.

BINOCULAR AND OCULOMOTOR CUES

In addition to the pictorial cues discussed above, depth perception also depends on oculomotor cues based on perceiving contractions of the muscles around the eyes. For example, there is **convergence**—this refers to the fact that the eyes turn inwards to focus on an object to a greater extent when it is very close than when it is further away. Another oculomotor cue is **accommodation**—this refers to the variation in optical power produced by a thickening of the lens of the eye when focusing on a close object.

There are two limitations with convergence and accommodation as depth cues. First, they are only effective with objects that are very close to the observer. For example, distance judgments based on accommodation are rather inaccurate even with nearby objects (e.g., Künnapas, 1968). Second, as Bruce, Green, and Georgeson (2003) pointed out, each cue only produces a *single* value at any given time, and so can at best provide information about the distance of only one object at a time.

Stereopsis is a more important cue than either convergence or accommodation. **Stereopsis** involves binocular cues—two slightly different pictures are presented at different locations so as to produce stereoscopic vision depending on the difference or disparity in the images projected on the retinas of the two eyes. The importance of stereopsis was shown by Wheatstone (1838), who probably invented the stereoscope. In a stereoscope, separate pictures or drawings are presented to an observer so that each eye receives essentially

KEY TERMS

Convergence: a cue to depth based on the eye turning inwards more when focusing on very close objects.

Accommodation: adjustment in the shape of the eye's lens when focusing on objects; a cue used in depth perception.

Stereopsis: a cue to depth based on binocular disparity.

the information it would receive if the object or objects depicted were actually presented. The simulation of the disparity or difference in the images presented to the two eyes produces a strong depth effect.

The limitation with stereopsis is that it rapidly becomes less effective at greater distances. This occurs because the disparity in the retinal images of an object decreases by a factor of 100 as its distance increases from 2 (6 feet) to 20 meters (65 feet) (Bruce et al., 2003).

One of the key processes involved in stereopsis is to match features in the input presented to the two eyes. Sometimes we make mistakes in doing this, which can lead to various visual illusions. For example, suppose you spend some time staring at wallpaper having a regular pattern. What you may find is that parts of the wallpaper pattern seem to float in front of the wall—this is known as the **wallpaper illusion**.

Something similar occurs with the autostereograms found in the well-known *Magic Eye* books. An **autostereogram** is a two-dimensional image containing depth information so that it appears as three-dimensional when viewed appropriately. If you only glance at an autostereogram, all you can see is a two-dimensional pattern. However, if you stare at it and strive *not* to bring it into focus, you can (sooner or later) see a three-dimensional image. Many people still have problems in seeing the three-dimensional image— what often helps is to hold the autostereogram very close to your face and then move it very slowly away while preventing it from coming into focus. The processes involved in seeing the three-dimensional image are complex (Tyler & Clarke, 1990). In essence, however, the dots that you link together differ from those linked before when seeing the two-dimensional image.

INTEGRATING CUE INFORMATION

As we have seen, psychologists often focus on the effects of a single cue on depth perception. However, in the real world we typically have access to several depth cues all at the same time. This raises the important issue of what we do when we have information available from two or more depth cues. Two possible strategies are the following (see Bruno & Cutting, 1988):

1. *Additivity*: All the information from different cues is simply added together.
2. *Selection*: Information from a single cue is used, with information from the other cue(s) simply being ignored.

Findings

Evidence for additivity was reported by Bruno and Cutting (1988). Observers viewed displays monocularly, and there were four sources of information about depth: relative size; height in the projection plane; interposition; and motion parallax. Depth judgments were based on combining information from all available cues. If two cues provide conflicting information, additivity would be shown if information from both cues was combined in making depth judgments. Supporting evidence was reported by Rogers and Collett (1989). When binocular disparity and motion parallax cues provided conflicting information about depth, observers resolved the conflict by taking both cues into account.

If you had to wear an eye patch your doctor may advise you to avoid driving for a while. Why is this a good idea?

KEY TERMS
Wallpaper illusion: a visual illusion in which staring at patterned wallpaper makes it seem as if parts of the pattern are floating in front of the wall.
Autostereogram: a complex two-dimensional image that is perceived as three-dimensional when it is *not* focused on for a period of time.

How do we combine various visual depth cues to form a single percept?

Observers generally make use of information from all available cues in depth perception (although we will discuss some exceptions soon). It can easily be argued that this is a reasonable strategy to adopt. Any depth cue can provide inaccurate information under some circumstances, and so relying exclusively on one cue would often lead to errors in depth perception.

In spite of the evidence for additivity of cues, there are several situations in which depth perception is influenced mainly (or exclusively) by only one cue. For example, Bruce et al. (2003) discussed evidence based on "pseudo-scopic" viewing in which the information presented to the left and right eyes is reversed using optical means. If stereoscopic information is all-important, pseudoscopic viewing should reverse perceived depth. That is precisely what happens with random-dot stereograms and with pictures of wire-frame objects. However, pseudoscopic viewing of photographed scenes rarely produces reversed depth for the objects (e.g., cars, buildings) shown in the photograph. What is happening here is that other cues (e.g., knowledge of objects, perspective, occlusion) dominate over stereoscopic cues.

The "hollow face" illusion (Gregory, 1973) is another example of stereo-scopic information being ignored. When a hollow mask of a face is seen from a few feet away, observers typically see it as a normal face. As Hill and Bruce (1993) found, this illusion is influenced by factors such as the familiarity of the face and observers' preference for convexity (perceiving object as bulging outwards).

As yet, we don't have a detailed understanding of these diverse findings. However Massaro (1985) has proposed an interesting theoretical approach based on fuzzy logic. **Fuzzy logic** is used when we are dealing with imprecise data and when we are concerned with degrees of truth rather than definite truth or falsity. In his fuzzy logical model of perception, Massaro (1985) argued for an approach rather different from the additivity or selection strategies. According to him, when evidence from different cues is combined, the influence of relatively unambiguous cues is greater than that of ambiguous ones. Information from the aggregate of the various cues is then used to calculate depth.

SIZE PERCEPTION

It has often been suggested that there are important connections between depth perception and size perception. For example, it is assumed in the size–distance invariance hypothesis (Kilpatrick & Ittelson, 1953) that for a given size of retinal image, the perceived size of an object is proportional to its perceived distance. One of the implications of this hypothesis is that accurate assessment of an object's distance allows us to judge its size accurately. This can help us to understand size constancy, which is the tendency for objects to appear the same size whether their size in the retinal image is large or small. For example, if someone walks towards you, their retinal image increases progressively, but their size seems to remain the same. Part of what is involved is that we take account of the reducing distance of the other person from us in judging their size.

KEY TERMS
Fuzzy logic: used to combine information from cues in perception when the available information is imprecise.

FINDINGS

If size judgments depend on perceived distance, then size constancy shouldn't be found when an object's perceived distance is very different from its actual distance. The Ames room provides a good example (see Figure 3.4). It has a peculiar shape: the floor slopes and the rear wall is not at right angles to the adjoining walls. In spite of this, the Ames room creates the same retinal image as a normal rectangular room when viewed through a peephole. The fact that one end of the rear wall is much farther from the viewer is disguised by making it much higher. The cues suggesting that the rear wall is at right angles to the viewer are so strong that observers mistakenly assume that two adults standing in the corners by the rear wall are at the same distance from them. This leads them to estimate the size of the nearer adult as being much greater than that of the adult who is further away. In other words, errors in perceived distance lead to errors in perceived size.

What types of cognitive problems may leave people susceptible to failures of size constancy?

The illusion effect with the Ames room is so great that an individual walking left and right in front of the rear wall appears to grow and shrink as he or she moves! However, it has been argued that observers are more likely to realize what is going on if the person walking backwards and forwards is someone they know very well. There is an anecdote about a researcher's wife who arrived at the laboratory to find him inside the Ames room. Her immediate reaction was to call out, "Gee, honey, that room's distorted!" (Ian Gordon, personal communication).

There is evidence indicating that size perception of objects often depends on factors other than perceptual information about their distance from the observer. According to Haber and Levin (2001), what is crucial is the observer's *memory* of the familiar size of the objects in question. In their first experiment, Haber and Levin (2001) found that observers were able to estimate the sizes of common objects with great accuracy purely on the basis of memory. They then presented observers with various objects at close viewing range (0–50 meters) or distant viewing range (50–100 meters), and asked them to make size judgments. Some objects came from categories of objects

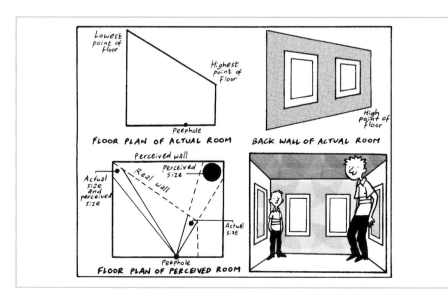

Figure 3.4 The Ames room

that are almost invariant in size or height (e.g., tennis rackets, guitars, bicycles). In contrast, other objects belonged to categories of objects varying in size (e.g., house plants, television sets, Christmas trees). Finally, there were some unfamiliar stimuli (ovals, rectangles, and triangles of various sizes).

What would we predict the findings would be? If familiar size is of major importance, then size judgments should be better for objects of invariant size than those of variable size, with size judgments being worst for unfamiliar objects. Suppose that distance perception is all-important. Distances are estimated more accurately for nearby objects than for more distant ones, so size judgments for all categories should be better at close than at distant viewing range. The actual findings indicated the importance of familiar size to accuracy of size judgments. However, we obviously cannot account for the fairly high accuracy of size judgments of unfamiliar objects in terms of familiar size. As Haber and Levin (2001, p. 1150) admitted, "We do not know how the subjects arrived at the size estimations for the unfamiliar objects in this experiment."

EVALUATION AND CHAPTER SUMMARY

Introduction
- Information from different depth cues is typically combined to produce accurate depth perception, and this often occurs in an additive way, but there are various situations in which one cue is dominant over others, and still other situations in which one cue is selected in preference to others.
- However, depth perception is most likely to be based almost entirely on one cue when different cues provide very conflicting information.
- This is sensible. If, for example, one cue suggests an object is 10 meters away and another cue suggests it is 90 meters away, it is probably a silly idea to split the difference and decide it is 50 meters away! What is more likely is that for some reason one of the cues is providing very misleading information.
- Note that large conflicts between cues are rarely found in naturalistic settings. As a consequence, relying almost exclusively on one cue in depth perception may occur much more often in the laboratory than in the real world.

Size perception
- Some of the factors responsible for size perception and size constancy have been identified.
- Two of the most important factors are perceived distance and memory for familiar size.
- However, as yet we don't have a coherent account of *how* these (and other) factors combine to produce size judgments. As Haber and Levin (2001, p. 1140) pointed out, "Explanations of the sources of information and processing mechanisms that human observers depend on for the perception of size have been very unsatisfying and share nothing of the complexity and completeness of the comparable descriptions for distance perception."

FURTHER READING

- Bruce, V., Green, P.R., & Georgeson, M.A. (2003). *Visual perception: Physiology, psychology and ecology* (4th ed.). Hove, UK: Psychology Press. Much relevant research on depth perception is discussed in Chapter 7 of this excellent textbook.
- Healy, A.F., & Proctor, R.W. (2003). *Handbook of psychology: Experimental psychology, vol. 4*. New York: Wiley & Sons. This edited book contains a chapter by Proffitt and Caudek on depth perception.
- Morgan, M. (2003). *The space between our ears: How the brain represents visual space*. London: Weidenfeld & Nicolson. There is entertaining coverage of issues relating to depth and size perception in this book.
- Sekuler, R., & Blake, R. (2006). *Perception* (5th ed.). New York: McGraw-Hill. This textbook contains good introductory coverage of depth and size perception.

CHAPTER 4

CONTENTS

Introduction 49

Unconscious perception and
perceptual defense 50

Blindsight 54

Conclusions 57

Evaluation and chapter summary 58

Further reading 59

Perception without awareness?

4

INTRODUCTION

Can we perceive aspects of the visual world in the absence of any conscious awareness that we are doing so? In other words, is there such a thing as **unconscious perception** (i.e., perception occurring even though the stimulus is below the threshold of conscious awareness)? Common sense suggests that the answer is, "No", in part because the notion of unconscious perception sounds like a contradiction in terms as does perception without awareness.

The issue of whether unconscious perception exists has been a matter of controversy for thousands of years. Many ancient Greeks (including Aristotle and Socrates) were perfectly happy with the notion of perception without awareness (see Dixon, 2004). However, for much of the twentieth century most experimental psychologists rejected the notion. This applied especially to an aspect of unconscious perception known as **perceptual defense**, in which emotionally loaded or taboo words are more difficult to perceive than neutral stimuli. What happened in studies on perceptual defense (see Dixon, 1981) was that rude or emotionally loaded words (e.g., whore, rape, shit) and neutral words (e.g., table, tree, cloud) were presented one a time. Initially, each word was presented so briefly that it couldn't be identified. After that, the exposure time was gradually increased until eventually the participants could name the word. The key finding was that emotionally loaded words had to be presented for significantly longer than neutral words before they could be identified, even when the two types of words were carefully matched for word frequency, length, and so on.

On the face of it, it seems hard to imagine we can defend ourselves against a taboo or emotionally loaded stimulus unless we have already perceived and identified it. The general skepticism among psychologists was expressed forcibly by Howie (1952, p. 311): "To speak of perceptual defense is to use a mode of discourse which must make any precise or even intelligible meaning of perceptual defense impossible, for it is to speak of perceptual process as somehow being both a process of knowing and a process of avoiding knowing."

The case for unconscious perception apparently received support from the notorious "research" carried out in 1957 by James Vicary, who was a struggling market researcher. He claimed to have flashed the words EAT POPCORN and DRINK COCA-COLA for 1/300th of a second (well below the threshold of conscious awareness) numerous times during showings of a film called *Picnic* at a cinema in Fort Lee, New Jersey. A grand total of 45,699 people allegedly received these messages over a 6-week period. The power of unconscious perception was apparently shown in the finding that there was an increase of 18% in the cinema sales of Coca-Cola and a 58% increase in popcorn sales. Alas, Vicary admitted in 1962 that the study was a fabrication. In addition, Trappery (1996) combined data from 23 studies in a meta-analysis and found that stimuli presented below the conscious threshold had little or no effect on consumer behavior.

These negative findings haven't stopped advertisers from trying to influence our buying habits by means of unconscious perception. For example, in 1990 Pepsi Cola was forced to withdraw one of its "Cool Can" designs. The reason was that when the cans were stacked in a certain way the red and blue lines on the design spelled out the word "SEX." It has also been alleged that there is a problem with the standard pack of Camel cigarettes. If you peer very closely at the left front leg of the camel shown on the pack, you can see the image of a naked man with an erect penis facing the rear of the camel!

The finding that subliminal stimuli don't influence buying behavior doesn't mean that subliminal stimuli have *no* effect whatsoever. In what follows, we consider two main strands of research on subliminal perception. First, we consider studies on individuals with normal vision presented with stimuli they report being unable to see. Second, we consider studies on brain-damaged patients who claim to have no conscious awareness of visual stimuli presented to parts of their visual field.

UNCONSCIOUS PERCEPTION AND PERCEPTUAL DEFENSE

There are three main ways in which researchers attempt to present people having normal vision with visual stimuli below the level of conscious awareness. First, they can present stimuli that are very weak or faint. Second, they can present stimuli very briefly. Third, there is masking, in which the target stimulus is immediately preceded by a masking stimulus that inhibits processing of the target stimulus.

Before considering the evidence for subliminal perception in normally sighted individuals, it is worth discussing the key issue of how to decide whether an observer is consciously aware of a given visual stimulus. As Merikle, Smilek, and Eastwood (2001) pointed out, there is an important distinction between two criteria or thresholds:

What is an objective threshold? *Why have many psychologists favored this measure of perception?*

1. *Subjective threshold*: This is defined by an individual's failure to report conscious awareness of a stimulus, and is the most obvious measure to use.
2. *Objective threshold*: This is defined by an individual's inability to make an accurate forced-choice decision about a stimulus (e.g., guess at above chance level whether it is a word).

Two issues arise with these threshold measures. First, as Reingold (2004, p. 882) pointed out, "A valid measure must index *all* of the perceptual information available to consciousness ... and *only* conscious, but not unconscious information." That is a tall order. Second, it is also easier said than done to show that either measure indicates zero conscious awareness given the difficulty (or impossibility) of proving the null hypothesis.

In practice, observers often show "awareness" of a stimulus assessed by the objective threshold even when the stimulus doesn't exceed the subjective threshold. Thus, what seems to be unconscious perception using the subjective threshold is often no longer subliminal when the objective threshold is used. What should we do in these circumstances? The objective threshold may seem unduly stringent, but many psychologists argue it is more valid than a reliance on people's possibly inaccurate or biased reports of their conscious experience. What seems indisputable is that evidence for subliminal perception based on the objective threshold is more convincing than evidence based on the subjective threshold.

FINDINGS

Dehaene et al. (1998) carried out a study using the objective threshold in which they showed that observers couldn't distinguish between trials on which a masked digit was or wasn't presented very briefly. After that, observers were presented on each trial with a masked digit followed by a clearly visible target digit, and they decided whether this target digit was larger or smaller than 5. The masked digit was either *congruent* with the target digit (both numbers on the same side of 5) or it was *incongruent*. The key finding was that performance was slower on incongruent trials than on congruent ones, indicating that information from the masked digit must have been processed.

Dehaene et al. (2001) used **functional magnetic resonance imaging (fMRI)** and **event-related potentials (ERPs)** to identify brain areas active during the processing of masked words that weren't consciously perceived, and unmasked words that were consciously perceived. In one condition, a masked word was followed by unmasked presentation of the same word. There were two main findings. First, there was detectable brain activity when masked words were presented. However, it was much less than when unmasked words were presented, especially in prefrontal and parietal areas. Second, the amount of brain activity produced by presentation of an unmasked word was reduced when preceded by the same word presented masked. This repetition suppression effect suggests that some of the processing typically found when a word is presented occurs even when it is presented below the conscious threshold.

Snodgrass, Bernat, and Shevrin (2004) carried out meta-analyses involving nine studies to assess the strength of the evidence for unconscious perception at the objective detection threshold. In their first meta-analysis, there was no significant evidence of above-chance performance on measures of conscious perception. However, in their second meta-analysis, there was very highly significant evidence of above-chance performance on measures designed to assess unconscious perception. As Snodgrass et al. (2004, p. 888) concluded, "Formal meta-analyses ... provide strong evidence for large, reliable unconscious perceptual effects."

KEY TERMS

Functional magnetic resonance imaging (fMRI): a technique providing information about brain activity based on the detection of magnetic changes; it has reasonable temporal and spatial resolution.

Event-related potentials (ERPs): the pattern of electroencephalograph (EEG) activity obtained by averaging the brain responses to the same stimulus presented repeatedly.

Many of the findings apparently supporting the notion of subliminal perception may be less convincing than they appear. For example, it is hard to eliminate the possibility that unconscious perception is simply a pale imitation of typical conscious perception based on responding to consciously perceived fragments of visual stimuli. More compelling evidence can be obtained if we can find situations in which the effects of subliminal perception are very *different* from those of normal perception rather than merely being weaker.

Is subliminal (unconscious) perception just a weaker form of normal perception? Explain your answer.

An example of a study conforming to the above specification is one by Groeger (1984). He presented target words followed immediately afterwards by a matrix of 24 words. Each target word was presented so briefly that it was undetected (unconscious perception condition) or it was presented sufficiently long for participants to report awareness of it (conscious perception condition). Participants were instructed to select the target word from the matrix. In fact, the target word was never included in the matrix, but words similar in meaning or in structure (same- or similar-shaped letters) to it were included. For example, suppose the target word was "change." "Differ" is a word similar in meaning and "orange" is a word similar in structure. In the conscious perception condition, participants tended to choose words *structurally* similar to the target word. In contrast, in the subliminal perception condition, participants tended to choose words similar in *meaning* to the target word.

Debner and Jacoby (1994) also focused on trying to show that unconscious perception can produce different effects to conscious perception. They assumed that information perceived with awareness permits us to control our actions, whereas information perceived without awareness doesn't. They tested these assumptions by presenting observers with a word for either 50 or 150 ms followed by a mask. Immediately after that, the first three letters of the word were presented again, and observers were instructed to think of the first word coming to mind starting with those letters, *except* for the word that had just been masked (exclusion condition). There was also a control condition, in which each word stem was preceded by an unrelated word.

When the masked word was presented for 150 ms, the participants followed instructions to avoid using that word on the word-stem completion task (see Figure 4.1). Presumably they perceived the masked word consciously, and so deliberately avoided using it. In contrast, when the masked word was presented for only 50 ms, it was often used to complete the word (see Figure 4.1). Presumably limited processing of the masked word below the conscious level automatically triggered activation of its representation in memory and made it accessible on the word-stem completion task.

As mentioned earlier, the phenomenon of perceptual defense (greater difficulty in perceiving threatening words) appears to involve a form of subliminal perception. Perceptual defense has a Freudian feel about it, because it suggests that

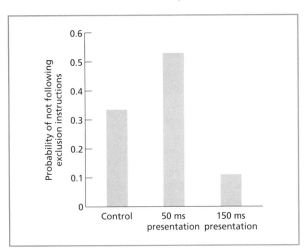

Figure 4.1 Probability of not following exclusion instructions in control (no relevant preceding word), 50 ms word presentation, and 150 ms word presentation conditions. Based on data in Debner and Jacoby (1994).

we "defend" ourselves against threatening material and so find it harder to recognize than neutral material.

Critics of the phenomenon of perceptual defense have argued that participants may *perceive* taboo or emotionally loaded words as rapidly as neutral ones, but are simply more reluctant to *say* them until they are certain. Dixon (1981) discussed several studies designed to handle this issue. For example, researchers asked participants to learn paired associates, some of which had an emotional word paired with a neutral one (e.g., table–rape, whore–tree). After that, the *first* word of each pair was presented for progressively longer periods, but the participants were instructed to say the *second* word. Thus, for example, if "whore" were presented, participants would say "tree." Perceptual defense was reported in some of these studies even though participants didn't have to say the taboo or emotionally loaded words. However, the findings tended to be rather inconsistent (see Dixon, 1981).

Hardy and Legge (1968) argued that the problem of response bias could be solved in a different way. They asked participants to detect the presence of a faint auditory stimulus while watching a screen on which emotional or neutral words were presented subliminally. Nearly all of the participants failed to notice that any words had been presented. However, the auditory threshold was higher when emotional words were being presented. Presumably the subliminal presentation of emotionally loaded words had an inhibitory effect on perceptual processing, and such inhibitory effects are responsible for producing the perceptual defense effect.

Most research on subliminal perception has focused on the *visual* modality. However, *smells* presented subliminally can also affect our reactions to stimuli. For example, Cowley, Johnson, and Brooksbank (1977) presented male participants with female **pheromones** (chemical substances produced by individuals and having a communicative function) that couldn't be detected consciously. The inhalation of these pheromones by the male participants increased the attractiveness of women whose photographs they rated.

An important issue that hasn't received much attention is whether unconsciously perceived information has long-lasting effects. Most laboratory experiments have focused on very short-term effects (i.e., 2–3 seconds), and clearly unconscious perception is of limited importance if its effects last no longer than that. Reassuring evidence was assembled by Merikle and Daneman (1996) in an analysis of numerous studies on the long-term effects of unconscious perception in the *auditory* modality. The studies were all carried out while the participants were under general anesthetic undergoing an operation. In most of these studies, the patients wore earphones while words were played repeatedly on a tape. After surgery, the patients claimed not to remember being presented with any words. However, they typically possessed some memory for the words when memory was assessed by indirect tests such as completing word stems (e.g., "p r o - -"). Memory for the words was greatest at short retention intervals, but was clearly present at all times up to 24 hours. Thus, unconsciously perceived information can have relatively long-lasting effects.

BLINDSIGHT

Numerous British soldiers in the First World War who had received head injuries in the course of battle were treated by an Army doctor by the name of George Riddoch. He found something fascinating in many of those with injuries to the primary visual cortex (Brodmann Area 17). This area is at the back of the occipital area of the brain (see Figure 1.4) and is involved in the early stages of visual processing. Unsurprisingly, these patients had a loss of perception in some parts of the visual field. What was much more surprising was that they could still detect motion in those parts of the visual field in which they claimed to be blind (Riddoch, 1917)! Brain-damaged patients having some visual perception in the absence of any conscious awareness are said to have **blindsight**, which neatly captures the apparently paradoxical nature of their condition. Patients with blindsight often possess various perceptual abilities: "Detection and localization of light, and detection of motion are invariably preserved to some degree. In addition, many patients can discriminate orientation, shape, direction of movement, and flicker. Color vision mechanisms also appear to be preserved in some cases" (Farah, 2001, p. 162).

The primary visual cortex plays a very important role in normal vision, and yet those parts of it corresponding to their blind field are severely damaged and unusable in patients with blindsight. How, then, do the patients manage to show evidence of some perceptual abilities? The first point that needs to be emphasized is that blindsight patients are very diverse in terms of the precise brain damage they have suffered. Thus, there can be no *single* answer to the question. Second, there are at least 10 pathways from the eye into the brain, and many of them can be used by blindsight patients (Cowey, 2004). Thus, there are several potential ways in which residual perceptual processing in blindsight patients could occur. Third, there is some evidence that cortical mechanisms aren't essential. Köhler and Moscovitch (1997) discussed findings from several patients who had had an entire cortical hemisphere removed, and thus could presumably only make use of subcortical mechanisms to process visual stimuli presented to their removed hemisphere. These patients showed evidence of blindsight for stimulus detection, stimulus localization, form discrimination, and motion detection. Fourth, blindsight patients having a cortical visual system (apart from primary visual cortex) can perform a wider range of perceptual tasks (e.g., making judgments about color) than those lacking a cerebral hemisphere (Stoerig & Cowey, 1997).

The phenomenon of blindsight becomes somewhat less paradoxical if we consider how it is assessed in a little more detail. There are generally two different measures. First, there are patients' subjective reports that they cannot see some stimulus presented to their blind region. Second, there is a forced-choice test, in which patients have to guess (e.g., stimulus present or absent?) or point at the stimulus they cannot see, or their eye movements are observed. Blindsight is defined by an absence of self-reported visual perception accompanied by above-chance performance on the forced-choice test. Note that the two measures are very different from each other.

There is a point to be emphasized before we turn to the research findings. As Cowey (2004, p. 588) pointed out, "The impression is sometimes given, however unwittingly, that blindsight differs from normal vision only in that it

How is subjective and objective threshold testing carried out with blindsight patients? What do the findings typically show?

KEY TERM
Blindsight: the ability of some brain-damaged patients to respond appropriately to visual stimuli in the absence of conscious visual perception.

is unaccompanied by any visual percept, as if it were like normal vision stripped of conscious visual experience. Nothing could be further from the truth, for blindsight is characterized by severely impoverished discrimination of visual stimuli."

FINDINGS

The most thoroughly studied patient with blindsight is DB. He underwent surgical removal of the right occipital cortex including most of primary visual cortex, and has been studied over a period of many years by Larry Weiskrantz. He showed some perceptual skills, including an ability to detect whether a visual stimulus had been presented to the blind area and to identify its location. In spite of DB's performance, he reported no conscious visual experience in his blind field. According to Weiskrantz, Warrington, Sanders, and Marshall (1974, p. 721), "When he was shown his results [by presenting them to a part of his visual field in which he had normal vision] he expressed surprise and insisted several times that he thought he was just 'guessing'. When he was shown a video film of his reaching and judging orientation of lines, he was openly astonished."

Some of the most impressive findings were reported by de Gelder, Vroemen, and Pourtois (2001). They found that GY could discriminate whether an unseen face had a happy or a fearful expression. It is not certain how best to interpret this finding, since it is improbable that GY was able to process the subtleties of facial expression. The likelihood is that he was responding to some distinctive facial feature (e.g., fearful faces have wide-open eyes).

The notion that blindsight is not at all like near-threshold normal vision would receive considerable support if it could be shown that they differ clearly from each other. Relevant evidence was reported by Kentridge, Heywood, and Weiskrantz (1999). They found that a blindsight patient (GY) could discriminate the location of low-contrast targets in his blind field, in the absence of a cue indicating approximately when the target would appear. However, GY performed at chance level when given a similar task in his spared visual field, in spite of reporting more awareness of these low-contrast stimuli in the spared field than the blind one. Kentridge et al. (1999, p. 479) concluded that, "GY's blindsight is qualitatively different from near-threshold normal vision."

There are uncertainties about what it means when a blindsight patient says he or she has no conscious awareness of a visual stimulus. Accordingly, it would be useful to study the perceptual abilities of blindsight patients *without* having to rely on their subjective reports of what they can see in the blind field. This was done by Marcel (1998). He found that a complete circle strad-dling the normal and blind areas was perceived as being more complete than a partial circle whose missing part was in the blind field.

Rafal, Smith, Krantz, Cohen, and Brennan (1990) also focused on the issue of whether perceptual performance in the intact visual field is influenced by stimuli presented to the blind field. Blindsight patients performed at chance when deciding whether a light had been presented to the blind area of the visual field. However, the time they took to direct their eyes at a light presented to the *intact* part of the visual field increased when a light was presented to the

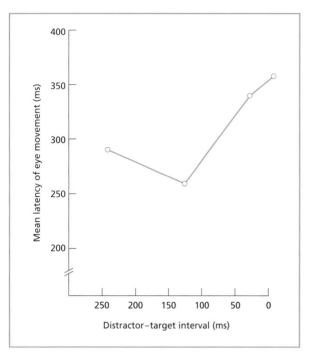

Figure 4.2 Mean latency of eye movement to target in intact visual field as a function of the time interval between onset of the unseen distractor and onset of the target in blindsight patients. Based on data in Rafal et al. (1990).

What criticisms have been made against blindsight research?

blind area at the same time (see Figure 4.2). Thus, the blindsight patients processed the light in the blind area to some extent even though they showed no evidence of detecting it when deciding whether it was present or absent.

In spite of all the evidence that blindsight is a genuine phenomenon, there have been numerous criticisms of the research. We will consider three such criticisms here. First, the reports of some blindsight patients suggest they may have residual conscious vision. We have focused on blindsight patients claiming to have no conscious awareness at all when presented with visual stimuli to their blind field. However, some patients claim to be aware that *something* is happening even though they cannot see anything. Weiskrantz (e.g., 2004) used the term blindsight Type 1 to describe patients with no conscious awareness, and the term blindsight Type 2 to describe those with awareness that something was happening. An example of Type 2 blindsight was found in patient EY, who "sensed a definite pinpoint of light," although "it does not actually look like a light. It looks like nothing at all" (Weiskrantz, 1980). Type 2 blindsight may sound suspiciously like residual conscious vision. However, what is probably involved is that patients who have been tested many times start to rely on indirect evidence (Cowey, 2004). For example, consider patients who have above-chance ability to guess whether a stimulus is moving to the left or to the right. Their performance may depend in part on a vague awareness of their own eye movements, and this is what produces Type 2 blindsight.

Second, Wessinger, Fendrich, and Gazzaniga (1997) argued that some blindsight patients have preserved "islands" of function within the primary visual cortex, and so don't really suffer from blindsight. As evidence, they found blindsight patients who had conscious awareness of visual stimuli presented to certain small regions of the visual field. However, this criticism doesn't apply generally to blindsight patients. As Cowey (2004, p. 580) pointed out, "Many patients with blindsight have now been structurally imaged by MRI, and in some of them ... there is not a shred of evidence that striate cortex [primary visual cortex] is spared in the region corresponding to the huge field defect."

Third, Campion, Latto, and Smith (1983) argued that stray light may fall into the intact visual field. As a consequence, the ability of blindsight patients to show above-chance performance on various detection tasks is due to processing within the intact visual field rather than the "blind" visual field. This criticism probably possesses some validity. However, blindsight is still observed when attempts are made to prevent stray light from affecting performance (see Cowey, 2004). In addition, if blindsight patients are actually processing within the intact visual field, it is unclear why they lack conscious awareness of such processing.

CONCLUSIONS

There has been a steady accumulation of evidence indicating the existence of unconscious perception or what used to be known as subliminal perception. Much of the early research was flawed and inconclusive, but the phenomenon has continued to be reported in well-controlled studies using various ingenious methods. The argument for unconscious perception is strengthened by the fact that studies on intact individuals and on brain-damaged patients with blindsight both point to the same conclusion.

Even though the evidence for unconscious perception is reasonably convincing, there is still the issue of making theoretical sense of the findings. If the truth be told, we haven't made much theoretical headway in understanding what is involved in unconscious perception. According to Holender and Duscherer (2004), the fact there has been only limited theoretical progress is a reason for being skeptical about the very existence of unconscious perception. However, that seems like an excessive reaction. As Snodgrass et al. (2004, p. 893) pointed out, "In the history of science, empirical phenomena are virtually always identified well before detailed explanations become available (e.g., gravity, genetics). Indeed, since nobody yet understands what makes conscious perceptions conscious, it makes little sense to demand analogous [comparable] explanations for unconscious perception at this time."

Why may a degree of unconscious perception be to our advantage on an everyday basis?

Do you find it perplexing that conscious awareness seems less important in visual perception than you had imagined? We can make a start to understanding what is happening by accepting that we are consciously aware of the *outcome* of our internal cognitive processes rather than of the processes themselves. For example, when you listen to someone speaking, you typically focus on the meaning of what they are saying. However, there is overwhelming evidence that several complex processes are involved in speech perception (see Chapter 18). The key point is that we are generally blissfully unaware of all these processes going on.

There is plenty of other evidence indicating that conscious awareness often occurs surprisingly late in processing (see Chapter 28). For example, we believe that our actions are caused by our conscious intentions. However, evidence that that is not the case was reported by Frith, Perry, and Lumer (1999). Their participants were presented with three rods and had to grasp the illuminated one. On some trials, the rod that was illuminated changed *after* participants had started to move their hand. They had been instructed to make a vocal response to indicate their conscious awareness of the target switch. The key finding was that participants often grasped the new target rod about 300 ms *before* making the vocal response. This suggests that participants were not consciously aware of the change in target rod when they altered their hand movement to accommodate the change in target.

An important milestone in our theoretical understanding of subliminal perception was an article by Erdelyi (1974). He argued persuasively that we should reject the notion of perception as a *single* event. Instead, we should think of perception as involving multiple processing stages or mechanisms, with consciousness possibly representing the final stage of processing. Thus, it is entirely possible for a stimulus input to receive sufficient perceptual processing to influence at least some aspects of behavior without conscious perceptual experience.

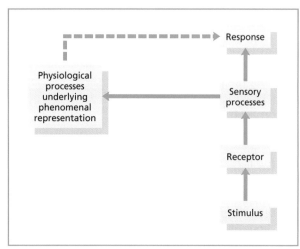

Figure 4.3 Processes involved in conscious (dotted line) and subliminal (solid line) perception. Adapted from Dixon (2004). From *Oxford Companion to the Mind* edited by R. Gregory (2004). By permission of Oxford University Press.

Dixon (2004) proposed a theoretical framework consistent with Erdelyi's (1974) earlier suggestions (see Figure 4.3). The major assumption incorporated into this framework is as follows: "The brain processes underlying conscious experience differ from those that mediate between incoming stimuli and outgoing responses ... information may be transmitted through the organism without ever achieving conscious representation" (Dixon, 2004, p. 885). Such a theoretical approach may lack the drama and complexity of Sigmund Freud's colorful views on the mysteries of the unconscious, but is much more likely to be in approximate accord with reality.

EVALUATION AND CHAPTER SUMMARY

Unconscious perception and perceptual defense
- We can use either a subjective threshold or a more stringent objective threshold to decide whether an observer is consciously aware of a visual stimulus.
- There is evidence for subliminal perception with both thresholds.
- Some of the strongest evidence has been obtained in studies in which the effects of unconscious perception are very different from those of normal perception.
- Additional evidence has come from studies on perceptual defense and research in the olfactory (smell) and auditory modalities.
- Research on anesthetized individuals indicates that the effects of subliminal perception can last for at least 24 hours.

Blindsight
- Patients with blindsight have severe damage to the primary visual cortex.
- They possess various perceptual abilities (e.g., detection and localization of light, detection of motion) even though they have no conscious awareness of the relevant stimuli.
- Some of the most convincing evidence for blindsight comes from studies in which perceptual information in the intact visual field is affected by stimuli presented to the blind field.
- Some blindsight patients report awareness that something is happening even though they cannot see anything (blindsight Type 2). This awareness is probably due to indirect information (e.g., from their own eye movements) rather than to residual conscious vision.
- Overall, the evidence is reasonably convincing that blindsight is a genuine phenomenon.

FURTHER READING

- Cowey, A. (2004). Fact, artefact, and myth about blindsight. *Quarterly Journal of Experimental Psychology*, *57A*, 577–609. This article by a leading researcher on blindsight provides a balanced and comprehensive account of our current knowledge about that condition.
- Merikle, P.M., Smilek, D., & Eastwood, J.D. (2001). Perception without awareness: Perspectives from cognitive psychology. *Cognition*, *79*, 115–134. There is good coverage of research on subliminal perception in individuals with intact vision in this article.
- Snodgrass, M., Bernat, E., & Shevrin, H. (2004). Unconscious perception at the objective detection threshold exists. *Perception & Psychophysics*, *66*, 888–895. The authors of this article carried out meta-analyses to provide good evidence for the existence of unconscious perception.
- Weiskrantz, L. (1997). *Consciousness lost and found*. Oxford: Oxford University Press. This is a readable book by one of the world's leading authorities on blindsight.

CHAPTER 5

CONTENTS

Introduction	61
Perceptual organization	62
Viewpoint-dependent or viewpoint-invariant?	64
Disorders of object recognition	68
Evaluation and chapter summary	72
Further reading	73

5

What is this I see before me?

INTRODUCTION

Something we all do tens of thousands of times a day is to identify or recognize objects in the world around us. At this precise moment, you are aware that you are looking at a book (possibly with your eyes glazed over). If you raise your eyes, then perhaps you can see a wall, windows, and so on in front of you. I imagine you would agree with me that it appears incredibly easy to recognize common objects—it doesn't seem to require any effort or thinking at all. In fact, there are various reasons for arguing that the processes involved in object recognition are actually far more complex than appears to be the case:

1. If you look around you, you will find that many of the objects in the environment overlap with each other. As a result, you have to decide where one object ends and the next one starts.
2. We can all recognize an object such as a chair without any apparent difficulty. However, chairs (and many other objects) vary enormously in their visual properties (e.g., color, size, shape), and it is not immediately clear how we manage to assign such diverse stimuli to the same category.
3. We recognize objects accurately over a wide range of viewing distances and orientations. For example, most plates are round but we can still identify a plate even when it is seen from an angle and so appears elliptical. We are also confident that the ant-like creatures we can see from the window of a plane as we begin our descent are actually people.

In spite of all these complexities, we can generally go beyond simply identifying objects in the visual environment. For example, we can typically describe what an object would look like if we viewed it from a different angle, and we also know its uses and functions. All in all, there is much more to object recognition than might initially be supposed (than meets the eye?).

PERCEPTUAL ORGANIZATION

A fundamental issue in visual perception is perceptual segregation, which is our ability to work out accurately which parts of the visual information presented to us belong together and thus form objects. The first systematic attempt to study perceptual segregation (and the perceptual organization to which it gives rise) was made by the Gestaltists. They were German psychologists (including Koffka, Köhler, and Wertheimer) many of whom emigrated to the United States before the Second World War. Their fundamental principle of perceptual organization was the law of Prägnanz: "Of several geometrically possible organisations that one will actually occur which possesses the best, simplest and most stable shape" (Koffka, 1935, p. 138).

The Gestaltists proposed several other laws, but most of them are specific examples of the law of Prägnanz (see Figure 5.1). The fact that three horizontal arrays of dots rather than vertical groups are seen in Figure 5.1(a) indicates that visual elements tend to be grouped together if they are close to each other (the law of proximity). Figure 5.1(b) illustrates the law of similarity, which states that elements will be grouped together perceptually if they are similar. Vertical columns rather than horizontal rows are seen because the elements in the vertical column are the same, whereas those in the horizontal rows are not. We see two crossing lines in Figure 5.1(c) because according to the law of good continuation we group together those elements requiring the fewest changes or interruptions in straight or smoothly curving lines. Finally, Figure 5.1(d) illustrates the law of closure, according to which missing parts of a figure are filled in to complete the figure. Thus, a circle is seen even though it is incomplete.

Describe the Gestalt principle of figure–ground segregation and give an example of a visual illusion that illustrates the concept.

The Gestaltists emphasized the importance of **figure–ground segregation**: one object or part of the visual field is identified as the figure (central object), whereas the rest of the visual field is less important and so forms the ground. The laws of perceptual organization permit this segregation into figure and ground to happen. According to the Gestaltists, the figure is seen as having a distinct form or shape, whereas the ground lacks form. In addition, the figure

Figure 5.1 Examples of some of the Gestalt laws of perceptual organization: (a) the law of proximity; (b) the law of similarity; (c) the law of good continuation; and (d) the law of closure.

KEY TERM
Figure–ground segregation: the perceptual organization of the visual field into a figure (object of central interest) and a ground (less important background).

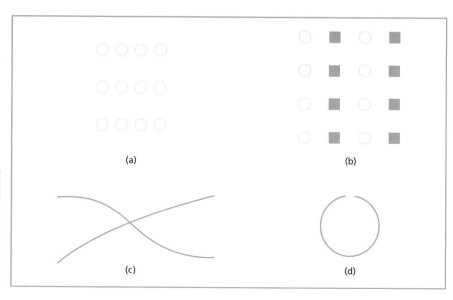

(a)

(b)

(c)

(d)

is perceived as being in front of the ground, and the contour separating the figure from the ground is seen as belonging to the figure.

You can check the Gestaltists' claims about figure and ground by looking at reversible figures such as the faces–goblet figure (see Figure 5.2). When the goblet is the figure, it seems to be in front of a dark background, whereas the faces are in front of a light background when forming the figure. Evidence that there is more attention to (and processing of) the figure than of the ground was reported by Weisstein and Wong (1986). They flashed vertical lines and slightly tilted lines onto the faces–goblet figure, and asked observers to decide whether the line was vertical. Performance on this task was much better when the line was presented to what the observers saw as the figure rather than to the ground.

Finally, we will briefly consider *four* limitations with the Gestaltists' approach to perceptual organization. First, they mostly studied *artificial* figures, and so we may well wonder whether their findings apply to more realistic stimuli. The evidence is mixed. Geisler, Perry, Super, and Gallogly (2001) used pictures to examine in great detail the contours of flowers, a river, trees, and so on. They found that the contours of objects could be worked out very well using two principles that were not the same as those emphasized by the Gestaltists:

Figure 5.2 An ambiguous drawing that can be seen either as two faces or a goblet.

1. Adjacent segments of any contour typically have very similar orientations.
2. Segments of any contour that are further apart generally have somewhat different orientations.

Elder and Goldberg (2002) used a similar approach to Geisler et al. (2001) in that they used pictures of natural objects. As predicted by the Gestaltists, proximity was a very powerful cue when deciding which contours belonged to which objects. In addition, the cue of good continuation also made a positive contribution.

Second, the Gestaltists argued that the various laws of perceptual grouping operate very *early* in visual processing. Clear evidence indicating that is not always the case was reported by Rock and Palmer (1990). Observers looked at luminous beads on parallel vertical strings presented in the dark. The beads were closer to each other in the horizontal direction than the vertical one. As the law of proximity predicts, the beads were seen as forming rows. The display was then tilted backwards so that the beads were now closer to each other in the vertical direction than in the horizontal one in the two-dimensional image. However, the beads remained closer to each other horizontally than vertically in three-dimensional space. The key finding was that observers still saw the beads organized in rows—grouping by proximity must have happened *after* depth perception, and so occurred later than assumed by the Gestaltists.

Third, the Gestaltists didn't focus enough on the complexities involved when different laws of grouping are in *conflict*. For example, consider a display such as the one in Figure 5.3, used by Quinlan and Wilton (1998).

Figure 5.3 Display involving a conflict between proximity and similarity.

How do you think most observers grouped the stimuli? In fact, about half grouped the stimuli by proximity and half by similarity. Alas, the Gestaltists didn't really indicate how we explain such individual differences!

Fourth, the Gestaltists tended to identify problems rather than solve them. More specifically, they discovered many interesting phenomena in visual perception but failed to provide adequate explanations of them.

VIEWPOINT-DEPENDENT OR VIEWPOINT-INVARIANT?

Form a visual image of a bicycle. I am reasonably confident that your visual image involves a side view in which the two wheels of the bicycle can be seen very clearly. We can use the example of a bicycle to raise an issue that has caused much controversy. Suppose some people were presented with a picture of a bicycle shown in the typical view as in your visual image, whereas other people were presented with a picture of the same bicycle viewed end on or from above. Both groups of people are instructed to identify the object as rapidly as possible. Would the group given the typical view of a bicycle perform this task faster than the other group, or would there be no difference between the groups?

Those who argue that object recognition is faster and easier when objects are seen from some angles rather than others favor the view that object recognition is **viewpoint-dependent**. In contrast, those who claim that object recognition is equally rapid and easy regardless of the angle from which an object is viewed favor the view that object recognition is **viewpoint-invariant**. We will briefly consider the reasons *why* some experts have proposed viewpoint-dependent theories whereas others have put forward viewpoint-independent theories.

Tarr and Bülthoff (1995, 1998) argued that changes in viewpoint typically (but not always) affect the speed and/or accuracy of object recognition. According to them, we have observed most common objects from several different angles or perspectives. As a result, we have several stored views of such objects in long-term memory, and object recognition is easier when the view we have of an object *corresponds* fairly directly to one of those stored views than when it does not.

In contrast, Biederman's (1987) recognition-by-components theory is an example of a viewpoint-invariant approach. According to him, objects consist of basic shapes or components known as "geons" (geometric ions). Examples of geons are blocks, cylinders, spheres, arcs, and wedges. According to Biederman (1987), there are about 36 different geons, which can be arranged in almost endless different ways. For example, a cup can be described by an arc

KEY TERMS
Viewpoint-dependent theories: theories of object recognition based on the assumption that objects can be recognized more easily from some angles than from others; see viewpoint-invariant theories.
Viewpoint-invariant theories: theories of object recognition based on the assumption that objects can be recognized equally easily from all angles; see viewpoint-dependent theories.

connected to the side of a cylinder, and a pail can be described by the same two geons, but with the arc connected to the top of the cylinder.

Geon-based information about common objects is stored in long-term memory. As a result, object recognition depends crucially on the identification of geons. Of key importance in the present context, an object's geons can be identified from numerous viewpoints. As a consequence, object recognition should generally be easy unless one or more geons are hidden from view.

We will shortly be discussing evidence relating to Biederman's (1987) prediction that object recognition is typically viewpoint-invariant. However, two limitations on the scope of his recognition-by-components theory deserve mention here. First, the theory only accounts for fairly unsubtle perceptual discriminations. Thus, it allows us to decide whether the animal in front of us is a dog or a cat, but not whether it is our dog or cat. Second, it seems to be assumed within the theory that objects consist of *invariant* geons, but object recognition is actually much more *flexible* than that. As Hayward and Tarr (2005, p. 67) pointed out, "You can take almost any object, put a working light-bulb on the top, and call it a *lamp* . . . almost *anything* in the image might constitute a feature in appropriate conditions."

What are the potential limitations of a strictly viewpoint-invariant approach to object perception?

FINDINGS

It is easy in principle to test the viewpoint-dependent and viewpoint-invariant theories. All that is required is to present the same object from several viewpoints and measure the time taken to identify it from each viewpoint. According to viewpoint-dependent theorists, the times should vary across viewpoints, whereas the times shouldn't vary according to viewpoint-invariant theorists. In reality, as you may have already guessed, the findings are somewhat inconsistent.

Biederman and Gerhardstein (1993) argued from their viewpoint-invariant theory that object naming should be facilitated as much by two different views of an object as by two identical views, provided the same geon-based object description could be constructed from both views. Their findings supported the prediction even when there was an angular difference of 135° between the two views. However, these findings are the exception rather than the rule.

Tarr and Bülthoff (1995) gave participants extensive practice at recognizing novel objects from certain specified viewpoints. What they found in each of several experiments was very consistent: "Response times and error rates for naming a familiar object in an unfamiliar viewpoint increased with rotation distance between the unfamiliar viewpoint and the nearest familiar viewpoint" (Tarr & Bülthoff, 1995, p. 1500). Thus, as predicted by viewpoint-dependent theories, it was easier to recognize objects presented from viewpoints that matched stored views than from viewpoints that did not.

One way of reconciling the different findings of Biederman and Gerhardstein (1993) and of Tarr and Bülthoff (1995) is to assume that as we develop expertise with given objects there is a gradual shift from viewpoint-dependent to viewpoint-invariant recognition. However, Gauthier and Tarr (2002) failed to find any evidence of such a shift (this study is also discussed in Chapter 7). They used artificial objects called Greebles belonging to various "families" (see Figure 5.4). The participants were given 7 hours of practice in learning to identify these Greebles. At several points during practice, the participants

Figure 5.4 Greebles can be grouped into two genders and come from various families. Reprinted with permission of Michael Tarr. Brown University, Providence, RI, www.tarrlab.org.

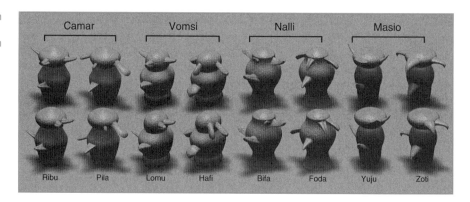

were presented with two Greebles in rapid succession, and decided whether the second Greeble was the same as the first. The second Greeble was presented at the same orientation as the first or at various other orientations up to 75°.

The findings obtained by Gauthier and Tarr (2002) are shown in Figure 5.5. As you can see, there was a general increase in speed as expertise developed, which is not surprising. However, the key finding was that object recognition throughout the experiment was faster when the orientation of the two stimuli was the same than when it differed. These findings indicate that object recognition remained strongly viewpoint-dependent throughout the course of the experiment and this was *not* reduced by practice.

It has often been argued (e.g., Tarr & Bülthoff, 1995) that viewpoint-dependent mechanisms are most likely to be used in object recognition when the task involves complex discriminations (e.g., between different makes of car), whereas viewpoint-invariant mechanisms may be used when the task is

Figure 5.5 Speed of Greeble matching as a function of stage of training and difference in orientation between successive Greeble stimuli. Based on data in Gauthier and Tarr (2002).

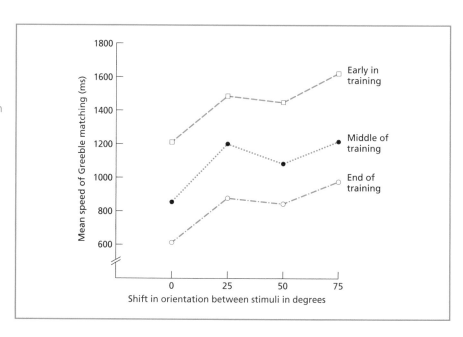

easy (e.g., discriminating between trees and flowers). Interesting evidence supporting this general perspective was reported by Vanrie, Béatse, Wagemans, Sunaert, and van Hecke (2002). Participants were presented with pairs of three-dimensional block figures in different orientations. They were given the task of deciding as rapidly as possible whether the two figures represented the same figure (i.e., matching vs. non-matching). There were two conditions differing in terms of how non-matches were produced (see Figure 5.6):

1. An easy invariance condition, in which the side components were tilted upward or downward by 10°.
2. A much harder rotation condition, in which one object was a mirror image of the other.

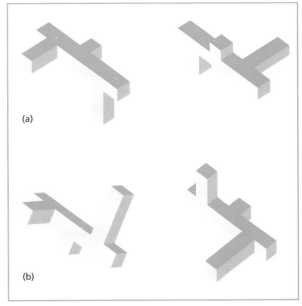

Figure 5.6 Non-matching stimuli in (a) the invariance condition and (b) the rotation condition. From Vanrie et al. (2002) with permission of Elsevier.

Vanrie et al. (2002) predicted that object recognition would be viewpoint-invariant in the much simpler invariance condition, but that it would be viewpoint-dependent in the more complex rotation condition. The findings were precisely in line with this prediction. First, performance in the invariance condition was viewpoint-invariant, that is, performance was not influenced by altering the angular difference between the two objects. Second, performance in the more complex rotation condition was strongly viewpoint-dependent; that is, performance was much faster when there was a small angular difference between the two figures than when there was a larger angular difference.

VIEWPOINT-DEPENDENT *AND* VIEWPOINT-INVARIANT

Most experts accept that it doesn't make much sense to argue that object recognition is either *always* viewpoint-dependent or *always* viewpoint-invariant. The most popular view nowadays (e.g., Vanrie et al., 2002) is that object recognition is viewpoint-dependent in some situations but viewpoint-invariant in others. However, what may well turn out to be the most fruitful theoretical approach is one based on the assumption that viewpoint-dependent and viewpoint-invariant information is generally combined *cooperatively* to produce object recognition (e.g., Foster & Gilson, 2002; Hayward, 2003).

Evidence that both kinds of information can be used at the same time in object recognition was reported by Foster and Gilson (2002). Participants saw pairs of simple three-dimensional objects constructed from connected cylinders (see Figure 5.7). Their task was to decide

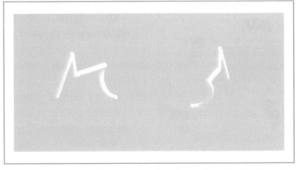

Figure 5.7 Example images of a "same" pair of stimulus objects. Adapted from Foster and Gilson (2002).

whether the two images showed the same object or two different objects. When two objects were different, they could differ in terms of a viewpoint-invariant feature (i.e., number of parts) and/or various viewpoint-dependent features (e.g., part length, angle of join between parts). The key finding was that participants used *both* kinds of information. This suggests that we make use of *all* available information in object recognition rather than confining ourselves to only some of the information, which makes a lot of sense.

DISORDERS OF OBJECT RECOGNITION

The central notion in research on object recognition is that successful object recognition involves a surprisingly large number of stages of processing. What are the implications of this notion when it comes to predicting the problems in object recognition experienced by brain-damaged patients? The most obvious implication is that there should be considerable differences from patient to patient in the nature of their problems—if object recognition involves five stages of processing, we might suppose that there would be some patients having impairments at each of these stages.

Historically, much importance was attached to a distinction between two forms of impairment in object recognition:

1. **Apperceptive agnosia**: Object recognition is impaired because of deficits in perceptual processing.
2. **Associative agnosia**: Perceptual processes are essentially intact, but there are difficulties in accessing relevant knowledge about objects from long-term memory.

According to this view, the problems with object recognition occur at an earlier stage of processing in apperceptive agnosia than in associative agnosia. More generally, apperceptive agnosia and associative agnosia are both forms of visual agnosia, which is "the impairment of visual object recognition in people who possess sufficiently preserved visual fields, acuity and other elementary forms of visual ability to enable object recognition, and in whom the object recognition impairment cannot be attributed to ... loss of knowledge about objects" (Farah, 1999, p. 181).

You can gain some idea of the severe problems experienced by patients with visual agnosia by considering the case of HJA, who had suffered damage to both occipital lobes after a post-operative stroke (Humphreys & Riddoch, 1987). HJA possessed considerable knowledge about common objects. For example, he described a carrot as follows: "The general shape of a carrot root is an elongated cone and its colour ranges between red and yellow" (Humphreys & Riddoch, 1987, p. 64). In addition, HJA could identify many objects by touch when blindfolded. However, when he was shown a line drawing of a carrot, this was what he said: "I have not even the glimmerings of an idea. The bottom point seems solid, and the other bits are feathery. It does not seem to be logical unless there is some sort of a brush" (Humphreys & Riddoch, 1987, p. 59).

The notion that there are only two major forms of visual agnosia (apperceptive agnosia and associative agnosia) is a gross oversimplification. For

KEY TERMS
Apperceptive agnosia: this is a form of visual agnosia in which there is impaired perceptual analysis of familiar objects.
Associative agnosia: this is a form of visual agnosia in which perceptual processing is fairly normal but there is an impaired ability to derive the meaning of objects.

example, HJA could copy drawings, which suggests he wasn't suffering from apperceptive agnosia. However, it often took him a very long time to copy a drawing because he found it hard to relate details of the object to the overall shape. We will return to HJA later, but note for now that his impairments in object recognition didn't neatly fit either apperceptive or associative agnosia.

What do apperceptive and associative agnosia have in common and what makes them different?

If we are to understand the various forms of visual agnosia, we really need to relate them to some model of the underlying processes involved in object recognition. Riddoch and Humphreys (2001) have provided just such a model (see Figure 5.8). Their hierarchical model of object recognition has the following stages or processes:

1. Edge grouping by collinearity (collinear means having a common line): This is an early stage of processing during which an object's edges are worked out.
2. Feature binding into shapes: During this stage, object features that have been extracted are combined to form shapes.
3. View normalization: During this stage, processing occurs to allow a viewpoint-invariant representation to be worked out. As we saw earlier in the chapter, this stage is controversial because object recognition often doesn't seem to involve viewpoint-invariant representations.

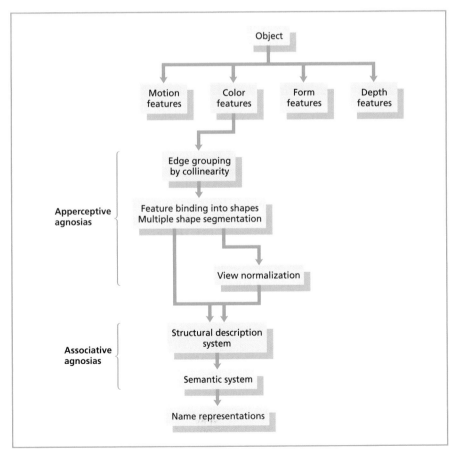

Figure 5.8 A hierarchical model of object recognition and naming, specifying different component processes which, when impaired, can produce varieties of apperceptive and associative agnosia. From Riddoch and Humphreys (2001).

4. Structural description: During this stage individuals gain access to stored knowledge about the structural descriptions of objects (i.e., their overall form and shape).

5. Semantic system: The final stage in object recognition involves gaining access to stored knowledge of semantic information relating to an object.

What predictions follow from this model? The most obvious one is that we might expect to find different patients with visual agnosia having problems in object recognition at each of the stages of processing identified in the model. If that is the case, that would reveal very clearly the limitations in the simple distinction between apperceptive and associative agnosia.

FINDINGS

We will follow Riddoch and Humphreys (2001) in working progressively through the five stages of the model, looking for patients who seem to have particular problems at each stage. We start with patients having problems with edge grouping. Milner et al. (1991) studied a patient, DF, who had very severely impaired object recognition (this patient is discussed in detail in Chapter 2). She recognized only a few real objects and couldn't recognize any objects shown in line drawings. She also had poor performance when making judgments about simple patterns grouped on the basis of properties such as proximity or collinearity.

We now turn to patients having particular problems with feature binding. The most-studied such patient is HJA, whose case was mentioned earlier. According to Humphreys (e.g., 1999), this patient suffers from **integrative agnosia**, a condition in which there are problems combining or integrating features of an object during object recognition. In one study, Giersch, Humphreys, Boucart, and Kovacs (2000) presented HJA with an array of three geometric shapes that were spatially separated, superimposed, or occluded (covered) (see Figure 5.9). Then a second visual array was presented, which was either the original array or a distractor array in which the positions of the shapes had been rearranged. HJA performed reasonably well with separated shapes but not with superimposed or occluded shapes. Thus, HJA has poor ability for shape segregation.

Patients having problems with view normalization would find it hard to recognize that two objects are the same when viewed from different angles. Such findings were reported by Warrington and Taylor (1978). They presented patients with pairs of photographs, one of which was a conventional or usual view and the other of which was an unusual view. For example, the usual view of a flat-iron was photographed from above, whereas the unusual view showed only the base of the iron and part of the handle. The

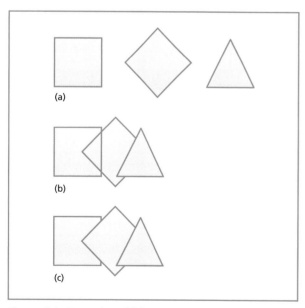

Figure 5.9 Examples of (a) separated, (b) superimposed, and (c) occluded shapes used by Giersch et al. (2000). From Riddoch and Humphreys (2001).

task was to decide whether the same object was shown in both photographs. The patients performed poorly on this task, finding it hard to identify an object shown from an unusual angle even when they had already identified it from the accompanying usual view. Such impaired performance suggests problems with view normalization.

Fery and Morais (2003) studied a patient (DJ) who had problems with using structural descriptions. In spite of his problems, several processes relating to object recognition seemed essentially intact. For example, he was correct on 93% of trials on a difficult animal-decision task requiring a decision as to which one out of various drawings was an animal (see Figure 5.10). However, DJ recognized only 16% of common objects presented visually, indicating that he could not easily access information about the structural descriptions of objects stored in memory from visual stimuli.

Finally, we consider patients who seem to find it hard to gain access to relevant stored semantic information about objects. Some of these patients suffer from **category-specific deficits**, meaning they have problems with certain semantic categories but not others. Many such patients have greater problems in identifying pictures of living than of non-living things. Martin and Caramazza (2003) reviewed the literature, and found that more than three times as many patients had greater problems with living than non-living things than had the opposite pattern. The interpretation of these findings is controversial (see Chapter 20 for a review). However, it is likely that the problems with object recognition experienced by patients with category-specific disorders center on accessing certain kinds of semantic knowledge about objects rather than on any of the earlier stages of processing.

Figure 5.10 Examples of animal stimuli with (from top to bottom) a part missing, the intact animal, with a part substituted, and a part added. From Fery and Morais (2003).

How has each stage of the Riddoch and Humphreys (2001) model been supported by evidence from patient studies?

KEY TERM
Category-specific deficits: problems in identifying members of certain semantic categories as a consequence of brain damage.

EVALUATION AND CHAPTER SUMMARY

Viewpoint-dependent or viewpoint-invariant?
- Real progress has been made in resolving the controversy as to whether object recognition is viewpoint-dependent or viewpoint-invariant. As Vanrie et al. (2002, p. 917) pointed out, "The key question is no longer *if* object recognition is viewpoint-dependent or viewpoint-independent [invariant], but rather *when*, i.e., under which circumstances."
- In other words, object recognition is sometimes viewpoint-dependent and sometimes viewpoint-invariant.
- The most important factor is the complexity of the task or discrimination the observer needs to make: object recognition is much more likely to be viewpoint-invariant when the task is a very easy one than when it is complex and involves fine discriminations.
- It seems reasonable to assume that there would often be a shift from viewpoint-dependent to viewpoint-invariant object recognition as observers develop expertise with the objects and so the task becomes easier. However, the evidence tends not to support that assumption (e.g., Gauthier & Tarr, 2002).
- Recently, there has been increasing emphasis on the notion that viewpoint-dependent and viewpoint-invariant information is combined in a cooperative fashion during object recognition.

Disorders of object recognition
- Riddoch and Humphreys' (2001) hierarchical model of object recognition has provided a useful framework within which to consider the various problems with object recognition shown by visual agnosics.
- The evidence is broadly supportive of the notion that there are separate stages of edge grouping, feature binding, view normalization, structural description, and access to semantic knowledge. The model certainly offers a more realistic account of visual agnosia than previous ones.
- According to the hierarchical model, the early stages of object recognition occur in a bottom-up way, starting with the presentation of a visual stimulus, with the last two stages being top-down.
- In fact, processes associated with later stages may influence the processing at earlier stages more than is implied by the model.
- Another limitation is that many details are omitted from the model. For example, it is assumed that each stage of processing uses the output from the previous one, but precisely *how* this is supposed to happen remains unclear.

FURTHER READING

- Bruce, V., Green, P.R., & Georgeson, M.A. (2003). *Visual perception: Physiology, psychology and ecology* (4th ed.). Hove, UK: Psychology Press. Chapter 9 of this outstanding textbook is devoted to object recognition.
- Hayward, W.G., & Tarr, M.J. (2005). Visual perception II: High-level vision. In K. Lamberts & R.L. Goldstone (Eds.), *The handbook of cognition*. London: Sage. This chapter provides a detailed (if complex) account of several issues in visual perception including object recognition.
- Morgan, M. (2003). *The space between our ears: How the brain represents visual space*. London: Weidenfeld & Nicolson. This book discusses what we know about visual perception in an entertaining and illuminating way.

CHAPTER 6

CONTENTS

Introduction 75

Who are you? 78

Theoretical approaches 83

Evaluation and chapter summary 86

Further reading 87

What's in a face?

INTRODUCTION

Recognizing faces is of immense importance in our lives. We can sometimes identify people from their physique, the way they walk, or their mannerisms. Most of the time, however, we simply look at their faces. Form a visual image of someone important in your life. It is very likely that your image contains fairly detailed information about their face and its special features.

Face recognition is also important in the real world. Hundreds (perhaps thousands) of innocent people are locked up in prison because eyewitnesses mistakenly claimed to recognize them as the person who committed a crime. We know this because DNA evidence has shown conclusively in hundreds of cases that the person found guilty of a crime didn't commit it (see Chapter 16). The misery caused by mistaken face recognition can be illustrated with the case of Arthur Lee Whitfield. He was sentenced to 63 years in prison for raping two women in August 1981 when he was 26 years old. However, he was released after 22 years on the basis of DNA evidence. He worked hard to avoid becoming too bitter during the long years in prison. As he pointed out, "If you're put in that position, you have to make the best of it, do things to keep your mind off what really has happened." Here are his thoughts on the investigator who helped to convict him and on the two women who said they were sure he had raped them: "It would be nice for them to say they made a mistake. It takes a big person to say they made a mistake."

Why do so many eyewitnesses make mistakes in face recognition? Gary Wells, a psychologist who has done much research on this issue, has this to say: "Why should people make good eyewitnesses? In the presence of danger, we're wired for fight or flight. What helped for survival was not a quick recall of details."

What do you think you know about faces? I will take the liberty of trying to guess some of your answers to that question.

1. You must have had the experience of finding someone facially attractive but discovering your friends simply didn't agree with your judgment. Of course, this may have been good news because it limited competition for the person you were interested in! That suggests the truth of the old saying that beauty is in the eye of the beholder, something we would expect to be even more the case with judgments of facial attractiveness across different cultures.

How good are people at recognizing faces? Why is it an important skill to possess?

2. To the extent that there is some measure of agreement concerning those having attractive faces, you would expect that there would be something striking or distinctive about their faces.

3. You may think that individuals who have attractive faces are luckier than those who don't. However, perhaps there is truth in the saying that beauty is only skin deep, meaning that individuals with attractive and unattractive faces don't differ in any important way other than facial attractiveness.

4. Most faces are broadly similar to each other, at least in the sense of having a chin, mouth, nose, eyes, and eyebrows in approximately the same arrangement within the face. When we look at a face, we make about four or five eye fixations per second, and are only able to extract detailed information from a very limited area close to the point of fixation. It seems reasonable to assume that it takes us a fair amount of time to recognize most of the people we meet in the course of our everyday lives.

5. People differ in terms of how good they are at recognizing faces. Anyone who is very poor at recognizing faces will also tend to be very poor at recognizing objects in the environment.

As we will see, *all* of the above assumptions are incorrect! Without more ado, let's turn to the evidence.

FINDINGS

What makes for an attractive face? Does the evidence support your intuitions?

The notion that we all have our own idiosyncratic views on what constitutes an attractive face has surprisingly little evidence to support it. Langlois, Kalakanis, Rubenstein, Larson, Hallam, and Smoot (2000) carried out a **meta-analysis** (combining the findings from numerous studies) to investigate this issue. Within any given culture, there was substantial agreement on the issue of who is attractive and who is unattractive. More surprisingly, a further meta-analysis revealed that there was also high agreement on facial attractiveness from one culture to another. Note that there isn't complete agreement on these issues, and some faces are regarded as much more attractive by some people than by others.

How do attractive faces differ from unattractive ones? Langlois, Roggman, and Musselman (1994) discovered that male and female computer-generated composites or "averaged" faces were regarded as more attractive than the individual faces forming the composite. Why is this? Averaged faces were regarded as more familiar than the individual faces, and this sense of familiarity made the averaged faces seem attractive. Averaged faces are also more symmetrical than individual faces, and symmetry is associated with attractiveness (Grammer & Thornhill, 1994). Mealey, Bridgstock, and Townsend (1999) carried out an interesting study on facial symmetry using monozygotic [identical] twins. The more symmetrical twin was rated as more attractive. In addition, the size of the difference between twins in rated attractiveness was directly related to the difference in symmetry. However, a note of caution is in order. Scheib, Gangestad, and Thornhill (1999) found that attractiveness ratings of faces were higher in women having symmetrical faces than those having asymmetrical faces, even when symmetry cues were eliminated by presenting only one half of each face. This suggests that cues associ-

KEY TERM
Meta-analysis: statistical analyses based on combining data from numerous studies on a given issue.

ated with symmetry may be more important than symmetry itself. Perhaps disappointingly, the secret of having an attractive face is rather banal: you need an average and symmetrical face. This may be bad news if your face happens to be striking or distinctive in some way!

We have argued that there is a reasonable consensus as to the attractiveness of any given face. However, there are some individual differences. For example, Perrett et al. (2002) studied the rated attractiveness of younger and older faces. The tendency to prefer the younger faces was less marked in adults who were the offspring of older parents than in those who were the offspring of younger parents.

Finally, females' judgments of the attractiveness of masculine male faces is influenced by the phase of the menstrual cycle. Masculine male faces are those in which there is "lateral [sideways] growth of the cheekbones, mandibles [lower jawbone], and chin; the forward growth of the bones of the eyebrow ridges; and the lengthening of the lower facial bone" (Fink & Penton-Voak, 2002, p. 155). Such faces are more likely to develop during puberty in young men having a high testosterone-to-estrogen ratio (greater dominance of "male" sex hormones). Females are more attracted to these masculine male faces during the phase of their menstrual cycle in which conception is most likely (Johnston, Hagel, Franklin, Fink, & Grammer, 2001). According to evolutionary psychologists, this may occur because men with masculine faces tend to have a high-quality immune system.

We turn now to the issue of whether facial attractiveness is more than skin deep; that is, related to other qualities. There is accumulating evidence that it is. Langlois et al. (2000) carried out a meta-analysis, and found several significant differences between physically attractive and unattractive adults. Below in brackets are the percentages having each characteristic (attractive people first). Attractive individuals had more self-confidence (56% vs. 44%), better social skills (55% vs. 45%), better physical health (59% vs. 41%), more extraversion (56% vs. 44%), and more sexual experience (58% vs. 42%).

Henderson and Anglin (2003) asked undergraduate students to rate the facial attractiveness of male and female students whose photographs had been taken from highschool yearbooks from the 1920s. The key finding was that these ratings of facial attractiveness predicted the longevity of the high-school students with an overall correlation of +.35. Soler et al. (2003) asked women to rate the attractiveness of men as a permanent partner on the basis of photographs of their faces. The women's ratings were perceptive in that sperm quality (in terms of fertility) was significantly greater in facially attractive men than in those who were not facially attractive. Such findings serve to make face processing an important topic!

How rapidly can we identify someone's face? Striking evidence was reported by Vinette, Gosselin, and Schyns (2004). Participants initially learned the identities of 10 faces. They were then presented with sequences of stimuli taken from individual faces at a rate of 24ms per stimulus. Participants used information from the eye on the left side of the face to identify the face between 47 and 94ms after stimulus onset, with information being used from the eye on the right side of the stimulus by about 94ms. The fact that information from the left side of the facial stimuli was used *before* information from the right side indicates that the right hemisphere of the brain is more efficient than the left hemisphere at processing faces.

Evidence that we process faces faster than other objects was reported by Carmel and Bentin (2002) in a study using event-related potentials (ERPs; regularities in the brain-wave record produced by repeated presentations of stimuli). They focused on a negative potential at 170ms (N170) that reflects stimulus processing. Carmel and Bentin's key finding was that various facial stimuli (photographs, paintings, sketches) produced larger N170s than several other kinds of stimuli including cars, human hands, items of furniture, and birds.

The most obvious reason why faces are processed so efficiently is because we are great experts at identifying faces—after all, it is a crucial skill in almost any social situation. Why do we have the ability to extract useful information from the eyes in under a tenth of a second? This is probably due to the fact that the eyes are a valuable source of information about the other person's intentions and state of mind as well as his or her identity.

WHO ARE YOU?

How can cases of prosopagnosia inform us about underlying neural pathways that guide face and object perception?

Imagine you have suffered brain damage, as a result of which you can no longer recognize the faces of any of your friends and relatives. Just think how distressing and sad that would be. Patients having enormous problems in recognizing familiar faces suffer from a condition known as **prosopagnosia** coming from two Greek words meaning "face" and "without knowledge." Prosopagnosia is sometimes commonly referred to as "face-blindness." What is surprising is that patients with prosopagnosia can recognize most objects reasonably well in spite of their enormous problems with faces. However, note that most prosopagnosics have *some* problems with object recognition, although a few (e.g., PS studied by Rossion, Caldara, Seghier, Schuller, Lazayras, & Mayer, 2003) have excellent object recognition.

Some idea of the problems faced by patients with prosopagnosia can be obtained by considering this report by one such patient: "At the club I saw someone strange staring at me, and asked the steward who it was. You'll laugh at me. I'd been looking at myself in the mirror." A young prosopagnosic Swedish woman called Cecilia Burman (2004, pp. 4–5) has described the strategies she uses to prevent the embarrassment of letting others know she doesn't recognize them:

> *Many face-blind people will greet within a second, in spite of not having had enough time to recognize someone ... We have to greet everyone who might be a friend, which can be pretty much everyone we meet ... Some face-blind people (I am one of them) become experts at pretending they knew all along who someone was when they finally learn about it. Since many people are offended by not being recognized, I would simply not let them know I had not recognized them ... Many face-blind people go to great lengths to avoid using names ... I probably use other people's names in their presence less than once a month, and always with a rush of adrenaline.*

KEY TERM
Prosopagnosia: a condition caused by brain damage in which patients cannot recognize familiar faces but can recognize familiar objects.

As we have seen, the crucial defining features of prosopagnosia are that there are great problems in recognizing familiar faces but not in recognizing familiar objects. However, even though familiar faces cannot be recognized at the conscious level, there may still be a reasonable amount of processing of such faces below the conscious level. For example, there is a phenomenon in which a name (e.g., "Stan Laurel") is recognized more rapidly when preceded by a related face (e.g., Oliver Hardy's) rather than an unrelated one (e.g., Robert Redford's). Some prosopagnosics show this pattern (known as semantic priming) in spite of the fact that they don't recognize the face (Young, Hellawell, & de Haan, 1988). This is an example of covert face recognition (excluding conscious processes) in the absence of overt face recognition (involving conscious processes).

How can we explain findings such as those of Young et al. (1988)? Schweinberger and Burton (2003) assumed that the same processing system is used in overt and covert recognition. However, *less* processing is required to produce covert recognition. Various predictions follow from this assumption. First, patients with reasonably good overt face recognition should have better covert face recognition than those with poor overt face recognition. Most of the evidence supports that prediction (see Schweinberger & Burton, 2003).

Second, it should be impossible for patients to have intact overt face recognition but impaired covert face recognition. The reason is that more processing is required for overt than for covert face recognition. According to Schweinberger and Burton (2003), no patients exhibiting this theoretically impossible pattern have been found.

Third, even though prosopagnosics have a weakly functioning face recognition system, they should show *some* overt face recognition if the task is sufficiently easy. Morrison, Bruce, and Burton (2003) found prosopagnosics exhibited overt face recognition when they were shown several faces at once and told they all belonged to the same category.

FACES ARE SPECIAL!

There are various reasons for supposing that faces are special. First, the existence of patients with prosopagnosia (impaired face perception but almost intact object perception) suggests that faces are processed differently from objects. Second, there is evidence of a brain region specialized for the processing of faces rather than objects. Indeed, the area in question (discussed further below) is sometimes known as the "fusiform face area." Third, it has been argued (e.g., by Farah, 1990, 1994) that faces differ from objects in terms of how they are processed. More specifically, faces are typically subject mainly to configural or holistic analysis, in which the *overall* structure of the face is processed with little attention paid to the details (e.g., face, mouth, eyebrows). In contrast, object processing generally also involves analysis by parts, in which the parts of the object are processed in turn.

Findings

We have seen that patients suffering from prosopagnosia have great difficulties in recognizing faces but can recognize objects reasonably well. The obvious interpretation of that finding is that prosopagnosics have suffered damage to a part of the brain specialized for processing faces. An alternative viewpoint is that we engage in more *detailed* processing to distinguish one face from another than to identify an object as a cat or a car. Face recognition involves distinguishing among members of the same category (i.e., faces), whereas object recognition generally involves only identifying the category to which an object belongs. Accordingly, some researchers have assessed the ability of prosopagnosics to make fine discriminations among objects belonging to the same category. Farah (1994) studied the ability of a prosopagnosic patient (LH) to discriminate among pairs of spectacles on a test of recognition memory. LH's performance in recognizing pairs of spectacles was comparable to that of healthy individuals. However, LH's recognition performance was much worse than that of healthy individuals with face recognition. These findings suggest there is something special about face recognition over and above the need to make fine discriminations.

Other studies (discussed by McNeil & Warrington, 1993) have produced different findings from those of Farah (1994). For example, an ornithologist (expert in the study of birds) who became prosopagnosic couldn't distinguish between similar species of birds. In similar fashion, a farmer who suffered brain damage resulting in prosopagnosia could no longer distinguish among his sheep.

As mentioned above, some researchers have argued that what is sometimes called the "fusiform face area" (especially the one in the right hemisphere) is specialized for the processing of faces. Some evidence fits that view. Kanwisher, McDermott, and Chun (1997) used fMRI (see Chapter 1) to compare brain activity to faces, scrambled faces, houses, and hands. Parts of the right fusiform gyrus [ridge] responded selectively to faces but not to other objects. In similar fashion, Pelphrey, Mack, Song, Guzeldere, and McCarthy (2003) used fMRI while observers viewed faces and common objects. They found that areas within the fusiform and inferior temporal gyri were activated only when faces were presented. In a review of PET and fMRI studies, Farah and Aguirre (1999) argued that the findings were somewhat inconsistent. However, parts of the fusiform gyrus were generally more active during face recognition than object recognition.

There is increasing evidence that the right fusiform face area may be less important than used to be thought. Rossion et al. (2003) considered a prosopagnosic patient, PS. Her right fusiform face area was intact, but she had damage to an area in the back of the brain called the "occipital face area." Rossion et al. suggested that normal face processing depends on integrated functioning of the right fusiform face area *and* the right occipital face area.

There are plausible reasons why face recognition might depend more than recognition of other objects on configural or global processing. Information about specific features can be unreliable because different individuals share similar facial features (e.g., eye color) or because an individual's features are subject to change (e.g., skin shade, mouth shape). In view of that unreliability of feature information, it may be desirable for us to use configural processing. One of the key findings is that faces are much harder to identify when presented inverted or upside-down rather than upright (see McKone, 2004, for a review). The Thatcher illusion is an interesting example of a problem with inverted faces when we rely too much on configural processing. When viewed as an inverted face we don't realize that the eyes and mouth are inverted relative to the face. However, the grotesque nature of the face becomes very clear when you view it the right way up.

Why is it much more difficult to identify inverted faces? It seems reasonable to interpret such findings by assuming that configural processing is pos-

What is the difference between configural and feature processing? Which applies to face perception?

sible mainly with upright faces, whereas feature processing is possible with upright *and* inverted faces. As predicted from the hypothesis that faces receive mainly configural processing, adverse effects of inversion on object recognition are much smaller with non-face objects. In addition, negative effects of inversion with ordinary objects disappear rapidly with practice (see McKone, 2004, for a review), whereas those with faces can persist for thousands of trials (McKone, Martini, & Nakayama, 2001).

As McKone (2004) pointed out, it is often difficult to interpret the findings obtained with faces because we typically use configural *and* feature processes when looking at them. Accordingly, she argued that we need to find some phenomenon that is present for upright faces but isn't found when only feature processing is possible. Participants initially learned to identify two fairly similar faces. After that, one face (upright or inverted) was presented very briefly on each trial, in a central position or at various locations out towards the periphery. Participants had to decide which face had been presented. When the face was presented towards the periphery, participants performed reasonably well with upright faces but at chance level with inverted faces (see Figure 6.1). These findings imply that participants used only configural information to identify faces presented to the periphery of vision.

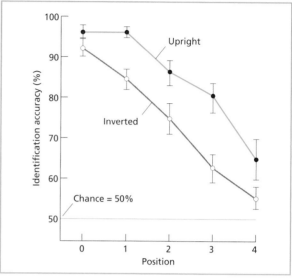

Figure 6.1 Accuracy of identification of upright and inverted faces presented centrally (position 0) or at various locations towards the periphery of vision.

FACES ARE *NOT* SPECIAL!

We have seen that there is apparently powerful evidence (much of it from patients with prosopagnosia) of important differences between face processing and object processing. However, Gauthier and Tarr (2002) have argued that some of these findings shouldn't be taken at face value (sorry!). According to them, there are *two* main reasons why faces appear special even though they aren't. First, we typically recognize faces at the individual level (e.g., "That's our William!"). In contrast, we often recognize objects at a much more general level (e.g., "That's a pretty car"; "That's a large bird"). Prosopagnosics may have special problems with face recognition simply because recognizing *specific* examples of a category is more difficult than recognizing the *general* category to which an object belongs.

Second, nearly all of us have considerably more experience (and thus *expertise*) in recognizing faces than in recognizing individual members of most other categories. The following predictions follow from the views of Gauthier and Tarr (2002): the processes and brain mechanisms claimed to be specific to faces are also involved in recognizing individual members of *any* object category for which we possess expertise. As Morgan (2003, pp. 114–115) expressed it, "There may not be a specialized 'face area' in the brain at all, but rather an area where practice has made perfect."

The notion that expertise is important in face recognition helps us to explain the "other face" effect. The nature of this effect is that we generally find it much more difficult to recognize faces from other races than from our own. Various factors may be involved. However, it is probable that our relative lack of experience with faces from other races is the most important one.

Findings

We have already mentioned that the perceptual problems of prosopagnosics aren't always limited to face recognition. There are various studies showing that prosopagnosics often have difficulty in identifying complex objects. For example, Gauthier, Behrmann, and Tarr (1999) presented prosopagnosics with faces and objects (e.g., synthetic snowflakes). Prosopagnosics had worse recognition performance than healthy individuals with objects as well as with faces. Their problems with objects were especially great when they had to recognize objects as belonging to a specific category rather than to a more general category. Henke, Schweinberger, Grigo, Klos, and Sommer (1998) studied two prosopagnosics. One had difficulties in recognizing members of living (e.g., fruit, vegetables) and non-living (e.g., cars) categories of objects, whereas the other prosopagnosic didn't. These findings suggest that at least some prosopagnosics have *general* problems with complex object recognition regardless of whether faces are involved.

The role of expertise in determining the involvement of the so-called fusiform face area was assessed in important research reported by Gauthier, Tarr, Anderson, Skudlarski, and Gore (1999). Participants were given several hours' practice in learning to identify Greebles (artificial objects belonging to various "families"; see Figure 5.4). As their expertise with Greebles increased, so did the amount of activation in the fusiform face area. Thus, the fusiform face area is involved in expert processing of a range of objects and is *not* limited to face processing.

Powerful support for the above conclusion was provided by Gauthier, Skudlarski, Gore, and Anderson (2000), using fMRI to assess activation of the fusiform face area during recognition tasks involving faces, familiar objects, birds, and cars. Some participants were experts on birds whereas others were experts on cars. Expertise influenced activation in the fusiform face area. There was more activation to cars when recognized by car experts than by bird experts, and more activation to birds when recognized by bird rather than car experts.

Suppose there is a part of the brain specialized for expert processing of most kinds of visually presented objects and faces, and that most people are experts in face processing. People who are experts in car identification should find it difficult to carry out face perception and car perception tasks together because the demands on that part of the brain would be very great. In contrast, non-experts in cars might be able to perform the two tasks together because the tasks would use different brain areas. Gauthier, Curran, Curby, and Collins (2003) obtained precisely those findings.

Finally, Farah's (1990, 1994) notion that holistic processing is much more associated with faces than with other objects has been challenged by Gauthier and Tarr (2002; see Chapter 5). Participants were given several hours' practice in identifying Greebles. As their expertise increased, so did their sensitivity to holistic changes in Greebles. This finding suggests that holistic processing occurs with *any* objects with which we have great familiarity and expertise.

Face perception is no different from object perception. Do you agree with this view?

THEORETICAL APPROACHES

We have discussed the accumulating evidence on face recognition, and it is now time to consider relevant theoretical approaches. We will start with the very influential model put forward by Bruce and Young (1986), in which eight components were identified (see Figure 6.2):

1. *Structural encoding*: This produces various representations or descriptions of faces.
2. *Expression analysis*: People's emotional states are inferred from their facial features.
3. *Facial speech analysis*: Speech perception is helped by observing a speaker's lip movements (see Chapter 18).
4. *Directed visual processing*: Specific facial information is processed selectively.
5. *Face recognition nodes*: These contain structural information about known faces.
6. *Person identity nodes*: These provide information about individuals (e.g., occupation, interests).
7. *Name generation*: A person's name is stored separately.
8. *Cognitive system*: This contains additional information (e.g., most actors and actresses have attractive faces), and influences which other components receive attention.

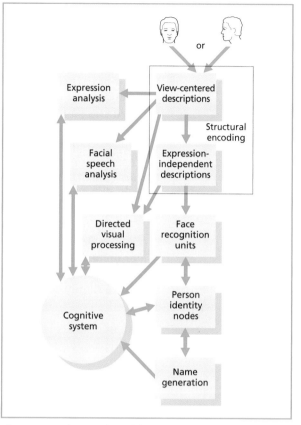

Figure 6.2 The model of face recognition put forward by Bruce and Young (1986).

What predictions follow from this model? First, there should be important differences in the processing of familiar and unfamiliar faces. Recognizing familiar faces depends mainly on structural encoding, face recognition units, person identity nodes, and name generation. In contrast, the processing of unfamiliar faces involves structural encoding, expression analysis, facial speech analysis, and directed visual processing.

Second, consider the processing of facial identity (who is the person?) and the processing of facial expression (what is he or she feeling?). According to the model, separate processing routes are involved in the two cases, with the key component for processing facial expression being the expression analysis component.

Third, when we look at a familiar face, familiarity information from the face recognition unit should be accessed first, followed by information about that person (e.g., occupation) from the person identity node, followed by that person's name from the name generation component. Thus, familiarity decisions about a face should be made faster than decisions based on person identity nodes.

FAMILIAR vs. UNFAMILIAR FACES

We can test the hypothesis that familiar faces are processed differently from unfamiliar ones by studying brain-damaged patients. We should find some patients with good recognition of familiar faces but poor recognition of unfamiliar faces, and other patients showing the opposite pattern. This double dissociation was obtained by Malone, Morris, Kay, and Levin (1982). They tested one patient who recognized the photographs of 82% of famous statesmen but was extremely poor at matching unfamiliar faces. A second patient performed normally at matching unfamiliar faces, but recognized the photographs of only 23% of famous people. However, Young, Newcombe, de Haan, Small, and Hay (1993) failed to replicate those findings in a study of 34 brain-damaged men. There was very weak evidence for selective impairment of either familiar or unfamiliar face recognition.

In spite of lack of support for Bruce and Young's (1986) model in the above findings, there must be major differences in the processing of familiar and unfamiliar faces. At the very least, we generally access various kinds of information about familiar faces (e.g., occupation, personal interests, name) that we simply don't know about unfamiliar faces.

FACIAL IDENTITY vs. FACIAL EXPRESSION

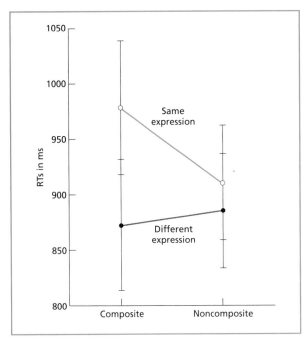

There is much support for the assumption that separate routes are involved in the processing of facial identity and facial expression. For example, we might expect to find some brain-damaged patients who can identify faces but cannot recognize facial expressions and others showing the opposite pattern. Such a double dissociation has been reported in various studies (e.g., Young et al., 1993).

Calder, Young, Keane, and Dean (2000) found suggestive evidence that different processes underlie recognition of facial identity and facial expression. When the top and bottom halves of faces of two different people showing the same expression were combined, facial expression (e.g., happiness) could easily be recognized even though there was no overall facial identity (see Figure 6.3). This led Calder et al. (2000) to construct three types of composite stimuli based on combining the top half of one picture with the bottom half of a second one:

1. The same person posing two different facial expressions.
2. Two different people posing the same facial expression.
3. Two different people posing different facial expressions.

Figure 6.3 Participants viewed the top and bottom halves of faces of two different people exhibiting the same expression or different expressions. The two halves were aligned (composite condition) or misaligned (noncomposite condition). The data show reaction times to identify the expression displayed in the bottom face. Calder et al., 2000, *Journal of Experimental Psychology: Human Perception and Performance, 26,* 527–551. Copyright © American Psychological Association.

The participants' task was to decide rapidly either the facial identity or the facial expression of the person shown in the bottom half of the composite picture.

What would we expect to happen if different processes are involved in recognition of facial identity and facial expression? Consider the task of deciding on the facial expression of the face shown in the bottom half. Performance should be slower when the facial expression is different in the top half, but there should be *no* additional cost when the two halves also differ in facial identity. In similar fashion, facial identity decisions shouldn't be slower when the facial expressions differ in the two halves. The predicted findings were obtained (see Figure 6.4).

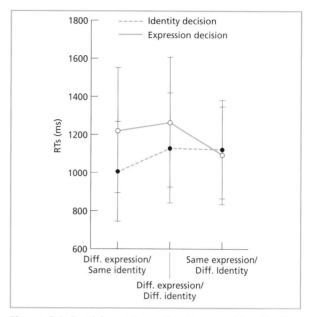

Figure 6.4 Participants' reaction times to identify the expression displayed (expression decision) or identity (identity decision) in the bottom segment of three types of composite images (different expression-same identity, different expression-different identity, and same expression-different identity). Calder et al., 2000, *Journal of Experimental Psychology: Human Perception and Performance*, 26, 527–551. Copyright © American Psychological Association. Reprinted with permission.

FAMILIARITY, PERSON IDENTITY, NAME

According to the model, when we look at a familiar face, we first access familiarity information, followed by personal information (e.g., the person's career), followed by the person's name. As predicted, Young, McWeeny, Hay, and Ellis (1986b) found the decision as to whether a face was familiar was made faster than the decision as to whether it was a politician's face. Also as predicted, Young et al. (1986a) found participants decided whether a face belonged to a politician much faster than they could produce the person's name.

According to the model, the name generation component can be accessed *only* via the appropriate person identity node. Thus, we should never be able to put a name to a face without also having available other information about that person (e.g., his or her occupation). Young, Hay, and Ellis (1985) asked people to keep a diary record of problems they experienced in face recognition. There were 1008 incidents in total, but people *never* reported putting a name to a face while knowing nothing else about that person. In contrast, there were 190 occasions on which someone remembered a reasonable amount of information about a person but not their name.

If the appropriate face recognition unit is activated but the person identity node isn't, there should be a feeling of familiarity but an inability to think of any relevant information about that person. In the incidents collected by Young et al. (1985), this was reported on 233 occasions.

The evidence discussed so far provides reasonable support for the model. However, other findings are inconsistent with the model. Rahman, Sommer, and Olada (2004) used pictures of eight males, plus names, telling the participants these males were inhabitants of either Aruba or Vanuatu and that their occupation was either a store-fitter or a sigillograph (a writer of satires). When the participants were tested with the male faces, they classified their names significantly faster than their occupations, a finding that cannot readily be explained on the Bruce and Young (1986) model.

Rahman et al.'s (2004) findings suggest that Bruce and Young's (1986) model is too rigid. This is certainly true of the assumption that information about faces is *always* accessed in the order familiarity, then personal information, and finally the name. What is needed is a more flexible approach. This has been provided in a series of interactive activation and competition models (Burton & Bruce, 1993; Burton, Bruce, & Hancock, 1999; Valentine, Bredart, Lawson, & Wood, 1991). What is of particular relevance here is the assumption that access to person information (e.g., occupation) and to people's names is via person identity nodes. The speed with which personal and name information is retrieved depends on the number of connections between that information and other information. These theoretical assumptions explain why name information is usually accessed more slowly than personal information, but is accessed faster when the personal information is very obscure (Rahman et al., 2004).

EVALUATION AND CHAPTER SUMMARY

Who are you?
- Nearly everyone involved in the controversy on whether faces are special or not agrees on various points: For example, prosopagnosics have great problems in recognizing faces; face processing is typically associated with activation of the fusiform face area; and face recognition involves holistic processing.
- However, there is less agreement concerning the appropriate interpretation of these findings.
- Nevertheless, the above findings provide weaker support for the faces-are-special view than was once thought.
- First, prosopagnosics often have problems in recognizing objects other than faces, especially when fine discriminations are required (e.g., Gauthier et al., 1999; Henke et al., 1998).
- Second, the so-called fusiform face area is also activated when people recognize objects within their area of expertise (e.g., Gauthier et al., 1999, 2000).
- Third, there is some evidence (e.g., Gauthier & Tarr, 2002) suggesting that holistic processing is associated with expert processing rather than being specific to face processing.
- Accordingly, there may *not* be anything intrinsically special about face processing.

Theoretical approaches
- Various theories starting with that of Bruce and Young (1986) have shown that the processes involved in face recognition are more numerous than might have been imagined.
- The processing of familiar faces differs from that of unfamiliar faces, partly because we possess certain information about familiar faces (e.g., personal information, name) that we don't have with unfamiliar faces.

- There is also much evidence to support the theoretical assumption that there are separate routes for processing information about facial identity and about facial expression.
- As predicted by the original Bruce and Young (1986) model, the processing of familiar faces typically leads first to accessing of familiarity information, followed by personal information, and then finally name information.
- However, name information is sometimes accessed before personal information when the personal information isn't connected to other information about the individual (Rahman et al., 2004).

FURTHER READING

- Bruce, V., & Young, A. (1998). *In the eye of the beholder: The science of face perception*. Oxford: Oxford University Press. There is comprehensive coverage of research on face recognition in this book by two leading authorities.
- Fink, B., & Penton-Voak, I. (2002). Evolutionary psychology of facial attractiveness. *Current Directions in Psychological Science, 11*, 154–158. This article provides a good discussion of the main factors determining facial attractiveness around the world.
- Morgan, M. (2003). *The space between our ears: How the brain represents visual space*. London: Weidenfeld & Nicolson. Face processing and recognition are discussed in Chapter 9 of this entertaining book.

CHAPTER 7

CONTENTS

Introduction	89
Does visual imagery resemble visual perception?	91
Brain systems in imagery	95
Evaluation and chapter summary	99
Further reading	101

Seeing with the mind's eye

7

INTRODUCTION

We are nearly all familiar with visual imagery in which we seem to "see with the mind's eye" even though the relevant visual stimuli are not present. Interest in visual imagery goes back over 2000 years to the ancient Greeks. For example, Aristotle regarded imagery as the main medium of thought. Others in ancient Greece used imagery-based mnemonic techniques to assist in memorizing speeches (see Yates, 1966). For example, there is the method of loci, in which someone who has to give a speech associates successive points in his or her forthcoming speech with locations ("loci") along a favorite walk. When it comes to giving the talk, he or she uses the locations on the walk as cues to assist recall of the key points.

It often feels as if our visual images have virtually all of the attributes of actual objects in the world. However, we frequently deceive ourselves about our own visual imagery. According to Schwitzgebel (2002, p. 36), our knowledge of our own visual imagery is actually rather poor: "Normal people in favorable circumstances make gross and enduring errors about the nature of their visual imagery experiences." He supported his argument by inviting readers to form a visual image of the front of their house and then answer various questions. How about doing as he suggests and see whether you are convinced? Form a clear visual image of your house and then ask yourself the following questions:

- How much of the scene are you able vividly to visualize at once?
- Can you keep the image of your chimney vividly in mind at the same time you vividly imagine (or "image") your front door? Or does the image of your chimney fade as your attention shifts to the door?
- If there is a focal part of your image, how much detail does it have? How stable is it? . . .

According to Schwitzgebel (2002), most people are not at all sure about the answers to several of these questions, suggesting that we don't know in detail what our visual images are really like.

Here is another imagery task. Imagine a cube balanced on one corner

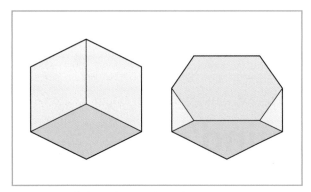

Figure 7.1 If the cube on the left is cut across its equator and the top is removed, the shape of the cut surface is (surprisingly) the regular hexagon shown on the right.

and then cut across its equator (see Figure 7.1). What is the shape of the cut surface when the top is removed? Most people say that it is a square (Ian Gordon, personal communication), but this isn't correct. In fact, it is a regular hexagon.

The first systematic research on visual imagery was reported in 1880 by the British scientist Francis (later Sir Francis) Galton. He asked several hundred people to visualize a scene (e.g., their breakfast table). They were then asked to rate their image for vividness, color, and breadth of field. To his great surprise, Galton discovered that many people (especially scientists) claimed to experience no visual imagery at all. For example, one person reported: "My powers are zero. To my consciousness there is almost no association of memory with objective visual impressions. I recollect the breakfast table, but do not see it" (Galton, 1880, p. 316). At the other extreme, someone else reported, "The image that arises in my mind is perfectly clear . . . I can see in my mind's eye just as well as if I was beholding the scene with my real eye" (Galton, 1880, p. 310).

Since Galton's time, several questionnaires to assess visual imagery have been developed. If such questionnaires provide an accurate assessment, then scores on them should predict performance on tasks involving visual imagery. McKelvie (1995) reported meta-analyses [involving combining numerous findings] based on studies using the Vividness of Visual Imagery Questionnaire (VVIQ). Scores on the VVIQ didn't predict performance on tests of spatial transformation, nor did they predict scores on tests of visual creativity. However, there was a small (but inconsistent) relationship between VVIQ scores and tests of visual memory. Overall, what people *say* about the vividness of their visual imagery generally doesn't predict their *behavior* on tasks involving visual imagery.

EIDETIC IMAGERY

What is eidetic imagery? *Does the evidence support its existence?*

We can pursue the issue of whether some people have genuinely vivid visual imagery by studying individuals with eidetic imagery. **Eidetic imagery** is known popularly as photographic memory. However, it can be defined more precisely as, "A mental image or memory that is extraordinarily clear and vivid, as though actually being perceived" (Colman, 2001, p. 236). It has often been argued that children are more likely than adults to possess eidetic imagery. However, studies on children have produced rather inconsistent and confusing results. Leask, Haber, and Haber (1969) studied children claiming to have eidetic imagery. After the children had viewed a picture, it was removed and they provided a verbal description of it. It has been claimed that individuals with eidetic imagery (known as eidetikers) report that the picture can still be seen, they have a high degree of confidence in their reports, they use the present tense, and they exhibit a pattern of eye movements corresponding to the features being reported. However, Leask et al. (1969) found

KEY TERM
Eidetic imagery: visual imagery resembling visual perception of the same scene or object.

there was little or no correlation between children's accuracy of recall and these various indicators of eidetic imagery. Thus, very few children provide clear evidence of eidetic ability.

Impressive findings using a more stringent test of eidetic imagery were reported by Stromeyer and Psotka (1970). They studied the powers of Elizabeth, a young and intelligent teacher at Harvard University. She was a skilled artist and claimed to project an exact image of a picture or scene onto her canvas. The researchers made use of pairs of computer-generated stereograms, each consisting of a 10,000-dot display (a simpler stereogram is shown in Figure 7.2).

Figure 7.2 An example of a stereogram in which you would see a square floating above the background if you viewed it through a stereoscope. Bruce et al. (2003).

If you look at these patterns through a stereoscope, which presents one pattern to each eye, you see a three-dimensional figure. However, if you look at one stereogram on its own, no pattern can be seen. In one study, Elizabeth viewed one stereogram for 1 minute through her right eye. After a 10-second interval, she looked at the other stereogram with her left eye. When she was asked to superimpose the eidetic image of the first pattern onto the visible stereogram, she immediately reported that she could see the letter "T."

Stromeyer and Psotka (1970) obtained even more dramatic findings in another study. This time Elizabeth formed eidetic images of four 10,000-dot patterns presented to her right eye. The next day she viewed a single pattern with her left eye. She combined this pattern in turn with all four of the patterns viewed the previous day, correctly identifying all the three-dimensional figures resulting from these combinations. Unfortunately, when this technique has been used with other individuals claiming to be eidetikers, the findings have nearly always been negative (see Eysenck, 1984). This has been the case even though much simpler patterns than those of Stromeyer and Psotka have generally been used, and the time interval between patterns has been much shorter. More generally, no one with eidetic powers remotely like those of Elizabeth has been uncovered even with the use of mass screening (Merritt, 1979). This has led many people to be skeptical about the powers claimed for Elizabeth.

DOES VISUAL IMAGERY RESEMBLE VISUAL PERCEPTION?

The somewhat inconclusive nature of most questionnaire-based research has led to the development of other methods of studying visual imagery, the fruits of which are discussed below.

Throughout recorded history, the most popular view of mental imagery has been that it is very similar to perception. As you will probably agree, our conscious experience when imaging resembles our conscious perception of the world around us. Theories of visual imagery will be discussed later in the chapter. However, note that some experts don't agree that visual imagery resembles visual perception. For example, according to Pylyshyn (2002,

2003), visual imagery depends on abstract propositional knowledge about the world rather than on perceptual processes.

The notion that visual imagery is very similar to visual perception receives support from the existence of hallucinations. **Hallucinations** involve experiences resembling ordinary visual perception in the absence of the appropriate environmental stimulus. Hallucinations are common in individuals with **Charles Bonnet syndrome**. This is a condition associated with eye disease in which detailed visual hallucinations not under the patient's control are experienced. Some of the hallucinations such patients experience are bizarre. For example, one sufferer reported the following hallucination: "There's heads of 17th century men and women, with nice heads of hair. Wigs, I should think. Very disapproving, all of them. They never smile" (Santhouse, Howard, & ffytche, 2000).

Do the hallucinations experienced by individuals with Charles Bonnet syndrome involve the same (or at least similar) brain processes as visual perception? ffytche, Howard, Brammer, David, Woodruff, and Williams (1998) discovered that the answer is, "Yes." They found using fMRI (see Glossary) that while patients with Charles Bonnet syndrome were hallucinating they had increased activity in brain areas specialized for visual processing. In addition, hallucinations in color were associated with increased activity in brain areas specialized for color, hallucinations of faces were related to increased activity in brain regions specialized for face processing, and so on.

Do visual perception and visual imagery involve the same underlying systems?

Very few people experience hallucinations. Indeed, anyone (other than those with eye disease) suffering from numerous hallucinations is unlikely to remain at liberty for long! This raises the following rather tricky question—if visual images closely resemble visual perception, why don't we confuse them? One reason is that we are often aware that we have *deliberately* constructed images, which isn't the case with perception. Another reason is that images typically contain much less detail than perception, as was reported by Harvey (1986). Participants studied the photograph of a face and focused on producing a visual image of it. When they had the visual image clearly in mind, they rated the similarity between their image and various photographs of the original face with some details removed. The visual images were rated as most similar to faces from which the sharpness of the edges and borders had been removed.

FINDINGS

Some support for the general notion that there are close links between imagery and perception comes from studies on mental rotation. We will consider a study by Cooper and Shepard (1973). They presented their participants with letters (test figures) in either their normal form or in reversed mirror-image form (see Figure 7.3). They had to judge whether the test figure was the normal or reversed version of the standard figure. The test figures were presented in various orientations (see Figure 7.3).

The key finding was that the farther the test figure was rotated from the upright standard figure, the more time the participants took to make their decisions (see Figure 7.4). Thus, visual imagery seems to resemble visual perception in that more time is required to imagine a greater rotation just as more time is needed in the real world to perceive a large rotation than a smaller one.

KEY TERMS

Hallucinations: visual experiences similar to visual perception occurring in the absence of the relevant environmental stimulus.

Charles Bonnet syndrome: a condition associated with eye disease involving recurrent and detailed hallucinations.

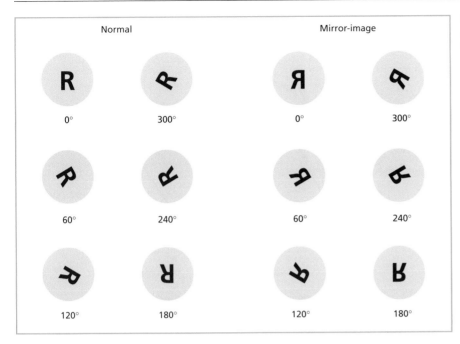

Additional evidence that there are important similarities between visual imagery and visual perception was reported by Finke and Kosslyn (1980).

Evidence that there are important similarities between visual imagery and visual perception was reported by Finke and Kosslyn (1980). Participants were presented with dots 6, 12, or 18 millimeters apart. They indicated how far into the visual periphery the dots could move until it was no longer possible to tell the dots were separate (this assesses what is known as the "field of resolution"). This task was performed either while looking at the dots or while imaging them, and it was performed in the vertical and horizontal directions.

Under both perception and imagery conditions, the fields of resolution increased at less than a constant rate as the distance separating the two dots increased (see Figure 7.5). Particip-

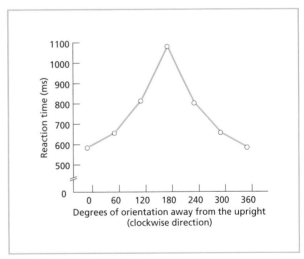

Figure 7.4 The mean time to decide whether a visual stimulus was in the normal or mirror-image version as a function of orientation. Data from Cooper and Shepard (1973).

ants with vivid imagery produced fields of resolution remarkably similar in size to the fields of resolution obtained in perception. In contrast, non-vivid imagers produced somewhat smaller fields of resolution in imagery than in perception. There was a tendency for the fields (perceptual and imaginal) to be elongated along the horizontal axis, with the upper half of the field being longer than the lower half.

Were the participants in the imagery conditions simply guessing the characteristics of the various fields of resolution? This seems very unlikely.

Figure 7.5 Horizontal and vertical fields of resolution in perception and imagery as a function of dot separation and vividness of imagery. Data from Finke and Kosslyn (1980).

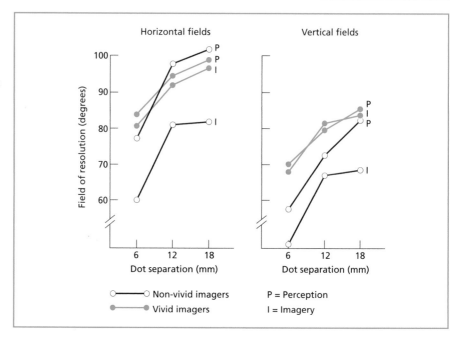

Finke (1980) found that participants asked to guess mistakenly argued that field size would increase in direct proportion to increasing dot size. They also claimed, wrongly, that the field of resolution would be symmetrical above and below the horizontal axis.

Two clear predictions follow from the assumption that visual imagery involves the same processes as visual perception. First, if the content of perception and of imagery tasks is the same, there should be a *facilitation* effect. The reason is that perceptual processing benefits imaginal processing (and vice versa) in those circumstances.

Second, if the content of perception and of imagery tasks is different, there should be an *interference* effect. Why is this? If imagery and perception use the same limited-capacity processes, then total demands are likely to exceed capacity when someone is performing different imagery and perception tasks together. As we will see, there is experimental support for both predictions.

McDermott and Roediger (1994) obtained a facilitation effect in a study in which participants were instructed auditorily to form visual images of objects (e.g., "apple"), or the object names themselves were presented. After that, they identified degraded pictures of those objects. As predicted, participants in the imagery condition were better than those in the name condition at identifying the degraded pictures, thus showing a facilitation effect of imagery on perception.

Baddeley and Andrade (2000) obtained interference effects when the content of perception and imagery differed. Participants formed visual or auditory images and rated the vividness of those images under control conditions (no additional task) or while performing a second task. This second task either involved visual and/or spatial processing (tapping a pattern on a keypad) or it involved auditory processing (counting aloud repeatedly from 1 to 10).

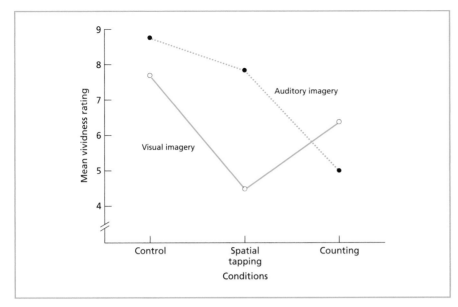

Figure 7.6 Vividness of auditory and visual imagery as a function of additional task (none in the control condition, spatial tapping, or counting). Data from Baddeley and Adrade (2000).

The findings obtained by Baddeley and Andrade (2000) are shown in Figure 7.6. Visual processing interfered with visual imagery, in that spatial tapping reduced the vividness of visual imagery more than the vividness of auditory imagery. In similar fashion, auditory processing interfered with auditory imagery, with the counting task reducing the vividness of auditory imagery more than the vividness of visual imagery.

BRAIN SYSTEMS IN IMAGERY

We have seen there is reasonable evidence that the same (or at least similar) processes are involved in visual imagery and visual perception. The case would be strengthened if it were found that the same brain areas are actively involved in imagery and perception. Kosslyn (e.g., 1980, 1994; Kosslyn & Thompson, 2003) argued that certain brain areas are of key importance in his very influential perceptual anticipation theory. Accordingly, we will discuss the essentials of his theory before turning to a consideration of the relevant evidence.

Kosslyn's approach is known as perceptual anticipation theory because the mechanisms used to generate images involve processes used to anticipate perceiving stimuli. According to the theory, there are close similarities between visual imagery and visual perception. Visual images are **depictive representations**—they are like pictures or drawings in that the objects and parts of objects contained in them are arranged in space. In other words, information within an image is organized spatially in the same way as information within a percept. Thus, for example, a visual image of a desk with a computer on top of it and a cat sleeping underneath it would be arranged so that the computer was at the top of the image and the cat at the bottom.

If visual images are organized spatially like pictures, they are presumably formed in some brain region in which the spatial organization of brain activity

KEY TERM
Depictive representations: representations (e.g., visual images) resembling pictures in that objects within them are organized spatially.

resembles that of the object or objects being imagined. This is the case with early visual cortex, which consists of primary visual cortex (also known as Area 17) and secondary visual cortex (also known as Area 18). Accordingly, Kosslyn and Thompson (2003) argued that Areas 17 and 18 play a key role in visual imagery. They used the term **visual buffer** to refer to the brain areas in which the depictive representations of imagery are formed. By the way, they assumed that the visual buffer is also used in the formation of depictive representations in visual perception.

By now you may be assuming that visual imagery and visual perception are essentially the same. However, there are actually important differences between them. The essential differences can be seen with reference to Figure 7.7. In perception, processing in the visual buffer depends mainly on *external* stimulation. In contrast, visual imagery in the visual buffer depends on non-pictorial information stored in long-term memory within the inferior temporal lobe.

Why is it potentially useful that there are differences between the characteristics of visual perception and visual imagery?

Figure 7.7 Structures and processes involved in visual perception and visual imagery. Based on Bartolomeo (2002).

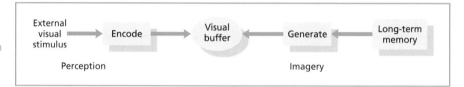

Not everyone agrees with the notion that visual imagery is basically similar to visual perception. Pylyshyn (e.g., 2002, 2003) has put forward a propositional theory (i.e., based on **propositions**). According to Pylyshyn, performance on mental imagery tasks doesn't involve depictive or pictorial representations. Instead, what is involved is tacit knowledge, which is knowledge not generally accessible to conscious awareness. More specifically, tacit knowledge is, "knowledge of *what things would look like* to subjects in situations like the ones in which they are to imagine themselves" (Pylyshyn, 2002, p. 161).

The exact nature of the tacit knowledge allegedly involved in visual imagery seems puzzling, because Pylyshyn hasn't provided a very explicit account of what is involved. For present purposes, however, the key implication of Pylyshyn's theoretical approach is that there is no reason to assume that early visual cortex would be involved when someone is forming a visual image. Kosslyn and Pylyshyn both agree that parts of the brain in which knowledge about the visual features of objects are stored are likely to be active during visual imagery.

There are two main ways in which we can investigate the issue of whether the brain areas involved in visual imagery and visual perception are very similar. First, we can obtain brain-imaging data while people engage in visual imagery or visual perception, and compare the brain areas activated on the two tasks. Second, we can study brain-damaged patients. If visual perception and visual imagery involve the same mechanisms, then brain damage should often have similar effects on perception and on imagery. We turn now to a consideration of both kinds of evidence.

KEY TERMS
Visual buffer: within Kosslyn's theory, the part of the brain involved in producing depictive representations in visual imagery and visual perception.
Proposition: a statement that makes an assertion or denial and which can be true or false.

BRAIN-IMAGING FINDINGS

Early visual cortex (Areas 17 and 18) is very important in the initial stages of visual perception, and so should be activated in visual imagery if imagery closely resembles perception. In contrast, if performance on visual imagery tasks involves tacit knowledge as Pylyshyn (2002) claims, there is no reason at all why early visual cortex would be activated on such tasks. Numerous brain-imaging studies have addressed the issue of whether early visual cortex is activated during visual imagery tasks. In their review, Kosslyn and Thompson (2003) discussed a total of 59 relevant studies. The bad news is that the findings superficially appear very inconsistent—tasks involving visual imagery were associated with activation of early visual cortex in one half of the studies, but not in the other half. The good news is that Kosslyn and Thompson successfully accounted for most of the apparent inconsistencies, as is discussed below.

Kosslyn and Thompson (2003) identified three factors that jointly determine the probability of finding that early visual cortex is activated during visual imagery:

1. *The nature of the task*: Imagery tasks requiring participants to inspect fine details of their visual images are much more likely to be associated with activity in early visual cortex than other imagery tasks are.
2. *Sensitivity of brain-imaging technique*: Early visual cortex is more likely to be shown to be involved in visual imagery when more sensitive brain-imaging techniques (e.g., fMRI) are used than when less sensitive ones (e.g., PET) are used.
3. *Shape-based vs. spatial/movement tasks*: Early visual cortex is more likely to be involved when the imagery task requires processing of an object's shape than when the emphasis is on imaging an object in motion (e.g., imaging an object rotating). There are complex issues here. In essence, however, there is convincing evidence that different brain areas are involved in processing the two types of information (see Kosslyn & Thompson, 2003).

Can we safely conclude that activation in early visual cortex plays an important role in the processing involved in a visual imagery task provided that the task requires processing of shape at a fairly fine level of detail? Not really. The evidence discussed so far only shows an *association* or correlation between visual imagery and activation of early visual cortex, and doesn't prove that early visual cortex is *essential* for visual imagery. As Kosslyn and Thompson (2003, p. 738) pointed out, "Activation in early visual cortex could be analogous to the heat from a light bulb used for reading, which plays no role in accomplishing the task."

We could decide whether early visual cortex is needed for visual imagery if we could prevent our participants from using it during an imagery task. If early visual cortex is needed, then imagery performance should be disrupted under those circumstances. That is precisely what was done by Kosslyn et al. (1999). Participants memorized a stimulus containing four sets of stripes, after which they formed a visual image of it and compared the stripes (e.g., in terms of their relative width) as rapidly as possible. Immediately before performing this task, some participants received repetitive transcranial magnetic stimulation (rTMS; see Chapter 1) applied to Area 17 in the occipital area at the back of the brain. rTMS has the effect of producing a temporary "lesion" and thus rendering an area of the brain inactive. The key finding was that rTMS significantly impaired performance on the imagery task, thus suggesting strongly that Area 17 is causally involved in imaginal processing.

Skeptics might still argue that the brain-imaging evidence discussed so far is not conclusive. It shows that the brain areas involved in visual imagery are often the same as those involved in visual perception. However, that certainly doesn't prove that imagery and perception make use of the same *processes*. An impressive step in the direction of showing that the same processes are involved in imagery and perception was taken by Klein et al. (2004) using fMRI. Participants were presented with flickering black-and-white, bow-tie shaped stimuli with either a horizontal or a vertical orientation in the perceptual condition. In the imagery condition, the participants imagined the same bow-tie shaped stimuli.

What did Klein et al. (2004) find? In the perception condition, brain activity in early visual cortex differed depending on the orientation of the stimulus. There was more activation in the vertical direction when the stimulus was in the vertical orientation and more in the horizontal direction when it was in the horizontal orientation. Dramatically, the same was the case in the imagery condition. In the words of Klein et al. (2004, p. 30), "Not only did the patterns of activation clearly differ for the horizontal and the vertical imagined stimuli, but the activated loci [areas] closely matched those activated during visual perception of similar objects."

EFFECTS OF BRAIN DAMAGE

The simple prediction from Kosslyn's perceptual anticipation theory is that brain damage should generally have similar adverse effects on perception and imagery. The relevant evidence has been well reviewed by Bartolomeo (2002), and the predicted pattern has been found in several studies. However, the overall picture is rather inconsistent and difficult to interpret. As Bartolomeo (2002, p. 372) concluded, "Despite the great variety of the methods used to assess perceptual and imagery abilities, recently published case studies have repeatedly confirmed that every type of dissociation [differing performance between perception and imagery] is possible between these functions."

Some brain-damaged patients have essentially intact visual perception but impaired visual imagery. In most of these patients, there is damage to the left temporal lobe (see Figure 1.4). For example, Sirigu and Duhamel (2001) studied a patient, JB, who had widespread damage to both temporal lobes. JB initially had severe problems with visual perception, but these problems disappeared subsequently, However, JB continued to have profound impairment of visual imagery.

It might seem that it is rather difficult to reconcile the existence of such patients with Kosslyn's emphasis on the similarity between perception and imagery. However, Kosslyn (e.g., 1994) argues that visual imagery differs from visual perception in that there is a process of *generation*—visual images have to be constructed from object information stored in long-term memory.

There is support for the notion that object information is stored in the temporal lobes. For example, Lee, Hong, Seo, Tae, and Hong (2000) applied electrical cortical stimulation to epileptic patients. The patients had conscious visual experience of complex visual forms (e.g., animals, people, landscapes) only when the temporal lobe was stimulated.

The opposite pattern of intact visual imagery but impaired visual perception has also been reported (see Bartolomeo, 2002). Some people suffer from **Anton's syndrome** in which a blind person is unaware he or she is blind and may confuse imagery for actual perception. Not surprisingly, this condition is sometimes known as "blindness denial." Goldenburg, Müllbacher, and Nowak (1995) described the case of a patient with Anton's syndrome, nearly all of whose primary visual cortex had been destroyed. In spite of that, the patient generated visual images so vivid they were mistaken for real visual perception.

Bartolomeo et al. (1998) studied a patient, D, with brain damage to parts of early visual cortex (Area 18) and to temporal cortex. She had severe perceptual impairment for object recognition, color identification, and face recognition. However, her imagery ability in every case seemed to be intact. According to Bartolomeo (2002, p. 365), "Madame D. performed the imagery tasks . . . in such a rapid and easy way as to suggest that her imagery resources were relatively spared by the lesions."

How can we account for patients such as Madame D and those with Anton's syndrome? The honest answer is that we don't have a clear understanding of why some patients have much worse perception than imagery. However, we do know that visual images are typically less detailed and precise than visual perception (e.g., Harvey, 1986). Perhaps limited brain damage prevents those affected from having detailed visual perception, without necessarily having much effect on visual images that lack detail even in healthy individuals.

KEY TERM
Anton's syndrome: a condition found in some blind people in which their visual imagery is misinterpreted as visual perception.

EVALUATION AND CHAPTER SUMMARY

Introduction
- Most early research on visual imagery involved the use of questionnaires to assess self-reported vividness of imagery.
- This research indicated that there are substantial individual differences in reported vividness of imagery. However, there are some doubts concerning the validity of such reports.
- More generally, our powers of visual imagery are sometimes not as good as we may like to think.
- Studies of eidetic imagery have generally proved rather disappointing, with convincing evidence of such imagery being lacking.

Does visual imagery resemble visual perception?
- There are various kinds of evidence indicating that visual imagery fairly closely resembles visual perception.
- First, some people experience hallucinations, in which visual images are mistaken for visual perception.

- Second, the hallucinations experienced by sufferers from Charles Bonnet syndrome involve the same brain areas as those involved in visual perception.
- Third, the sizes of the field of resolution in visual imagery and visual perception are remarkably similar.
- Fourth, there is a facilitation effect when the content of imagery and of perception is the same.
- Fifth, there is an interference effect when the content of imagery and of perception is different.
- We are seldom confused as to whether what we are experiencing is imagery or perception, because we can control imagery more than perception and images are typically less detailed and clear than perception.

Brain systems in imagery
- The central assumption of Kosslyn's perceptual anticipation theory (i.e., that very similar processes are involved in imagery and perception) has received much convincing support.
- The prediction that perceptual and imagery tasks will have facilitatory effects on each other if their content is the same has been confirmed.
- It has also been found that perceptual and imagery tasks interfere with each other if their content differs.
- The findings from brain-imaging research are also strongly supportive.
- Visual imagery involving attention to high-resolution details consistently involves early visual cortex (Kosslyn & Thompson, 2003), a finding hard to account for on Pylyshyn's theory.
- Of particular importance, the detailed patterns of activation in early visual cortex are very similar with imagery and perception tasks (Klein et al., 2004).
- On the negative side, the evidence from brain-damaged patients is messy and difficult to interpret.
- The most puzzling finding in Kosslyn's theory is the existence of patients with intact visual imagery but severely impaired visual perception. As yet, we don't have a convincing explanation for that finding.
- More generally, we need to develop more of an understanding of why dissociations or differences occur between perception and imagery in brain-damaged patients.

FURTHER READING

- Bartolomeo, P. (2002). The relationship between visual perception and visual mental imagery: A re-appraisal of the neuropsychological evidence. *Cortex*, *38*, 357–378. The light that findings from brain-damaged patients has shed on the relationship between visual perception and visual imagery is discussed in this review article.
- Kosslyn, S.M., & Thompson, W.L. (2003). When is early visual cortex activated during visual mental imagery? *Psychological Bulletin*, *129*, 723–746. This excellent article makes coherent sense of the brain-imaging literature on visual imagery.
- Pylyshyn, Z.W. (2002). Mental imagery: In search of a theory. *Behavioral and Brain Sciences*, *25*, 157–238. The case against the notion that visual imagery closely resembles visual perception is put strongly in this article.

CHAPTER 8

CONTENTS

Introduction   103

When is change blindness found?   106

What causes change blindness?   109

Evaluation and chapter summary   113

Further reading   113

In sight but out of mind

INTRODUCTION

Suppose you are watching a film in which students are passing a ball to each other. At some point a woman in a gorilla suit walks right into camera shot, looks at the camera, thumps her chest, and then walks off. Altogether she is on the screen for 9 seconds. I am sure you feel it is absolutely certain that you would spot the woman dressed up as a gorilla almost immediately. Simons and Chabris (1999) carried out an experiment along the lines just described (see Figure 8.1). What percentage of their participants do you think failed to spot the gorilla? Think about your answer before reading on.

It seems reasonable to assume that practically no one would fail to spot a gorilla taking 9 seconds to stroll across a scene. In fact, the findings were very surprising: 50% of observers didn't notice the woman's presence at all! We will consider possible explanations for this finding shortly.

Simons and Levin (1998) carried out similar research in which people walking across a college campus were asked by a stranger for directions. About 10 or 15 seconds into the discussion, two men carrying a wooden door passed between the stranger and the participants. While that was happening, the stranger was substituted with a man of different height, build, and voice wearing different clothes. In spite of that, approximately half the participants failed to realize their conversational partner had changed!

Before going any further, we will consider the terms used to describe the phenomena just discussed. First, there is **inattentional blindness**, the failure to notice an unexpected object appearing in a visual display (e.g., the gorilla in the midst of students). Second, there is **change blindness**, the failure to detect that an object has moved, changed, or disappeared (e.g., one stranger being replaced with a different one). Change blindness is the more general phenomenon, which is why the focus in this chapter is more on change blindness than on inattentional blindness.

The above findings challenge some of our basic assumptions. For example, we assume we have a clear and detailed visual representation of the world around us. As a consequence, we also assume we would immediately detect any change in the visual environment provided that it was sufficiently great. In fact, our perception of the environment is much less complete than we like to think.

Evidence that we greatly overestimate our ability to detect visual changes was shown by Levin, Drivdahl, Momen, and Beck (2002). Participants saw

Figure 8.1 Frame showing a woman in a gorilla suit in the middle of a game of passing the ball. From Simons and Chabris (1999). Reproduced with permission from D.J. Simons.

What is the difference between inattentional blindness *and* change blindness? *Can you think of examples of both from your own life?*

various videos involving two people having a conversation in a restaurant. In one video, the plates on their table changed from red to white, and in another a scarf worn by one of them disappeared. A third video showed a man sitting in his office and then walking into the hall to answer the telephone. When the view switches from the office to the hall, the first person has been replaced by another man wearing different clothes. These videos had previously been used by Levin and Simons (1997), who found that none of their participants detected any of the changes. Levin et al. (2002) asked their participants to indicate whether they thought they would have noticed the changes if they had not been forewarned about them. The percentages claiming they would have noticed the changes were as follows: 78% for the disappearing scarf; 59% for the changed man; and 46% for the change in color of the plates. Levin et al. (2002) used the term **change blindness blindness** to describe our wildly optimist beliefs about our ability to detect visual changes.

Inattentional blindness and change blindness are both phenomena occurring fairly frequently in everyday life. For example, when you are in a hurry to get somewhere, you may walk right past a friend of yours without seeing them at all, or you may trip up because you failed to spot an irregularity in the pavement. As Simons and Chabris (1999, p. 1059) pointed out, "We have all had the embarrassing experience of failing to notice when a friend or colleague shaves off a beard, gets a haircut, or starts wearing contact lenses."

The fact that our belief that we perceive and remember nearly everything in the world around us is mistaken sounds like bad news. However, it is definitely good news for conjurors, whose livelihood depends on that mistaken belief. Most magic tricks involve **misdirection**, in which the magician directs spectators' attention away from some action crucial to the success of the trick. When this is done skillfully, spectators fail to see how the magician is doing his or her tricks, while thinking they have seen everything that is going on.

Jakobsen (2004) discussed various ways of misdirecting an audience, of which we will consider three below. First, if you make a larger and a smaller movement at the same time, spectators will attend to the larger movement. As a result, you can prepare the trick with the smaller movement. Second, spectators will typically look wherever the magician is looking. That means you can direct their attention away from the crucial action you want to perform without their knowledge. Third, if you ask a spectator a question such as "Remember your card?" he or she will look you in the eyes, thus moving their attention away from the action central to the success of the trick.

We can illustrate some of the above points by considering the French drop, which forms the basis for many coin tricks. In the French drop, a coin seems to be passed from one hand to the other while actually remaining in

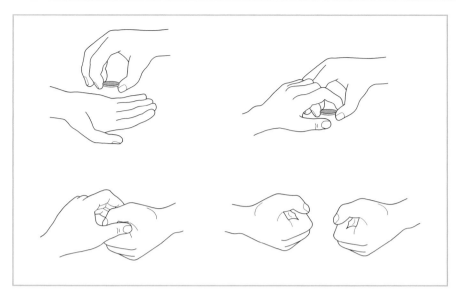

Figure 8.2 The four stages involved in performing the French drop (see text for explanation).

the first hand. What you do is hold a coin by its edge in your right hand between the tips of your fingers and thumb, with the flat side of the coin parallel to your palm. You hold your right hand still and move your left hand with the palm downwards towards your right hand. The fingers of your left hand go above the coin and the thumb of your right hand goes under the coin. As soon as the coin is hidden from view, you should release it so that it falls into your right hand, resting on the second joints of the fingers. What you do next is to bring your left thumb along your right fingertips and close your left hand to convey the impression that it holds the coin. As you move your left hand away from your right hand, drop your left hand casually by your side and focus your eyes on your left hand. The pronounced movements of your left hand and your attentional focus on the left hand will help to convince spectators that the coin is now in your left hand.

As a brief aside, *not* all magic tricks involve misdirection. For example, consider the tricks performed by Harry Houdini (1874–1926). He was frequently encased in chains, padlocks, and handcuffs, having had his clothes and body thoroughly searched beforehand by skeptical spectators to ensure he wasn't concealing any keys. In spite of this careful scrutiny, the Great Houdini escaped triumphantly every time. How did he do it? He held a key suspended in his throat, and regurgitated it when he was unobserved. Since the natural response to having an object stuck in your throat is to gag, it is not surprising that no one thought of Houdini's throat as a possible hiding place for keys. Houdini's real trick was that he could control his gag reflex as a result of painstaking practice with a small piece of potato attached to a piece of string.

Change blindness is also present when we see movies in the movie theater. Levin and Simons (2000) found that observers tended to perceive events as continuous in movies and in staged real-world interactions even when the reality was very different. As they concluded, "Perception of continuity may be an inference that proceeds in spite of impossible between-view changes, both in motion pictures and real-world scenes" (Levin & Simons, 2000, p. 357).

The existence of change blindness is good news for those making movies. It means we rarely spot visual changes when the same scene has been shot more than once with parts of each shot being combined in the finished version of the movie. I will take the risk of appearing nerdy by providing a few examples. In *Grease*, while John Travolta is singing "Greased Lightning," his socks change color several times between black and white. In *Speed*, a bus jumps over an unfinished part of a motorway. Initially you can clearly see several people in the bus, but everyone including the driver has disappeared when it lands. In *Basic Instinct*, there is the famous scene in which Sharon Stone crosses her legs to reveal her lack of underwear. During that scene, the cigarette she was holding suddenly disappears and then re-appears. In the movie *Diamonds Are Forever*, James Bond tilts his car on two wheels to drive through an alleyway. As he enters the alleyway, the car is balanced on its *right* wheels, but when it emerges on the other side it is miraculously on its *left* wheels! If you have seen any of these movies, ask yourself whether you noticed any of these mistakes!

WHEN IS CHANGE BLINDNESS FOUND?

What factors could lead you to fail to notice a change in your visual environment?

The extent to which observers show change blindness or inattentional blindness depends on several factors. Not surprisingly, one relevant factor is the observer's *intention*. At one extreme, there are studies involving the incidental approach (e.g., Simons & Levin, 1998; Simons & Chabris, 1999), in which there is no mention of any possible change. In such studies, it is only some time *after* the change has occurred that observers are asked whether they noticed a change. At the other extreme, there is the intentional approach, in which observers are told beforehand to expect a change in the visual display. As you would imagine, observers are much more likely to show change blindness or inattentional blindness when the incidental approach is used rather than the intentional one (see Rensink, 2002, for a review). For example, it is probable that 100% of observers would have detected the gorilla in the study by Simons and Chabris if instructed to look out for something unexpected. Indeed, observers who watched the film a second time were very surprised they had missed the gorilla on first viewing. Some of them even claimed that the film had been tampered with!

Mack and Rock (1998) reported a series of experiments on inattentional blindness showing the importance of whether the intentional or incidental approach is used. In some experiments, observers judged which of two arms of a briefly displayed large cross was longer when the cross was presented in the area in which the eyes were fixated. On the fourth trial, an unexpected object appeared in the periphery of vision at the same time as the cross. Observers in this incidental condition were then asked whether they saw anything other than the cross, with about 25% of them showing inattentional blindness. Before the following trial, observers were instructed to report if they saw anything other than the cross (intentional condition). Practically all of the observers detected the critical object on this trial.

Another important factor determining whether inattentional blindness occurs is the *similarity* between an unexpected object and other objects in the visual display. For example, Most, Simons, Scholl, Jimenez, Clifford, and

Chabris (2001) asked observers to count the number of either white or black shapes bouncing off the edges of the display window. What Most et al. were interested in was the percentage of observers noticing an unexpected object that could be white, light gray, dark gray, or black. The detection rates for unexpected objects were much higher when they were similar in luminance (brightness) to the target objects (see Figure 8.3). Presumably this happened because unexpected objects resembling target objects were more likely to receive attention than those not resembling target objects.

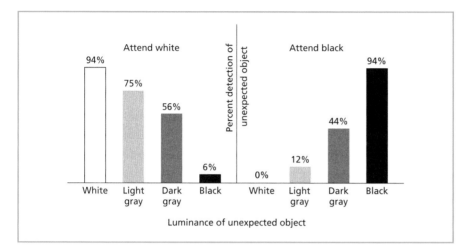

Figure 8.3 Percent of participants detecting unexpected objects as a function of similarity between their luminance or brightness and that of target objects. From Most et al. (2001) with permission from Blackwell Publishing.

You will remember the surprising finding of Simons and Chabris (1999) that 50% of observers failed to detect a woman dressed as a black gorilla. As we will see, similarity was an important factor in their research. There were two teams of students in the film (one dressed in white and the other dressed in black), and the observers were given the task of counting the passes of the team of students dressed in white. Presumably, the observers focused on people dressed in white, which led to them ignoring the black gorilla.

Simons and Chabris (1999) carried out a further experiment in which observers counted the passes made by either members of the team dressed in white or of the one dressed in black. The gorilla's presence was detected by only 42% of observers when the attended team was the one dressed in white, thus replicating the previous findings. However, the gorilla's presence was detected by 83% of observers when the attended team was the one dressed in black. The difference between 42% and 83% shows the importance of the similarity between the unexpected stimulus (gorilla) and task-relevant stimuli (members of attended team).

Finally, we turn to an important study by Hollingworth and Henderson (2002), who considered the role of attention in change blindness. They emphasized the importance of a distinction between two kinds of changes to an object (see Figure 8.4):

1. Type change, in which an object is replaced by an object from a *different* category (e.g., a plate is replaced by a bowl).
2. Token change, in which an object is replaced by an object from the *same* category (e.g., a plate is replaced by a different plate).

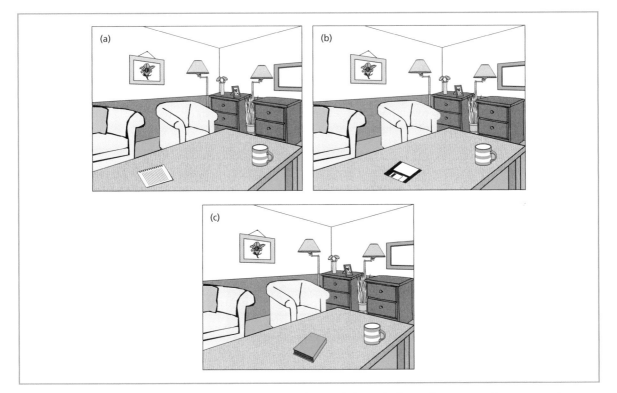

Token changes are smaller and less obvious than type changes, and so we would predict there would be more change blindness with token changes.

Hollingworth and Henderson (2002) recorded eye movements while participants looked at a visual scene (e.g., kitchen, living room) for several seconds. It was assumed that the object fixated at any given moment was being attended to. Participants were told to press a button if they detected any change in the scene. As predicted, changes in objects were much more likely to be detected when the changed object had received attention (been fixated) before the change occurred (see Figure 8.5(a)). The findings suggest that attention to the to-be-changed object is necessary (but not sufficient) for change detection, because there was change blindness for about 60% of changed objects fixated before being changed.

It seems reasonable to assume that change detection would be greater for objects fixated immediately before they were changed than for objects fixated some time before they changed. Surprisingly, that was *not* the case. Hollingworth and Henderson (2002) found that the number of fixations on other objects occurring after the last fixation on the to-be-changed object had no systematic effect on change detection (see Figure 8.5(b)).

Hollingworth and Henderson (2002) also compared performance with type and token changes. As can be seen in Figures 8.5(a) and (b), change detection was much better when there was a change in the type of object rather than merely swapping one member of a category for another (token change).

Finally, we need to consider the methods used to assess change blindness and inattentional blindness. Observers are generally asked to indicate whether they saw any changes in a scene (i.e., reliance is placed on observers' self-reports). This approach is somewhat limited, because observers who deny

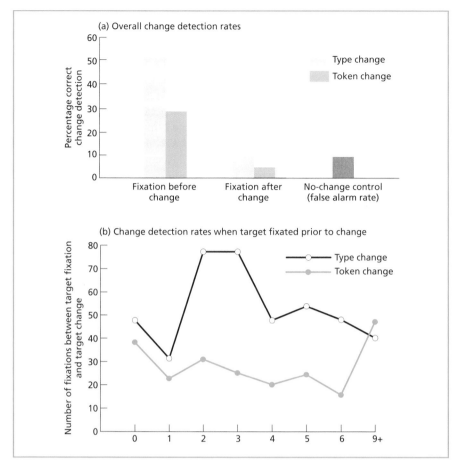

Figure 8.5 (a) percent correct change detection as a function of form of change (type vs. token) and time of fixation (before vs. after change); also false alarm rate when there was no change. From Hollingworth and Henderson (2002). (b) Mean percent correct change detection as a function of the number of fixations between target fixation and change of target and form of change (type vs. token). From Hollingworth and Henderson (2002). Copyright © 2002 by the American Psychological Association. Reprinted with permission.

detecting any changes might nevertheless reveal evidence of detection if more sensitive measures were used. For example, Hollingworth, Williams, and Henderson (2001) used eye-movement data as well as self-report. They compared gaze duration on changed objects when the change wasn't reported by observers with gaze duration on unchanged objects. The key finding was that gaze duration was 250 ms longer on the former objects than on the latter ones. Thus, the change was actually detected in some sense even though conscious awareness of the change was lacking.

Additional evidence that self-report measures can underestimate our ability to detect change was reported by Fernández-Duque and Thornton (2000). Observers failing to detect a change at the conscious level were asked to guess the location at which the change had occurred. Their guesses were accurate more often than chance would allow.

In what ways may our representations of our environment not be as complete and coherent as we believe?

WHAT CAUSES CHANGE BLINDNESS?

There is general agreement that change blindness (and its opposite, change detection) depend on attentional processes. As a first approximation, we detect changes when we are attending to an object that changes, and we show change blindness when *not* attending to that object. Rensink (2002) proposed *coherence theory*, which is based on those assumptions. According to this theory, focused attention on an object produces a very detailed representation that lasts only briefly. Thus, the object will be perceived as having changed when a new stimulus replaces it, even with a short delay between attending to the object and it being replaced. When focused attention is removed from an object, its representation disintegrates fairly rapidly. When that happens, the object will be subject to change blindness.

Why do we have the illusion that we have a fairly complete visual representation of our immediate environment? According to Rensink (2002), the answer is that we have weak representations of most objects in the environment that do not have attention focused on them. These representations (weaker than we believe them to be) lack stability, and so we fail to note when objects within these representations are changed. In contrast, we form very detailed and coherent representations of objects that are the direct focus of attention. Such representations last for a few seconds, and during that time changes to the object will be detected. When focused attention is removed from an object, its representation disintegrates, at which point changes to it are no longer detected.

Rensink's coherence theory sounds plausible. As predicted by the theory, observers are much more likely to detect change in an object when it was fixated prior to the change (e.g., Hollingworth & Henderson, 2002). However, several predictions from coherence theory have been falsified. First, it is assumed within the theory that observers possess very detailed information about objects currently being attended to, but very imprecise information about objects attended to a short time ago. It follows that the probability of detecting change to an object should decrease rapidly as the time since it was last fixated increases. In fact, as we have seen (Figure 8.5), moderately detailed information about previously attended objects is available for at least a few seconds after they cease to receive attention.

Second, it is predicted by coherence theory that observers should have essentially no long-term memory for objects they fixated and attended to several minutes previously. This prediction was tested by Hollingworth and Henderson (2002). Between 5 and 30 minutes after viewing various scenes, observers were presented with two scenes:

1. The original scene with a target object marked with a green arrow.
2. A distractor scene identical to the original scene except that there was a different object in the location of the target object.

The observers had to decide which was the original object. Hollingworth and Henderson found that 93% of type changes were detected as well as 81% of token changes. These percentages are much higher than predicted from coherence theory.

Hollingworth (2004) provided additional evidence that there is good long-term visual memory for objects. He used a "follow-the-dot" method in which observers fixated a dot as it moved from object to object. Observers were then given a test of change detection in which two versions of an object (the original and a token change) were presented and they decided which was the original. Change-detection performance was good even when 402 objects were fixated between the original presentation of an object and its presentation on the change-detection test (see Figure 8.6).

Third, Rensink's (2002) theoretical assumption that focused attention leads to the creation of highly detailed point-by-point representations of visual scenes has been disproved by Henderson and Hollingworth (2003). They presented observers with complex real-world scenes in which half of each scene was hidden by vertical gray bars (see Figure 8.7). The entire scene changed whenever an observer's gaze crossed either of two invisible cross-hatched vertical lines, so that the previously visible parts of the scene were hidden and the hidden parts became visible. Even though the observers were told the precise nature of the changes that might occur, they detected only 2.7% of them. The findings were similar when the researchers (John Henderson and Andrew Hollingworth) tested themselves: "Despite our own familiarity with the images and complete understanding of when the changes take place, we regularly experience the phenomenon" (Henderson & Hollingworth, 2003, p. 496).

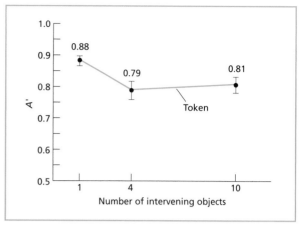

Figure 8.6 Change-detection performance as a function of the number of objects intervening between original object presentation and test. A′ is a measure of performance going from .5 (chance) to 1.0 (perfect sensitivity).

In view of the limitations of coherence theory, we obviously need to look for an alternative theoretical account of change blindness. Such an account was provided by Hollingworth and Henderson (2002). They argued that fairly detailed visual representations are formed of objects that are the focus of attention. These representations are fitted into a mental map providing a spatial layout of the overall scene. These representations are more abstract and less detailed than assumed by Rensink (2002). Information about these visual representations and the overall spatial layout is stored in long-term memory. As a result, "Over multiple fixations on a scene, local object information accumulates in LTM [long-term memory] from previously fixated and attended regions and is indexed within the scene map, forming a detailed representation of the scene as a whole" (Hollingworth & Henderson, 2002, p. 132).

Hollingworth and Henderson's (2002) theoretical position is preferable to that of Rensink (2002). Our ability to detect many changes in objects several seconds (or even minutes) after the original object was attended to is readily explained if fairly detailed representations of most scenes are stored in long-term memory. The finding (Henderson & Hollingworth, 2003) that we sometimes fail to detect substantial changes to visual scenes indicates strongly that Hollingworth and Henderson were correct to argue that our representations of visual scenes are less detailed than assumed by Rensink (2002).

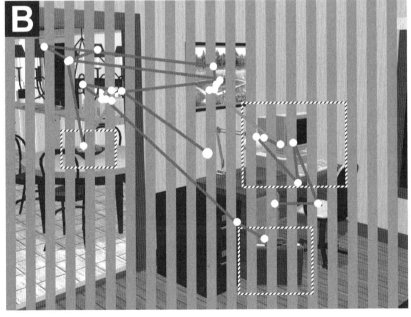

Figure 8.7 This figure shows a scene used in the study by Henderson and Hollingworth (2003) with the eye movements of two observers (A and B). The larger central dot in each panel corresponds to the first fixation, white lines indicate saccades (eye movements) that initiated image change and black lines indicate saccades not initiating an image change. Observers could not see the cross-hatched lines, and the actual stimuli were in color.

EVALUATION AND CHAPTER SUMMARY

When is change blindness found?
- Change blindness and inattentional blindness (especially the latter) are found more often when observers aren't informed beforehand that there may be some change in the visual display.
- Inattentional blindness also depends on the similarity between the unexpected object and the other objects in the display, being more common when it is dissimilar.
- Change blindness is much more likely to occur when the object that changes doesn't receive attention prior to the change.
- Sometimes there is more evidence of change blindness when self-report measures are used rather than more sensitive measures (e.g., gaze duration).

What causes change blindness?
- Hollingworth and Henderson's (2002) theoretical approach is more in line with the available evidence than is Rensink's (2002) coherence theory.
- According to coherence theory, observers possess very detailed information about objects currently being attended to, but very imprecise information about objects attended to a short time ago.
- In fact, the evidence suggests (in line with Hollingworth and Henderson's prediction) that moderately detailed information about previously attended objects is available for at least a few seconds after they cease to receive attention.
- In addition, and also as predicted by Hollingworth and Henderson, some information about previously attended objects is stored in long-term memory.
- In sum, our belief that we have a clear and detailed representation of our visual environment is exaggerated but not entirely incorrect.
- What we actually have is a fairly clear and detailed representation of those parts of the visual environment to which we have paid attention in the recent past.
- As everyone agrees, change blindness is especially likely to be found when the part of the visual scene that is changed hasn't previously been the focus of attention.

FURTHER READING

- Mack, A., & Rock, I. (1998). *Inattentional blindness*. Cambridge: MA: MIT Press. This book was an important landmark for research in this area, and contains details of many fascinating studies on inattentional blindness.
- Rensink, R.A. (2002). Change detection. *Annual Review of Psychology*, *53*, 245–277. This article provides a good overview of theory and research on change detection.
- Simons, D.J. (2000). Current approaches to change blindness. *Visual Cognition*, *7*, 1–15. There is a useful discussion of various theoretical approaches to the phenomenon of change blindness in this article.

CHAPTER 9

CONTENTS

Introduction 115

Do we attend to locations or objects? 118

Disorders of attention:
Unattended stimuli 119

Cross-modal effects 122

Evaluation and chapter summary 124

Further reading 125

What do we attend to in vision?

INTRODUCTION

According to the American psychologist and philosopher William James (1890, pp. 403–404), "Everyone knows what attention is. It is the taking possession by the mind, in clear and vivid form, of one out of what seem several simultaneously possible objects or trains of thought. Focalization, concentration, of consciousness are of its essence. It implies withdrawal from some things in order to deal effectively with others." As James (1890) suggested, we need focused attention because most of the time we are confronted by an enormous amount of sensory input, from which we must select only that fraction that is of most relevance.

What is focused visual attention like? Before answering that question, take a look around you and observe for yourself. As James (1890) pointed out, you probably found yourself attending to one object at a time or at one part of the visual space around you. Several psychologists (e.g., Posner, 1980) argue that visual attention is like a spotlight: It illuminates a small part of the visual field; little can be seen outside its beam; and it can be redirected flexibly to focus on any object of interest. Other psychologists (e.g., Eriksen & St. James, 1986) have developed the notion of an attentional beam by comparing focused attention to a zoom lens. The basic idea here is we have the ability to increase or decrease the area of focal attention at will, just as a zoom lens can be moved in or out to alter the visual area it covers. This certainly makes sense. For example, when driving a car it is typically desirable to attend to as much of the visual field as possible to anticipate danger. However, when we detect a potential hazard, we focus specifically on it to avoid having a crash.

LaBerge (1983) reported findings supporting the notion that visual attention resembles a zoom lens. Five-letter words were presented, and a probe requiring a rapid response was occasionally presented instead of (or immediately after) the word. This probe could appear in the spatial position of any of the five letters of the word. In one condition, an attempt was made to focus participants' attention on the middle letter of the five-letter word by asking them to categorize that letter. In another condition, participants categorized the entire word. It was expected that this would lead them to adopt a broader attentional beam.

The findings on speed of detection of the probe are shown in Figure 9.1.

Figure 9.1 Mean reaction time to the probe as a function of probe position. The probe was presented at the time that a letter string would have been presented. Data from LaBerge (1983).

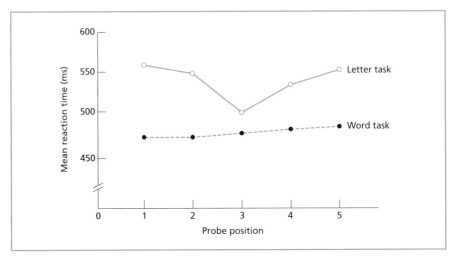

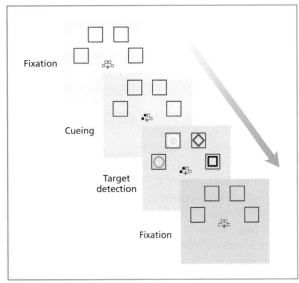

Figure 9.2 Schematic illustration of the experimental design. Cues were presented for 4, 7, or 10 sec and indicated the possible locations of the target (white circle). Either one, two (as in this example), or four locations were cued, determining the size of the attended region. Müller et al. (2003). Copyright © Society for Neuroscience.

"For many, attention acts like a zoom lens." Why is this a potentially misleading belief?

KEY TERM
Split attention: allocation of attention to two non-adjacent regions of visual space.

LaBerge (1983) assumed that the probe would be responded to faster when it fell within the central attentional beam than when it did not. On this assumption, the attentional spotlight or zoom lens can have either a very narrow (letter task) or rather broad beam (word task).

Müller, Bartelt, Donner, Villringer, and Brandt (2003b) also reported findings supporting the zoom-lens theory. On each trial, participants were presented with four squares arranged as in Figure 9.2. They were cued to focus their attention on one given square, on two given squares, or on all four squares. After that, four objects were presented (one in each square), and participants decided whether a target (e.g white circle) was among them. When a target was present, it was always in one of the cued squares. Müller et al. (2003b) used fMRI (see Glossary) to assess brain activation in the various conditions.

There were two key findings. First, as predicted by zoom-lens theory, targets were detected fastest when the attended region was small (i.e., only one square), and slowest when the it was large (i.e., all four squares) (see Figure 9.3). Second, fMRI revealed that activation in early visual areas was most widespread when the attended region was large, and was most limited when the attended region was small. This finding supports the notion of an attentional beam that can be either wide or narrow.

Are you convinced by now that visual attention can accurately be described as resembling a spotlight or zoom lens? If so, you are mistaken! There is increasing evidence that we can use visual attention in a more *flexible* way than implied by the analogy with a spotlight or zoom lens. More specifically, we can show **split attention**, in which attention is directed to two regions of space *not* adjacent to each other. Awh and Pashler (2000) carried out a study on split attention. Participants were presented with a 5×5 visual display containing 23 letters and two digits, and had to report the identity of the two digits. Just before the display was presented, participants were given two cues indicating the probable locations of the two digits. However, these cues were invalid on 20% of trials. Part of what was involved is shown in Figure 9.4(a). The crucial condition was one in which the cues were invalid, with one of the digits being presented in between the cued locations.

How good would we predict performance to be for a digit presented between the two cued locations? If the spotlight or zoom-lens theory is correct, focal attention should include the two cued locations *and* the space in between. In that case, performance should be high for that digit because it receives full attention. In contrast, if split attention is possible, performance should

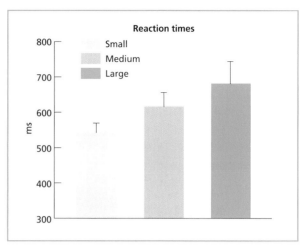

Figure 9.3 Reaction times to detect targets as a function of the attended region in the study by Müller et al. (2003). Copyright © Society for Neuroscience.

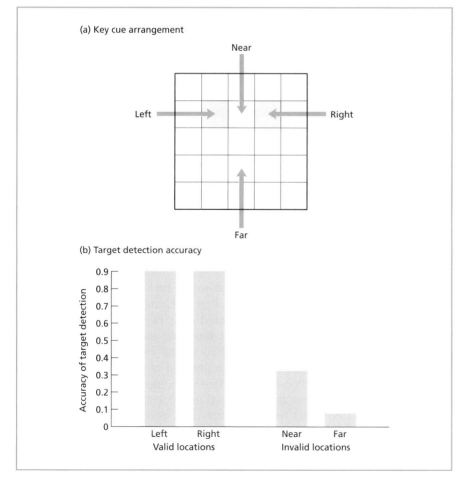

Figure 9.4 (a) Shaded areas indicate the cued locations and the near and far locations are not cued. Based on information in Awh and Pashler (2000); (b) Probability of target detection at valid (left or right) and invalid (near or far) locations. Based on information in Awh and Pashler (2000).

be poor because only the cued locations should receive full attention. As can be seen in Figure 9.4(b), performance was much lower for digits presented *between* cued locations than for digits presented *to* cued locations. Thus, split attention is possible and the spotlight/zoom-lens approach is inadequate. The existence of split attention suggests that attention can be shaped like a donut, with nothing in the middle.

Müller, Malinowski, Gruber, and Hillyard (2003a) obtained further support for the notion that visual attention can be donut-shaped. There was a display consisting of four horizontally arranged rectangles, and a rapidly flashing series of symbols was presented in each rectangle. Participants were instructed to attend to the two left rectangles (1 + 2), the two right rectangles (3 + 4), or to two separated rectangles (1 + 3 or 2 + 4). The task was to detect the simultaneous presentation of a target symbol within the two attended rectangles. They used an EEG-based measure known as steady-state visual evoked potentials to assess the amount of attentional processing directed to each rectangle.

The most important findings of Müller et al. (2003a) were obtained when attention was directed to separated rectangles. The EEG measure indicated that participants attended much more to the separated rectangles than to the one in the middle. This is another demonstration of split attention.

DO WE ATTEND TO LOCATIONS OR OBJECTS?

Spotlight and zoom-lens theories of visual attention have proved moderately successful in spite of their problems in accounting for split attention. Such theories share an emphasis on the notion that visual attention is directed to a given location or area within the visual field. However, there is also convincing evidence that visual attention can be directed to *objects* rather than to a particular *region*. For example, Marshall and Halligan (1994) presented ambiguous displays to a patient who failed to respond to stimuli in the left visual field. Each display could be seen as a black shape against a white background or as a white shape on a black background. There was a jagged edge dividing the two shapes at the center of each display. The patient copied this jagged edge when drawing the shape on the left side of the display, but couldn't copy exactly the same edge when drawing the shape on the right side. Thus, the patient attended to objects rather than simply to a region of visual space.

Additional evidence that visual attention can be directed to objects rather than to a particular region was reported by O'Craven, Downing, and Kanwisher (1999). Participants were presented with two stimuli (a face and a house) that overlapped transparently at the same location, with one of the objects moving slightly. They were told to attend *either* to the direction of motion of the moving stimulus *or* to the position of the stationary stimulus. Suppose attention is location-based. In that case, participants would have to attend to both stimuli, because both were in the same location. In contrast, suppose attention is object-based. In that case, processing of the attended stimulus should be more thorough than processing of the unattended stimulus.

O'Craven et al. (1999) tested the above competing predictions by using fMRI (see Glossary) to assess activity in brain areas selectively involved in processing faces or houses. There was more activity in the face-specific brain area when the face stimulus was attended, and more activity in the house-specific brain area when the house stimulus was attended. Thus, visual attention seemed to be object-based rather than location-based.

DISORDERS OF ATTENTION: UNATTENDED STIMULI

We can learn much about the processes involved in attention by studying brain-damaged individuals suffering from attentional disorders. Here we consider two of the main attentional disorders: neglect and extinction. **Neglect** (or unilateral neglect) is typically found after brain damage in the right parietal lobe, and is often the result of a stroke. Neglect patients with right-hemisphere damage don't notice (or fail to respond to) objects presented to the left side of the visual field. This occurs because of the nature of the visual system—information from the left side of the visual field proceeds to the right hemisphere of the brain. According to Driver and Vuilleumier (2001, p. 40), "Neglect patients often behave as if half of their world no longer exists. In daily life, they may be oblivious to objects and people on the neglected side of the room, may eat from only one side of their plate … and make-up or shave only one side of their face."

How is neglect *distinct from* extinction?

Extinction is a phenomenon often found in neglect patients. However, the two disorders are distinct. The main reason they are found in the same patients is because they involve damage to anatomically close brain areas (Karnath, Himmelbach, & Küker, 2003). In cases of extinction, a *single* stimulus on either side of the visual field can be judged as well as by healthy individuals. However, when *two* stimuli are presented together, the one further toward the side of the visual field that is neglected tends to go undetected. Some patients only show extinction when the objects presented simultaneously are the same. Extinction is a serious condition, because we are typically confronted by multiple stimuli at the same time in everyday life.

How can we explain extinction? Most experts assume that *competition* among stimuli is of key importance. For example, Marzi, Girelli, Natale, and Miniussi (2001, p. 1354) argued as follows:

The presence of extinction only during bilateral [on both sides] stimulation is strongly suggestive of a competitive mechanism, whereby the presence of a more salient [prominent] stimulus presented on the same side of space as that of the brain lesion (ipsilesional side) captures attention and hampers the perception of a less salient stimulus on the opposite (contralesional) side.

The fact that neglect and extinction patients often show no conscious awareness of certain stimuli suggests that these unattended stimuli are not being processed. However, there is much evidence indicating a reasonable amount of processing of unattended stimuli by neglect and extinction patients. For example, McGlinchey-Berroth, Milber, Verfaellie, Alexander, and Kilduff (1993) gave neglect patients the task of deciding rapidly whether letter strings formed words. Decision times on this task were faster on "yes" trials when a semantically related object rather than an unrelated one

KEY TERMS
Neglect: a disorder of visual attention in which stimuli or parts of stimuli presented to the side opposite the brain damage are undetected and not responded to; the condition resembles extinction, but is more severe.
Extinction: a disorder of visual attention in which a stimulus presented to the side opposite the brain damage is not detected when another stimulus is presented at the same time.

preceded the letter string. This effect was the same size regardless of whether the object was presented to the left (neglected) or to the right (attended) visual field. These findings indicate that there was some semantic processing of left-field stimuli by neglect patients.

Rees, Wojciulik, Clarke, Husain, Frith, and Driver (2000) carried out an fMRI study to assess the processing of extinguished stimuli. Extinguished stimuli produced moderate levels of activation in the primary visual cortex and some nearby areas. These findings suggest that these stimuli of which the patient was unaware were nevertheless processed reasonably thoroughly.

EXPLAINING NEGLECT

Why do some patients experience neglect?

It is difficult to explain neglect, in part because the precise symptoms vary from one patient to another. However, we can develop an understanding of neglect in the context of the theory proposed by Corbetta and Shulman (2002). Their theory is based on the assumption that there are two major attentional systems. One attentional system is voluntary or goal-directed, whereas the other system is involuntary or stimulus-driven. According to Corbetta and Shulman (2002), the goal-directed or top-down system is involved in the selection of sensory information and responses. This system is influenced by expectation, knowledge, and current goals. In contrast, the stimulus-driven or bottom-up system is involved in the detection of salient or conspicuous unattended visual stimuli (e.g., flames appearing under the door of your room). This system has a "circuit-breaking" function, meaning that visual attention is redirected from its current focus.

Corbetta and Shulman (2002) went further theoretically, and identified the main brain areas associated with these two attentional systems. The goal-directed system consists of a dorsal fronto-parietal network (see Figure 9.5), whereas the stimulus-driven system (see Figure 9.6) consists of a right-hemisphere ventral fronto-parietal network. These two systems generally influence and interact with each other to determine what is attended at any moment.

How is this theory relevant to an understanding of neglect? According to Corbetta and Shulman (2002), neglect patients typically have damage to the stimulus-driven attentional system. This view is supported by the finding that many neglect patients have damage to the right temporo-parietal junction (Vallar & Perani, 1987), an important part of the stimulus-driven system. In addition, neglect is much more common after damage to the right hemisphere than to the left one. This fits with the evidence that the stimulus-driven system is located in the right hemisphere.

Bartolomeo and Chokron (2002) agreed that neglect is due to an impaired stimulus-driven

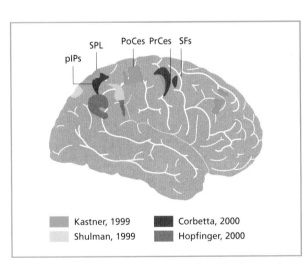

Figure 9.5 The brain network involved in the goal-directed attentional system, based on findings from various brain-imaging studies in which participants were expecting certain visual stimuli. PIPs = posterior intraparietal sulcus; SPL = superior parietal lobule; PoCes = postcentral sulcus; PrCes = precentral sulcus; and SDS = superior frontal sulcus. From Corbetta and Shulman (2002). Copyright © 2002 by the Nature Publishing Group. Reproduced with permission.

system, and argued that the goal-directed system is reasonably intact in neglect patients. As predicted, the attentional performance of neglect patients is generally much better when they can use the goal-directed or top-down attentional system to assist them. Smarnia et al. (1998) compared the time taken to detect stimuli when the side of the visual field was predictable (thus permitting use of the goal-directed system), and when it was determined at random (thus *not* permitting use of that system). Neglect patients responded faster in the attended field *and* the unattended (neglect) field when the side to which stimuli would be presented was predictable.

Duncan, Bundesen, Olson, Humphreys, Chavda, and Shibuya (1999) presented arrays of letters briefly, and asked neglect patients to recall either all the letters or only the ones in a pre-specified color. It was assumed that the goal-directed or top-down attentional system could only be used effectively when target letters were identified by color. As expected, recall of letters presented to the left (neglect) side was much worse than recall of letters presented to the right side when all letters had to be reported. However, neglect patients resembled healthy controls in showing comparable recall of letters presented to each side of the visual field when only letters in a certain color were reported. Thus, neglect patients showed reasonably good top-down attentional control.

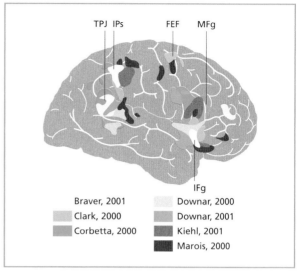

Figure 9.6 The brain network involved in the stimulus-driven attentional system, based on findings from various brain-imaging studies in which participants detected low-frequency target stimuli. TPJ = temporo-parietal junction; IPS = intra-parietal sulcus; FEF = frontal eye field; and MFg = middle frontal gyrus. From Corbetta and Shulman (2002). Copyright © 2002 by the Nature Publishing Group. Reproduced with permission.

UNATTENDED VISUAL STIMULI IN HEALTHY INDIVIDUALS

So far we have considered unattended visual stimuli in the context of research on patients with neglect or extinction. What happens to stimuli not attended to by healthy individuals? There is a considerable amount of neurophysiological evidence indicating that there is reduced processing of such stimuli (see Umiltà, 2001, for a review). For example, Martinez et al. (1999) compared event-related potentials (ERPs; see Glossary) to attended and unattended visual displays. The attended displays produced a greater first positive wave (P1) about 70–75 ms after stimulus presentation and a greater first negative wave (N1) about 130–140 ms after stimulus presentation. These findings indicate that attended stimuli are processed more thoroughly than unattended ones. However, ERPs 50–55 ms after stimulus presentation showed no difference between attended and unattended displays. Thus, attentional processes don't influence the very early stages of processing.

Further evidence that there is reduced processing of unattended visual stimuli was reported by Wojciulik, Kanwisher, and Driver (1998). Participants were presented with displays containing two faces and two houses. On any given block of trials, they had to attend to the faces or to the houses, with the other type of stimulus being unattended. There was significantly more brain activity in a part of the brain involved in face processing when the faces needed to be attended to than when they did not. This indicates that the faces received less processing when unattended.

CROSS-MODAL EFFECTS

Virtually all of the research discussed so far in this chapter is limited in that the visual modality was studied on its own. In a similar fashion, research on auditory attention typically ignores visual perception. This approach has been justified on the grounds that attentional processes in each sensory modality (e.g., vision, hearing) operate *independently* from those in all other modalities. However, that assumption is wrong and in the real world we often co-ordinate information from two or more sense modalities at the same time (known as **cross-modal attention**). For example, when listening to someone speaking, we often observe their lip movements at the same time. Information from the auditory and visual modalities is combined to facilitate our understanding of what they are saying.

Before turning to research on cross-modal effects, we need to draw a distinction between endogenous spatial attention and exogenous spatial attention. **Endogenous spatial attention** involves an individual voluntarily directing his or her visual attention to a given spatial location. This generally happens because he or she anticipates that a target stimulus will be presented at that location. In contrast, **exogenous spatial attention** involves the "involuntary" direction of visual attention to a given spatial location determined by aspects of the stimulus there (e.g., intensity or high level of threat). Cross-modal effects occur when directing visual attention to a given location also attracts auditory and/or tactile (touch-based) attention to the same location. Alternatively, directing auditory or tactile attention to a given location can attract visual attention to the same location.

FINDINGS

We will start our discussion of cross-modal effects by considering the **ventriloquist illusion**. In this illusion, which everyone who has been to the movie theater or seen a ventriloquist will have experienced, sounds are misperceived as coming from their apparent visual source. Ventriloquists try to speak without moving their lips, while at the same time manipulating the mouth movements of a dummy. The dominance of visual over auditory information means that it seems as if the dummy rather than the ventriloquist is speaking. Something very similar happens in the movie theater. We look at the actors and actresses on the screen and see their lips moving. The sounds of their voices are actually coming out of loudspeakers to the side of the screen, but we hear those voices coming from their mouths.

We turn now to research on endogenous or "voluntary" spatial attention. Suppose we present participants with two streams of lights (as was done by Eimer and Schröger, 1998), with one stream of lights being presented to the left and the other to the right. At the same time, we also present participants with two streams of sounds, with one stream of sounds being presented to each side. In one condition, the instructions inform participants to detect

In what ways can information from separate modalities influence each other?

KEY TERMS

Cross-modal attention: the coordination of attention across two or more modalities (e.g., vision and hearing).

Endogenous spatial attention: attention to a given spatial location determined by voluntary or goal-directed mechanisms; see exogenous spatial attention.

Exogenous spatial attention: attention to a given spatial location determined by "involuntary" mechanisms triggered by external stimuli (e.g., loud noise); see endogenous spatial attention.

Ventriloquist illusion: the mistaken perception that sounds are coming from their apparent visual source, as in ventriloquism.

deviant *visual* events (e.g., longer than usual stimuli) presented to one side only. In the other condition, participants have to detect deviant *auditory* events in only one of the streams.

Event-related potentials (ERPs) were recorded to obtain information about the allocation of attention. Not surprisingly, Eimer and Schröger (1998) found that ERPs to deviant stimuli in the relevant modality were greater to stimuli presented on the to-be-attended side than those presented on the to-be-ignored side. This finding simply shows that participants allocated their attention as instructed. What is of more interest is what happened to the allocation of attention on the irrelevant modality. Suppose participants were given the task of detecting *visual* targets on the left side. What happened was that ERPs to deviant *auditory* stimuli were greater on the left side than on the right side. Thus, we have here a cross-modal effect in which the voluntary or endogenous allocation of visual attention also affected the allocation of auditory attention. In similar fashion, when participants had to detect *auditory* targets on one side, ERPs to deviant *visual* stimuli on the same side were greater than ERPs on the opposite side. Thus, the allocation of auditory attention influenced the allocation of visual attention as well.

Finally, we turn to exogenous or "involuntary" spatial attention. Clear evidence of cross-modal effects was reported by Spence and Driver (1996). Participants fixated straight ahead with hands uncrossed, holding a small cube in each hand. There were two light-emitting diodes, with one light at the top and one at the bottom of each diode. In one condition, loudspeakers were placed directly above and below each hand close to the light sources. There was a sound from one of the loudspeakers shortly before one of the four lights was illuminated. The key finding was that visual judgments were more accurate when the auditory cue (which didn't predict which light would be illuminated) was on the *same* side as the subsequent visual target. Thus, "involuntary" or exogenous auditory attention influenced the allocation of visual attention.

Spence and Driver (1996) also had a condition in which the roles of the visual and auditory modalities were reversed. In other words, a light was illuminated shortly before a sound was presented, and the task involved making auditory judgments. Auditory judgments were more accurate when the non-predictive visual cue was on the *same* side as the subsequent auditory target. The implication is that involuntary visual attention influenced the allocation of auditory attention.

We have seen that voluntary and involuntary visual attention can influence auditory attention, and vice versa. In addition, visual attention to a given location can influence attention to tactile stimuli (involving touch), and attention to tactile stimuli at a given location can influence visual attention (see Eysenck & Keane, 2005).

What produces these various cross-modal effects? They depend at least in part on multimodal neurons, which are responsive to stimuli in various modalities. These multimodal neurons respond strongly to multimodal stimulation at a given location. However, they show reduced responding when there is multimodal stimulation involving more than one location (see Stein & Meredith, 1993, for a review).

EVALUATION AND CHAPTER SUMMARY

Do we attend to locations or objects?
- Visual attention is often object-based. This is not surprising given that the goal of visual perception is generally to identify objects in the environment.
- Remember that the grouping processes (e.g., law of similarity, law of proximity) occurring fairly early in visual processing divide the visual environment into figure (central object) and ground (see Chapter 5).
- The major limitation of object-based accounts of visual attention is that attention can also be location-based.
- Thus, we need theoretical accounts to indicate the circumstances in which visual attention is either object-based or location-based.
- Whatever the nature of such theoretical accounts, it is clear that they will need to emphasize the *flexibility* of the human visual attentional system.

Disorders of attention: Unattended stimuli
- Extinction and neglect are two major attentional disorders in which some visual stimuli are not detected.
- Extinction is probably best explained by assuming that stimuli on the side opposite the lesion are not detected because stimuli on the same side as the lesion capture attention.
- However, even extinguished stimuli receive some processing.
- Neglect often involves damage to the stimulus-driven attentional system rather than the goal-directed attentional system.
- Indeed, the attentional performance of neglect patients is often reasonably good when they can make use of the goal-directed attentional system.
- Brain-imaging studies on normal individuals indicate that unattended visual stimuli receive some processing, but less than that received by attended stimuli.

Cross-modal effects
- Cross-modal attention is very important in everyday life and has recently started to be studied seriously by psychologists.
- Future theories of focused visual attention need to incorporate assumptions about the ways in which stimuli in other sensory modalities influence visual attention.
- Attention directed towards stimuli in one modality presented at a given location typically attracts attention to stimuli in other modalities presented to the same location.
- These cross-modal effects occur regardless of whether endogenous (voluntary) or exogenous (involuntary) attention is involved.
- Cross-modal effects depend in part on multimodal neurons.
- What does the future hold for research on cross-modal effects?
- First, we know much about cross-modal effects in spatial attention but little about cross-modal effects in the *identification* of stimuli and objects. In other words, is information from different sense modalities combined to facilitate object recognition?

- Second, several important cross-modal effects have been reported, but as yet we lack a detailed theoretical understanding of the processes involved. For example, we cannot predict ahead of time how strong any cross-modal effects are likely to be.

FURTHER READING

- Driver, J. (2001). A selective review of selective attention research from the past century. *British Journal of Psychology*, *92*, 53–78. This article provides a good overview of the history of research on visual attention.
- Spence, C. & Driver, J. (Eds.) (2004). *Cross-modal space and cross-modal attention*. Oxford: Oxford University Press.
- Umiltà, C. (2001). Mechanisms of attention. In B. Rapp (Ed.), *The handbook of cognitive neuropsychology*. Philadelphia, PA: Psychology Press. Attentional processes in brain-damaged patients are discussed in detail in this interesting chapter.

CHAPTER 10

CONTENTS

Introduction	127
What determines dual-task performance?	131
Theoretical perspectives	136
Evaluation and chapter summary	140
Further reading	141

Multitasking

INTRODUCTION

It is a matter of everyday observation that most people's lives are becoming busier and busier. We can see this in the increased tendency for people to try to do two things at once. Examples include holding a conversation on a mobile phone while buying bus or train tickets and chatting with friends while watching television. The pressured and stressful nature of our daily lives was described recently by Darrah, English-Lueck, and Freeman (2001): "That the pace of life is fast and is getting faster has become a truism for the new century. Several effects combine to create the maelstrom [powerful whirlpool]—the flurry of rapidly occurring activities in lives already crowded with activities; and the constant looming threat of minor catastrophe."

There is general agreement that more and more is demanded of people at work. According to the *Wall Street Journal*, 45% of American workers contacted in a recent survey claimed they were expected to work on too many different tasks at the same time. The central issue discussed in this chapter is the effectiveness (or otherwise!) of our attempts to juggle two or more tasks at the same time. A key term is **multitasking**, which was originally used in the context of computer functioning. According to the Webopedia (2004), multitasking is, "The ability to execute more than one task at the same time, a task being a program ... In multitasking, only one CPU [central processing unit] is involved, but it switches from one program to another so quickly that it gives the appearance of executing all of the programs at the same time."

The fact that most of us engage in multitasking much of the time suggests we believe ourselves capable of performing two tasks at once. The main reason we multitask is because we think it will save us precious time compared to the traditional approach of doing one thing at a time. If that isn't the case, then we are simply wasting time and incurring higher stress levels by continuing to engage in multitasking!

There is a common belief that women are better than men at multitasking. This belief may owe something to the fact that women engage in much more multitasking than men. Floro (1999) studied two-adult Australian households. Women involved in child care were much more likely than men to be multitasking (e.g., doing household work at the same time). There are surprisingly few studies in which the multitasking abilities of men and women were compared directly. However, Rubinstein, Meyer, and Evans (2001)

KEY TERM

Multitasking: performing two or more tasks at the same time by switching rapidly between tasks.

How can individual differences affect the ability to multitask?

found no gender differences in multitasking performance in a series of experiments discussed in detail shortly.

There is also a common belief that unintelligent people are less able to multitask effectively. This notion was given vivid expression by American President Lyndon Johnson. He claimed that Gerald Ford (a slow-witted Congressman who subsequently became President), "can't fart and chew gum at the same time." There is support for the notion that intelligence is related to the ability to perform two tasks at the same time. In a study by Engle, Tuholski, Laughlin, and Conway (1999), participants sometimes performed one task at a time (e.g., immediate serial recall of words in the order presented). At other times, participants performed two tasks at a time (e.g., sentences presented for comprehension + serial recall of the last word in each sentence). The key finding was that intelligence was a good predictor of dual-task performance, but was unrelated to single-task performance.

FINDINGS

How good are we at multitasking? We can address this question more precisely if we consider two different situations. In the first situation (single-task condition), we perform each of two tasks (A and B) on its own. In the second situation (dual-task condition), we perform both tasks (A and B) at the same time. In an ideal world, we would perform both tasks as rapidly and as accurately in the dual-task condition as in the single-task condition. The fact that most of us engage in multitasking much of the time suggests we believe ourselves capable of performing two tasks at once. Many people argue that we approach the ideal state of affairs when the tasks we perform together are well-practiced and so involve automatic skills. In other words, "Practice makes perfect." For example, skilled drivers can drive while listening to the radio, air-traffic controllers can monitor the positions of numerous aircraft at once, and a one-man band can play several instruments together.

Evidence supporting commonsensical views on the value of practice was reported by Spelke, Hirst, and Neisser (1976). Two students (Diane and John) received 5 hours' training a week for 3 months on various tasks. Their first task was to read short stories for comprehension while writing down words to dictation. Initially they found it very difficult to combine these tasks, with their reading speed and handwriting both suffering considerably. After 6 weeks of training, however, Diane and John could read as rapidly and with as much comprehension when taking dictation as when only reading. In addition, the quality of their handwriting had also improved.

Spelke et al. (1976) were still not satisfied with the students' performance. For example, Diane and John could recall only 35 out of the thousands of words they had written down at dictation. Even when 20 successive dictated words formed a sentence or came from the same semantic category (e.g., four-footed animals), the students were unaware of that. With further training, however, they could write down the names of the categories to which the dictated words belonged while maintaining normal reading speed and comprehension.

Does training improve our ability to multitask?

Not everyone is convinced we are good at multitasking. For example, the Roman sage Publilius Syrus said that, "To do two things at once is to do neither." In similar vein, the American commentator David Weinberger argued recently that slicing your attention is like slicing a plum—"You lose some of the juice." Evidence that the costs of multitasking can be high even with simple tasks was reported by Rubinstein et al. (2001). Let us consider one of their experiments in some detail. Participants were presented with a deck of 24 cards, each of which had on it a pattern of identical geometrical objects. The cards differed in terms of shapes (triangle, circle, star, cross), number of shapes, shape size, and shape shading. There were four main conditions:

1. *Low rule complexity; no task switching*: Each card had to be sorted with respect to one stimulus dimension (e.g., shape).
2. *Low rule complexity; task switching*: Cards in odd serial positions had to be sorted with respect to one stimulus dimension (e.g., shape), whereas those in even positions had to be sorted with respect to a different stimulus dimension (e.g., number of shapes).
3. *High rule complexity; no task switching*: Each card had to be sorted with respect to *two* stimulus dimensions at the same time (shape + number or size + shading).
4. *High rule complexity; task switching*: Cards in odd serial positions had to be sorted with respect to one rule (e.g., based on shape + number) and cards in even serial positions had to be sorted with respect to the other rule (e.g., based on size + shading).

In sum, tasks 2 and 4 involve multitasking, because there is rapid alternation between two different tasks. In contrast, tasks 1 and 3 don't involve multitasking, because only a single task is performed with any deck of cards. The findings obtained by Rubinstein et al. (2001) are shown in Figure 10.1. As you can see, performance was much slower under multitasking than single-task conditions (975 ms per card on average). It was also much slower when the sorting rule was high in complexity than when it was low (724 ms per card on average). Finally, the slowing of performance associated with multitasking was much greater when the sorting rule was high in complexity.

Rubinstein et al.'s (2001) findings indicate that multitasking can incur surprisingly great costs, especially when the tasks involved are relatively complex. More specifically, task performance was approximately 50% slower on average when two tasks were alternated compared to single-task performance. These findings should make us ponder the wisdom of continuing to spend much of our lives multitasking.

Why did Rubinstein et al. (2001) find much more evidence than Spelke et al. (1976) that multitasking can create substantial costs? At least part of the answer is that participants in the Spelke et al. (1976) study had far more practice. It would be interesting to see what would

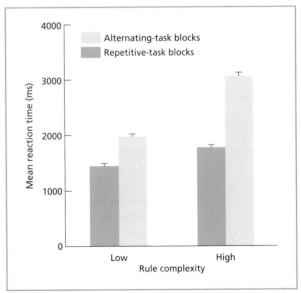

Figure 10.1 Mean reaction times (RTs) as a function of rule complexity (low vs. high) and trial-block type (alternating vs. repetitive). Copyright © American Psychological Association. Reprinted with permission.

happen to performance on Rubinstein et al.'s (2001) tasks if massive practice were provided.

CAN WE THINK AND DRIVE?

Does the evidence support a ban on using handheld mobile phones whilst driving?

When we consider multitasking in everyday life, an issue of considerable practical importance is whether the ability to drive a car is impaired when the driver uses a mobile phone. There has been much controversy on this issue. More than a dozen countries have passed laws restricting the use of mobile phones while driving, but millions of irate motorists complain that such legislation infringes their civil liberties. We turn to a consideration of the relevant evidence.

Redelmeier and Tibshirani (1997) studied the mobile-phone records of 699 drivers who had been involved in a car accident. They discovered that 24% of them had used their mobile phone within 10 minutes of the accident, with the percentage being similar for those using handheld and hands-free phones. They concluded that use of a mobile phone (whether handheld or hands-free) was associated with a four-fold increase in the likelihood of being involved in a car accident.

David Strayer and William Johnston (2001) pointed out that the above findings don't prove that use of mobile phones plays a part in causing accidents. Perhaps people who drive while using mobile phones tend to engage in risky behavior. If so, their tendency to impulsive behavior may explain the association or correlation between mobile-phone use and probability of having an accident. Accordingly, Strayer and Johnston carried out an experiment using a simulated-driving task. The participants had to brake as rapidly as possible when they detected a red light. This task was carried out on its own or while the participants held a conversation using a handheld or hands-free mobile phone.

What did Strayer and Johnston (2001) find? First, performance on the driving task was the same in the handheld and hands-free conditions. Second, participants missed significantly more red lights when using a mobile phone at the same time (7% vs. 3%, respectively). Third, the mean time taken to respond to the red light was about 50 ms longer in the mobile-phone conditions. That may sound trivial. However, consider what that means for a motorist driving at 70 mph (110 kph). The additional 50 ms taken to brake would mean that the motorist's car would travel an extra 5 feet (1.5 meters) before stopping. That could mean the difference between stopping just short of a child in the road or hitting and killing that child.

Lesch and Hancock (2004) reviewed several findings on the effects of mobile-phone use. It leads to an increase in brake response time, impaired ability to maintain lane position, and greater variability in speed control. It also leads to reduced frequency of rear-view mirror checking, and a decreased ability to respond to other drivers.

Even if mobile-phone use reduces driving performance, the consequences may not be too serious if drivers are aware that is the case. Lesch and Hancock (2004) addressed this issue in a study in which male and female drivers expressed their confidence to deal with distractors while driving. In addition, they performed a driving task while using a mobile phone. Male drivers were reasonably accurate in their assessment of how well they would cope with the distraction of using a mobile phone, but female drivers tended to be unrealistically confident.

We have scratched the surface in terms of identifying the factors determining the extent to which multitasking is (or isn't) effective. In the next section, we consider the issue in much more detail.

WHAT DETERMINES DUAL-TASK PERFORMANCE?

Some theorists (e.g., Pashler, Johnston, & Ruthruff, 2001; Welford, 1952) argue we will *always* find evidence of interference in dual-task performance if we use sensitive techniques. One such technique involves presenting participants with two stimuli (e.g., two lights) each of which is associated with a different response (e.g., pressing different buttons). Their task is to respond to each stimulus as rapidly as possible. When the second stimulus is presented very shortly after the first one, there is generally a marked slowing of the response to the second stimulus. This interference effect is known as the **psychological refractory period (PRP) effect** (see Pashler et al., 2001, for a review). This effect does *not* occur simply because people aren't used to responding to two immediately successive stimuli. For example, Pashler (1993) discussed one of his studies in which the effect was still observable after more than 10,000 practice trials.

Several researchers have tried to show that it is possible to eliminate the psychological refractory period effect. For example, Van Selst, Ruthruff, and Johnston (1999) pointed out that the two tasks used in many previous studies of the PRP effect both involved manual [hand] responses. They suggested that this may have produced a PRP effect because people find it hard to control their two hands separately. Van Selst et al. used two tasks, one of which required a vocal response and the other a manual response. After extended practice, the PRP effect reduced to only 50 ms. This was a much smaller effect than when they repeated the experiment with both tasks requiring manual responses.

More dramatic findings were reported by Schumacher et al. (2001). They used two tasks: (1) say "one," "two," "three" to low-, medium-, and high-pitched tones; (2) respond with different fingers to four stimuli (O - - -, - O - -, - - O -, and - - - O) having a disc (O) in different locations. These two tasks were performed on over 2000 trials, at the end of which 5 of the 11 participants performed them virtually as well together as singly (see Figure 10.2). In contrast, four of the participants had high levels of dual-task interference (150 ms or more) even after extensive practice (see Figure 10.2). According to Schumacher et al. (2001, p. 107), "Participants may use a variety of task-scheduling strategies

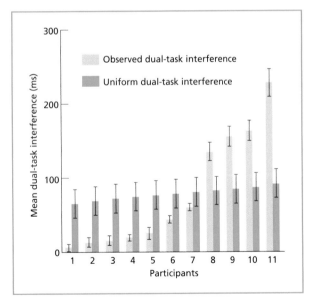

Figure 10.2 Observed (light bars) and expected uniform (dark bars) amounts of dual-task interference in ms at the end of practice rank-ordered from smallest to largest for 11 participants. Shumacher et al. (2001). Copyright © American Psychological Association. Reprinted with permission.

(e.g., a cautious one with minimal temporal overlap in processing for the two tasks, or a daring strategy with a great deal of processing overlap) during the course of practice, and so exhibit various amounts of dual-task interference."

Greenwald (2003) showed that it is possible for two tasks to be performed at the same time with no disruption or interference. One task involved vocal responses to auditory stimuli: saying "A" or "B" in response to hearing those letter names. The other task involved manual responses to visual stimuli: moving a joystick switch to the left to an arrow pointing left and moving it the right to an arrow pointing right. In view of the simplicity of these two tasks, it is perhaps not surprising that participants could perform them as well together as on their own.

Greenwald (2004) provided an explanation of the various findings. He argued that what is most important for each task is whether the relationship between stimuli and responses is *direct* and obvious. For example, both tasks used by Greenwald possess a very direct relationship between stimuli and responses (e.g., saying "A" when you hear "A" and saying "B" when you hear "B"). According to Greenwald (2004), two tasks can readily be performed together without disruption when both involve direct stimulus–response relationships. Most studies have found some disruption when two tasks are performed together because one or both of the tasks involves *indirect* stimulus–response relationships. The experiment by Schumacher et al. (2001) is exceptional in finding an absence of disruption even though neither task involved direct stimulus–response relationships. However, this atypical finding only occurred after very extensive practice—there was substantial disruption under dual-task conditions early in practice.

PRACTICE AND AUTOMATICITY

We have seen evidence that practice often has a dramatic effect on people's ability to perform two tasks at the same time (e.g., Schumacher et al., 2001; Spelke et al., 1976). It is often assumed that this happens because practice allows some processing activities to become automatic. This may help to explain why two tasks involving very direct relationships between stimuli and responses can be performed together with no disruption. Here are the main criteria for automatic processes:

- they are fast
- they don't require attention, and so don't reduce the capacity to perform other tasks at the same time
- they are unavailable to consciousness
- they are unavoidable, meaning they always occur when an appropriate stimulus is presented.

Few processes are fully automatic in the sense of conforming to all of the above criteria. For example, let's consider the **Stroop effect**, in which naming the colors in which words are printed is slowed down by using competing color words (e.g., the word BLUE printed in red). This sounds like a good example of automatic processing since we apparently cannot avoid processing the word. However, Kahneman and Henik (1979) found the Stroop effect was

KEY TERM
Stroop effect: the finding that naming the colors in which words are printed is slower when the words are conflicting color words (e.g., the word RED printed in green).

much larger when the color name was in the same location as the to-be-named color rather than in an adjacent location. Thus, the processes producing the Stroop effect are *not* entirely unavoidable and so not completely automatic.

Important studies on automatic processing were reported by Shiffrin and Schneider (1977) and Schneider and Shiffrin (1977). They used a task in which participants memorized up to four letters (the memory set) and were then shown a visual display containing up to four letters. Their task was to decide rapidly whether one of the letters in the visual display was the same as any of the letters in the memory set. The crucial manipulation was the type of mapping used:

1. *Consistent mapping*: Only consonants were used as members of the memory set, and only numbers were used as distractors in the visual display (or vice versa).
2. *Varied mapping*: A mixture of numbers and consonants was used to form the memory set and to provide distractors in the visual display.

In order to clarify the difference between these two types of mapping, we will consider a few examples of each:

Consistent mapping

Memory set	Visual display	Response
H B K D	4 3 B 7	Yes
H B K D	9 2 5 3	No
5 2 7 3	J 5 D C	Yes
5 2 7 3	B J G H	No

Varied mapping

Memory set	Visual display	Response
H 4 B 3	5 C G B	Yes
H 4 B 3	2 J 7 C	No
5 8 F 2	G 5 B J	Yes
5 8 F 2	6 D 1 C	No

What do you think happened in terms of speed of performance? You probably guessed that consistent mapping led to faster performance than varied mapping. However, the actual difference may be even greater than you thought. As can be seen in Figure 10.3, the numbers of items in the memory set and visual display greatly affected decision speed in the varied mapping conditions but not in the consistent mapping conditions. According to Shiffrin and Schneider (1977), the participants performed well with consistent mapping because they used automatic processes operating at the same time (parallel processing). These automatic processes have evolved through many years of practice in distinguishing between letters and numbers. In contrast, performance with varied mapping required controlled processes, which are of limited capacity and require attention. As a result, participants had to compare each item in the memory set with each item in the visual display one at a time (serial processing) until a match was found or every comparison had been made.

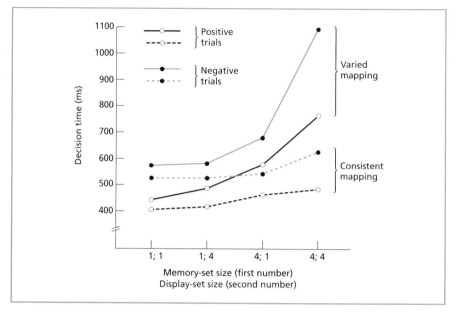

Figure 10.3 Reaction times on a decision task as a function of memory-set size, display-set size, and consistent vs. varied mapping. Data from Shiffrin and Schneider (1977).

The findings discussed so far don't really prove that automatic processes develop through practice. However, that was shown in a further experiment by Shiffrin and Schneider (1977). They used consistent mapping with the consonants B to L forming one set and the consonants Q to Z forming the other set. As before, items from only one set were always used in the construction of the memory set, and the distractors in the visual display were all selected from the other set. Thus, for example, if the memory set was "G," then that was the only consonant between B and L that could possibly appear in the visual display. There was a dramatic improvement in performance speed over 2100 trials, apparently reflecting the development of automatic processes.

From what has been said so far, it may seem that automatic processes are more useful than controlled ones. However, automatic processes suffer from the serious limitation that they are *inflexible* whereas controlled processes are not. As a result, performance based on automatic processes suffers following a change in what is required. Shiffrin and Schneider (1977) demonstrated this in the second part of the experiment discussed above. The initial 2100 trials with one consistent mapping were followed by a further 2100 trials with the reverse consistent mapping. Thus, the items in the memory set were now always drawn from the consonants Q to Z if they had previously been drawn from the set B to L. This reversal of the mapping conditions greatly disrupted performance. Indeed, it took nearly 1000 trials before performance recovered to the level at the very start of the experiment!

In sum, we can draw the following conclusions: "Automatic processes function rapidly and in parallel but suffer from inflexibility; controlled processes are flexible and versatile but operate relatively slowly and in a serial fashion" (Eysenck, 1982, p. 22). However, there is a problem with Shiffrin and Schneider's (1977) explanation of their findings. Their assumption that automatic processes operate in parallel and don't require capacity means that decision time with consistent mapping shouldn't depend on the number of items in the memory set or visual display. In fact, however, decision speed with consistent mapping was slower when the memory set and the visual display both contained several items (see Figure 10.3).

SIMILARITY

Think of tasks you can perform reasonably well together and of others you can't. You will probably find that tasks easily performed together typically differ considerably from each other. For example, you may be able to study while listening to music, or to hold a conversation while dancing. In contrast, it can be remarkably difficult to rub your stomach with one hand while patting your head with the other.

How can the nature of the task affect your ability to multitask?

There are various ways in which two tasks can be similar. First, they can be similar in terms of stimulus modality (e.g., both involving visual or auditory presentation). Second, they can be similar in terms of central processing (e.g., both involving spatial processing). Third, tasks can be similar in terms of responding (e.g., both requiring manual responses). Think back to the studies by Schumacher et al. (2001) and by Greenwald (2003), in which they found that two tasks could be performed at the same time without interference. In both studies, the two tasks differed in stimulus modality (visual vs. auditory) and in type of response (manual vs. vocal).

There is much evidence that similarity of stimulus modality is important. For example, Treisman and Davies (1973) found that two monitoring tasks interfered with each other much more when the stimuli on both tasks were in the same modality (visual or auditory). Response similarity is also important. We saw earlier that Van Selst et al. (1999) obtained much more dual-task interference when both tasks required a manual response than when one required a verbal response and the other a manual response. McLeod (1977) asked participants to perform a continuous tracking task with manual responding, together with a tone-identification task. Some participants responded vocally to the tones, whereas others responded with the hand not involved in the tracking task. Performance on the tracking task was worse with high response similarity (manual responses on both tasks) than low response similarity (manual responses on one task and vocal ones on the other).

It is often hard to decide just how similar or dissimilar two tasks are. For example, how similar are piano playing and poetry writing, or driving a car and watching a football match? Only when there is a better understanding of the processes involved in the performance of such tasks will sensible answers be forthcoming.

TASK DIFFICULTY

Common sense suggests that our ability to perform two tasks at the same time depends on their difficulty level, and there is much supporting research. For example, Sullivan (1976) asked participants to repeat back (shadow) an auditory message and to detect words on a non-shadowed message at the same time. The key manipulation involved varying the complexity of the shadowed message. When the shadowing task was difficult, fewer targets were detected on the non-shadowed message than when the shadowing task was easy.

Greenwald's (2004) account of the factors determining whether there is dual-task interference was discussed earlier and is relevant here. He distinguished between easy tasks involving *direct* stimulus–response relationships and difficult tasks involving *indirect* stimulus–response relationships. As he pointed out, two tasks can be performed at the same time with little or no disruption if both tasks are easy ones involving direct stimulus–response relationships. In contrast, disruption is almost inevitable if both tasks are difficult ones involving indirect stimulus–response relationships.

It is perhaps natural to assume that the demands for resources of two tasks performed together simply equal the demands of the two tasks when performed separately. In fact, however, the necessity of performing two tasks together often introduces new demands. Relevant evidence was reported by D'Esposito, Detre, Alsop, Shin, Atlas, and Grossman (1995). Participants performed a semantic judgment task and a spatial rotation task, either separately or together. The key finding was that there was significant activity in the prefrontal cortex and the anterior cingulate (both in the frontal lobe—see Figure 1.4) *only* in the dual-task condition. The importance of this finding is that these brain areas are associated with attentional and other related processes.

THEORETICAL PERSPECTIVES

Plenty of theories are designed to account for how well (or how poorly) we manage to cope with the need to perform two tasks at the same time. Here we focus on two major theoretical approaches that have influenced much thinking in this area: central capacity theories and multiple-resource theories.

CENTRAL CAPACITY THEORIES

A simple way of accounting for many dual-task findings is to assume there is some central capacity (e.g., an attentional system such as the central executive discussed in Chapter 12). This theoretical approach has been adopted by several theorists including Kahneman (1973) and Baddeley (1986). This central capacity has strictly limited resources, and the extent to which two tasks can be performed together depends on the demands each task makes on those resources. If the combined demands of the two tasks don't exceed the total resources of the central capacity, the two tasks won't interfere with each other. However, if the resources are insufficient, then performance disruption will occur.

Predictions of central capacity theory were tested by Bourke, Duncan, and Nimmo-Smith (1996) using four different tasks. These tasks were performed in all possible pairings, with one task being identified as more important than the other. According to the theory, the task making most demands on the central capacity should interfere most with all three of the other tasks. In contrast, the task making fewest demands on central capacity should interfere least with all the other tasks. Here are the four tasks in order from most demanding to least demanding:

1. *Random generation*: Generating letters at random.
2. *Prototype learning*: Working out the features of two patterns or prototypes from seeing various examples.

3. *Manual task*: Screwing a nut down to the bottom of a bolt and back up to the top, and then down to the bottom of a second bolt and back up, and so on.
4. *Tone task*: Detecting the occurrence of a target tone.

What did Bourke et al. (1996) find? The key findings were in line with predictions (see Figure 10.4). The most demanding task (random generation) consistently interfered most with the prototype, manual, and tone tasks, and did so whether it was the primary or secondary task. The least demanding task (tone task) consistently interfered least with each of the other three tasks.

Findings from dual-task studies are not always as supportive as those of Bourke et al. (1996). For example, consider a study by Hegarty, Shah, and Miyake (2000) in which they used three primary tasks:

1. *Paper folding*: Participants had to fold a piece of paper mentally, imagine a hole punched through it, and then decide what the paper would look like when unfolded.
2. *Card rotation*: Participants viewed a target figure and indicated which of the test figures represented rotations of the target.
3. *Identical pictures*: Participants viewed a target figure and decided which test figure was identical to it.

These tasks were performed together with various secondary tasks, two of which were random number generation and the two-back tasks (listen to a series of consonants, indicating when a consonant was identical to the one presented two items earlier).

Which primary task would we expect to be most disrupted by the secondary tasks? Hegarty et al. (2000) had previously found that the paper-folding task seemed to make the greatest demands on central capacity and the identical-pictures task the least. Thus, the obvious prediction from central capacity theory is that the secondary tasks should disrupt paper folding the most and identical pictures the least. In fact, the findings were precisely the opposite (see Figure 10.5). Why was this? According to Hegarty et al. (2000), there are two reasons. First, participants found the paper-folding task the most difficult primary task, and so allocated more of their available processing resources to it than other primary

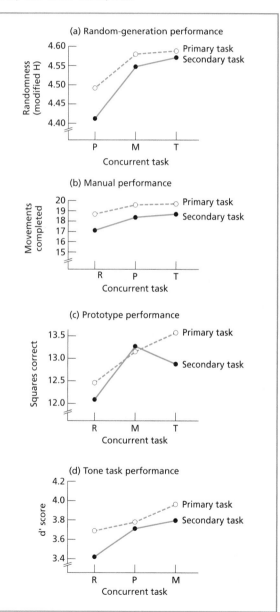

Figure 10.4 Performance on random generation, R, prototype learning, P, manual, M, and tone, T, tasks as a function of concurrent task. Adapted from Bourke et al. (1996).

Figure 10.5 Mean disruption or decrement on three primary tasks (identical pictures; card rotations; paper folding) as a function of secondary task (random number generation; two-back task). Data from Hegarty et al. (2000).

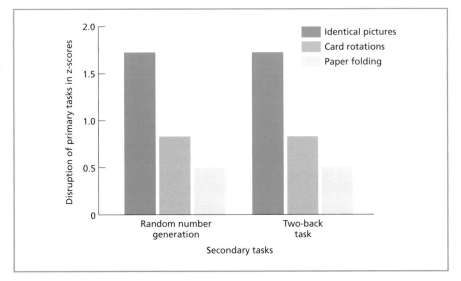

Figure 10.5 Mean disruption or decrement on three primary tasks (identical pictures; card rotations; paper folding) as a function of secondary task (random number generation; two-back task). Data from Hegarty et al. (2000).

tasks. Second, there is evidence that selecting a response on one task inhibits the ability to perform a second task (Pashler, 1993). The paper-folding task involved the least response selection and the identical-pictures task the most.

Just, Carpenter, Keller, Emery, Zajac, and Thulborn (2001) reported a very interesting study using functional magnetic resonance imaging (fMRI; see Chapter 1) lending support to central capacity theories. They used two tasks performed together or on their own. One task was auditory sentence comprehension (e.g., deciding whether "The pyramids were burial places and they are one of the seven wonders of the ancient world" is true or false). The other tasks involved mentally rotating three-dimensional figures to decide whether they were the same. These tasks were selected deliberately so they would involve very different processes in different parts of the brain.

What did Just et al. (2001) find? First, performance of both tasks was significantly impaired under dual-task conditions compared to single-task conditions. Second, the language task mainly activated parts of the temporal lobe, whereas the mental rotation task mostly activated parts of the parietal lobe (see Figure 1.4). Third, and most importantly, Just et al. (2001) compare the amount of the activation associated with each task under single- and dual-task conditions. Brain activation in regions associated with the language task decreased by 53% under dual-task conditions compared to single-task conditions. In similar fashion, brain activation in regions involved in the mental rotation task decreased by 29% under dual-task conditions. The need to distribute a limited central capacity (probably attention) across two tasks meant the amount each task could receive was reduced compared to the single-task condition.

The tasks used by Just et al. (2001) were very different from each other and didn't require extensive attentional control and coordination for them to be performed together. However, attentional control and coordination are generally required when two tasks are performed together. As discussed in Chapter 12, Baddeley (1986, 2001) assumed in his working memory model that there is a central capacity (the central executive) whose functions include attentional control and coordination. There is evidence that brain areas within the prefrontal cortex at the front of the brain are associated with its use. For example, D'Esposito et al. (1995) found that areas within the dorso-lateral prefrontal cortex were activated under dual-task conditions but not under single-task conditions. In similar fashion, Bunge, Klingberg, Jacobsen, and Gabrieli (2000) reported there was significantly more activation in parts of the prefrontal cortex in dual-task conditions than in single-task ones.

MULTIPLE-RESOURCE MODEL

Some theorists (e.g., Wickens, 1984) have argued that the processing system consists of independent processing mechanisms in the form of multiple resources, each of which has limited capacity. If this is the case, then it is clear why the degree of similarity between two tasks is so important: similar tasks compete for the same specific limited resources, and thus produce interference. In contrast, dissimilar tasks involve different resources, and so don't interfere with each other.

Wickens (1984) put forward a three-dimensional structure of human processing resources (see Figure 10.6). According to his model, there are three successive stages of processing (encoding, central processing, and responding). Encoding involves the perceptual processing of stimuli, and typically makes use of the visual or auditory modality. Encoding and central processing can involve spatial or verbal codes. Finally, responding involves manual or vocal responses. There are two key assumptions in this model:

1. There are several pools of resources based on the distinctions among stages of processing, modalities, codes, and responses.
2. If two tasks make use of different pools of resources, then people should be able to perform both tasks without disruption.

There is much support for this multiple-resource model and its prediction that several kinds of task similarity influence dual-task performance. For example, we have seen there is more interference when two tasks share the same modality (Treisman & Davies, 1973) or when they share the same type of response (McLeod, 1977; Van Selst et al., 1999). However, the model has some limitations. First, it focuses only on visual and auditory inputs or stimuli, but

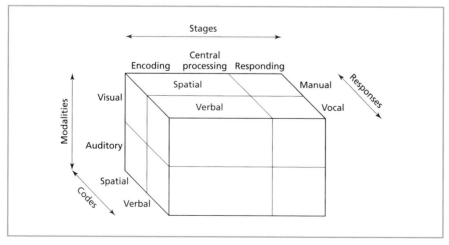

Figure 10.6 A proposed dimensional structure of human processing resources. From "Processing resources in resources in attention" by Wickens, C.D. in *Varieties of Attention*, edited by R. Parasuraman and D.R. Davies © 1984 by Academic Press, reproduced by permission of the publisher.

tasks can be presented in other modalities (e.g., touch). Second, there is often some disruption to performance even when two tasks make use of different modalities (e.g., Treisman & Davies, 1973). Third, the model assumes that several tasks could be performed together without interference provided each task used different pools of resources. However, Just et al. (2001) found that two very different tasks (auditory sentence comprehension and mental rotation) couldn't be performed together without interference. Their brain-imaging data suggested there was a limitation on the capacity of some general capacity available for processing, but such a capacity is not included in Wickens' model.

EVALUATION AND CHAPTER SUMMARY

Introduction
- There is no clear evidence that women are better than men at multitasking, but more intelligent people can multitask more effectively than less intelligent ones.
- The ability to multitask often increases dramatically with practice (Spelke et al., 1976).
- However, the costs associated with multitasking can be very high even when the two tasks involved are relatively simple (Rubinstein et al., 2001).
- Problems with multitasking are important in the real world. For example, mobile-phone use impairs driving performance in several ways.
- It also appears that hands-free mobile phones impair driving performance as much as handheld ones. This is presumably because the use of any mobile phone distracts the motorist's attention away from the task of driving.
- It follows that the law should prohibit the use of hands-free mobile phones as well as handheld ones.
- Those disputing the need for such a law often point out that no one has proposed banning conversations between the driver and other occupants of the vehicle. However, conversational activity inside a car is reduced when the driving conditions become more difficult (Parks, 1991). This is less likely to happen with mobile phone conversations, because one of the participants in the conversation has no knowledge of the current driving conditions.

What determines dual-task performance?
- Numerous studies have obtained evidence of dual-task interference via the psychological refractory period effect.
- However, this effect can sometimes be largely (or entirely) eliminated by extensive practice or when both tasks involve direct stimulus–response relationships.
- More generally, dual-task performance typically exhibits minimal interference when one or both tasks involve automatic processes developed through practice.
- Convincing evidence that people can process several stimuli much faster when automatic rather than controlled processes are involved was reported by Shiffrin and Schneider (1977).

- However, automatic processes have the disadvantage of being inflexible when the situation changes.
- It is easier to perform two tasks at the same time when they are dissimilar in terms of stimulus modality and/or type of response required.
- Two tasks can be performed more easily together when they are relatively simple rather than complex. However, we need to take account of the complexity of coordinating performance on the two tasks as well as the difficulty of each task considered separately.

Theoretical perspectives
- Many of the findings from dual-task studies can be accounted for by central capacity theories.
- We can "explain" dual-task interference by arguing that the resources of some central capacity have been exceeded; and the absence of interference by assuming the two tasks didn't exceed those resources.
- However, unless we can measure central processing capacity properly, we may simply be re-describing the findings rather than providing an explanation. In that connection, the use of brain-imaging data to clarify the involvement of attentional processes in single- and dual-task conditions represents an important step forward.
- More specifically, brain areas associated with the central executive are significantly more active when considerable attentional control is required (e.g., dual-task conditions) than when it is not (e.g., single-task conditions).
- Another tricky issue is that it is very difficult to assess the total demands on central capacity imposed by performing two tasks at the same time. Each task imposes its own demands.
- However, there are also additional demands from coordinating processing on two tasks at the same time, preventing interference between competing responses, and so on.
- Finally, even if we have evidence that some central capacity has impaired dual-task performance, it still remains to clarify the nature of that central capacity.

FURTHER READING

- Pashler, H., Johnston, J.C., & Ruthroff, E. (2001). Attention and performance. *Annual Review of Psychology*, *52*, 629–651. This chapter discusses dual-task performance, practice effects, and the development of automatic processes in detail.
- Rubinstein, J.S., Meyer, D.E., & Evans, J.E. (2001). Executive control of cognitive processes in task switching. *Journal of Experimental Psychology: Human Perception and Performance*, *27*, 763–797. The authors provide an interesting evaluation of theoretical approaches to multitasking performance and also report a series of important experiments.

PART II

CONTENTS

11 The long and the short of human memory   146

12 Short-term or working memory   164

13 Learning without awareness?   178

14 It's slipped my mind   190

15 The story of my life   206

16 Should we believe eyewitnesses?   220

Learning and memory

Learning and memory have always been regarded as two of the most important topics within psychology. There are obvious reasons why that is the case. If we were unable to learn, then we wouldn't have any information available to remember. In the absence of both learning and memory, we wouldn't recognize anyone or anything as familiar. We wouldn't be able to talk, read, or write, because we would no knowledge of language. We would have extremely limited personalities, because we would know nothing about the events of our own lives and, therefore, would have no sense of self. The devastating effects associated with the progressive destruction of the human memory system can be seen in patients suffering from Alzheimer's disease.

Learning and memory are closely connected to each other. Learning involves the accumulation of knowledge or skills and would be impossible in the absence of memory. In similar fashion, memory would be impossible in the absence of learning, because we can only remember things learned previously. In spite of their strong connections, learning and memory have surprisingly often been treated separately in the history of psychology. For example, consider the American behaviorists such as John Watson, Fred Skinner, and Clark Hull. Their central focus was on learning and on trying to predict changes in behavior using the principles of conditioning. In contrast, cognitive psychologists have for the most part focused on memory rather than learning, which helps to explain why most of the topics discussed in this part of the book relate more directly to memory than to learning.

There are more topics in the areas of memory and learning than you can shake a stick at, so I have had to be very selective. Chapter 11 is a scene-setting chapter, in which the emphasis is on the distinction between short-term memory and long-term memory. This distinction has been regarded as of fundamental importance since the very beginnings of research into memory towards the end of the nineteenth century. Our understanding of both short-term and long-term memory has become more sophisticated over the years. It was assumed originally that short-term memory is *only* useful when we try to remember some information for a few seconds. As is discussed in Chapter 12, two British psychologists (Alan Baddeley and Graham Hitch) in the mid-1970s came up with an extremely influential broader perspective. According to them, in everyday life we mostly use short-term memory in the context of some non-memory task we are carrying out. For example, if trying to solve a mathematical problem in our heads, we need to hold part of the accumulating answer in short-term memory while processing other parts of the problem. Baddeley and Hitch used the term "working memory" to refer to a system combining temporary storage and processing.

Imagine trying to learn something (e.g., a chapter in a psychology textbook) so that you can remember it later. Probably you imagined yourself thinking about the material, trying to identify key points, link those points together, and so on. In very general terms, you regard learning as something requiring the use of various conscious processes. In fact (spooky as it sounds), there is increasing evidence we can acquire certain kinds of information *without* conscious awareness that learning has occurred! This is known as *implicit learning*, and is the focus of Chapter 13.

As we all know to our cost, the flip side of remembering is forgetting. Why do we tend to forget information as time goes by? Why is recognition memory (e.g., for someone's face) generally better than recall (e.g., for someone's name)? These and other issues are addressed in Chapter 14 in the context of various theories of forgetting. For example, it has been argued that forgetting occurs because memory traces interfere with each other, because the information available when we are trying to remember something differs from the information contained in the memory trace, or because of basic physiological processes within the brain. According to Freud, memories of traumatic events are so upsetting that they are repressed (driven into the unconscious mind). As we will see, all of these theoretical ideas possess some validity.

Most research in the chapters discussed so far was carried out under laboratory conditions, and typically involved studying phenomena discovered in the laboratory. This led Ulric Neisser (1978, p. 4) to argue in despair, "If X is an interesting or socially significant aspect of memory, then psychologists have hardly ever studied X." This statement has been regarded as a plea for researchers to study everyday memory under naturalistic conditions even at the cost of abandoning experimental control. In my opinion, this would be foolish for various reasons. First, realism for its own sake has no great value. Aronson and Carlsmith (1968) used the term *mundane realism* to refer to boring and unimportant real-world activities. Second, as Koriat and Goldsmith (1996, p. 168) pointed out, "Many everyday memory topics can be studied in the laboratory, and memory research in naturalistic settings may be amenable to strict experimental control." Third, what really matters is ecological validity, which involves the two aspects of generalizability and representativeness. Generalizability refers to the extent to which the findings of a study are applicable to the real world, whereas representativeness refers to the naturalness of the experimental situation. Generalizability is much more important than representativeness.

Neisser (1996) identified a crucial difference between memory as studied traditionally and memory in everyday life. Participants in traditional memory studies are generally motivated to be as accurate as possible in their memory performance. In contrast, in everyday life, "remembering is a form of purposeful action" (Neisser, 1996, p. 204). For example, when telling a friend what we did at a recent party, we may well focus on making our account entertaining and showing ourselves in a good light (or a bad light!) rather than on being strictly accurate. Marsh and Tversky (2004) asked participants about naturally occurring retellings of real events. Participants admitted that 61% of the stories they told about their own lives were distorted.

The two everyday memory topics discussed in this section of the book are autobiographical memory (Chapter 15) and eyewitness testimony (Chapter 16). It is reasonable to argue that autobiographical memory is the most important topic within everyday memory. Our sense of who we are and what kind of personality we have depends on autobiographical memory. In addition, the kinds of information in autobiographical memory often reflect our most important goals in life. If you think of personal experiences that have made you especially happy or unhappy, this may shed some light on whether your main life goals focus on personal relationships or on academic success.

The study of eyewitness testimony is important in part because of its potential applicability to the legal process. Psychologists have discovered that eyewitnesses' memories for criminal events can be much more inaccurate than most jurors believe. Such memories are fragile, and can easily be distorted by the questions that eyewitnesses are asked. The good news is that the use of psychologists as expert witnesses has undoubtedly prevented many innocent defendants from going to prison. Psychologists have also played an important role in developing interview techniques to increase the amount of accurate information about events recalled by eyewitnesses.

CHAPTER 11

CONTENTS

Introduction	147
Short-term vs. long-term memory	149
Amnesia	153
Evaluation and chapter summary	160
Further reading	163

The long and the short of human memory

INTRODUCTION

What would you say if someone asked you to compare human memory to some common object? Numerous suggestions have been forthcoming over the past 2000 years. For example, the Greek philosopher Socrates asked whether possessing knowledge in long-term memory is not "like a man who has caught some wild birds—pigeons or what not—and keeps them in an aviary he has made for them at home ... let us suppose that every mind contains an aviary stocked with birds of every sort, some in flocks apart from the rest, some in small groups, and some solitary and flying in any direction among them all" (Hamilton, 1961, p. 904).

The above bird-brain analogy is embarrassing for contemporary cognitive psychologists because some fairly recent theories of memory are remarkably similar, especially in their focus on memories as objects contained within a space. However, technological advances have led to some interesting changes in the precise analogies used. For example, memory has been compared to switchboards, gramophones, tape recorders, conveyer belts, underground maps, and the stores found in computers (see Roediger, 1980, for a review).

One of the major contributions that cognitive psychologists have made to our understanding of memory can be shown by considering the following apparently simple question: How do you know you have memory for some event that happened in the past? I'm confident that your answer is along the lines that memory for past events depends on conscious recollection of that event. Patients suffering from **amnesia** (a condition caused by brain damage in which there are severe problems with long-term memory) are often very poor at consciously recollecting the past. For example, when they meet someone they may not remember they saw that person only 1 hour ago, or they re-read a newspaper having forgotten that they had already read it earlier that morning. If long-term memory depends on conscious recollection, then amnesic patients simply have very poor long-term memory.

In fact, memory for the past is more complex than indicated so far. We can obtain some inkling of that complexity by considering a hackneyed anecdote from Edouard Claparède (1873–1940) reported by him in 1911. He studied a female patient (living in what Claparède described as a lunatic asylum!) who suffered from amnesia due to chronic alcoholism. She couldn't recognize doctors and nurses she had seen virtually every day over a period of several years, and she didn't know what day it was or her age.

One day Claparède hid a pin in his hand before shaking hands with the patient. The following day, she was very sensibly reluctant to shake hands with him. However, she felt very embarrassed because she couldn't explain her reluctance.

What does this anecdote tell us? First, the patient had no conscious recollection of what had happened the previous day. Second, in spite of that, her *behavior* indicated very clearly that she *did* possess some long-term memory for what happened. Thus, long-term memory can depend less on conscious recollection than we suppose.

Similar findings to those of Claparède (1911) have been obtained in much more recent studies on amnesic patients (see Parkin, 1996, for a review). For example, patients who are given a series of piano-playing lessons may have no conscious recollection of having received any previous lessons. However, their piano-playing ability typically improves as rapidly as that of normal controls—thus, their behavior shows that their long-term memory is very good in some ways. Such findings indicate that we must distinguish between explicit and implicit memory: "**Explicit memory** is revealed when performance on a task requires conscious recollection of previous experiences ... **Implicit memory** is revealed when performance on a task is facilitated in the absence of conscious recollection" (Graf & Schacter, 1985, p. 501). In those terms, amnesic patients have impaired explicit memory but intact implicit memory.

Ryan, Althoff, Whitlow, and Cohen (2000) wondered whether the common view that amnesic patients have problems with explicit memory but not with implicit memory was strictly correct. More specifically, they predicted that amnesics would have problems with implicit memory if the memory task involved *relating* different pieces of information.

Ryan et al. (2000) tested the above hypothesis by presenting amnesic patients and healthy controls with color images of real-world scenes belonging to three conditions:

1. *Novel scenes*: The scene had not been presented before.
2. *Repeated old scenes*: The identical scene had been presented before.
3. *Manipulated old scenes*: The scene had been presented before, but the positions of some of the objects had been altered.

The participants' eye fixations were recorded, and the key measure was the proportion of eye fixation in the critical region (i.e., the part of the scene that had been systematically altered in the manipulation condition). It was assumed that participants' implicit memory could be inferred from their patterns of eye movements.

What did Ryan et al. (2000) find? The healthy controls had significantly more fixations in the critical region in the manipulated condition than in the other two conditions (see Figure 11.1), presumably because they had implicit memory for the relations among the objects in the original scene. In contrast, the amnesic patients did *not* devote more fixations to the critical regions; presumably they had no implicit memory for the relations among the elements of presented scenes.

KEY TERMS
Explicit memory: retrieval of information from long-term memory based on the use of conscious recollection; see implicit memory.
Implicit memory: retrieval of information from long-term memory that doesn't depend on conscious recollection; see explicit memory.

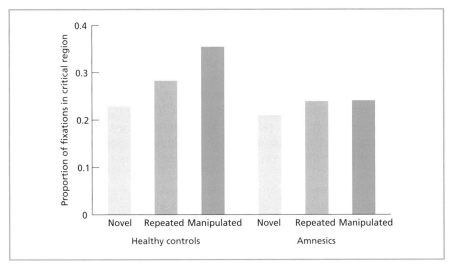

Figure 11.1 Proportion of eye fixations in the critical region in healthy controls and amnesic patients as a function of condition (novel, repeated, manipulated). Data from Ryan et al. (2000).

SHORT-TERM vs. LONG-TERM MEMORY

Our focus so far has been on long-term memory. However, most people draw a distinction between the information stored away in our brains for periods of time running into months or years and information that is held very briefly in memory (e.g., a telephone number, the number needed to open a combination lock). Somewhat surprisingly, the bearded Viennese psychoanalyst Sigmund Freud provided an apt analogy based on the distinction between short-term and long-term memory. Freud (1925/1961) argued that memory is like a "mystic writing pad" consisting of celluloid on top of a hard slab. When you write on the celluloid it leaves a clear record on the celluloid and a faint record on the slab. When you pull the pad most of the way out of its container, the record on the celluloid disappears leaving only the one on the slab. In this analogy, the celluloid is short-term memory and the hard slab is long-term memory.

Short-term memory has been assessed in several ways (see Cowan, 2000, for a review). For example, there is **digit span**: participants listen to a random series of digits and then try to repeat them back immediately in the correct order. Other span measures are letter span and word span. The maximum number of units (e.g., digits) that can be recalled without error is usually "seven plus or minus two" (Miller, 1956). However, there are two qualifications that need to be put on that finding. First, Miller (1956) argued that the capacity of short-term memory should be assessed in terms of the number of **chunks** (integrated pieces or units of information). For example, "IBM" is *one* chunk for those familiar with the company name International Business Machines, but *three* chunks for everyone else. It has often been found that the capacity of short-term memory is about seven chunks. However, Simon (1974) found that the span in chunks was less with larger chunks (e.g., eight-word phrases) than with smaller chunks (e.g., one-syllable words).

Second, Cowan (2000, p. 88) argued that Miller's (1956) estimate of the capacity of short-term memory was too high: "The evidence provides broad support for what can be interpreted as a capacity limit of substantially fewer than Miller's 7 plus or minus 2 chunks; about four chunks on the average." How can we explain this discrepancy? Cowan (2000) argued that estimates of short-term memory capacity are often inflated because participants' performance depends on rehearsal and on long-term memory as well as on "pure" short-term memory capacity. When these additional factors aren't allowed to come into play, the capacity of short-term memory is only four chunks.

Not everyone is convinced by the above line of argument (e.g., Baddeley, 2000). However, for present purposes what matters most is that there is a huge difference between the essentially unlimited capacity of long-term memory and the very limited capacity of short-term memory (whether four or seven chunks).

Why is short-term memory so limited in the amount of information it can process?

Another (and very obvious difference) between short-term and long-term memory is in the length of time for which information is remembered. We all know that information can remain in long-term memory for years, or even decades, whereas information in short-term memory is lost rapidly. In a classic study, Peterson and Peterson (1959) studied the duration of short-term memory by using the task of remembering a three-letter stimulus while counting backwards by threes. The ability to remember the three letters in the correct order reduced to only about 50% after 6 seconds and forgetting was almost complete after 18 seconds (see Figure 11.2).

Findings such as those of Peterson and Peterson (1959) are typically explained by assuming that unrehearsed information disappears rapidly from short-term memory through a process of decay (see Nairne, 2002, for a review). However, Nairne, Whiteman, and Kelley (1999) argued that rapid forgetting from short-term memory is *not* inevitable. They argued that the rate of forgetting observed by Peterson and Peterson (1959) was especially rapid for two reasons. First, they used all the letters of the alphabet repeatedly and this may have caused considerable confusion and interference. Second, the memory task was difficult in that participants had to remember both the items themselves and the order in which they were presented. Nairne et al. (1999) presented different words on each trial to reduce interference, and they tested memory only for order information and not for the words themselves. Even though there was a rehearsal-prevention task (reading aloud digits presented on a screen) during the retention interval, there was remarkably little forgetting even over 96 seconds (see Figure 11.3). This finding casts doubt on the notion that decay causes forgetting in short-term memory.

Finally, we turn to the strongest evidence that short-term and long-term memory are distinct. Surprisingly, this evidence comes from brain-damaged patients. Suppose for a moment there is only *one* memory system dealing with short-term and long-term memory. If that one and only memory system were damaged, the natural prediction is that performance would be impaired on memory tasks regardless of whether they involved short-term or long-term memory. In contrast, suppose there are separate short-

Figure 11.2 Forgetting over time in short-term memory. Data from Peterson and Peterson (1959).

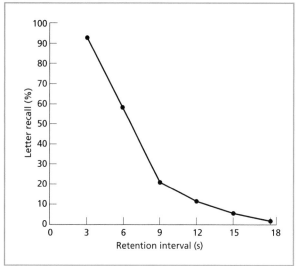

term and long-term memory systems located in different parts of the brain. It follows that some brain-damaged patients should have impaired long-term memory but intact short-term memory, whereas others should have impaired short-term memory but intact long-term memory. If these findings are obtained, they would form what is known as a *double dissociation* (see Glossary).

The actual findings from brain-damaged patients are complex but provide evidence of a double dissociation. As we have seen, amnesic patients have severely impaired long-term memory (at least when explicit memory is involved). However, the overwhelming majority of amnesic patients have essentially intact short-term memory. In their review of 147 amnesic patients, Spiers, Maguire, and Burgess (2001) concluded that *none* of them had a significant problem with short-term memory. There are also some brain-damaged patients having severely impaired short-term memory but intact long-term memory. For example, consider the case of KF, who suffered brain damage after a motorcycle accident. He had no problems with long-term learning and recall, but his digit span was greatly impaired (Shallice & Warrington, 1970). Subsequent research by Warrington and Shallice (1972) and by Shallice and Warrington (1974) revealed a more complex picture. It turned out that KF's problems with short-term memory were less widespread than initially assumed—his forgetting of *visual* stimuli was much less than his forgetting of *auditory* stimuli, and his forgetting of auditory stimuli consisting of meaningful sounds (e.g., telephones ringing) was much less than his forgetting of letters, words, or digits.

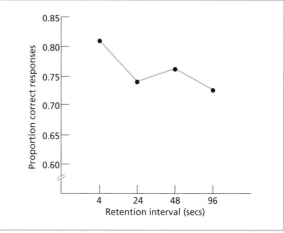

Figure 11.3 Proportion of correct responses as a function of retention interval. Data from Nairne et al. (1999).

Is forgetting inevitable?

MULTI-STORE MODEL

One of the key theoretical issues is to decide how short-term and long-term memory are related to each other. An influential answer was provided by Atkinson and Shiffrin (1968) in their multi-store model (see Figure 11.4). They assumed that stimulation from the environment is initially received by the sensory stores. These stores are modality-specific, meaning that there is a separate one for each sensory modality (e.g., vision, hearing). Information is held briefly in the sensory stores, with some fraction of this information being attended to and processed further within the short-term store. The short-term

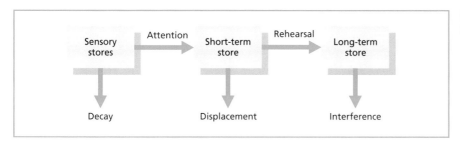

Figure 11.4 The multi-store model of memory.

store itself has very limited capacity. Some information processed in the short-term store is transferred to the long-term store, which has essentially unlimited capacity. Long-term storage of information often depends on rehearsal, with a direct relationship between the amount of rehearsal in the short-term store and the strength of the stored memory trace.

As we have seen, Atkinson and Shiffrin (1968) argued that short-term memory is involved before long-term memory. However, an increasingly popular view is that short-term memory is only involved after long-term memory. For example, Ruchkin, Grafman, Cameron, and Berndt (2003, p. 711) argued that, "Short-term memory corresponds to activated long-term memory and information is stored in the same systems that initially processed the information." For once, a theoretical controversy can be resolved without discussing experimental findings in detail. The information processed in short-term memory *must* have already made contact with information in long-term memory (Logie, 1999). For example, our ability to engage in verbal rehearsal of visually presented words depends on *prior* contact with stored information concerning pronunciation. In similar fashion, we can only rehearse "IBM" as a single chunk in short-term memory by using relevant information stored in long-term memory. Thus, access to long-term memory occurs *before* information is processed in short-term memory.

What objections could there be to Atkinson and Shiffrin's notion that short-term memory precedes long-term memory?

There is another reason why Atkinson and Shiffrin's (1968) assumption that information is processed in short-term memory prior to reaching long-term memory should be rejected (Marc Brysbaert, personal communication). It was assumed by Atkinson and Shiffrin that information in short-term memory represents "the contents of consciousness," strongly implying that *only* information that is processed consciously can be stored in long-term memory. However, there is reasonable (if not conclusive) evidence for the existence of learning without conscious awareness of what has been learned (as in Claparède's story). This is known as implicit learning and is discussed in Chapter 13. It would seem that implicit learning would be impossible in terms of Atkinson and Shiffrin's (1968) model.

SHORT-TERM MEMORY—ACTIVATED LONG-TERM MEMORY

Several theorists (e.g., Ruchkin et al., 2003) have assumed that short-term memory is simply that fraction of long-term memory activated at any given time. As we have seen, that assumption provides an explanation of how it is that we can process information accessed from long-term memory in short-term memory.

There is strong evidence indicating that various kinds of information stored in long-term memory influence rehearsal in short-term memory. For example, consider studies in which participants see a short visually presented word list and then have to recall the words in the correct order. A key finding is that recall performance is worse when the words are phonologically similar [sounding similar] than when they are phonologically dissimilar: this is known as the *phonological similarity effect*. For example, FEE, HE, KNEE, LEE, ME, SHE form a list of phonologically similar words, whereas BAY, HOE, IT, ODD, SHY, UP form a list of phonologically dissimilar words. Larsen, Baddeley, and Andrade (2000) used those lists, and found that serial recall was 25% worse with the phonologically similar list. The existence of the phonological similarity effect indicates that information about the sounds of words stored in long-term memory affects processing in short-term memory.

Evidence that semantic [meaning] information from long-term memory influences processing in short-term memory was reported by Ruchkin, Berndt, Johnson, Grafman, Ritter, and Canoune (1999). Words and pseudo-words designed to sound very similar to words were presented aurally, followed by serial recall. If participants processed only phonological information in short-term term memory, then brain activity should have been very similar for the words and the pseudo-words. In fact, Ruchkin et al. (1999) found using event-related potentials (ERPs) that there were large differences in brain activity associated with words and pseudo-words, indicating that semantic information from long-term memory was processed when words were presented.

AMNESIA

We have already seen that research on amnesic patients has proved very important in supporting the distinction between explicit and implicit memory. It has also provided the most convincing evidence for the distinction between short-term and long-term memory. We will consider other ways in which the study of amnesic patients has increased our understanding of long-term memory after a brief account of the causes of amnesia and the impact it can have on the lives of those affected.

Many people in the world suffer from amnesia. The reasons why patients have become amnesic are very varied. Bilateral stroke is one factor causing amnesia, but closed head injury is the most common cause. However, patients with closed head injury often have other cognitive impairments, and this makes it hard to interpret their memory deficit. As a result, most experimental work has focused on patients who have become amnesic due to chronic alcohol abuse (this is known as **Korsakoff's syndrome**).

Describe the range of causes of symptoms associated with amnesia.

When discussing the long-term memory problems of amnesic patients, it is important to distinguish between anterograde and retrograde amnesia. **Anterograde amnesia** involves poor long-term memory for information learned *after* the onset of the amnesia. In contrast, **retrograde amnesia** involves poor long-term memory for information acquired *before* the onset of amnesia. The extent of retrograde amnesia varies considerably from patient to patient. However, there is generally a *temporal gradient*, with forgetting being greater for memories acquired closer to the onset of the amnesia than those acquired longer ago.

Amnesic patients vary in the precise areas of the brain damaged. However, the key structures are in a sub-cortical brain region (the diencephalon) and a cortical region (the medial temporal lobe), see Figure 11.5. Patients with Korsakoff's syndrome have brain damage in the diencephalon (especially the medial thalamus and the mamillary body), but typically the frontal cortex is also damaged. There are significant differences among amnesic patients, but we shouldn't exaggerate these differences. As Aggleton and Brown (1999, p. 426) argued, "The traditional distinction between temporal lobe and diencephalon is misleading; both groups have damage to the same functional system."

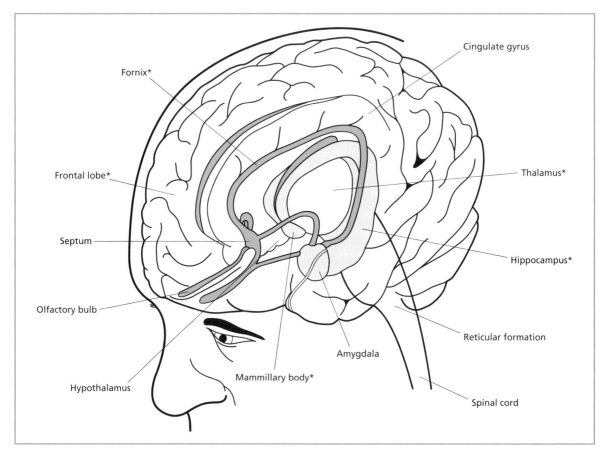

Fornix*

Cingulate gyrus

Frontal lobe*

Thalamus*

Septum

Hippocampus*

Olfactory bulb

Reticular formation

Hypothalamus

Mammillary body*

Amygdala

Spinal cord

Figure 11.5 Diagram of the brain with those areas known to be associated with memory function indicated with an asterisk. Areas including the hippocampus and amygdala are in the temporal lobe, and areas such as the thalamus and mammillary body are in the diencephalon. From Parkin (2001).

As you can imagine, suffering from amnesia can greatly affect people's lives. The effects can be devastating as can be seen in the case of Clive Wearing, who is one of the most extreme cases of amnesia ever recorded (see French, 2005, for a detailed discussion). He was a successful 46-year-old musician and Renaissance music scholar. On Tuesday March 26, 1985, he suddenly developed a high temperature. The doctor said it was flu, but he actually had encephalitis (infection of the brain) caused by herpes simplex, the cold-sore virus. A part of the brain known as the hippocampus is of central importance in long-term memory, and the encephalitis completely destroyed the left hippocampus and parts of the right hippocampus. As a result, Clive Wearing had to move from the smart flat he shared with his wife Deborah in central London to a care home. He can remember practically nothing of his daily activities and cannot even remember the names of his children from his first marriage.

When Clive Wearing began to have a vague awareness there was something terribly wrong with him, he wept almost non-stop for over a month. One of his favorite questions was, "What's it like to have one long night lasting . . . how long? It's like being dead."

We can see more clearly what it is like for Clive Wearing to live constantly in the present in the following extract from his diary (French, 2005):

7.46am: I wake for the first time. 7.47am: This illness has been like death till NOW. All senses work. 8.07am: I AM awake. 8.31am: Now I am really, completely awake. 9.06am: Now I am perfectly, overwhelmingly awake. 9.34am: Now I am superlatively, actually awake.

The problems of living with someone with practically no memory of the past led Deborah to divorce Clive Wearing. However, the story has a happy ending. They remained in love with each other, and decided to renew their marriage vows on Easter Sunday 2002.

The most-studied amnesic patient of all time is HM. He suffered from frequent epileptic seizures, and so it was decided to carry out brain surgery. Accordingly, on 23 August 1953, William Scoville operated on HM, who was 27 years old at the time. As a result of the operation, there was extensive damage to his medial temporal lobe including the hippocampus. His IQ is above average, but he simply cannot remember the events and experiences he has had since the operation. In the words of Scoville and Milner (1957), HM "forgets the events of his daily life as fast as they occur." In addition, he has extensive retrograde amnesia stretching back for the 11 years preceding the operation. However, HM has intact memories of his life up to the age of 16 (Ogden & Corkin, 1991). In addition, he learned various skills such as mirror drawing (i.e., tracing a figure seen only in mirror image) almost as rapidly as normal individuals, indicating that he retained the ability to form some long-term memories.

One of the crucial issues in memory research is to decide on the *number* and the *nature* of long-term memory systems. The distinction between explicit and implicit memory is useful here, but attempts have been made to go beyond that distinction. You should be warned that we are moving into controversial territory, in which there is nothing like complete agreement on the systems of long-term memory. For now, what is important is to understand how the study of amnesic patients can shed light on these issues. In essence, suppose someone argues that memory systems X and Y are entirely separate from each other, whereas someone else claims that X and Y are merely different aspects of a single memory system. If we found that amnesic patients' memory performance was consistently poor on tasks apparently requiring memory system X but was at normal levels on tasks involving memory system Y, that would be strong (but not conclusive) evidence that X and Y are separate memory systems.

In what follows we will be discussing the theoretical approach of Schacter, Wagner, and Buckner (2000). They argued that there are *four* long-term memory systems: episodic memory, semantic memory, perceptual representation system, and procedural memory. How does the distinction between explicit and implicit memory relate to these four long-term memory systems? In approximate terms, episodic memory and semantic memory both involve explicit memory, whereas the perceptual representation system and procedural memory both involve implicit memory.

EPISODIC AND SEMANTIC MEMORY

There has been much interest in the notion that episodic and semantic memory form two rather separate long-term memory systems. The distinction was introduced into psychology by Tulving (1972, p. 386), who defined **semantic memory** as follows:

> *It is a mental thesaurus, organized knowledge a person possesses about words and other verbal symbols, their meanings and referents, about relations among them, and about rules, formulas, and algorithms [rules for solving problems] for the manipulations of these symbols, concepts, and relations.*

In contrast, the main feature of **episodic memory** is, "its dependence on a special kind of awareness that all healthy human adults can identify. It is the type of awareness experienced when one thinks back to a specific moment in one's personal past and consciously recollects some prior episode or state as it was previously experienced" (Wheeler, Stuss, & Tulving, 1997, p. 333).

In essence, then, semantic memory is concerned with our general knowledge, whereas episodic memory is concerned with our personal experiences in a given place at a given time. Do amnesic patients with anterograde amnesia always have impaired episodic *and* semantic memory for memories acquired after the onset of amnesia? This is an important question—if the answer is "No," that would imply episodic and semantic memory form separate long-term memory systems.

Perhaps the most definitive answer to the above question was provided by Spiers et al. (2001) in their extensive review of 147 cases of amnesia involving damage to the hippocampus or fornix. Episodic memory was impaired in *all* cases, and many (but by no means all) of the cases also had poor ability to form new semantic memories. For example, most amnesics have very poor recognition memory for the faces of people who have become famous fairly recently. Gabrieli, Cohen, and Corkin (1988) found that HM had an almost complete inability to acquire new vocabulary. However, he has some remaining ability to acquire new semantic memories. He was given pairs of names, one famous and one not (O'Kane, Kensinger, & Corkin, 2004). The famous individual became famous either before the onset of HM's amnesia or afterwards. He correctly identified the famous name on 92% of trials when the person became famous prior to the onset of his amnesia, and this only dropped to 88% for those who became famous afterwards.

The evidence assembled by Spiers et al. (2001) indicates that episodic memory in amnesic patients is more vulnerable than semantic memory. However, what we are really looking for are amnesic patients who have very poor episodic memory but intact semantic memory. Vargha-Khadem et al. (1997) found precisely that. Beth and Jon had suffered bilateral [on both sides] hippocampal damage at an early age before they had had the chance to develop semantic memories. Beth suffered brain damage at birth, and Jon did so at the age of 4. Both these patients had very poor episodic memory for the day's activities, television programs, and telephone conversations. In spite of this, Beth and Jon both attended ordinary schools, and their levels of speech and language development, literacy, and factual knowledge (e.g., vocabulary)

What are episodic, semantic, and procedural memories? Give an example of your own for each category.

KEY TERMS

Semantic memory: a form of long-term memory consisting of general knowledge about the world, language, and so on; see episodic memory.

Episodic memory: a form of long-term memory concerned with personal experiences or episodes that happened in a given place at a specific times; see semantic memory.

were within the normal range. Vargha-Khadem, Gadian, and Mishkin (2002) carried out a follow-up study on Jon when he was 20. As a young adult, he had a high level of intelligence (IQ = 114), and his semantic memory continued to be markedly better than his episodic memory.

If episodic and semantic memory are really separate from each other, *why* do so many amnesics have great problems with both of them? There are two main answers. First, the two memory systems don't function entirely independently of each other, with many memories combining episodic and semantic information. Second, Vargha-Khadem et al. (1997) argued that the brain areas of central importance to episodic memory and semantic memory are very close to each other. Episodic memory depends mainly on the hippocampus, whereas semantic memory depends on its underlying cortices [outer layers]. Thus, brain damage sufficient to impair episodic memory will typically also impair semantic memory.

We turn now to retrograde amnesia (impaired memory for learning occurring before the onset of amnesia). Tulving (2002, p. 13) discussed the case of a patient (KC), whose "retrograde amnesia is highly asymmetrical: he cannot recollect any personally experienced events . . . , whereas his semantic knowledge acquired before the critical accident is still reasonably intact. His knowledge of mathematics, history, geography, and other 'school subjects', as well as his general knowledge of the world is not greatly different from others' at his educational level."

The opposite pattern was reported by Yasuda, Watanabe, and Ono (1997). A female amnesic patient had very poor ability to remember public events, cultural items, historical figures, and some items of vocabulary from the time prior to the onset of amnesia. However, she was reasonably good at remembering personal experiences from episodic memory dating back to the pre-amnesia period.

PERCEPTUAL REPRESENTATION SYSTEM AND PROCEDURAL MEMORY

As was mentioned earlier, the two memory systems discussed in this section (perceptual representation system and procedural memory) are both thought to depend on implicit memory. According to Schacter et al. (2000, pp. 635–636), the **perceptual representation system** "can be viewed as a collection of domain-specific modules that operate on perceptual information about the form and structure of words and objects." This system is involved in **priming**, which is "a facilitation or biasing of performance occurring for the specific stimuli encountered in a task" (Poldrack, Selco, Field, & Cohen, 1999, p. 208). The perceptual representation system is specifically relevant to **perceptual priming**, in which degraded stimuli are processed and identified faster and/or more accurately when they have been processed previously than when they have not.

Here are some examples of perceptual priming. First, there is word-stem completion. Participants initially learn a list of words (e.g., "toboggan"). Some time later they are presented with word fragments (e.g., "_O_O_GA_") and simply asked to fill in the blanks to form words. For some participants, a word that will complete a given fragment was presented on the previous list, whereas that it is not the case for other participants. Perceptual priming is revealed when word completions tend to correspond to words previously presented.

Second, there is word-stem completion. This is very similar to word-fragment completion except that on the test word stems (e.g., "TOB_____") are presented instead of word fragments. Perceptual priming is indicated when the words formed from the word stems correspond to words previously presented.

Third, there is visual word recognition in which words are presented very briefly, with the exposure duration increasing slightly on successive trials. The minimum exposure duration needed to identify each word is recorded. Perceptual priming is shown when words that have been presented previously are identified at shorter exposure durations than words not presented previously.

The other memory system to be discussed here is **procedural memory**, which "refers to the learning of motor and cognitive skills, and is manifest across a wide range of situations. Learning to ride a bike and acquiring reading skills are examples of procedural memory" (Schacter et al., 2000, p. 636). Reading mirror-reversed script is an example of a skill involving procedural memory. What happens is that you have to read script reflected in a mirror, and there is a gradual increase in the speed and accuracy with which this can be done.

Priming and skill learning both involve implicit memory and some experts (e.g., Poldrack & Gabrieli, 2001) have argued that they both involve the operation of a single memory system. However, there are real differences between priming and skill learning. Priming involves enhanced performance on *specific* stimuli that are presented on more than one occasion. In contrast, skill learning is typically much more general, in that a skill learned in one situation can be applied to other situations. For example, when you have acquired the skill of car driving, you can rapidly adjust to the demands of driving a car you have never driven before.

If perceptual priming and procedural memory involve different memory systems, there is no particular reason why individuals good at perceptual priming should also be good at procedural memory, and vice versa. Much of the evidence indicates that there is practically no correlation between performance on these two types of tasks. For example, Schwartz and Hashtroudi (1991) found there was no correlation between performance on word-identification (perceptual priming) and inverted-text reading (procedural memory) tasks.

There is brain-imaging research to support the notion that perceptual priming and skill learning involve different memory systems. Schacter et al. (2000, pp. 637–638) discussed the relevant research and concluded as follows:

> *There appears to be a tendency for [skill-learning] tasks that require extensive prefrontal and/or premotor contributions in their naive state to shift to more automated pathways with practice, although the specific transition noted in any individual study appears highly dependent on the exact task that is performed . . . Investigations of priming within the PRS [perceptual representation system] have consistently revealed activation reductions in posterior cortical regions.*

KEY TERM

Procedural memory: a long-term memory system concerned with motor and cognitive skills; it may also be involved in priming.

There are two important take-home messages from the above conclusions. First, perceptual priming and procedural memory involve different brain regions. Second, what happens to brain activation as a result of practice differs between perceptual priming and procedural memory. Perceptual-priming tasks are simple and so less brain activation is required as processing becomes more efficient. In contrast, procedural-memory tasks are generally more complex and this is reflected in the use of more brain areas during practice.

FINDINGS

As mentioned earlier, Spiers et al. (2001) considered memory performance in 147 amnesic patients. Here are their conclusions concerning those aspects of memory that remained intact in all patients: "None of the cases was reported to be impaired on tasks which involve learning skills or habits, priming, simple classical conditioning and simple category learning" (Spiers et al., 2001, p. 359). In the terms we have been used, that means that amnesics' perceptual representation system and procedural memory are both intact.

There is plenty of evidence that amnesic patients have intact priming. For example, Graf, Squire, and Mandler (1984) presented word lists followed by one of four memory tests. Three of the tests were conventional memory tests of explicit memory (free recall, cued recall, and recognition memory) but the fourth memory test (word-stem completion) assessed perceptual priming. On this last test, participants were given three-letter word fragments (e.g., STR ___) and simply wrote down the first word they thought of starting with those letters (e.g., STRAP, STRIP). Priming was assessed by the extent to which the word completions corresponded to words from the list previously presented. As expected, amnesic patients did much worse than healthy controls on all the tests of explicit memory. However, the two groups didn't differ in the size of their perceptual priming effect on the word-completion task (see Figure 11.6).

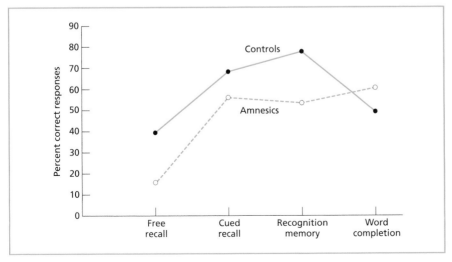

Figure 11.6 Free recall, cued recall, recognition memory, and word completion in amnesic patients and controls. Data from different experiments reported by Graf et al. (1984).

Hamann and Squire (1997) studied an amnesic patient, EP, who seemed to have no explicit memory at all following herpes simplex encephalitis. For example, on a test of recognition memory he was correct on only 52% of items (chance = 50%) compared to 65% for other amnesic patients and 81% for normal controls. In spite of his lack of explicit memory, his perceptual priming was normal.

What kinds of skill learning involving procedural memory have been found to be intact in amnesic patients? Corkin (1968) reported that the amnesic patient, HM, could learn mirror drawing. HM also showed learning on the pursuit rotor, which involves manual tracking of a moving target (a small metal circle in a rotating disk). However, his rate of learning was slower than that of healthy individuals. In contrast, Cermak, Lewis, Butters, and Goodglass (1973) found that amnesic patients learned the pursuit rotor as rapidly as healthy participants.

Reading mirror-reversed script is another task involving procedural memory that has been studied in amnesics. We can distinguish between a *general* improvement in speed of reading produced by practice on this task and a more *specific* improvement produced by re-reading the same groups of words of sentences. Cohen and Squire (1980) reported general and specific improvement in reading mirror-reversed script in amnesics, and some of this improvement was maintained over a period of 3 months. Martone, Butters, Payne, Becker, and Sax (1984) also reported evidence of general and specific improvement in amnesics. However, although the general practice effect was as great in amnesics as in healthy individuals, the specific practice effect was not.

EVALUATION AND CHAPTER SUMMARY

Short-term vs. long-term memory
- There is strong evidence that the distinction between short-term and long-term memory is important.
- This is shown most convincingly by findings from brain-damaged patients.
- However, it is also shown by differences in capacity and in forgetting rate.
- We have seen glimpses of evidence suggesting that there is more than one type of long-term memory (explicit vs. implicit memory).
- We have also seen that there may be complexities associated with short-term memory (e.g., auditory verbal memory vs. visual memory), an issue discussed in detail in Chapter 12.

Multi-store model
- Atkinson and Shiffrin's (1968) multi-store model has had a major impact, but has clearly gone past its sell-by date for several reasons.
- First, its account of long-term memory is oversimplified. According to the model, there is a *single* long-term memory store. This seems highly dubious when we consider the amazing wealth of informa-

tion stored in our long-term memory, including knowledge that Russell Crowe is a film star, that $2 + 2 = 4$, that we had muesli for breakfast, and perhaps information about how to ride a bicycle.

- We have already seen that long-term memory can be subdivided into explicit memory and implicit memory, and there are ways of dividing long-term memory into several systems.
- Second, the model's account of short-term memory is oversimplified.
- For example, it is assumed that the main way information is transferred from the short-term store to the long-term store is via rehearsal. However, a moment's thought will probably convince you that the role of rehearsal in our everyday lives is very limited.
- The most influential contemporary view is that of Baddeley (e.g., 2001), who has replaced the concept of a *single* short-term memory store with a working memory system having *four* components (see Chapter 12). This level of complexity is needed to explain the findings.
- Third, as we have seen, it doesn't make sense to assume that processing in the short-term store occurs before contact is made with long-term memory.
- However, in fairness to Atkinson and Shiffrin, it should be noted that they subsequently changed their minds—Atkinson and Shiffrin (1971) proposed that short-term memory is the temporarily activated part of long-term memory.

Short-term memory—activated long-term memory
- There are good reasons for assuming that activation of part of long-term memory plays an important role in short-term memory or working memory. However, that doesn't mean that short-term memory is *only* activated long-term memory.
- Baddeley (2003, p. 729) dismissed that notion, arguing that, "We reject the generalization that WM [working memory] is activated LTM [long-term memory] . . . because such a view offers a simplistic answer to a complex question. LTM influences WM in a range of different ways that go beyond the concept of simple activation."
- In essence, we can manipulate activated long-term memory in flexible ways and such manipulations go well beyond simply activating some fraction of long-term memory.
- Logie and Della Sala (2003) gave two examples of ways in which we can manipulate information in short-term memory—backward digit recall (recalling digits in the opposite order to the one in which they are presented) and generating novel visual images.

Episodic and semantic memory
- The study of amnesic patients has provided strong support for the hypothesis that episodic and semantic memory form separate memory systems.
- Some patients with anterograde amnesia have reasonable semantic memory in spite of having greatly impaired episodic memory.
- Some patients with retrograde amnesia have good pre-amnesia

semantic memories but very limited episodic memories, and others show the opposite pattern.

- Brain-imaging studies on normal individuals also provide support.
- Wheeler et al. (1997) reviewed the evidence from numerous such studies, finding that the left prefrontal cortex was more active during the encoding of episodic than of semantic memories in 90% of studies.
- At the time of retrieval, the right prefrontal cortex was more active when episodic memories were being retrieved than semantic ones in 95% of studies.

Perceptual representation system and procedural memory
- Real progress has been made in discovering the number and nature of long-term memory systems, as can be seen if you consider that Atkinson and Shiffrin (1968) identified a single long-term memory store.
- Many of the details remain unclear, but there is reasonable support for Schacter et al.'s (2000) notion that there are four long-term memory systems: episodic memory, semantic memory, perceptual representation system, and procedural memory.
- Schacter et al. (2000) treat these systems as separate from each other, but there are some linkages between episodic and semantic memory, and between the perceptual representation system and procedural memory.
- For example, all episodic memories contain semantic information, and episodic and semantic memory both typically involve explicit memory.
- Perceptual priming and procedural memory both involve improvement in performance as a result of practice, and both typically involve implicit memory.
- What is needed for the future is a more complex theory of long-term memory that clarifies the similarities as well as the differences among the various memory systems.

FURTHER READING

- Emilien, G., Durlach, C., Antoniadis, E., Van der Linden, M., & Maloteaux, J.-M. (2004). *Memory: Neuropsychological, imaging, and psychopharmacological perspectives*. Hove, UK: Psychology Press. The first chapter of this book provides a useful overview of memory research.
- Healy, A.F., & Proctor, R.W. (2003). *Handbook of psychology: Experimental psychology, Vol. 4.* New York: Wiley & Sons. Several topics relevant to this chapter are covered in this edited book, including semantic memory, priming, episodic memory, and procedural memory.
- Schacter, D.L., Wagner, A.D., & Buckner, R.L. (2000). Memory systems of 1999. In E. Tulving & F.I.M. Craik (Eds.), *The Oxford handbook of memory*. New York: Oxford University Press. This chapter provides an excellent introduction to the issue of the number of memory systems we possess.
- Wearing, D. (2005). *Forever today—A memoir of love and amnesia*. New York: Doubleday. This book contains a fascinating account of the well-known amnesic patient Clive Wearing.

CHAPTER 12

CONTENTS

Introduction 165

Baddeley's working memory model 166

Phonological loop 167

Visuospatial sketchpad 169

Central executive 170

Working memory and intelligence 173

Evaluation and chapter summary 175

Further reading 177

Short-term or working memory

INTRODUCTION

What is the point of short-term memory in everyday life? Textbook writers sometimes answer the question by pointing out that it allows us to remember a telephone number for the few seconds that it takes to dial it. However, even that use of short-term memory is rapidly becoming obsolete now most people have mobile phones that store all the phone numbers needed regularly.

In 1974, two British psychologists, Alan Baddeley and Graham Hitch, came up with a convincing answer to the question above. In essence, they argued that we generally use short-term memory when engaged in the performance of complex tasks. You have to carry out various processes to complete the task. However, you also have to briefly store information about the outcome of early processes in short-term memory as you move on to later processes. For example, suppose you were given the addition problem $13 + 18 + 24$. What you would probably do is to add 13 and 18 and keep the answer (i.e., 31) in short-term memory. You would then add 24 to 31 and produce the correct answer of 55. Baddeley and Hitch (1974) used the term **working memory** to refer to a system combining processing and short-term memory functions. More specifically, according to Baddeley and Logie's (1999, p. 28) definition, "Working memory comprises multiple specialized components of cognition that allow humans to comprehend and mentally represent their immediate environment, to retain information about their immediate past experience, to support the acquisition of new knowledge, to solve problems, and to formulate, relate, and act on current goals."

As discussed in Chapter 11, Atkinson and Shiffrin (1968) and other theorists in the 1960s emphasized the importance of verbal rehearsal in short-term memory. Baddeley (e.g., 1986, 2000) accepted that verbal rehearsal is of importance, but argued that other kinds of information can also be stored in short-term memory. For example, suppose you are driving along focusing on steering the car, avoiding pedestrians, and keeping a safe distance behind the car in front. In addition, you may be holding some visual and spatial information in short-term memory (e.g., speed limit on the road, width of the road, the distance of the car behind you) to assist you in driving.

In what follows, we will mainly consider the theoretical approach to working memory put forward by Baddeley and his colleagues. You should note there are various other approaches to working memory, some based on different theoretical assumptions. These other approaches are discussed in a book edited by Miyake and Shah (1999).

BADDELEY'S WORKING MEMORY MODEL

Baddeley's original basic working memory model consisted of three components:

- *Central executive*: This is a limited capacity processing system resembling attention. It is modality-free, meaning it can process information from any sensory modality (e.g., visual, auditory).
- *Phonological loop*: This is a temporary storage system holding verbal information in a phonological (speech-based) form.
- *Visuospatial sketchpad*: This is a temporary memory system holding spatial and/or visual information.

The working memory system is hierarchical in nature (see Figure 12.1). The phonological loop and the visuospatial sketchpad are both "slave" systems at the base of the hierarchy. They are slave systems in the sense that they are used by the central executive of the attention-like system for various purposes.

All three components of the basic working memory system have limited capacity. However, each component can function relatively independently of the other components except when a slave system is influenced by the dictates of the central executive. These assumptions permit us to predict whether or not two tasks can be performed successfully at the same time. There are two predictions:

1. If two tasks make use of the *same* component of working memory, they cannot be performed successfully together, because that component's limited capacity will be exceeded.
2. If two tasks make use of *different* components, it should be possible to perform them as well together as separately.

Figure 12.1 The major components of Baddeley's working memory system. Figure adapted from Baddeley (2001).

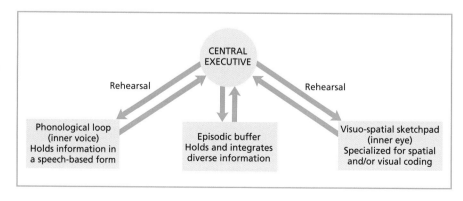

We can see how this works in practice by considering which components of working memory are involved in playing chess. This issue was addressed by Robbins et al. (1996), who gave weaker and stronger players the task of selecting continuation moves from various chess positions. The chess players carried out this chess task while performing one of the following secondary tasks at the same time:

- Random number generation: This task requires participants to try to produce a random series of digits and involves the central executive.
- Pressing keys on a keypad in a clockwise pattern: This task makes use of the visuospatial sketchpad.
- Rapid repetition of the word "see-saw": This uses the phonological loop.
- Repetitive tapping: This very simple task places minimal demands on working memory.

The findings obtained by Robbins et al. (1996) are shown in Figure 12.2. Random number generation and pressing keys in a clockwise fashion both reduced the quality of the chess moves selected compared to the control condition. Thus, selecting good chess moves involves the central executive and the visuospatial sketchpad. In contrast, rapid word repetition didn't reduce the quality of chess moves, and so the phonological loop is *not* involved in selecting chess moves. The effects of the various secondary tasks on the quality of the chess moves selected were similar for weaker and stronger players. This suggests that both groups used the working memory system in the same way when choosing moves. Note that there is more coverage of dual-task performance in Chapter 10 on multitasking.

PHONOLOGICAL LOOP

Most of the early research on the **phonological loop** focused on the notion that verbal rehearsal (i.e., saying words over and over to oneself) is of central

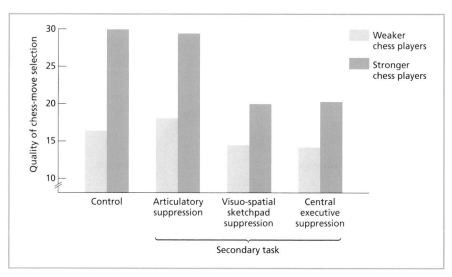

Figure 12.2 Effects of secondary tasks on quality of chess-move selection in stronger and weaker players. Adapted from Robbins et al. (1996).

KEY TERM
Phonological loop: a component of working memory in which speech-based information is held and subvocal articulation occurs.

*What effects have been
used to support the
notion of the
phonological loop?*

importance. Two phenomena providing reasonable support for this view are
the phonological similarity effect and the word-length effect. The **phonological similarity effect** is found when a short list of visually presented words has
to be recalled immediately in the correct order. What happens is that recall
performance is worse when the words are phonologically similar (i.e., having
similar sounds) than when they are phonologically dissimilar. For example,
FEE, HE, KNEE, LEE, ME, and SHE form a list of phonologically similar
words, whereas BAY, HOE, IT, ODD, SHY, and UP form a list of phonologically dissimilar words. Larsen, Baddeley, and Andrade (2000) used those
lists, finding that the ability to recall the words in order was 25% worse with
the phonologically similar list. This phonological similarity effect occurred
because the participants used speech-based rehearsal processes within the
phonological loop. This study was discussed in connection with a different
theory in Chapter 11.

The **word-length effect** is based on memory span (the number of words or
other items recalled immediately in the correct order). It is defined by the
finding that memory span is lower for words taking a long time to say than for
those taking less time. For example, Baddeley, Thomson, and Buchanan (1975)
found that participants could recall as many words presented visually as they
could read out loud in 2 seconds. The findings discussed so far don't show clearly
that the word-length effect depends on the phonological loop. More convincing
evidence was reported by Baddeley, Thomson, and Buchanan (1975) in a study
on memory span. Some participants had to repeat the digits 1 to 8 out loud while
being presented visually with short or long words. The argument was that the
task of repeating digits (known as articulatory suppression) uses up the
resources of the phonological loop and so prevents it being used on
the memory-span task. As predicted, articulatory suppression eliminated
the word-length effect, suggesting that the effect involves the phonological loop.

As so often in psychology, reality turns out to be more complex than was
originally thought. Note that the research discussed so far involved the *visual*
presentation of words. Baddeley et al. (1975) obtained the usual word-length
effect when there was *auditory* presentation of word lists. Puzzlingly,
however, there was still a word-length effect with auditorily presented words,
even when articulatory suppression was used! This suggested the need to re-
think the phonological loop. This was done by Baddeley (1986, 1990), who
distinguished between a phonological or speech-based store and an articulatory control process (see Figure 12.3). More specifically, there is a *passive*

Figure 12.3
Phonological loop
system as envisaged by
Baddeley (1990).

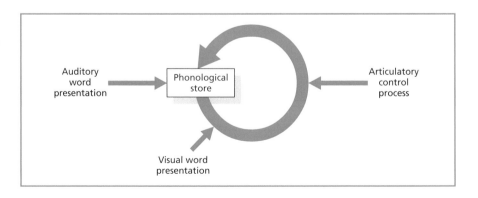

phonological store directly concerned with speech perception, and an articulatory process linked to speech production giving access to the phonological store.

How does this account of the phonological loop explain findings on the word-length effect? Visual presentation of words permits only *indirect* access to the phonological store through subvocal articulation. As a consequence, articulatory suppression prevents the phonological loop from being used and so there is no word-length effect. In contrast, auditory presentation of words produces *direct* access to the phonological store regardless of whether there is articulatory suppression. As a result, the word-length effect is found with auditory presentation even with articulatory suppression.

The above account of the phonological loop is supported by evidence from brain-damaged patients. Some patients (e.g., JB, PV) have very poor short-term memory for words presented auditorily but nevertheless have essentially normal speech production (Shallice & Butterworth, 1977; Vallar & Baddeley, 1984). These patients have a damaged phonological store but an intact articulatory control process. In contrast, other patients (e.g., TO) have an intact phonological store but a damaged articulatory control process shown by a lack of evidence for rehearsal (Vallar, Di Betta, & Silveri, 1997).

What is the value of the phonological loop? According to Baddeley, Gathercole, and Papagno (1998), it is very useful when learning new words. Supporting evidence comes from a study by Papagno, Valentine, and Baddeley (1991). Native Italian speakers learned pairs of Italian words and pairs of Italian–Russian words. Articulatory suppression (which reduces use of the phonological loop) greatly slowed down the learning of foreign vocabulary. However, it had little effect on the learning of pairs of Italian words. Thus, the negative effects of articulatory suppression on learning were limited to new words.

VISUOSPATIAL SKETCHPAD

The **visuospatial sketchpad** is used for the temporary storage and manipulation of visual patterns and spatial movement. It is used in many situations in everyday life (e.g., finding the route when walking, playing computer games). Logie, Baddeley, Mane, Donchin, and Sheptak (1989) studied performance on a complex computer game called Space Fortress, which involves maneuvering a space ship around a computer screen. Early in training, performance on Space Fortress was severely impaired when participants had to perform a secondary visuospatial task. After 25 hours' training, the adverse effects on the computer game of carrying out a visuospatial task at the same time were greatly reduced, being limited to those aspects directly involving perceptuomotor control. Thus, the visuospatial sketchpad was used throughout training on Space Fortress, but its involvement decreased with practice.

One of the key issues is whether there is a *single* system combining visual and spatial processing or whether there are partially or completely *separate* visual and spatial systems. According to Logie (1995; see Figure 12.4), the visuospatial sketchpad consists of two components:

Is visual memory distinct from spatial memory in the working memory model?

KEY TERM
Visuospatial sketchpad: a component of working memory that is involved in visual and spatial processing of information.

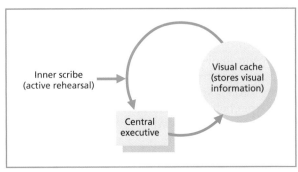

Figure 12.4 The visuo-spatial sketchpad or working memory as envisaged by Logie. Adapted from Logie (1995).

1. **Visual cache**: This stores information about visual form and color.
2. **Inner scribe**: This processes spatial and movement information. It rehearses information in the visual cache and transfers information from the visual cache to the central executive (attention-like system).

Klauer and Zhao (2004) explored the above issue, and we will consider one of their experiments in detail. There were two main tasks, one a spatial task (memory for dot locations) and the other a visual task (memory for Chinese ideographs). There were also three secondary task conditions:

1. a movement discrimination task (spatial interference)
2. a color discrimination task (visual interference)
3. a control condition involving no secondary task.

What would we predict if there are separate spatial and visual components? First, the spatial interference task should disrupt performance more on the spatial main task than on the visual main task. Second, the visual interference task should disrupt performance more on the visual main task than on the spatial main task. As can be seen in Figure 12.5, both predictions were confirmed.

Additional evidence supporting the notion of separate visual and spatial systems was reported by Smith and Jonides (1997) in an ingenious study. Two visual stimuli were presented together followed by a probe stimulus. Participants decided whether the probe was in the same location as one of the initial stimuli (spatial task) or had the same form (visual task). Even though the stimuli were identical in the two tasks, there were clear differences in patterns of brain activation as revealed by PET (see Glossary). There was more activity in the right hemisphere during the spatial task than the visual task, but there was more activity in the left hemisphere during the visual task than the spatial task. Several other studies have indicated that different brain areas are activated during visual and spatial working memory tasks (see Sala, Rämä, & Courtney, 2003, for a review).

CENTRAL EXECUTIVE

The **central executive**, which resembles an attentional system, is the most important and versatile component of the working memory system. Alas, it is also the least well understood. As Baddeley (1996, p. 6) admitted with total honesty, "Our initial specification of the central executive

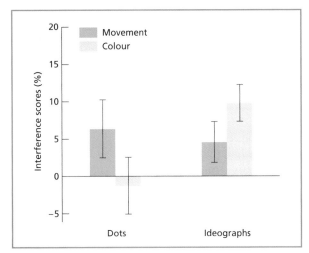

Figure 12.5 Amount of interference on a spatial task (dots) and a visual task (ideographs) as a function of secondary task (spatial: movement distribution vs. visual: color discrimination). From Klauer and Zhao (2004).

was so vague as to serve as little more than a ragbag into which could be stuffed all the complex strategy selection, planning, and retrieval checking that clearly goes on when subjects perform even the apparently simple digit span task."

What is the purpose of the central executive?

There have been various attempts to identify the main functions of the central executive. For example, here is the list put forward by Smith and Jonides (1999):

1. Switching attention between tasks.
2. Planning sub-tasks to achieve some goal.
3. Selective attention and inhibition.
4. Updating and checking the contents of working memory.
5. Coding representations in working memory for time and place of appearance.

Baddeley assumes that there is a single central executive serving various functions. However, he has entertained the possibility that things might actually be more complex than that. Shah and Miyake (1996) disagreed with that assumption. According to them, there are separate verbal and spatial working memory systems. This issue remains unresolved, but we will shortly consider some relevant evidence.

FINDINGS

Which regions of the brain are associated with processing in the central executive? The frontal lobes (and especially the prefrontal cortex) are often involved. Relevant evidence has been obtained from studies in which two tasks are performed together or singly. The basic assumption is that there is greater need for attentional control and coordination of attentional resources in dual-task conditions than in single-task ones. D'Esposito et al. (1995) used functional magnetic resonance imaging (fMRI; see Glossary) to identify the brain regions specifically associated with dual-task processing. The two tasks were deciding whether each word presented was a vegetable and deciding whether two visual displays differed only in rotation. The key finding was that areas within the dorsolateral prefrontal cortex were activated under dual-task conditions but not under single-task conditions. Presumably these areas were involved in coordinating processing on the two tasks.

Similar findings were reported by Bunge, Klingberg, Jacobsen, and Gabrieli (2000). Participants performed two tasks (sentence reading, recall of the last word in each sentence) either together or singly. The same brain areas were activated under single- and dual-task conditions. However, the key difference was that there was significantly more activation in parts of the prefrontal cortex in dual-task conditions than in single-task ones, reflecting the greater involvement of the central executive under dual-task conditions.

Is the central executive unitary in the sense that there is a single executive mechanism, or are there two or more different executive mechanisms? Evidence supporting the latter position was reported by Miyake et al. (2000). They used several tasks involving one of three main executive functions (i.e., shifting attention, updating information, and inhibition). These three functions were moderately correlated with each other, but were nevertheless clearly separable. The implication is that the various executive functions differ in terms of the processes involved, even though they share some common process (e.g., controlled attention).

We need to be careful about simply assuming that all central executive functioning involves parts of the frontal cortex. Andres and Van der Linden (2002) studied patients with damage to the frontal cortex. Two central executive tasks were used with these patients:

1. A directed forgetting task in which they had to inhibit information that was no longer relevant.
2. Dual-task conditions, in which processing and storage operations had to be carried out together.

Andres and Van der Linden (2002, p. 835) reported the following findings: "Frontal patients performed the dual task and inhibited the no-longer relevant information as well as control participants. These findings suggest that not all executive processes are exclusively sustained by the frontal cortex."

Collette and Van der Linden (2002) reviewed numerous brain-imaging studies involving several central executive functions. The evidence indicated that such functions most often involve prefrontal cortex, but various other areas are sometimes involved (Collette & Van der Linden, 2002, p. 120):

> Some prefrontal areas ... are systematically activated by a large range of executive tasks, suggesting their involvement in rather general executive processes. However, other frontal areas ... and even parietal regions ... are also frequently found during the execution of executive tasks. Since these regions are involved less systematically in the different executive processes explored in this review, we can hypothesize that they have more specific functions.

Shah and Miyake (1996) obtained evidence supporting the notion that there are separate verbal and spatial working-memory systems. They assessed verbal processing with a reading span task—participants read several sentences for meaning and then recalled the final word of each sentence. Reading span is the maximum number of sentences for which they could do this. They assessed spatial processing with a spatial span task. On this task, participants decided whether each of a set of letters was in normal or mirror-image orientation and then indicated the direction in which the top of each letter had been pointing. Spatial span is the maximum number of letters for which participants could do this.

Several of Shah and Miyake's (1996) findings indicated that verbal and spatial working memory are separate. First, there was only a modest relationship between reading span and spatial span, as was indicated by a correlation of +.23. Second, reading span correlated +.45 with verbal IQ but hardly at all with spatial IQ. Third, spatial span correlated highly with spatial IQ (+.6), but didn't correlate with verbal IQ.

The participants in the study by Shah and Miyake (1966) were nearly all of high intelligence, and this may have reduced the correlation between verbal and spatial working memory. However, Mackintosh and Bennett (2003) replicated the key findings of Shah and Miyake (1996) with participants having a broader range of ability.

BRINGING THE STORY UP TO DATE: EPISODIC BUFFER

What I have done so far is to describe and discuss Baddeley's working memory model as it existed up until the end of the twentieth century. In 2000, however, Baddeley decided to add a fourth component to the model. Why did he decide to do this? In essence, the phonological loop and the visuospatial sketchpad permit the processing and temporary storage of information of *specific* kinds of information only, and the central executive is involved in *general* processing but has no storage capacity. Something is missing, since none of these three components is a general storage system that can combine several kinds of information. It is precisely this gap that the fourth component (the episodic buffer) is designed to fill. More specifically, the **episodic buffer** is a limited-capacity storage system. The central executive integrates information from the phonological loop and the visuospatial sketchpad into "a unitary multi-dimensional representation" (Baddeley & Wilson, 2002, p. 1738) within the episodic buffer (see Figure 12.1).

The value of the notion of an episodic buffer can be seen in a study by Baddeley and Wilson (2002) on immediate recall of prose. It used to be argued that good immediate prose recall involves the ability to store some of the relevant information in long-term memory. According to this position, amnesic patients with very impaired long-term memory should have very poor immediate prose recall. In contrast, Baddeley and Wilson argued that the ability to perform well on a task involving immediate recall of prose depends on two factors: (1) the capacity of the episodic buffer; and (2) an efficiently functioning central executive creating and maintaining information in the buffer. According to this argument, even severely amnesic patients should have good immediate prose recall provided they have an efficient central executive. As predicted, immediate prose recall was much better in amnesics having little deficit in executive functioning than in those with a severe executive deficit.

Why do you think Baddeley proposed the additional episodic buffer component to the working memory model?

WORKING MEMORY AND INTELLIGENCE

Another way of considering working memory is to focus on individual differences in working memory capacity, an approach that is very popular, especially in the United States. This approach is related to Baddeley's in that it is assumed that working memory is a system used for both storage and processing. It follows that individuals with the greatest ability to combine those functions have the greatest working memory capacity. For example, Daneman and Carpenter (1980) used a task in which participants read several sentences for comprehension (processing task) and then recalled the final word of each sentence (storage task). The largest number of sentences from which a participant could recall all the final words more than 50% of the time was his or her **reading span**, and was taken as a measure of working memory capacity. It was assumed that the processes used in comprehending the sentences require a smaller proportion of the available working memory capacity of those with a large capacity. As a result, they have more capacity available for retaining the last words of the sentences.

Various other ways of measuring working memory capacity have been proposed. For example, Turner and Engle (1989) presented participants with a series of items such as "IS $(4 \times 2) - 3 = 5$? TABLE." They had to answer each arithmetical question and remember the last word. The data were used to calculate a measure of working memory capacity known as **operation span**: the maximum number of items for which the participants could remember all the last words.

It has usually been assumed that reading span and operation span reflect the capacity of a *single* resource used for processing and storage, with increasing demands on processing reducing the capacity available for storage, and vice versa. In contrast, it would seem more likely within Baddeley's working memory model to assume that these spans depend on *two* separate resources: processing relies on the central executive, whereas storage of the final words relies on the phonological loop. These contrasting views were put to the test by Duff and Logie (2001). There were three conditions: (1) processing only (arithmetic verification such as $8 + 7 = 17$: correct or incorrect?); storage only (memory span for words presented individually); and (3) processing *and* storage (operation span in which arithmetic verification and memory span were combined). If arithmetic verification and memory span both depend on a single processing resource, performance on each task should be much worse when they are performed together (Condition 3) than when they are performed separately (Conditions 1 and 2). In contrast, if the two tasks involve separate resources, then combining the tasks should *not* severely impair performance. The findings provided reasonably strong evidence that the two tasks involve separate resources.

INTELLIGENCE

An important issue in this area of research is the relationship between working memory capacity and general intelligence (often referred to as "g"). This issue came to the fore when Kyllonen and Christal (1990) administered various tests of reasoning ability to assess general intelligence and also measured working memory capacity. The key finding was that correlations between reasoning ability and working memory capacity were mostly around +.8 to +.9. These correlations were so high that they suggested working memory capacity is essentially the same as general intelligence. Colom, Rebollo, Palacios, Juan-Espinosa, and Kyllonen (2004) used a wider range of intelligence tests than Kyllonen and Christal and obtained very similar findings: "WM [working memory capacity] is (almost) perfectly predicted by g (92% of explained variance)" (Colom et al., 2004, p. 287).

Conway, Kane, and Engle (2003) reviewed the research on working memory capacity and general intelligence. They found the typical correlation between working memory capacity and general intelligence was about +.6, indicating that the two constructs are similar but by no means identical. For example, Süß, Oberauer, Wittman, Wilhelm, and Schulze (2002) carried out a comprehensive study in which several aspects of working memory (e.g., coordination, integration, updating, task switching) were assessed. Overall, the correlation between working memory capacity and general intelligence was +.65.

In a review article, Barrett, Tugade, and Engle (2004) focused on differences in cognitive processes between individuals high and low in working memory capacity. The central hypothesis was that those high in working memory capacity have superior attentional control than those low in that capacity. It follows from that hypothesis that individuals low in working memory capacity should be more susceptible to distraction than those high in working memory capacity. Conway, Cowan, and Bunting (2001) found that individuals low in working memory capacity were much more likely to attend to their name within the unattended message during a listening task. Kane, Bleckley, Conway, and Engle (2001) found that attention to distracting peripheral cues was greater among participants low in working memory capacity.

In sum, research on individual differences in working memory capacity is of real relevance to an understanding of intelligence in view of the moderately high (or very high) correlation between the two constructs. This research indicates that attentional control is an important factor associated with working memory capacity (Feldman Barrett et al., 2004) and by implication it may also help to explain at least some individual differences in intelligence. It is also necessary to identify differences between working memory capacity and intelligence. In that connection, there is some evidence that processing speed is of more direct relevance to working memory capacity than to intelligence (Ackerman, Beier, & Boyle, 2002).

Is working memory capacity a good predictor of general intelligence?

EVALUATION AND CHAPTER SUMMARY

Phonological loop
- The phonological loop is involved when people have to recall a set of words in the correct order immediately after hearing them.
- Two phenomena providing evidence that the phonological loop is used for immediate serial recall of words are the phonological similarity effect and the word-length effect.
- The phonological loop consists of a phonological store and an articulatory control process.

Visuospatial sketchpad
- It is now generally accepted that the visuospatial sketchpad consists of somewhat separate visual and spatial components.
- Some of the evidence consists of findings showing there is less interference when a visual and a spatial task are performed together than when both tasks are visual or spatial (e.g., Klauer & Zhao, 2004).
- Additional evidence comes from neuroimaging studies indicating that visual tasks activate different regions of the brain from those activated by spatial tasks (Sala et al., 2003).
- In spite of the evidence for separate visual and spatial components, many tasks require both components to be used in combination.

- It still remains unclear precisely how processing and information involving the two components are combined and integrated on such tasks.
- In addition, As Baddeley and Logie (1999, p. 36) admitted, "The precise nature of the mechanisms underlying the capacity limitations for spatial and visual information is not clear yet."

Central executive
- The central executive is an attention-like system involved in various functions (e.g., selective attention and inhibition; switching attention).
- According to Shah and Miyake (1996), there are separate verbal and spatial working-memory systems. Some of the evidence supports this view.

Working memory and intelligence
- Measures of working memory capacity (e.g., reading span; operation span) correlate moderately highly with intelligence.
- Individual differences in attentional control are important in accounting for individual differences in working memory capacity and may also help to explain some individual differences in intelligence.

The working memory model overall summary
- The working memory model has proved very successful. We spend much of our time engaged in tasks requiring both active processing and temporary storage of information, and the working memory model provides an account of how this is accomplished.
- The working memory model is applicable to numerous tasks and situations. As a result, the model's scope is substantially greater than that of the short-term store component of Atkinson and Shiffrin's (1968) multi-store model (see Chapter 11).
- Another advantage of the working memory model over the multi-store model is that verbal rehearsal is regarded as an optional process within the phonological loop. This is much more realistic than the enormous significance accorded to rehearsal within the multi-store model.
- What are the limitations of the working memory model? First, as Baddeley and Hitch (2000, p. 129) admitted, "The central executive is the least well understood component of the Baddeley and Hitch model." For example, the central executive has limited capacity, but it is difficult to measure that capacity.
- Second, and related to the first point, it remains controversial whether the central executive is unitary or whether we should distinguish two or more central executive systems.
- Third, the relationship between the episodic buffer and the other components of the working memory system is unclear. We still lack a detailed account of how the episodic buffer integrates information from the other components and from long-term memory.

FURTHER READING

- Andrade, J. (2001). *Working memory in perspective*. Hove, UK: Psychology Press. The chapters in this edited book provide a good overview of theory and research on working memory.
- Baddeley, A.D., & Logie, R.H. (1999). Working memory: The multiple-component model. In A. Miyake & P. Shah (Eds.), *Models of working memory: Mechanisms of active maintenance and executive control*. Cambridge: Cambridge University Press. This chapter provides a very clear account of the key assumptions of Baddeley's working memory model.
- Healy, A.F., & Proctor, R.W. (2003). *Handbook of psychology: Experimental psychology, Vol. 4.* New York: Wiley & Sons. There are good reviews of several topics in memory in this edited book, including one on working memory.
- Miyake, A., & Shah, P. (1999). *Models of working memory: Mechanisms of active maintenance and executive control*. New York: Cambridge University Press. This edited book contains various alternative theoretical approaches to the one put forward by Baddeley.

CHAPTER 13

CONTENTS

Introduction 179

Complex normal learning 181

Learning in amnesics 184

Brain-imaging research 185

Evaluation and chapter summary 186

Further reading 188

Learning without awareness?

13

INTRODUCTION

Do you think you could learn something without being aware of what you have learned? On the face of it, it sounds improbable that that could happen. For example, suppose you attended a lecture on social psychology yesterday. No matter how boring the lecture was, I imagine (perhaps optimistically!) that you learned *some* useful new information about social psychology. Of most relevance to the present discussion, it is virtually certain that you can bring to mind some of that information and that you have a strong conscious awareness of having learned. Such considerations may lead you to think that the entire notion of learning without conscious awareness is very suspect. Even if we *did* acquire information without any conscious awareness, it might seem somewhat pointless and wasteful—if we don't realize we have learned something, then it seems unlikely that we are going to make much use of it.

In the terminology used by psychologists, we have been considering **implicit learning**, which has been defined as, "Learning without conscious awareness of having learned" (French & Cleeremans, 2002, p. xvii). Implicit learning has been contrasted with **explicit learning**, which involves conscious awareness of what has been learned. We have just dismissed the notion of implicit learning, but there is another side to the story. Consider a fuller definition of implicit learning offered by Cleeremans and Jiménez, 2002, p. 20): "Implicit learning is the process through which we become sensitive to certain regularities in the environment (1) in the absence of intention to learn about these regularities, (2) in the absence of awareness that one is learning, and (3) in such a way that the resulting knowledge is difficult to express." A moment's reflection probably allows you to think of skills you possess that are difficult to express in words. For example, it is notoriously difficult to express what we know about riding a bicycle. Indeed, the verbal descriptions most people give of how to steer a bicycle around a corner are inaccurate and would lead anyone following them to fall off pretty quickly! Another example is that most of us speak reasonably grammatically even though we have little or no conscious access to the grammatical rules in the English language.

One of the most-used tasks used by psychologists to study implicit learning is artificial grammar learning. In a typical study on artificial grammar learning (Reber, 1967), participants memorize meaningless letter strings (e.g., PVPXVPS, TSXXTVV). After that, they are told that the memorized letter strings all follow the rules of an artificial grammar, but they are not told the natures of these rules. Next, the participants classify *novel* strings as grammatical or ungrammatical. Finally, they are asked to describe the rules of the artificial grammar.

What are the typical findings from studies on artificial grammar learning? First, the classification task is performed significantly above chance level, thus indicating that some learning has occurred. Second, the participants cannot describe the grammatical rules when asked to do so. This combination of learning plus an inability to express what has been learned seems superficially to fit Cleeremans and Jiménez's (2002) definition of implicit learning very neatly. Alas, as we will see shortly, there have been considerable disagreements about the proper interpretation of findings from the artificial grammar task.

Reber (1993) argued that the systems involved in implicit learning and memory differ from those involved in explicit learning and memory. He proposed five major differences between the two systems (but note that *none* of them has been established definitely):

1. *Robustness*: Implicit systems are relatively unaffected by disorders (e.g., amnesia) affecting explicit systems.
2. *Age independence*: Implicit learning is less influenced by age or developmental level than is explicit learning.
3. *Low variability*: There are smaller individual differences in implicit learning and memory than in explicit learning and memory.
4. *IQ independence*: Performance on implicit tasks is less affected by IQ than is performance on explicit tasks.
5. *Commonality of process*: Implicit systems are common to most species whereas explicit systems are not.

ROLE OF CONSCIOUSNESS

At the heart of the controversy over implicit learning is the issue of whether conscious awareness is as important in human learning and behavior as we like to think it is. Evidence that the information available to conscious awareness is often grossly deficient was reported by Nisbett and Wilson (1977). In one study, participants were presented with a display of five essentially identical pairs of stockings, and decided which pair was the best. After they had made their choice, they indicated *why* they had chosen that particular pair. Most participants chose the right-most pair, and so their decisions were actually influenced by relative spatial position. However, the participants strongly denied that spatial position played any part in their decision. They argued instead that their choice was determined by slight differences in color, texture, and so on among the pairs of stockings.

Cleeremans and Jiménez (2002) identified two extreme positions on the issue of the relationship between consciousness and cognition (including learning). One extreme is the notion of a "Commander Data" type of consciousness based on *Star Trek*'s character Data. He is an android [robot resembling a human being] who can describe his internal states in enormous detail. Commander Data theorists assume that consciousness has great power and that any knowledge expressed through behavior is available to it. The opposite extreme is the notion of a zombie consciousness, in which we have no conscious awareness of the knowledge influencing our behavior. According to zombie theorists, "There is a zombie within you and ... it could be responsible for most of your actions ... Your zombie is unconscious ... cognition is inherently opaque, and consciousness, when present, offers but a very incomplete and imperfect perspective on internal states of affairs."

Are we more like Data or more like zombies? The key point that Cleeremans and Jiménez (2002) were making is that neither extreme position is plausible, even though some theorists adhere to one or other of these positions. Thus, the most reasonable assumption is that consciousness is sometimes (but by no means always) of relevance to learning and to human cognition in general.

It is now time to turn to more of the evidence on implicit learning. We can identify *three* main experimental approaches, each of which is considered in what follows. First, there are studies (e.g., on artificial grammar learning) designed to see whether normal participants can learn fairly complex material in the absence of conscious awareness of what they have learned. Second, there are studies on brain-damaged patients with amnesia. Here the focus is on whether their implicit learning is essentially intact even though their explicit learning is severely impaired. If that is the case, it suggests that different processes underlie implicit and explicit learning. Third, there are brain-imaging studies. The basic rationale here is as follows: If implicit and explicit learning are very different forms of learning, then different brain areas should be active during implicit learning and explicit learning. You should be warned here and now that the findings from all three approaches are nothing like clear-cut!

COMPLEX NORMAL LEARNING

Why has it proved difficult to decide whether or not normal individuals exhibit implicit learning? A major reason is because the failure of participants when questioned to indicate conscious awareness of what they have learned (e.g., on an artificial grammar learning task) does *not* necessarily prove that the learning was implicit. This issue was addressed by Shanks and St. John (1994), who proposed two criteria that need to be met to show implicit learning:

Is it possible to learn something and have no explicit knowledge of what you have learned?

1. *Information criterion*: The information participants are asked to provide on the awareness test must be the information responsible for the improved level of performance.
2. *Sensitivity criterion*: "We must be able to show that our test of awareness is sensitive to all of the relevant knowledge" (Shanks & St. John, 1994, p. 374). People may be consciously aware of more task-relevant knowledge than appears on an insensitive awareness test, and this may lead us to underestimate their consciously accessible knowledge.

In principle, numerous tasks could be used to test for the existence (or non-existence!) of implicit learning. In practice, however, much of the research has focused on two tasks: artificial grammar learning and serial reaction. We already considered the former task and the latter is discussed below.

The serial reaction time task consists of dozens or hundreds of trials, and has been used by many researchers (e.g., Nissen and Bullemer, 1987). On each trial, a stimulus appears at one out of several locations on a computer screen, and the participant responds as rapidly as possible with the response key corresponding to its location. There is typically a complex, repeating sequence over trials in the various stimulus locations, but the participants are not told this. Towards the end of the experiment, there is a block of trials conforming to a *novel* sequence. Participants typically respond more rapidly to stimuli in the repeating sequence than to stimuli in the novel sequence, indicating they have learned information about the repeating sequence. However, when questioned at the end of the experiment, participants usually show *no* conscious awareness that there was a sequence or pattern in the stimuli presented to them.

The above findings may seem to provide strong support for the notion of implicit learning. After all, as Wilkinson and Shanks (2004, p. 354) pointed out, "If participants can be shown to perform well on a task while at the same time performing poorly on a test of awareness, then this is good evidence that they learned implicitly." Unfortunately, however, most studies on artificial grammar learning and the serial reaction time task fail to adequately fulfill the information and sensitivity criteria discussed above. There is also what Shanks and St. John (1994) referred to as the "retrospective problem." Participants may be consciously aware of what they are learning at the time, but have forgotten when they are questioned about their conscious awareness at the end of the experiment.

Research on artificial grammar learning has proved inconclusive because it fails to meet the information and sensitivity criteria discussed above. In essence, people's ability to discriminate above chance between grammatical and ungrammatical letter strings does *not* prove that they have acquired knowledge of the underlying grammatical rules. For example, Channon, Shanks, Johnstone, Vakili, Chin, and Sinclair (2002) found that decisions on the grammaticality of letter strings didn't depend at all on knowledge of grammatical rules. Instead, participants classified letter strings as grammatical when they shared letter pairs (bigrams) with the letter strings memorized initially, and as ungrammatical when they did not. Thus, participants' above-chance performance when classifying letter strings may depend on conscious awareness of two-letter fragments relevant to the grammatical rules, with no direct knowledge (explicit or implicit) of the rules themselves.

How can we satisfy the information and sensitivity criteria with the serial reaction time task? One reasonable approach is to make the awareness test very similar to the learning task. Precisely this was done by Howard and Howard (1992). In their version of the task, an asterisk appeared in one of four positions on a screen, under each of which was a key. The task was to press the key corresponding to the position of the asterisk as rapidly as possible. Participants showed clear evidence of learning the underlying sequence by responding faster and faster to the asterisk. However, when given the awareness test of predicting where the asterisk would appear next, their performance was at chance level.

Contrary findings indicating that participants have *some* conscious aware-

ness of what they have learned on a serial reaction time task were reported in an important
study by Wilkinson and Shanks (2004). Participants were given either 1500 (15 blocks) or 4500
(45 blocks) trials on the task and showed clear
evidence of sequence learning. They were then
told there was a repeated sequence in the
stimuli, following which they were presented on
each of 12 trials with part of the sequence under
one of two conditions. In the *inclusion* condition,
they were told to guess the next location in the
sequence. In the *exclusion* condition, they were
told they should *avoid* guessing the next location
in the sequence. If sequence knowledge is wholly
implicit, then performance shouldn't differ
between the inclusion and exclusion conditions.
In contrast, if it is partly explicit, then the
guesses generated in the inclusion condition
should be more likely to conform to the
repeated sequence than those in the exclusion
condition. As can be seen in Figure 13.1, the
findings indicated that explicit knowledge was
acquired on the serial reaction time task.

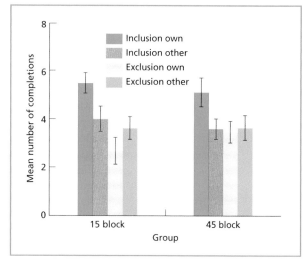

Figure 13.1 Mean number of completions (guessed
locations) corresponding to the trained sequence
(own) or the untrained sequence (other) in inclusion
and exclusion conditions as a function of number of
trials (15 vs. 45 blocks). Wilkinson and Shanks (2004).
Copyright © American Psychological Association.
Reprinted with permission.

Heuer and Schmidtke (1996) also used the serial reaction time task. They
compared performance when this task was performed on its own or at the
same time as a second, attentionally demanding task (remembering a verbal
or spatial sequence). Heuer and Schmidtke found that the presence of an
attentionally demanding secondary task had *no* effect on performance on the
serial reaction time task. The implication is that implicit learning differs from
explicit learning in not requiring attentional resources.

Shea, Wulf, Whitacre, and Park (2001) tried to demonstrate implicit
learning using a different task. Participants stood on a platform and tried to
move it to mimic the movements of a line displayed on a computer screen.
They performed the task several times. On each occasion, the middle
segment was identical, but the first and third segments varied. However, the
participants weren't told that the middle segment would remain the same.
Performance on the middle segment improved more than performance on the
other segments, indicating that the participants had benefited from having
that segment repeated. There was evidence that this learning was implicit
rather than explicit. Two-thirds of the participants reported that they didn't
think that part of the pattern had been repeated. In addition, they performed
at chance level when trying to recognize the repeated segment on a subsequent recognition test.

In a second experiment, Shea et al. (2001) repeated two out of the three
segments, and participants were told explicitly about one of the repeated segments. Surprisingly, performance on this segment was significantly *worse* than
on the repeated segment about which participants had not been told. This
finding supports the notion that there is a clear distinction between implicit
and explicit learning. However, as Perruchet, Chambaron, and Ferrel-Chapus
(2003) pointed out, the provision of explicit information about one of the

segments may have led participants to attend to information that was irrelevant for good task performance.

In sum, there is superficially strong evidence in favor of implicit learning. In spite of that, there are reasons for skepticism, with the most powerful evidence against implicit learning being provided by Wilkinson and Shanks (2004). It is very important to note that it would be illogical to argue that because explicit learning typically plays some role in producing improvements in performance therefore there is no such thing as implicit learning. For example, Sun, Slusarz, and Terry (2005) argued that skill learning involves both explicit and implicit learning—implicit learning is specific to any given learning environment and explicit learning is more general and can be used more flexibly than implicit learning.

LEARNING IN AMNESICS

As we saw in Chapter 11, amnesic patients have severe impairments in explicit memory (involving conscious recollection) but not in implicit memory (not involving conscious recollection). If amnesic patients have impaired explicit learning but intact implicit learning, this would support those claiming implicit learning is very different from explicit learning. You may well wonder why implicit learning and implicit memory have not been discussed together in the same chapter. After all, there are close connections between learning and memory. There are two main reasons. First, studies of implicit learning have typically used relatively complex, novel stimuli, whereas most studies of implicit memory have used simple and familiar stimuli. Second, surprisingly little research has considered the relationship between implicit learning and implicit memory.

Is implicit learning separable from implicit memory? Why?

One of the earliest studies on implicit learning in amnesic patients was by Knowlton, Ramus, and Squire (1992). Amnesics' performance in artificial grammar learning was comparable to that of healthy controls when asked to distinguish between grammatical and ungrammatical letter strings (63% vs. 67%, respectively). This finding suggests that amnesic patients had intact implicit learning. In contrast, when the amnesic patients were given the explicit test of recognizing the letter strings presented during training, their performance was worse than that of healthy individuals (62% vs. 72%, respectively).

Channon et al. (2002), in a study mentioned earlier, devised complex versions of the artificial grammar learning task permitting separate assessment of the learning of grammatical rules and of fragments of letter strings. Neither normal participants nor amnesic patients showed any evidence of abstract rule learning. However, both groups learned about fragments, and tended to categorize familiar two-letter fragments as grammatical. However, amnesic patients learned fewer fragments than the normal controls. These findings are out of step with previous studies, many of which found that amnesic patients have essentially intact implicit learning. The discrepancy may have occurred because Channon et al. (2002) used longer and more complex letter strings than those used in previous research.

Findings apparently contradicting those of Channon et al. (2002) were reported by Meulemans and Van der Linden (2003). They used an artificial grammar learning task in which the test of implicit learning was such that fragment knowledge couldn't influence the accuracy of grammaticality judgments. In addition, they used a test of explicit learning in which participants wrote down 10 letter strings they considered to be grammatical. The amnesic patients performed as well as the normal controls on *implicit* learning, but their performance was much worse than that of the controls on *explicit* learning.

Some studies have focused on amnesics' performance on the serial reaction time task. Nissen, Willingham, and Hartman (1989) found comparable implicit learning in amnesic patients and control participants, and this was also the case on a second test 1 week later. In contrast, the amnesic patients showed worse explicit learning than controls when questioned about the presence of a repeating sequence.

Other studies using the serial reaction time task have obtained similar findings (see Meulemans & Van der Linden, 2003, for a review). A limitation with most of these studies is that any implicit learning may only have involved simple associations between pairs of stimuli. Reber and Squire (1994) used a version of the serial reaction time task on which the repeating sequence could *not* be learned by forming associations between successive stimuli. The implicit learning performance of the amnesic patients was as good as that of the control participants, thus showing they can learn relatively complex associations.

BRAIN-IMAGING RESEARCH

Suppose there are somewhat separate cognitive systems involved in explicit and implicit learning. If that is the case, then it seems reasonable to predict that different brain regions should be activated more on explicit-learning tasks than on implicit-learning tasks. We can also make a more specific prediction given that only explicit learning involves conscious awareness of what is being learned. It is known (e.g., Dehaene & Naccache, 2001) that conscious awareness is associated with activation in many regions. Some of the main brain areas are within the prefrontal cortex (e.g., the anterior cingulate and the dorsolateral prefrontal cortex). Thus, these areas should be more active during explicit learning than during implicit learning.

Does brain-imaging research support a dissociation between implicit and explicit learning?

The evidence is somewhat inconsistent. Grafton, Hazeltine, and Ivry (1995) obtained PET scans during the learning of motor sequences. There were two conditions, one of which made it easier for participants to become consciously aware of the sequence. Grafton et al. (1995) found that several brain areas were more activated during explicit learning, including the dorsolateral prefrontal cortex and the anterior cingulate. In addition, explicit learning was associated with more activation in areas within the parietal cortex associated with voluntary attention and working memory, both of which involve conscious awareness.

Additional positive evidence was reported by Aizenstein et al. (2004) using a version of the serial reaction time task. The explicit task involved learning a sequence of shapes. At the same time, the colors of the shapes used in the explicit task formed a sequence used on the implicit learning task. Some brain regions were activated during both explicit and implicit learning. However, the key finding was that there was greater prefrontal activation with explicit than with implicit learning. This is as expected if conscious processes are more important in explicit learning.

Negative evidence was reported by Schendan, Searl, Melrose, and Stern (2003) in a study on implicit and explicit sequence learning. In contrast to the studies by Grafton et al. (1995) and Aizenstein et al. (2004), implicit and explicit learning both activated the same brain areas. Schendan et al. (2003, p. 1020) concluded that, "Both implicit and explicit learning of higher order sequences involve the MTL [medial temporal lobe] structures implicated in memory functions."

What remains for the future? First, more research should focus on possible *interactions* between implicit and explicit learning. Second, we need more sophisticated techniques for identifying the roles played by explicit and implicit processes in performing complex tasks (e.g., artificial grammar learning). Third, and more speculatively, we may need to move away from the simple division of learning into implicit or explicit. As Kelly (2003, p. 1389) suggested, "Knowledge is not necessarily implicit or explicit per se but may be dynamic in nature, with accessibility to explicit consciousness being dependent on the quality of the underlying representation (determined by three characteristics: stability, distinctiveness, and strength)." Thus, representations that are stable, distinctive, and strong are more likely than those that are unstable, non-distinctive, and weak to become accessible to conscious awareness.

EVALUATION AND CHAPTER SUMMARY

Complex normal learning
- In my opinion, most of the studies discussed in this section are frustrating.
- On the one hand, many of the findings seem superficially to provide strong evidence in favor of implicit learning. On the other hand, careful consideration of the evidence (especially from the artificial grammar learning task) reveals reasons for doubt and skepticism.
- This is especially the case with the study by Wilkinson and Shanks (2004). However, they used far more trials on the serial reaction task than most other researchers—it is likely that the probability of *some* explicit learning occurring would be enhanced by increasing the number of trials.
- It often seems to be assumed that finding that explicit learning plays some part in explaining performance improvement with practice means *no* implicit learning occurred.
- Sun, Slusarz, and Terry (2005) put forward a theoretical approach (supported by several computer simulations) based on the notion that skill learning involves an interaction between explicit and implicit knowledge.
- More specifically, implicit learning often precedes explicit learning, with explicit knowledge being "extracted" from implicit skills.
- It is useful for us to combine implicit and explicit learning because they make different contributions. Implicit learning is specific to the learning environment and isn't adaptable to changing conditions. In contrast, explicit learning is more general and can be used flexibly when conditions change.

Learning in amnesics
- Most of the findings from artificial grammar learning and the serial reaction time task suggest that amnesic patients have intact implicit learning but impaired explicit learning.
- Such a pattern is consistent with the notion that explicit and implicit learning involve different mechanisms.
- In spite of the positive findings, there are some grounds for caution.
- First, the implicit learning performance of amnesic patients is sometimes worse than that of normal controls (e.g., Channon et al., 2002). Gooding, Mayes, and van Eijk (2000) found in a review of the literature that amnesic patients tended to perform at the same level as healthy individuals on implicit tests with familiar material, but performed worse with novel material.
- Second, it is sometimes not clear *what* information is being used to perform implicit learning tasks (especially with artificial grammar learning). If we lack this information, it is difficult to assess whether implicit or explicit learning is involved.
- Third, some findings seeming to point to the existence of separate explicit and implicit learning systems can be interpreted in simpler ways.

- For example, consider the findings of Knowlton et al. (1992) discussed above. Kinder and Shanks (2001) managed to account for these findings by assuming that there is only *one* learning system, with amnesic patients having a slower learning rate than healthy individuals.

Brain-imaging research
- There has been too little brain-imaging research on explicit and implicit learning to draw any sweeping conclusions.
- All that can be said at present is that the predicted greater prefrontal activation during explicit than implicit learning is generally present (Aizenstein et al., 2004; Grafton et al., 1995).
- The fact that there is also reasonable evidence that implicit learning differs from explicit learning in studies on healthy individuals and on amnesics means that implicit learning is probably distinctively different from explicit learning.
- Some of the apparent inconsistencies in the literature can be explained by assuming that most tasks involve a mixture of implicit and explicit learning.

FURTHER READING

- French, R.M., & Cleeremans, A. (2002). *Implicit learning and consciousness: An empirical, philosophical and computational consensus in the making*. Hove, UK: Psychology Press. This edited book contains contributions by several of the leading researchers on implicit learning.
- Frensch, P.A., & Rünger, D. (2003). Implicit learning. *Current Directions in Psychological Science*, *12*, 13–18. This short article provides a good overview of research on implicit learning.
- Shanks, D.R. (2004). Implicit learning. In K. Lamberts and R. Goldstone (Eds.), *Handbook of cognition*. London: Sage. David Shanks puts forward a powerful case for being skeptical of the existence of implicit learning in this chapter.

CHAPTER 14

CONTENTS

Introduction 191

Are traumatic memories repressed? 196

Memories interfere with each other 198

Encoding specificity 200

Consolidation theory 201

What about the future? 202

Evaluation and chapter summary 203

Further reading 205

It's slipped my mind

INTRODUCTION

Our ability to remember information and the events of our own lives is of tremendous importance. In the absence of memory, we would find ourselves in a similar position to a newborn infant, with everything seeming to be completely novel and surprising. In view of the great significance of having a good memory, it is valuable to consider the factors leading to forgetting so that we can try to minimize the amount of information we forget. The central focus of this chapter is on factors determining whether we remember or forget.

We will start by considering some commonsensical views about human memory. First, most people say they have a really poor memory and are always forgetting things. This view may owe something to the fact that forgetting things can often be embarrassing. Examples that spring to mind are forgetting your partner's birthday, people's names, or the punchline of a joke. Many years ago now, the British royal family went on an extended tour of South America. As they were leaving by plane from one airport to continue their tour, a member of the crowd waving them off realized with a sinking feeling that he should have been on the plane rather than the tarmac!

Some evidence that our memories can be poor for important information comes from the study of passwords. Brown, Bracken, Zoccoli, and Douglas (2004) found that 31% of their sample of American students admitted to having forgotten one or more passwords. As Brown et al. (2004, p. 650) pointed out, "We are faced with a continuing dilemma in personal password construction between security and convenience: fool the password hacker and you are likely to fool yourself." They found that 45% of students avoided this dilemma by using their own name in password construction, which hardly seems the way to have a secure password!

Brown et al. (2004) provided tips to people constructing passwords. If security is important, select a password that is a transformation of some memorable cue involving a mixture of letters and symbols. In addition, keep a record of passwords in a place to which only you have access (e.g., a safe deposit box). Of course, you then need to remember where you have put your passwords!

Second, in spite of the pessimistic view we have of our memory abilities, we feel that we have excellent long-term memory for dramatic events (e.g., death of Princess Diana; September 11, 2001). These memories of very significant and surprising world events are known as **flashbulb memories** and will be discussed shortly.

KEY TERM
Flashbulb memories: vivid and detailed memories of dramatic events (e.g., September 11, 2001).

Third, most people have only a vague idea of *why* they forget. It is generally known that we lose what sounds like a frighteningly large number of brain cells every day, and many people imagine this causes our memories to decay or fade away over time.

Some of the evidence relating to the three commonsensical views discussed above is considered below. In essence, we will see that none of these views can be regarded as more than partially correct.

POOR MEMORY?

We start by considering the notion that we have poor memories. Evidence that we may underestimate our own abilities comes in studies by Standing, Conezio, and Haber (1970) and Bahrick, Bahrick, and Wittlinger (1975). Standing et al. (1970) presented a total of 2560 color pictures for 10 seconds each to participants. Several days later the participants were presented with pairs of items (one new and one old), and asked to decide which one had been presented previously. In spite of the huge number of pictures they had seen, the participants made the correct choice on 90% of the trials. Bahrick et al. (1975) tested adults' ability to remember information about their classmates at school. There was remarkably little forgetting at retention intervals of up to 25 years. Performance was 90% for recognizing a name as being that of a classmate, for recognizing a classmate's photograph, and for matching a classmate's name to his or her school photograph. Performance remained very high on the last two tests even at a retention interval of almost 50 years, but performance on the name recognition task declined.

FLASHBULB MEMORIES

Are flashbulb memories really as accurate as we think they are? That was certainly the view of Brown and Kulik (1977), who claimed that flashbulb memories are much more accurate and long-lasting than other memories. They argued that dramatic world events activate a special neural mechanism, provided that the events are surprising and have real consequences for the individual. This mechanism "prints" the details of such events permanently in the memory system. Details are often stored away about the person who supplied the information, the place where the news was heard, the ongoing event when the news was heard, the individual's own emotional state, the emotional state of others, and the consequences of the event for the individual. For example, I was in the Psychology Department at Royal Holloway on September 11, 2001. I went down to the office of Rosemary Westley (the Departmental Superintendent) to ask her something, and she gave me the terrible news of the attack on the World Trade Center in New York.

Is flashbulb memory a uniquely accurate form of memory?

If flashbulb memories are special and involve permanent storage of information about dramatic world events, they should show *consistency* (lack of change) over time. Some evidence supports the view that flashbulb memories are special. Conway et al. (1994) studied flashbulb memories for the resignation of the former British Prime Minister, Margaret Thatcher, in 1990. This event was regarded as surprising and consequential by most British people, and so should theoretically have produced flashbulb memories. Memory for this event was tested within a few days, after 11 months, and after 26 months. Flashbulb memories were found in 86% of British participants after 11 months, and remained consistent even after 26 months. Kvavilashvili, Mirani, Schlagman, and Kornbrot (2003) found that British participants had detailed flashbulb memories of the death of Princess Diana. Indeed, their 51-month-old memories of her death were as detailed and specific as their 3-month-old memories of September 11 (9/11). In addition, their memories of the death of Princess Diana were comparable to those obtained very shortly after September 11 from other groups of participants.

In spite of some impressive findings, most research on flashbulb memories suggests there is nothing very special about such memories. For example, Talarico and Rubin (2003) assessed students' memories for the events of September 11 one day afterwards. At the same time, they assessed their memory for a very recent everyday event. The students were then tested again 7, 42, or 224 days later. There were two key findings (see Figure 14.1). First, the reported vividness of flashbulb memories remained very high over the entire 32-week period. Second, flashbulb memories showed no more consistency or lack of change than did everyday memories. Thus, there is a major discrepancy between people's beliefs in the strength of their flashbulb memories and the actual accuracy of those memories. As Talarico and Rubin (2003, p. 460) concluded, "The true 'mystery' is not why flashbulb memories are so accurate for so long ... but why people are so confident for so long in the accuracy of their flashbulb memories."

If you think your memories of September 11 are accurate, try answering the following questions: (1) "On September 11, did you see the videotape on television of the first plane striking the first tower?"; (2) "Was the Pentagon struck before the first tower collapsed?" Precisely these questions were asked of American students by Pezdek (2003). With the first question, 73% said "Yes," which is incorrect (there was videotape of the *second* tower being hit). Interestingly, even President George W. Bush mistakenly claimed to have seen a videotape of the first tower being hit. With the second question, 39% incorrectly answered, "No" (the Pentagon was struck at 9:41 and the first tower collapsed at 10:28.

Now try this question: "Have you seen the film of the car crash in which Princess Diana was killed?" I hope your answer was, "No," because there is no film of the car crash! However, Ost, Vrij, Costall, and Bull (2002) found that 45% of a British sample claimed to have seen the non-existent film.

Why is there much stronger evidence for flashbulb memories in some studies than in others? Winningham, Hyman, and Dinnel (2000) provided an important part of the answer. They studied memory for the unexpected acquittal of O.J. Simpson (a retired American football star) who had been accused of murdering his ex-wife and her friend. They found that people's memories changed considerably in the first few days after hearing about the acquittal but became consistent thereafter. This finding threatens the notion that flashbulb memories are fully formed at the moment when individuals learn about a dramatic event. It also makes sense of the literature. Conway et al. (1994) found consistent memories over time, but they first tested their participants several days after Mrs Thatcher's resignation. In contrast, Talarico and Rubin (2003) found inconsistent memories over time with

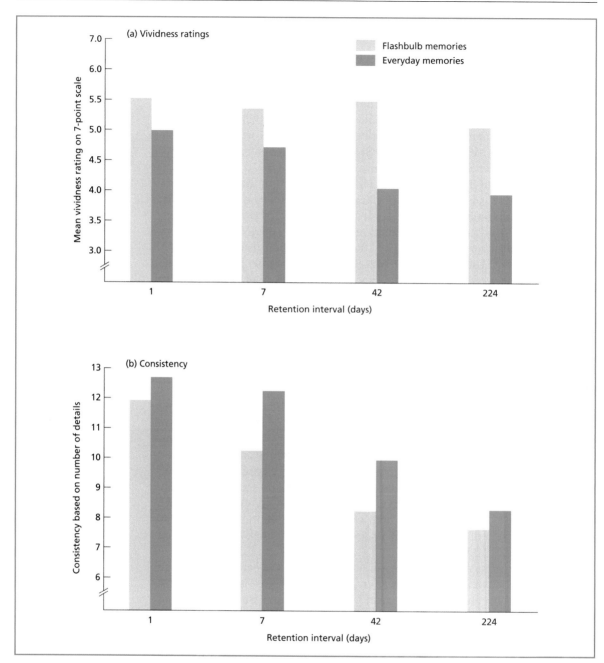

Figure 14.1 (a) Vividness ratings and (b) consistency of memory as a funtion of type of memory (flashbulb vs. everyday) and length of retention interval. Based on data in Talarico and Rubin (2003).

an initial memory test the day after September 11. In sum, it seems that the long-term memories we have of dramatic world events were constructed over the first few days after the event rather than at the time.

DOES DECAY CAUSE FORGETTING?

Why do we forget?

Everyday experience tells us that most forgetting can't be due to decay. Consider the embarrassing situation in which you want to introduce an acquaintance to a friend of yours but realize you have forgotten their name. Does that mean that the name has disappeared from the memory system? Not at all, because you probably recognized the name as soon as you heard it.

Clear evidence that much forgetting is due to a failure to retrieve information rather than to loss of information from long-term memory was provided by Tulving and Pearlstone (1966). Participants were presented with a list of words belonging to various categories (e.g., four-footed animals, articles of furniture). They then tried to recall as many of the words as possible in any order (**free recall**). The participants' free recall showed evidence of considerable forgetting. However, they were then given a test of **cued recall**, in which the category names were presented as cues. The key finding was that many more words were recalled in cued recall than in free recall, especially when numerous categories were represented in the list. For example, consider what happened when there were 48 categories with one word per category. About 30 words were recalled with cued recall compared to only about 18 in free recall. Thus, much apparent "forgetting" is due to problems in retrieving information rather than to decay.

The study by Tulving and Pearlstone (1966) made it very clear that forgetting does *not* depend only on the state of the memory traces within our brains. In addition, forgetting depends crucially on the information available to us at the time we are trying to remember something. When much information is available (e.g., cued recall), there is much less forgetting than when little information is available (e.g., free recall). This theoretical idea is discussed in more detail later in the chapter.

WHAT DO WE NEED TO EXPLAIN?

The key phenomenon is that the rate of forgetting is generally fastest shortly after learning, and decreases progressively as the time that has elapsed after learning increases. This was first demonstrated by the German psychologist Hermann Ebbinghaus (1885/1913). He carried out extensive studies with himself as the only participant (not a practice to be recommended!). His basic approach involved learning a list of nonsense syllables having little or no meaning. At various intervals of time, he re-learned the list. He assessed forgetting by means of the savings method (the reduction in the number of trials during re-learning compared to original learning). The forgetting he observed over time is shown in Figure 14.2. Rubin and Wenzel (1996) obtained a similar forgetting curve (well described by a logarithmic function) when they analyzed the forgetting functions taken from 210 data sets.

KEY TERMS
Free recall: a memory test in which the to-be-remembered items are recalled in any order; see cued recall.
Cued recall: recall in which relevant cues are presented to assist retrieval; see free recall.

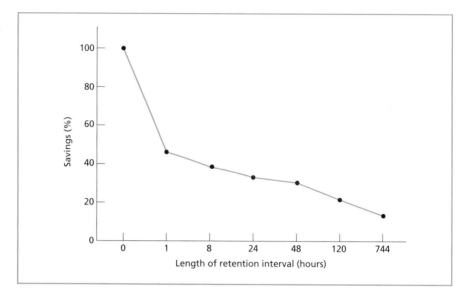

ARE TRAUMATIC MEMORIES REPRESSED?

One of the best-known theories of forgetting owes its origins to the bearded Austrian psychologist Sigmund Freud (1856–1939). He claimed that very threatening or traumatic memories are often unable to gain access to conscious awareness, and he used the term **repression** to refer to this phenomenon. According to Freud (1915/1963, p. 86), "The essence of repression lies simply in the function of rejecting and keeping something out of consciousness." However, Freud sometimes used the concept to refer merely to the inhibition of the capacity for emotional experience (Madison, 1956). Even though it is generally believed that Freud regarded repression as unconscious, Erdelyi (2001) has shown convincingly that Freud accepted that repression is sometimes an active and intentional process. It is difficult to test the notion of repression if we accept that it can be unconscious or conscious.

There are obvious ethical reasons why we cannot create repressed memories in the laboratory. As a result, most evidence relating to repression is based on adult patients who have apparently recovered repressed memories of childhood sexual and/or physical abuse. As you probably know, there has been fierce controversy as to whether these recovered memories are genuine or false.

RECOVERED MEMORIES

We will start by considering evidence supporting the view that many recovered memories are genuine before discussing evidence suggesting they may be false. Findings supportive of the notion that recovered memories are genuine were reported by Andrews, Brewin, Ochera, Morton, Bekerian, and Davies (1999), who obtained detailed information from over 200 patients with claimed recovered memories. They found that 41% of the patients had supporting evidence for their claims (e.g., someone else had also reported being abused by the alleged perpetrator). In addition, 22% of the patients claimed that the trigger for the first recovered memory occurred before therapy had started. This is important, because it is often assumed that direct pressure from the therapist plays a role in patients' false memories. Lief and Fetkewicz (1995) found that 80% of patients who admitted reporting false memories of childhood abuse had therapists who made direct suggestions that they had been the victims of sexual abuse.

How much can you trust recovered memories?

There are two main lines of evidence suggesting that most recovered memories may not be genuine. First, there are a few relevant laboratory studies. Second, there are numerous studies showing that most people can be misled into believing in the existence of events that never happened. Clancy, Schacter, McNally, and Pitman (2000) used a memory task (called the Deese–Roediger–McDermott paradigm after its inventors) that reliably produces false memories. In essence, people are given lists of words all of which are related in meaning. They are then found to falsely "recognize" another word related in meaning to the words actually presented. For example, a list might consist of the following words: thread, pin, eye, sewing, sharp, point, pricked, thimble, haystack, pain, hurt, and injection. Many participants would subsequently "recognize" the word "needle" as having been presented in the list.

Clancy et al. (2000) compared women with recovered memories of childhood abuse with women who believed they had been sexually abused but couldn't recall the abuse, women who had always remembered being abused, and control women. As can be seen in Figure 14.3, women reporting recovered memories showed higher levels of false recognition than any of the other groups. As Clancy et al. (2000, p. 30) concluded, "The results are consistent with the hypothesis that women who report recovered memories of sexual abuse are more prone than others to develop certain types of illusory memories."

In many studies, adults have received strong suggestions that various unpleasant things had happened to them when they were children, even

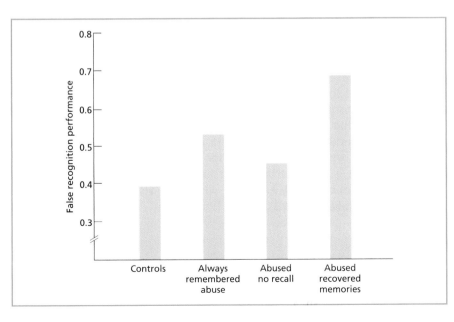

Figure 14.3 False recognition of words not presented in four groups of women with lists containing eight associates. Data from Clancy et al. (2000).

though this was not the case. For example, many adults have been made to believe incorrectly that as children they had been hospitalized overnight, lost in a shopping mall for a long time, or involved in an accident at a family wedding (see Loftus, 2004, for a review). Dramatic findings were reported by Lindsay, Hagen, Read, Wade, and Garry (2004b). They tried to persuade participants that at the age of 6 or 7 they had put Slime (a colored jelly-like substance) in their teacher's desk. The suggestion was made more convincing by providing a narrative describing the incident allegedly from their teacher at the time, and a photograph of the participant allegedly supplied by his or her parents. Lindsay et al. found that over 65% of the participants reported false memories of this event when tested subsequently. Even when they told their memories were false, some participants expressed surprise (e.g., "You mean that didn't happen to me?" and "No way! I remember it! That's so weird!").

MEMORIES INTERFERE WITH EACH OTHER

If any of your female acquaintances are married, you may have found yourself remembering their maiden name rather than their married name. In other words, what used to be their name interferes with (or disrupts) your ability to recall their current name. The notion that interference is important in forgetting can be traced back at least to the nineteenth century and to German psychologist Hugo Münsterberg (1863–1916). Men had pocket watches in those days, and Münsterberg kept his watch in one particular pocket. When he started to keep it in a different pocket for reasons lost in the mists of history, he found he was often fumbling around in confusion when asked for the time.

The above story shows the key features of what became known as interference theory. Münsterberg had learned an association between the stimulus, "What's the time, Hugo?," and the response of removing the watch from his pocket. Subsequently the stimulus remained the same, but a different response was now associated with it. This is an example of **proactive interference**, in which previous learning disrupts later learning and memory (see Figure 14.4). There is also **retroactive interference**, in which later learning disrupts memory for earlier learning (see Figure 14.4). For example, suppose you have learned to play tennis, which involves little wrist action, and then you learn to play squash, which requires much more wrist action. You might find afterwards that learning squash has interfered with your shot making at tennis. As a general rule of thumb, both proactive and retroactive interference are greatest when two different responses have been associated with the same stimulus (e.g., Münsterberg with his watch), intermediate when two similar stimuli are involved, and least when two very different stimuli are involved (e.g., Underwood & Postman, 1960).

KEY TERMS
Proactive interference: disruption of memory by previous learning (often of similar material); see retroactive interference.
Retroactive interference: disruption of memory by learning of other material during the retention interval; see proactive interference.

FINDINGS

If we go back some 50 or 60 years, there were numerous studies showing large proactive and retroactive interference effects. Many of these studies involved   paired-associate   learning   (e.g.,   participants   initially   learn

	Proactive interference		
Group	Learn	Learn	Learn
Experimental	A–B (e.g., Cat–Tree)	A–C (e.g., Cat–Dirt)	A–C (e.g., Cat–Dirt)
Control	–	A–C (e.g., Cat–Dirt)	A–C (e.g., Cat–Dirt)

	Retroactive interference		
Group	Learn	Learn	Test
Experimental	A–B (e.g., Cat–Tree)	A–C (e.g., Cat–Dirt)	A–B (e.g., Cat–Tree)
Control	A–B (e.g., Cat–Tree)	–	A–B (e.g., Cat–Tree)

Note: for both proactive and retroactive interference, the experimental group exhibits interference. On the test, only the first word is supplied, and the participants must provide the second word.

Figure 14.4 Methods of testing for proactive and retroactive interference.

"Cat–Tree" and then have to respond "Tree" when "Cat" is presented on its own; see Figure 14.4). Perhaps you can see a problem with all these studies—they show large interference effects with very artificial laboratory tasks. Of course, that doesn't prove that proactive and retroactive interference are important in everyday life. However, Isurin and McDonald (2001) argued that retroactive interference may help to explain why people forget parts of their first language when acquiring a second language. Their participants were first presented with various pictures and the corresponding words in either Russian or Hebrew. Some of them were then presented with the same pictures and the corresponding words in the other language. Finally, they were tested for their recall of the words in the first language. There was substantial retroactive interference: recall of the first-language words became progressively worse the more learning trials there were with the second-language words.

Suppose you took part in a memory experiment, and found your performance was being disrupted by interference. It is generally assumed (implicitly rather than explicitly) that individuals in that situation simply *passively* allow themselves to suffer from interference. However, doesn't it seem likely that you would adopt some *active* strategy to try to minimize any interference effects? This notion was explored by Kane and Engle (2000). They argued that individuals with high attentional or working-memory capacity would be better able to resist proactive interference than those with low capacity. However, even such individuals wouldn't be able to resist proactive interference if they had to perform an attentionally demanding task at the same time as the learning task. As predicted, high-capacity participants with no additional task showed the least proactive interference (see Figure 14.5).

What causes proactive interference? Jacoby, Debner, and Hay (2001) argued that there is a competition between two responses: the correct one and the incorrect one. As a result, there are two major possible reasons why

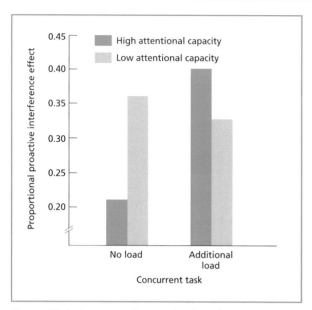

Figure 14.5 Amount of proactive interference as a function of attentional capacity (low vs. high) and concurrent task (no vs. additional load). Data from Kane and Engle (2000).

How can context affect our ability to later recall or recognize information?

proactive interference occurs: (1) the incorrect response is very strong; or (2) the correct response is very weak. Jacoby et al. found that proactive interference was due much more to the strength of the incorrect response than to the weakness of the correct response.

ENCODING SPECIFICITY

One of the most influential ideas in the history of memory research is Tulving's **encoding specificity principle**). According to Tulving (1979, p. 408), "The probability of successful retrieval of the target item is a monotonically increasing function of *informational overlap* between the information present at retrieval and the information stored in memory" [my italics]. For the benefit of bewildered readers, "monotonically increasing function" refers to a generally rising function that doesn't decrease at any point. The key idea is that we are more likely to remember something when the information available at the time of retrieval *matches* the information contained in the memory trace. The memory trace typically includes various kinds of contextual information (e.g., the learner's mood state, details of the room in which learning occurs) as well as information about the to-be-remembered material.

The major prediction from the encoding specificity principle is as follows: memory performance will be worse (and so forgetting will be greater) when the contextual information present at retrieval *differs* from the contextual information stored in memory. According to this view, your memory for an event should be better when your mood state at the time of testing is the same as your mood state at the time of learning. This effect (not surprisingly called **mood-state-dependent memory**) was shown amusingly in the film, *City Lights*. In this film, Charlie Chaplin saves a drunken millionaire from attempted suicide and is befriended in return. When the millionaire sees Charlie again, he is sober and fails to recognize him. However, when the millionaire becomes drunk again, he catches sight of Charlie, treats him like a long-lost friend, and takes him home with him. The next morning, when the millionaire is sober again, he forgets that Charlie is his invited guest, and gets his butler to throw him out.

Kenealy (1997) provided evidence of mood-state-dependent memory. In one study, the participants looked at a map and learned a set of instructions concerning a particular route until their learning performance exceeded 80%. The following day they were given tests of free recall and cued recall (the cue consisted of the visual outline of the map). Context was manipulated by using music to create happy or sad mood states at learning and at test. As predicted, free recall was better when the context (mood state) was the same at learning and at testing than when it differed (see Figure 14.6). However, there was no context effect with cued recall. Thus, context in the form of

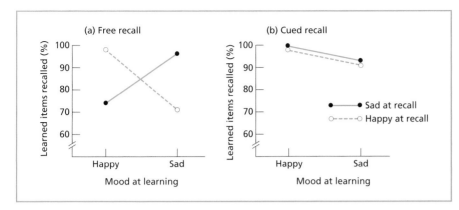

Figure 14.6 Free and cued recall as a function of mood state (happy or sad) at learning and at recall. Based on data in Kenealy (1997).

mood state can affect memory but only when no other powerful cues are available.

Ucros (1989) reviewed 40 studies on mood-state-dependent memory. Overall, there was a moderate tendency for people to remember information better when the mood at learning and at test matched. However, the effects were stronger when participants were in a positive mood rather than a negative one. They were also greater when people remembered personal events rather than information lacking personal relevance.

We all know that recognition memory is generally better than recall. For example, we may be unable to recall an acquaintance's name, but if someone mentions their name we recognize it instantly. According to Tulving's encoding specificity principle, memory depends on the overlap between information in the memory trace and information available at retrieval. Recognition memory is typically better than recall because this overlap is usually greater on a recognition test (after all, the entire item is presented) than on a recall test. However, it follows from the encoding specificity principle that recall *can* on occasion be superior to recognition memory. For this to happen, the information in the recall cue should overlap more with the information stored in the memory trace than the information in the recognition cue does.

Muter (1978) carried out a study based on the above requirement. Participants were presented with names of people (e.g., DOYLE) and circled those they "recognized as a person who was famous before 1950." They were then given recall cues in the form of brief descriptions plus first names of the famous people whose surnames had appeared on the recognition test. Here is an example: "Author of the Sherlock Holmes stories: Sir Arthur Conan ____." You may well have found the recall item easier than the recognition one because so much more information was supplied. Muter (1978) found that participants recognized only 29% of the names but recalled 42% of them.

CONSOLIDATION THEORY

One of the most important approaches to forgetting is based on **consolidation**, which is a long-lasting process fixing information in long-term memory. A crucial assumption is that recently formed memories in an early

KEY TERM
Consolidation: a process that is mostly completed within several hours, but can last for years, and that fixes information in long-term memory.

stage of consolidation are especially vulnerable to interference and forgetting. More specifically, "New memories are clear but fragile and old ones are faded but robust" (Wixted, 2004, p. 265).

The process of consolidation involves two major phases (Eichenbaum, 2001). The first phase occurs over a period of hours and is centered on the hippocampus. The second phase takes place over a period ranging from days to years, and involves interactions between the hippocampal region, adjacent entorhinal cortex, and the neocortex. This second phase only applies to episodic memories (memories for specific events or episodes) and semantic memories (stored knowledge about the world).

FINDINGS

Has consolidation theory completely explained the way we forget?

Consolidation theory provides an explanation of the basic shape of the forgetting curve (see Figure 14.2). According to the theory, memory traces are most vulnerable in the period of time shortly after learning. Thus, the rate of forgetting should be most rapid initially but should *decrease* as the length of time after learning increases.

Some of the best evidence for consolidation theory comes from the study of patients with *retrograde amnesia*, in which there is impaired memory for events occurring before the onset of the amnesia. Many of these patients have suffered damage to the hippocampus as the result of an accident (or through surgery in the case of the well-known amnesic HM). Since the hippocampus is of central importance to the first phase of consolidation, the most recently formed memories should be the ones most impaired in these patients. As predicted, this pattern has been found in numerous patients with retrograde amnesia (Manns, Hopkins, & Squire, 2003).

The assumption that memories are most vulnerable during the early stages of consolidation has also been tested in a different way. We saw earlier in the chapter that retroactive interference can cause forgetting. According to consolidation theory, people should be more susceptible to retroactive interference early in the retention interval than they are later. Several relevant studies reported findings in line with this prediction (see Wixted, 2004, for a review).

Support for the assumption that consolidation consists of two phases was reported by Haist, Gore, and Mao (2001) in a study in which participants identified faces of people famous in the 1980s or 1990s. Selective activation in the hippocampus for famous faces relative to non-famous ones was only found for those famous in the 1990s. In contrast (and also as predicted), there was greater activation in the entorhinal cortex connected to widespread neocortical areas for famous faces from the 1980s than from the 1990s.

WHAT ABOUT THE FUTURE?

The various theoretical approaches we have considered have all contributed to our understanding of forgetting. However, they all provide only partial explanations and each one accounts for only a fraction of the phenomena associated with forgetting. It would seem a superior theory could be produced by combining elements of different theories. Below we will briefly consider two such combinations.

First, it would be interesting to combine the encoding specificity principle with interference theory. The encoding specificity principle generally works reasonably well when we consider a single memory trace in isolation. In contrast, interference theory focuses primarily on *competition* among memory traces. In crude terms, a new theory (proposed by Eysenck, 1979) could be based on the following two notions:

1. The probability of remembering a given event depends in part on the overlap between the information in the relevant memory trace and the information available in the retrieval environment. The greater is this overlap, the higher is the probability of successful memory performance.
2. The probability of remembering a given memory depends in part on the overlap between the information in other competing memory traces and the information available in the retrieval environment. The greater is this overlap, the lower is the probability of successful memory performance.

Second, it would be possible to combine the consolidation and interference theories. As predicted by interference theory, much forgetting can be understood in terms of proactive and retroactive interference. However, interference theory doesn't really explain why retroactive interference is greater when interfering learning occurs early in the retention interval rather than later. This greater vulnerability to interference soon after learning is precisely what is predicted on consolidation theory. Therefore, a combined theory would provide a more powerful explanatory framework than either of the theories on their own.

EVALUATION AND CHAPTER SUMMARY

Are traumatic memories repressed?
- The controversy as to the genuineness or otherwise of recovered memories of traumatic childhood experiences has not been resolved.
- In some cases, there is supporting evidence for recovered memories, and they have been produced in the absence of any pressure from the therapist (e.g., Andrews et al., 1999).
- However, some laboratory evidence (e.g., Clancy et al., 2000) suggests that women reporting recovered memories are prone to produce false memories.
- In addition, it has proved surprisingly easy to persuade most people that they experienced various childhood events that were suggested to them.

Memories interfere with each other
- There are literally dozens (if not hundreds) of laboratory studies showing the existence of proactive and retroactive interference.
- There is also increasing evidence that much forgetting in everyday life is due to interference.
- Earlier we considered a study (Isurin & McDonald, 2001) in which learning a second language interfered with recall of words from participants' first language.

- Another relevant example comes from research on eyewitness testimony (Chapter 16).
- It has been found many times (e.g., Loftus & Palmer, 1974) that information provided after seeing an incident can cause retroactive interference for details of the incident.
- Eyewitnesses' memory is also subject to proactive interference when they are exposed *beforehand* to information similar to that contained in the subsequent incident (Lindsay, Allen, Chan, & Dahl, 2004a).
- Interference theory possesses various limitations.
- First, while the existence of proactive and retroactive interference is indisputable, relatively little is known of the specific *processes* responsible. However, the study by Jacoby et al. (2001) is a step in the right direction.
- Second, the natural prediction from interference theory is that all memory traces are susceptible to proactive and retroactive interference. However, as is discussed later, retroactive interference is actually greater when the interfering learning occurs early in the retention interval rather than later on (see Wixted, 2004).
- Third, there has until recently been a neglect of the active processes that people use to minimize interference effects (e.g., Kane & Engle, 2000).

Encoding specificity
- Whether we remember or forget something depends in part on the overlap between the information in the memory trace and that in the retrieval environment.
- Much evidence (e.g., from studies on mood-state-dependent memory) indicates that contextual information is stored in the memory trace and influences memory performance.
- In addition, it was a major success for Tulving's approach that he demonstrated recall can be superior to recognition memory.
- What are the limitations of the encoding specificity principle?
- First, the extent to which retrieval information allows us to *discriminate* the correct response from incorrect responses is important, but is ignored by the principle.
- As research on interference shows, information easy to recall in the absence of interference (presumably due to substantial informational overlap) becomes much harder to recall when similar material has been presented.
- Second, Tulving apparently assumed that the information available at the time of test is compared *directly* with the information stored in memory to assess informational overlap.
- This can't be the whole story. If I were to ask you, "What did you do six days ago?," you would probably engage in a complex problem-solving strategy to reconstruct the relevant events. However, the encoding specificity principle has nothing to say about such strategies.
- Third, Tulving (1979) assumed that *context* influences recall and recognition in the same way.

- Godden and Baddeley (1975, 1980) tested this assumption by having people learn a list of words on land or 20 feet under water and then testing them on land or under water. Recall was 50% higher when learning and recall took place in the same context (Godden & Baddeley, 1975), but recognition memory was not affected by context (Godden & Baddeley, 1980).

Consolidation theory
- Consolidation theory has various successes to its credit.
- First, unlike most other theories of forgetting, it provides an explanation of *why* the rate of forgetting decreases over time.
- Second, consolidation theory successfully predicts that retrograde amnesia is greater for recently formed memories, and that retroactive interference effects are greatest shortly after learning. No other theory provides a plausible explanation of these effects.
- Third, consolidation theory identifies the brain areas most associated with the two major phases of consolidation.
- Consolidation theory has various limitations.
- First, we lack strong evidence that all of the effects described above are actually due to effects on consolidation processes. For example, there are various possible reasons why newly formed memories are more easily disrupted than older ones.
- Second, consolidation theory (emphasizing the fragility of new memory traces) indicates in a *general* way why newly formed memory traces are especially susceptible to interference effects. However, it doesn't explain the more *specific* finding that retroactive interference is greatest when two different responses are associated with the same stimulus.
- Third, forgetting is much more likely when there is little informational overlap between the memory trace and the information available in the retrieval environment than when there is substantial overlap. However, it is unclear how this robust finding could be explained within consolidation theory.

FURTHER READING

- Baddeley, A.D. (1997). *Human memory: theory and practice* (Rev. ed.). Hove, UK: Psychology Press. The leading British memory researcher evaluates theory and research on forgetting.
- Intons-Peterson, M.J., & Best, D.L. (1998). *Memory distortions and their prevention*. Mahwah, NJ: Lawrence Erlbaum Associates. Several factors producing forgetting and inaccurate memory are discussed in this edited book.
- Loftus, E.F. (2004). Memories of things unseen. *Current Directions in Psychological Science, 13*, 145–147. Elizabeth Loftus considers ways in which our memories can be distorted.
- Wixted, J.T. (2004). The psychology and neuroscience of forgetting. *Annual Review of Psychology, 55*, 235–269. A convincing case is made that neuroscience has much to contribute to our understanding of forgetting.

CHAPTER 15

CONTENTS

Introduction 207

What do elderly people remember? 211

Emotional personal memories 214

Model of autobiographical memory 215

Evalution and chapter summary 218

Further reading 219

The story of my life

INTRODUCTION

Of all the hundreds of thousands of memories we possess, those relating to our own past, to the experiences we have had, and to the people who have really mattered to us have a special importance and significance. This is the territory we will be exploring in this chapter. Our own autobiographical memories are of consuming interest to us because they relate to our major life goals, to our most powerful emotions, and to our personal meanings. As Conway, Pleydell-Pearce, and Whitecross (2001, p. 493) pointed out, autobiographical knowledge has the function of "defining identity, linking personal history to public history, supporting a network of personal goals and projects across the life span, and ultimately in grounding the self in experience."

We can draw a distinction between autobiographical memory and episodic memory (see Chapter 11). Episodic memory allows us to remember events and the context (location, time) in which they occurred. The two forms of memory clearly overlap in that they both relate to personally experienced events. However, there are various important differences between them. First, autobiographical memory is concerned with events of personal significance, whereas episodic memory is often concerned with trivial events (e.g., was the word "chair" in the first list or the second list?). Second, autobiographical memory extends back over years or decades, whereas episodic memory (at least for events in the laboratory) often extends back only for minutes or hours. Third, autobiographical memory typically deals with complex memories selected from a huge collection of personal experiences, whereas episodic memory is much more limited in scope.

If you are not convinced by the previous paragraph, then perhaps you will be by the meta-analysis of many studies carried out by Gilboa (2004). He considered brain-imaging studies on autobiographical memory and episodic memory (mostly involving standard recall or recognition memory for word lists, word pairs, and so on). The key finding was that there were some clear differences in patterns of activation of the prefrontal cortex between the two forms of memory. There was substantially more activation in the right mid-dorsolateral prefrontal cortex in episodic memory than in autobiographical memory (see Figure 15.1(a)). This probably happens because episodic memory requires conscious monitoring to avoid errors. In contrast, there was much more activation in the left ventromedial prefrontal cortex in autobiographical memory than in episodic memory (see Figure 15.1(b)).

Figure 15.1(a) shows more activation in the right mid-dorsolateral (top and to the side) prefrontal cortex in episodic than in autobiographical memory.

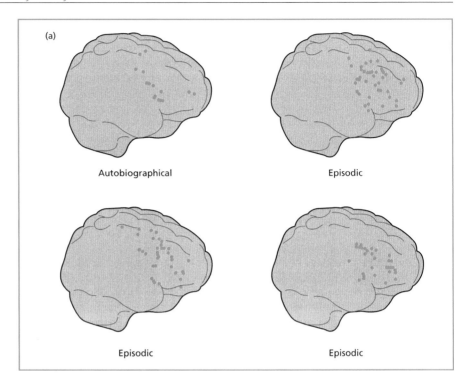

Figure 15.1(b) shows more activation in the left ventromedial (bottom middle) prefrontal cortex in autobiographical than in episodic memory. Gilboa (2004). Copyright © Elsevier.

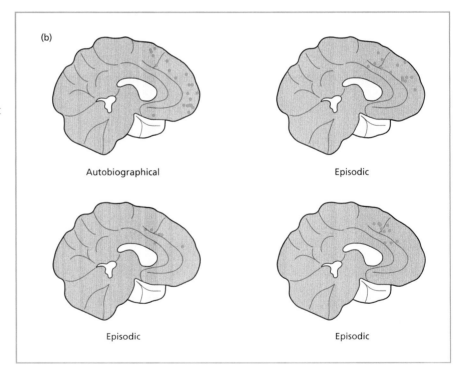

This probably happens because autobiographical memory involves monitoring the accuracy of retrieved memories in relation to activated knowledge of the self.

What have we learned about autobiographical memory from diary studies? What limits them as a research tool?

DIARY STUDIES

Basic information about autobiographical memory was obtained by Wagenaar (1986), who kept a diary record of over 2000 events over a 6-year period. For each event, he recorded information about who, what, where, and when, plus the rated pleasantness, emotionality, and salience or rarity of each event. He then tested his memory by using the who, what, where, and when information either one at a time or in combination. "What" information provided the most useful retrieval cue, perhaps because our autobiographical memories are organized in categories. "What" information was followed in order of decreasing usefulness by "where," "who," and "when" information. The more cues presented, the higher was the probability of recall (see Figure 15.2). However, even with three cues, almost half the events were forgotten over a 5-year period. When these forgotten events involved another person, that person provided additional information. This was typically sufficient for Wagenaar to remember the event, suggesting that the great majority of life events may be stored in long-term memory. Finally, high levels of salience, emotional involvement, and pleasantness were all associated with high levels of recall.

Wagenaar (1994) reconsidered 120 very pleasant and unpleasant memories from his 1986 study. He recalled pleasant events much better than unpleasant ones when someone else played the major role in an event. However, the opposite was the case for events in which Wagenaar himself played the major role. According to Groeger (1997), this latter finding may reflect Wagenaar's self-critical personality.

Burt, Kemp, and Conway (2003) identified a significant limitation with diary studies such as that of Wagenaar (1986). They pointed out that the

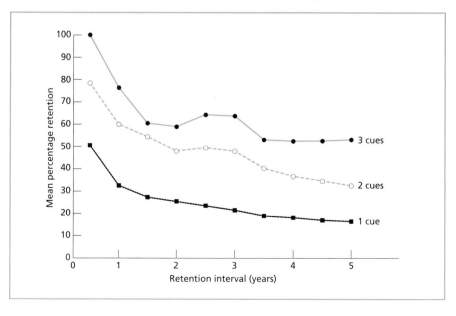

Figure 15.2 Memory for personal events as a function of the number of cues available and the length of the retention interval. Adapted from Wagenaar (1986).

emphasis in such studies is on specific on-one-day events. However, these don't correspond well with the autobiographical events we generally remember, which tend to be more general in nature. For example, Barsalou (1988) asked college students to recall events of the previous summer. The students recalled relatively few on-one-day memories, but numerous general events extended in time.

ARE AUTOBIOGRAPHICAL MEMORIES ACCURATE?

One of the problems psychologists face when studying autobiographical memory (unless carrying out an exhaustive diary study) is that it is often very hard to know whether the memories are genuine. If you have read any autobiographies, you have probably wondered whether the authors have provided an unduly positive view of themselves and what they have accomplished. Wilson and Ross (2003) reviewed the available evidence on the accuracy of autobiographical memories. They concluded that, "People's constructions of themselves through time serve the function of creating a coherent—and largely favorable—view of their present selves and circumstances" (Wilson & Ross, 2003, p. 137). For example, Karney and Frye (2002) found that spouses often recalled their past contentment as lower than their present level of satisfaction. However, this apparent improvement over time was generally illusory, because they mostly underestimated their past contentment. Ross and Wilson (2002) asked students to remember the course in the previous semester on which they had obtained their best (or their worst) mark. Students felt that previous failure happened longer ago than previous success, even though the time interval was the same in both cases. Thus, people's autobiographical memories for *what* happened and *when* it happened are both subject to systematic distortion.

BELIEFS ABOUT AUTOBIOGRAPHICAL MEMORY

We will be considering some of the beliefs most people have about autobiographical memory. First, there is the belief that most elderly people spend much of their time recalling childhood events in great detail, but find it difficult to remember recent events.

Second, there is the belief that the kinds of autobiographical memories we tend to recall are selected almost at random and tell us little or nothing about ourselves. For example, if a friend comes back from a holiday in a place where we have been too, this often leads us to remember a few amusing but basically trivial incidents about our own holiday there.

Third, there is the notion that odors provide particularly powerful cues to remind us of vivid and emotional personal experiences that happened a very long time ago. This is known as the **Proust phenomenon** in honor of the French novelist Marcel Proust. He described the way in which the smell and taste of a tea-soaked pastry evoked childhood memories:

> *I raised to my lips a spoonful of the tea in which I had soaked a morsel of the cake. No sooner had the warm liquid, and the crumbs with it, touched my palate than a shudder ran through my entire body, and I stopped, intent upon the extraordinary changes that were taking place*

KEY TERM

Proust phenomenon: the tendency for odors to be especially strong cues for recalling very old vivid and emotional personal memories.

... I was conscious that it was connected with the taste of tea and cake, but that it infinitely transcended those savors, could not, indeed, be of the same nature as theirs. (Proust, 1922/1960, p. 58)

We will see shortly that the first two beliefs (common though they are) are both incorrect. However, there is some substance to the Proust phenomenon, and we will start by discussing that. Laird (1935) surveyed 254 eminent men and women. Seventy-six percent of the women and 47% of the men claimed that memories triggered by odors were among their most vivid ones. In contrast, only 7% of the women and 16% of the men claimed their odor-triggered memories were emotionally neutral.

Chu and Downes (2000, 2004) asked people in their late 60s and early 70s to think of autobiographical experiences when presented with olfactory [relating to the sense of smell] or verbal cues. One feature of the Proust phenomenon is that the memories triggered by odors are typically very old. Chu and Downes found that more odor-cued autobiographical memories came from the period when participants were between the ages of 6 and 10 than any other period. In contrast, the peak for memories triggered by verbal cues was the period between the ages of 11 and 25.

Chu and Downes (2000) asked participants to think of autobiographical events triggered by verbal cues corresponding to the names of odorous objects. After that, they were presented with the appropriate odor, an inappropriate odor, a picture of the odorous object, or the verbal label of the object. The participants then recalled further details of the autobiographical event. There were two main findings. First, the appropriate odor triggered recall of more additional details than any other cue. Second, the appropriate odor led to a greater increase in the rated emotionality of the autobiographical memories than did any other cue.

WHAT DO ELDERLY PEOPLE REMEMBER?

Suppose we ask 70-year-olds to recall personal memories triggered by cue words (e.g., nouns referring to common objects). From which parts of their lives would most of the memories come? Is it really true that they mostly recall distant childhood memories? The short answer is "No." As can be seen in Figure 15.3, there are three key features when we look at the periods of their life from which 70-year-olds recall more and fewer memories:

How does our memory for autobiographical events change as we age?

- Childhood amnesia (also known as **infantile amnesia**): This is shown by the almost total lack of memories from the first three years of life.
- A **reminiscence bump**, consisting of a surprisingly large number of memories coming from the years of adolescence and early adulthood, especially between the ages of 15 and 25.
- A *retention function* for memories up to 20 years old, with the older memories being less likely to be recalled than more recent ones.

Most interest has focused on childhood amnesia and the reminiscence bump. In what follows, we consider possible explanations of both of these phenomena. We will not discuss the retention function, which is generally assumed merely to reflect the normal course of forgetting (see Chapter 14).

KEY TERMS

Infantile amnesia: the inability of adults to recall autobiographical memories from early childhood (also known as childhood amnesia).

Reminiscence bump: the tendency of older people to recall a disproportionate number of autobiographical memories from the years of adolescence and early adulthood.

Figure 15.3 Idealized representation of the age at which autobiographical memories were formed in elderly people recalling the past. © American Psychological Association. Reprinted with permission.

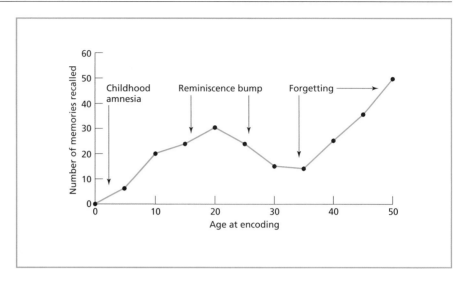

INFANTILE OR CHILDHOOD AMNESIA

Why do we have so few memories from when we were very young?

There is convincing evidence that older adults (as well as adolescents and younger adults) recall very few autobiographical memories from their early childhood. Rubin (2000) combined data from numerous studies. He concluded as follows: "Childhood amnesia ... is a robust phenomenon that is nearly identical in studies using different methods and different populations. Of the autobiographical memories reported as occurring before age 11, only 1.1% occurred before the age of 3, with a sharp rise after that point" (Rubin, 2000, p. 268).

The most famous (or notorious) account of childhood amnesia is that of Freud (1915/1963). He argued that childhood amnesia occurs through repression, with threat-related experiences in early childhood being consigned to the unconscious. Alas, there is practically no support for this theoretical position, and it doesn't explain why *pleasant* memories of early childhood cannot be recalled. The social–cultural–developmental theory (e.g., Fivush & Nelson, 2004) provides a much more convincing account of childhood amnesia. According to this theory, language and culture both play central roles in the early development of autobiographical memory. Language is important because we use language to communicate our memories, and experiences occurring before children develop language are difficult for them to express in language later on.

The parents' use of language is also very important. According to Fivush and Nelson (2004), parents vary along a dimension of elaboration when discussing the past with their children. Some parents discuss the past in great detail, whereas others do not. It is predicted that children whose parents have an elaborative reminiscing style will report more and fuller early childhood memories. Culture is relevant at this point—mothers from Western cultures tend to talk about the past in a more elaborated and emotional way than mothers from Eastern cultures (Leichtman, Wang, &

Pillemer, 2003). It has also been found (Fivush & Buckner, 2003) that Western mothers are more elaborative with daughters than with sons when discussing the past.

There is much support for the social–cultural–developmental theory. First, there is evidence that the language skills available to children at the time of an experience determine what can be recalled about it subsequently. Two- and 3-year-old children described their memories for complex play activities up to 12 months later. They *only* used words they had known at the time of the event, even though they had acquired hundreds of new words during the retention interval (Simcock & Hayne, 2002).

Second, the mother's reminiscing style has been shown to be important. Children's very early ability to talk about the past was much better among those whose mothers had an elaborative reminiscing style than among those whose mothers rarely talked about the past (e.g., Harley & Reese, 1999). This remained the case even when account was taken of children's language and non-verbal memory skills.

Third, cross-cultural research indicates that adults from Eastern cultures have a later age of first autobiographical memory than adults from Western cultures (Pillemer, 1998). In addition, the reported memories of early childhood are much more elaborated and emotional in American children than in those from Korea or China (Han, Leichtman, & Wang, 1998).

Fourth, adult females in Western cultures have an earlier age of first autobiographical memory than adult males (Pillemer, 1998). Western females also report more detailed and emotional autobiographical memories of childhood events than Western males (Pillemer, 1998). These findings are consistent with the theory in view of the fact that girls tend to be slightly ahead of boys in language development.

In sum, the development of autobiographical memory is greatly influenced by both language and culture. The notion that children need to acquire a reasonable grasp of language to form long-lasting autobiographical memories explains the phenomenon of infantile or childhood amnesia, and suggests it is poorly named. An issue that deserves consideration is whether children's and adults' reports of early childhood memories reflect their actual memories. Perhaps social and cultural expectations lead people to distort their reported memories and other memories can't be expressed in language. Another prediction is that deaf children (who generally develop language late) should have fewer early memories than children who can hear.

REMINISCENCE BUMP

The reminiscence bump has not generally been found in adults younger than 30 years old, and has infrequently been observed in 40-year-olds. However, it is nearly always found among older people. Rubin and Schulkind (1997) used far more cue words than had been used in previous studies. They found, "no evidence that any aspect of the distribution of autobiographical memories is affected by having close to 1,000 as opposed to 100 memories queried" (Rubin & Schulkind, 1997, p. 863) It has also been found that 70-year-olds have a reminiscence bump for particularly memorable books, memories they would want included in a book about their lives, and memories for current events (Rubin, Rahhal, & Poon, 1998).

Rubin et al. (1998) argued that a sense of adult identity develops in early adulthood, and this heralds a period of stability. They also claimed that early adulthood is a time of life in which many important novel events occur. These two factors (i.e., stability and novelty) produce the reminiscence bump for the following reasons:

- *Novelty*: This causes more effort after meaning.
- *Novelty*: There is a relative lack of proactive interference (interference from previous learning; see Chapter 14).
- *Novelty*: This produces distinctive memories standing out from other memories.
- *Stability*: Events from a stable period of life are more likely to serve as models for future events.
- *Stability*: If the structure of autobiographical memory established in early adulthood remains fairly stable throughout the rest of one's life, it provides an effective way of cueing memories of early adulthood.

How important is novelty? Evidence that it really does matter was reported by Pillemer, Goldsmith, Panter, and White (1988). When they asked middle-aged participants to recall four memories from their first year at college over 20 years before, 41% of their autobiographical memories came from the first month of the course. However, we shouldn't exaggerate the importance of novelty. For example, Fitzgerald (1988) found that fewer than 20% of the memories from the reminiscence bump recalled by older adults were of first-time experiences.

EMOTIONAL PERSONAL MEMORIES

Do the personal memories we store and recall have special significance? Even though it may seem as if the answer is "No," many experts claim that the correct answer is "Yes." For example, Conway and Pleydell-Pearce (2000, p. 266) argued that, "Autobiographical memories are primarily records of success or failure in goal attainment." Some of the strongest evidence comes from Woike, Gershkovich, Piorkowski, and Polo (1999). They distinguished between two types of personality:

1. *Agentic* personality type, with an emphasis on independence, achievement, and personal power;
2. *Communal* personality type, with an emphasis on interdependence and similarity to others.

In their first experiment, Woike et al. (1999) asked participants with agentic and communal personality types to write about a positive or negative personal experience. When the experience was positive, 65% of the agentic participants recalled agentic memories (e.g., involving success), whereas 90% of the communal participants recalled communal memories (e.g., involving love or friendship). The same pattern was found for negative personal experiences: 47% of the agentic individuals recalled agentic memories (e.g., involving failure), whereas 90% of the communal individuals recalled communal memories (e.g., involving betrayal of trust). Even when agentic and communal individuals recalled negative communal memories relating to betrayal of trust, there were still differences between the two groups. Agentic individuals emphasized losing face and the social embarrassment associated with betrayal, whereas communal individuals focused on hurt feelings and the lack of trust between people.

In a second study, Woike et al. (1999) considered differences between agentic and communal individuals when recalling autobiographical memories associated with six different emotions. Three emotions were positive (happiness, pride, relief) and the others were negative (anger, fear, sadness). There were consistent differences between the agentic and communal groups with all six emotions. Those with an agentic personality recalled more autobiographical memories concerned with agency (e.g., success, absence of failure, failure) than those with a communal personality (see Figure 15.4). In contrast, individuals with a communal personality recalled more memories concerned with communion (e.g., love, friendship, betrayal of trust) than those with an agentic personality.

In sum, the emotional autobiographical memories we readily bring to mind reflect our personalities and our major life goals. That may not sound surprising, but bear in mind that probably 99% of studies on human memory are of no obvious relevance to either personality or life goals! The memory tasks used by Woike et al. (1999) probably maximized the involvement of personality in influencing what autobiographical memories were recalled. It would be interesting to see whether personality continued to predict the kinds of memories recalled if several memories associated with each emotion or only mildly emotional memories were asked for.

MODEL OF AUTOBIOGRAPHICAL MEMORY

In order to understand the various findings on autobiographical memory, it is useful to consider them in the context of Conway and Pleydell-Pearce's (2000) influential theory of autobiographical memory. According to them, we possess a self-memory system having two major components:

How do we remember our personal lives according to the Conway and Pleydell-Pearce (2000) model? Does the evidence support their theory?

1. *Autobiographical knowledge base*: This contains personal information at three levels of specificity:

   - Lifetime periods: These generally cover substantial periods of time defined by major ongoing situations (e.g, time at secondary school, time spent living with someone).
   - General events: These include repeated events (e.g., visits to a sports club) and single events (e.g., a holiday in South Africa). General events are often related to each other as well as to lifetime periods.
   - Event-specific knowledge: This knowledge consists of images, feelings, and other details relating to general events, and spanning time periods from seconds to hours. Knowledge about a specific event is usually organized in the correct temporal order.

Figure 15.4 Percentages of recalled autobiographical memories that were agentic (a), or communal (b), as a function of personality type (agentic vs. communal) and type of emotion. Data from Woike et al. (1999).

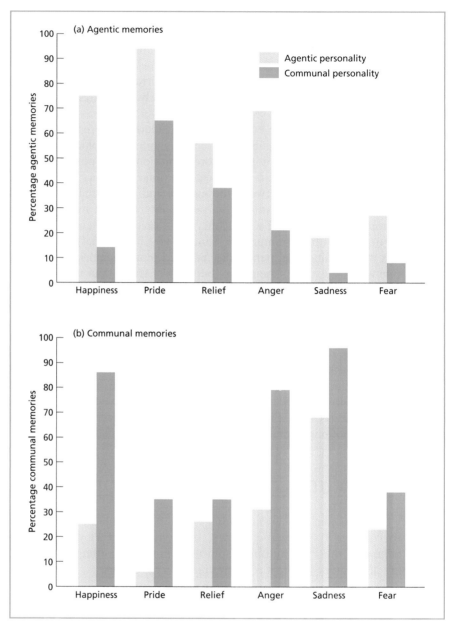

Figure 15.4 Percentages of recalled autobiographical memories that were agentic (a), or communal (b), as a function of personality type (agentic vs. communal) and type of emotion. Data from Woike et al. (1999).

2. *Working self*: This is concerned with the self, what it may become in future, and with the individual's current set of goals. The goals of the working self influence the kinds of memories stored within the autobiographical knowledge base. They also help to determine which autobiographical memories we recall (e.g., Woike et al., 1999).

According to the theory, autobiographical memories can be accessed through *either* generative retrieval *or* direct retrieval. We use **generative retrieval** when we deliberately construct autobiographical memories by combining the resources of the working self with information contained in the autobiographical knowledge base. As a result, autobiographical memories produced via generative retrieval often relate to the individual's goals as contained within the working self. In contrast, **direct retrieval** does *not* involve the working self. Autobiographical memories produced by direct retrieval are triggered by specific cues (e.g., hearing the word "Venice" on the radio may produce direct retrieval of a memory of a holiday there). Remembering autobiographical memories via generative retrieval is more effortful and involves more active involvement by the rememberer than does direct retrieval.

FINDINGS

Evidence for the notion that there are three types of autobiographical knowledge has been obtained from brain-damaged patients with *retrograde amnesia*, which involves widespread forgetting of events preceding brain injury (see Chapter 11). Such patients often cannot recall specific memories but can recall general events and knowledge of lifetime periods (Conway & Rubin, 1993). Other patients can recall only information about lifetime periods. Thus, event-specific knowledge is most vulnerable to loss or disruption, whereas knowledge of lifetime periods is least vulnerable.

When people are asked to produce autobiographical memories, most of the memories produced tend to consist of general events. Why is this? Autobiographical memories based on lifetime periods are rather general and relatively uninformative, whereas memories based on event-specific knowledge are often very specific and lack general significance. Autobiographical memories based on general events provide a happy medium between these two extremes. When people recall general events, they usually start with the most distinctive details, and then work through the event in the order in which various incidents occurred (Anderson & Conway, 1993).

According to the theory, our generative retrieval of autobiographical memories is influenced by the goals of the working self. As a consequence, when we produce such autobiographical memories, they should reflect success or failure with respect to our current goals. As we saw in the previous section, Woike et al. (1999) found that most autobiographical memories recalled by individuals in response to emotional cues are consistent with their major goals.

Evidence supporting the distinction between generative or voluntary retrieval of autobiographical memories and direct or involuntary retrieval was reported by Berntsen (1998) and Berntsen and Hall (2004). Berntsen (1998) argued that autobiographical memories elicited by cues involve generative or voluntary retrieval. In contrast, those coming to mind without any deliberate attempt to recall them involve direct or involuntary retrieval. More of the autobiographical memories produced by direct retrieval than by generative retrieval were of specific events (89% vs. 63%, respectively). Berntsen and Hall (2004) repeated these findings. In addition, the cues most associated with direct retrieval of autobiographical memories were specific ones, such as being in the same place as the original event (61% of cases) or being in the same place engaged in the same activity (25% of cases).

According to the theory, autobiographical memories produced by generative retrieval are constructed by an effortful process rather than simply reproduced. Support for this assumption was obtained by Conway (1996).

KEY TERM
Direct retrieval:
involuntary recall of autobiographical memories triggered by a specific retrieval cue (e.g., being in the same place as the original event); see generative retrieval.

Participants took four times longer to retrieve autobiographical memories than to verify personal information (e.g., name of their bank). In addition, the information contained in autobiographical memories produced on two occasions a few days apart differed considerably. This is as expected if such memories are constructed, whereas memories would presumably be highly similar if they were simply reproduced.

Conway and Pleydell-Pearce (2000) argued that generative retrieval initially involves the control processes of the working self followed by activation of parts of the autobiographical knowledge base. They speculated that processes within the working self involve activation in the frontal lobes (see Figure 1.4), whereas processes within the autobiographical knowledge base involve activation in more posterior regions of the brain. These assumptions were tested by Conway, Pleydell-Pearce, and Whitecross (2001). As predicted, there was extensive activation in the left frontal lobe during the initial stages of generative retrieval of autobiographical memories. After that, when an autobiographical memory was being held in conscious awareness, there was activation in the temporal and occipital lobes especially in the right hemisphere. According to Conway et al. (2001, p. 517), "The working self sited in left frontal networks ... generates a retrieval model that is subsequently used to direct searches of the knowledge base ... The knowledge base is distributed within networks in the (right) temporal and occipital lobes, which is where a specific memory is eventually formed."

What differences in brain activation might we expect to find between memory for experienced events and for imagined ones? First, if the initial construction processes are more difficult for imagined memories than for experienced ones, there should be greater activation of prefrontal cortex for imagined memories. Second, if experienced memories involve the retrieval of more detailed information, there should be greater activation in occipito-temporal regions with experienced memories than with imagined ones. Both of these predictions were confirmed by Conway, Pleydell-Pearce, Whitecross, and Sharpe (2003).

EVALUATION AND CHAPTER SUMMARY

The story of my life
- The approach of Conway and Pleydell-Pearce (2000) is the most comprehensive theory of autobiographical memory currently available.
- Several key assumptions, such as the hierarchical structure of autobiographical memory and the intimate relationship between autobiographical memory and the self, are well supported.
- In addition, the fact that several brain regions are involved in the generative retrieval of autobiographical memories is consistent with the theoretical notion that such retrieval is complex.
- What are the main limitations of the theory?
- First, little is known about the precise ways in which the working self interacts with the autobiographical knowledge base to produce autobiographical recall.

- Second, the theory draws a sharp distinction between generative and direct retrieval, but recalling autobiographical memories often involves elements of both modes of retrieval.
- Third, our understanding of the conscious self is based mainly on consciously accessible information. However, it is entirely possible that aspects of the working self (e.g., some of its goals) are not consciously accessible.

FURTHER READING

- Conway, M.A., & Pleydell,-Pearce, C.W. (2000). The construction of autobiographical memories in the self-memory system. *Psychological Review*, *107*, 261–288. This article provides the most thorough theory of autobiographical memory currently available.
- Healy, A.F., and Proctor, R.W. (2003). *Handbook of psychology: Experimental psychology, Vol. 4.* New York: Wiley & Sons. Episodic and autobiographical memory are compared in detail in a chapter by Roediger and Marsh.
- *Memory* (2003). Special issue on autobiographical memory. *Memory*, 2003, *11*, 113–224. This issue of the journal Memory contains several articles by leading experts on key aspects of autobiographical memory.

CHAPTER 16

CONTENTS

Introduction 221

What influences eyewitness accuracy? 222

Eyewitness identification 225

Interviewing eyewitnesses 227

Evaluation and chapter summary 230

Further reading 231

Should we believe eyewitnesses?

INTRODUCTION

You are a juror in a murder case. You are finding it difficult to decide whether the defendant is indeed the murderer because nearly all the evidence is indirect or circumstantial. However, one piece of evidence *does* seem to be very direct and revealing. An eyewitness was present at the time of the murder, and he identified the defendant as the murderer in an identification line-up. When you see the eyewitness being questioned in court, you are impressed by the fact that he appears very confident he has correctly identified the murderer. As a result, you and your fellow jurors all decide the defendant is guilty of murder, and he is sentenced to death or to life imprisonment.

There is plenty of evidence that most jurors are strongly influenced by eyewitness testimony, especially when the eyewitness is very confident that he or she has correctly identified the culprit. It is important to decide how much to believe eyewitnesses, because there are literally thousands of cases in which defendants have been found guilty solely on the basis of eyewitness identification. It is not an encouraging sign that most judges and jurors have relatively little knowledge about the numerous limitations of eyewitness testimony. Wise and Safer (2004) carried out a survey in which 160 American judges indicated their agreement or disagreement with various statements about eyewitness testimony on which psychologists have obtained relevant evidence. Worryingly, judges on average were correct on only 55% of the items, and most believed that jurors knew less about the limitations of eyewitness testimony than they did themselves. Judges generally minimized the factors causing eyewitness testimony to be inaccurate. As a result, only 23% of them agreed with the following statement: "Only in exceptional circumstances should a defendant be convicted of a crime solely on the basis of eyewitness testimony."

Until fairly recently, there was no satisfactory way of proving that innocent people have been found guilty on the basis of inaccurate eyewitness testimony. However, the advent of DNA tests means that we can often establish whether the person convicted of a crime was actually responsible. In the United States, more than 100 convicted people have been shown to be innocent by means of DNA tests, and more than 75% of them were found guilty on the basis of mistaken eyewitness identification. The 100th innocent person freed following DNA testing was Larry Mayes of Indiana. He was convicted of raping a cashier at a filling station after she identified him in court. Thomas Vanes, the lawyer who prosecuted Mayes, believed at the time of the trial that Mayes was guilty. However, the DNA evidence changed his mind, leading him to conclude that, "He [Mayes] was right, and I was wrong."

There have been hundreds of studies on eyewitness testimony, and the key findings from such studies are discussed below. Early research focused on the issue of identifying eyewitness errors *after* they had occurred. In contrast, more recent research has attached more weight to the issue of how to prevent eyewitness errors occurring in the first place. This distinction is reflected in the distinction between estimator variables and system variables. **Estimator variables** are those not under the control of the criminal justice system. They include the lighting conditions at the scene of the crime and the amount of stress suffered by the eyewitness. In contrast, **system variables** are under the control of the criminal justice system. They include the kinds of questions asked of eyewitnesses and the instructions given to them prior to seeing a line-up.

The legal system in most countries has taken a long time to accept the important findings of psychologists on eyewitness testimony. However, things are starting to change. For example, in 1999 the United States Department of Justice published a document entitled "Eyewitness evidence: A guide for law enforcement." This document (discussed by Wells et al., 2000) provides guidelines for the most effective use of eyewitness evidence, and its contents were strongly influenced by the research of psychologists.

WHAT INFLUENCES EYEWITNESS ACCURACY?

How can information received after an event affect our memory for the event itself?

We have seen that there are many real-life cases in which eyewitness testimony is inaccurate. Why do you think that is the case? Perhaps the most obvious explanation is that eyewitnesses often fail to pay sufficient attention to the crime and to the criminal or criminals. They are typically thinking their own thoughts and pursuing their own goals when suddenly and unexpectedly a crime occurs in front of them. It is only to be expected that their recollection of what they have seen and heard should lack detail and be prone to error.

POST-EVENT INFORMATION

It is undeniable that failures of attention often play a part in explaining the inaccurate memories of eyewitnesses. However, Elizabeth Loftus and John Palmer argued that what matters is not only what happens at the time of the crime. They claimed that eyewitness memories are somewhat fragile and can surprisingly easily be distorted by subsequent questioning. In their well-known study (Loftus & Palmer, 1974), participants were shown a film of a multiple-car accident. After viewing the film, they described what had happened, and then answered specific questions. Some were asked, "About how fast were the cars going when they hit each other?," whereas for other participants the verb "hit" was substituted for "smashed into." Control participants were not asked a question about car speed. The estimated speed was affected by the verb used in the question, averaging 41 mph when the verb "smashed" was used versus 34 mph when "hit" was used. Thus, the information implicit in the question affected how the accident was remembered.

One week later, all of the participants were asked, "Did you see any broken glass?" There wasn't actually any broken glass in the accident. However, 32% of those who had previously been asked about speed using the verb "smashed" said they had seen broken glass (see Figure 16.1). In contrast, only 14% of the participants asked using the verb "hit" said they had seen broken glass, and the figure was 12%

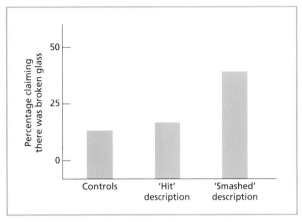

Figure 16.1 Results from Loftus and Palmer's (1974) study showing how the verb used in the initial description of a car accident affected recall of the incident after one week.

for the control participants. Thus, our memory for events is so fragile that it can be distorted by changing *one* word in *one* question!

The tendency for eyewitness memory to be influenced by misleading post-event information is very strong. Eakin, Schreiber, and Sergent-Marshall (2003) showed participants slides of a maintenance man repairing a chair in an office and stealing some money and a calculator. As predicted, eyewitness memory was impaired by misleading post-event information. More strikingly, memory was impaired even when the eyewitnesses were warned immediately about the presence of misleading information.

The above findings indicate that information acquired between original learning (the event or crime) and the subsequent memory test can disrupt performance on that memory test. What we have here is a clear example of retroactive interference, defined as disruption of memory by learning of other material occurring during the retention interval (see Chapter 14). Loftus (1992) emphasized the notion of *misinformation acceptance*: eyewitnesses "accept" misleading information presented after an event, and subsequently regard it as forming part of their memory for that event. There is a greater tendency to accept post-event information in this way as the time since the event increases.

Studies of forgetting have shown the importance of proactive interference, in which memory for some information is disrupted by learning occurring *prior* to the acquisition of that information (see Chapter 14). Evidence that eyewitness memory can be distorted by proactive interference was reported by Lindsay, Allen, Chan, and Dahl (2004a). Participants were shown a video of a museum burglary. On the previous day, they listened to a narrative *either* thematically similar (a palace burglary) *or* thematically dissimilar (a school field-trip to a palace) to the video. Eyewitnesses made many more errors when recalling information from the video when the narrative was thematically similar than when it was thematically dissimilar. This is potentially an important finding. In the real world, eyewitnesses often have some experiences of relevance to the questions they are asked about the event or crime, and these experiences distort their answers.

How concerned do we need to be about the distorting effects of information presented either before or after the crucial event seen by eyewitnesses? Such distorting effects may be less damaging than might be imagined. Memory distortions are more common for peripheral or minor details (e.g., presence of broken glass) than for central details (e.g., features of the criminal) (e.g., Heath & Erickson, 1998).

WEAPON FOCUS

The accuracy of eyewitness testimony is influenced by **weapon focus**: "The weapon appears to capture a good deal of the victim's attention, resulting in, among other things, a reduced ability to recall other details from the environment, to recall details about the assailant, and to recognize the assailant at a later time" (Loftus, 1979, p. 75). Loftus, Loftus, and Messo (1987) asked participants to watch one of two sequences:

1. A person pointing a gun at a cashier and receiving some cash.
2. A person handing a check to the cashier and receiving some cash.

The first finding was that participants looked more at the gun than at the check. The second finding was that (as predicted) memory for details unrelated to the gun/check was poorer in the weapon condition.

There is evidence suggesting that weapon focus may be less important with real line-ups than in the laboratory. Valentine, Pickering, and Darling (2003) considered the findings from over 300 real line-ups. The presence of a weapon had no effect on the probability of an eyewitness identifying the suspect.

EYEWITNESS CONFIDENCE

If an eyewitness is confident, does it necessarily follow that their testimony is accurate?

It seems reasonable to assume that eyewitnesses who are confident they have correctly identified the culprit are more likely to be accurate than those lacking confidence. However, Kassin, Tubb, Hosch, and Memon (2001) found that over 80% of eyewitness experts agreed that an eyewitness's confidence is *not* a good predictor of his or her identification accuracy. The poor relationship between eyewitness confidence and accuracy matters, because jurors are generally most influenced by an eyewitness's confidence when assessing his or her credibility. However, there is not *always* a poor relationship between eyewitness confidence and accuracy. Sporer, Penrod, Read, and Cutler (1995) integrated the findings from numerous studies in which an eyewitness's confidence was assessed immediately after the eyewitness had chosen a suspect from a line-up. They distinguished between choosers (eyewitnesses making a positive identification) and non-choosers (those not making a positive identification). There was practically no correlation between confidence and accuracy among non-choosers. However, the mean correlation was +.41 among choosers, indicating that choosers' confidence predicted their accuracy to a moderate extent.

Why is eyewitness confidence often a poor predictor of identification accuracy? This issue was addressed by Perfect and Hollins (1996). Participants were given recognition memory tests for the information contained in a

KEY TERM
Weapon focus: the finding that eyewitnesses pay so much attention to the weapon that they tend to ignore other details.

film about a girl who was kidnapped and also for general knowledge questions. Participants' confidence didn't predict accuracy with questions about the film, but did predict accuracy with the general knowledge questions.

Perfect and Hollins (1996) argued that eyewitness confidence doesn't predict accuracy because eyewitnesses don't know whether their ability to remember a witnessed event is better or worse than that of others. Accordingly, they have no solid basis for being low or high in confidence. In contrast, most people know whether their general knowledge compares well or badly with that of others, and this is reflected in their confidence.

BARTLETT'S SCHEMA THEORY

Many of the inaccuracies in memory shown by eyewitnesses can be interpreted within Bartlett's (1932) schema theory (see Chapter 19). According to this theory, we possess numerous schemas or packets of knowledge stored in long-term memory. Recall involves a process of *reconstruction* in which all relevant information (including schema-based information) is used to reconstruct the details of that event in terms of "what must have been true." On that account, new information relevant to a previously experienced event can affect recall of that event by providing a different basis for reconstruction. Such reconstructive processes may be involved in eyewitness studies on post-event information.

More direct support for Bartlett's schema theory was reported by Tuckey and Brewer (2003a, 2003b). Tuckey and Brewer (2003a) first of all established what information is contained in most people's bank robbery schema. Here is what they found: robbers are male, they wear disguises, they wear dark clothes, they make demands for money, and they have a getaway car with a driver in it. Tuckey and Brewer (2003a) showed participants a video of a simulated bank robbery followed by a test of memory.

What did Tuckey and Brewer (2003a) find? As predicted by Bartlett's theory, eyewitnesses had better recall for information *relevant* to the bank robbery schema than for *irrelevant* information (e.g., the color of the getaway car). Thus, eyewitnesses used schematic information to assist in their recall of the bank robbery. In the study by Tuckey and Brewer (2003b), eyewitnesses recalled the details of a simulated crime they had observed, with the researchers focusing on how eyewitnesses remembered ambiguous information. As predicted, eyewitnesses generally interpreted the ambiguous information as being consistent with their crime schema. Thus, their recall was systematically distorted by including information from their crime schema *not* present in the crime they had observed.

EYEWITNESS IDENTIFICATION

The performance of eyewitnesses is very fallible when they try to select the suspect from a number of individuals in an identification line-up (see Wells & Olson, 2003, for a review). Valentine, Pickering, and Darling (2003) studied the findings based on 640 eyewitnesses who tried to identify suspects in 314 real line-ups organized by the Metropolitan Police in London. About 40% of witnesses identified the suspect, 20% identified a non-suspect, and 40% failed to make an identification.

In the United States and the United Kingdom (and elsewhere), there has been a dramatic increase in the number of closed-circuit television (CCTV) cameras. It seems reasonable to assume that it would be an easy matter to identify someone on the basis of CCTV images. In fact, that is not necessarily the case. Bruce, Henderson, Greenwood, Hancock, Burton, and Miller (1999) presented participants with a target face taken from a CCTV video, together with an array of 10 high-quality photographs (see Figure 16.2). Their task was to select the matching face or to indicate that the target face was not present in the array. Performance was relatively poor. When the target face was present in the array, it was selected only 65% of the time. When it was not present, 35% of participants nevertheless claimed that one of the faces in the array matched the target face. Allowing participants to watch a 5-sec. video segment of the target person as well as a photograph of their faces failed to improve identification performance.

IMPROVING MATTERS

What can be done to improve the identification performance of eyewitnesses? It has often been argued that warning eyewitnesses that the culprit may not be present in the line-up reduces the chances of mistaken identification.

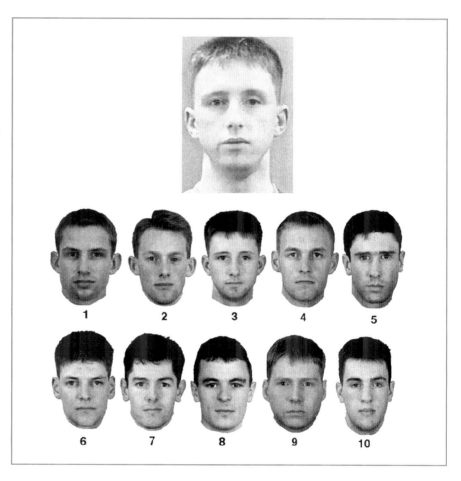

Figure 16.2 Example of full-face neutral target with an array used in the experiments. Readers may wish to attempt the task of establishing whether or not target is present in this array and which one it is. The studio and video images used are from the Home Office Police Information Technology Organisation. Bruce et al. (1999). Copyright © American Psychological Association. Reprinted with permission.

This was explored by Steblay (1997) in a meta-analysis of numerous studies. Such warnings reduced mistaken identification rates in culprit-absent line-ups by 42%, while reducing accurate identification rates in culprit-present line-ups by only 2%.

Line-ups are generally simultaneous, meaning the eyewitness is presented with everyone in the line-up at the same time. The alternative is to have sequential line-ups, in which the eyewitness sees only one person at a time. Steblay, Dysart, Fulero, and Lindsay (2001) considered 25 studies in which simultaneous and sequential line-ups were compared. Sequential line-ups reduced the chances of mistaken identification when the culprit was absent by almost 50%. However, sequential line-ups also produced a significant reduction in accurate identification rates when the culprit was present. What happens is that eyewitnesses adopt a more *stringent* criterion for identification with sequential than with simultaneous line-ups.

INTERVIEWING EYEWITNESSES

Until about 20 years ago, the interviewing techniques used by the police when questioning eyewitnesses were often inadequate and severely limited the amount of information elicited. Some of the limitations in the traditional approach taken by the police in the United States and the United Kingdom were discussed by Wells et al. (2000). First, there was a tendency to ask closed-ended questions (e.g., "What color was the car?"), which typically elicit only very specific information. Open-ended questions (e.g., "What can you tell me about the car?") are likely to elicit more information. Second, police often interrupted eyewitnesses in the middle of saying something. This forced the eyewitness to turn his or her attention to the interviewer and away from the retrieval of relevant information. Third, police frequently asked questions in an inflexible, predetermined order, taking no account of the answers provided by the eyewitness.

How have techniques for interviewing eyewitnesses advanced? Do you think that the changes have improved accuracy?

In sum, as Wells et al. (2000, p. 583) concluded, "By dint of their assertive questioning style, which is replete with rapid-fire, closed-ended questions, police often create a passive eyewitness from whom information is extracted rather than an active eyewitness who freely generates information."

Several attempts have been made to develop alternative ways of eliciting more information from eyewitnesses than obtained using traditional police interviewing techniques. We turn now to a discussion of two of those ways: (1) hypnosis; and (2) cognitive interviews.

HYPNOSIS

Police forces in several countries have made extensive use of hypnosis as a method for improving the effectiveness of their interviews with eyewitnesses. There has been considerable controversy as to whether or not the hypnotic state differs substantially from ordinary consciousness. On balance, the evidence suggests that hypnosis *does* represent an altered state of consciousness (see Eysenck, 2004).

Findings

It has often been found (e.g., Geiselman, Fisher, MacKinnon, & Holland, 1985) that hypnotized eyewitnesses recall more information about an incident than do non-hypnotized ones. Hypnosis has also proved effective in increasing eyewitnesses' memory for details of real-life crimes. For example, Westen (1996) discussed a case from the late 1970s in which a busload of children and the bus driver were kidnapped at gunpoint. The driver found it difficult to remember key details until he was hypnotized. Under hypnosis, he recalled enough information about the number plate of the kidnappers' car for the police to track down the kidnappers.

The key problem with hypnosis is that it can lead eyewitnesses to become much less cautious in their reporting and so to introduce more errors into their recall. For example, Putnam (1979) showed eyewitnesses a videotape of an accident involving a car and a bicycle. They were then asked a series of questions, some of which contained misleading information. Hypnotized eyewitnesses made more errors in their answers than did non-hypnotized ones, and this was especially the case with the misleading questions. These findings led Putnam (1979, p. 444) to conclude that eyewitnesses are "more suggestible in the hypnotic state and are, therefore, more easily influenced by the leading questions."

Similar findings were reported by Buckhout, Eugenio, and Grosso (1981). They asked eyewitnesses to recall the number on the shirt worn by someone involved in a simulated crime. Nearly all (90%) of the hypnotized eyewitnesses produced a number, compared to only 20% of those not hypnotized. However, that doesn't mean that hypnosis was effective—none of the hypnotized eyewitnesses recalled the number correctly!

COGNITIVE INTERVIEW

Psychologists have found it fairly easy to devise interviewing techniques that are more effective than the traditional police approach. More specifically, two psychologists (Fisher and Geiselman) used well-established findings in memory research to develop the cognitive interview (see Fisher & Geiselman, 1992). Their central assumption was that memory traces are usually complex and contain various kinds of information (e.g., the person's mood state at the time of learning, contextual information). As a result, various different retrieval cues may permit access to any given memory trace.

What does all this mean in practice? Here are some of the main features of the cognitive interview:

- The eyewitness re-creates the context at the time of the crime including environmental and internal (e.g., mood state) information.
- The eyewitness reports everything he or she can think of about the incident, even if the information is fragmented.
- The eyewitness reports the details of the incident in various orders.
- The eyewitness reports the event from various perspectives (e.g., those of other eyewitnesses).

Fisher, Geiselman, Raymond, Jurkevich, and Warhaftig (1987) devised an enhanced cognitive interview. It includes all of the features discussed already, but adds the following recommendations (Roy, 1991, p. 399):

Investigators should minimize distractions, induce the eyewitness to speak slowly, allow a pause between the response and next question, tailor language to suit the individual eyewitness, follow up with interpretive comment, try to reduce eyewitness anxiety, avoid judgmental and personal comments, and always review the eyewitness's description of events or people under investigation.

Findings

Geiselman et al. (1985) found that the average number of correct statements produced by eyewitnesses was 41.1 using the cognitive interview against only 29.4 using the standard police interview (see Figure 16.3). Hypnosis produced an average of 38.0 correct statements, so it was less effective than the cognitive interview.

Fisher et al. (1987) found that the enhanced cognitive interview was more effective than the basic cognitive interview. Eyewitnesses produced an average of 57.5 correct statements with the enhanced cognitive interview compared to only 39.6 with the basic cognitive interview. However, there were 28% more incorrect statements with the enhanced interview.

The studies by Geiselman et al. (1985) and by Fisher et al. (1987) were limited because they were conducted under laboratory conditions and involved mock crimes. However, Fisher, Geiselman, and Amador (1990) tested the enhanced cognitive interview by training detectives working for the Robbery Division of Metro-Dade Police Department in Miami in its techniques. Strikingly, Fisher et al. (1990) found that this training produced an increase of 46% in the number of statements obtained from eyewitnesses. When it was possible to check the accuracy of these statements with a second eyewitness, over 90% proved accurate.

Kohnken, Milne, Memon, and Bull (1999) combined the findings from over 50 studies into a meta-analysis. The cognitive interview consistently elicited more correct information than standard police interviews. Indeed, the average eyewitness given a cognitive interview produced more correct items of information than 81% of eyewitnesses given a standard interview. However, there was a small cost in terms of reduced accuracy—the average eyewitness given a cognitive interview produced more errors than 61% of those given a standard interview.

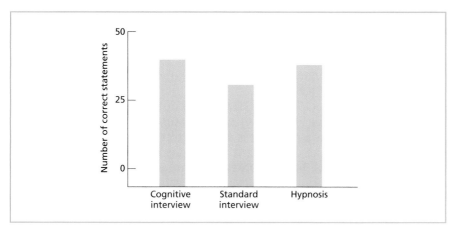

Figure 16.3 Number of correct statements using different methods of interview. Based on data in Geiselman et al. (1985).

EVALUATION AND CHAPTER SUMMARY

Eyewitness identification
- We have seen that there are various simple ways of setting up identification line-ups to improve the performance of eyewitnesses.
- For example, the eyewitness should be warned that the culprit may not be present in the line-up, and it is preferable for the line-up to be sequential rather than simultaneous.
- The main limitation of research in this area is that, "The eyewitness identification literature has been driven much less by theoretical frameworks than by practical perspectives" (Wells & Olson, 2003, p. 290).

Interviewing eyewitnesses
- The original cognitive interview and the enhanced cognitive interview have both contributed much to improving the system of justice in several countries including the United States and the United Kingdom.
- The substantial increase in correct information obtained from eyewitnesses with these interview techniques has led to the conviction of many guilty defendants and to courts finding more innocent defendants not guilty. This is quite an achievement for cognitive psychology, which is often regarded as too laboratory-based and remote from everyday life!
- In spite of its great success, the cognitive interview (whether enhanced or not) possesses several limitations.
- First, the increase in the amount of incorrect information reported by eyewitnesses given the cognitive interview is a cause of concern. Admittedly, the increase is typically small, but it makes it harder to assess the validity of the testimony provided by eyewitnesses.
- Second, a key ingredient in the cognitive interview is the attempt to re-create the context at the time of the incident.
- However, context typically has more effect on recall than on recognition memory (see Chapter 14). As a result, the cognitive interview doesn't improve person identification from photographs or line-ups (see Fisher, 1999).
- Third, the cognitive interview is typically less effective at enhancing recall when used at longer intervals of time after an incident has occurred (Geiselman & Fisher, 1997). Thus, eyewitnesses should be interviewed as soon as possible after the incident or event.
- Fourth, as Fisher (1999, p. 551) pointed out, "Most experiments on the C.I. [cognitive interview] have presented the technique as a 'package' and, as a result, it is difficult to tease apart the contribution of each of the component techniques."
- It follows that we have a somewhat limited understanding of precisely *why* the cognitive interview is so effective.

FURTHER READING

- Fisher, R.P. (1999). Probing knowledge structures. In D. Gopher & A. Koriat (Eds.), *Attention and performance XVII: Cognitive regulation of performance: Interaction of theory and application*. Cambridge, MA: MIT Press. The strengths and limitations of the cognitive interview as a technique for obtaining information from eyewitnesses is discussed in detail.
- Loftus, E.F. (2004). Memories of things unseen. *Current Directions in Psychological Science*, *13*, 145–147. Some of the reasons why eyewitness testimony is fallible are considered in this article.
- Wells, G.L., & Olson, E.A. (2003). Eyewitness testimony. *Annual Review of Psychology*, *54*, 277–295. This article provides a good account of several factors influencing the accuracy of eyewitness identification.

PART III

CONTENTS

17 Read all about it!   **236**

18 What are you saying?   **252**

19 What does this mean?   **270**

20 Talking the talk   **288**

21 What's in a concept?   **306**

Language

If you doubt the importance of language in your life, just consider for a moment how incredibly limited it would be to live without language. Our social interactions with friends and acquaintances depend very heavily on language, and a good command of language is vital for all students. People nowadays are generally much more knowledgeable than those of previous generations. The main reason is because knowledge is passed on from one generation to the next with most of this knowledge being in the form of language.

What is language? According to the *Dictionary of Psychology* (Colman, 2001), language is, "a conventional system of communicative sounds and sometimes (though not necessarily) written symbols." In that definition, the crucial words is "communicative," because the primary function of language is to communicate. However, language also fulfills other functions. Crystal (1997) identified *eight* functions of language, of which communication was one. In addition, we use language for thinking, to record information, to express emotion (e.g., "I love you"), to pretend to be animals (e.g., "Woof! Woof!"), to express identity with a group (e.g., singing in church), and so on.

Language is an impressive human achievement. Are there other species that make use of language? Parrots say certain words. Even if they are trying to communicate, this is not language in the full sense, because they don't use rules or show the flexibility in use of language that humans do. It seems more promising to try to teach language to apes. The earliest attempts to do so were almost farcical. After several years, Keith and Katharine Hayes taught a female chimpanzee Vicki to say a grand total of *four* words. They hoped that Vicki would learn language by being exposed to their young child. In fact, what happened was that their child learned to grunt like a chimpanzee!

Progress was made when it was realized that chimpanzees' vocal apparatus is not suited to speaking English and that language should be taught in other ways. For example, consider the research of Savage-Rumbaugh with a bonobo chimpanzee called Panbanisha (see Leake, 1999). She uses a specially designed keypad with about 400 geometric patterns on it. When she presses a sequence of keys, a computer translates the sequence into a synthetic voice. Panbanisha learned 3000 words by the age of 14, and became very good at combining a series of symbols in the grammatically correct order. For example, she can construct a sentence such as, "Please can I have an iced coffee?"

Panbanisha's achievements are considerable. However, her command of language is much less than that of most fairly young children. For example, she doesn't produce many novel sentences, her sentences are mostly rather simple, and she only rarely refers to objects that are not visible. As Noam Chomsky (quoted in Atkinson, Atkinson, Smith, & Bem, 1993) remarked, "If animals had a capacity as biologically advantageous as language but somehow hadn't used it until now, it would be an evolutionary miracle, like finding an island of humans who could be taught to fly."

In our everyday lives, most of us make extensive use of four main language skills. These are as follows: listening to speech; reading; speaking; and writing. It is perhaps natural to assume that any given person's four main language skills will be generally strong or weak. That assumption may often (but certainly not always) be correct with respect to first language acquisition. Even there, however, many people develop special expertise with respect to just one language skill because it is of particular relevance to their interests or career. For example, novelists and textbook writers need to have highly developed writing skills, and comedians, politicians, and lawyers require expert speaking skills. Differences in the four main language skills are often fairly pronounced when we focus on second language acquisition. For example, I spent 10 years at school learning French. I can just about read newspapers and easy novels in French, and I am also able to write French reasonably well (although my writing skills lag behind my reading ones). However, I find it agonizingly difficult to understand rapid spoken French, and often can't even work out the topic being discussed. Finally, my ability to speak French is poor, and I find myself limited to very simple and uninteresting sentences.

Three of the chapters in this section of the book are concerned with the main language skills. Chapter 17 deals with basic processes involved in reading. These processes include those involved in reading aloud, working out the grammatical structure of sentences, and understanding the meaning of sentences that we read. Much progress has been made in understanding what is involved in reading by carrying out studies in which readers' eye movements are carefully analyzed as they read text. Chapter 18 focuses on the basics of speech perception. One of the key issues in speech perception is to identify the words being spoken by another person, a task that is more difficult than it might appear. Another issue concerns the extent to which speech perception is influenced by our expectations as to what we are about to hear. Much understanding has occurred as a result of studying brain-damaged patients having various problems with speech perception. Chapter 20 is concerned with speech production. One approach to identifying the processes involved in speech production is to study the errors that occur while we are speaking. Another approach (as with speech perception) is to study brain-damaged patients having particular problems with speech production. As we will see, speech production generally proceeds from some notion of the idea or ideas we want to communicate through to the detailed pronunciation of the words we decide to use to express those ideas.

You may have noticed that nothing has been said so far about writing. Writing is not discussed because it has been studied much less thoroughly than the other main language skills. If you are interested in finding out about the processes involved in writing, then you could have a look at Chapter 12 of Eysenck and Keane (2005).

Our understanding or comprehension of language is very similar regardless of whether the language input is *visual* (an entire text) or *auditory* (someone is talking to us). The processes involved are discussed in detail in Chapter 19. Of particular importance is the way in which we make use of our pre-existing knowledge in the comprehension process.

Finally, we turn to Chapter 21. That chapter deals with concepts, which are important in any full discussion of language. Language is concerned with words and with the meanings we attach to them. The relevance of concepts is that all words have an underlying concept, and the meaning that we attach to any given word depends in part on its underlying concept. Note that concepts play a vital role in virtually all our dealings with the world. For example, we use concepts when we recognize objects in our environment. We also use conceptual knowledge when we think about a problem or plan our future.

CHAPTER 17

CONTENTS

Introduction 237

Reading aloud 238

Parsing 243

It's in the eyes 246

Evaluation and chapter summary 249

Further reading 250

Read all about it!

INTRODUCTION

Why is it important to study reading? Skilled reading has much value in contemporary society, and adults without effective reading skills are at a great disadvantage. Another major reason is that reading involves several perceptual and other cognitive processes, as well as a good knowledge of language and of grammar. In fact, most mental activities are related to reading, and so it can appropriately be regarded as "visually guided thinking."

We can study reading in many ways. At one extreme, we can present people with a single word and see how long it takes them to decide which word has been presented (word identification task) or to read the word out aloud (word naming). At the other extreme, we could ask people to read a lengthy text, and then ask them several comprehension questions to assess what information they had acquired from their reading. This chapter is concerned with basic reading processes operating mainly at the level of the individual word within sentences. However, we do also consider the processes involved in working out the syntactical or grammatical structure of sentences. Other processes involved in reading sentences, and those involved in reading paragraphs and entire texts are discussed in Chapter 19.

SOUND AS WELL AS VISION?

It is natural to think of reading as being almost exclusively a *visual* skill, in that all the information the reader is presented with is visual in nature. However, when you read a complicated text, you may well find yourself muttering some of the words in the text to yourself. According to Huey (1908), "It is of the greatest service to the reader or listener that at each moment a considerable amount of what is being read should hang suspended in the primary memory [short-term memory] of the inner speech."

Such considerations have led to an interest in the role of **phonology** (the sound of words) in the reading process. Frost (1998, p. 76) put forward an extreme theoretical position (the strong phonological model): "A phonological representation is a necessary product of processing printed words, even though the explicit pronunciation of their phonological structure is not required. Thus, the strong phonological model would predict that phonological processing will be mandatory [obligatory], perhaps automatic."

The available evidence indicates that phonology is often (but not always)

KEY TERM
Phonology: information about the sounds of words and parts of words.

What role does phonology play in reading?

used in reading. For example, Jared, Levy, and Rayner (1999) recorded eye movements during proof-reading. They found that the use of phonology depended on the nature of the words and participants' reading ability. The eye-movement data indicated that phonological processing was used to access the meaning of low-frequency words but not high-frequency ones. In addition, poor readers were more likely than good readers to engage in phonological processing as a way of accessing meaning.

Further evidence of phonological processing in reading was reported by Pexman, Lupker, and Reggin (2002). They used a **lexical decision task**, on which participants had to decide as rapidly as possible whether letter strings formed words or non-words. Among the words used by Pexman et al. (2002) were **homonyms** (e.g., "maid", "made'); that is, words having one pronunciation but two spellings. Suppose that seeing a homonym activates its phonological representation, and this in turn activates both of its spellings. In that case, activation of the "wrong" spelling would slow down performance of homonyms compared to non-homonyms. That is precisely what was found by Pexman et al. (2002).

Hanley and McDonnell (1997) reported reasonably convincing evidence that word meaning can be accessed without access to phonology. They studied a patient, PS, who understood the meanings of words while reading even though he couldn't pronounce them accurately. PS didn't even seem to have access to an internal phonological representation of words. For example, he couldn't work out both meanings of homonyms when he saw one of the spellings in print.

In sum, the findings indicate that the strong phonological model is incorrect in its assumption that phonological processing always occurs when reading. In fact, the involvement of phonological processing in reading depends on the nature of the stimulus material, the nature of the task, and the individual's reading ability. Thus, the strong phonological model should be rejected in favor of the weak phonological model, according to which phonological processing is often used in reading.

We all know that the goal of reading is to understand the texts we encounter every day. In so thinking, we may argue that it is of little value to focus (as many psychologists have done) on the processing of individual words presented in sentences. In fact, however, that argument isn't very persuasive. As we will see, a substantial amount has been learned about the main processes involved in reading from studies on words presented one at a time.

READING ALOUD

Reading aloud familiar words (and even many non-words) seems about as easy a task as you can imagine. Indeed, I would be surprised if you had any difficulty at all in reading out the following list of words and non-words:

CAT   FOG   COMB   PINT   MANTINESS   FASS

However, close inspection of what you have just done reveals some hidden complexities. For example, how do you know the "b" in "comb" is silent, and

that "pint" doesn't rhyme with "hint"? Presumably you have specific information about how to pronounce these words stored in long-term memory.
However, this cannot explain your ability to pronounce non-words such as
"mantiness" and "fass." Perhaps non-words are pronounced by analogy with
real words (e.g., "fass" is pronounced to rhyme with "mass"). Alternatively,
we may use rules governing the translation of letter strings into sounds to
generate pronunciations for non-words.

How do we know how to pronounce non-words?

DUAL-ROUTE CASCADED MODEL

The take-home message from the above paragraph is that reading aloud is
probably a sufficiently complex task in that there is more than one way it can
be achieved. Precisely this insight is at the heart of the dual-route model proposed by Coltheart, Rastle, Perry, Langdon, and Ziegler (2001; see Figure
17.1). According to this model, there are three routes between the printed
word and speech. All of these routes start with orthographic analysis (used
for identifying and grouping letters in printed words). You may well be
puzzled why a model with *three* routes is called a
dual-route model. The explanation is that the
key distinction is between a lexical look-up route
based on a lexicon or mental dictionary (Routes
2 and 3) and a non-lexical route (Route 1). The
non-lexical route involves converting spelling
(graphemes or basic units of written language)
into sound (phonemes or basic units of sound).
To oversimplify somewhat, people reading aloud
will typically use mainly the lexical or dictionary
look-up route when reading words. However,
they will use the non-lexical route when reading
non-words, because non-words don't have dictionary entries.

How can we test the dual-route model? One
approach that has proved very successful is to
identify different groups of patients with brain
damage who are largely reliant on only *one* of
the three routes. Below we consider this
approach in action. What would happen if a
patient had access only to Route 1? The use of
rules for converting letters into sound should
permit accurate pronunciation of *regular* words
(i.e., the pronunciation is predictable from the
letters) that can be read with no special knowledge of the word (e.g., "tint", "save"). The use
of grapheme–phoneme conversion rules also
allows non-words to be pronounced accurately.
The main problem would come with *irregular*
words. These are words in which the pronunciation is *not* predictable from the spelling
(e.g., "island", "yacht"). Patients conforming
most closely to these predictions suffer from

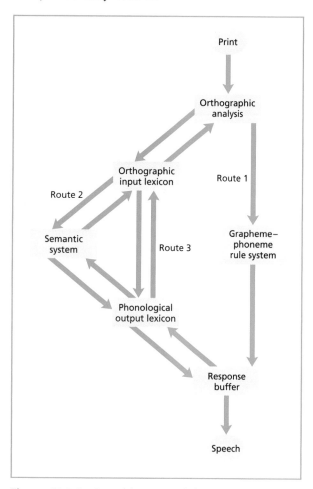

Figure 17.1 Basic architecture of the dual-route
cascaded model. Adapted from Coltheart et al.
(2001).

surface dyslexia, a condition in which regular words can be read but irregular words cannot. For example, McCarthy and Warrington (1986) studied a surface dyslexic, KT. He read 100% of non-words accurately as well as 81% of regular words. However, he was successful with only 41% of irregular words, with over 70% of his errors involving treating irregular words as if they were regular.

What would happen if a patient had access only to Route 2, which involves the lexicon or mental dictionary and the semantic system? He or she should be able to pronounce familiar words, whether regular or irregular, and to understand them. This is because Route 2 goes through the semantic or meaning system and each word's sound pattern is generated in the phonological output lexicon. In contrast, the patient should find it hard to pronounce unfamiliar words and non-words, because he or she would be unable to use grapheme–phoneme conversion. Patients with phonological dyslexia fit this pattern. **Phonological dyslexia** involves problems with reading unfamiliar words and non-words. For example, Beauvois and Dérouesné (1979) carried out an experiment in which a phonological dyslexic, RG, read 40 words and 40 non-words. RG read 100% of the real words accurately but only 10% of the non-words.

What would happen if a patient had access only to Route 3, in which the lexicon is used but not the semantic system or grapheme–phoneme conversion? Such a patient could pronounce regular and irregular words accurately. However, he or she wouldn't understand the meaning of regular or irregular words, and should also have great problems with non-words. Some phonological dyslexics exhibit this pattern. For example, Funnell (1983) found that WB could read about 85% of words, but had a poor ability to make semantic judgments about these words. These findings support the notion that WB was bypassing the semantic system when reading words. As predicted, WB couldn't pronounce any non-words.

We have seen that evidence from different kinds of brain-damaged patients provides support for the dual-route model. From what has been said so far, you may have formed the view that Coltheart et al. (2001) assume the lexical and non-lexical routes operate totally *independently* of each other. In fact, that is *not* the case. In normal individuals, it is assumed that words and non-words activate *both* routes, and what people say is determined by which route first provides a pronunciation. Convincing support for the dual-route model based on this assumption was provided by Coltheart et al. (2001), who developed a detailed computational model to test their theoretical approach. They presented the model with 7981 words, and found that 7898 (99.5%) were read accurately. When the model was presented with 7000 one-syllable non-words, it read 98.9% of them correctly.

DISTRIBUTED CONNECTIONIST APPROACH

As we have seen, it is assumed within the dual-route model that pronouncing irregular words and non-words is based mainly on different routes. This assumption can be contrasted with the single-route connectionist approach of Plaut, McClelland, Seidenberg, and Patterson (1996). At the risk of oversimplification, we can describe the key differences between the two approaches as follows. According to the dual-route approach, the processes involved in reading words and non-words differ from each other and are relatively neat and tidy. According to the connectionist approach, in contrast, the various processes involved in reading are used more flexibly than assumed within the dual-route model. In crude terms, it is a matter of "all hands to the pump," with identical processes underlying the reading of words and non-words.

How does the connectionist approach of Plaut et al. (1996) characterize the processes involved in reading? "All of the system's knowledge of spelling-sound correspondences is brought to bear in pronouncing all types of letter strings [words and non-words]. Conflicts among possible alternative pronunciations of a letter string are resolved ... by co-operative and competitive interactions based on how the letter string relates to all known words and their pronunciations" (Plaut et al., 1996).

It follows from this approach that an important factor determining speed of word reading should be its *consistency*; that is, the extent to which its pronunciation agrees with that of similarly spelled words. Well-known examples of words having very low consistency are the following similarly spelled words: BOUGH, THROUGH, COUGH, DOUGH, ROUGH. Highly consistent words should be pronounced faster and more accurately than inconsistent ones, because more of the available knowledge supports the correct pronunciation of such words. The evidence indicates that word naming *is* generally predicted well by consistency (e.g., Glushko, 1979).

Plaut et al. (1996) argued that pronouncing words depends on word frequency as well as on consistency. High-frequency or common words are encountered more often than low-frequency or rare words and so have more impact on the pronunciation of a given word. These notions were incorporated into a computer model involving a network. Learning occurred by the use of **back-propagation**, in which the responses (i.e., pronunciations) produced by the system are compared against the correct ones. The network was given extensive training with 2998 words, and its performance at the end of training closely resembled that of adult readers:

1. Consistent words were named faster than inconsistent ones.
2. High-frequency or common words were named faster than low-frequency or rare ones.
3. The network pronounced over 90% of non-words "correctly," which is comparable to the performance of adult readers. This finding is especially impressive because the network received no direct training on non-words.

We saw that Coltheart et al.'s (2001) dual-route model was really successful at accounting for the reading performance of patients suffering from surface dyslexia and phonological dyslexia. What does the Plaut et al. (1996) model have to say about these conditions? Surface dyslexics have particular problems in pronouncing irregular words not pronounced in line with rules governing the translation of letter strings into sounds. According to Plaut et al. (1996), surface dyslexics have an impairment to the semantic system and so their reading of words occurs mainly through the use of phonological information. Phonological dyslexics have problems in reading non-words. According to Plaut et al. (1996), these problems arise because phonological dyslexics have a general impairment of phonological processing and of course lack semantic knowledge about non-words.

KEY TERM
Back-propagation: a learning mechanism in which the responses produced by a computer network are compared against the correct responses.

Findings

We have already mentioned that there is support for the model's prediction that consistent words should be pronounced faster than inconsistent words. However, the findings are less supportive of the related prediction that consistent non-words (having spellings resembling those of words pronounced consistently) should be named faster than inconsistent non-words. This issue was addressed by Job, Peressotti, and Cusinato (1998). Consistent non-words were named significantly faster than inconsistent non-words when words and non-words were both presented in the list. However, there was *no* consistency effect when only non-words were present. It is not clear how we could use the connectionist model to explain the absence of a consistency effect in the latter condition. According to the dual-route model, participants given only non-words to read may well have relied mainly on the non-lexical route based on converting spellings to sounds. In that case, no consistency effect would be expected.

Some support for the connectionist model's assumptions about surface dyslexia was reported by Plaut et al. (1996). They made "lesions" to their computer-based network to reduce or eliminate the contribution from semantics and thus mimic the effects of brain damage in surface dyslexics. The network's reading performance was very good on regular high- and low-frequency words and on non-words, worse on irregular high-frequency words, and worst on irregular low-frequency words. This performance matches the pattern found with surface dyslexics. On the negative side, it follows from the model that patients with severe damage to the semantic system should have very poor reading of irregular words (a key symptom of surface dyslexia). In fact, however, some patients with severe semantic impairments read irregular words very well (e.g., WLP studied by Schwartz, Saffran, & Marin 1980, and DRN studied by Cipolotti & Warrington, 1995).

The explanation of phonological dyslexia offered by the connectionist approach is very different from that offered by the dual-route approach. According to the connectionist approach, phonological dyslexics have a *general* impairment in the representation of phonological information. In contrast, the dual-route model assumes that phonological dyslexics have a *specific* impairment to the non-lexical route that translates spellings into sounds, although more general phonological impairments may also be involved. Thus, the crunch issue is whether phonological deficits are *always* found in phonological dyslexics (predicted by Plaut et al., 1996) or are not (predicted by Coltheart et al., 2001).

Clear support for the dual-route model over the connectionist model was reported by Caccapoppolo-van Vliet, Miozzo, and Stern (2004). They studied two phonological dyslexics. IB is a 77-year-old female who had worked as a secretary; MO is a 48-year-old male accountant. Both patients showed the typical pattern of phonological dyslexics. Their performance on reading regular and irregular words exceeded 90%, compared to under 60% with non-words. Crucially, the performance of IB and MO on various phonological tasks (e.g., deciding whether two words rhymed, finding a rhyming word) was above 95% and as good as healthy individuals. As Caccapppolo-van Vliet et al. (2004, p. 583) concluded, "These results challenge the ideas, proposed in the context of connectionist ... theories, that phonological dyslexia originates from a phonological deficit."

PARSING

As we read a sentence, it is very important to identify its syntactical (grammatical) structure; this is technically known as **parsing**. What exactly is grammar? It is concerned with the way in which words are combined. However, as Altmann (1997, p. 84) pointed out, "It [the way in which words are combined] is important, and has meaning, only insofar as both the speaker and the hearer (or the writer and the reader) share some common knowledge regarding the significance of one combination or another. This shared knowledge is *grammar*."

Which comes first when we read a sentence; the meaning (semantics) or the structure (syntax)?

A central issue in parsing concerns the relationship between syntactic and semantic (meaning) analysis. There are at least four major possibilities:

1. Syntactic analysis generally precedes (and influences) semantic analysis.
2. Semantic analysis usually occurs *prior* to syntactic analysis.
3. Syntactic and semantic analysis occur at the same time.
4. Syntax and semantics are very closely associated, and have a hand-in-glove relationship (Altmann, personal communication).

Most of the time, it seems to us that parsing or assigning grammatical structure to sentences is fairly easy. However, numerous sentences (e.g., "They are flying planes") pose problems because their grammatical structure is ambiguous. Some sentences are syntactically ambiguous at the *global* level, meaning the whole sentence has two or more possible interpretations. For example, "They are cooking apples", is ambiguous because it may or may not mean that apples are being cooked. Other sentences are syntactically ambiguous at the *local* level, meaning that various interpretations are possible at some point during parsing.

Much research on parsing has focused on ambiguous sentences. Why is that the case? Parsing typically occurs very rapidly, and this makes it difficult to study the processes involved. However, observing the problems readers have with ambiguous sentences can provide revealing information about parsing processes. Note that most of the processes involved in parsing during reading are also used in parsing when listening to speech (see Chapter 18).

Theoretical approaches to parsing can be divided into one-stage and two-stage models (Harley, 2001). According to one-stage models, all sources of information (syntactic and semantic) are used at the same time to construct a syntactic model of sentences. In contrast, the first stage of processing in two-stage models uses *only* syntactic information, with semantic information being used during the second stage. We will mainly consider the most influential two-stage approach (the garden-path model) and the most influential one-stage approach (the constraint-based theory of MacDonald, Pearlmutter, & Seidenberg, 1994). As you read about these theories, bear in mind that a key issue concerns *when* semantic information is used in parsing.

GARDEN-PATH MODEL

Frazier and Rayner (1982) put forward a garden-path model. It was given that name because readers can be misled or "led up the garden path" by ambiguous sentences.

The model is based on the following assumptions:

- Only one syntactical structure is initially considered for any sentence.
- Meaning is not involved in the selection of the initial syntactical structure.
- The simplest syntactical structure is chosen based on two general principles: minimal attachment and late closure.
- According to the principle of minimal attachment, the grammatical structure producing the fewest nodes (major parts of a sentence such as noun phrase and verb phrase) is preferred.
- The principle of late closure is that new words encountered in a sentence are attached to the current phrase or clause if grammatically permissible.

Findings

There is much evidence that readers typically follow the principles of late closure and minimal attachment (see Harley, 2001). However, there are exceptions. Carreiras and Clifton (1993) found that readers don't always follow the principle of late closure. They presented complicated sentences such as, "The spy shot the daughter of the colonel who was standing on the balcony." According to the principle of late closure, readers should interpret this as meaning that the colonel (rather than the daughter) was standing on the balcony. In fact, they didn't strongly prefer either interpretation. When an equivalent sentence was presented in Spanish, most readers assumed the daughter was standing on the balcony. This is diametrically opposite to the prediction of the garden-path model.

What is most crucial for the model is the assumption that semantic factors don't influence the construction of the initial syntactic structure. Support for this prediction was reported by Ferreira and Clifton (1986). Eye movements were recorded while participants read sentences such as the following:

- The defendant examined by the lawyer turned out to be unreliable.
- The evidence examined by the lawyer turned out to be unreliable.

According to the principle of minimal attachment, readers should initially treat the verb "examined" as the main verb, and should thus experience ambiguity for both sentences. However, if readers initially make use of semantic information, they would experience ambiguity for the first sentence but not the second. The reason is that the defendant could possibly examine something, but the evidence could not. In fact, the eye-movement data suggested that readers experienced ambiguity equally for both sentences. This implies that semantic information did *not* influence the formation of the initial syntactic structure.

Trueswell, Tanenhaus, and Garnsey (1994) argued that the semantic manipulations used by Ferreira and Clifton (1986) were too weak to allow semantic information to influence the early stages of parsing. Accordingly, they used sentences with stronger semantic constraints. With their sentences, semantic information *was* used at an early stage to facilitate rapid identification of the correct syntactic structure. However, the water has become muddy again. Clifton et al. (2003) used the same sentences as Trueswell et al., but analyzed their data more thoroughly than Trueswell et al. had done. Their findings suggested that semantic information was of relatively little use in removing ambiguity.

Evaluation

The garden-path model provides a simple and coherent account of key processes involved in sentence processing. There is much evidence suggesting that readers follow the principles of late closure and minimal attachment. However, there are various limitations with the model. First, the assumption that meaning plays no part in the initial assignment of grammatical structure to a sentence seems implausible. Second, semantic information is often involved at an early stage in the construction of syntactic structure (Trueswell et al., 1994) when reading and also when listening to sentences (see Chapter 18). Third, readers sometimes don't adhere to the principle of late closure (e.g., Carreiras & Clifton, 1993).

CONSTRAINT-BASED THEORY

According to the constraint-based theory put forward by MacDonald et al. (1994), *all* relevant sources of information or constraints are available immediately to the parser. Competing analyses of the current sentence are activated at the same time, with these analyses being ranked according to the strength of their activation. The syntactic structure receiving the most support from the various constraints is highly activated, with other syntactic structures being less activated. Readers become confused when reading ambiguous sentences if the correct syntactic structure is less activated than one or more incorrect structures.

According to the theory, the following are some of the language characteristics used to resolve sentence ambiguities:

1. Grammatical knowledge constrains possible sentence interpretations.
2. Words may be less ambiguous in some ways than in others (e.g., ambiguous for tense but not for grammatical category).
3. The various interpretations permissible according to grammatical rules generally differ considerably in frequency and probability on the basis of past experience.

Findings

The study by Trueswell et al. (1994; discussed above) suggested that semantic information is used early in parsing. That is exactly as predicted by constraint-based theory. However, the findings of Clifton et al. (2003) are less consistent with the theory.

Boland and Blodgett (2001) tested predictions of constraint-based theory using noun/verb homographs (e.g., duck, train). These are words that can be used as nouns or verbs. For example, if you read a sentence starting, "She saw her duck and . . .," you wouldn't know whether "duck" was being used as a noun (". . . and chickens near the barn") or as a verb (". . . and stumble near the barn"). According to the theory, readers should initially try to form a syntactic structure in which the homograph is used as its more common part of speech. For example, "duck" is a verb more often than a noun, whereas "train" is more often a noun. As predicted, readers had greater problems in parsing when noun/verb homographs were used in their less common form.

Another prediction from constraint-based theory tested by Boland and Blodgett (2001) is that readers should use information from preceding context very early on in parsing. The context was sometimes misleading and sometimes not. Consider the following example in which the context is misleading:

As they walked around, Kate looked at all of Jimmy's pets.
She saw her duck and stumble near the barn.

As predicted theoretically, it took longer to read the second sentence when the context was misleading than when it was not. However, context influenced parsing *later* in processing than predicted by the theory. Thus, the notion that all relevant sources of information are used immediately in parsing was not correct so far as previous context was concerned.

Evaluation

It seems efficient that readers should use all the relevant information from the outset when trying to work out the syntactic structure of sentences. Much of the evidence is consistent with that notion (e.g., Trueswell et al., 1994; studies on parsing heard sentences reviewed in Chapter 19: Spivey, Tanenhaus, Eberhard, & Sedivy, 2002; Tanenhaus, Spivey-Knowton, Eberhard, & Sedivy, 1995).

One of the limitations with constraint-based theory is that it is not always correct that all relevant constraints or sources of information are used immediately (e.g., Boland & Blodgett, 2001). Another limitation is that little is said within MacDonald et al.'s (1994) theory about the detailed processes involved in generating syntactic structures for complex sentences. Finally, it is difficult to obtain data that distinguish clearly between this theory and the garden-path model: "Proponents of the garden-path model argue that the effects that are claimed to support constraint-based models arise because the second stage of parsing begins very quickly, and that many experiments that are supposed to be looking at the first stage are in fact looking at the second stage of parsing" (Harley, 2001, p. 264).

IT'S IN THE EYES

One of the major goals of research into reading is to obtain a detailed understanding of the processes involved. A good way of making progress towards this goal is by recording eye movements during reading. This approach has at least two significant strengths: (1) it provides a reasonably precise record of attention-related processes; and (2) it is unobtrusive. Indeed, the only restriction on readers whose eye movements are being recorded is that they must keep their heads fairly still.

Are there any disadvantages with relying on eye movements to identify what is happening during reading? There is one, namely that it is hard to know precisely *what* processing occurs during each fixation made by readers. In spite of that limitation, the use of eye movements during reading has proved extremely useful.

Our eyes seem to move smoothly across the page when we are reading. In fact, they actually move in rapid jerks (**saccades**), as you can see if you look closely at someone else reading. Once a saccade is initiated, its direction cannot be changed. There are fairly frequent regressions in which the eyes move backwards in the text, accounting for about 10% of all saccades. Reading saccades take 20–30 milliseconds to complete, and they are separated by fixations lasting for 200–250 milliseconds. The length of each saccade is about eight letters or spaces. Information is extracted from the text only during each fixation, and not during the intervening saccades.

Readers typically fixate about 80% of content words (nouns, verbs, and adjectives), whereas they only fixate about 20% of function words (articles, conjunctions, and pronouns). More generally, words not fixated tend to be common, short, or predictable. In contrast, words fixated for longer than average are generally rare words or words unpredictable in the sentence context. In general, words easy to process are most likely not to be fixated, whereas those especially hard to process are fixated for the longest time. Finally, there is the **spillover effect**: the fixation time on a word is longer when preceded by a rare word rather than a common word.

What kinds of effects have typically been recorded during reading? Why do they happen?

How does the reading system function to produce these effects? The most obvious model is that readers fixate on a word until they have processed it adequately, after which they immediately fixate the next word until it has been adequately processed. Alas, there are two major problems with such a model, and it cannot be regarded as satisfactory. First, it takes about 85–200 ms to execute an eye-movement program. If readers operated according to the simple model described above, they would waste time waiting for their eyes to move to the next word. Second, it is hard on the basis of the model to see how readers could skip words, because they would know nothing about the next word until they had fixated it.

E-Z READER MODEL

Thankfully, we have an eye-movement model that has overcome the problems with the simple model. This is the E-Z Reader model put forward by Reichle, Pollatsek, Fisher, and Rayner (1998) and Reichle, Rayner, and Pollatsek (2003). The title of the model is a spoof on the title of the film *Easy Rider*, but this only becomes apparent if you know that Z is pronounced "zee" in American English! According to Reichle et al. (1998, 2003), the next eye movement is programmed after only *part* of the processing of the currently fixated word has occurred. This assumption makes a lot of sense, because it greatly reduces the time between completion of processing on the current word and movement of the eyes to the next word. Any spare time is used to start processing the next word. There is typically less spare time available with rare words than with common words, and that accounts for the spillover effect described above. If the processing of the next word is completed rapidly enough (e.g., it is highly predictable in the sentence context), it is skipped.

KEY TERMS
Saccade: a fast eye movement or jump that cannot be altered after being initiated.
Spillover effect: any given word is fixated longer during reading when it is preceded by a rare word rather than a common word.

The main development of the E-Z Reader model in Reichle et al. (2003) compared to Reichle et al. (1998) is that a tentative account of the brain areas involved in reading is presented. In essence, Reichle et al. (2003) argue that several processes are applied to a fixated word in sequence, and they identify the brain areas associated with each process. According to this part of the model, reading a fixated word starts with processing of the features of the fixated word in the primary visual cortex (in the occipital area at the back of the brain) about 90 ms after word fixation. Reading a fixated word finishes with accessing its meaning using Wernicke's area in the posterior temporal lobe and various regions of associative cortex.

Findings

Some of the strongest support for the most recent version of the model (E-Z Reader 7) was reported by Reichle et al. (2003). They compared 11 models of reading in terms of whether each one could account for each of eight phenomena (e.g., frequency effects; spillover effects, word predictability effects, costs of skipping). E-Z Reader accounted for all eight phenomena, whereas eight of the other models accounted for two or fewer of the phenomena.

It is assumed within the E-Z Reader model that word frequency and word predictability are both important factors in determining how long we fixate on a word during reading. Problems with these assumptions were reported by McDonald and Shillcock (2003). Common words tended to be more predictable than rare words, making it important to disentangle the effects of word frequency and word predictability. When they did this, the effects of word frequency often disappeared. Thus, many of the apparent effects of word frequency on length of eye fixations are actually due to word predictability.

In spite of their emphasis on word frequency and word probability as factors influencing how long we fixate any given word in reading, Reichle et al. (2003) admitted that other factors are also probably of some importance. Evidence that additional factors need to be considered was reported by Juhasz and Rayner (2003). They found a significant effect of word concreteness on gaze duration in reading.

According to the E-Z Reader model, the length of fixations on individual words depends in part on the word's predictability within the sentence in which it appears. It is natural to wonder whether sentence context influences word fixations in other ways. For example, Rayner, Warren, Juhasz, and Liversedge (2004) considered the effects of plausibility. Some sentences were plausible (e.g., "John used a knife to chop the large carrots for dinner"); some sentences were implausible (e.g., "John used an axe to chop the large carrots for dinner"; and some sentences were very implausible or anomalous (e.g., "John used a pump to inflate the large carrots for dinner").

There were only modest differences in eye fixations between the plausible and implausible sentences. However, when readers were presented with very implausible sentences (i.e., the anomalous ones), there was a large, immediate increase in duration of eye fixations on the critical part of the sentence. Thus, eye fixations when reading depend in part on plausibility, especially when very implausible sentences are presented.

EVALUATION AND CHAPTER SUMMARY

The dual-route model

- The dual-route model provides a very good account of reading disorders such as surface dyslexia and phonological dyslexia.
- It has also proved useful in accounting for the naming performance and lexical-decision performance (i.e., deciding rapidly whether a letter string forms a word) of healthy individuals. More specifically, the computational model has successfully simulated 18 effects with naming or reading aloud, plus 5 effects associated with lexical decision.
- On the negative side, while the model names words and non-words very accurately, it is much less successful in accounting for naming *times*.
- The model accounts for almost 40% of variation or variance in non-word naming times, but for a very modest 4.5% of the variance in word naming times.
- Another issue is that the dual-route model can't be applied to several major languages: "The Chinese, Japanese, and Korean writing systems are structurally so different from the English writing system that a model like the [dual-route model] would simply not be applicable: for example, monosyllabic non-words cannot even be written in the Chinese script or in Japanese kanji, so the distinction between a lexical and non-lexical route for reading aloud cannot even arise" (Coltheart et al., 2001, p. 236).

Distributed connectionist approach

- Plaut et al.'s (1996) connectionist model has the advantage of being based on the assumption that reading processes are flexible and interactive. That assumption has much support.
- It is noteworthy that the latest version of the dual-route model (Coltheart et al., 2001) is significantly more flexible and interactive than earlier versions (e.g., Coltheart, Curtis, Atkins, & Haller, 1993).
- In addition, there is much evidence that word consistency is an important factor.
- Finally, the model provides an account of the reading problems of surface dyslexics and phonological dyslexics.
- On the negative side, the model is rather limited.
- For example, it has very little to say about the role of semantic processing in reading. In addition, it has only been tested with one-syllable words (as is the case with the dual-route model).
- It remains to be seen whether the model can be applied successfully to multisyllable words.
- More worryingly, the model provides somewhat sketchy accounts of the impairments suffered by surface dyslexics and by phonological dyslexics.
- With respect to phonological dyslexia, the key assumption that it is always accompanied by a phonological deficit is incorrect (e.g., Caccappolo-van Vliet et al., 2004). In my opinion, the dual-route model has shed more light on surface and phonological dyslexia than has the connectionist model of Plaut et al. (1996).

E-Z Reader model
- The E-Z Reader model is probably the most successful attempt to date to specify the major factors determining eye movements in reading.
- More specifically, the model indicates the processes determining *when* we move our eyes in reading and *where* we move them.
- It is especially impressive that the E-Z Reader model accounts for many more reading phenomena than any other model (Reichle et al., 2003).
- The attempt by Reichle et al. (2003) to identify the brain areas involved in the various reading-related processes has added significantly to the value of the model.
- What are the model's limitations?
- First, it could be argued that the model focuses excessively on explaining eye-movement data, which is not the same as providing an explanation of human reading performance. What is needed is a systematic attempt to integrate the findings from eye-movement studies more closely with general theories of reading.
- Second, and related to the first point, eye-movement data provide very detailed information about *where* the eyes are looking at any given moment. However, we also want to know *what* kinds of processing readers are engaged in during reading, and eye-movement data provide only indirectly relevant evidence.
- Third, it is assumed within the E-Z Reader model that word frequency and word predictability have *independent* effects on the length of fixation on words in text.
- However, the findings of McDonald and Shillcock (2003) suggest that the importance of word frequency in determining fixation duration is exaggerated in the model.

FURTHER READING

- Harley, T. A. (2001). *The psychology of language: From data to theory* (2nd. ed.). Hove, UK: Psychology Press. Chapters 6 and 7 of this excellent textbook provide clear accounts of the basic processes involved in reading.
- Lamberts, K., & Goldstone, R. (2004). *Handbook of cognition.* London: Sage. There are a number of chapters on language in this edited book, and the one by Pollatsek and Rayner on reading is of particular relevance to this chapter.
- Reichle, E.D., Rayner, K., & Pollatsek, A. (2003). The E-Z Reader model of eye-movement control in reading: Comparisons to other models. *Behavioral and Brain Sciences, 26,* 445–526. This article contains an updated version of an excellent theory of reading, as well as much useful discussion of major issues in reading research. It is followed by commentaries on the model by the authors of most of the competing models.

- Van Gompel, R.P.G., Pickering, M.J., & Traxler, M.J. (2001). Reanalysis in sentence processing: Evidence against current constraint-based and two-stage models. *Journal of Memory and Language*, *45*, 225–258. If you are feeling adventurous, this article points the way to a new theoretical approach to parsing based on elements of the garden-path and constraint-based approaches discussed in the chapter.

CHAPTER 18

CONTENTS

Introduction	253
What difference does context make?	255
TRACE model	256
Cohort model	258
Disorders of speech perception	261
Parsing	263
Understanding the message	265
Evaluation and chapter summary	266
Further reading	269

What are you saying?

INTRODUCTION

Most of us are very good at understanding what other people are saying to us even when they speak in a strange dialect and/or ungrammatically. In our everyday lives we take our ability to understand the speech of others for granted. Indeed, in view of the enormous experience we have all had in using the English language and in listening to other people, speech perception seems very easy and straightforward.

Can you think of any reasons why speech perception might actually be much more complex than it appears? Think about the problems you have experienced trying to understand foreigners speaking in a language you studied for several years at school. If your experience is anything like mine, what you hear is someone who appears to be speaking incredibly rapidly without any pauses for breath. This illustrates two of the problems listeners have to contend with all the time. First, language is typically spoken at a rate of about 10 **phonemes** (basic speech sounds conveying meaning) per second, so we have to process spoken language very rapidly. Second, there is the **segmentation problem**, the difficulty of separating out or distinguishing words from the pattern of speech sounds. This problem occurs because speech typically consists of a continuously changing pattern of sound with few periods of silence. This makes it hard to know when one word ends and the next begins.

How do we cope with the segmentation problem? First, we use our knowledge of what is possible and impossible in the English language. For example, a stretch of speech lacking a vowel cannot form a word. Evidence that we use this knowledge was reported by Norris, McQueen, Cutler, and Butterfield (1997). Listeners found it fairly easy to detect the word "apple" in "vuffapple," because "vuff" could conceivably be an English word. In contrast, listeners found it hard to identify the word "apple" in "fapple," because the [f] couldn't possibly be an English word.

Second, there is stress. In the English language, the initial **syllable** (a rhythmic unit of speech) of most content words (e.g., nouns, verbs) is stressed. If listeners assume the first syllable of words they hear will be stressed, they should find it difficult to identify strings of words in which the stress is *not* on the first syllable. When such strings of words (e.g., "conduct ascents uphill") were presented very faintly, they were often misheard (Cutler & Butterfield, 1992). However, we mustn't exaggerate the importance

When listening to normal speech, how do we cope with variations in speed and people's accents?

of stress as a cue. Stress is very useful as a cue to identifying word boundaries when the speech signal is impoverished by superimposed noise, but is of little value when the speech signal is intact (Mattys, 2004).

So far we have discussed the problems created by the speed at which language is spoken and by the almost continuous nature of speech. Two other problems deserve mentioning at this point. First, there is the problem of **co-articulation**. This refers to the fact that the way in which a speaker produces a given phoneme depends in part on the phonemes preceding and following it. In other words, the pronunciation of any phoneme is not invariant, and the listener has to adjust to variations in pronunciation. Second, as mentioned at the outset, listeners have to cope with large individual differences between speakers. Sussman, Hoemeke, and Ahmed (1993) found considerable differences among speakers saying the same short words starting with a consonant. How do we deal with such differences? In essence, each speaker has his or her own characteristic speech pattern, and listeners learn to use this information to identify what the speaker is saying.

Our ability to understand speech obviously depends very heavily on the sound signal produced by the speaker. However, deaf people make extensive use of visual information in the form of lip-reading to assist them in understanding speech. What is less well known is that people whose hearing is entirely intact also use lip-reading. Clear evidence of this was reported by McGurk and MacDonald (1976). They prepared a videotape of someone saying "ba" repeatedly. The sound channel then changed so there was a voice saying "ga" in synchronization with lip movements still indicating "ba." Listeners reported hearing "da," which is a blending of the visual and auditory information. This combining of visual and auditory information when the two sources of information are in conflict is known as the **McGurk effect**. This effect doesn't *always* occur when the visual and auditory signals are discrepant.

We will conclude this section by considering an unresolved mystery in research on speech perception—what is the basic unit (or building block) in speech perception? The two main contenders are the phoneme and the syllable. However, as Goldinger and Azuma (2003, p. 307) pointed out, "30 years of speech-unit research has generated little apparent progress. If the goal was to decide a 'winner', the enterprise has clearly failed: despite dozens of studies, the candidate list has actually grown."

Goldinger and Azuma (2003) argued that there is no basic unit of speech perception. Instead, the perceptual unit varies flexibly depending on the precise circumstances. They presented listeners with lists of two-syllable non-words and asked them to decide whether each non-word contained a target. The target was sometimes a phoneme and sometimes a syllable. The volunteers who recorded the lists of non-words were told either that phonemes are the basic units of speech perception or that syllables are the basic units. These instructions influenced the way they read the non-words, and this in turn affected the listeners' performance. Listeners detected phoneme targets faster than syllable targets when the speaker believed phonemes are the fundamental units in speech perception. In contrast, they detected syllable targets faster than phoneme targets when the speaker believed syllables are the basic perceptual units. Thus, either phonemes or syllables can form the basic perceptual units in speech perception.

KEY TERMS

Co-articulation: the finding that the production of a phoneme in speech is influenced (and distorted) by the production of the previous sound and preparations for the next sound.

McGurk effect: the phoneme perceived in speech is influenced by visual and acoustic information when the two are in conflict.

In what follows, we will be focusing mainly on the processes involved in identifying words and sentences in spoken language. Issues concerning listeners' overall comprehension or understanding of what a speaker is saying are considered in Chapter 19.

WHAT DIFFERENCE DOES CONTEXT MAKE?

When listeners are trying to identify the sounds or words they are hearing, they often make use of additional contextual information to assist them in that task. For example, consider the following study by Warren and Warren (1970). Listeners heard a sentence in which a small portion had been removed and replaced with a meaningless sound. The sentences used were as follows (the asterisk indicates a deleted portion of the sentence):

- It was found that the *eel was on the axle.
- It was found that the *eel was on the shoe.
- It was found that the *eel was on the table.
- It was found that the *eel was on the orange.

Listeners' perception of the crucial element in the sentence (i.e., "*eel") was influenced by sentence context. Those listening to the first sentence heard "wheel," those listening to the second sentence heard "heel," and those exposed to the third and fourth sentences heard "meal" and "peel," respectively. The auditory stimulus (i.e., "*eel") was always the same, so *all* that differed was the contextual information. This phenomenon is known as the **phonemic restoration effect**.

What causes the phonemic restoration effect? According to Samuel (1997), there are two main possibilities:

1. Sentence context has a *direct* effect on speech processing (i.e., the missing phoneme is processed almost as if it were present).
2. Sentence context has an *indirect* effect involving guessing the identity of the missing phoneme *after* basic speech processing has occurred.

Most of the evidence (e.g., Samuel, 1981, 1987) is inconsistent with the first possibility, and so supports the second one. Samuel either added noise to the crucial phoneme or replaced the missing phoneme with noise. If listeners process the missing phoneme as usual, they would have heard the crucial phoneme plus noise in both conditions. As a result, they would have been unable to tell the difference between the two conditions. In fact, the listeners could readily distinguish between the conditions. This suggests that sentence context affects only post-perceptual processing in line with the second possibility above.

Similar findings were reported by Connine (1990), who found the identification of an ambiguous phoneme was influenced by the meaning of the sentence in which it was presented. This effect of sentence context was due to processes occurring *after* the completion of perceptual processing of the ambiguous phoneme but *before* responding.

WORD CONTEXT

We have seen that the effects of sentence context on missing or ambiguous phonemes don't occur during their initial processing but instead depend on post-perceptual processes. However, the identification of ambiguous sounds involves perceptual processes when we are dealing with *word* context rather than *sentence* context. Consider, for example, an important study by Ganong (1980). Listeners were presented with various sounds ranging between a word (e.g., "dash") and a non-word (e.g., "tash"). He obtained a contextual effect. An ambiguous initial sound was more likely to be assigned to a given phoneme category if it produced a word than when it didn't. This phenomenon is known as the **lexical identification shift**.

Pitt (1995) argued that the lexical identification shift is due to perceptual processes rather than to post-perceptual processes occurring after the perceptual processes are complete. Post-perceptual processes can be influenced by providing rewards for correct responses and penalties for incorrect ones. Pitt found that rewards and penalties had *no* effect on the lexical identification shift, suggesting it depends on perceptual processes.

TRACE MODEL

One of the most influential theoretical approaches to speech perception is the TRACE model proposed by McClelland and Elman (1986). Its key assumption is that bottom-up processes triggered by the speech input and top-down processes based on expectations interact flexibly in spoken word recognition. It is a matter of, "All hands to the pump," with *all* sources of information being used at the same time to assist in the task of identifying spoken words.

We will briefly mention the other main assumptions of the TRACE model before considering the relevant evidence. First, processing units or nodes exist at three different levels:

1. sound features (e.g., voicing—the larynx vibrates for voiced but not for voiceless phonemes)
2. phonemes (basic speech sounds conveying meaning)
3. words.

Second, feature nodes are connected to phoneme nodes, and phoneme nodes are connected to word nodes. Third, connections between levels operate in both directions. All of these connections are facilitatory and produce increased activation. Fourth, the word recognized or identified by the listener is the one having the highest level of activation.

Bottom-up processing within the model occurs as activation proceeds from the feature level up to the phoneme level, and then up to the word level. In contrast, top-down processing occurs as activation proceeds from the word level down to the phoneme level, and from the phoneme level down to the feature level.

FINDINGS

The TRACE model has several successes to its credit. First, it provides a reasonable explanation of the lexical identification shift (Ganong, 1980) discussed earlier in the chapter. In this effect, there is a bias towards perceiving an ambiguous sound so as to form a word. According to the TRACE model, top-down activation from the word level is responsible for this effect.

Second, Norris, McQueen, and Cutler (2003) obtained convincing evidence that phoneme identification can be directly influenced by top-down processing. Listeners were initially presented with words ending in the phoneme /f/ or /s/. For different groups, an ambiguous phoneme equally similar to /f/ and /s/ replaced either the final /f/ or /s/ in these words. After that, listeners categorized phonemes presented *on their own* as either /f/ or /s/. Listeners who had heard the ambiguous phoneme in the context of /s/-ending words strongly favored the /s/ categorization. In contrast, those who had heard the same phoneme in the context of /f/-ending words favored the /f/ categorization. Thus, top-down learning at the word level affected phoneme categorization as predicted by the TRACE model.

Third, Cutler, Mehler, Norris, and Segui (1987) used a phoneme monitoring task in which listeners had to detect a target phoneme. There was a word superiority effect in which phonemes were detected faster when presented in words rather than in non-words. According to the TRACE model, this occurred because there is top-down activation from the word level to the phoneme level.

The most serious limitation with the TRACE model is that it *exaggerates* the influence of top-down processes on spoken word recognition. Speech processing can easily be impaired if there is too much emphasis on top-down processing and not enough on bottom-up processing based on information in the acoustic signal. According to Norris, McQueen, and Cutler (2000), "Models [such as TRACE] run the risk of hallucinating. Particularly when the input is degraded, the information in the speech input will tend to be discarded and phonemic decisions may then be based mainly on lexical [word] knowledge."

Frauenfelder, Segui, and Dijkstra (1990) showed that top-down effects can be less important than assumed within the TRACE model. Listeners detected a given phoneme, and the key condition was one in which a non-word was presented that closely resembled an actual French one (e.g., "vocabutaire" instead of "vocabulaire"). According to the model, top-down effects from the word node corresponding to "vocabulaire" should have inhibited the task of identifying the "t" in "vocabutaire." In fact, however, they did not.

More evidence that the model predicts greater top-down effects than are actually found was reported by McQueen (1991). Listeners were presented with ambiguous phonemes at the end of auditory stimuli, and asked to categorize them. Each ambiguous phoneme could be perceived as completing either a word or a non-word. According to the TRACE model, top-down effects from the word level should have produced a tendency to perceive the phonemes as completing words. This prediction was confirmed when the stimulus was degraded. However, there was no support for the prediction when the stimulus was not degraded.

Finally, we consider a study by Davis, Marslen-Wilson, and Gaskell (2002). They challenged the assumption of the TRACE model that recognizing a spoken word is based on identifying the *phonemes* of which it is formed. Listeners heard only the first syllable of a word. They decided whether this was the *only* syllable of a short word (e.g., "cap") or the first syllable of a longer word (e.g., "captain"). The two words between which listeners had to choose were cunningly selected so that the first phoneme was the same for both words. Since listeners couldn't use phonemic information to make the correct decision, the prediction from the TRACE model is that the task should have been very difficult. In fact, performance was good. Listeners used non-phonemic information ignored by the TRACE model (e.g., small differences in syllable duration) to discriminate between short and longer words (see Figure 18.1).

Figure 18.1 Percentage of decisions that the initial syllable of short and long words belonged to short and long words. Data from Davis et al. (2002).

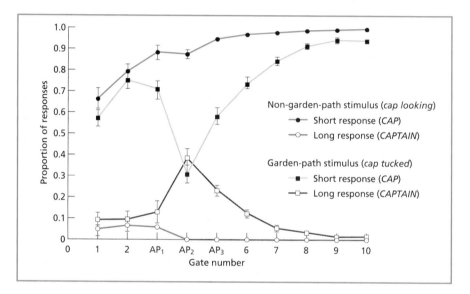

In sum, the TRACE model has various strengths. For example, the basic assumption that spoken word recognition depends on both bottom-up and top-down processes is consistent with most of the evidence. In addition, the TRACE model provides a reasonable account of several phenomena associated with spoken word recognition. These phenomena include the lexical identification shift, the word superiority effect, and top-down effects of learning on phoneme categorization.

The TRACE model also has various limitations. The most serious limitation is that the impact of top-down processes on spoken word recognition is generally significantly less than is assumed by the model. Another limitation is that the model seems to exaggerate the role of phonemic information in determining spoken word recognition (Davis et al., 2002).

COHORT MODEL

Another very influential theoretical approach to speech perception is the cohort model originally put forward by Marslen-Wilson and Tyler (1980) and based on the following four assumptions:

1. Early in the auditory presentation of a word, all the words conforming to the sound sequence to that point become active; this set of words is known as the "word-initial cohort."
2. Words belonging to this word-initial cohort are subsequently eliminated if they don't match additional information from the word being presented, or if they are inconsistent with the semantic or other context.
3. Various knowledge sources (e.g., lexical, syntactic, semantic) are processed in parallel (at the same time); these knowledge sources interact and combine with each other.
4. Processing of the presented word continues up until the moment at which information from the word itself and contextual information have eliminated all but one of the words in the word-initial cohort. This is the "recognition point" or "uniqueness point."

Describe the Trace and Cohort models of speech perception. Which does a better job of describing the process of everyday speech perception?

FINDINGS

Support for the original version of the cohort model was reported by Marslen-Wilson and Tyler (1980). Listeners had to detect specified targets (a given word, a member of a given category, a word rhyming with a given word) presented within spoken sentences. The sentences were normal (providing useful semantic and syntactic context), syntactic (providing useful grammatical information only), or random (unrelated words lacking any useful context). Listeners used the contextual information available to reduce the time taken to detect targets, often identifying them before the entire word had been presented (see Figure 18.2).

O'Rourke and Holcomb (2002) tested the prediction that a spoken word is identified when the point is reached (the recognition or uniqueness point) at which only *one* word is consistent with the acoustic signal. Listeners heard words and non-words, and decided whether each one was a word. The words were selected so that some had an early recognition point whereas others had a late recognition point. As predicted, listeners worked out faster that a word had been presented when its recognition point was early. In addition, there

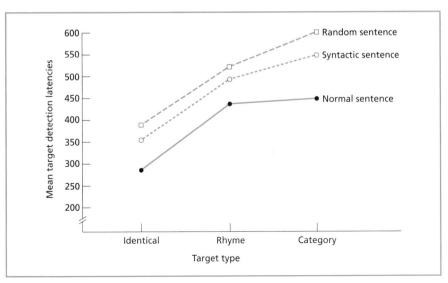

Figure 18.2 Detection times for word targets presented in sentences. Adapted from Marslen-Wilson and Tyler (1980).

was evidence that listeners realized that a word had been presented shortly after its uniqueness point had been reached.

In the original cohort model, considerable importance was attached to the processing of the *initial* part of a word. Indeed, it was assumed that a spoken word would generally not be recognized if its initial phoneme was unclear or ambiguous. However, this assumption was too strong. Accordingly, Marslen-Wilson (1990) revised the cohort model so the word-initial cohort can contain words having *similar* initial phonemes to the presented word, rather than being limited to words having exactly the same initial phoneme. The evidence supports the revised version. For example, Allopenna, Magnuson, and Tanenhaus (1998) found a tendency for listeners to activate words rhyming with the auditory input (e.g., "beaker" activated "speaker"). Thus, some words *not* sharing an initial phoneme with the auditory input are nevertheless included in the word cohort.

According to the original version of the cohort model, context influences word recognition very early in processing. In contrast, the effects of context on word recognition are much more limited in the revised version, occurring only at a fairly late stage of processing. Some of the evidence discussed earlier in the chapter is more consistent with the assumptions of the revised version of the model. For example, the effects of sentence context on the phonemic restoration effect occur late in processing (e.g., Samuel, 1981, 1987). In similar fashion, sentence context influences the identification of ambiguous phonemes late in processing (Connine, 1990).

In spite of the above findings, sentence context sometimes affects the early stages of word processing. Van Petten, Coulson, Rubin, Plante, and Parks (1999) used sentence contexts allowing listeners to predict the final word before it was presented. For example, guess what the last word is going to be in this sentence used in their study: "Sir Lancelot spared the man's life when he begged for _____." It was "mercy" when the last word was *congruent* with the sentence context, whereas it was "mermaid" when the last was *incongruent* with the context. The event-related potentials (ERPs; see Glossary) to congruent and incongruent words differed 200 ms *before* the recognition or uniqueness point was reached. This suggests that context can influence spoken word processing earlier than expected within the revised version of the cohort model.

In sum, the cohort model (especially the revised version) provides a more adequate account of spoken word recognition than does the TRACE model. The revised version correctly predicts that most effects of context on spoken word recognition will occur fairly late in processing, whereas it was assumed that such effects would occur early in processing in the original version. The revised version of the model is also an improvement on the original version in that it correctly predicts that misidentification of the initial phoneme of a word often nevertheless leads to accurate word identification. Both versions of the cohort model are limited in that they do not attempt to provide a full account of all the processes involved in spoken word recognition. For example, little is said about how we manage to identify the starting point of each word we hear on the basis of the acoustic signal.

DISORDERS OF SPEECH PERCEPTION

Consider the task of repeating a spoken word immediately after hearing it. In spite of the apparent simplicity of this task, many brain-damaged patients who are not deaf experience difficulties with it. As we will see, much has been learned about speech perception from studies on brain-damaged patients. The fact that they show *different* patterns of impairment has proved useful in identifying the processes involved in the task of repeating spoken words. It has also proved useful in deciding whether repeating familiar words involves the same processes as repeating unfamiliar words, and whether spoken words can be repeated without accessing their meaning.

Figure 18.3 provides a framework for making sense of the findings from brain-damaged patients. The most striking feature of this framework is the notion that saying a spoken word can be achieved using *three* different routes. This is probably two more than most people would have guessed. In essence, Routes 1 and 2 are designed to be used with familiar words, whereas Route 3 is for use with unfamiliar words. When Route 1 is used, a heard word activates relevant stored information about it including its meaning and its spoken form. Route 2 closely resembles Route 1 except that information about the meaning of heard words is *not* accessed. As a result, someone using Route 2 can say familiar words accurately, but doesn't have access to their meaning. Finally, Route 3 involves using rules about the conversion of the acoustic information contained in heard words into the appropriate spoken

Do we have different routes for processing speech?

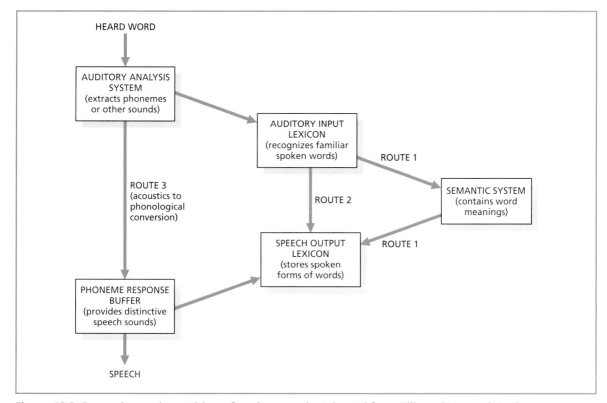

Figure 18.3 Processing and repetition of spoken words. Adapted from Ellis and Young (1988).

forms of those words. We don't know in detail how this happens, but it is assumed that such conversion processes must be involved when listeners repeat back unfamiliar words and non-words.

FINDINGS

What would happen if someone had damage *only* to the auditory analysis system (used to extract phonemes or other sounds from the speech wave)? Such a patient would have a deficit in phoneme processing. As a result, he or she would have impaired speech perception for words and non-words, especially those containing phonemes hard to discriminate. However, this patient should have normal perception of non-verbal environmental sounds (e.g., coughs, whistles) not containing phonemes, and his or her hearing would be unimpaired. In addition, the patient's other language abilities (e.g., speech production, reading) would be unaffected.

Patients apparently conforming to the pattern described above are said to suffer from **pure word deafness** (see Poeppel, 2001, for a review). However, there is increasing evidence that such patients do *not* have normal perception of non-speech sounds. Pinard, Chertkow, Black, and Peretz (2002) reviewed 63 cases of pure word deafness, and found normal non-verbal processing in only 5 of them. In every other case, there were additional impairments of music perception and/or environmental sounds. As Pinard et al. (2002, p. 51) concluded, "'Apparent' pure word impairment is usually an epiphenomenon [by-product] arising from the limited environmental stimuli hitherto available for testing."

If the model shown in Figure 18.3 is broadly correct, there should be brain-damaged patients who make use of only one or two routes when repeating heard words. Various patients seem to fit the bill. Patients who can use Routes 1 and 2 but not Route 3 would be able to perceive and to understand spoken familiar words, but would be impaired at perceiving and repeating unfamiliar words and non-words. This pattern is found in patients with **auditory phonological agnosia**. Such a patient was studied by Beauvois, Dérouesné, and Bastard (1980). Their patient, JL, had almost perfect repetition and writing to dictation of spoken familiar words, but his repetition and writing of non-words was very poor. He had an intact ability to distinguish between words and non-words, indicating there were no problems with access to the input lexicon. Similar findings were reported by McCarthy and Warrington (1984) whose patient, ORF, repeated words much more accurately than non-words (85% vs. 39%, respectively), indicating that Route 3 was severely impaired.

Patients who can only use Route 2 would be able to repeat familiar words but would often not understand their meaning. In addition, they should have problems in saying unfamiliar words and non-words, because non-words cannot be processed through Route 2. Finally, since such patients would use the input lexicon, they should be able to distinguish between words and non-words. Patients with **word meaning deafness** fit the above description. One of the clearest cases of word meaning deafness was Dr O, who was studied by Franklin, Turner, Ralph, Morris, and Bailey (1996). His ability to repeat words was dramatically better than his ability to repeat non-words, 80% vs. 7%, respectively. Dr O was very good at distinguishing between words and non-words presented auditorily, making the correct decision on 94% of trials. However, his ability to *understand* the meaning of words (especially abstract ones) was impaired. Another patient with word meaning deafness (KW) spelled 60% of auditorily presented words correctly compared to only 35% of non-words. He showed poor comprehension of words, but was 89% accurate in distinguishing between auditorily presented words and non-words.

In sum, there is reasonable evidence from brain-damaged patients to support the three-route model of the processing and repetition of spoken words. Much of this evidence comes from patients having auditory phonological agnosia or word meaning deafness. It would be very useful in future research to find brain-damaged patients who mainly use Route 3, which involves using rules to convert the acoustic information in heard words into the correct spoken form.

PARSING

So far we have focused mainly on the processes involved in identifying individual words in speech perception. However, there is obviously much more than that to speech perception. For example, it is important to identify the *How do we parse* processes involved in assigning a syntactical or grammatical structure to sen- *spoken language?* tences that are read. This is known as parsing. The processes involved in parsing while reading were discussed in Chapter 17. Many of the processes involved in parsing spoken language are the same as those involved in reading. However, it is worth considering some of the relevant research evidence based specifically on listening to speech.

Listeners make use of prosodic cues when trying to work out the grammatical structure of spoken sentences. These prosodic cues include stress, intonation, and so on (discussed further in Chapter 20). For example, in the ambiguous sentence, "The old men and women sat on the bench," the women may or may not be old. If the women are not old, then the spoken duration of the word "men" will be relatively long, and the stressed syllable in "women" will have a steep rise in pitch contour. Neither of these prosodic features will be present if the sentence means the women are old.

How rapidly is prosodic information used by listeners? Snedeker and Trueswell (2003) addressed this question by recording listeners' eye movements as they listened to ambiguous sentences. It may seem odd to record eye movements when sentences are presented auditorily. However, it was done to find out when listeners focused attention on the relevant objects mentioned in the sentences. Snedeker and Trueswell found that listeners used information from prosodic cues at a very early stage. Indeed, listeners' interpretation of ambiguous sentences was influenced by prosodic cues even *before* the start of the ambiguous phrase. Thus, prosodic cues are used to predict information to be presented later in the sentence.

One of the key theoretical issues is whether semantic (meaning) information is used at an early stage to influence the formation of the initial syntactic structure. According to the garden-path model (Frazier & Rayner, 1982), meaning plays no role in the selection of the initial syntactic structure. In contrast, it is assumed within the constraint-based theory (MacDonald et al., 1994) that all relevant kinds of information (including semantic) are used to construct the initial syntactic structure. Below we consider some of the evidence.

FINDINGS

The two theories discussed above make different predictions concerning the impact of prior context on the initial parsing of an ambiguous sentence. According to the garden-path model, prior context should *not* influence initial parsing. In contrast, prior context should affect initial parsing according to the constraint-based theory.

The above issue was addressed by Tanenhaus et al. (1995). They presented participants auditorily with the ambiguous sentence, "Put the apple on the towel in the box." Eye movements were recorded to assess how the sentence was interpreted. According to the garden-path model, "on the towel" should initially be understood as the place where the apple should be put. The reason is that that is the simplest syntactic structure. That is what Tanenaus et al. found when the context failed to remove the ambiguity. However, the findings were different when the visual context consisted of two apples, one on a towel and the other on a napkin. With that context, participants rapidly interpreted "on the towel" as a way of identifying which apple was to be moved. As a result, they didn't make the mistake of focusing on the towel presented on its own.

Spivey et al. (2002) carried out a similar experiment to that of Tanenhaus et al. (1995). The main difference was that they used pre-recorded digitized speech to prevent speech intonation from influencing participants' interpretations. Context had a large effect on eye movements (see Figure 18.4). There were far fewer eye movements to the incorrect object (e.g., towel on its own) when the context disambiguated ambiguous sentences than when it did not. Indeed, the pattern of eye movements was very similar for ambiguous sentences and for ambiguous sentences with a disambiguating context.

In sum, the studies by Tanenhaus et al. (1995) and Spivey et al. (2002) indicated that the meaning contained in a prior contextual sentence is used at

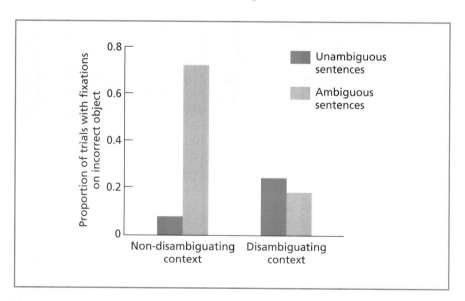

Figure 18.4 Proportion of trials with eye fixations on the incorrect object as a function of sentence type (unambiguous vs. ambiguous) and context (non-disambiguating vs. disambiguating). Based on data in Spivy et al. (2002).

an early stage of parsing. These findings are much more consistent with constraint-based theory than with the garden-path model.

UNDERSTANDING THE MESSAGE

Even when listeners identify every word the speaker is saying, they often fail to understand fully what he or she is trying to say. What is important here is the **common ground**, which is the shared knowledge and beliefs between speaker and listeners (see Chapter 19). Consider what happens when you overhear a conversation on a bus or train. You probably find it very hard to understand what is being said because you lack the common ground shared by those involved in the conversation.

In view of its importance, we might well assume that listeners strive to work out the common ground existing between them and the speaker. However, Keysar (e.g., Keysar, Barr, Balin, & Brauner, 2000) argued this can be very effortful. Accordingly, listeners often use a rapid and non-effortful **egocentric heuristic**. This involves them interpreting what is said only in the light of their own knowledge rather than shared knowledge. Information about common ground is calculated more slowly, and can be used to correct any misunderstandings resulting from use of the egocentric heuristic.

FINDINGS

Keysar et al. (2000) used a situation in which a speaker and a listener were on opposite sides of a vertical array containing 16 slots arranged in a 4×4 pattern. Some slots contained objects (e.g., candles, toy cars), and the listener's task was to obey the speaker's instructions to move one object. Some slots were blocked so the listener could see the objects in them but the speaker could not. For example, in one display, the listener could see three candles of different sizes, but the speaker could see only two, with the smallest candle blocked from view. Note that the listener could see which slots were blocked, so he or she could work out what the speaker could and couldn't see.

What happened when the speaker said, "Now put the small candle above it"? If the listener used only common ground information, he or she would move the smaller of the two candles that the speaker could see. However, if the listener used the egocentric heuristic, he or she might initially have considered the candle the speaker couldn't see. The initial eye movements of listeners were often directed to the object only they could see, thus ignoring the common ground. In addition, listeners reached for that object on 20% of trials, and actually picked it up on 75% of those trials.

Barr and Keysar (2002) carried out a two-phase experiment. In the first phase, listeners were presented with two pictures on each trial (e.g., car and flower), the speaker used a *specific* term to refer to one of them (e.g., sports car, carnation), and the listener rapidly selected the appropriate picture. In the second phase, the task was the same. However, the speaker (same as or different from the speaker in phase one) used *general* terms (e.g., car) to describe the picture.

KEY TERMS

Common ground: the mutual knowledge and beliefs shared by a speaker and a listener.

Egocentric heuristic: a comprehension strategy in which listeners interpret what they hear based on their own knowledge rather than on knowledge they share with the speaker.

How much of a speaker's meaning do we interpret using our own knowledge?

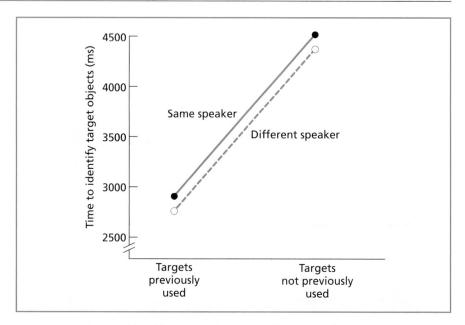

Figure 18.5 Time to identify target objects as a function of whether the speaker is the same as earlier in the experiment or different and whether or not the targets have been used previously. Data from Barr and Keysar (2002).

If common ground or mutual knowledge is of crucial importance, the participants should have been slowed down when the speaker was the same throughout. This is because they would have expected the speaker to continue to use specific terms. However, there should have been no slowing down with a different speaker, because no common ground had been established previously. In fact, participants' performance was comparable in the same speaker and different speaker conditions (see Figure 18.5). Thus, listeners relied on the egocentric heuristic rather than the common ground.

Hanna, Tanenhaus, and Trueswell (2003) argued that listeners are most likely to take account of the common ground when it is salient or prominent. For example, listeners in the study by Keysar et al. (2000) made limited use of the common ground because it is so unusual for objects between speaker and listener to differ in their perceptual accessibility. Hanna et al. used a situation similar to that of Keysar et al. (200). They found that information about the common ground was used almost immediately provided it was sufficiently salient or conspicuous.

EVALUATION AND CHAPTER SUMMARY

What difference does context make?
- Word and sentence context both influence speech perception but do so in different ways.
- Word context has a *direct* effect on perceptual processes, whereas sentence context has an *indirect* effect operating only on post-perceptual processes.

- This makes sense given that it is more complex and time-consuming to use information from the sentence context than from within the word itself.

TRACE model
- The general assumption within the TRACE model that bottom-up and top-down processes both contribute to spoken word recognition is correct.
- The model has proved its value by providing reasonable explanations of various findings, including the lexical identification shift, top-down effects of learning on phoneme categorization, and the word superiority effect.
- On the negative side, the model possesses several limitations. First, it exaggerates the importance of top-down effects (e.g., Frauenfelder et al., 1990; McQueen, 1991).
- Second, the findings of Davis et al. (2002) indicate that spoken word recognition involves non-phonemic information in addition to the phonemic information emphasized in the model.
- Third, tests of the model have relied heavily on computer simulations involving a small number of one-syllable words. It is unclear how well the model would perform if applied to the dramatically larger vocabularies of most people.

Cohort model
- The revised version of the cohort model is an improvement over the original version.
- One advantage is that it predicts accurately that most contextual effects on spoken word recognition occur relatively late in processing.
- In contrast, it was assumed that such effects occur early in processing in the original version.
- In addition, there is more scope for correcting errors (e.g., misidentification of the initial phoneme) in the revised version.
- The reason is that words are less likely to be eliminated from the cohort at an early stage in the revised model. This is in line with the available evidence (e.g., Allopenna et al., 1998).
- The assumptions of the revised cohort model are more consistent with the available evidence than are those of the TRACE model with its emphasis on extensive interactive processing.
- As with any theoretical approach, the revised cohort model has limitations.
- The revised model is more realistic than the original version, but some of its predictions are less precise.
- In addition, the identification of the starting point of each spoken word is very important within the model, because that triggers processing specific to that word.
- However, the task of identifying a word's starting point from the acoustic signal is complex (remember our earlier discussion of the segmentation problem), and the model doesn't make it clear how it is accomplished.

Disorders of speech perception
- The available evidence from brain-damaged patients provides some support for the three-route model of the processing and repetition of spoken words.
- More specifically, patients with auditory phonological agnosia use mainly Routes 1 and 2, and those with word meaning deafness use mainly Route 2.
- There would be more support for the model if patients could be found who used mainly Route 3, but no clear cases have been reported in the literature. As a result, the three-route model remains somewhat conjectural.
- It is also a matter for concern that it has proved very difficult to find patients with damage only to the auditory analysis system.
- It has been claimed that patients with pure word deafness fit the bill. However, closer examination indicates that nearly all of them have additional problems in perceiving non-speech sounds. This indicates that the damage isn't limited to the auditory analysis system.

Parsing
- Listeners make use of prosodic cues when parsing spoken sentences, and seem to do this early in processing.
- Most of the evidence indicates that semantic information is used early in the construction of syntactic structure as predicted by the constraint-based theory.
- As Pickering (1999, p. 140) argued, "Semantic factors can have very rapid effects on ambiguity resolution. If a restricted account [e.g., garden-path model] is correct, then the initial stage that ignores these factors must be very brief indeed."

Understanding the message
- Listeners sometimes use the egocentric heuristic even though it can lead to error. As Keysar et al. (2000, p. 37) pointed out, "The typical benefit of egocentric interpretation outweighs the typical cost of making an error ... [Listeners] use a strategy that is relatively effective though prone to errors, in order to accommodate a limited mental capacity."
- This somewhat error-prone approach works well, because common ground or mutual knowledge can be used to correct errors.
- Keysar has used rather artificial situations. As a result, it is not altogether clear that the egocentric heuristic is generally used in everyday life.
- For example, we may make more use of the common ground (and less of the egocentric heuristic) when listening to someone with whose beliefs we are very familiar (e.g., a good friend) than to a stranger in the laboratory.
- In addition, information about the common ground is most likely to be used when it is salient or prominent (Hanna et al., 2003).

FURTHER READING

- Cutler, A., & Clifton, C. (1999). Comprehending spoken language: A blueprint of the listener. In C.M. Brown & P. Hagoort (Eds.), *The neurocognition of language.* Oxford: Oxford University Press. This chapter provides a very informative account of the processes involved in speech perception.
- Diehl, R.L., Lotto, A.J., & Holt, L.L. (2004). Speech perception. *Annual Review of Psychology*, *55*, 149–179. The authors evaluate major theoretical perspectives designed to account for key phenomena in speech perception.
- Harley, T.A. (2001). *The psychology of language: From data to theory* (2nd ed.). Hove, UK: Psychology Press. Speech perception is discussed in detail in Chapter 8 of this excellent textbook.
- Jay, T.B. (2003). *The psychology of language*. Upper Saddle River, NJ: Prentice Hall. This textbook has good basic coverage of theory and research on speech perception.
- McQueen, J.M. (2004). Speech perception. In K. Lamberts & R. Goldstone (2004). *The Handbook of cognition*. London: Sage. This chapter provides good coverage of theory and research on speech perception.

CHAPTER 19

CONTENTS

Introduction	271
Schemas	275
Pragmatics	279
Construction–integration model	281
Evaluation and chapter summary	284
Further reading	287

What does this mean?

INTRODUCTION

We spend most of our time trying to understand language. We listen to what our friends and acquaintances have to say, we read magazines, newspapers, and books, we see movies at the movie theater, we watch television, and we track down information on the internet. As with some of our other language skills (e.g., listening, speaking), reading often seems an easy and fairly automatic process—but perhaps not when we are grappling with complex material such as that between the covers of some textbooks in psychology!

If our normal reading rate is leisurely and undemanding of processing resources, presumably we could increase that rate dramatically if we used all our processing resources and operated with maximal efficiency. Precisely that has been argued by many psychologists and others keen to sell people their speedreading courses. **Speedreading** involves increasing your reading speed from about 300 words per minute to 2000 words or more per minute. People on speedreading courses zigzag their finger rapidly down through each page of text to increase the speed of visual processing. It is claimed this leads readers to take in more information per eye fixation and to eliminate inner speech (muttering what we are reading to ourselves). If you use the internet, you may well have found yourself speedreading as you search for interesting information.

How effective is speedreading? Sadly, the answer is, "Not very." The main problems with speedreading were discussed by Rayner and Pollatsek (1989). They pointed out that performance after a speedreading course is generally measured by the Reading Efficiency Index: reading rate in words per minute × proportion correct on a comprehension test. If someone after a speedreading course reads at 3000 words per minute and has a comprehension score of 60% they would have a Reading Efficiency Index of 1800 words per minute. In contrast, suppose someone who hasn't taken the course and reads at the normal 300 words per minute scores 100% on the Reading Efficiency Index. Even though their comprehension is excellent (perfect performance on the test), they have a Reading Efficiency Index of only 300! Even more worryingly, someone who hasn't even read the text might score, say, 50% on the comprehension test on the basis of their knowledge. If that person then "reads" the text at the rate of 6000 words per minute while understanding absolutely nothing, they would have a Reading Efficiency Index of 3000! The take-home message is that we need to assess how much comprehension has *increased* as a result of reading the text, but this is rarely done.

KEY TERM
Speedreading: a technique for reading that is about seven times faster than normal reading but allegedly results in no loss of understanding.

Is it possible to increase the rate at which you read?

Clarification of the limitations of speedreading was reported by Just, Carpenter, and Masson (1982). They found that speedreaders performed as well as normal readers when tested on questions about the gist of the passage. However, they performed much worse than normal readers when asked about details in the text. More specifically, speedreaders couldn't answer detailed questions about the text unless they had fixated on the region of the text containing the answer. This finding (and much other evidence) suggests that speedreaders can't obtain more information per eye fixation simply by reading very rapidly.

There is one positive message from research on speedreading. Speedreading or skimming through a text can be effective if two conditions hold. First, you already know a lot about the topic discussed in the text and so it isn't necessary to read all the material. Second, your goal is to extract the gist of the text to see whether your previous knowledge needs updating. Apart from that, the typical situation is not too far removed from Woody Allen's line: "I took a speedreading course and read *War and Peace* [a novel almost 2000 pages long] in two minutes. It's about Russia."

LIMITED UNDERSTANDING?

It is generally agreed that the processes involved in understanding texts and spoken language are very similar. However, theorists disagree among each other as to precisely what processes are involved. Nevertheless, most theorists assume that we finish up with a reasonably detailed and accurate representation of the information contained in them. That assumption is often wrong. For example, consider the Moses illusion (Erickson & Mattson, 1981). When asked, "How many animals of each sort did Moses put on the ark?" many people reply, "Two," but the correct answer is, "None" (think about it!). There are many other examples, Wason and Reich (1979) found most people misinterpreted the following sentence taken from a notice in a hospital casualty department: "No head injury is too trivial to be ignored." Most people interpret this as meaning, "However trivial a head injury might appear, it should not be ignored." In fact, it actually means, "However trivial a head injury is, it should be ignored." You can see this is the correct meaning if you consider the following sentence: "No missile is too small to be banned," which means, "However small a missile is, it should be banned."

Ferreira (2003) presented sentences auditorily, and found that our sentence representations are often inaccurate. A sentence such as, "The mouse was eaten by the cheese," was sometimes misinterpreted as meaning the mouse ate the cheese, and, "The man was visited by the woman," was sometimes mistakenly misinterpreted to mean the man visited the woman.

Ferreira (2003) found that people were especially prone to error when processing passive sentences such as those discussed above. According to Ferreira (2003), we misinterpret sentences because we often use heuristics or rules of thumb to simplify the task of understanding sentences. One much-used heuristic is to assume the subject of a sentence is the agent of some action, whereas the object of the sentence is the recipient of the action. This heuristic generally works well, because a substantial majority of sentences in English conform to this pattern. However, it produces misinterpretations of passive sentences in which the subject of the sentence is *not* the agent.

INFERENCE DRAWING

What happens when we read texts or listen to speech for understanding? The obvious answer is that we focus on the words and sentences presented to us and try to make sense of them. In terms of our conscious experience, that is certainly what we seem to be doing. According to this view, understanding language involves stimulus-driven or bottom-up processes almost totally dependent on linguistic stimuli to which we attend. For example, we read the sentence, "The cat sat on the mat," and we find it easy to understand its meaning.

In fact, the ways in which we understand language are more complex than suggested so far. We can see very clearly that top-down processes are also involved if we consider the following very short story taken from Rumelhart and Ortony (1977):

1. *Mary heard the ice-cream van coming.*
2. *She remembered the pocket money.*
3. *She rushed into the house.*

You probably made various assumptions or inferences while reading the story: Mary wanted to buy some ice-cream; buying ice-cream costs money; Mary had some pocket money in the house; and Mary had only a limited amount of time to get hold of this money before the ice-cream van arrived. None of these assumptions is explicitly stated in the three sentences. Thus, these inferences *cannot* depend on stimulus-driven or bottom-up processes but instead must involve top-down processes based on our knowledge and experience. It is simply so common for us to draw inferences that we are generally unaware of doing so.

We have established that we often draw inferences when reading a text or listening to someone talking to us. However, we need to distinguish various types of inferences. **Logical inferences** depend only on the meanings of words. For example, we can infer that anyone who is a widow is female. **Bridging inferences** are made to establish coherence between the current part of the text and preceding text. In contrast, **elaborative inferences** serve to add details to the text but are less important than bridging inferences.

What types of interferences do we make when reading? Are some inferences more automatic than others?

It is generally accepted that we draw logical and bridging inferences because both are essential for a proper understanding of what we are listening to or reading. What is more controversial is the extent to which non-essential or elaborative inferences are drawn automatically. Singer (1994) compared the time taken to verify a test sentence (e.g., "A dentist pulled a tooth") following one of three contexts:

1. The information had already been explicitly presented.
2. A bridging inference was needed to understand the test sentence.
3. An elaborative inference was needed to make sense of the test sentence.

Verification times in conditions (1) and (2) were fast and very similar, suggesting that bridging inferences are drawn automatically during comprehension. In contrast, verification times were slower in condition (3), presumably because the elaborative inference was *not* drawn automatically.

> **KEY TERMS**
> **Logical inferences:** inferences depending solely on the meaning of words.
> **Bridging inferences:** inferences that are drawn to increase the coherence between the current and preceding parts of a text.
> **Elaborative inferences:** inferences that add details to a text that is being read.

There has been much controversy on the issue of precisely *which* inferences (especially elaborative ones) are drawn when readers try to understand a text. At one extreme, there is the constructionist approach proposed by Bransford (e.g., Bransford, Barclay, & Franks, 1972). According to Bransford, numerous elaborative inferences are typically drawn. Graesser, Singer, and Trabasso (1994) put forward a modified constructionist theory. They argued in their search-after-meaning theory that readers typically search after meaning, but won't do so if their goals don't require this (e.g., if they are proof-reading). Search-after-meaning theory is a toned-down version of Bransford et al.'s (1972) constructionist theory in that it is assumed that several kinds of inference aren't generally drawn. Those inferences *not* drawn include ones about future developments, the precise way in which actions are accomplished, and the author's intent.

At the other extreme, there is the minimalist hypothesis put forward by McKoon and Ratcliff (1992, p. 440): "In the absence of specific, goal-directed strategic processes, inferences of only two kinds are constructed: those that establish locally coherent representations of the parts of a text that are processed concurrently [i.e., bridging inferences] and those that rely on information that is quickly and easily available." Thus, constructionists claim that many inferences are drawn automatically in reading, whereas supporters of the minimalist hypothesis argue there are very definite constraints on the number of such inferences. Some of the predictions are the same. However, it is assumed by search-after-meaning theory that more types of inference are generally made than is predicted by the minimalist hypothesis.

Findings

Evidence supporting the minimalist position over Bransford et al.'s constructionist one was reported by Dosher and Corbett (1982). They used instrumental inferences (e.g., "Mary stirred her coffee" has "spoon" as its instrumental inference). In order to decide whether readers generated these instrumental inferences during reading, Dosher and Corbett used an unusual procedure. The time taken to name the color in which a word is printed is slowed down if the word has recently been activated. Thus, if presentation of the sentence, "Mary stirred her coffee," activates the word "spoon," this should slow the time to name the color in which the word "spoon" is printed. The predicted findings (i.e., slowed color naming) were obtained when the readers were told to guess the instrument in each sentence as it was presented. However, there was *no* evidence that instrumental inferences were formed with normal reading instructions.

What do the above findings mean? First, whether or not an inference is drawn can depend on the reader's intentions or goals, one of the central assumptions made by McKoon and Ratcliff (1992). Second, the findings go against Bransford et al.'s constructionist position. We need to infer the instrument used in stirring coffee to gain full understanding, but such instrumental inferences are *not* typically drawn.

Other evidence is less favorable to the minimalist position. People often draw more inferences than predicted by the minimalist hypothesis. For example, Suh and Trabasso (1993) used texts in which a character's initial goal was or wasn't satisfied. In one text, Jimmy wants a bicycle, and his mother either buys him one immediately or doesn't buy him one. Later on, Jimmy has earned a lot of money, and sets off for a department store. In the condition in which Jimmy hasn't satisfied his goal of having a bicycle, readers inferred that his intention was to buy one in the store. However, the minimalist hypothesis wouldn't have predicted that such inferences would be drawn.

Finally, we consider **predictive inferences**, which are drawn when readers infer what event will happen next on the basis of the current situation. Predictive inferences are of special interest because they aren't generally drawn according to the search-after-meaning theory and the minimalist hypothesis. Campion (2004) presented readers with texts such as the following:

> It was a pitch black night and a gigantic iceberg floated in the ocean, emerging by only 5 meters. The helmsman was attentive, but the ship advanced towards the iceberg and ran into it, causing a terrible noise.

What do you think happened next? Campion found that readers drew the predictive inference that the ship sank. However, this inference was stored as a hypothesis rather than as an established fact. This was shown by the additional finding that readers were slow to read the follow-up sentence, "What a big mistake, as the ship went down at sea."

Predictive inferences are only drawn in certain circumstances. They are most likely to be drawn when the reader's attention is focused on the predictable event and that event is strongly associated with text information in the reader's knowledge (see Campion, 2004, for a review). An additional relevant factor was identified by Murray and Burke (2003). They considered the drawing of predictive inferences by readers having low, moderate, or high reading skill. All three groups showed evidence of drawing predictive inferences. However, these inferences were only drawn automatically by those with high reading skill.

In sum, some inferences are typically drawn whereas others are drawn relatively infrequently. The evidence probably supports the search-after-meaning theory more than other theories of inference drawing. However, there is considerable variation in the number of inferences drawn as a function of the reader's goals and interests and his/her level of reading and intellectual ability.

What are schemas? How may they influence our reading?

SCHEMAS

As we have seen, our stored knowledge and experience play an important role in reading and listening because they allow us to fill in the gaps in what we read or hear and so enhance our understanding. Bartlett (1932) argued in a very influential book that our knowledge and experience can have much more dramatic effects. His central claim was that the knowledge we possess can produce systematic *distortions* in what we remember about what we have read. According to Bartlett, this knowledge is in the form of **schemas**, which are organized packets of knowledge about the world, events, or people.

We can see what schemas look like by considering a study by Bower, Black, and Turner (1979). They focused on a type of schema known as **scripts**, which are used to store information about typical events. For example, Bower

KEY TERMS
Predictive inferences: making assumptions about what will happen next on the basis of what is currently happening.
Schemas: organized packets of information about the world, events, or people that are stored in long-term memory.
Scripts: organized information or schemas that represent typical events (e.g., going to a restaurant).

et al. asked people to list 20 actions or events that usually occur when eating in a restaurant. In spite of the varied restaurant experiences of their participants, there was much agreement on the actions associated with the restaurant script. At least 73% of the participants mentioned sitting down, looking at the menu, ordering, eating, paying the bill, and leaving. In addition, at least 48% included entering the restaurant, giving the reservation name, ordering drinks, discussing the menu, talking, eating a salad or soup, ordering dessert, eating dessert, and leaving a tip.

Bartlett's approach emphasized that remembering is a process of reconstruction in which we use schematic knowledge to organize and make sense of the information in a previously read text. In his own words, "Remembering is not the re-excitation of innumerable fixed, lifeless and fragmentary traces. It is an imaginative reconstruction, or construction, built out of the relation of our attitude towards a whole active mass of organized past reactions or experience and to a little outstanding detail . . . It is thus hardly ever really exact, . . . and it is not at all important that it should be so" (Bartlett, 1932, p. 213).

You may think that Bartlett's notion that remembering is practically never accurate is over the top. Interestingly, Bartlett himself had doubts about that notion, as is shown in an article by Ost and Costall (2002). Bartlett (1932) referred to various examples of extremely accurate recall. These included a woman who remembered accurately two of the names from a story called *The War of the Ghosts* 10 years after reading it and the "wonderful memory" of the Bantu. Bartlett was forced to admit that recall can be accurate when there is no conflict between the information presented and the individual's schematic knowledge.

FINDINGS

Bartlett (1932) had the ingenious idea of presenting people with stories involving *conflict* between the information contained in the story and their prior schematic knowledge. His participants were mostly students from Cambridge University and the stories (e.g., *The War of the Ghosts*) were often folk tales from the very different North American Indian folk culture. He argued that the students would read each folk tale from their English cultural perspective. As a result, their prior knowledge would produce distortions in the remembered version of the story, making it more conventional and acceptable from the standpoint of their own cultural background. Bartlett's findings supported his predictions. A substantial proportion of the recall errors were in the direction of making the story read more like a conventional English story. He used the term **rationalization** to refer to this type of error. He also found other kinds of errors, including flattening (failure to recall unfamiliar details) and sharpening (elaboration of certain details).

Bartlett (1932) made a further prediction. He argued that memory for the precise information contained in the story would be forgotten over time, whereas participants' relevant schematic knowledge would not. As a result, rationalization errors (dependent on the participants' knowledge) should increase at longer retention intervals. Bartlett's findings supported this prediction.

Bartlett's (1932) experimental approach can be criticized. The instructions he gave his participants were rather vague and he practically never used

KEY TERM
Rationalization: in Bartlett's theory, the tendency in recall of stories to produce errors that conform to the cultural expectations of the rememberer.

any statistical tests on his data! More worryingly, many of the distortions in recall observed by Bartlett were due to conscious guessing rather than genuine problems in memory. Perhaps the participants were trying to be helpful by guessing when they couldn't remember some aspect of the story. Convincing evidence that this is a problem was produced by Gauld and Stephenson (1967). Clear instructions emphasizing the need for accurate recall (and so presumably reducing deliberate guessing) eliminated almost half the errors obtained using Bartlett's vague instructions.

In spite of the various problems with Bartlett's procedures, there is convincing support for his major findings from well-controlled studies. For example, Sulin and Dooling (1974) presented some participants with a story about Gerald Martin: "Gerald Martin strove to undermine the existing government to satisfy his political ambitions . . . He became a ruthless, uncontrollable dictator. The ultimate effect of his rule was the downfall of his country" (Sulin & Dooling, 1974, p. 256). Other participants were given the same story, but the main actor was called Adolf Hitler. Those participants told the story was about Adolf Hitler were much more likely than the other participants to believe incorrectly they had read the sentence, "He hated the Jews particularly and so persecuted them." Their schematic knowledge about Hitler distorted their recollections of what they had read (see Figure 19.1). As Bartlett (1932) predicted, this type of distortion was more common at a long than a short retention interval.

Many of Bartlett's critics have pointed out that his experiments were very artificial and removed from everyday life. What happens when we study memory under naturalistic conditions? Wynn and Logie (1998) tested students' recall of "real-life" events experienced during their first week at university at various intervals of time up to 6 months. What they found was as follows: "The initial accuracy sustained throughout the time period, together with the relative lack of change over time, suggests very limited use of reconstructive processes" (Wynn & Logie, 1998, p. 1).

A key issue is whether schemas influence the process of *comprehension* when people are reading a text or whether they influence the subsequent processes of *retrieval*. Bartlett (1932) argued that schemas influence retrieval. However, many other psychologists (e.g., Bransford & Johnson, 1972) claim the main impact of schemas is on comprehension. Evidence supporting the latter position was reported by Bransford and Johnson (1972). They

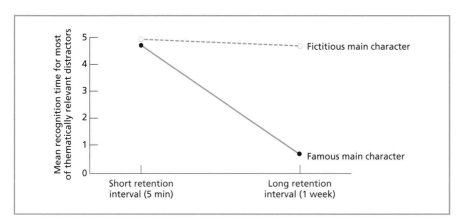

Figure 19.1 Correct rejection of thematic distractor as a function of main actor (fictitious: Gerald Martin or famous: Adolf Hitler) and of retention interval. Data from Sulin and Dooling (1974).

presented a passage in which in which it was hard to work out which schemas were relevant. Part of it was as follows:

> The procedure is quite simple. First, you arrange items into different groups. Of course one pile may be sufficient depending on how much there is to do. If you have to go somewhere else due to lack of facilities that is the next step; otherwise, you are pretty well set. It is important not to overdo things. That is, it is better to do too few things at once than too many. In the short run this may not seem important but complications can easily arise.

What on earth was that all about? Participants hearing the passage in the absence of a title rated it as incomprehensible and recalled very little of it. In contrast, those supplied beforehand with the title, "Washing clothes," found it easy to understand and recalled twice as much. The title indicated the nature of the underlying schema and helped comprehension of the passage rather than retrieval. We know this because participants receiving the title *after* hearing the passage (but *before* recall) had as poor recall as those never receiving the title.

Anderson and Pichert (1978) found that schemas can influence the retrieval of information from long-term memory. They asked participants to read a story from the perspective of a burglar or of someone interested in buying a home. After the participants had recalled the story, they were told to shift to the alternative perspective (e.g., from burglar to home buyer or vice versa) before recalling the story again. On the second recall, participants recalled more information important only to the second perspective or schema than they had done on the first recall (see Figure 19.2).

How can we explain the findings of Anderson and Pichert (1978)? Altering the perspective produced a shift in the schematic knowledge accessed by the participants (e.g., from burglar-relevant knowledge to home-buyer-relevant knowledge). Accessing different schematic knowledge enhanced recall, and this provides support for the notion of schema-driven retrieval.

Figure 19.2 Recall as a function of perspective at the time of retrieval. Based on data from Anderson and Pichert (1978).

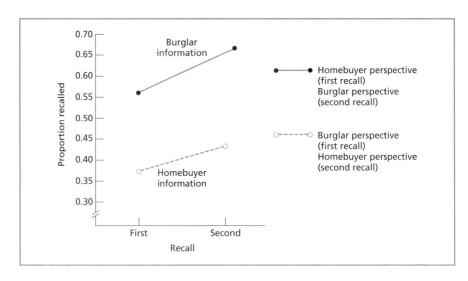

SCHEMA-INCONSISTENT INFORMATION

We have seen that schema-consistent information tends to be recalled even when not actually presented in the text. What is the fate of schema-*inconsistent* information? Davidson (1994) discovered that the answer to that question depends on the nature of the inconsistency. Some schema-inconsistent information is simply *irrelevant* to the story, whereas other schema-inconsistent information *interrupts* the story. For example, in a story about going to the cinema, "Sarah mentions to Sam that the screen is big" is irrelevant to the story. In contrast, "Another couple, both of whom are very tall, sits in front of them and blocks their view," interrupts the story as well as the view.

Davidson (1994) found both kinds of schema-inconsistent information were better recalled than schema-consistent information 1 hour later. The reason is that such information is *distinctive* in memory. However, the findings were different 1 week later. At that time, interruptive information was still better recalled than schema-consistent information, but irrelevant information was worse recalled than schema-consistent information. Recall after 1 week was determined more by the underlying schemas than was recall after 1 hour, and interruptive information was more directly relevant to those schemas than was irrelevant information. These complex findings would not have been predicted by Bartlett's (1932) schema theory.

In sum, we generally make use of schematic knowledge when we are trying to understand a text or what someone is saying to us. This knowledge is sometimes used subsequently at the time of recall as well as at the time of comprehension. The use of schematic knowledge can produce errors and distortions in memory when there is a conflict between our schematic knowledge and the information presented to us in a text. The main limitation of schema theories is that it is very difficult to identify precisely the information contained in schemas. In addition, the circumstances in which any given schema will be activated are not entirely clear.

PRAGMATICS

What aspects of language are described by the term pragmatics? *How good are we at processing pragmatics?*

Pragmatics deals with practical language and comprehension, especially those aspects going beyond the literal meaning of what is said and taking account of the current social context. Thus, pragmatics is concerned with *intended* rather than *literal* meaning as expressed by speakers and understood by listeners, and it often involves drawing inferences. Cases in which the intended meaning is *not* the same as the literal meaning include irony, sarcasm, and understatement. For example, we assume that someone who says, "The weather's really great!" when it has been raining non-stop for several days actually thinks the weather is terrible. The term **figurative language** is often used to refer to language not intended to be taken literally. A **metaphor** is a form of figurative language in which a word is used to describe something it merely resembles. For example, someone who is always cheerful is described as a ray of sunshine.

How do we process figurative language? The traditional view (the standard pragmatic model) originated with Aristotle but was brought up to date by Searle (1979). According to this model, we go through three stages when processing figurative expressions:

KEY TERMS

Pragmatics: the study of the ways in which language is used and understood in the real world, including a consideration of its intended meaning.

Figurative language: forms of language (e.g., metaphor) that are not intended to be taken literally.

Metaphor: a figure of speech in which a word is said to mean something that it only resembles; for example, a timid person is described as a sheep.

1. The literal meaning is accessed. For example, the literal meaning of, "David kicked the bucket," is that David struck a bucket with his foot.
2. The listener or reader decides whether the literal meaning makes sense in the context in which it is encountered.
3. If the literal meaning doesn't make sense, the listener or reader searches for a non-literal meaning making sense in the context.

Two main predictions follow from the standard pragmatic model. First, literal meanings are *always* accessed before non-literal or figurative ones. Second, literal interpretations are accessed automatically, whereas non-literal interpretations are optional and thus not necessarily accessed.

Giora (1997, 2002) put forward the graded salience hypothesis, according to which initial processing is determined by *salience* or prominence rather than by the type of meaning (literal vs. non-literal). Thus, a sentence's salient meaning is accessed rapidly. After that, its non-salient meaning may be accessed more slowly, but this typically requires facilitation from the sentence context.

FINDINGS

Most evidence fails to support the prediction that non-literal meanings take longer to understand than literal ones. The typical finding is that non-literal or metaphorical meanings are understood as rapidly as literal ones (see Glucksberg, 2003, for a review) even when metaphors are not familiar. For example, Blasko and Connine (1993) presented participants with relatively unfamiliar metaphors (e.g., "Jerry first knew that loneliness was a desert when he was very young"). The non-literal meanings of such metaphors were understood as rapidly as the literal ones.

The prediction from the standard pragmatic model that figurative or metaphorical meanings aren't accessed automatically was shown to be incorrect in a study reported by Glucksberg (2003). The task was to decide as rapidly as possible whether various sentences were literally true or false. Among the sentences were the following types: literally false (e.g., "Some fruits are tables"), metaphors (e.g., "Some surgeons are butchers"), and scrambled metaphors (e.g., "Some jobs are butchers"). According to the model, the figurative meaning of metaphors shouldn't be accessed (because it isn't required by the task), and so there should be no problem in deciding they are literally false. In contrast, if people automatically process the figurative meaning of metaphors, metaphor sentences should take longer to judge as false because of *competition* between the "true" non-literal meaning and the false literal meaning. The findings supported the notion that figurative meanings are accessed automatically (see Figure 19.3), thus providing evidence against the standard pragmatic model.

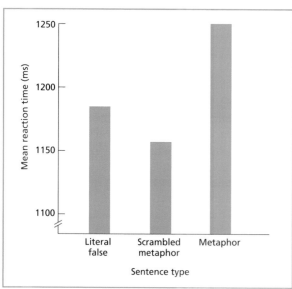

Figure 19.3 Time to decide that a sentence was literally false as a function of sentence type (literal false; scrambled metaphor; metaphor). Adapted from Glucksberg (2003).

Kazmerski, Blasko, and Dessalegn (2003) carried out a similar study to that of Glucksberg (2003). However, they also considered individual differences in intelligence or IQ. Glucksberg's finding that it took longer to decide that sentences are literally false with metaphors than with scrambled metaphors was replicated with high-IQ participants. However, it wasn't replicated with low-IQ participants. These findings suggest that high-IQ individuals access metaphorical meanings automatically but low-IQ ones don't.

Most theories of figurative language processing don't allow sufficiently for *flexibility* of processing in different situations. For example, consider the question of how long it will take to understand the metaphor, "My lawyer was a shark." Our knowledge of sharks includes literal properties (e.g., "has fins," "has sharp teeth," "can swim") and metaphorical properties (e.g., "vicious," "predatory," "aggressive"). If so, perhaps it would take longer to understand the above metaphor if preceded by a contextual sentence emphasizing the literal meaning (e.g., "Sharks can swim") rather than by a metaphor-irrelevant sentence (e.g., "Some lawyers are married"). That is precisely what was found by McGlone and Manfredi (2001).

Giora's (1997, 2002) graded salience hypothesis received support in a study by Giora and Fein (1999). Participants were presented with familiar metaphors (having salient or prominent literal and metaphorical meanings) and less familiar metaphors (having only a salient literal meaning). These metaphors were presented in a context that was biased towards either their metaphorical or their literal meaning. If (as the hypothesis assumes) salience is the most important factor, then the literal and metaphorical meanings of familiar metaphors should have been activated regardless of context. With less familiar metaphors, the literal meaning should have been activated regardless of context. However, the non-salient metaphorical meaning should only have been activated in the context biasing that meaning. All of these predictions were confirmed.

In sum, the notion that literal meanings will always be accessed faster and more easily than non-literal or figurative ones has been disproved. The graded salience hypothesis provides a superior account of the processing of figurative language. according to that hypothesis (which is consistent with most of the evidence), the meaning of a sentence that is accessed initially will be the most salient one. The most salient interpretation (depending on context) will sometimes be the literal meaning but sometimes it will be the figurative meaning.

CONSTRUCTION–INTEGRATION MODEL

So far we have considered some of the main factors involved in comprehension of text and speech. It is now time to consider language comprehension in a more general way. We will do this by considering the leading theoretical approach, which is Kintsch's (1988, 1992, 1998) construction–integration model (see Figure 19.4).

What types of representations do we form when we read text? Does this depend on the situation?

Here are the key assumptions of the model:

- The sentences in the text are turned into *propositions* (statements making an assertion or a denial and which can be true or false).

Figure 19.4 The construction–integration model. Adapted from Kintsch (1992).

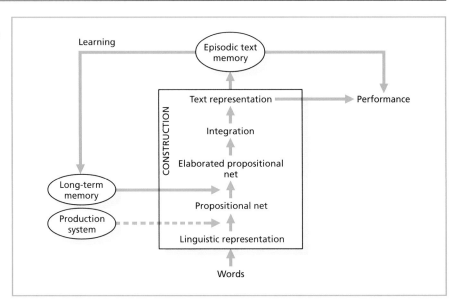

Figure 19.4 The construction–integration model. Adapted from Kintsch (1992).

- *Construction process*: Readers use their knowledge base to retrieve propositions related to the text propositions (e.g., inferences). These propositions and text propositions both form an *elaborated propositional net*. This may seem inefficient, because many propositions in this net are only marginally relevant to the theme of the text.
- *Integration process*: Contextual information provided by the previous parts of the text is used to select from the elaborated propositional net only those propositions most relevant to the theme of the text.
- Three levels of text representation are constructed:
  1. Surface representation (the text itself); this representation lasts for the shortest time.
  2. Propositional representation (propositions formed from the text).
  3. Situational representation (a mental model describing the situation referred to in the text). Schemas can be used as the building blocks for the construction of situational representations or models. This representation lasts for the longest time.

The construction–integration model may sound rather complex, but its key assumptions are straightforward. The initial construction process uses semantic knowledge to form a large number of propositions. After that, the integration process uses contextual information from the text to weed out those propositions of little relevance while retaining those most related to the theme of the text.

FINDINGS

One of the most striking assumptions of the construction–integration model is that no fewer than *three* representations are formed when we read a text. This assumption was investigated by Kintsch, Welsch, Schmalhofer, and Zimony (1990). Participants were presented with brief descriptions of very stereotyped situations (e.g., going to see a movie), and then their recognition memory was tested immediately or at times ranging up to 4 days later.

The forgetting functions for the surface, propositional, and situational representations differed considerably (see Figure 19.5). There was rapid and complete forgetting of the surface representation, whereas information from the situational representation showed no forgetting over 4 days. Propositional information differed from situational information in that there was only partial forgetting. Thus, the findings were precisely in line with predictions from the model.

Other research indicates that readers don't *always* construct all three forms of text representation. Zwaan and van Oostendop (1993) gave readers part of an edited mystery novel describing the details of a murder scene, including the locations of the body and various clues. Most readers did *not* construct a situational or spatial representation when they read normally, something of which a legion of detective story writers since Agatha Christie have taken advantage. However, situational representations were formed (at the cost of a substantial increase in reading time) when the initial instructions emphasized the importance of constructing a spatial representation. Thus, limited processing capacity may often restrict the formation of situational representations.

Kaup and Zwaan (2003) obtained evidence that propositional representations aren't always formed. They pointed out that a key feature of propositional representations is that they contain information about *all* the objects referred to in a sentence, regardless of whether they are present or absent. In contrast, situational representations only contain information about entities that are present. Consider the following sentence: "Sam was relieved that Laura was not wearing her pink dress." Information about the absent pink dress would be included in the propositional representation of this sentence but not in the situational representation.

According to the construction–integration model, information about absent objects should be as accessible as information about present objects for some time after the presentation of a sentence. However, Kaup and Zwaan (2003) found that information about absent objects was less accessible than that about present objects only $1\frac{1}{2}$ seconds after a sentence had been

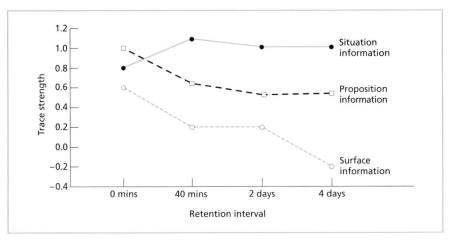

Figure 19.5 Forgetting functions for situation, proposition, and surface information over a four-day period. Adapted from Kintsch et al. (1990).

read. The implication is that readers simply generated a situational representation without previously constructing a propositional representation.

We now consider a final assumption of the construction–integration model. According to the model, textual information is first linked with general world or semantic knowledge, after which it is linked to contextual information from the rest of the text. Cook and Myers (2004) tested this assumption using various passages. Here are excerpts from one of those passages:

> The movie was being filmed on location in the Sahara Desert. It was a small independent film with a low budget and small staff, *so everyone involved had to take on extra jobs and responsibilities*. On the first day of filming, "Action!" was called by the *actress* so that shooting could begin . . .

What was of interest was how long the readers fixated the word "actress." This word is inappropriate in terms of our knowledge, which tells us that the director says, "Action!" However, the context of the passage (shown in italics) provides a reason why it might not be the director who is in charge. According to the construction–integration model, readers' knowledge that actresses don't direct films should have caused them to dwell a long time on the unexpected word "actress." In fact, the word was *not* fixated for long. Presumably readers immediately used the contextual justification for someone other than the director being in charge. Thus, in opposition to the model, contextual information can be used *before* general world knowledge during reading.

In sum, the construction–integration model has proved successful, in that there seem to be successive stages of construction and integration. In addition, the three levels of representation assumed within the model all seem to exist. However, the situational representation is not always constructed, and the propositional representation sometimes doesn't include information about absent objects although it is supposed to according to the model. The model's assumption that general knowledge is accessed by readers before contextual information from the text is accessed has been found to be incorrect at least sometimes (Cook & Myers, 2004). Finally, there may be other levels of representation in addition to the three assumed within the construction–integration model. One possibility is the text genre level, which relates to the nature of the text (e.g., narration).

EVALUATION AND CHAPTER SUMMARY

Introduction
- The evidence suggests that the minimalist hypothesis predicts too few inferences, whereas Bransford et al.'s constructionist approach predicts too many.
- Overall, the findings are probably most consistent with the search-after-meaning theory.
- According to this theory, fewer inferences are drawn than predicted by Bransford, but more than predicted by the minimalist hypothesis.

- However, the precise inferences drawn vary considerably from one situation to another.
- This is reflected in the conclusion reached by Graesser, Millis, and Zwaan (1997, p. 183): "We suspect that each of the ... models is correct in certain conditions. The minimalist hypothesis is probably correct when the reader is very quickly reading the text, when the text lacks global [overall] coherence, and when the reader has very little background knowledge. The constructionist [or search-after-meaning] theory is on the mark when the reader is attempting to comprehend the text for enjoyment or mastery at a more leisurely pace."
- There is an important final point, which is that there are considerable individual differences in the number and type of inferences drawn when reading a text.
- We have seen that individual differences in reading ability influence how easily predictive inferences are drawn (Murray & Burke, 2003).
- More generally, individuals of greater intellectual ability typically draw more inferences than those of lesser ability (see Eysenck & Keane, 2005, for a review).
- In the future, we need to develop more of an understanding of *how* text processing differs across individuals.

Schemas
- Our schematic knowledge is used during comprehension and retrieval.
- The use of this knowledge can create errors and distortions when there is a conflict between our schematic knowledge and information presented in the text.
- There are greater numbers of such errors and distortions as the retention interval increases.
- On the negative side, schema theories find it hard to explain differences in recall between various kinds of schema-inconsistent information (Davidson, 1994).
- More generally, it has proved hard to identify precisely the characteristics of schemas in spite of the efforts of researchers such as Bower et al. (1979).
- If we want to explain text comprehension and memory in terms of the activation of certain schemas, we need clear evidence that these schemas exist and are activated.
- However, such evidence is not generally available. This led Harley (2001, p. 331) to conclude that, "The primary accusation against schema and script-based approaches is that they are nothing more than re-descriptions of the data."

Pragmatics
- The standard pragmatic model has been shown to be inadequate.
- Its assumption that literal meanings will always be accessed faster than non-literal ones is wrong.
- The assumption that non-literal interpretations are optional and are never accessed automatically is also incorrect.

- More generally, the standard pragmatic model is inflexible. It doesn't take sufficient account of the effects of context on processing (e.g., McGlone & Manfredi, 2001) and it ignores individual differences (e.g., Kazmerski et al., 2003).
- Giora's graded salience hypothesis is more flexible than the standard pragmatic model. For example, it includes the assumption that context determines whether or not non-salient meanings are processed.
- Its crucial assumption that the meaning of a sentence initially accessed is the most salient one (which may or may not be its literal meaning) is consistent with most of the evidence (e.g., Giora & Fein, 1999). Overall, the graded salience hypothesis represents a promising theoretical approach.

Construction–integration model
- The construction–integration model has been very influential because it provides a detailed account of how information in the text is combined with the reader's relevant knowledge.
- There are reasonable grounds for arguing that there are successive stages of construction and of integration.
- In addition, there is evidence for the three levels of representation (surface, propositional, and situational) specified in the model.
- There are various limitations with the model.
- First, the situational representation is sometimes not constructed (Zwaan & van Oostendop, 1993).
- Second, the propositional representation is supposed to contain information about absent objects as well as ones present, but sometimes does not (Kaup & Zwaan, 2003).
- That may mean that the propositional representation can be less complete than assumed theoretically. Alternatively, people may sometimes ignore the propositional representation and move straight to the situational representation.
- Third, the assumption that general knowledge is accessed before contextual information from the text during comprehension is sometimes incorrect (Cook & Myers, 2004).
- Fourth, Graesser, Millis, and Zwaan (1997) argued that Kintsch's proposed three levels of representation are insufficient. For example, Kintsch ignored the *text genre* level, which is concerned with the nature of the text (e.g., narration, description, jokes).
- The kinds of information presented, how the information is presented, and the ways in which the information is to be interpreted differ greatly as a function of the type or genre of text.

FURTHER READING

- Butcher, K.R., & Kintsch, W. (2003). Text comprehension and discourse processing. In A.F. Healy & R.W. Proctor (Eds.), *Handbook of psychology: Experimental psychology, Vol. 4*. New York: Wiley & Sons. This chapter provides a good overview of theory and research on language comprehension.
- Garnham, A. (2004). Language comprehension. In K. Lamberts & R. Goldstone (Eds.), *Handbook of cognition*. London: Sage. Theories and experiments in the area of language comprehension are analyzed in detail in this chapter by Alan Garnham.
- Giora, R. (2003). *On our mind: Salience, context and figurative language*. New York: Oxford University Press. Key issues in language (especially in pragmatics) are discussed comprehensively in this book.
- Harley, T. (2001). *The psychology of language: From data to theory* (2nd ed.). Hove, UK: Psychology Press. Most of the topics covered in this chapter are dealt with in a very well-informed way in this excellent textbook.

CHAPTER 20

CONTENTS

Introduction	289
Speech errors	293
Word processing: Ordered or disordered?	296
Speech disorders	300
Evaluation and chapter summary	303
Further reading	305

Talking the talk

INTRODUCTION

On the face of it (or should that be by the sound of it?), speech production is a straightforward business. Most of the time it seems almost effortless as we chat with friends or acquaintances about the topics of the day. Indeed, we often seem to speak without much preparation or planning. We typically speak at three words a second or almost 200 words a minute, and this rapid speech rate fits the notion that speaking is very undemanding of processing resources. It is sometimes true that we open our mouths before putting our brain into gear, as can be seen in this example (Svartvik & Quirk, 1980, 1.5.416–1.5.421):

> *but what functions, do people variously fill, I mean are you . all members of a research . project, or just a group, I mean is . Marilyn, . uh: uh assistant le uh I mean is she a lecturer?*

In fact, the reality is often very different from the account of speech production in the previous paragraph. Smith (2000) pointed out that we use various strategies when talking to reduce the processing demands on us while we plan what to say. One example is **preformulation**, which involves reducing processing costs by producing phrases used before. About 70% of our speech consists of word combinations we use repeatedly (Altenberg, 1990). Convincing evidence for the importance of preformulation was reported by Kuiper (1996). He analyzed the speech of two groups of people (auctioneers and sports commentators) who often need to speak very rapidly. Speaking quickly led them to make very extensive use of preformulation (e.g., "They're on their way"; "They're off and racing now").

Another strategy we use to make speech production easier is **underspecification**, which involves using simplified expressions. Smith (2000) illustrated underspecification with the following: "Wash and core six cooking apples. Put them in an oven." In the second sentence, the word "them" underspecifies the phrase "six cooking apples."

The research discussed so far (and most other research on speech production) focuses on *monologue*, in which one person talks to another person. However, as Pickering and Garrod (2004, p.169) pointed out, "The most natural and basic form of language use is dialogue [conversation] . . . Therefore, a central goal of psycholinguistics [the study of psychological processes

KEY TERMS

Preformulation: this is used in speech production to reduce processing costs by using phrases often used previously.

Underspecification: a strategy used to reduce processing costs in speech production by producing simplified expressions.

What kinds of cues and strategies do we typically use to help speech perception?

underlying language use] should be to provide an account of the basic processing mechanisms that are employed during natural dialogue." Psychologists focusing on dialogue have generally assumed that, "dialogue simply involves chunks of monologue stuck together" (Pickering & Garrod, 2004, p. 170).

Most psychologists argue that speech production is harder in interactive dialogue than monologue because speakers have to adjust what they say to fit what the previous speaker just said. However, Pickering and Garrod (2004) argued that exactly the opposite is generally the case. According to them, speakers often copy phrases and even sentences they heard when the other person was speaking. Thus, the other person's words serve as a prime or prompt. As a result, dialogue is often much more repetitive than monologue. In addition, speakers delivering a monologue must generate their own ideas. In contrast, speakers within a dialogue make extensive use of the ideas communicated by the other person.

FACILITATING COMMUNICATION

We have seen that speech production can be more demanding than might have been imagined. One reason why it is often demanding is because as speakers we generally try to talk so as to facilitate communication with our listener or listeners. One way we do that is by using discourse markers (e.g., "well"; "oh"; "anyway"). **Discourse markers** are spoken words or phrases that help the process of communication in spite of not being directly relevant to what the speaker is saying. Flowerdew and Tauroza (1995) found a video-taped lecture was understood better when the discourse markers were left in rather than edited out. However, the lecture was in the participants' second language. As a result, we can't necessarily assume that the findings would generalize to first-language listening. Fox Tree (2000, p. 393) identified the functions of various specific markers: "Discourse markers like *oh, then, now*, and *well* can help listeners deal with speakers' shifts of topic and focus by indicating when a topic shift will occur ... *Anyway* and *anyway be that as it may* can be used to mark the end of a digression and the return to the prior topic."

Another way we as speakers can make life easier for our listeners is by providing **prosodic cues** (e.g., rhythm, stress, and intonation). It has sometimes been assumed that speakers make extensive use of such cues. However, the evidence suggests prosodic cues are not used as a matter of course. Snedeker and Trueswell (2003) argued that prosodic cues are much more likely to be provided when the context fails to clarify the meaning of an ambiguous sentence. As predicted, speakers saying ambiguous sentences (e.g., "Tap the frog with the flower") provided many more prosodic cues when the context was consistent with both sentence interpretations. In case you are wondering, the above sentence is ambiguous because it may mean that you should tap the frog that has the flower or that you should use the flower to tap the frog.

We have seen that speakers make use of discourse markers and prosodic cues in the attempt to communicate effectively. In fact, speakers go much further than that to try to ensure their message is understood by the listener. According to Clark (e.g., Clark & Carlson, 1981; Clark & Krych, 2004),

KEY TERMS
Discourse markers: spoken words and phrases that don't contribute directly to the content of what is being said but still serve various functions (e.g., clarification of the speaker's intentions).
Prosodic cues: features of spoken language such as stress and intonation.

speakers and listeners typically work together to maximize the *common ground*: "Common ground for two people refers to the sum of their mutual knowledge, beliefs, and suppositions, in other words, what they mutually know" (Holtgraves, 2002, p. 123). Friends have much more common ground between them than do strangers, and so they don't need to provide so much background information when chatting.

Horton and Keysar (1996) argued that speakers find it easier (i.e., less effortful) to plan what they say using *only* information available to them rather than taking account of the common ground. Participants had to describe moving objects so the listener could identify them, and these descriptions had to be produced rapidly or slowly. Speakers used the common ground in their descriptions when they had plenty of time but tended not to use it when speed was required. These findings suggest that it *is* effortful for speakers to focus on the common ground between them and their listeners when they are planning what to say.

An important limitation in the study by Horton and Keysar (1996) is that there was no dialogue between speaker and listener—the listener simply listened to what the speaker had to say. Clark and Krych (2004) used a more realistic situation in which interaction and dialogue were permitted. They arranged their participants into pairs. One member of each pair was a director who told the other member (the builder) how to construct 10 Lego models. The directors often changed very rapidly what they were saying to maximize the common ground between them and the builders. For example, consider what happened when Ken (one of the builders) held a block over the right location while Jane (one of the directors) was speaking. She almost instantly took advantage by interrupting herself by saying "yes": "and put it on the right hand half of the—yes—of the green rectangle." Another finding was that the builders produced much non-verbal behavior (e.g., pointing, nodding) that influenced the directors' spoken language. This behavior served the function of increasing the common ground between the director and the builder.

SPEECH PLANNING

It's not really clear so far whether we typically plan what we are going to say before saying it. Accordingly, we will now address that issue. As we will see, speakers generally plan what they are going to say to some extent. However, there is controversy concerning the extent of such planning.

How far ahead do we plan our speech?

Several theorists (e.g., Garrett, 1980) have argued that the planning of speech may extend over an entire **clause**, a part of a sentence containing a subject and a verb. There is support for this view from the study of speech errors (see Garrett, 1980). For example, word-exchange errors involve two words changing places. Of importance, the words exchanged often come from different phrases but belong to the same clause (e.g., "My chair seems empty without my room"). The fact that word-exchange errors rarely involve words from different clauses strengthens the argument that the clause is a key unit in speech planning.

Additional evidence that planning may be at the level of the clause was reported by Holmes (1988). Speakers talked spontaneously about various topics, and then other participants read the utterances the speakers

KEY TERM
Clause: part of a sentence that contains a subject and a verb.

had produced. Speakers (but not readers) often had hesitations and pauses before the start of a clause, suggesting they were planning the forthcoming clause.

Other evidence suggests that speech planning may be at the level of the **phrase**, a group of words expressing a single idea and smaller in scope than a clause. Martin, Miller, and Vu (2004) asked participants to produce sentences to describe moving pictures. The sentences either had a simple initial phrase (e.g., "The ball moves above the tree and the finger") or they had a complex initial phrase (e.g., "The ball and the tree move above the finger"). Speakers took longer to initiate speech when using complex initial phrases than when using simple ones. These findings indicate they were planning the initial phrase before starting to speak.

Not everyone agrees that speech planning operates at the level of the phrase or clause. Griffin (2001) presented participants with displays containing three pictured objects and instructed them to respond according to the following sentence frame: "The A and the B are above the C." The time taken to start speaking was influenced by the difficulty in finding the right word to describe the first object (i.e., A) but was *not* affected by the difficulty in finding the right words to describe the second and third objects (i.e., B and C). Thus, participants started to talk when they had prepared a name for only *one* object, suggesting that speech planning is much more limited than it was in other studies.

How can we make sense of the various findings? We can draw an analogy with diving from the high board in a swimming pool. If you ask how much preparation and planning a diver engages in prior to diving, the answer is clearly that this is variable. If time permits, there will be careful planning, but a skilled diver can dive reasonably well with little or no planning. It may well be that the amount of planning preceding speech is *flexible* and varies as a function of the demands of the situation in which the speaker finds himself/herself.

Support for the above view was reported by Ferreira and Swets (2002). Participants answered mathematical problems varying in difficulty level, and the time taken to start speaking and the length of time spent speaking were recorded. These measures were taken to test various predictions. If there is complete planning before speaking, the time taken to start speaking will be longer for more difficult problems than for easier ones, but the time spent speaking won't vary. In contrast, if people start speaking before planning their responses, then the time taken to start speaking will be the same for all problems. However, the duration of speech should be longer with more difficult problems.

Ferreira and Swets (2002) found that task difficulty affected the time taken to start speaking but not the time spent speaking. This indicated that participants fully planned their responses before speaking. However, the findings differed in a second experiment in which participants had to start producing their answers to mathematical problems very rapidly for them to count. In these circumstances, some planning occurred before speaking, with additional planning occurring during speaking. Thus, speakers are *flexible*. They do only as much prior planning as is feasible in the time available before starting to speak.

In sum, studies in which speakers are free from constraints as to *what* to say and *when* to say it (e.g., Garrett, 1980; Holmes, 1988) indicate that speech

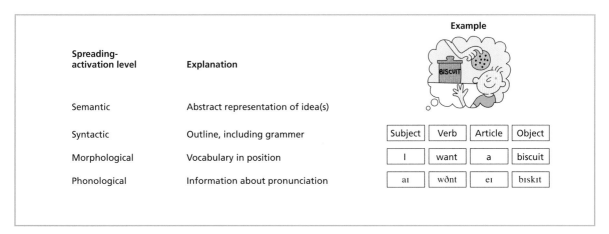

Spreading-activation level	Explanation			Example	
Semantic	Abstract representation of idea(s)				
Syntactic	Outline, including grammer	Subject	Verb	Article	Object
Morphological	Vocabulary in position	I	want	a	biscuit
Phonological	Information about pronunciation	aɪ	wɒnt	eɪ	bɪskɪt

Figure 20.1 The sentence "I want a biscuit" broken down into spreading-activation levels.

planning is fairly extensive and probably includes entire clauses. When the task is more artificial and the same sentence frame is used repeatedly (e.g., Griffin, 2001; Martin et al., 2004), planning is more limited in scope. Such variability in findings is as expected if speakers operate in the flexible ways suggested by Ferreira and Swets (2002).

SPEECH PRODUCTION LEVELS

Most theorists assume there are several levels or stages of processing involved in speech production. So far we have focused on the initial level or stage of processing, during which the meaning of what the speaker wants to say is worked out. The main levels or stages were identified by Dell (1986) and are shown in Figure 20.1. Initial planning of the message to be communicated is considered at the semantic level. At the syntactic level, the grammatical structure of the words in the planned utterance is decided. At the morphological level, the **morphemes** (basic units of meaning or word forms) in the planned sentence are worked out. At the phonological level, the *phonemes* or basic units of sound within the sentence are added.

Figure 20.1 implies that the processes involved in speech and word production proceed in an orderly way from the semantic level through the syntactic and morphological levels down to the phonological level. In fact, however, there is much disagreement as to the extent to which the processes concerned do occur in this neat sequential way. This issue is discussed at length later in the chapter.

SPEECH ERRORS

We know from experience that our speech is imperfect and prone to various kinds of errors. Many psychologists have argued we can learn much about the processes involved in speech production by studying the types of errors made and their relative frequencies. There are various reasons why the study of speech errors is important:

1. We can obtain insights into how the complex cognitive system involved in speech production works by focusing on what happens when it malfunctions.

2. Speech errors can shed some light on the extent to which speakers plan ahead. For example, there is a type of speech error known as the *word-exchange error*, in which two words in a sentence switch places (e.g., "I must let the house out of the cat" instead of "I must let the cat out of the house"). As discussed before, the existence of such errors strongly suggests that speakers engage in forward planning of their utterances.

3. Comparisons between different types of speech errors can be revealing. For example, we can compare word-exchange errors with *sound-exchange errors* in which two sounds exchange places (e.g., "barn door" instead of "darn bore"). Of crucial importance, the two words involved in word-exchange errors are typically further apart in the sentence than the two words involved in sound-exchange errors. This suggests (but doesn't prove) that planning of the words to be used occurs at an earlier stage than planning of the sounds to be spoken.

How do we know what errors are made in speech? The evidence consists mainly of those personally heard by the researcher concerned (Stemberger, 1982). You might imagine this would produce distorted data, since some errors are easier to detect than others. However, the types and proportions of speech errors obtained in this way are very similar to those obtained from analyzing tape-recorded conversations (Garnham, Oakhill, & Johnson-Laird, 1982).

TYPES OF ERROR

What can typical speech errors tell us about normal speech? Give an example, with one such error.

One of the best-known types of error is the so-called **Freudian slip**, a motivated error in speech or action revealing the speaker's true desires. Freud, being Freud, emphasized speech errors related to sex. For example, Freud (1901/1975) gave as an example a man who intended to say "Alabasterbüchse" (alabaster box) but instead said "Alabüsterbachse" (woman's bust). Freud's ideas were generally discounted for many years, but were revived by Motley. His focus was on spoonerisms. A **spoonerism** occurs when the initial letter or letters of two or more words are switched. It is named after the Reverend William Archibald Spooner, who is credited with several memorable examples (e.g., "You have hissed all my mystery lectures"; "The Lord is a shoving leopard to his flock"). Alas, most of the Rev. Spooner's gems were the result of much painstaking effort.

Motley (1980) carried out an experiment in which male participants said out loud pairs of items such as *goxi furl* and *bine foddy*. The experimenter was either a male or a female, "who was by design attractive, personable, very provocatively attired, and seductive in behavior" (Motley, 1980, p. 140). Motley predicted that the number of sex-related spoonerisms (e.g., turning *goxi furl* into *foxy girl*; turning *bine foddy* into *fine body*) would be greater when the passions of the male participants were inflamed by the female experimenter. That was exactly what he found.

In other experiments (see Motley, Baars, & Camden, 1983, for a review), Motley considered further sexual spoonerisms. Participants were given word pairs such as *tool kits*; *fast luck*. The key measure was the extent to which these

KEY TERMS
Freudian slip: an error in speech (or action) that is motivated and reveals the speaker's underlying desires or thoughts.
Spoonerism: a speech error where the initial letter or letters of two words are switched.

word pairs were turned into sexually explicit spoonerisms (e.g., *cool tits*). As Motley (1980) had found, more sexual spoonerisms were produced when the situation was designed to increase sexual arousal in the male participants. They seemed to be aware of the emotionality of what they were going to say because there was a greater delay in saying taboo responses than neutral ones.

Morpheme-exchange errors involve inflections or suffixes remaining in place but attached to the wrong words (e.g., "He has already trunked two packs"). An implication of morpheme-exchange errors is that the positioning of inflections is dealt with by a rather separate process from the one responsible for positioning word stems (e.g., "trunk"; "pack"). The word stems (e.g., trunk, pack) seem to be worked out *before* the inflections are added. This is the case because the spoken inflections or suffixes are generally altered to fit with the new word stems to which they are linked. For example, the "s" sound in the phrase "the forks of a prong," is pronounced in a way appropriate within the word "forks." However, this is different to the "s" sound in the original word "prongs" (Smyth, Morris, Levy, & Ellis, 1987).

Finally, there are *semantic substitution errors*, in which the correct word is replaced by a word of similar meaning (e.g., "Where is my tennis bat?" instead of "Where is my tennis racket?"). In 99% of cases, the substituted word is of the same form class as the correct word (e.g., nouns substitute for nouns). Verbs are much less likely than nouns, adjectives, or adverbs to undergo semantic substitution (Hotopf, 1980).

INTERPRETING SPEECH ERRORS

Various theories are designed to account for speech errors. However, we will focus on the spreading-activation theory put forward by Dell (1986) and by Dell and O'Seaghdha (1991). We start with the key notion of **spreading activation**. It is assumed that the nodes within a network (many corresponding to words) vary in their activation or energy. When a node or word is activated, activation or energy spreads from it to other related nodes. For example, strong activation of the node corresponding to "tree" may cause some activation of the node corresponding to "plant."

As we saw earlier, Dell (1986) identified four levels of speech production: semantic, syntactic, morphological, and phonological. Processing during speech planning occurs at the same time at all four levels. However, it is typically more advanced at the semantic and syntactic levels than at the morphological and phonological ones. Thus, the system operates flexibly. It also operates in parallel, meaning that several processes can all occur at the same time. Two kinds of rules are of particular importance:

1. *Categorical rules* impose constraints on the categories of items produced at each level. This ensures that selected items belong to the appropriate category (e.g., noun or verb at the syntactic level).
2. *Insertion rules* select the items for inclusion in the representations at each level according to the following criterion: the most highly activated node or word belonging to the appropriate category (e.g., noun) is selected.

After an item has been selected, its activation level immediately reduces to zero, thus ensuring it will not be selected repeatedly.

KEY TERM
Spreading activation: the notion that activation or energy spreads from an activated node (e.g., word) to other related nodes.

Spreading-activation theory provides a straightforward account of many speech errors. According to the theory, speech errors occur whenever an incorrect item is more activated than the correct item. The existence of spreading activation means that several nodes are typically *all* activated at the same time—this increaes the likelihood of errors creeping into our speech. Below we briefly consider findings on speech errors that support spreading-activation theory.

First, the existence of categorical rules means that errors should typically belong to the appropriate category (e.g., an incorrect noun replacing the correct one). As predicted, precisely this is the case with 99% of semantic substitution errors.

Second, many sounds and words within a sentence being planned will all be activated at the same time. As a result, there will be anticipation errors, in which a sound or word is spoken earlier in the sentence than is appropriate. This is found with sound-exchange errors, word-exchange errors, and spoonerisms.

Third, and related to the second point, exchange errors mostly involve sounds or words moving only a relatively short distance within the sentence. Those words relevant to the part of the sentence under current consideration will tend to be more activated than those relevant to more distant parts of the sentence. Thus, these findings are also consistent with spreading-activation theory.

Fourth, and of special importance, spreading-activation theory can account for the **mixed error effect**. This occurs when an incorrect spoken word is semantically *and* phonemically related to the correct word. Dell (1986) quoted the example of someone saying "Let's stop" instead of "Let's start." The spoken word and the correct word are generally more similar in sound than would be expected by chance alone (Dell & O'Seaghdha, 1991). According to spreading-activation theory, activation often occurs at the semantic and phonological levels at the same time, and this helps to produce the mixed error effect.

WORD PROCESSING: ORDERED OR DISORDERED?

There is reasonable agreement on the kinds of processing involved in speech production. For example, it is generally accepted that speakers need to engage in processing at the semantic, syntactic, morphological, and phonological levels. However, there has been considerable controversy concerning the ways in which these various processes relate to each other in the production of individual words. One major possibility is that everything happens in a neat and tidy fashion as proposed by Levelt, Roelofs, and Meyer (1999) in their influential WEAVER++ model. According to Levelt et al., word production involves a series of processing stages following each other in serial (i.e., one at a time) fashion. The key notion here is that each processing stage is completed before the next one starts. In addition, WEAVER++ is based on the assumption that the system is a feedforward one. This means that processing proceeds in a strictly forward (i.e., from meaning to sound) direction.

Another major possibility is that the processes involved in word production occur in much more flexible and variable ways. According to Dell's (e.g.,

KEY TERM
Mixed error effect:
speech errors that are semantically and phonologically related to the intended word.

1986) spreading-activation theory (discussed above), processing during speech production (including the production of words) occurs *at the same time* at all levels (e.g., semantic, syntactic). In other words, processing occurs in parallel. In addition, processing is *interactive*, meaning that processes at any level can influence processes at any other level.

In sum, the serial processing and feedforward assumptions of WEAVER++ imply that the processes involved in speech production are highly regimented and structured. In contrast, the parallel processing and interactive assumptions of spreading-activation theory imply that the processes involved in speech production are, if not chaotic, then at least very flexible. In fact, however, the differences between the two theoretical approaches are less extreme than indicated so far. For example, it is indeed assumed within spreading-activation theory that processing can occur at all levels at the same time. However, Dell (1986) accepted that processing is generally more advanced at some levels (e.g., semantic) than at others (e.g., phonological). Thus, the notion that initial processing is mainly at the semantic and syntactic levels whereas later processing is mainly at the morphological and phonological levels is subscribed to by Levelt et al. (1999) and by Dell (1986).

As we will see, there is no clear winner in this controversy. What we will do is consider evidence supporting each theoretical position and then draw some conclusions.

PROCESSING: SERIAL!

According to Levelt et al.'s (1999) WEAVER++ model, what is of central importance in word production is the process by which word meaning is translated into word sound. It is assumed that we possess lemmas containing the meaning we want to convey. More specifically, **lemmas** are abstract words containing semantic and syntactic (grammatical) information. A key assumption is that the process of lemma or abstract word selection is completed *before* phonological information about the word is accessed.

This view of what is involved receives support from a fairly common experience known as the **tip-of-the-tongue phenomenon**. In this phenomenon, we have a concept or idea in mind but search in vain for the right word to describe it. Brown and McNeill (1966) presented participants with dictionary definitions of rare words and asked them to identify the words defined. In many cases, participants were put into the tip-of-the-tongue state, in which they, "would appear to be in a mild torment, something like the brink of a sneeze" (Brown & McNeill, 1966, p. 325). In terms of Levelt et al.'s theory, it seems likely that the tip-of-the-tongue state occurs when the lemma or abstract word has been activated but the word itself cannot be accessed.

You may remember that Levelt et al. (1999) assumed that the lemma includes syntactic as well as semantic information. Accordingly, individuals in the tip-of-the-tongue state should have access to syntactic (grammatical) information. In many languages (e.g., Italian), part of the syntactic information about nouns is in the form of grammatical gender (e.g., masculine, feminine). Vigliocco, Antonini, and Garrett (1997) carried out a study on Italian participants who guessed the grammatical gender of words they couldn't produce. When they were in the tip-of-the-tongue state, they guessed the grammatical gender correctly about 85% of the time. Thus, these participants had access to syntactic information about words they couldn't bring to mind.

According to WEAVER++, speakers have access to semantic and syntactic information about words *before* they have access to phonological information. Support for these assumptions has been obtained in studies using event-related potentials (ERPs; see Glossary). van Turennout, Hagoort, and Brown (1998) measured ERPs while their Dutch participants produced noun phrases (e.g., "rode tafel" meaning "red table"). Their key finding was that syntactic information about the noun's gender was available about 40 ms before its initial phoneme. Schmitt, Münte, and Kutas (2000) used ERPs on a picture-naming task. A crucial component of the ERP (N200) peaked 89 ms earlier when participants could make decisions on the basis of semantic information rather than phonological information.

Evidence consistent with the assumptions of WEAVER++ has been obtained from other brain-imaging studies. Indefrey and Levelt (2004) used data from dozens of picture-naming experiments to carry out a *meta-analysis* (involving combining data from many studies on a given issue). Lexical selection occurs within about 175 ms of picture presentation, with the appropriate phonological (sound) code being retrieved between 250 and 300 ms of stimulus presentation. After that, a phonological word is generated at about 455 ms. Finally, after a further 145 ms or so, the sensori-motor areas involved in word articulation become active (see Figure 20.2)

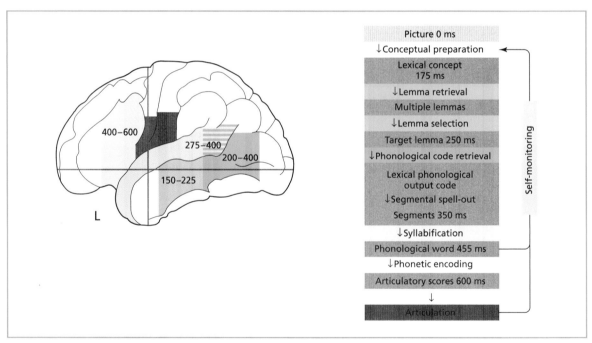

Figure 20.2 Time taken (in ms) for different processes to occur in picture naming. The specific processes are shown on the right and the relevant brain regions are shown on the left. From Indefrey and Levelt (2004). Reprinted with permission of Elsevier.

PROCESSING: PARALLEL!

Suppose that Dell (1986) is correct. If so, various levels of processing involved in speech production, and specifically in word production, interact flexibly at the same time. It follows that word errors can be multiply determined; that is, influenced by more than one source of information. Precisely this has been observed in the mixed error effect (discussed above). This occurs when a spoken word is both semantically *and* phonemically related to the correct word.

Some studies have been designed to test conflicting predictions from the two theoretical approaches we have been comparing. Suppose we present participants with pictures having a dominant (e.g., rocket) and a non-dominant name (e.g., missile), and ask them to name the picture as rapidly as possible. According to WEAVER++, the stage of lemma retrieval typically produces the dominant name (e.g., rocket). Accordingly, there should be little or no phonological processing of the non-dominant name (e.g., missile). Suppose, however, there is considerable parallel and interactive processing as assumed within Dell's spreading-activation theory. If so, there would generally be much phonological processing of the dominant *and* non-dominant words.

Peterson and Savoy (1998) tested the above predictions. On key trials, a word appeared in the middle of the picture (e.g., of a rocket or missile) and the participants had to name that word out loud as rapidly as possible rather than name the picture. As both models would predict, word naming was speeded up when the word was related in sound to the *dominant* picture name (e.g., rocket). More importantly, word naming was also speeded up when the word was related in sound to the *non-dominant* picture. The finding that there was activation of the sounds of *both* pictures at the same time seems inconsistent with Levelt et al.'s (1999) serial processing model.

Morsella and Miozzo (2002) reported similar findings. Participants were presented with two colored pictures, with one superimposed on the other. They had to name the pictures in a given color (target pictures) while ignoring the pictures in a different color (distractor pictures). Some distractor pictures were related in sound to the target pictures (e.g., bell as a distractor presented with bed), but others weren't related in sound (e.g., hat as a distractor presented with bed). According to WEAVER++, the phonological features of the names for distractor pictures shouldn't have been activated. As a result, the speed of naming target pictures shouldn't be influenced by whether or not the names of the two pictures were phonologically related. In contrast, Dell's (1986) spreading-activation model predicts that the phonological features of distractors are often activated. As a result, target pictures should be named faster when accompanied by phonologically related distractors rather than by unrelated ones. The findings supported the prediction of spreading-activation theory and disconfirmed that of WEAVER++.

We have seen that speech production often involves parallel processing. However, the extent of such processing has sometimes been exaggerated. According to spreading-activation theory, for example, speech errors occur when the wrong word is more highly activated than the correct one and so is selected. It follows that there should be numerous errors when incorrect words are readily available. This prediction was tested by Glaser (1992), who studied the time taken to name pictures (e.g., a table). Theoretically, there should have been a large increase in errors when each picture was accompanied by a semantically related distractor word (e.g., chair). In fact, there was only a modest increase in the error rate. This clearly implies that there was more limited processing of the distractor words than expected on Dell's theory.

SPEECH DISORDERS

As we have seen in several chapters of this book, we can often learn much about normal human cognition by studying brain-damaged patients. That is certainly the case so far as speech production is concerned. Some language-disordered patients have relatively intact access to syntactic information but impaired access to content words (e.g., nouns, verbs), whereas other language-disordered patients have the opposite pattern. The existence of such *patterns* is consistent with theories (e.g., spreading-activation theory, WEAVER++) assuming that speech production involves separable stages of syntactic processing and word finding. As you read this section, focus on the issue of whether you are convinced that patients with a given disorder actually show clear patterns of strengths and weaknesses in their speech-production abilities. Alas, you may well conclude that the findings in this area are very inconsistent, with no clear picture emerging.

HISTORICAL PERSPECTIVE

Back in the nineteenth century, studies on brain-damaged patients produced an important distinction between Broca's aphasia and Wernicke's aphasia. Patients with **Broca's aphasia** have slow, non-fluent speech. They also have a poor ability to produce syntactically correct sentences, even though their speech comprehension is relatively intact. Here is the speech (in italics) of a man with Broca's aphasia having a conversation (Gardner, 1977):

Compare and contrast Broca's and Wernicke's aphasia. What can these cases tell us about normal speech perception and production?

"What happened to make you lose your speech?"
"Head, fall, Jesus Christ, me no good str ... str ... Oh Jesus ... stroke."
"I see. Could you tell me, Mr. Ford, what you've been doing in the hospital?"
"Yes, sure. Me go, er, uh, P.T. nine o'cot, speech ... two times ... read ... wr ... ripe, er, write ... practice ... getting better."

In contrast, patients with **Wernicke's aphasia** have fluent and apparently grammatical speech which often lacks meaning. They also typically have severe problems with speech comprehension. Here is the speech (in italics) of a patient with Wernicke's aphasia as reported by Gardner (1977):

"What brings you to the hospital?" I asked the 72-year-old retired butcher four weeks after his admission to the hospital.
"Boy, I'm sweating, I'm awful nervous, you know, once in a while I get caught up, I can't mention the tarripoi, a month ago, quite a little, I've done a lot well, I impose a lot, while, on the other hand, you know what I mean ..."

KEY TERMS
Broca's aphasia: a form of language disorder in brain-damaged patients involving non-fluent speech and grammatical errors.
Wernicke's aphasia: a form of language disorder in brain-damaged patients involving impaired comprehension and fluent speech with many content words missing.

It was claimed by those giving their names to these two language disorders (Paul Broca and Carl Wernicke) that areas within the left hemisphere were damaged (see Figure 20.3). More specifically, it was argued that Broca's aphasia occurs because of damage within a small area of the frontal lobe (Broca's area). In contrast, Wernicke's aphasia involves damage within a small area of the posterior temporal lobe (Wernicke's area).

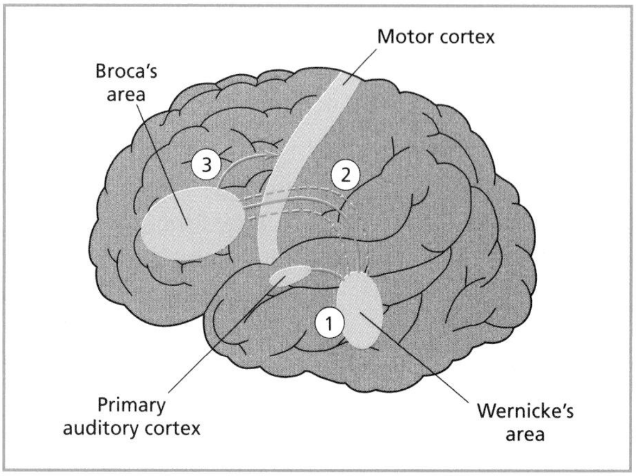

The evidence indicates that the brain damage suffered by patients with Broca's aphasia and Wernicke's aphasia is very often *not* specific to the classic brain areas. For example, Willmes and Poeck (1993) found that only 59% of patients with Broca's aphasia had damage in Broca's area, and 35% of patients with damage in Broca's area had Broca's aphasia. De Bleser (1988) studied seven very clear cases of Broca's aphasia and six very clear cases of Wernicke's aphasia. Of the seven patients with Broca's aphasia, four had damage to Broca's area, but the others had damage to Wernicke's area. Of the six patients with Wernicke's aphasia, four had damage primarily to Wernicke's area, but the other two had damage to Broca's area as well.

Figure 20.3 The location of Wernicke's area (1) and Broca's area (3) are shown. When someone speaks a word, activation proceeds from Wernicke's area through the arcuate fasciculus (2) to Broca's area.

Dick et al. (2001) pointed out that there are many **inflecting languages** in which important grammatical relationships (e.g., tense of verbs; single vs. plural of nouns) are indicated by changing the endings of words. For example, adding -ed to "show" indicates the verb is in the past tense. There are many inflections in the English language, but far fewer than in inflecting languages such as German, Italian, or Hungarian.

The above differences among languages help to explain why English-speaking patients with Wernicke's aphasia seem to speak reasonably grammatically. There are two major possibilities:

1. Patients with Wernicke's aphasia genuinely suffer few grammatical problems.
2. Patients with Wernicke's aphasia have severe grammatical problems, but these are not obvious in a non-inflecting language like English.

Dick et al. (2001, p. 764) considered findings from patients speaking various inflecting languages, and obtained clear support for the second possibility: "Studies of speech production in richly inflecting languages show that Wernicke's aphasic patients make grammatical errors similar in quantity and severity to the errors produced by Broca's aphasic patients . . . The English system of grammatical morphology [form and structure of words] is so impoverished that it offers few opportunities for grammatical substitution errors."

AGRAMMATISM

Most theories of speech production assume there are separate stages for working out the syntax or grammar of utterances and for producing content

KEY TERM
Inflecting language: a language in which grammatical relationships are shown by altering word endings (e.g., -s to indicate plural nouns).

words to fit that grammatical structure (e.g., Dell, 1986). It follows that some patients should be able to produce content words in spite of having problems with syntax. Brain-damaged patients who can generally find the right words but can't order them grammatically suffer from **agrammatism**, a condition associated with damage to Broca's area. Patients with agrammatism typically produce short sentences containing content words (e.g., nouns, verbs) but lacking function words (e.g., the, in, and) and word endings. In addition, it has often been assumed that patients with agrammatism have problems in understanding syntactically complex sentences.

Guasti and Luzzati (2002) provided a detailed account of the spontaneous speech of agrammatic patients. The patients had very impaired syntactic processing especially as revealed in their inappropriate use of verbs. They often failed to adjust the form of verbs to take account of person or number, mostly used only the present tense of verbs, and omitted many verbs altogether. In addition, they rarely used a **subordinate clause**, a minor clause that cannot stand on its own to form a sentence. For example, in the sentence "A pop star who had taken drugs was arrested at his hotel," "who had taken drugs" is the subordinate clause.

The greatest weakness with the notion of agrammatism is that it implies that patients with the disorder are much more similar to each other than is actually the case. For example, Miceli, Silveri, Romani, and Caramazza (1989) studied the speech productions of 20 patients classified as agrammatic. Some patients omitted many more **prepositions** (grammatical words such as "with" and "from" indicating a relation) than definite articles ("the") when speaking, but others showed the opposite pattern. Berndt, Mitchum, and Haendiges (1996) used data from numerous studies to address the issue of whether agrammatic aphasics have impaired language comprehension for active and passive sentences. In 30% of studies, comprehension was above chance on both kinds of sentences. In 36% of studies, there was reasonable performance on active sentences but chance performance on passive sentences. In the remaining 34% of studies, comprehension performance was at (or close to) chance on both kinds of sentences.

JARGON APHASIA

We have seen that patients with agrammatism can find the content words they want to say, but cannot produce grammatically correct sentences. Patients suffering from **jargon aphasia** show the opposite pattern, apparently speaking fairly grammatically but being unable to find content words. Jargon aphasics experience great difficulty in finding the right words. They often substitute one word for another, and often produce **neologisms**, which are made-up words. Most jargon aphasics have very severe problems with language comprehension. In addition, jargon aphasics are typically unaware that their speech contains numerous errors, indicating that they are very poor at self-monitoring (Marshall, Robson, Pring, & Chiat, 1998).

Patients with jargon aphasia would often have been diagnosed as having Wernicke's aphasia in the past, and such patients often have severe problems with grammatical processing (Dick et al., 2001). However, Butterworth (1985) found that when jargon aphasics used invented or made-up words in their speech, they typically added prefixes or suffixes to them to make them fit into the syntactic structure of the sentence. For example, if an invented word referred to the past participle of a verb, then it would generally end in -ed.

Ellis, Miller, and Sin (1983) studied a jargon aphasic, RD. Here is his description of a picture of a scout camp with the words he seemed to be looking for in brackets: "A b-boy is swi'ing (SWINGING) on the bank with his hand (FEET) in the stringt (STREAM). A table with orstrum (SAUCEPAN?) and ... I don't know ... and a three-legged stroe (STOOL) and a strane (PAIL)—table, table ... near the water." RD, in common with most jargon aphasics, produced more neologisms or invented words when the word he wanted was not a common one.

What factors determine the particular neologisms produced by jargon aphasics? Robson, Pring, Marshall, and Chiat (2003) provided part

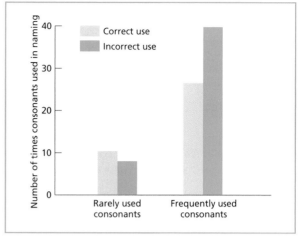

Figure 20.4 Mean number of times rarely used and frequently used consonants were produced correctly and incorrectly on a picture-naming task. Based on data in Robson et al. (2003).

of the answer in a study of a jargon aphasic LT, whose speech consisted almost entirely of neologisms. He named pictures, and most of the phonemes he used were related to those in the correct answer. However, LT had a strong tendency to produce consonants common in the English language regardless of whether or not they were correct (see Figure 20.4). This finding can be explained on Dell's spreading-activation theory (discussed earlier). In essence, the resting activation of frequently used consonants is greater than that of rarely used consonants. This increases the probability of producing frequently used consonants correctly and incorrectly.

EVALUATION AND CHAPTER SUMMARY

Introduction
- Speakers make use of various strategies such as preformulation and underspecification to reduce the demands on them.
- However, they typically communicate fairly effectively, by using discourse markers, prosodic cues, and by establishing the common ground with their listener or listeners.
- The amount of planning engaged in by speakers before starting an utterance is flexible and responsive to situational demands.
- When there are few constraints on what they should say or when they should say it, speakers' planning often extends to an entire clause. However, when the time and/or other demands are great, there is much less pre-planning of utterances.
- Speech production involves semantic, syntactic, morphological, and phonological processing.
- Processing tends to proceed from the semantic and syntactic levels to the morphological and phonological ones. However, there are many exceptions, and the reality is rarely neat and tidy.

Speech errors
- The study of speech errors sheds light on speech production by revealing what happens when there is partial malfunctioning of the mechanisms involved.
- For example, the fact that many speech errors are anticipation errors provides evidence that we engage in forward planning when speaking.
- Most of the findings on speech errors can be understood within Dell's spreading-activation theory.
- According to this theory, speech production involves four levels of processing (semantic, syntactic, morphological, and phonological), with processing occurring flexibly and in parallel across all levels.
- Speech errors occur when the most activated node or item is incorrect, a common situation in a parallel system in which several nodes are typically activated at the same time.
- The finding that most exchange errors involve sounds or words moving only a short distance within the sentence suggests that there is limited forward planning of speech.

Word processing: Ordered or disordered?
- There has been controversy as to whether the processes involved in word production occur serially or in parallel.
- On the one hand, it is assumed within WEAVER++ that the precise word meaning is decided on before phonological information only relating to that word is activated. This is a serial model.
- In contrast, it is assumed within spreading-activation theory that phonological information of two or more words could be activated at the same time. This is a parallel theory.
- The tip-of-the-tongue phenomenon indicates that semantic (and syntactic) information can be available in the absence of information about the sound of the sought-after word.
- In addition, studies using event-related potentials (ERPs) have shown that semantic and syntactic information is processed before phonological information.
- However, the existence of the mixed error effect suggests that semantic and phonological information can be activated at the same time.
- Studies designed to compare predictions from the two competing approaches (Morsella & Miozzo, 2002; Peterson & Savoy, 1998) have supported spreading-activation theory over WEAVER++.
- There is more parallel processing of word meaning and sound than assumed within WEAVER++, but the extent of such processing may be less than assumed within spreading-activation theory.

Speech disorders
- Research in this area provides general support for the notion that there are separate stages of syntactic processing and word finding in speech production.
- More specifically, it has been argued that patients with Broca's

aphasia or agrammatism have impaired syntactic processing, but relatively intact ability to produce content words.
- In contrast, patients with Wernicke's aphasia or jargon aphasia have the opposite pattern.
- What we have here is a double dissociation, and double dissociations are often regarded as providing especially strong evidence that two processes or mechanisms are genuinely separate.
- There is some validity in the above argument, but there are two problems with it.
- First, the pattern of intact and impaired language abilities in any given patient is typically rather complex.
- Second, and related to the first point, it is a serious oversimplification to assume that all patients assigned to the same category (e.g., jargon aphasia) have the same impairments.

FURTHER READING

- Harley, T. (2001). *The psychology of language: From data to theory* (2nd ed.). Hove, UK: Psychology Press. Chapter 12 of this truly excellent textbook contains good coverage of key issues in speech production.
- Holtgraves, T.M. (2002). *Language as social action: Social psychology and language use*. Mahwah, NJ: Lawrence Erlbaum Associates. A central theme in this book is the notion that speech allows us to share our social world with other people.
- Jay, T.B. (2003). *The psychology of language*. Upper Saddle River, NJ: Prentice Hall. Chapter 6 of this textbook provides a useful introduction to the topic of speech production.
- Vigliocco, G., & Hartsuiker, R.J. (2002). The interplay of meaning, sound, and syntax in sentence production. *Psychological Bulletin*, *128*, 442–472. This chapter contains a thorough analysis of the main processes involved in speech production.
- Wheeldon, L.R. (2000). *Aspects of language production*. Hove, UK: Psychology Press. This edited book covers a wide range of key topics within speech production.

CHAPTER 21

CONTENTS

Introduction 307

Prototype approach 310

Exemplar approach 313

Concept learning 315

Evaluation and chapter summary 318

Further reading 321

What's in a concept?

INTRODUCTION

As I sit here in the morning sunshine dreaming my dreams, I am vaguely aware of certain concepts such as those of a "computer," a "computer screen," a "keyboard," and "cup" (I have just made myself a cup of coffee). It is perhaps easy to imagine that **concepts** (mental representations of classes or objects or other entities) are relatively uninteresting and perhaps even unimportant. Nothing could be further from the truth, as was shown by the South American writer Jorge-Luis Borges (1964, pp. 93–94). He described a fictional man called Funes who had perfect memory for every second of his life, but had no ability to categorize his experience or to use concepts:

> Funes remembered not only every leaf of every tree of every wood, but also every one of the times he had perceived or imagined it . . . He was, let us not forget, almost incapable of ideas of a general, Platonic sort. Not only was it difficult for him to comprehend that the generic symbol dog embraces so many unlike individuals of diverse size and form; it bothered him that the dog at three fourteen (seen from the side) should have the same name as the dog at three fifteen (seen from the front). His own face in the mirror, his own hands, surprised him every time he saw them.

As the quotation from Borges suggests, concepts are of vital importance in our lives, and are centrally involved in perception, learning, memory, and our use of language. Why is that the case? The answer was provided by Murphy (2002, p. 1):

> Concepts are the mental glue that holds our mental world together . . . When we walk into a room, try a new restaurant, go to the supermarket to buy groceries, meet a doctor, or read a story, we must rely on our concept of the world to help us understand what is happening . . . Concepts are a kind of mental glue in that they tie our past experiences to our present interactions with the world, and because the concepts themselves are connected to our larger knowledge structures.

KEY TERM

Concepts: mental representations of categories of objects or items.

TYPES OF CONCEPTS

What are concepts? How many types are there?

It has often been assumed that concepts are organized into hierarchies. Rosch, Mervis, Gray, Johnson, and Boyes-Braem (1976) identified *three* levels within such hierarchies: superordinate categories at the top, basic-level categories in the middle, and subordinate categories at the bottom. For example, "furniture" is a superordinate category, "chair" is a basic-level category, and "easy chair" is a subordinate category.

Rosch et al. (1976) asked people to list all the attributes of concepts or categories at each level. Very few attributes were listed for the superordinate categories, presumably because the categories are rather abstract. Many attributes were listed for the categories at the other two levels. However, at the lowest level very similar attributes were listed for different categories. The basic-level categories are of most general usefulness, having the best balance between informativeness and distinctiveness. Informativeness is missing at the highest level of the hierarchy, and distinctiveness is missing at the lowest level.

Rosch et al. (1976) asked people to name pictures of objects. They obtained strong evidence that we generally use basic-level categories rather than superordinate or subordinate ones. Basic-level names were used 1595 times in the course of the experiment, with subordinate names being used 14 times and superordinate names only once. However, we might imagine that experts would focus more on subordinate categories than on basic-level ones. For example, we would expect a botanist to refer to the various kinds of plants in a garden rather than simply describing them as plants! Relevant evidence was reported by Tanaka and Taylor (1991) in a study on birdwatchers and dog experts shown pictures of birds and dogs. Both groups used subordinate names (i.e., specific species or breeds) much more often in their expert domain than in their novice domain.

ORGANIZATION OF CONCEPTS

The classical approach to concept organization (known as the defining-attribute approach) owes its origins to Aristotle, the great ancient Greek philosopher and scientist. According to this approach, a concept can be characterized by a set of **defining attributes**, which are those semantic features necessary and sufficient for something to be an instance of the concept (see Panel 21.1). Thus, for example, the defining attributes of the concept "bachelor" might be as follows: male; single; and adult. According to this defining-attribute view, concepts should divide up individual objects in the world into distinct classes so that the boundaries between categories are well-defined and rigid.

Another prediction from the defining-attribute view is that conceptual hierarchies should be neat and tidy. For example, suppose the defining attributes of the concept "bird" are feathered, animate, and two-legged. We would then expect that every species of bird (e.g., sparrows, robins) should possess *all* of the attributes of the "bird" concept, plus other attributes specific to that species. Since most species of birds we can readily think of are basically fairly similar, that expectation may seem perfectly reasonable.

The defining-attribute approach was highly regarded for hundreds (if not thousands) of years, and superficially seems to make sense. However, it is now dismissed as woefully inadequate. We will consider three kinds of evid-

Panel 21.1 Defining-attribute theories of concepts

- The meaning of a concept can be captured by a conjunctive list of attributes (i.e., a list of attributes connected by ANDs).
- These attributes are atomic units or primitives which are the basic building blocks of concepts.
- Each of these attributes is necessary and all of them are jointly sufficient for something to be identified as an instance of the concept.
- What is and is not a member of the category is clearly defined; thus, there are clear-cut boundaries between members and non-members of the category.
- All members of the concept are equally representative.
- When concepts are organized in a hierarchy then the defining attributes of a more specific concept (e.g., sparrow) in relation to its more general relative (its superordinate; e.g., bird) include all the defining attributes of the superordinate.

ence disproving the defining-attribute approach. First, according to that approach, any given object is definitely a member of a given category or definitely not. However, many of our concepts are nothing like that. They are often fuzzy rather than neat and tidy, and we may be unsure whether a given object is (or is not) a member of a given category. For example, McCloskey and Glucksberg (1978) gave 30 participants tricky questions such as, "Is a stroke a disease?" and "Is a pumpkin a fruit?" They found that 16 said a stroke was a disease, but 14 said it was not. A pumpkin was regarded as a fruit by 16 participants but not as a fruit by the remainder. More surprisingly, when McCloskey and Glucksberg tested the same participants 1 month later, 11 of them had changed their minds about "stroke" being a disease, and 8 had altered their opinion about "pumpkin" being a fruit!

Second, it follows from the defining-attribute approach that every instance of a category is an equally strong or representative member of that category. This is simply *not* the case. For example, we can construct a **typicality gradient** for any category, in which members of that category are ordered in terms of their typicality as category members. There is generally a high level of agreement among people as to which category members are more or less typical, For example, a "robin" is a much more typical member of the bird category than "canary," which in turn is more typical than "penguin." Note that the entire notion of typicality gradients is alien to the defining-attribute approach.

Third, according to the defining-attribute view, concepts are static and unchanging. In fact, as Barsalou (1987, 1989) pointed out, how we represent a concept *changes* as a function of the context in which it appears. For example, when we read the word "frog" in isolation, the phrase "eaten by humans" probably remains inactive in our memory system. However, "eaten by humans" *does* become active when reading about frogs in a French restaurant. Thus, concepts are unstable or flexible to the extent that different information is incorporated into the representation of a concept in different situations.

Barsalou (2003) provided another interesting example of concept instability. Participants carried out two tasks at the same time:

1. They used their hands to imagine performing various factory operations.
2. They identified the properties of concepts.

Sometimes the actions performed by the participants were relevant to the property generation task. For example, they produced the properties of

KEY TERM

Typicality gradient: the ordering of the members of a category in terms of how typical of that category they seem to be.

"dresser" while at the same time pretending to open a drawer. Concept instability was shown, because more internal properties of a dresser (e.g., "socks"; "sweater") were produced when the action revealed the inside of the drawer than when it did not.

Fourth, some categories (known as *ad hoc* categories) are formed spontaneously in certain situations. For example, suppose you wanted to sell off your unwanted possessions. You might construct an *ad hoc* category of "things to sell at a garage sale."

In view of the enormous limitations of the defining-attribute approach, numerous other theoretical approaches to concepts have been developed. We turn now to two of the best-known of such approaches.

PROTOTYPE APPROACH

How well does the prototype approach explain concept structure and organization?

Rosch and Mervis (1975), whose research is discussed shortly, played a major role in the development of the prototype approach. According to this approach, categories have a central description or **prototype** that in some sense stands for the whole category. There are various prototype-based approaches. However, it is often assumed that the prototype is a set of characteristic attributes or a summary representation in which some attributes are weighted more than others. Note that within this approach there are *no* defining attributes, but rather only characteristic ones.

It follows from the prototype approach that an object is a member of a given category if there is a reasonably good match between its attributes and those of the prototype. Category members share **family resemblances**, meaning they have some features in common with other category members. Why are family resemblances important? According to prototype theory, category members having the highest family resemblance scores come closer than other category members to representing the category's prototype. Thus, category members with high family resemblance scores are "better" or more typical category members than those having low family resemblance scores. A fairly complete listing of the main assumptions of prototype theories is presented in Panel 21.2.

Panel 21.2 Prototype theory of concepts

- Concepts have a prototype structure; the prototype is either a collection of characteristic attributes or the best example (or examples) of the concept.
- There is no delimiting set of necessary and sufficient attributes for determining category membership; there may be necessary attributes, but they are not jointly sufficient; indeed membership often depends on the object possessing some set of characteristic, non-necessary attributes that are considered more typical or representative of the category than others.
- Category boundaries are fuzzy or unclear; what is and is not a member of the category is ill-defined; so some members of the category may slip into other categories (e.g., tomatoes as fruit or vegetables.)
- Instances of a concept can be ranged in terms of their typicality; that is, there is a typicality gradient which characterizes the differential typicality of examples of the concept.
- Category membership is determined by the similarity of an object's attributes to the category's prototype.

FINDINGS

Impressive evidence of the importance of family resemblances within categories was reported by Rosch and Mervis (1975). They used six categories with 20 members varying in their typicality representing each category (see Table 21.1). The participants' task was to list the attributes of the category members. Most of the attributes of any given category member were shared by at least some of the other members of the same category, and this information was used to calculate family resemblance scores for each member. For example, suppose a category member had two attributes, one possessed by 16 category members and the other possessed by 14 category members. This would give a family resemblance score of $16 + 14 = 30$.

Rosch and Mervis's (1975) key finding was that typical category members had much higher family resemblance scores than did atypical category members. The correlation between typicality and family resemblance ranged between $+.84$ (for vegetables) and $+.94$ (for weapons). Rosch and Mervis also considered the numbers of attributes shared by the five most typical and the five least typical members of each category. We will discuss the findings from the vehicle category, but similar results were obtained with all the other categories as well. The five most typical members of the vehicle category (car, truck, bus, motorcycle, and train) had 36 attributes in common (e.g., wheels, engine, driver). In contrast, the five least typical members (horse, blimp, skates, wheelbarrow, and elevator) had only 2 attributes in common.

Prototype theory predicts it should be easier to learn concepts when exposed only to typical instances than when exposed only to atypical ones not

Table 21.1 Typicality of items belonging to six categories. From Rosch and Mervis (1975). Reproduced with permission from Elsevier.

Typicality	Furniture	Fruit	Vehicle	Weapons	Clothing	Vegetables
1	Chair	Orange	Car	Gun	Pants	Peas
2	Sofa	Apple	Truck	Knife	Shirt	Carrots
3	Table	Banana	Bus	Sword	Dress	String beans
4	Dresser	Peach	Motorcycle	Bomb	Skirt	Spinach
5	Desk	Pear	Train	Hand grenade	Jacket	Broccoli
6	Bed	Apricot	Trolley	Spear	Coat	Asparagus
7	Bookcase	Plum	Bicycle	Cannon	Sweater	Corn
8	Footstool	Grape	Aeroplane	Bow and arrow	Underpants	Cauliflower
9	Lamp	Strawberry	Boat	Club	Socks	Brussels sprouts
10	Piano	Grapefruit	Tractor	Tank	Pyjamas	Lettuce
11	Cushion	Pineapple	Cart	Tear gas	Bathing suit	Beets
12	Mirror	Blueberry	Wheelchair	Whip	Shoes	Tomato
13	Rug	Lemon	Tank	Ice pick	Vest	Lima beans
14	Radio	Watermelon	Raft	Fists	Tie	Eggplant
15	Stove	Honeydew	Sled	Rocket	Mittens	Onion
16	Clock	Pomegranate	Horse	Poison	Hat	Potato
17	Picture	Date	Blimp	Scissors	Apron	Yam
18	Closet	Coconut	Skates	Words	Purse	Mushroom
19	Vase	Tomato	Wheelbarrow	Foot	Wristwatch	Pumpkin
20	Telephone	Olive	Elevator	Screwdriver	Necklace	Rice

resembling the prototype. This prediction was confirmed by Mervis and Pani (1980) in a study in which children were initially presented with a typical or atypical exemplar of a novel category. Their performance with other category members was much worse when they had previously seen the atypical exemplar than when they had seen the typical exemplar. This finding makes sense—for example, you wouldn't teach a young child the concept of "bird" by exposing him or her only to ostriches and penguins!

The prototype approach works well with most categories, but not with all. For example, Hampton (1981) found that some abstract concepts (e.g., "a crime"; "a work of art"; "a science") exhibited a prototypic structure, but others (e.g., "a rule"; "a belief"; "an instinct") did not. Why do some abstract concepts lack prototypes? Membership of some abstract categories seems to be almost endlessly flexible in a way not true of concrete categories. For example, we cannot begin to specify the complete set of possible rules or beliefs. This marked lack of constraint on the membership of many abstract categories may be partially responsible for their apparent absence of structure.

According to prototype theory, we group certain objects together in the same category because they are *similar* to each other and share common attributes. This may well be true of most categories. However, we all form categories based only very loosely on shared attributes. For example, Murphy and Medin (1985) discussed the biblical categories of clean and unclean animals. Clean animals include most fish, grasshoppers, and some locusts, whereas unclean animals include camels, ostriches, crocodiles, mice, sharks, and eels. It's hard to see what determines whether any given animal is deemed to be clean or unclean. In fact, the underlying notion is that creatures of the water should have fins and scales and should swim, whereas creatures of the land should have four legs and be well suited for moving on land. Creatures conforming to this theory are clean, whereas those not equipped for the "right" kind of locomotion are unclean.

KEY TERM
Goal-derived categories: categories in which all the members of the category satisfy some goal (e.g., increasing human happiness).

Rosch and Mervis (1975) found that family resemblance scores were very highly correlated with typicality scores. This is as predicted by prototype theory, according to which family resemblances are very important. However, family resemblances are much less important with what are known as **goal-derived categories**. These are categories in which all category members satisfy a given goal (e.g., birthday presents that make the recipient happy). Barsalou (1985) found that family resemblance scores didn't predict typicality scores for members of goal-derived categories (see Figure 21.1). What is going on here? Typical members of goal-derived categories are those best satisfying the goal (e.g., providing pleasure to someone celebrating his or her birthday) rather than sharing attributes with other category members.

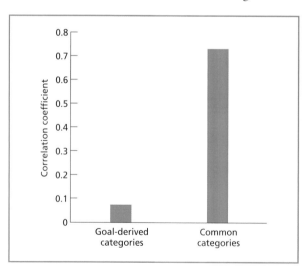

Figure 21.1 Partial correlations (removing statistically the effects of other factors) between family resemblance and typicality for two types of categories (common vs. goal-derived). Data from Barsalou (1985).

EXEMPLAR APPROACH

There has been fierce controversy between those advocating the prototype approach and those who prefer the exemplar approach. Exemplar-based theorists (e.g., Kruschke, 1992; Nosofsky, 1991) paint a very different picture of categories from prototype-based theorists (compare Panels 21.2 and 21.3). Instead of there being some abstracted description of a bird acting as a central prototype, the assumption is one of a memory system storing large numbers of specific instances. Thus, we don't have a prototype for "bird" that is a list of all the characteristic features taken from members of this category (e.g., *has wings*, *flies*, etc.). Instead, we just have a store of all the instances of birds encountered in the past (e.g., the robin you see every morning).

What are the main differences between prototype and exemplar models?

Panel 21.3 The exemplar-based view of concepts

- Categories are made up of a collection of instances or exemplars rather than any abstract description of these instances (e.g., a prototype summary description).
- Instances are grouped relative to one another by some similarity metric.
- Categorization and other phenomena are explained by a mechanism that retrieves instances from memory given a particular cue.
- When exact matches are not found in memory the nearest neighbor to the cue is usually retrieved.

There is a final important assumption associated with the exemplar approach. The instances of a category that come to mind at any given time depend on the specific context. Thus, for example, thinking of the concept of "snails" may be more likely to conjure up images of platefuls of snails cooked in garlic when we are in France than when we are in England. Thus, exemplar theories are better placed than prototype theories to account for flexibility in our use of concepts.

FINDINGS

We saw earlier that category members differ in terms of their typicality. According to the exemplar approach, typicality ratings reflect the number of times that the members of the category have been encountered in the past. For example, a robin is a more typical instance of a bird than is a penguin, because we have many more stored instances of robins than of penguins.

It will be remembered that Barsalou (1987, 1989) found that the representation of concepts (e.g., "frog") varied as a function of the context in which they appeared. Such influences of context are easily accounted for within exemplar theories, because context helps to determine which members of the category are accessed.

According to the exemplar approach, the information about a category we have stored in long-term memory preserves information about the *variability* of instances in that category. In contrast, a prototype is a kind of average across the instances of a category and so excludes information about variability. Rips and Collins (1993) showed that variability information sometimes influences categorization. The categories they considered included pizzas and rulers. Most pizzas in the United States are 12 inches across but can vary between about 2 and 30 inches. Most rulers are also 12 inches in size and vary in size much less than pizzas. Participants decided whether a new object 19 inches in size was a pizza or a ruler. If they had prototypes, then there should have been a 50–50 split between pizza and ruler, because the prototype average is 12 inches for each. However, if information about size variability was used (as predicted by exemplar-based theories), then participants should always have said the object was a pizza. The findings supported the exemplar approach over the prototype approach.

Storms, De Broeck, and Ruts (2000) carried out an especially interesting study comparing the exemplar and prototype approaches for common categories such as "furniture," "fruit," and "birds." Participants carried out the following four tasks:

1. Category naming: Participants were given exemplars and had to name the category.
2. Exemplar generation: Participants were given the category name and had to name exemplars.
3. Typicality ratings: Participants rated the typicality of various exemplars of each category.
4. Speeded categorization: Participants were shown a category name followed by various words. They decided as rapidly as possible whether each word was or wasn't a member of the category.

What did Storms et al. (2000) find? As can be seen in Figure 21.2, performance on all four tasks was predicted reasonably well by both approaches. However, the predictions of the exemplar-based approach were consistently more accurate, especially on the exemplar-generation task.

The exemplar approach emphasizes the similarity among members of any given category. This poses problems with respect to some categories. For example, it would be difficult to provide an adequate exemplar-based account of *ad hoc* and goal-derived categories. This is because the members of such categories are generally not very similar at all.

Smith and Minda (2000) consistently obtained less support for exemplar theories when relatively simple concepts were learned rather than complex

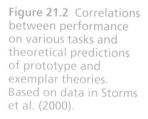

Figure 21.2 Correlations between performance on various tasks and theoretical predictions of prototype and exemplar theories. Based on data in Storms et al. (2000).

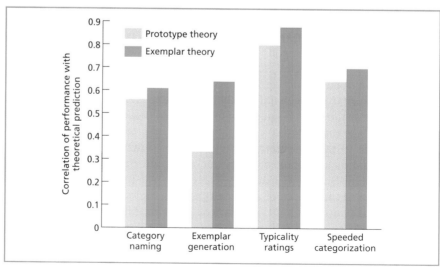

ones. According to Feldman (2003), simple concepts are learned by extracting their *common regularities* (e.g., all even numbers are divisible by 2). In contrast, we cannot learn complex concepts in that way because they lack common regularities, and so we rely on exemplars. Feldman found that exemplar theories greatly underestimate how much easier people find it to learn simple concepts than complex ones. This is because they omit the key role of common regularities or generalizations in the acquisition of simple concepts.

CONCEPT LEARNING

So far we have focused on the organization of concepts in long-term memory. In order to understand more fully *why* concepts are organized as they are, it is important to consider the processes involved in concept learning. Indeed, many attempts to test the exemplar and prototype theories have involved studies in which participants learned various artificial concepts.

In this section, we will focus on two important issues related to concept learning. First, is there a *single* concept-learning mechanism (as is implied by the exemplar and prototype approaches) or are there several? Second, there is the issue of the role played by prior knowledge in concept learning.

ONE vs. SEVERAL LEARNING MECHANISMS

Would we expect concept learning to involve a single learning mechanism or is it more reasonable to expect there to be two or more learning mechanisms? Ashby and Maddox (2005, p. 172) made an excellent point directly relevant to that question: "This issue—of whether there are one or more category-learning systems—is tied to the historically older issue of whether there are one or more memory systems. Learning is, by definition, the process of laying down some sort of memory trace, and there is certainly no reason to suspect that any of the separate memory systems that have been hypothesized are incapable of storing memories about categories." Since the current best estimate is that there are four long-term memory systems (see Chapter 11), the strong implication of Ashby and Maddox's point is that the number of category-learning systems exceeds one. We turn now to research providing support for that viewpoint.

Ashby and Maddox (2005) drew a distinction between rule-based and information-integration category-learning tasks. In rule-based tasks, the categories can be learned by using some explicit reasoning process. The underlying rule is typically easy to describe verbally (e.g., stimuli small on dimension x and small on dimension y belong to category A). In contrast, information-integration tasks generally require complex integration of information from two or more stimulus dimensions. With such tasks it is generally hard or even impossible to verbalize the best strategy to use. A real-world example of an information-integration task is deciding whether an X-ray shows a tumor. This is a complex task requiring years of training, and even expert radiologists find it difficult to describe their categorization strategies.

According to Maddox and Ashby (2004) and Ashby and Maddox (2005), different category-learning systems underlie performance on these two types of tasks. Rule-based category learning mainly depends on attentional processes and working memory (see Chapter 12). Among the parts of the brain claimed to underlie rule-based category learning are the anterior cingulate and the prefrontal cortex, areas associated with working memory and attention. Performance on rule-based category learning tasks is strongly influenced by explicit memory (see Chapter 11) and so there is generally conscious awareness of what has been learned.

In contrast, performance on information-integration tasks involves an implicit system based on procedural learning. It is thus linked to the procedural memory system discussed in Chapter 13. As a result, there is little or no conscious awareness of what has been learned. It has been claimed that brain areas such as the basal ganglia and the medial temporal lobe are involved in category learning on information-integration tasks.

Findings

Evidence concerning the parts of the brain involved in rule-based and information-integration tasks was reviewed by Ashby and Ell (2001). First they discussed findings obtained from brain-damaged patients. There was consistent evidence that patients with damage to the frontal lobe (especially the prefrontal cortex) performed very poorly on rule-based tasks. However, these patients performed as well as non-patients on category learning tasks involving information integration. In contrast, patients with damage to the medial temporal lobe performed poorly on some information-integration tasks, but performed as well as non-patients on rule-based tasks.

Ashby and Ell (2001) went on to discuss the findings from neuroimaging studies. In general terms, the findings from these studies were consistent with those from neuropsychological studies of brain-damaged patients. There was much more evidence of activation in the prefrontal cortex when participants were performing a rule-based task than when performing an information-integration task. In contrast, there was generally much more activation in the medial temporal lobe during category learning on an information-integration task than on a rule-based task.

What would impair performance on information-integration learning tasks but not on rule-based tasks? According to Ashby and Maddox's (2005) theory, people use procedural learning on information-integration tasks and attentional processes, and explicit memory on rule-based tasks. The former type of learning is more rigid or inflexible than the latter type, and so should be more easily disrupted by small changes to the response requirements. Ashby, Ell, and Waldron (2003) tested this hypothesis in a study in which at the end of category training the assignment of categories to response keys was switched. This disrupted performance for participants performing the information-integration task but not for those carrying out the rule-based task.

What would impair performance more on rule-based learning than on information-integration learning? Rule-based learning makes much more use of attentional processes and so should be much more easily disrupted by some irrelevant task demanding attentional resources. This hypothesis was tested by Maddox, Ashby, Ing, and Pickering (2004). Participants performing rule-based and information-integration category learning tasks were provided with feedback. This feedback was followed immediately by an attentionally demanding irrelevant task in one condition. As predicted, this attentionally demanding task was associated with a decrement in performance on the rule-based task but not on the information-integration task (see Figure 21.3).

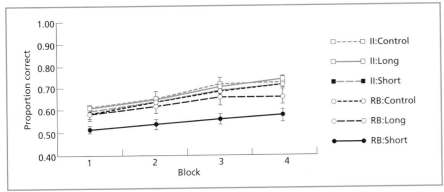

Figure 21.3 Proportion correct for the rule-based (RB, circles) and information-integration (II, squares) category structures under control, short (feedback followed immediately by an attentionally demanding task), and long (feedback followed after an interval by an attentionally demanding task) conditions for each of four blocks of trials. Maddox et al. (2004). Copyright © Psychonomic Society.

KNOWLEDGE-BASED VIEWS

How does our previous knowledge affect our concept learning/ formation?

Exemplar and prototype theories don't take account of knowledge effects, which are "influences of prior knowledge of real objects and events that people bring to the concept-learning situation" (Murphy, 2002, p. 146). The key point was made with great clarity by Murphy (2002, p. 183): "Neither prototype nor exemplar models have attempted to account for knowledge effects ... The problem is that these models start from a kind of *tabula rasa* [blank slate] representation, and concept representations are built up solely by experience with exemplars."

According to Murphy and Medin (1985), what actually happens during concept learning is that we use various explanatory frameworks based on our prior knowledge. For example, there is the biblical distinction (discussed earlier) between clean and unclean animals. Animals belonging to the category of clean animals are equipped for the "appropriate" kind of locomotion for their natural habitat (e.g., land), whereas unclean animals are not.

Findings

Lin and Murphy (1997) showed how knowledge can influence decisions about categorizations made after concept learning has occurred. Participants had the task of learning about objects in a foreign country, with different participants being taught different things about each object. For example, consider the "tuk" shown in Figure 21.4. One group was told the tuk is used for

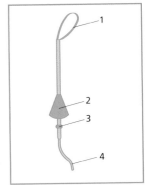

Figure 21.4 A "tuk." The numbers are used to describe its parts (see text). From Lin and Murphy (1997). Copyright © by the American Psychological Association. Reprinted with permission.

hunting. The hunter slips the noose (1) over the animal's head, and pulls on the end of the rope (4) while holding the handle (3) with one hand, and having a hand guard (2) to provide protection from the animal. A second group was told the tuk was a fertilizing tool. Liquid fertilizer is held in the tank (2), the knob (3) is turned to allow it to flow through the outlet pipe (4), and there is a loop (1) which is used to hold the tuk up.

After the participants had learned various concepts, Lin and Murphy (1997) created objects lacking one or more of the parts of the original objects. For example, participants might be presented with a tuk lacking the loop at the top. Those for whom a tuk was a hunting tool were much less likely than those who had learned it was a fertilizing tool to classify this altered object as a tuk. Thus, knowledge of which parts of an object are of crucial importance influences concept learning and subsequent categorization.

Ahn, Kim, Lassaline, and Dennis (2000) argued that we use features providing *causal* explanations when learning concepts. Participants were told that members of a category tend to have three features (e.g., blurred vision, headaches, insomnia). They were also told that blurred vision causes headaches and that headaches cause insomnia. After that, participants indicated the likelihood that an item belonged to the category if one of its features was absent. The rated likelihood of membership was lowest when the initial cause (e.g., blurred vision) was absent and highest when the terminal effect (e.g., insomnia) was missing. Thus, people believe that if the cause is missing, then it is unlikely that an item is a member of the category.

Keil (2003) argued that we typically possess much less causal knowledge about concepts than we think we do. He called this phenomenon the "illusion of explanatory depth." Evidence for this phenomenon was reported by Rozenblit and Keil (2002). Participants were initially presented with a list of phenomena and devices (e.g., helicopters) and rated their overall understanding of how each phenomenon or device works. After that, they read an expert's description of each phenomenon and device and then re-rated their initial level of understanding. The illusion of explanatory depth was shown by the dramatic decrease in participants' ratings of their own knowledge after reading expert descriptions. Indeed, many participants expressed astonishment at how little they knew compared to what they thought they knew.

EVALUATION AND CHAPTER SUMMARY

Prototype approach

- The prototype approach provides a reasonable account of the structure or organization of many concepts.
- Of particular importance, it provides a convincing account of the typicality ratings found with the members of most categories.
- It is likely that summary descriptions or prototypes of most concepts are stored in long-term memory.
- The prototype approach has several limitations, three of which will be mentioned here.

- First, many researchers have failed to provide a precise definition of the key term "prototype." As Murphy (2002, p. 45) pointed out, "Many statements about prototypes in the literature are somewhat vague, making it unclear exactly what the writer is referring to—a single best example? a feature list? if a feature list, determined how?"
- Second, prototype theories work much better with some kinds of concepts than with others. As we have seen, the prototype approach doesn't seem very applicable to some abstract concepts (Hampton, 1981), to some complex concepts (Murphy & Medin, 1985), or to goal-derived categories (Barsalou, 1985).
- Third, as is discussed later, our learning of concepts is influenced by prior knowledge. However, prototype theories are virtually silent in terms of accounting for such effects of knowledge on concept learning.

Exemplar approach
- According to Murphy (2002, p. 114), "Exemplar models have the edge in the current battle of category-learning experiments—certainly if one just counts up the number of experiments in which exemplar models outperform prototype models." For example, Storms et al. (2000) found the exemplar approach predicted performance better than the prototype approach on each of four tasks.
- However, the "victory" of the exemplar-based approach may not be decisive. It is more successful when applied to the learning of very complex concepts rather than simple ones (e.g., Feldman, 2003; Smith & Minda, 2000), and less research attention has been paid to the learning of simple concepts.
- Exemplar theories can account for many findings (e.g., the phenomenon of concept instability; effects attributable to the variability of instances within a category). However, we generally lack detailed accounts of what an exemplar-based account might look like.
- What are the limitations of exemplar theories?
- Simply ask yourself the question, "Is all my knowledge of any given concept provided by the dozens or hundreds or examples of that concept and related concepts stored in my long-term memory?" Hopefully you agree that the answer must be "No!"
- As Murphy (2002, p. 490) pointed out, "One major problem with the [exemplar] approach is that it has been far too narrow, focusing on a small number of paradigms." For example, it is not clear how exemplar-based accounts could explain how we know that cats are mammals or how concept learning is influenced by prior knowledge.
- Is every instance of a category stored in memory?
- If the answer is "Yes," then we have a huge amount of stored information about many categories. If so, it would be very difficult to access most of that information.
- If the answer is "No," then we need a theoretical understanding of the factors determining *which* instances are stored in memory.

- At present, no exemplar-based account provides a convincing explanation of how we prevent information (and storage) overload.

One vs. several concept learning mechanisms
- There is respectable evidence that category learning can involve two very different learning mechanisms.
- As Maddox and Ashby (2004) and Ashby and Maddox (2005) argued, rule-based learning involves attentional processes and depends on explicit memory.
- In contrast, information-integration involves an implicit system based on procedural learning. There are several lines of support for that theory.
- First, some brain-damaged patients have intact performance on rule-based learning but impaired performance on information-integration learning, whereas others show the opposite pattern. The areas of brain damage in both cases are as predicted by the theory.
- Second, neuroimaging studies also indicate that different brain areas are most involved in the two types of category learning. The brain areas identified correspond reasonably well to those based on brain-damaged patients.
- Third, there are significant (and predicted) differences in the effects of various manipulations (e.g., response switching, attentionally demanding irrelevant task) on category learning.
- These differences can be explained by assuming that different processing mechanisms underlie rule-based and information-integration learning.

Knowledge-based views of concept learning
- There is convincing evidence that most (or all) aspects of concept learning are influenced by knowledge effects.
- As we have seen, among the kinds of knowledge influencing concept learning is causal knowledge (Ahn et al., 2000).
- Any adequate theory of everyday concept learning would have to take full account of the numerous ways it is affected by prior knowledge.
- There are various limitations with knowledge- and explanation-based accounts of concept learning.
- First, we lack a comprehensive theory applicable to most knowledge effects.
- Second, we generally can't predict the extent to which relevant prior knowledge will be used on a concept-learning task.
- Third, we lack a knowledge-based theory specifying the processes involved in producing knowledge effects. For example, how do we combine our knowledge of causal relationships with the information available in presented exemplars to produce concept learning?

FURTHER READING

- Ashby, F.G., & Maddox, W.T. (2005). Human category learning. *Annual Review of Psychology*, *56*, 149–178. The central message of this review chapter is that multiple systems underlie category learning.
- Moss, H., & Hampton, J. (2003). *Conceptual representations*. Hove, UK: Psychology Press. This edited book provides several interesting accounts of various important theoretical approaches to concepts.
- Murphy, G.L. (2002). *The big book of concepts*. Cambridge, MA: MIT Press. The author provides a well-written and comprehensive (sometimes too comprehensive!) account of theory and research on concepts.

PART IV

CONTENTS

22 How accurate are our judgments?   326

23 What am I going to do?   340

24 Finding the solution   356

25 How do you become an expert?   374

26 Reasoning   386

Thinking and reasoning

Most of us spend the great majority of our waking lives engaged in thinking and reasoning. It is probably true that other species can engage in a certain amount of thinking and reasoning. However, it is indisputable that no other species begins to match ours in terms of the complexity of our thinking behavior. A moment's consideration will convince you that the ways in which we think (and reason and make decisions) are incredibly varied. These ways range from solving puzzles in newspapers to troubleshooting when the car breaks down to developing a new theory of the universe. Here we will just consider two very different examples of thinking.

First, a fragment of Molly Bloom's sleepy thoughts about Mrs Riordan taken from James Joyce's (1922/1960, pp. 871–872) very famous (if infrequently read!) book *Ulysses*:

> *. . . God help the world if all the women in the world were her sort down on bathingsuits and lownecks of course nobody wanted her to wear I suppose she was pious because no man would look at her twice I hope I'll never be like her a wonder she didn't want us to cover our faces but she was a welleducated woman certainly and her gabby talk about Mr. Riordan here and Mr. Riordan there I suppose he was glad to be shut of her . . .*

Second, here is the impatient author trying to use PowerPoint:

> *Why has the Artwork put the title in the wrong part of the slide? Suppose I try to put a frame around it so I can drag it up to where I want it. Ah-ha, now if I just summon up the arrows I can move the top bit up, and then I can do the same with the bottom bit. If I move the bottom bit up more than the top bit, then the title will fit in OK. (A few expletives have been deleted!)*

Both of the above examples illustrate various general aspects of thinking. First, the individuals concerned are *conscious* of their thoughts. Note, however, that we tend to be conscious of the products of thinking rather than the processes themselves, and many of these processes occur below the level of conscious awareness. Second, thinking varies in the extent to which it is *directed*. At one extreme, it can be very undirected, as in the case of Molly Bloom letting one thought slide into another as she is on the point of slipping into a dream. At the other extreme, the goal is much clearer and well-defined, as in the case of me trying to make PowerPoint work effectively. Third, the amount and nature of the knowledge in different thinking tasks vary enormously. The knowledge required in the PowerPoint case is quite limited, even though it took me a fair amount of time to acquire it! In contrast, Molly Bloom is using a vast amount of knowledge about people's beliefs and prejudices.

The five chapters in this part are concerned with the higher-level cognitive processes involved in thinking and reasoning. The topics dealt with are judgment, decision making, problem solving, expertise, and reasoning. Bear in mind that we use the *same* cognitive system to deal with all these types of task. As a result, many distinctions among different forms of thinking and reasoning are somewhat arbitrary and can hide underlying similarities in cognitive processes.

In spite of what has just been said, some distinctions among types of task *are* important and worth making (see Panel 1). For example, problem solving involves generating various possibilities and then choosing among them to make progress towards a goal. Expertise involves highly-skilled problem solving based on a considerable amount of relevant knowledge. In contrast, in decision making the possibilities are presented, and the task only involves choosing one of them. Judgment is that part of decision making concerned with working out the probability of occurrence of one or more events. Finally, reasoning involves calculating which inferences or conclusions follow from a given set of information.

One of the issues running through the five chapters in this part of the book is that of determining the extent to which human thinking and reasoning are impressive or unimpressive. This issue is often associated with the key question, "Are humans rational?" There has been fierce controversy concerning the answer to that question. However, as you can probably guess, the essence of the answer favored by the author is, "Yes and no," rather than a definite "Yes" or "No"!

Panel 1 Forms of thinking

Judgment: (Chapter 22)	The component of decision making which involves calculating the likelihood of various possible events; what is of most concern is the accuracy (or inaccuracy) of the judgments that are made. There is much evidence that people use heuristics (rules of thumb when required to make judgments.
Decision making: (Chapter 23)	Selecting one out of a number of presented options or possibilities, with the decision having consequences for the individual concerned. Decision making often seems irrational, with people being much more concerned to avoid losses than to make gains.
Problem solving: (Chapter 24)	Cognitive activity which involves moving from recognition that there is a problem through a series of steps to the solution or goal state. Past experience is generally (but not always) advantageous in problem solving, and problem solvers sometimes have sudden insight into the solution to a current problem. Most other forms of thinking involve some problem solving.
Expertise (Chapter 25)	Expertise is the specific knowledge that an expert has with a given area or domain. For example, chess experts have a huge knowledge of chess moves and patterns stored in long-term memory. Expertise can only be acquired as a result of substantial amounts of deliberate practice. It is generally assumed that a high level of intelligence is also needed to attain real expertise.
Deductive reasoning (Chapter 26)	Deciding what conclusions follow necessarily, provided that various statements are assumed to be true.

CHAPTER 22

CONTENTS

Introduction 327

Our judgments are OK! 329

Do heuristics make us smart? 332

Kahneman and Tversky: More heuristics 333

Evaluation and chapter summary 337

Further reading 339

How accurate are our judgments?

INTRODUCTION

In everyday life, we spend much of our time making judgments about the likelihood of various events, using whatever information is available. For example, you may use information about your examination performance over the years to work out your chances of succeeding in a forthcoming examination. You also make numerous judgments about your friends and acquaintances. For example, you use your knowledge of their behavior and what they have said in the past to decide how trustworthy, honest, loyal, and so on they are. You probably think that you are reasonably good at making accurate judgments (certainly most people do!), but I may be about to prove you wrong.

You can assess your own ability to make correct judgments by considering what answer you would give to the following problem, which is taken from Casscells, Schoenberger, and Graboys (1978):

> If a test to detect a disease whose prevalence [occurrence] is 1/1000 has a false positive rate of 5% [chance of indicating the disease is present when it is not], what is the chance that a person found to have a positive result actually has the disease, assuming that you know nothing about the person's symptoms or signs?

What is your answer to the above problem in judgment? If you think that 95% is the correct answer, then you are in good company, because that is easily the most common answer. Unfortunately, however, you have got the answer *wrong* if you said 95%! Casscells et al. (1978) gave the problem to staff and students at Harvard Medical School. Forty-five percent of them produced the wrong answer of 95%, and only 18% of them produced the correct answer, which is 2%. Why is 2% correct? The information provided indicates that 999 people out of every 1000 do *not* suffer from the disease. The additional fact that the test mistakenly indicates in 5% of cases that someone who is perfectly healthy has the disease means that 50 out of every 1000 people tested would give a misleading positive finding. Thus, 50 times as many people give a false positive result as give a true positive result (the one person in 1000 who actually has the disease). As a result, there is only a 2% chance that a person testing positive has the disease.

In essence, the main mistake made by most people who get the answer wrong is not paying enough attention to the fact that only one person in 1000 has the disease. The relative frequency with which an event occurs in the population is known as **base-rate information**, and we often neglect such information when making judgments. We will return to issues relating to base-rate information later.

Below is another judgment problem taken from Tversky and Kahneman (1983) for you to consider:

> Linda is 31 years old, single, outspoken and very bright. She majored in philosophy. As a student, she was deeply concerned with issues of discrimination and social justice, and also participated in anti-nuclear demonstrations.

Do you think it is more likely that Linda is a bank teller or a feminist bank teller? Most people (including you?) argue that it is more likely that Linda is a feminist bank teller than a bank teller. If you did so, I am afraid you have got the answer wrong! Every single feminist bank teller must necessarily also be a bank teller. It is thus impossible for the probability that Linda is a feminist bank teller to be greater than the probability she is a bank teller. The mistaken belief that the conjunction or combination of two events (A and B) is more likely than one of the events on its own is the **conjunction fallacy**.

Is there any basis for the idea that we are actually quite bad at making decisions?

We conclude this section with a third judgment problem taken from Redelmeier, Koehler, Liberman, and Tversky (1995). Suppose expert doctors have to decide on a diagnosis for a woman suffering with abdominal pain. What is of interest is the doctors' estimated probability that the woman is suffering from something other than gastroenteritis or ectopic pregnancy. Would it make any difference how this problem was phrased? I guess you feel it probably wouldn't make any difference since those being given the problem are all experts. In fact, however, it *did* make a difference. Doctors who assigned probabilities to gastroenteritis, ectopic pregnancy, and a residual category of everything else assigned an average probability of .50 to her disease falling into the residual category. Other equally expert doctors assigned probabilities to five specified diseases (including gastroenteritis and ectopic pregnancy) and a residual category of everything else. These doctors decided that the probability that the woman was suffering from a disease other than gastroenteritis or ectopic pregnancy was .69, which is much higher than the other group (.50).

Why were these medical experts so influenced by the precise wording of the question about the woman with abdominal pain? The key idea is that an event described explicitly and in detail typically seems more likely than the same event described less explicitly. We can consider a concrete example of this. I imagine you assume that the probability you will die on your next summer holiday is extremely low. However, I dare say it would seem somewhat more likely if I asked you the following question: "What is the probability that you will die on your next summer holiday from a disease, a sudden heart attack, a car accident, a plane crash, an earthquake, a terrorist incident, or from any other cause?"

Tversky and Koehler (1994) put forward support theory as a way of explaining findings such as those just discussed. According to this theory,

KEY TERMS
Base-rate information: the relative frequency with which an event occurs in a population.
Conjunction fallacy: the mistaken belief that the probability of a conjunction of two events (A and B) is greater than the probability of one of them (A or B).

there are two main reasons why a more explicit description of an event has greater subjective probability than the same event described less explicitly:

1. An explicit description may draw attention to aspects of the event that are less obvious in the non-explicit description.
2. Memory limitations may mean that people don't remember all of the relevant information if it is not supplied.

Support theory has considerable relevance in the real world. For example, Johnson, Hershey, Meszaros, and Kunreuther (1993) reported evidence consistent with support theory. Some participants were offered hypothetical health insurance covering hospitalization for any reason, whereas others were offered health insurance covering hospitalization for any disease or accident. These offers are the same, but participants were willing to pay a higher premium in the latter case! The explicit references to disease and accident made it seem more likely that hospitalization would be required, and so increased the value of being insured.

Support theory provides a plausible account of many findings. However, it has some limitations. According to the theory, probability judgments are based on an assessment of the evidence for and against various hypotheses. However, as Keren and Teigen (2004) pointed out, the factors determining precisely *how* the evidence is evaluated are unclear.

In sum, various kinds of evidence suggest we are rather poor at making judgments. However, that is not the whole story, and so we shouldn't get depressed at our deficiencies just yet. As we will see shortly, many experts have argued that the findings are misleading and that we can make very accurate judgments in the right circumstances. Before we move on, it is worth clarifying the relationship between judgment and decision making (which is the central focus of the next chapter). Judgment typically forms a small part of the overall decision-making process, and generally occurs fairly early on during decision making. In more detail, "Decision making refers to the entire process of choosing a course of action. Judgment refers to the components of the larger decision-making process that are concerned with assessing, estimating, and inferring what events will occur and what the decision-maker's evaluative reactions to those outcomes will be" (Hastie, 2001, p. 657).

OUR JUDGMENTS ARE OK!

We can reduce the impact of the findings discussed so far by claiming that performance would have been much better if the problems had been expressed differently. For example, perhaps we find it hard to think in terms of probabilities and percentages. According to Gigerenzer and Hoffrage (1999, p. 430), "Humans seem to be developmentally and evolutionarily prepared to handle natural frequencies. In contrast, many of us go through a considerable amount of mental agony to learn to think in terms of fractions, percentages and other forms of normalized counts." For example, suppose you try to estimate how many intelligent people there are in the population. You might do this by considering the frequencies of intelligent and unintelligent people encountered over the past week or month; these are known as natural frequencies. As you may be thinking, this will only produce a reasonable answer provided that the people you meet are not generally more or less intelligent than the average of the population!

Let us now return to the problem by Casscells et al. (1978) about a test to detect a disease. Cosmides and Tooby (1996) argued that we are much better at using information about frequencies (e.g., how many people fall into each category?) than at using information about probabilities (as in the Casscells et al., 1978, problem). Accordingly, Cosmides and Tooby used the same problem but emphasized the frequencies of individuals in the various categories:

> One out of 1000 Americans has disease X. A test has been developed to detect when a person has disease X. Every time the test is given to a person who has the disease, the test comes out positive. But sometimes the test also comes out positive when it is given to a person who is completely healthy. Specifically, out of every 1000 people who are perfectly healthy, 50 of them test positive for the disease. Imagine that we have assembled a random sample of 1000 Americans. They were selected by a lottery. Those who conducted the lottery had no information about the health status of any of these people. How many people who test positive for the disease will actually have the disease? (___ out of ___).

This version of the medical problem made life much easier for the participants. Cosmides and Tooby (1996) found that 76% of them produced the correct answer with this frequency version of the problem. In contrast, only 12% of participants produced the correct answer with the original version of the problem.

Fiedler (1988) obtained rather similar findings with the Linda problem discussed earlier. He compared performance on the original version of that problem with that on a frequency version, in which the participants indicated how many of 100 people fitting Linda's description were bank tellers, and how many were bank tellers and active feminists. As you can see in Figure 22.1, the percentage of participants showing the conjunction fallacy and so getting the answer wrong dropped dramatically with the frequency version. Note, however, that some people still failed to make accurate judgments—about one quarter of those given the frequency version showed the conjunction fallacy.

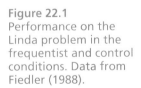

Figure 22.1
Performance on the Linda problem in the frequentist and control conditions. Data from Fiedler (1988).

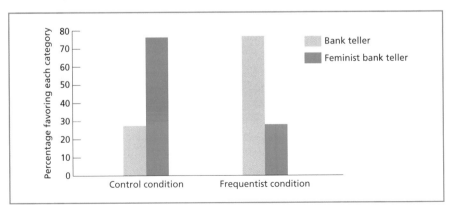

PROBLEMS WITH NATURAL FREQUENCIES

Is it really true that difficulties in making judgments disappear when we use frequencies and the natural sampling of events? The short answer is, "No!" There are many situations in which frequency information is of little or no use in making accurate judgments. Consider the **planning fallacy**. This involves underestimating how long it will take to complete a given task, even though we know that similar tasks in the past have taken longer than expected. Most students have found to their cost the problems in terms of stress and lost marks resulting from the planning fallacy! Griffin and Buehler (1999) asked students to list 10 projects. After that, the students estimated a "best-guess" completion date for each task, the probability that each project would be completed in time, and the number (frequency) of tasks that would meet the deadline.

Griffin and Buehler (1999) converted the estimates into percentages. Students expected 73% of the projects to be finished on time when using probabilities, compared to 65% when using frequencies. In fact, only 48% of the projects were actually completed on time, so there was convincing evidence of a planning fallacy in both cases. Of most importance, judgments based on frequencies were only marginally more accurate than those based on probabilities.

Gigerenzer and Hoffrage (1999) argued that our judgments will typically be accurate when based on our natural sampling of different kinds of events in everyday life. It is difficult to evaluate that argument, because there is a chasm between the neat-and-tidy frequency data provided in laboratory experiments and people's actual sampling behavior. One of the few attempts to study how effectively people sample events was reported by Fiedler, Brinkmann, Betsch, and Wild (2000) using the following problem in various forms. There is an 80% probability that a woman with breast cancer will have a positive mammogram compared to a 9.6% probability that a woman without breast cancer will have a positive mammogram. The base rate of breast cancer in women is 1%. The task is to decide the probability that a woman has breast cancer, given a positive mammogram (the correct answer is 7.8%).

Fiedler et al. (2000) were interested in people's sampling behavior when they were allowed to make their own choices. Accordingly, they didn't give them the problem in the form described above. Instead, some participants were provided with index card files organized into the categories of women with breast cancer and those without. They had to select cards, with each selected card indicating whether the woman in question had had a positive mammogram. The key finding was that participants' sampling was heavily *biased* towards women with breast cancer. As a result, the participants produced an average estimate of 63% that a woman had breast cancer given a positive mammogram (remember the correct answer is 7.8%).

In sum, natural sampling and the use of frequency data do *not* magically produce accurate judgments. When people are free to sample events, their sampling can be very biased and misleading (e.g., Fiedler et al., 2000). When people use frequency data, their judgments can still be very inaccurate (e.g., Griffin & Buehler, 1999). Even when frequency data produce a substantial improvement in performance (e.g., Cosmides & Tooby, 1996), this may not simply be because of the use of frequencies. It may be more because the frequency versions of problems make the underlying structure much easier to grasp (see Sloman & Over, 2003, for a review).

KEY TERM

Planning fallacy: the tendency to underestimate the time it will take to complete a task resembling similar tasks completed in the past.

DO HEURISTICS MAKE US SMART?

What are heuristics? Could they potentially help or hinder problem solving?

Gigerenzer, Todd, and the ABC Research Group (1999) and Todd and Gigerenzer (2000) focused on how people make judgments. They argued that we often use various **heuristics** or rules of thumb, and that these heuristics are typically very effective. Indeed, Gigerenzer et al. entitled their 1999 book, *Simple heuristics that make us smart.* One of the main heuristics they have studied is the take-the-best heuristic or strategy, which involves "take the best, ignore the rest," We can illustrate use of this strategy with the example of deciding whether Herne or Cologne has the larger population. You might assume that the most valid cue to city size is that cities whose names you recognize generally have larger populations than those whose names you don't recognize. However, you recognize both names. Then you think of another valid cue to city size, namely, that cities with cathedrals are usually larger than those without. Since you know Cologne has a cathedral but are unsure about Herne, you say, "Cologne."

If we consider the take-the-best strategy in detail, we can see it has three components:

1. Search rule: search cues (e.g., name recognition; cathedral) in order of validity.
2. Stopping rule: stop after finding a discriminatory cue (one that is positively associated with only *one* possible answer).
3. Decision rule: choose outcome.

Much research on the take-the-best strategy has focused on the **recognition heuristic**: "If one of two objects is recognized and the other is not, then infer that the recognized object has the higher value with respect to the criterion" (Goldstein & Gigerenzer, 2002, p. 76). We can illustrate what this means by considering the example just discussed. If you recognize the name "Cologne" but not "Herne," then you use the recognition heuristic to guess (correctly) that Cologne is the larger city, without taking account of any other information.

Why might people use the take-the-best and recognition heuristics? First, these heuristics often produce accurate predictions. For example, Goldstein and Gigerenzer (2002) reported correlations or associations of +.60 and +.66 in two studies between the number of people recognizing a city and its population. In other words, cities with larger populations are fairly consistently recognized by more people than are cities with smaller populations. Second, the recognition heuristic takes very little time to use and imposes practically no demands on our cognitive processes.

WHAT HAS BEEN FOUND?

Evidence supporting the notion that the recognition heuristic is important was reported by Goldstein and Gigerenzer (2002) in a series of experiments. In one experiment, American students decided which in each pair of German cities was the larger. The participants were told at the outset that German cities with football teams tend to be larger than those without. They were also told the names of well-known cities with and without football teams. Of key importance were the judgments when participants decided whether a recog-

KEY TERMS
Heuristics: rules of thumb that often (but not invariably) solve any given problem.
Recognition heuristic: using the knowledge that only one out of two objects is recognized to make a judgment.

nized city without a football team was larger or smaller than an unrecognized city. Participants used the recognition heuristic 92% of the time in spite of the fact that recognized cities lacked a football team.

In another experiment, Goldstein and Gigerenzer (2002) presented American and German students with pairs of American cities and pairs of German cities. They were all asked to select the larger city in each pair. Common sense suggests that performance would be better when the students judged cities in their own country, since they would obviously have much more information about such cities. However, you cannot apply the recognition heuristic when you recognize both cities in a pair, and this should have an adverse effect on participants' performance. The findings were very much in line with theoretical expectation: American and German students both performed *worse* when deciding on the larger city in pairs of cities in their own country than when making the same decision on pairs of cities in the other country! Thus, the recognition heuristic can be more useful than a substantial amount of additional knowledge. In the words of Goldstein and Gigerenzer (2002, p. 7), "Under certain conditions, a counterintuitive less-is-more effect emerges, in which a lack of knowledge is actually beneficial for inference."

Oppenheimer (2003) carried out an ingenious study showing convincingly that sometimes the recognition heuristic is *not* used when theoretically it should be. In his crucial condition, students at Stanford University decided whether recognized cities known to be small were larger than unrecognized cities. The small cities were close to Stanford University and the unrecognized cities were fictitious but sounded plausible (e.g., Las Besas, Rio Del Sol). The students generally failed to use the recognition heuristic, because the recognized city was judged to be larger than the unrecognized city on only 37% of trials. What these results mean is that knowledge of city size can override the recognition heuristic.

More bad news for Gigerenzer and his colleagues was reported by Newell, Weston, and Shanks (2003). They asked people to choose between the shares of two fictitious companies (Share A and Share B) on the basis of various cues. Only 33% of the participants conformed fully to the take-the-best strategy. Many participants searched for more information than they should have done on the take-the-best strategy. This presumably happened because they thought they would make better decisions if they had access to additional information.

KAHNEMAN AND TVERSKY: MORE HEURISTICS

The most influential psychologists who have worked in the area of judgment are Danny Kahneman and the late Amos Tversky. Indeed, they were mainly responsible for establishing judgment as a field of research back in the 1970s. They initially discovered several interesting heuristics or rules of thumb that we seem to use frequently in everyday life. Later on, both of them (but especially Kahneman) developed theoretical approaches within which to understand the limitations of human judgment.

REPRESENTATIVENESS HEURISTIC

We will start by considering the representativeness heuristic, which is probably the most important of the heuristics identified by Kahneman and

Tversky. When people use the **representativeness heuristic**, "Events that are representative or typical of a class are assigned a high probability of occurrence. If an event is highly similar to most of the others in a population or class of events, then it is considered representative" (Kellogg, 1995, p. 385). The representativeness heuristic is used when people judge the probability that an object or event A belongs to a class or process B. Suppose you are given the description of an individual, and have to estimate the probability he or she has a certain occupation.

You would probably estimate the probability mostly in terms of the *similarity* between that individual's description and your stereotype of that occupation. Indeed (the argument goes) you will do this even when it means ignoring other relevant information.

Let's turn to a concrete example of people's use of the representativeness heuristic. Kahneman and Tversky (1973, p. 241) gave participants the following description:

> Jack is a 45-year-old man. He is married and has four children. He is generally conservative, careful, and ambitious. He shows no interest in political and social issues and spends most of his free time on his many hobbies which include home carpentry, sailing, and numerical puzzles.

The participants' task was to decide the probability that Jack was an engineer or a lawyer. They were all told the description had been selected at random from a total of 100 descriptions. Half the participants were told 70 of the descriptions were of engineers and 30 of lawyers, whereas the other half were told there were descriptions of 70 lawyers and 30 engineers. The participants decided on average that there was a .90 probability that Jack was an engineer regardless of whether most of the 100 descriptions were of lawyers or of engineers. Thus, the participants took no account of the base-rate information (i.e., the 70:30 split of the 100 descriptions). Suppose they had used based-rate information. If so, the estimated probability that Jack was an engineer would have been less when the description was selected from a set of descriptions mainly of lawyers.

What can we do to persuade people to make use of base-rate information? Griffin and Buehler (1999) adopted various strategies. For example, they used a large transparent plastic box containing 100 balls, 70 of which were white and 30 of which were green, with white indicating either the descriptions of engineers or of lawyers. Participants guessed the relative numbers of white and green balls (base-rate information) and then chose a ball at random with their eyes closed. They then received the description of Jack. Finally, they estimated either the probability that Jack was an engineer or how many descriptions out of 10 resembling the one of Jack would be engineers. Base-rate information had much more effect on frequency judgments than on probability judgments (see Figure 22.2). This shows (as we saw in some research discussed earlier) that frequency formats are sometimes useful in improving judgmental accuracy.

Some experts (e.g., Mueser, Cowan, & Mueser, 1999) argue that full information is not provided on the lawyer–engineer and other similar problems. More specifically, participants don't know what mechanism causes the base rate to vary. In addition, they don't know whether the description they are given is

KEY TERM
Representativeness heuristic: the assumption that representative or typical members of a category are encountered most frequently.

informative because they have no knowledge of the 99 other descriptions. As a consequence, it is simply unclear whether or not participants typically place insufficient weight on base rates.

AVAILABILITY HEURISTIC

Tversky and Kahneman (1974) identified the **availability heuristic**, which involves estimating the frequencies of events on the basis of how easy or difficult it is to retrieve relevant information from long-term memory. You can try your luck on one of the questions used by Tversky and Kahneman (1974):

> If a word of three letters or more is sampled at random from an English text, is it more likely that the word starts with "r" or has "r" as its third letter?

Most participants answered that a word starting with "r" was more likely to be selected at random than a word with "r" as its third letter. If you did the same, you are wrong, because there are actually more words with "r" as the third letter. According to Tverksy and Kahneman (1974), participants made the wrong decision because they relied on the availability heuristic, and words starting with "r" can be retrieved more easily from memory (i.e., are more available) than those with "r" as the third letter.

In their study, Tversky and Kahneman (1974) used five consonants (K, L, N, R, and V), each of which was more frequent as third letter than as first letter. Sedlmeier, Hertwig, and Gigerenzer (1998) argued that this may have produced distorted findings, because a majority of consonants are more common as first letters than as third letters. Accordingly, they used all the letters in the German alphabet, and asked participants to estimate the relative frequency of each one as the first or second letters in words. Participants' estimated relative frequencies corresponded reasonably well to the actual frequencies, suggesting that they were not making use of the availability heuristic.

Tversky and Kahneman (1983) reported a study in which apparent use of the availability heuristic led to error. Participants rated the frequency of seven-letter words ending in "ing" and "-n-" out of 2000 words taken from a novel. Most of them claimed (on the basis of using the availability heuristic) that there would be many more words ending in "ing." This is clearly the wrong answer in view of the fact that all words ending in "ing" also end in "-n-"!

There is evidence that our use of the availability heuristic in everyday life often produces errors in judgment. For example, Lichtenstein, Slovic, Fischhoff, Layman, and Combs (1978) asked people to judge the relative likelihood of different causes of death. Causes of death attracting considerable publicity (e.g., murder) were judged more likely than those that don't (e.g., suicide), even when the opposite was actually the case.

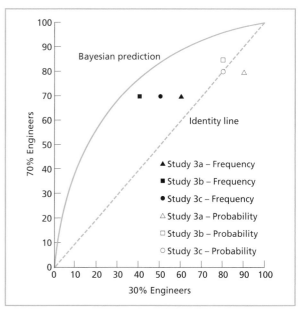

Figure 22.2 Median probability and frequency estimates (engineer) as a function of base rates (30% Engineers vs. 70% Engineers). The identity line indicates complete neglect of base rates. The curved line indicates base rates used according to Bayes' rule. Griffin and Buehler (1999). Copyright © Elsevier.

KEY TERM
Availability heuristic: the assumption that the frequencies of events can be estimated accurately by their accessibility in memory.

Oppenheimer (2004) provided convincing evidence that we don't *always* use the availability heuristic. He presented participants with pairs of names (one famous, one non-famous), and asked them to indicate which surname was more common in the United States. For example, one pair consisted of the names "Bush" and "Stevenson"—which name do you think is more common? Here is another one: Which surname is more common: "Clinton" or "Woodall"? If participants had used the availability heuristic, they would have said, "Bush" and "Clinton." In fact, however, only 12% said Bush and 30% Clinton. They were correct to avoid these famous names, because the non-famous name in each case is slightly more common.

How did participants make their judgments in the above study? According to Oppenheimer (2004, p. 100), "People not only spontaneously recognize when familiarity of stimuli comes from sources other than frequency (e.g., fame), but also overcorrect, so that in an effort to be uninfluenced by irrelevant sources of familiarity they end up underestimating the frequency of such stimuli."

THEORETICAL ISSUES

We have seen that people seem to rely heavily on heuristics or rules of thumb when making judgments. On the face of it, this seems somewhat puzzling given that these heuristics are prone to error. Two plausible explanations for our extensive use of heuristics were provided by Hertwig and Todd (2003). First, they have the advantage of speed, allowing us to produce approximately accurate judgments very rapidly. Second, heuristics are robust in that they can be used effectively almost regardless of the amount of information we have available. In contrast, complex cognitive strategies can produce very accurate judgments when a substantial amount of information is available, but are of very limited usefulness when information is sparse.

Another explanation for our widespread use of heuristics is simply that we don't like thinking hard if we can avoid it. A problem commonly used to show our aversion to thinking hard is the following: "A bat and a ball cost $1.10 in total. The bat costs $1 more than the ball. How much does the ball cost?" If you didn't think it through, you may have come up with the answer, "10 cents," which unfortunately is wrong!

Another argument in favor of the use of heuristics in everyday life was advanced by Maule and Hodgkinson (2002, p. 71): "Often . . . people have to judge situations or objects that change over time, making it inappropriate to expend a good deal of effort to make a precise judgment at any particular point in time. Under these circumstances, an approximate judgment based on a simpler, less effortful heuristic may be much more appropriate."

Kahneman and Fredrick (2002) and Kahneman (2003) argued that heuristics can be understood within their dual-process model. According to them, probability judgments depend on processing occurring within two systems:

1. System 1: This system is intuitive, automatic, and immediate. More specifically, "The operations of System 1 are typically fast, automatic, effortless, associative, implicit [not open to introspection] and often emotionally charged; they are also difficult to control or modify" (Kahneman, 2003). Most heuristics are produced by the first system.

2. System 2: This system is more analytical, controlled, and rule-governed. According to Kahneman (2003), "The operations of System 2 are slower, serial [one at a time], effortful, more likely to be consciously monitored and deliberately controlled; they are also relatively flexible and potentially rule-governed."

A clearer idea of how we use these two systems to make judgments can be gleaned from Kahneman and Fredrick's (2002, p. 51) own words: "In the particular dual-process model we assume, System 1 quickly proposes intuitive answers to judgment problems as they arise, and System 2 monitors the quality of these proposals, which it may endorse, correct, or override." Both systems can be active at the same time, and we often decide not to make much use of System 2.

We would expect usage of System 2 to depend on the nature of the task and on individual differences in ability. More specifically, if it is really important to produce the correct judgment, then System 2 is more likely to be used than it is if the task is a trivial one. In addition, highly intelligent individuals can use System 2 more effectively than those of lesser intelligence, and so have a higher probability of using it on judgment tasks (see Kahneman, 2003, for a review). In addition, System 2 is less likely to be used when there is time pressure or when individuals are performing a second cognitive task at the same time (Kahneman, 2003).

What kind of individual differences and biases make it difficult to apply general heuristic rules?

EVALUATION AND CHAPTER SUMMARY

Do heuristics make us smart?

- There is reasonably convincing evidence that people often use simple heuristics such as the recognition heuristic and the take-the-best strategy.
- Simple heuristics can be surprisingly effective, with people having little knowledge who use them outperforming those with greater knowledge.
- On the negative side, simple heuristics are sometimes *not* used. This is especially so when people want plenty of information before making a judgment (e.g., Newell et al., 2003) or when they have ready access to other kinds of information (e.g., Oppenheimer, 2003).
- We are most likely to use the heuristics identified by Gigerenzer et al. (1999) when making judgments in areas where we are relatively ignorant, which greatly limits their applicability.
- Even when we use simple heuristics, there are still complex issues to be addressed.
- As Goldstein and Gigerenzer (1999, p. 188) admitted, "There is the large question which kept us arguing days and nights, lunches and dinners, coffees and teas: Which homunculus [tiny man inside our heads] selects among heuristics, or is there none?" In other words, some cognitive processes presumably occur before we decide to use a given heuristic, but we know very little about these processes.
- Finally, it seems improbable that simple heuristics are used when it comes to making important judgments.

- Consider a woman deciding which of two men would make the better husband. She will surely consider *all* the relevant evidence before getting married rather than making a judgment as soon as she thinks of one difference between the two men!
- More generally, as Ben-Zeev (2002, p. 655) pointed out, "There are circumstances in which a take-your-time-and-think-about-complexity heuristic may be advantageous. Which circumstances require the latter and what reasoning allows us to make such an observation?"

Kahneman and Tversky: More heuristics

- Kahneman and Tversky have shown clearly that several general heuristics or rules of thumb (e.g., representativeness heuristic, availability heuristic) underlie judgments in many different contexts.
- These biases may well be of great practical significance in helping to account for errors of judgment in everyday life.
- Kahneman and Fredrick's (2002) dual-system model is an advance in that it allows us to see how heuristics can be incorporated into a more general theoretical approach.
- What are the main limitations with Kahneman and Tversky's approach?
- First, some of the errors of judgment reported in the literature occurred because participants misunderstood parts of the problem presented to them. For example, between 20% and 50% of participants presented with the Linda problem interpret, "Linda is a bank teller," as implying that she is not active in the feminist movement (see Gigerenzer, 1996).
- However, we mustn't exaggerate the role played by such misunderstandings in producing incorrect judgments.
- Sides, Osherson, Bonini, and Vitale (2002) found that there was still significant evidence of systematic errors on the Linda problem even when almost everything possible was done to ensure that participants didn't misinterpret the problem.
- Second, in spite of the theoretical efforts of Kahneman and Fredrick (2002), we have a very limited theoretical understanding of heuristics.
- Consider, for example, the representativeness and availability heuristics. There is some validity in the criticism that these terms merely provide labels or descriptions of observed phenomena and thus fail to provide a proper explanation. Indeed, "Critics . . . have pointed out that the proposed heuristics are vague and hence not readily testable" (Keren & Teigen, 2004, p. 100).
- Third, more attention needs to be paid to cultural differences, which have been almost totally ignored.
- For example, consider the **overconfidence bias**, which involves overestimating the probability that one has given a correct answer. Participants can be given general knowledge questions such as the following: "Which is longer? (a) Panama Canal; (b) Suez Canal. Now indicate the probability (50%–100%) that your chosen answer is correct."

KEY TERM
Overconfidence bias: overestimating the probability that an answer to a general knowledge or other question is correct.

- Somewhat surprisingly, it has been found in several studies that Asians' judgments are significantly more overconfident than those of Americans (see Choi, Choi, & Norenzayan, 2004, for a review).
- The reason for the above cultural difference was identified by Yates, Lee, Shinotsuka, Patalano, and Sieck (1998), who asked participants to list arguments for and against each potential answer.
- Americans were almost twice as likely as Chinese individuals to list arguments disagreeing with the alternatives they chose as the correct answer. Thus, the American tendency to think critically reduced overconfidence bias compared to the Chinese tendency to engage in respectful learning in which counter-arguments are de-emphasized.
- Fourth, much research on heuristics and biases is somewhat remote from the realities of real life.
- Our everyday judgments are often influenced by emotional and motivational factors rarely studied under laboratory conditions.
- For example, Hewstone, Benn, and Wilson (1988) used a judgment problem in which a fallible witness claimed that a burglary had been carried out by a white or a black youth. Hypothetical base-rate information in the form of the numbers of white and black youths committing burglaries was provided. The participants (all of whom were white) used the base-rate information, but did so in a prejudiced way.
- When the actual probability (using the witness's claim + base-rate information) was .41 that the burglary was committed by a black youth, the average estimated probability was .60. However, when the actual probability was .41 that the burglary was committed by a white youth, the average estimated probability was only .21.

FURTHER READING

- Gilovich, T., Griffin, D., & Kahneman, D. (2002). *Heuristics and biases: The psychology of intuitive judgement*. Cambridge: Cambridge University Press. This edited book contains chapters covering all the main issues in judgment research.
- Hardman, D., & Macchi, L. (2003). *Thinking: Psychological perspectives on reasoning, judgment and decision making*. Chichester, UK: Wiley. This edited book contains an interesting section on judgment with chapters by various experts.
- Hastie, R. (2001). Problems for judgment and decision making. *Annual Review of Psychology, 52*, 653–683. This article identifies the main issues that are currently the focus of research in the area of judgment.
- Kahneman, D. (2003). A perspective on judgment and choice: Mapping bounded rationality. *American Psychologist, 58*, 697–720. Danny Kahneman provides an interesting overview of his research with Amos Tversky on judgment and decision making.
- Koehler, D.J., & Harvey, N. (2004). *Blackwell handbook of judgment and decision making*. Oxford: Blackwell. This book contains chapters by most of the world's leading authorities on judgment.

CHAPTER 23

CONTENTS

Introduction 341

Losses and gains 342

What will people think? 348

Complex decision making 351

Evaluation and chapter summary 354

Further reading 355

What am I going to do?

INTRODUCTION

Life is full of decisions. Which movie will I go to see tonight? Would I rather go out with Dick or Harry? Which subject will I study at university? Who will I share an apartment with next year? Some experts such as Barry Schwartz believe we live in a society in which decision making is becoming more difficult because of an explosion of choice. He developed his ideas in a book called *The paradox of choice: Why more is less* (2004). You can see where he's coming from in the following anecdote. He was in a shop called The Gap, and he wanted to buy a pair of jeans. "I told them my size, and they asked if I wanted relaxed fit, easy fit, slim fit, boot cut, button-fly, zipper-fly, acid-washed, or stone-washed. And I said, 'I want the kind that used to be the only kind'" (Schwartz, 2004).

Evidence that we sometimes simply give up when confronted by too many choices was reported by Iyengar and Lepper (2000). They set up a tasting booth in Draeger's supermarket in Menlo Park, California. On one weekend, this booth offered 6 kinds of jam, and it offered 24 kinds of jam on another weekend. Nearly 30% of shoppers confronted by 6 choices bought some jam but the figure slumped to only 3% when there were 24 choices.

Psychologists studying decision making have often addressed the crucial issue of the extent to which people make the best decisions given the information available to them. There is considerable evidence that people's decisions are influenced by all kinds of factors, many of which may seem of little or no direct relevance. Not surprisingly, the factors involved vary depending on the precise nature of the decision that has to be made. For example, the processes involved in deciding which career path to follow are much more complex and time-consuming than those involved in deciding whether to buy a can of *Coca-Cola* or *Pepsi*!

Let's start with an apparently easy question: Would you expect Americans to be more inclined to make risky financial decisions than Asians? I hazard a guess that your answer is, "Yes." In fact, the correct answer is, "No." Weber and Hsee (2000) discussed several of their studies in which they found Americans less inclined than Chinese individuals to make risky financial decisions. They explained these findings by means of the cushion hypothesis—Chinese individuals can afford to take greater financial risks than Americans because they enjoy more protection from their family and social networks. As predicted, Americans with strong networks were more willing than those with weak ones to make risky financial decisions, and Chinese individuals with weak networks were risk-averse.

According to the cushion hypothesis, the Chinese would not be more risk-seeking than the Americans when making decisions about issues where family and social support was irrelevant. Weber and Hsee (2000) asked participants to make three kinds of decisions:

1. *Financial*: Invest in shares (high risk) or in a savings account (low risk).
2. *Academic*: Write a term paper on a provocative topic (high risk) or a conservative topic (low risk).
3. *Medical*: Use a pain reliever of very variable effectiveness (high risk) or with moderate but sure effectiveness (low risk).

As predicted, Chinese participants were more risk-seeking than American ones on the financial decision. However, they weren't more risk-seeking on the academic or medical decisions where poor outcomes couldn't be salvaged by their families or social networks.

The study of decision making is of direct relevance to everyday life. Consider, for example, worrying evidence that the decision making of jurors may be biased. Carlson and Russo (2001) showed potential jurors a video explaining the importance of refraining from making decisions before all the evidence has been presented. After that, they were presented with affidavits [written declarations made under oath], case backgrounds, and opening arguments. As soon as each new piece of evidence was presented, the participants were asked to decide whether it benefited the plaintiff or the defendant. The key finding was that 85% of the participants showed "pre-decisional distortion." In other words, they were too inclined to consider new evidence as supporting whichever party (plaintiff or defendant) they favored already. Pre-decisional distortion may help the jurors to create a coherent account of what they think happened but can obviously be very bad news for innocent defendants!

A central theme in this chapter is that it is often surprisingly hard to decide whether or not a decision is the best one. Consider a middle-aged male contestant taking part in the television show, *Who wants to be a millionaire?* He has won £250,000 (about $425,000) and has to decide whether to answer the next question. He has eliminated two of the four answers, and has no idea which of the two remaining possibilities is correct. If he wants, he can refuse to answer the question and walk away with £250,000 ($425,000). If he guesses correctly, he will gain a further £250,000 ($425,000). If he guesses incorrectly, he will lose £218,000 (about $375,000), because he would still go away with £32,000 ($55,000). What should he do? If he focuses only on the money, it seems like a reasonable bet. The chances of winning and losing are equal, and he stands to gain more than he would lose. However, his family may be livid if he goes home having needlessly lost £218,000 ($375,000)! Thus, what appears like a good decision from one perspective doesn't appear so from a different one.

LOSSES AND GAINS

All of us spend much of our time striving to achieve gains (e.g., emotional, financial, at work) while avoiding losses. As a first approximation, it seems likely that we make decisions so as to maximize the chances of making a gain and minimize the chances of making a loss. For example, suppose someone offered you $200 if a tossed coin came up heads and a loss of $100 if it came up tails. You would jump at the chance (wouldn't you?), given that the bet provides an average expected gain of $50 per toss.

How are decisions affected by the potential outcomes (i.e., potential gain vs. potential losses)?

Here are two more decisions. Would you prefer to make a sure gain of $800 or an 85% probability of gaining $1000 and a 15% probability of gaining nothing? Since the expected value of the latter decision is greater than that of the former decision ($850 vs. $800, respectively), you might well choose the latter alternative. Finally, would you prefer to make a sure loss of $800 or an 85% probability of losing $1000 with a 15% probability of not incurring any loss? The average expected loss is $800 for the former choice and $850 for the latter one, so you go with the former choice, don't you?

The first problem was taken from Tversky and Shafir (1992) and the other two problems were come from Kahneman and Tversky (1984). In all three cases, most participants did *not* make what appear to be the best choices. Two-thirds of participants refused to bet on the toss of a coin, and a majority preferred the choice with the smaller expected gain, and the choice with the larger expected loss! What on earth is going on here? Kahneman and Tversky accounted for these findings (and many more besides) on the basis of two theoretical assumptions incorporated into prospect theory:

1. People identify a reference point generally representing their current state.
2. People are much more sensitive to potential losses than to potential gains; this is known as **loss aversion**.

Both of these assumptions are shown in Figure 23.1. The reference point is the point at which the line labeled "losses" and "gains" intersects the line labeled "value." As you can see, the positive value associated with gains increases relatively slowly as gains become greater. In contrast, the negative value associated with losses increases relatively rapidly as losses become greater.

There is a further prediction following from prospect theory. When people make decisions, they attach *more* weight to low-probability events than these events merit according to their actual probability of occurrence. In contrast, high-probability events receive *less* weight than they deserve.

How does prospect theory account for the findings discussed earlier? If people are much more sensitive to losses than to gains, they should be unwilling to accept bets involving potential losses, even though the potential gains outweigh the potential losses. They would also prefer a sure gain to a risky but potentially greater gain. Finally, note that prospect theory does *not* predict that people will always seek to avoid risky decisions. If offered the chance of avoiding a loss (even if it means the average

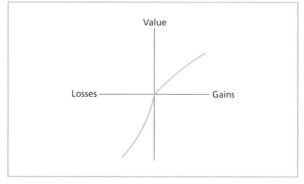

Figure 23.1 A hypothetical value function. From Kahneman and Tversky (1984). Copyright © by the American Psychological Association. Reprinted with permission.

expected loss increases from $800 to $850), most people will take that chance because they are so concerned with avoiding losses.

We can contrast prospect theory with older theoretical views. For example, at one time many economists based their theories on the notion of "rational man" (or "rational person"). According to this notion, when we consider a financial decision, we work systematically through all the evidence and make the decision most likely to produce a desirable outcome. Psychologists incorporated the idea that we typically behave rationally and select the best option in **normative theories**. These theories focused on how people *should* make decisions rather than on how they *actually* make them. For example, according to von Neumann and Morgenstern's (1947) utility theory, we try to maximize *utility*, which is the subjective value we attach to an outcome. When we choose between simple options, we assess the expected utility or expected value of each one by means of the following formula:

$$\text{Expected utility} = (\text{probability of a given outcome}) \times (\text{utility of the outcome})$$

We will be turning shortly to the experimental evidence. As we will see, there isn't much support for the notion that we make decisions in an entirely rational and logical way. In spite of its limitations, prospect theory clearly represents an advance in understanding the mechanics of human decision making.

FINDINGS: POSITIVE

We have seen that there is convincing evidence for loss aversion. There is also evidence for a related phenomenon known as the **sunk-cost effect**. This is "a greater tendency to continue an endeavor once an investment in money, effort, or time has been made" (Arkes & Ayton, 1999, p. 591). This effect is captured by the expression "throwing good money after bad." A study on the sunk-cost effect based on the following problem was reported by Arkes and Blumer (1985, p. 126):

> Assume that you have spent $100 on a ticket for a weekend ski trip to Michigan. Several weeks later you buy a $50 ticket for a weekend ski trip to Wisconsin. You think you will enjoy the Wisconsin ski trip more than the Michigan ski trip. As you are putting your just-purchased Wisconsin ski trip ticket in your wallet you notice that the Michigan ski trip and the Wisconsin ski trip are for the same weekend. It's too late to sell either ticket, and you cannot return either one. You must use one ticket and not the other. Which ski trip will you go on?

You might imagine that everyone would choose to go on the Wisconsin ski trip (the one expected to be more enjoyable). In fact, however, over 50% of the participants opted for the ski trip they would enjoy less! They thought it was less "wasteful" to go on the more expensive ski trip even though they expected to enjoy it less than the cheaper one.

Intriguingly, children and various species of animals (e.g., ducks, blackbirds, mice) are much less affected than adult humans by the sunk-cost effect. This is surprising, because we regard ourselves (with some justification!) as

KEY TERMS

Normative theories: as applied to decision making, theories focusing on how people should make decisions.

Sunk-cost effect: expending additional resources to justify some previous commitment (e.g., throwing good money after bad).

much smarter than birds and mice. Arkes and Ayton (1999, p. 598) provided a plausible explanation: "We suggest that over-generalization of the eminently sensible rule, 'Don't waste', contributes to the manifestation of the sunk-cost effect. Non-human animals and young humans do not know this rule, so its over-generalization is not an issue for them."

The problems discussed so far have dealt with hypothetical issues in the laboratory. Does prospect theory work with real-world decision making? Evidence that it does was reported by Banks et al. (1995). They studied the effectiveness of two videotapes in persuading women to undergo a mammogram (breast examination). Both videotapes contained the same medical facts. However, one emphasized the gains of mammography, whereas the other focused on the risks of not undergoing a mammogram. As predicted by prospect theory, more of the women watching the risk-focused videotape obtained a mammogram within the following year.

Suppose we provided different groups of participants with precisely the same problem phrased in different ways. In one version, the potential gains associated with various decisions are emphasized, whereas the potential losses associated with the decisions are emphasized in the other version. Since the problem remains the same, common sense would suggest that people would make the same decisions regardless of problem phrasing. According to prospect theory, changing the wording should matter because people are more motivated to avoid losses than to achieve gains. This is known as a **framing effect**, meaning the decision is influenced by irrelevant aspects of the situation.

The Asian disease problem has often been used to study the framing effect. Tversky and Kahneman (1987) told participants there was likely to be an outbreak of an Asian disease in the United States, and it was expected to kill 600 people. Two programs of action had been proposed: Program A would allow 200 people to be saved; Program B would have a 1/3 probability that all 600 people would be saved, and a 2/3 probability that none of the 600 would be saved. When the issue was expressed in this form, 72% of the participants favored Program A, although both programs (if carried out several times) would on average lead to the saving of 200 lives. This is a clear example of a framing effect, with the participants being influenced by loss aversion to avoid certain losses.

Other participants in the study by Tversky and Kahneman (1987) were given the same problem, but it was negatively framed: Program A would lead to 400 people dying, whereas Program B carried a 1/3 probability that no one would die and a 2/3 probability that 600 would die. In spite of the fact that the problem was the same, 78% chose Program B. This is another framing effect, and is also due to loss aversion.

Framing effects have sometimes been found to be important in real-world situations. McNeil, Pauker, Sox, and Tversky (1982) asked patients and experienced doctors to choose between surgery and radiation for lung cancer. A higher percentage in both groups chose radiation if the mortality from surgery was presented as a 10% chance of dying rather than a 90% chance of survival.

FINDINGS: NEGATIVE

Prospect theory provides a good account of the findings of Tversky and Kahneman (1987). However, the theory is limited, as was shown by Wang (1996)

What types of bias or decision-making behaviors are not accounted for by prospect theory?

using various versions of the Asian disease problem. Participants chose between definite survival of two-thirds of the patients (the deterministic option) and a 1/3 probability of all patients surviving and a 2/3 probability of none surviving (the probabilistic option). In terms of minimizing the number of deaths, the deterministic option is much superior, because on average it leads to the survival of twice as many patients. As expected, the overwhelming majority of participants chose the deterministic option when the problem was phrased in terms of 600 unknown patients (see Figure 23.2).

The other conditions used by Wang (1996) were phrased in terms of six unknown patients, three unknown patients, or six close relatives. As can be seen in Figure 23.2, the findings were very different in these conditions. There was a large increase in the percentage of participants choosing the probabilistic option with small group size. Indeed, more participants chose the probabilistic option than the deterministic one when the decision involved six close relatives. Why did this happen? Presumably the social context and psychological factors relating to *fairness* were regarded as more important in those conditions, especially when close relatives were involved.

Additional evidence that emotional and social factors not included within prospect theory influence decision making was reported by Ritov and Baron (1990). Participants were told to assume that their child had 10 chances in 10,000 of dying from flu during an epidemic if not vaccinated. The vaccine was certain to prevent the child from catching flu, but had potentially fatal side effects. The participants indicated the maximum death rate from the vaccine they were willing to tolerate to have their child vaccinated. The average maximum acceptable risk was five deaths per 10,000. Thus, people would choose not to have their child vaccinated when the likelihood of the vaccine causing death was much lower than the death rate from the disease against which the vaccine protects! This is puzzling from the perspective of prospect theory, according to which people should make the decision minimizing the risk of loss.

Ritov and Baron's (1990) participants argued they would feel more *responsible* for the death of their child if it resulted from their own actions rather than from their inaction. This is an example of **omission bias**, a tendency to prefer inaction over action when engaged in decision making.

Figure 23.2 Choice of option (deterministic vs. probabilistic) as a function and number of patients and type of patient (unknown vs. close relatives). Data from Wang (1996).

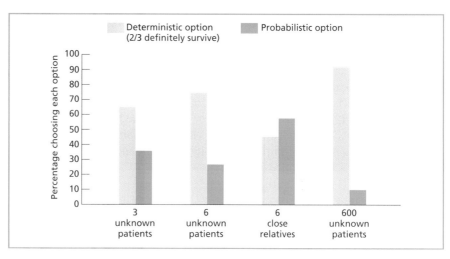

An important factor in omission bias is anticipated regret. This is typically greater when an unwanted outcome has been caused by an individual's own actions rather than by inaction. However, evidence for omission bias with vaccination decisions has not always been obtained. For example, Connolly and Reb (2003) found that most students and non-student adults chose to vaccinate when the risks from vaccination equaled those from the disease.

Most studies on omission bias may be limited in that people's decisions when confronted by a hypothetical situation in the laboratory may differ from the decisions they make in everyday life. Some reassurance was provided by Chapman (2004). First, participants imagined they had a 10% chance of contracting a disease. A vaccine was available that would always prevent the disease but could also cause the disease itself. Second, participants made the real-life decision as to whether they wanted an injection. Those who showed omission bias with respect to the hypothetical vaccine were the ones most likely to refuse the flu injection.

Prospect theory doesn't consider individual differences in people's willingness to engage in risky decision making (e.g., deciding to go rock climbing). Evidence of such individual differences was reported by Josephs, Larrick, Steele, and Nisbett (1992), who compared individuals high and low in self-esteem. These individuals chose between two options of equal utility but differing in risk (e.g., a sure win of $10 versus a 50% chance of winning $20 on a gamble). Individuals low in self-esteem were 50% more likely than those high in self-esteem to choose the sure gain. People with low self-esteem are concerned that negative or threatening events will reduce their self-esteem.

According to prospect theory, people should overweight the probability of rare events when making decisions. This prediction has been supported in several studies, but there are some exceptions (see Hertwig, Barron, Weber, & Erev, 2004, for a review). Hertwig et al. (2004) argued that we should distinguish between decisions based on descriptions and those based on experience. In the laboratory, people are typically provided with a neat summary description of the possible outcomes and their associated probabilities. In contrast, in the real world people typically make decisions (e.g., to go out on a date) purely on the basis of personal experience.

Hertwig et al. (2004) compared decision making based on descriptions with decision making based on experience (i.e., personal observation of events and their outcomes). When decisions were based on descriptions, people overweighted the probability of rare events as predicted by prospect theory. However, when decisions were based on experience, people underweighted the probability of rare events, which is opposite to theoretical prediction. This happened in part because participants in the experience condition often failed to encounter the rare event at all.

Finally, evidence that there are cross-cultural differences in the willingness to take financial risks was discussed earlier (Weber & Hsee, 2000; see Choi, Choi, & Norenzayan, 2004, for a review). The relevance of this research here is that prospect theory doesn't explicitly consider cross-cultural differences at all.

WHAT WILL PEOPLE THINK?

We begin this section by considering an interesting study on decision making reported by Tversky and Shafir (1992). American students imagined they had the chance to buy a very cheap holiday in Hawaii, but the special offer expired the next day. They had three choices:

1.   buy the holiday immediately
2.   decide not to buy the holiday
3.   pay a $5 non-refundable fee to retain the chance to buy the holiday two days later.

All the students were told to assume they had just taken a difficult examination. Some knew they had passed the examination; some knew they had failed; and some would only find out the next day whether they had passed or failed. What did the three groups of students decided to do? Think what answer you would give to that question before seeing the actual answer below.

You may have guessed that most people in all three groups decided to buy the holiday immediately because it is an extremely appealing idea to have a very cheap holiday in Hawaii. This was true of the groups knowing they had passed or failed the examination. However, only 32% of those who didn't know their examination result decided to buy the holiday immediately (see Figure 23.3). We can explain these results by focusing on people's need to justify their decisions. Those who have passed an examination "deserve" a holiday, and those who have failed an examination "deserve" some consolation to cheer themselves up. In contrast, those who don't know whether they have passed or failed have no strong justification for going on holiday.

The study by Tversky and Shafir (1992) points us in the direction of an extremely important difference between decision making in most laboratory experiments (but not theirs) and in real life. This difference was expressed very clearly by Tetlock (1991, p. 453): "Subjects in laboratory studies ... rarely feel accountable to others for the positions they take. They function in a social vacuum ... in which they do not need to worry about the interper-

Figure 23.3 Percentage choosing to buy a holiday immediately as a function of having passed an examination, failed an examination, or not knowing whether the examination has been passed or failed. Data from Tversky and Shafir (1992).

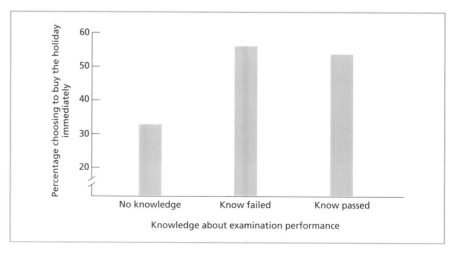

sonal consequences of their conduct." For example, suppose that 1 year ago you bought shares in a company. You were so convinced the shares would increase in value that you boasted about your purchase to all your friends. The shares are now worth only 50% of what you paid for them, and all the indications are that the company is in serious trouble. It is probably a good idea to sell the shares immediately, but you may well decide to hang on to them because it would be so embarrassing to explain to your friends why you have sold them. If you keep them, you can justify this decision by telling everyone it is only a matter of time before the share price moves upwards.

SOCIAL FUNCTIONALIST APPROACH

Tetlock (2002) put forward a social functionalist approach based on some of the ideas we have been discussing. He argued that our decision making in everyday life is strongly influenced by the social and cultural context in which we live. More specifically, people often behave like intuitive politicians, whose "long-term success at managing impressions hinges on their skill at anticipating objections that others are likely to raise to alternative courses of action and at crafting accounts that pre-empt those objections" (Tetlock, 2002, p. 454). Thus, people acting as intuitive politicians need to be able to justify their decisions to other people.

Tetlock (2002) argued that people sometimes behave like intuitive theologians or intuitive prosecutors when engaged in decision making. Intuitive theologians, "believe that the prevailing accountability and social control regime is not arbitrary but rather flows naturally from an authority that transcends accidents of history" (Tetlock, 2002, p. 453). In contrast, intuitive prosecutors, "place accountability demands on others who might be tempted to derive the benefits of collective interdependence without contributing their fair share" (Tetlock, 2002, p. 453).

People probably spend more of their time behaving like intuitive politicians than intuitive theologians or prosecutors. Accordingly, we will focus on studies concerned with the ways in which intuitive politicians justify their decisions to others.

Justifying our decisions

Think back to the study by Tversky and Shafir (1992). In that study, students who didn't know whether they had passed the examination tended not to buy the holiday in Hawaii immediately because it was difficult to justify buying the holiday to themselves or to others. In contrast, students who did know whether they had passed or failed could use this information to justify buying a holiday.

How may a degree of accountability affect our decisions?

Tetlock's (2002) theoretical approach focuses on justifying our decisions to others in everyday life. However, the study by Tversky and Shafir (1992) was laboratory-based, and it could be argued that the students in their study were mainly concerned to justify their decision to themselves. A study more directly relevant to Tetlock's social functionalist approach was reported by Camerer, Babcock, Loewenstein, and Thaler (1997). They examined the factors determining how long New York cab drivers decided to work on any given day. From a purely economic perspective, the cab drivers should work fewer hours when business is slack and longer hours when business is good. In fact, many cab drivers do the opposite. They set themselves a target income for each day, and stop work when they have reached it. As a result, they work unnecessarily long hours when business is poor and miss out on easy money on days when business is good.

How can we account for the apparently illogical behavior of New York cab drivers? A persuasive answer was provided by Tetlock and Mellers (2002, p. 98): "Should Camerer's cabbies be taught to escape from their slavishly rigid work policies? Or is such rigidity an adaptive response to no-excuses accountability pressures from the home front to bring home the bacon? Many effects that look like biases from a strictly individual level of analysis may be sensible responses to interpersonal and institutional pressures for accountability."

Additional support for Tetlock's approach comes from a study by Simonson and Staw (1992) on the sunk-cost effect (throwing good money after bad) discussed earlier. Participants were initially given information about a beer company selling light beer and non-alcoholic beer. They had to recommend which product should receive an additional $3 million for advertising purposes. When they had made their recommendation, they were told that the president of the company had made the same decision, but that this had produced disappointing results. Finally, they were told that the company had decided to allocate an additional $10 million from the advertising budget, which could be divided between the two products. Their task was to decide how to use this budget. Three of the conditions (varying in the emphasis given to justifying the decision to others) were as follows:

1. *High-accountability condition*: Participants were told that information about their decision might be shared with other students and instructors. They were also asked to give permission to record an interview about their decision.
2. *Medium-accountability condition*: Participants were told that the information provided to them should be sufficient to allow a good decision to be made.
3. *Low-accountability condition*: Participants were informed that their decisions would be confidential, and that there was no connection between their performance on the task and their managerial effectiveness or intelligence.

Simonson and Staw (1992) were interested in the extent to which participants decided to put substantial additional advertising money into the product that had already received previous advertising money to little avail. This is a measure of the sunk-cost effect. As you can see in Figure 23.4, the tendency towards a sunk-cost effect was greatest in the high-accountability condition and lowest in the low-accountability condition. Participants in the high-accountability condition needed to justify their previously ineffective course of action (i.e., fruitless investment in one type of beer) by increasing their commitment to it.

You might assume that *experts* (especially medical experts) would be more likely to make sound and unbiased decisions when held accountable for their decisions. Both of these assumptions were disconfirmed by Schwartz, Chapman, Brewer, and Bergus (2004). Doctors were told about a patient with osteoarthritis for whom many anti-inflammatory drugs had proved ineffective. In the two-option condition, they chose between simply referring the patient to an orthopedic specialist to discuss surgery, or combining referral with prescribing an untried anti-inflammatory drug. In the three-option condition, there were the same options as in the two-option condition, plus referral combined with prescribing a different untried anti-inflammatory drug. The doctors either simply made their decisions or were made accountable for their decisions (they wrote an explanation for their decision and agreed to be contacted later to discuss it).

The doctors showed a bias in their decision making regardless of whether they were made accountable. They were *more* likely to select the referral-only option in the three-option condition than in the two-option condition, which seems contrary to common sense. This bias was significantly greater when doctors were made accountable for their decisions. What is going on here? In the three-option condition, it is very hard to justify selecting one anti-inflammatory drug over the other one. As a result, the easy way out is to select the remaining option (i.e., referral only).

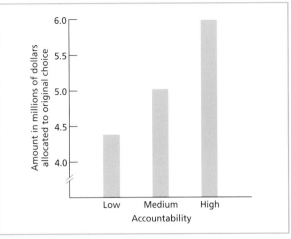

Figure 23.4 Millions of dollars allocated to original choice (sunk-cost effect) as a function of accountability. Data from Simonson and Staw (1992).

COMPLEX DECISION MAKING

So far we have focused mainly on decision making applied to fairly simple problems. In real life, however, we are often confronted by very complex decisions (e.g., shall I marry John?; shall I move to Australia?). How do we deal with such decisions? According to multi-attribute utility theory (Wright, 1984), the decision maker should go through the following stages:

How do we make complex decisions?

1. identify dimensions relevant to the decision
2. decide how to weight those dimensions
3. obtain a total **utility** (i.e., subjective desirability) for each option by summing its weighted dimensional values
4. select the option with the highest weighted total.

We can illustrate how multi-attribute utility theory works in practice by considering that someone has to decide which apartment to rent. First, consideration is paid to the relevant dimensions (e.g., number of rooms, location, rent per week). Second, the relative utility of each dimension is calculated. Third, the various apartments being considered are compared in terms of their total utility, and the person chooses the one with the highest total utility.

You can probably guess that people rarely adopt the above decision-making procedure in real life. There are various reasons for this. The procedure can be very complex, the set of relevant dimensions can't always be worked out, and the dimensions themselves may not be clearly separate from each other.

KEY TERM
Utility: the subjective desirability of a given outcome in decision making.

BOUNDED RATIONALITY

A much more realistic approach to complex decision making owes its origins to Herb Simon (1957). He drew a distinction between unbounded rationality and bounded rationality. Within models of unbounded rationality, it is assumed that all relevant information is available for use (and is used) by the decision maker. In other words, the notion is that we engage in a process of **optimization**, in which the best choice or decision is made. There are two problems with the notion of optimization. First, as Klein (2001, p. 103) pointed out, "In the majority of field settings, there is no way to determine if a decision choice is optimal owing to time pressure, uncertainty, ill-defined goals, and so forth." Second, whatever definition of optimization we prefer, most people typically fail to select the optimal choice on a regular basis.

According to Simon (1957), we possess **bounded rationality**. This means we produce reasonable or workable solutions to problems, in spite of our limited processing ability by using various short-cut strategies including heuristics. More specifically, decision making can be "bounded" by constraints in the environment (e.g., information costs) or by constraints in the mind (e.g., limited attention, limited memory). What is important is the degree of fit or match between the mind and the environment. According to Simon (1990, p. 7), "Human rational behavior is shaped like a scissors whose blades are the structure of task environments and the computational capabilities of the actor." If we consider only one blade (i.e., the task environment or the individual's abilities) we will have only a partial understanding of how we make decisions. In similar fashion, we would be unable to understand how scissors cut if we focused on only one blade.

Simon (1978) argued that bounded rationality is shown by the heuristic known as satisficing. The essence of **satisficing** (formed from the words satisfactory and sufficing) is that individuals consider various options one at a time and select the first one meeting their minimum requirements. This heuristic doesn't guarantee at all that the decision is the best one. However, it is especially useful when the various options become available at different points in time. An example would be the vexed issue of deciding who to marry. Someone using the satisficing heuristic would set a minimum acceptable level, and the first person reaching (or exceeding) that level would be chosen. If the initial level of acceptability is set too high, the level is adjusted downwards. Of course, if you set the level too low, you may spend many years bitterly regretting having used the satisficing heuristic!

We can distinguish between individuals who are satisficers (content with making reasonable decisions) and those who are maximizers (perfectionists). Is it preferable to be a satisficer or a maximizer? This question was addressed by Schwartz et al. (2002), who found that there are various advantages associated with being a satisficer. Satisficers are happier and more optimistic than maximizers, they have greater life satisfaction, and they experience less regret and self-blame.

Tversky (1972) put forward a theory of complex decision making resembling Simon's approach. According to Tversky's elimination-by-aspects theory, decision makers eliminate options by considering one relevant attribute after another. For example, someone buying a house may first of all consider the attribute of geographical location, eliminating from consideration all those houses not lying within a given area. They may then consider the attribute of price, eliminating all properties costing above a certain figure. This process continues attribute by attribute until only one option remains. This is a reasonably undemanding strategy, but suffers from the limitation that the option selected can vary as a function of the order in which the attributes are considered. As a consequence, the best choice will sometimes not be made.

FINDINGS

Payne (1976) carried out an interesting study to see the extent to which decision makers actually use the various strategies discussed above. They had to decide which apartment to rent on the basis of information about various attributes, such as rent, cleanliness, noise level, and distance from campus, presented on cards. The information describing each apartment was printed on the back of the cards, which had to be turned over to reveal its value. There were different tasks, varying in the number of apartments (between 2 and 12) and the number of attributes (between 4 and 12).

When there were many apartments to consider, participants typically started by using a simple strategy such as satisficing or elimination-by-aspects. Here is one participant's account of using elimination-by-aspects: "I'm going to look at landlord attitude. In H it's fair. In D it's poor. In B it's fair, and in A it's good. In L, the attitude is poor. In K it's poor. In J it's good, and in I it's poor ... So, that's important to me ... So, I'm not going to live any place where it's poor" (Payne, 1976, p. 379). When only a few apartments remained to be considered, there was often a switch to a more complex strategy corresponding to the assumptions of multi-attribute utility theory.

Another factor determining how people approach decision making is time pressure. Payne, Bettman, and Johnson (1988) found that moderate time pressure led people to speed up their processing and to become slightly more selective in their processing. When the time pressure was severe, people speeded up their processing, focused their attention on only a fraction of the available information, and changed their processing strategies.

It was assumed within many of the older theories of decision making (e.g., multi-attribute utility theory) that a given individual's assessment of the utility or preference (desirability × importance) of any given attribute remains constant. In fact, our preferences are subject to change. Simon, Krawczyk, and Holyoak (2004) asked participants to decide between job offers from two department store chains, "Bonnie's Best" and "Splendor." There were four relevant attributes (salary, holiday package, commute time, and office accommodation). Each job offer was preferable to the other on two attributes and inferior on two attributes. Participants assessed their preference for each attribute. They were then told that one of the jobs was in a much better location than the other, which often tipped the balance in favor of choosing the job in the better location. The participants then assessed their preference for each attribute again. Preferences for desirable attributes of the chosen job increased and preferences for undesirable attributes of that job decreased. As Simon et al. (2004, p. 335) concluded, "Preferences used in decision making are not fixed, as assumed by classic theories of rational choice, but rather are reconstructed in the course of decision making."

Finally, let's consider what happens in the real world with real decisions.

Frisch and Jones (1993) asked participants to answer numerous questions relating to a recent decision they had made that had proved to be very successful or unsuccessful. The most important difference was that participants were much more likely to be have considered alternative courses of action before making successful decisions.

EVALUATION AND CHAPTER SUMMARY

Losses and gains
- There is considerable support for the main assumptions of prospect theory.
- It provides a more accurate account of human decision making than previous normative theories such as utility theory.
- The notion that people attach more weight to losses than to gains allows us to account for many phenomena, including the framing effect and the sunk-cost effect.
- Indeed, the single assumption that we are much more sensitive to potential losses than to potential gains is perhaps the most powerful and well-supported one in research on decision making.
- In spite of its numerous successes, prospect theory suffers from five important limitations.
- First, the theory fails to address the impact of social and emotional factors on decision making (e.g., Ritov & Baron, 1990; Wang, 1996).
- Second, there is insufficient recognition of the importance of individual differences in the willingness to make risk decisions (e.g., Josephs et al., 1992).
- Third, the theory doesn't take account of cross-cultural differences in risk-taking (Choi et al., 2004).
- Fourth, many studies on prospect theory haven't involved any *real* gains or losses. People may make different decisions in everyday life when they stand to lose some of their own money.
- Fifth, the most powerful criticism of prospect theory is perhaps the one made by Hardman and Harries (2002, p. 76): "There is no apparent rationale for . . . the value function . . . The value function is descriptive of behavior but does not go beyond this." Thus, we are not given a convincing explanation of *why* people are more sensitive to losses than to gains.

Social functionalist approach
- The central assumption of the social functionalist approach is that the decisions we make in everyday life are often influenced by social and cultural factors.
- That assumption is absolutely correct.
- Of particular importance, we typically feel under some pressure to justify our decisions to other people as well as to ourselves. That may seem like an obvious point. However, it was not incorporated into prospect theory that was discussed earlier.
- These pressures to account for our decisions can even lead experts into biased decision making (Schwartz et al., 2004).

- There are some limitations to the social functionalist approach that are worth bearing in mind.
- First, important factors emphasized within prospect theory (e.g., our greater sensitivity to losses than to gains) are ignored.
- Second, there are large individual differences in the extent to which people feel the need to justify themselves to other people. For example, we would expect individuals having low self-esteem to be more concerned about the views of others than those having high self-esteem.
- Third, Tetlock and others favoring the social functionalist approach have often criticized other researchers for their reliance on laboratory tasks not involving real gains or losses and not making any real demands on social responsibility. Ironically, much the same can be said about their own research!

Complex decision making
- There is general agreement that humans possess bounded rationality, and that their typical approach to decision making involves some form of satisficing.
- Elimination-by-aspects theory is one example of a theoretical approach based on satisficing, but there are many other similar theories.
- It is very difficult to construct a theory of decision making that is generally applicable, given the wide range of decisions that people make and the great individual differences in strategies.
- Decision-making strategies are also influenced by the number of choices remaining to be considered and the extent of any time pressure.
- Decision making is influenced by our preferences for various aspects of the choices before us. It is important to note that those preferences are not constant but rather are flexible and subject to change.

FURTHER READING

- Gigerenzer, G., & Selten, R. (2001). *Bounded rationality: The adaptive toolbox*. Cambridge, MA: MIT Press. Many of the chapters in this edited book focus on simple heuristics used in decision making.
- Hardman, D., & Macchi, L. (2003). *Thinking: Psychological perspectives on reasoning, judgment and decision making*. Chichester, UK: Wiley. There are several informative chapters on decision making in this edited book.
- Kahneman, D. (2003). A perspective on judgment and choice: Mapping bounded rationality. *American Psychologist*, *58*, 697–720. The approach to decision making developed by Kahneman and Tversky is discussed in a clear way in this article.
- Koehler, D.J., & Harvey, N. (2004). *Blackwell handbook of judgment and decision making*. Oxford: Blackwell. This book contains interesting chapters by several well-known experts on decision making.

CHAPTER 24

CONTENTS

Introduction	357
Does insight exist?	361
How useful is past experience?	364
General Problem Solver	368
Evaluation and chapter summary	372
Further reading	373

Finding the solution

24

INTRODUCTION

Life is full of problems, although thankfully the great majority of them are fairly trivial ones. We have the problem of working out how to mend our bicycle, how to get hold of a crucial reference for an essay that needs to be handed in on Friday, how to analyze the data from last week's laboratory exercise or practical, and so on. Before going any further, we should consider what we mean by a problem and by problem solving. In essence, there are three aspects to problem solving:

1. It is purposeful in the sense of being goal-directed (we are trying to achieve something).
2. It involves controlled cognitive processes rather than automatic ones.
3. A problem only exists when someone lacks the relevant knowledge to produce an immediate solution. Thus, a mathematical calculation may be a problem for most of us but not for a professional mathematician.

There are major differences among problems. For example, some problems are well-defined and others are ill-defined. **Well-defined problems** are ones in which all aspects of the problem are clearly specified, including the initial state or situation, the range of possible moves or strategies, and the goal or solution. The goal is well specified in the sense that it is clear when the goal has been reached. For example, a maze is a well-defined problem in which reaching the center is the goal. In contrast, **ill-defined problems** are under-specified. Suppose you have locked your keys inside your car, and want to get into it without causing any damage. However, you have very urgent business to attend to elsewhere, and there is no one around to help you. In such circumstances, it may be difficult to identify the best solution to the problem. For example, breaking a window will solve the immediate problem, but will obviously create additional ones.

Most of the problems we encounter every day are ill-defined, but psychologists have focused mainly on well-defined problems. Why is this? One important reason is that well-defined problems have a best strategy for their solution. Thus, we can identify the errors and deficiencies in the strategies adopted by human problem solvers.

It is also important to distinguish between knowledge-rich and knowledge-lean problems. **Knowledge-rich problems** can only be solved by

What can sabotage our attempts to solve a problem? What may help?

individuals having a considerable amount of relevant specific knowledge. In contrast, **knowledge-lean problems** don't require such knowledge, because most of the information required to solve the problems is contained in the initial problem statement. Most traditional research on problem solving has involved the use of knowledge-lean problems, in part because individual differences in relevant knowledge don't complicate matters with such problems. However, research on expertise (discussed in Chapter 25) has generally involved knowledge-rich problems.

MONTY HALL PROBLEM

We like to think we are good at problem solving. On those occasions when we fail to solve a problem, we expect to understand why our thinking was wrong when we are told the correct answer. Let me put this to the test by giving you the Monty Hall problem, named after the host of an American television show called *Let's Make a Deal*. Here is the most common version of the problem:

> Suppose you're on a game show and you're given the choice of three doors. Behind one door is a car, behind the others, goats. You pick a door, say, Number 1, and the host, who knows what's behind the doors, opens another door, say Number 3, which has a goat. He then says to you, "Do you want to switch to door Number 2?" Is it to your advantage to switch your choice?

If you decided to stay with your first choice, you're in good company. Burns and Wieth (2004) reported that across several studies an average of 85% of participants (mostly intelligent university students) made that decision. Unfortunately, it is the wrong answer! It seems as if either choice has a 50% chance of being correct, but in fact there is a two-thirds chance of being correct if you switch your choice. When this problem and its correct answer appeared in *Parade* magazine, it triggered thousands of indignant letters from readers disagreeing with the correct answer. Even Paul Erdõs, one of the greatest twentieth-century mathematicians, rejected the correct answer to the Monty Hall problem until he was convinced by a computer simulation.

I will use three ways of trying to convince you that switching doubles your chances of winning the car compared to not switching. First, when you make your initial choice by picking one door out of three at random, you clearly only had a one-third chance of winning the car. Regardless of whether your initial choice was correct, the host can open a door that doesn't have the prize behind it. Thus, the host's action sheds *no light* at all on the correctness of your initial choice, which remains a one-third chance.

Second, as Krauss and Wang (2003) pointed out, there are basically only three possible scenarios with the Monty Hall problem (see Figure 24.1). With scenario 1, your first choice was correct, and you would win by refusing to switch. With scenario 2, your first choice was incorrect, and so Monty Hall opens the only remaining door with a goat behind it. As a result, switching is certain to succeed. With scenario 3, again your first choice was incorrect. As with scenario 2, Monty Hall opens the only other door with a goat behind it,

KEY TERM
Knowledge-lean problems: problems that can be solved without the use of much prior knowledge, with most of the necessary information being provided by the problem statement; see knowledge-rich problems.

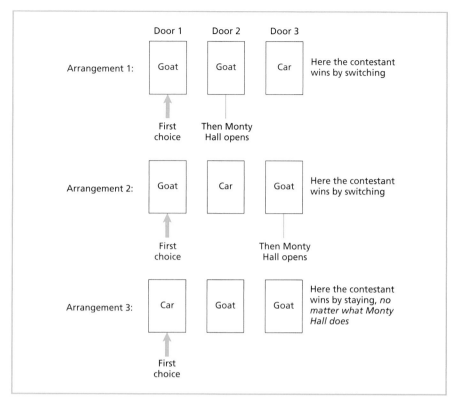

Door 1   Door 2   Door 3

Arrangement 1:

| Goat | Goat | Car |

Here the contestant wins by switching

First choice   Then Monty Hall opens

Arrangement 2:

| Goat | Car | Goat |

Here the contestant wins by switching

First choice   Then Monty Hall opens

Arrangement 3:

| Car | Goat | Goat |

Here the contestant wins by staying, *no matter what Monty Hall does*

First choice

Figure 24.1 Explanation of the solution to the Monty Hall problem: In two out of three possible car–goat arrangements the contestant would win by switching; therefore she should switch. Copyright © by the American Psychological Association. Reprinted with permission.

which guarantees that switching would be successful. Thus, switching succeeds with two out of three scenarios (2 and 3) and fails with only one scenario (1), producing a two-thirds chance that switching will succeed.

Third, it seems natural to focus on the *randomness* contained within the problem. For example, the location of the car is randomly determined, as is your initial choice (at least in the sense that you have no knowledge to guide your choice). As a result, it seems plausible that it is equally likely that the car is behind the door you chose initially and the other unopened door. However, this line of thinking ignores the fact that the host's behavior is *not* at all random—two-thirds of the time, his selection of a door to open makes it 100% certain that the car is behind the only door that is unopened and wasn't the participant's initial choice. As Burns and Wieth (2004) pointed out, a central difficulty people have with the Monty Hall problem is that they make errors when thinking about causality—the actions of the host cause switching to be a much better choice than not switching.

Burns and Wieth (2004) argued that people would do much better on the Monty Hall problem if it were presented in such a way that its causal structure was clearer. They did this with a boxer version of the problem (Burns & Wieth, 2004). There are three boxers, one of whom was so good that he was certain to win any bout. You select one boxer and then the other two boxers fight each other. The winner of the first bout then fights the boxer initially selected, and you win if you choose the winner of this second bout. You decide whether you want to stay with your initial choice or switch to the winner of the first bout. With this version of the problem, 51% of the participants made the correct decision to switch compared to only 15% with the standard three-door version. This difference occurred because it is easy to see that the boxer who won the first bout did so because of skill rather than any random factors.

INSIGHT?

What is involved in problem solving? What typically seems to happen is that we need to show persistence as we work slowly but surely through a problem until we reach the solution. We are all very familiar with such "grind-out-the-solution" problems. For example, solving a complicated problem in multiplication involves several processing operations that need to be performed in the correct sequence. Another example might be if you need urgently to go somewhere 50 miles from home, and you have the problem of getting there as soon as possible. However, the trains generally run late or are cancelled, your friend's car is old and unreliable and he may be unable or unwilling to take you, and the buses are slow.

Do you agree that most problems resemble the ones described above? If you do, then you are in for a rude shock! There are many problems in which the solution depends on **insight** or "aha" experience, which involves a sudden transformation of the problem. For example, let's consider the mutilated checkerboard (or draughtboard) problem (see Figure 24.2). The board is initially completely covered by 32 dominoes occupying two squares each. Then two squares from diagonally opposite corners are removed. Can the remaining 62 squares be filled by 31 dominoes? What nearly everyone does when given this problem is to start by mentally covering squares with dominoes (Kaplan & Simon, 1990). Alas, this strategy is not terribly effective, because there are 758,148 permutations of the dominoes!

Since very few people solve the mutilated checkerboard problem without assistance, I'll assume you are in that large majority. However, if I tell you something you already know, the chances are much greater that you will rapidly solve the problem. Remember that each domino covers one white and one black square. If that clue doesn't do the trick, think about the colors of the two squares that have been removed—they must have been the same color. Thus, the answer is that the 31 dominoes *cannot* cover the mutilated board.

The take-home message from the mutilated checkerboard problem is that how we think about a problem (the **problem representation**) is often of great importance in problem solving. Many psychologists (e.g., Köhler, 1925;

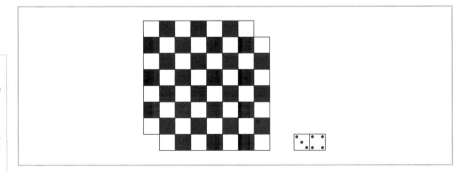

Figure 24.2 The mutilated checkerboard problem.

Ohlsson, 1992) argue that what happens with many problems is that we initially construct one or more problem representations. Eventually we form the correct problem representation, which involves a sudden restructuring of the problem (known as insight). In the next section, we consider whether the available evidence indicates that insight is important in problem solving.

DOES INSIGHT EXIST?

During the 1930s and 1940s, the Gestaltists (a group of German psychologists who emigrated to the United States) claimed to have found evidence for insightful problem solving. For example, Köhler (1925) studied an ape called Sultan. He (the ape rather than Köhler!) was kept inside a cage, and could only reach a banana outside the cage by joining two sticks together. Sultan seemed lost at first. However, he then seemed to realize how to solve the problem and rapidly joined the sticks together. According to Köhler, Sultan had shown insight.

There is a major problem with Köhler's claimed demonstrations of insight in Sultan and other apes. These apes had spent the early months of their lives in the wild, and so could have learned useful information about sticks and how they can be combined. Birch (1945) found that apes raised in captivity showed very little evidence of insightful problem solving. Thus, the apparent insight shown by Sultan may have been due to a slow learning process rather than a sudden flash of insight.

FINDINGS

There are several studies in which the processes involved in insightful problem solving differed substantially from those involved in ordinary non-insightful or incremental problem solving. For example, Metcalfe and Weibe (1987) recorded participants' feelings of "warmth" (closeness to solution) while engaged in insight and non-insight problems. There was a progressive increase in warmth during non-insight problems, as would be expected if they involve a sequence of processes. With insight problems, on the other hand, the warmth ratings remained at the same low level until suddenly increasing dramatically just before the solution was reached.

What is insight? Is this subjective experience matched by our underlying cognitive processes?

It is often assumed that non-insight problems involve gradual processes of which the problem solver is aware, whereas insight problems do not. What would happen if we asked people to provide an ongoing commentary of their attempts to solve a problem? Since this would not change the basic nature of the processes involved in non-insight problems, it shouldn't interfere with participants' ability to solve such problems. In contrast, verbalizing the steps involved is very different from what normally happens with insight problems, and so would be expected to interfere with performance. Schooler, Ohlsson, and Brooks (1993) found that the effects of verbalization of problem-solving steps had precisely the predicted effects.

Additional evidence of important differences between insightful and non-insightful problem solving was reported by Bowden, Jung-Beeman, Fleck, and Kounios (2005). Their participants performed the Remote Associates Test in which three words were presented (e.g., "fence"; "card"; and "master") and they had to think of a word (e.g., "post") that would go with each of them to form a compound word. Participants pressed a button to indicate whether they solved each problem using insight. In the first experiment, Bowden et al. used fMRI (see Glossary). The anterior superior temporal gyrus [ridge] in the right hemisphere was activated *only* when solutions involved insight. In the second experiment, event-related potentials (ERPs; see Glossary) were recorded. There was a burst of high-frequency brain activity one-third of a second before the participants indicated they had achieved an insightful solution. This brain activity was centered on the right anterior superior temporal gyrus. According to Bowden et al., this area is vital to insight because it is involved in processing general semantic (meaning) relationships.

Bowden and Beeman (1998) had previously found that the right hemisphere plays an important role in insight. Participants were presented with problems resembling those found on the Remote Associates Test. Before solving each problem, they were shown either the solution word or an unrelated word and had to decide whether the word provided the solution. The word was presented to either the left or the right hemisphere. Participants responded much faster when the word (solution or unrelated) was presented to the right hemisphere than to the left one.

Our subjective experience tells us that insight occurs suddenly and unexpectedly. In the words of one participant describing his experience of producing an insightful solution on an anagram-solving task, "The solution came to mind suddenly, seemingly out of nowhere. I have no awareness of having done anything to try get the answer" (Novick & Sherman, 2003). The crucial question is whether what is true of our subjective experience is also true of the underlying processes. In other words, do these underlying processes show the same sudden transformation from having made no progress to solving the problem that characterizes our experience of insight? As we will see, Novick and Sherman argued fairly convincingly that the answer is "No."

Novick and Sherman (2003) presented expert and non-expert anagram solvers with five-letter anagrams. They asked solvers to indicate whether the solutions "popped-out" in an insightful way. In the first experiment, "pop-out" solutions (produced mainly by expert solvers) were typically produced very rapidly (within 2–3 seconds of anagram presentation) whereas non-insightful solutions took much longer. This suggests that insight occurs suddenly and doesn't involve the gradual accumulation of information. However, conflicting evidence was obtained in a further experiment. Strings of five letters that could be rearranged to form words (anagrams) or couldn't be rearranged to form words (non-anagrams) were presented very briefly (for 469 or 953 ms). After that, the participants indicated very rapidly whether each letter string could be rearranged to form an English word. Note that the time available was so short that practically none of the anagrams could be solved. In spite of that, expert and non-expert anagram solvers both had above-chance levels of performance, with the experts performing significantly better than the non-experts. Thus, *partial* information was available to the participants at times much shorter than those needed to produce pop-out or insight solutions.

What is the importance of the above findings? The strong implication is that relevant processing occurs *before* "insight" anagram solutions, even though people have no conscious awareness of such processing. If so, how can we account for the fact that pop-out solutions differ from non-insightful solutions in speed and subjective experience? Novick and Sherman argued that pop-out solutions are based on *parallel* processing (several processes occurring at the same time). In contrast, non-insightful solutions are a more plodding business based on *serial* processing (only *one* process at a time).

WHAT PRODUCES INSIGHT?

What factors help to produce insight? This question was addressed by Ohlsson (1992) in his representational change theory. When trying to solve a problem, we often encounter a block or impasse because the way we have represented the problem is inappropriate. In order for insight to occur, we need to change the problem representation. This can occur in at least three ways:

1. *Constraint relaxation*: Inhibitions on what is regarded as permissible are removed.
2. *Re-encoding*: Some aspect of the problem representation is reinterpreted.
3. *Elaboration*: New problem information is added to the representation.

We saw how important it can be to change the problem representation via re-encoding in our earlier discussion of the mutilated checkerboard problem. The key to insight in that problem is the realization that each domino covers a black square and a white one. Evidence that insight can involve relaxing constraints we have needlessly imposed on our possible moves was reported by Knoblich, Ohlsson, Haider, and Rhenius (1999). They gave participants mathematical problems involving Roman numerals with sticks. Each problem represented was false, and the task was to move *one* stick to turn it into a true statement. For example, $VI = VII + I$ ($6 = 7 + 1$) becomes true by turning it into $VII = VI + 1$ ($7 = 6 + 1$).

What is the correct answer to the following problem: $IV = III - I$ ($4 = 3 - 1$)? If you are like the participants in the study by Knoblich et al. (1999), you probably found this problem harder than the previous one. The correct answer is $IV - III = I$ ($4 - 3 = 1$). According to Knoblich et al., our experience of arithmetic tells us that many operations change the *values* (numbers) in an equation (as in our first example). In contrast, relatively few operations change the *operators* (i.e., plus, minus, and equal signs) as in our second example. Thus, insight on problems of the second types requires us to relax the normal constraints of arithmetic.

Several theorists (e.g., Wallas, 1926) have argued that a block or impasse in solving a problem can often be overcome by simply ignoring it for some time. This is the essence of incubation. **Incubation** was originally thought to depend on processes below the conscious level operating during a period when the conscious mind was focused on other issues. Research on incubation has often involved comparing an experimental group having an incubation period away from an unsolved problem with a control group working continuously. Dodds, Ward, and Smith (2004) reviewed 39 studies on incubation. Incubation effects were obtained in 29 of these studies, and there were non-significant findings in the remaining 10 studies. Only a few factors influencing the extent of the incubation effects have been found. First, when the incubation period is short, a period of 30 minutes seems to be more effective than one that is less or more than that. Second, incubation generally has a more beneficial effect on participants of high ability than on ones of low ability.

It has often been claimed that "sleeping on a problem" can be a very effective form of incubation in problem solving. For example, the dreams of August Kekulé led to the discovery of a simple structure for benzene and those of Dmitri Mendeleyev initiated the development of the periodic table of elements. For experimental evidence of the value of sleep, we turn to a study by Wagner, Gais, Haider, Verleger, and Born (2004). Their participants performed a complex mathematical task and were subsequently retested several hours later. The mathematical problems were designed so they could be solved in a much simpler way than the one used initially by nearly all the participants. What was of interest was to see how many of them discovered the short-cut solution. Of those who slept between training and testing, 59% found the short cut compared to only 25% of those who did not.

How can we explain incubation effects? According to Simon (1966), incubation involves a special type of forgetting. More specifically, what tends to be forgotten over time is control information relating to the strategies tried by the problem solver. This forgetting makes it easier for problem solvers to adopt a new approach to the problem after the incubation period.

Support for the above viewpoint was reported by Smith and Blankenship (1991). They used the Remote Associates Test (e.g., finding a word ("chair") that links "wheel," "electric," and "high"). In the crucial interference condition, clues were presented that emphasized the differences in meanings of the three words (e.g., indicating that "high" is the opposite of "low"). There was also a control condition in which no misleading clues were presented. The participants either tried to solve the problems with a 5-minute break for incubation, or without a break. Participants in the interference condition given an incubation period solved 57% of the problems, compared to only 27% in the control condition. In the control condition, there was no effect of allowing a 5-minute break. Thus, there was an incubation effect only when the break allowed information about misleading clues to be forgotten.

HOW USEFUL IS PAST EXPERIENCE?

How can past experience both impair and promote problem solving?

Common sense indicates that our ability to solve a problem is much better if we have relevant past experience with similar problems than if we do not. Indeed, the crucial reason why adults can solve problems much faster than children and can solve a much wider range of problems is because of their enormous relevant past experience.

Is past experience *always* useful? Psychologists argue that the answer is, "No!" For example, Duncker (1945) obtained evidence of what he termed **functional fixedness**. This is observed when we fail to solve problems because we assume from past experience that any given object has only a limited number of uses. Duncker gave participants a candle, a box of nails, and several other objects (see Figure 24.3). Their task was to attach the candle to a wall by a table so it didn't drip onto the table below. Most participants tried to nail the candle directly to the wall or to glue it to the wall by melting it. Only a few came up with the correct answer, which was to use the inside of the nail-box as a candle holder and then to nail it to the wall.

According to Duncker (1945), his participants "fixated" on the box's function as a container rather than as a platform. This interpretation was supported by the finding that more correct solutions were produced when the nail-box was empty (rather than full) at the start of the experiment. Presumably having the nail-box empty made the box seem less like a container.

Duncker (1945) assumed that functional fixedness occurred in his study because of the participants' past experience with boxes.

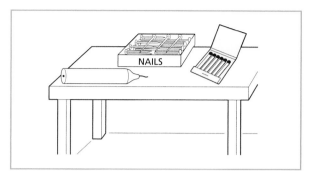

Figure 24.3 Some of the materials provided for participants instructed to mount a candle on a vertical wall in the study by Duncker (1945).

However, there was no *direct* evidence that past experience was the key factor. Luchins (1942) and Luchins and Luchins (1959) adopted the superior approach of *manipulating* participants' relevant past experience by providing it within the experiment. They presented water-jar problems involving three water jars of varying capacity. They asked participants to imagine pouring water from one jar to another to finish up with a specified amount of water in one of the jars.

The striking findings obtained by Luchins can be illustrated by considering one of his studies in detail. One problem was as follows: Jar A can hold 28 quarts of water, Jar B 76 quarts, and Jar C 3 quarts (see Figure 24.4). The task is to end up with exactly 25 quarts in one of the jars. The solution is not difficult as I'm sure you will agree: Jar A is filled, and then Jar C is filled from it, leaving 25 quarts in Jar A. Not surprisingly, 95% of participants who had previously been given similar problems solved it. Other participants were trained on a series of problems all of which had the same complex three-jar solution. Of these participants, only 36% managed to solve this extremely simple problem! The previous problems had created a mental set or "mechanized state of mind" (Luchins, 1942, p. 15), which prevented the participants from seeing the obvious.

More dramatic evidence of how mental set can prevent us from thinking clearly was reported by Levine (1971). He presented participants with a series of cards, each bearing the letters A and B. They had been instructed to work out the hypothesis he had in mind. One letter was on the left and the other was on the right. On each trial, the participant said "A" or "B", and the experimenter said whether this correct. For the first few problems, the solution involved a position sequence (e.g., the letter on the left should be selected on the first trial, the letter on the right on the second trial, and so on, alternately). After several problems involving position sequences, participants were given a very simple problem not involving a position sequence. The simple problem Levine used was one in which saying "A" was always correct and saying "B" was always incorrect. About 80% of university students failed to solve this problem

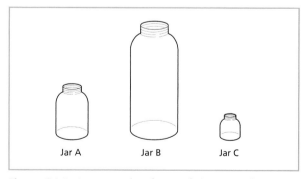

Figure 24.4 An example of one of the water jar problems use by Luchins (1942) and Luchins and Luchins (1954); Jar A holds 28 quarts, Jar B holds 76 quarts, and Jar C holds 3 quarts.

within 100 trials! The explanation was that they assumed that the answer must be some kind of position sequence, and there are almost endless possible position sequences.

POSITIVE TRANSFER

So far we have been discussing what is known as **negative transfer**, meaning disruptive and interfering effects of previous problem solving on a current problem. In the real world, of course, the effects of past experience on problem solving are mostly positive, and the term **positive transfer** is used to describe that state of affairs.

Your eyes may be starting to glaze over if you think positive transfer is of very little practical interest and importance. You may be pleased to learn that nothing could be further from the truth (as we will see shortly)! For example, nearly everyone involved in education firmly believes that what students learn at school or university facilitates learning later in life. In other words, it is assumed there is substantial positive transfer from the classroom or lecture theater to subsequent forms of learning (e.g., work-related skills).

One of the main ways in which positive transfer has been studied is via analogical problem solving. This involves participants using similarities between the current problem and one or more problems solved in the past. For example, consider a study by Gick and Holyoak (1980) using the radiation problem devised by Duncker (1945). A patient has a malignant stomach tumor and can only be saved by a special kind of ray. However, a ray strong enough to destroy the tumor will also destroy the healthy tissue, whereas a ray that won't harm healthy tissue will be too weak to destroy the tumor.

What is the answer to the radiation problem? If you haven't found it yet, here is an analogy to help you. A general wants to capture a fortress but the roads leading to it are too narrow to allow the entire army to march along any one of them. Accordingly, the general had his army converge at the same time on the fortress by walking along several different roads. Gick and Holyoak (1980) found that about 80% of participants solved the radiation problem when told that this story was relevant (the solution is to direct low-intensity rays at the tumor from several different directions). Only 40% of participants solved the problem when *not* informed of the story's relevance, and even fewer (10%) of those who weren't exposed to the story.

The above findings indicate that having a relevant analogy stored in long-term memory is no guarantee it will be used. The main reason was that there were few superficial similarities between the story and the problem. Keane (1987) found that participants were much more likely to spontaneously recall a previous story with superficial similarities to the radiation problem (story about a surgeon using rays on a cancer) than one that didn't (the general-and-fortress story).

In order for people to make successful use of a previous problem to solve a current problem, it is crucial they detect *similarities* between the two problems. As Chen (2002) pointed out, there are *three* main types of similarity between problems:

1. *Superficial similarity*: Solution-irrelevant details (e.g., specific objects) are common to both problems.

2. *Structural similarity*: Causal relations among some of the main components are shared by both problems.
3. *Procedural similarity*: Procedures for turning the solution principle into concrete operations are common to both problems.

It has often been argued that detecting structural similarities between a past and a current problem is sufficient to solve the current problem. However, Chen (2002) argued that procedural similarity is also important. He supported this argument by studying the weigh-the-elephant problem: A boy has to weigh an elephant, but his scales only weigh objects up to 200 pounds. Before proceeding, see if you can think how the boy solved the problem. In general terms, what is required is to use smaller objects to balance the weight of the elephant, and then to weigh the smaller objects separately on the scales. For example, you could put the elephant into a boat (perhaps easier said than done!) and mark the water level on the boat. After the elephant has been removed from the boat, put smaller objects into it until the water level is the same. Finally, weigh the objects one by one and work out the total weight.

Chen (2002) provided participants with an analogy resembling the weigh-the-elephant problem in both structural and procedural similarity or an analogy having only structural similarity. Participants in the latter condition performed worse. They understood the importance of finding objects of equivalent weight to the elephant, but couldn't find the right procedures to solve the problem. Thus, effective analogies often need to possess procedural as well as structural similarity to a current problem.

FAR TRANSFER

A limitation of most laboratory research is that the emphasis has been on **near transfer**. This typically involves the immediate application of knowledge and skills from one situation to a rather similar one. In real life, in contrast, we are often interested in **far transfer**. This involves positive transfer to a dissimilar context that may be far removed in time from the original learning.

There is increasing evidence that far transfer does exist and that the effects are sufficiently large to be of practical importance. For example, let's consider an important study by Chen and Klahr (1999). Children between the ages of 7 and 10 received training in designing and evaluating experiments in the domain of physical science. Of central importance in the children's learning was the control-of-variables strategy, involving the ability to create sound experiments and to distinguish between confounded and unconfounded experiments.

Chen and Klahr (1999) carried out a test of far transfer 7 months after the training, including a control group of children who had not received training. This test assessed mastery of the control-of-variables strategy in five new domains (plant growth, biscuit making, model airplanes, drink sales, and running speed). The children who had received the previous training were much more likely than control children to perform well on the test (see Figure 24.5).

Convincing evidence of far transfer over a period of several years was

KEY TERMS
Near transfer: beneficial effects of previous learning on current learning in a similar context; a form of positive transfer.
Far transfer: beneficial effects of previous learning on current learning in a dissimilar context; a form of positive transfer.

Why is far transfer a problem for lab-based studies of problem solving?

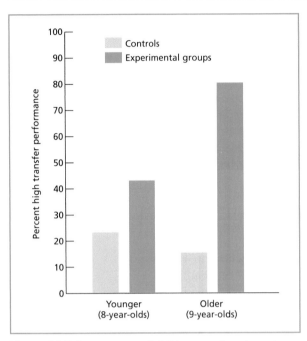

Figure 24.5 Percentage of children performing at a high level on the transfer test (13 or more out of 15) as a function of age (8 vs. 9) and previous relevant training (control vs. experimental). Based on data from Chen and Klahr (1999).

reported by Chen, Mo, and Honomichl (2004). In one experiment, American and Chinese university students were given a problem in which a treasure hunter travels into a cave and then has to find his way out without using a map or compass. The solution (leaving a trail of small objects while travelling through the cave) can be found with reference to the Hansel and Gretel story. In this story, a brother and sister find their way out of a forest by creating a trail with bread crumbs and pebbles. This story is much better known in America than China, and so it was predicted that American students would outperform Chinese ones on this problem. In fact, 75% of the American students solved the problem compared to only 25% of the Chinese students. Thus, far transfer based on a story typically encountered several years previously was obtained.

De Corte (2003) asked whether far transfer depends on **metacognition**, which is concerned with the beliefs and knowledge we have about our own cognitive processes and strategies. Students studying business economics were given 7 months of training in two metacognitive skills: orienting and self-judging. Orienting involves preparing oneself to solve problems by thinking about possible goals and cognitive activities. Self-judging is a motivational activity designed to assist students to accurately assess the effort required for successful task completion.

Far transfer was assessed when students subsequently learned statistics. Students who had received metacognitive training performed better than those who had not. Within the group that had received training, academic performance in statistics correlated positively with orienting and self-judging behavior.

GENERAL PROBLEM SOLVER

What types of heuristics are described by the Newell and Simon (1972) approach to problem solving?

One of the greatest landmarks in research on problem solving was the publication in 1972 of a book by Allen Newell and Herb Simon entitled *Human problem solving*. Their central insight was that the strategies we use when tackling complex problems take account of our limited ability to process and store information. They assumed we have strictly limited short-term memory capacity and that complex information processing is typically serial (one process at a time). These assumptions were incorporated into their General Problem Solver, which is a computer program designed to solve a large number of well-defined problems (discussed in more detail later).

How do we cope with our limited processing capacities? According to Newell and Simon (1972), we rely heavily on heuristics or rules of thumb (discussed in Chapter 22). Heuristics have the advantage that they don't require

KEY TERM
Metacognition: an individual's beliefs and knowledge about his or her own cognitive processes and strategies.

extensive information processing. However, they have the significant disadvantage that they aren't guaranteed to lead to problem solution. We can contrast heuristics with **algorithms**, which are generally complex methods or procedures that will definitely lead to problem solution. For example, the rules of multiplication form an algorithm—no matter how complex the problem, you are certain to get the right answer provided your follow the rules of multiplication. Algorithms have the advantage that you are guaranteed to solve the problem if used correctly. However, they have the disadvantage that they are often so complex that we lack the processing capacity to use them properly.

The most important of the various heuristics identified by Newell and Simon (1972) is **means–ends analysis**:

- Note the difference between the current state of the problem and the goal state.
- Form a sub-goal that will reduce the difference between the current and goal states.
- Select a mental operator that will permit attainment of the sub-goal.

Another important heuristic is hill climbing. **Hill climbing** involves changing the present state within the problem into one that is closer to the goal or problem solution. As Robertson (2001, p. 38) pointed out, "Hill climbing is a metaphor for problem solving in the dark." In other words, it is used when the problem solver has no clear understanding of the structure of a problem. It is thus a more primitive heuristic than means–ends analysis.

Newell and Simon (1972) obtained some of their key insights into problem solving by asking people to solve people while thinking aloud. These verbal reports were used to decide what general strategy people were adopting on each problem. After that, Newell and Simon specified the problem-solving strategy in sufficient detail for it to be programmed in their General Problem Solver. In the General Problem Solver, problems are represented as a problem space. The **problem space** consists of the following:

1. the initial state of the problem
2. the goal state
3. all of the possible mental operators (i.e., moves) that can be applied to any state to change it into a different state
4. all of the intermediate states of the problem.

Thus, the process of problem solving involves a sequence of different knowledge states. These knowledge states intervene between the initial state and the goal state, with mental operators producing the shift from one knowledge state to the next.

It will be helpful to consider a concrete example of what Newell and Simon (1972) had in mind. In the Tower of Hanoi problem (see Figure 24.6), the initial state of the problem consists of up to five disks piled in decreasing size on the first of three pegs. The goal state involves

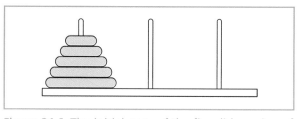

Figure 24.6 The initial state of the five-disk version of the Tower of Hanoi problem.

having all the disks piled in the same arrangement on the last peg. Only one disk can be moved at a time, and a larger disk cannot be placed on top of a smaller one. These rules serve to restrict the possible mental operators on each move.

FINDINGS

There is much evidence that people use heuristics such as hill climbing and means–ends analysis when solving well-defined problems. However, they also make use of a range of other strategies. For example, Simon and Reed (1976) used a complex version of the missionaries and cannibals problem. In their problem, missionaries and cannibals have to be transported across a river without the number of cannibals on either side of the river ever exceeding the number of missionaries. The problem can be solved in 11 moves, but on average participants took 30 moves to solve it. Initially, they adopted a *balancing strategy*, in which they tried to ensure there were equal numbers of missionaries and cannibals on each side of the river. After a while, participants shifted to *means–ends analysis*, in which the focus was on moving more people to the goal side of the river. Finally, participants used an *anti-looping heuristic* designed to avoid any moves reversing the immediately preceding move.

Means–ends analysis is generally a useful heuristic that assists people in their attempts to solve problems. Suppose, however, that we set up a problem in which use of means–ends analysis would consistently lead problem solvers to make the *wrong* move. In such circumstances, people using means–ends analysis should perform much worse than those not using that heuristic. Dramatic evidence supporting that prediction was reported by Sweller and Levine (1982). Participants were given the maze shown in Figure 24.7, but most of it was not visible to them. All participants could see the current problem state (i.e., where they were in the problem); some could also see the goal state (goal-information group), whereas the others could not (no-goal-information group).

What do you think happened on this relatively simple problem (simple because its solution only involved alternating left and right moves)? Use of means–ends analysis requires knowledge of the location of the goal, so only the goal-information group could have used that heuristic. However, the problem was designed so that means–ends analysis would not be useful, because every move involved turning *away* from the goal. As predicted, participants in the goal-information group performed very poorly—only 10% solved the problem in 298 moves! In contrast, participants in the no-goal-information group solved the problem in a median of only 38 moves. Thus, people seem to be powerfully attached to means–ends analysis. They continue to use it even when it prevents them discovering the structure of the problem and so greatly impairs problem-solving performance.

Why do most people engage in only a modest amount of planning when engaged in problem

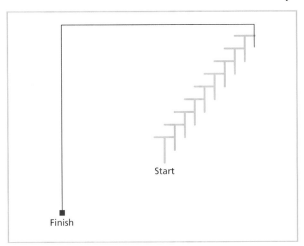

Figure 24.7 The image used in the study by Sweller and Levine (1982). Adapted from Sweller and Levine (1982).

solving? According to Newell and Simon (1972), the main problem is our limited short-term memory capacity. However, another possibility is that planning incurs costs in terms of time and effort, and is often unnecessary because simple heuristics suffice. Evidence favoring the latter possibility was reported by Delaney, Ericsson, and Knowles (2004) using water-jar problems in which the task was to finish up with specified amounts of water in each of three water jars. Half of the participants were instructed to generate the complete solution before making any moves, whereas the other half (control group) were free to adopt whatever strategy they wanted.

Delaney et al. (2004) found that the control participants showed little evidence of planning. However, the key finding was that those in the planning group showed very clear evidence of being able to plan, and solved the problems in far fewer moves than control participants. Thus, people have a greater ability to plan than is usually assumed, but often choose not to plan unless required to do so.

Newell and Simon (1972) assumed that people would shift strategies or heuristics if the ones they were using proved ineffective, but this idea was developed by MacGregor, Ormerod, and Chronicle (2001). According to them, strategy change often occurs because people keep track of their performance. More specifically, they use a heuristic known as **progress monitoring**, in which the rate of progress towards the goal is assessed, and criterion failure occurs if progress is too slow to solve the problem within the maximum number of moves. The basic idea is that criterion failure acts as a "wake-up call" that leads people to change strategy.

MacGregor et al. (2001) obtained support for the usefulness of progress monitoring in a study on the nine-dot problem (see Figure 24.8(a)). In this problem, you have to draw four straight lines connecting all nine dots without taking your pen off the paper. The solution is shown in 24.8(b), and one reason why many people fail to solve it is because they mistakenly assume the lines must stay within the square. The key conditions used by MacGregor et al. (2001) are shown in Figure 24.8(c) and (d). We might expect participants given (c) to perform better than those given (d) because it makes it clear that the lines have to go outside the square. In contrast, MacGregor et al. (2001) argued that individuals given Figure 24.8(c) can cover more dots with the next two lines than those given Figure 24.8(d) while remaining within the square. As a result, they are less likely to experience criterion failure, and so will be less likely to shift to a superior strategy.

The findings obtained by MacGregor et al. (2001) supported the prediction. Only 31% of those given Figure 24.8(c) solved the nine-dot problem, compared to 53% of those given Figure 24.8(d). The take-home message is that if the strategy you are using cannot allow you to solve a problem, the sooner you realize that that is the case the better.

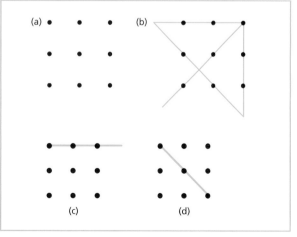

Figure 24.8 The nine-dot problem (a) and its solution (b); two variants of the nine-dot problem (c) and (d) presented in MacGregor et al. (2001). Copyright © 2001 by the American Psychological Association. Reprinted with permission.

EVALUATION AND CHAPTER SUMMARY

How useful is past experience?
- Much has been learned about the factors determining whether people will use relevant past knowledge when engaged in analogical problem solving.
- However, there are important differences between most laboratory studies and everyday life.
- In the laboratory, the fit or match between previous knowledge and the current problem is generally *precise*. In addition, that knowledge is typically presented very shortly before the problem.
- In real life, analogies are mostly *imprecise* and may have been encountered months or even years previously.
- Another limitation of most laboratory research is the neglect of individual differences.
- Spearman (1927) found that performance on analogical reasoning correlated about +.7 with IQ, indicating that highly intelligent individuals are much better than less intelligent ones at analogical problem solving.
- A final limitation of most of the studies carried out under laboratory conditions is that they have focused on near transfer (the immediate application of what has been learned previously to a current situation).
- In real life, in contrast, what is typically of more importance is far transfer, which involves positive transfer to a dissimilar context that may occur a long time after the original learning. For example, educationalists hope that that what students learn at school or university will make it easier for them to learn useful career skills many years later.

General Problem Solver
- The Newell and Simon approach has been shown to work well with several well-defined problems.
- Their approach also has the advantage that it allows us to specify the shortest sequence of moves from the initial state to the goal state. Thus, we can see exactly *when* and *how* an individual's performance deviates from the ideal.
- The theoretical approach is generally consistent with our knowledge of human information processing. For example, our limited processing capacity helps to explain why we typically use heuristics or rules of thumb such as means–ends analysis and hill climbing rather than algorithms.
- In spite of its successes and its impact on the field of problem solving, Newell and Simon's approach has some limitations.
- First, the General Problem Solver is better than humans at remembering what has happened on a problem. However, it is inferior to humans at planning future moves: it focuses on only a single move, whereas people often plan small sequences of moves (Greeno, 1974).

- Second, the General Problem Solver is designed to solve well-defined problems. It is essentially irrelevant to the ill-defined problems of everyday life, which depend on possession of relevant knowledge rather than use of heuristics.
- Third, in spite of our limited short-term memory capacity, we may be better able to plan several moves ahead in problem solving than was assumed by Newell and Simon (1972).
- Fourth, Newell and Simon (1972) didn't focus enough on the motivational factors causing us to shift strategies. This gap was filled to some extent by MacGregor et al. (2001) with their progress monitoring heuristic.

FURTHER READING

- Barnett, S.M., & Ceci, S.J. (2002). When and where do we apply what we learn? A taxonomy for far transfer. *Psychological Bulletin*, *128*, 612–637. The authors provide a very useful framework for transfer research.
- Robertson, S.I. (2001). *Problem solving*. Hove, UK: Psychology Press. This book provides good introductory coverage of all the main topics in problem solving.
- Sternberg, R.J., & Ben-Zeev, T. (2001). *Complex cognition: The psychology of human thought*. Oxford: Oxford University Press. Chapter 7 in this textbook provide good coverage of key issues in problem solving.

CHAPTER 25

Introduction   375

Chess-playing expertise   377

Deliberate practice   382

Evaluation and chapter summary   384

Further reading   385

How do you become an expert?

25

INTRODUCTION

In Chapter 24, we focused on certain kinds of problem solving. The studies considered were mainly those in which the time for learning was short, the tasks involved were relatively limited, and prior specific knowledge was not required. In the real world, however, much problem solving is very different. Millions of people spend several years acquiring knowledge and skills in a given area (e.g., psychology, medicine, law). The end point is the development of **expertise**, which can be defined as "highly skilled, competent performance in one or more task domains [areas]" (Sternberg & Ben-Zeev, 2001, p. 365).

What makes an expert? Most people (including many psychologists) would argue that a high level of intelligence is of key importance in the achievement of real expertise. Just think for a moment whether you agree. If you do, you may be surprised to discover that there is evidence suggesting some real experts have only average levels of intelligence. For example, Ceci and Liker (1986) studied individuals with great expertise about harness racing. For those unfamiliar with harness racing (popular in the United States), it involves horses pulling a sulky (a light two-wheeled cart) holding one person (the driver). They identified 14 experts and 16 non-experts. However, the term "non-experts" is a relative one, because the non-experts knew a vast amount about harness racing and attended horse races nearly every day. The IQs of the experts ranged from 81 to 128, and those of the non-experts from 80 to 130. Four of the experts had IQs in the low 80s, which is well below the population mean of 100.

The groups of experts and non-experts were given information about 50 unnamed horses and one unnamed standard horse. Fourteen pieces of information were provided in each case (e.g., each horse's lifetime speed, race driver's ability, track size). The participants worked out the probable odds for 50 comparisons, with each horse in turn being compared against the standard horse. Not surprisingly, the experts performed better than the non-experts. The performance of the experts was outstanding. For example, they took account of complex interactions among up to seven variables at the same time. What that means is that it was only possible to interpret the significance

*What does it take to
become an expert?*

of any one piece of information about a horse by considering it in the context of the other pieces of information about the same horse. It would require complicated statistical formulae to express these interactions mathematically.

The key finding was that the experts' high level of performance did not depend at all on a high IQ—the correlation between their performance and their IQ scores was −.07. Thus, experts with very low IQs were very successful at combining information in extremely complex ways. Indeed, if anything, experts with low IQs used more complex cognitive models than non-experts with high IQs when processing information about horses and horse racing.

What can we conclude from this study by Ceci and Liker (1986)? They claimed that the findings mean that, "IQ is unrelated to real-world forms of cognitive complexity that would appear to conform to some of those that scientists regard as the hallmarks of intelligent behavior" (Ceci & Liker, 1986, p. 255). However, this is probably something of an overstatement.

Dramatic findings have also been obtained from individuals who are rather patronizingly known as **idiots savants** (knowledgeable idiots) (see Howe, 1998, for a review). Idiots savants generally have mental retardation and low IQs but they possess some special expertise. For example, they can work out in a few seconds the day of the week corresponding to any specified date in the past or the future, or they perform complex multiplications at high speed, or they know what *pi* is to thousands of places of decimals.

More evidence that outstanding levels of expertise can be achieved through hard work and practice was reported by Ericsson and Chase (1982). They carried out a study on a student, SF. He was given extensive practice on the digit-span task, on which random digits have to be recalled in the correct order. Initially, his digit span was about 7 digits, which is only an average level of performance. He was then paid to practice the digit-span task for 1 hour a day for 2 years. At the end of that time, SF reached a digit span of 80 digits! This is extraordinary, because hardly anyone has a digit span of more than about 10 or 11 digits.

How did SF do it? He reached a digit span of about 18 items by using his extensive knowledge of running times. For example, if the first few digits presented were "3594," he might note that this was Bannister's world-record time for the mile. As a result, those four digits would be stored as a single unit or *chunk* (a stored unit integrating two or more smaller pieces of information; see Chapter 11). SF then increased his digit span by organizing these chunks into a hierarchical retrieval structure, with the top levels of the hierarchy serving as retrieval cues for information at lower levels of the hierarchy.

In spite of impressive findings like those just described, we need to be aware of their limitations. In all cases, the expertise (harness racing, exceptional memory or calculating power, digit span) is very narrow and specific. Clear evidence for this comes from SF. Even when he had reached a digit span of 80, his letter and word spans were no greater than those of most other people! What happens when we consider expertise that is much broader in scope, such as career success? Common sense (which can of course be very fallible!) would suggest that innate talent and/or high intelligence is essential if someone is to have an outstandingly successful career. As Sternberg and Ben-Zeev (2001, p. 302) argued, "Is one to believe that anyone could become a Mozart if only he or she put in the time? . . . Or that becoming an Einstein is just a matter of deliberate practice?"

KEY TERM
Idiots savants: individuals who have limited outstanding expertise in spite of being mentally retarded.

Support for the commonsensical view that innate ability (at least as assessed by IQ) predicts long-term career success in many occupations was provided in a review article by Gottfredson (1997). However, the strength of the relationship depended on the complexity of the jobs being considered. The correlation between intelligence and work performance was only +.23 with low-complexity jobs (e.g., shrimp picker, corn-husking machine operator). With high-complexity jobs (e.g., biologist, city circulation manager), however, the correlation between intelligence and job performance rose to +.58. Mackintosh (1998) reviewed evidence showing that the mean IQ of those in very complex occupations (e.g., accountants, lawyers, doctors, even academics) is about 120 to 130, which puts most of them in the top 15% in terms of IQ. Thus, high intelligence is of real importance for obtaining (and succeeding in) occupations of high complexity requiring high levels of expertise.

CHESS-PLAYING EXPERTISE

This section of the chapter is devoted to chess-playing expertise, and so we'll make a start by considering the value (or otherwise) of focusing on chess. There are at least two reasons why studying chess-playing expertise might not be very informative about expertise in general. First, the stereotype of keen chess players is that they are rather nerdy and unworldly and so not representative of the rest of the population. Second, chess is an artificial game and so we might imagine that the skills acquired by expert chess players have little relevance in everyday life.

Gobet, Voogt, and Retschitzki (2004) provided several arguments for the notion that we can learn much of general importance about expertise from studying chess players. First, chess has the advantage that we can access very precisely chess players' level of skill. Second, expert chess players develop specific cognitive skills (e.g., pattern recognition, selective search) that are useful in many other areas of expertise. Third, information about chess experts' remarkable memory for chess positions generalizes very well to most other types of expertise.

You may have wondered why so few of the world's best chess players are female. For example, in July 2003, there was only one female player (Judith Polgar) among the 100 best players in the world. In fact, there is nothing sinister about this—it depends mainly on the fact that the overwhelming majority of serious chess players are male. Charness and Gerchak (1996) predicted the respective numbers of high-ranking male and female players by developing a simple mathematical model taking account of the total number of male and female players. All of this begs the question as to the reasons *why* there are so few female chess players.

Why are some people much better than others at playing chess? Solso (1994) discussed the obvious answer: "Several years ago the late Bill Chase gave a talk on experts in which he promised to tell the audience what it would take to become a grandmaster chess player. His answer: 'Practice.' After the talk, I asked Chase how much practice. 'Did I forget to say how much?' he asked quizzically. 'Ten thousand hours.'"

It is indisputable that practice is of vital importance in the development of the chess-playing skills of a grandmaster. However, working out *exactly* what expert chess players know that non-expert players don't is hard to do. A breakthrough in our understanding of chess expertise came with the influential research of De Groot (1965). Initially, he found that chess masters differed surprisingly little from less expert players in terms of the number of moves considered, how many moves ahead they tried to look, or the ways in which they searched for the best move. However, De Groot eventually found that expert players were much better than non-expert ones at remembering chess positions. He gave his participants brief presentations (between 2 and 15 seconds) of board positions from actual games. After removing the board, De Groot asked them to reconstruct the positions. Chess masters recalled the positions very accurately (91% correct), whereas less expert players made many more errors (41% correct.).

What conclusions can we draw from De Groot's (1965) research? The fact that the experts' ability to remember chess positions was much better than that of non-experts strongly suggests that they have much more relevant knowledge about chess stored in long-term memory. However, the findings discussed so far leave two issues unaddressed. First, expert chess players may simply have generally better memories than non-experts. However, De Groot found that expert players were no better than non-expert ones at remembering random chess positions. Second, even if we assume that expert chess players have much more chess-relevant knowledge than non-experts stored in long-term memory, we still don't know in detail what that knowledge looks like.

WE LEARN CHUNKS!

What role does memory play in the development of chess expertise? Do the memory improvements transfer outside chess?

In one of the best-known studies on chess, Chase and Simon (1973) developed the experimental approach used by De Groot (1965). They argued that chess players memorizing chess board positions would break them down into about seven chunks or units in which information about a number of pieces would be integrated. Their key assumption was that the chunks formed by expert players contain more information than those of other players because they can bring more chess knowledge to bear on the memory task. Accordingly, they were looking for ways of working out how many chunks were being used by players varying in expertise, and came up with two tasks:

1. *Recall task*: The players inspected a chess position for 5 seconds before it was removed from view. They then tried to reconstruct as much of the chess position as possible. They assumed that pieces placed with less than 2 seconds' interval between them belonged to the same chunk.
2. *Copy task*: The players reconstructed a chess board position onto an empty board while the board remained in view. Chase and Simon assumed that the pieces placed on the empty board after a glance at the board position formed a chunk.

Chase and Simon (1973) used the above tasks with three players (a master, a class A player, and a beginner). The most expert player seemed to encode about 2.5 pieces per chunk, whereas the weakest player encoded only 1.9 pieces per chunk. They also argued that all chess players regardless of ability level can store about seven chunks in short-term memory. We will shortly see that these conclusion are suspect because of the flawed nature of Chase and Simon's research.

WE LEARN TEMPLATES!

Gobet and Waters (2003) argued that there are three major weaknesses with chunking theory. First, the theory focuses on what is happening at the fairly low chunk level. However, it de-emphasizes the various higher-level representations used by expert chess players to integrate and make use of information accumulating at the chunk level. Second, chunking theory predicts that it will take longer to encode [form representations of] chess positions than is actually the case. Third, it was assumed in chunking theory that the chunks were stored in short-term memory. As we will see, that would make memory for chess positions more fragile than it has been found to be.

The above weaknesses with chunking theory have been overcome in template theory (Gobet & Simon, 1996a; Gobet & Waters, 2003). The key assumption in template theory is that the chunks used frequently by chess players develop into more complex structures known as templates. What is a template? A **template** is a schematic structure more general than actual board positions. Each template consists of a *core* (very similar to the fixed information stored in chunks) plus *slots* (containing variable information about pieces and locations). The notion that templates contain slots means they are more flexible and adaptable than chunks. Templates also differ from chunks in being larger: each template stores information relating to about 10 pieces, although it can be larger than that. Finally, it is assumed that much of the information contained in any given template is stored in long-term memory. This contrasts with chunking theory, it which it was assumed that chunks are mainly stored in short-term memory.

Template theory makes various testable predictions. First, template theory predicts that the chunks into which information about chess positions is organized are larger and fewer in number than is assumed by chunking theory. More specifically, it is assumed that chess positions will be stored in three chunks or templates, with some of these chunks being relatively large.

Second, it is assumed that outstanding chess players owe their excellence mostly to their superior template-based knowledge of chess. This knowledge can be accessed rapidly, thus allowing them to narrow down with great speed the possible moves they need to consider.

Third, the theory predicts that expert chess players will have better recall of random chess positions than non-experts. The thinking behind this prediction is that some patterns occur by chance even in random positions, and these patterns relate to template-based information.

Fourth, the theory assumes that information in templates is stored mainly in long-term memory. As a result, it is predicted that template memory is largely resistant to interference.

FINDINGS

The first prediction received strong support in a study by Gobet and Clarkson (2004). They started by pointing out two limitations in the research of Chase and Simon (1973). Chase and Simon used only three players, and their master

KEY TERM

Template: as applied to chess—an abstract, schematic structure consisting of a mixture of fixed and variable information about chess pieces.

was out of practice and in his forties. More importantly, the players in their study had to move the pieces physically, and it is possible that the limited capacity of the hand for holding chess pieces may have made chunk size seem smaller than is actually the case. Gobet and Clarkson removed these problems by using 12 chess players and a computer display so that chess pieces didn't have to be moved by hand but were moved by using a mouse.

Gobet and Clarkson's (2004) findings supported the predictions of template theory more than those of chunking theory. The superior recall of chess board positions by expert players was due to the larger size of their chunks or templates: the maximum chunk size was about 13–15 for masters compared to only about 6 for beginners. The number of chunks didn't vary as a function of playing strength and averaged out at about two. That is much closer to the prediction of template theory (i.e., three) than to the prediction of chunking theory (i.e., seven).

The evidence provides some support for the second prediction, especially the notion that expert chess players assess chess positions very rapidly. For example, Charness, Rheingold, Pomplun, and Stampe (2001) asked expert and intermediate chess players to study chess positions and identify the best move. Their first five eye fixations (lasting in total for only about 1 second) were recorded. Even at this very early stage in considering each board position, the experts were more likely than the intermediate layers to fixate on tactically relevant pieces (80% vs. 64% of fixations).

Burns (2004) reported an interesting study to decide whether individual differences in chess-playing ability are due more to their template-based knowledge or to the ability to search successfully through possible moves. He used information about expert chess players' performance in normal competitive games and in blitz chess, in which the entire game has to be completed in 5 minutes (less than 5% of the time available in normal chess). The basic assumption was that any player's performance in blitz chess must depend mainly on his or her template-based knowledge because there is so little time to engage in relatively slow search processes. Thus, template-based knowledge is readily available to players in both blitz and normal chess, whereas search processes are much more available in normal chess than in blitz chess. If template theory is correct, then players who perform best in normal chess should also tend to perform best in blitz chess—the reason is that the key to successful chess (i.e., template-based knowledge) is available in both forms of chess.

What did Burns (2004) find? The key finding was that performance in blitz chess correlated highly with performance in normal chess. In three samples, the correlation varied between +.78 and +.90, indicating that template theory is correct in emphasizing the importance of template-based knowledge.

However, we must *not* draw the conclusion that slow search processes are irrelevant—Burns (2004) found that the same players playing chess under normal conditions and under blitz conditions made superior moves in the former condition, which provided time for much slow searching. It could be argued that blitz conditions didn't allow the players enough time to access all of their template-based knowledge. This is much less likely to have been the case in a study by Chabris and Hearst (2003). They identified the blunders made by grand masters in normal tournaments (about 3 minutes per move), in rapid tournaments (less than 1 minute per move), and rapid blindfold tournaments (less than 1 minute per move). Grand masters made 5.02 blunders per 1000 moves in normal tournaments compared to 6.85 in rapid games and 7.63 in rapid blindfold games. The significant increase in blunders when chess had to be played more rapidly almost certainly reflects problems with searching ahead for good moves rather than problems in accessing template knowledge.

More evidence that search processes are important was reported by Charness (1981). He compared chess players of differing levels of expertise in terms of the number of moves ahead they considered. Experts and grand masters considered about five moves ahead, by each player, whereas class D players (who have a low level of skill) considered only an average of 2.3 moves ahead by each player.

The third prediction from template theory is that expert players will have better recall than non-experts of random chess positions. This contrasts with chunking theory, according to which there should be no effects of chess expertise on the ability to remember random chess positions. Support for template theory was reported by Gobet and Simon (1996b), who combined the findings from several studies into a meta-analysis. They concluded that there was a small (but statistically significant) effect of skill on random board positions.

Gobet and Waters (2003) identified a real limitation with the studies considered by Gobet and Simon (1996b)—the so-called random board positions were not truly random! More precisely, the positions of the pieces were random, but the pieces placed on the board were not selected at random (e.g., two kings were always present). Gobet and Waters used completely random board positions (i.e., random pieces as well as random piece locations). Their findings supported template theory, because the number of pieces recalled varied from 14.8 for the most expert players to 12.0 for the least expert ones.

The fourth prediction receives support from an early study by Charness (1976). He looked at what happened to recall when the delay between the presentation and the recall of a chess position was filled with a demanding task (e.g., counting backwards; finding the best move on another board). The reduction in recall performance was surprisingly small, rarely exceeding more than about 6%–8%.

WHAT ARE THE LIMITATIONS OF TEMPLATE THEORY?

We conclude our discussion of template theory by considering its main limitations. First, as we have seen, outstanding chess players think more moves ahead than inferior players, and this can't readily be accounted for simply in terms of template knowledge. Second, there is an important distinction between routine and adaptive expertise (Hatano & Inagaki, 1986). **Routine expertise** is involved when a chess player can solve familiar problems rapidly and efficiently. In contrast, **adaptive expertise** is involved when a player has to develop strategies for deciding what to do when confronted by a novel board position. Template theory provides a convincing account of what is involved in routine expertise. However, it is less clear that it sheds much light on adaptive expertise. For example, consider what happens when expert players compete against chess-playing computers with limited time available.

KEY TERMS

Routine expertise: using acquired knowledge to solve familiar problems efficiently.

Adaptive expertise: using acquired knowledge to develop strategies for dealing with novel problems.

When the game must be completed in 25 minutes, computers gain about 100 Elo points (a measure of playing strength) relative to their human opponents (Lassiter, 2000). More strikingly, computers gain 200 or more Elo points when the game is limited to 5 minutes (Lassiter, 2000). Presumably expert players need to evaluate novel moves as well as gain rapid access to relevant templates in order to play chess effectively. This evaluative process involves adaptive expertise and is not accounted for by template theory.

DELIBERATE PRACTICE

What do you need to fulfill the criteria for deliberate practice? Why is it important in expertise?

We have just seen that expert chess players differ from non-expert ones in terms of the amount of practice devoted to learning chunks and/or templates. Earlier we saw that practice can enable people to increase their digit span dramatically (Ericsson & Chase, 1982) or to acquire an excellent awareness of the ways in which different factors interact to determine odds at harness racing (Ceci & Liker, 1986). We can go further. Everyone knows that prolonged and carefully organized practice is essential in the development of *any* kind of expertise. That is a useful starting point, but what we really need is a theory in which the details of what is involved in effective practice are spelled out. Precisely that was done by Ericsson and Lehmann (1996). They emphasized that a wide range of expertise can be developed through deliberate practice. **Deliberate practice** has four aspects:

1. The task is at an appropriate level of difficulty (not too easy or too hard).
2. The learner is given informative feedback about his or her performance.
3. The learner has adequate chances to repeat the task.
4. The learner has the opportunity to correct his or her errors.

What exactly happens as a result of prolonged deliberate practice? According to Ericsson and Kintsch (1995), experts can get round the limited capacity of working memory. They proposed the notion of **long-term working memory**: experts learn how to store relevant information in long-term memory so that it can be accessed readily through retrieval cues held in working memory. This does *not* mean that experts have greater working memory capacity than the rest of us. Instead, they are more efficient at combining the resources of long-term memory and working memory. Note that Ericsson and Kintsch claimed that long-term working memory is useful for all kinds of expertise, not just those directly dependent on memory.

Where the approach adopted by Ericsson and Lehmann (1996) becomes controversial is in the additional assumption that deliberate practice is *all* that is needed to develop expert performance—innate talent or ability is said to have practically no influence on expert performance.

FINDINGS

One of the central assumptions of the theory is that what is important in acquiring expertise is the amount of *deliberate* practice rather than simply the sheer amount of practice. Charness, Krampe, and Mayr (1996) found that amount of chess playing failed to predict chess skill when they controlled statistically for the amount of chess study or deliberate practice. The best players were those who had engaged in the most deliberate practice, for example by using published games to predict the moves made by chess masters. Similar findings were reported by Ericsson, Krampe, and Tesch-Römer (1993), who studied violinists in a German music academy. The key difference between 18-year-old students having varying levels of expertise on the violin was the amount of deliberate practice they had had over the years. The most expert violinists had spent on average nearly 7500 hours engaged in deliberate practice, compared to the mere 5300 hours clocked up by the good violinists.

The main limitation with studies such as those by Charness et al. (1996) and by Ericsson et al. (1993) is that they focused on correlations or associations between amount of deliberate practice and level of performance. This is a limitation, because it doesn't prove that the deliberate practice *caused* the higher level of performance. With respect to the study by Ericsson et al., perhaps those musicians with the greatest innate talent and/or musical success decided to spend more time practicing than did those with less talent or previous success. However, some evidence goes against that interpretation. Sloboda, Davidson, Howe, and Moore (1996) compared highly successful young musicians with less successful ones. The two groups didn't differ in terms of the amount of practice time they required to achieve a given level of performance. This suggests that the advantage possessed by the very successful musicians is *not* due to their greater level of natural musical ability.

We turn now to the controversial view that innate ability is almost irrelevant to the acquisition of expertise. We saw earlier in the study by Ceci and Liker (1986) that expertise in calculating odds at harness racing was unrelated to IQ, and that the mean IQ of the greatest experts was only around the average of the population. We also saw that some of the most striking evidence comes from studies on individuals (idiots savants) who are mentally retarded but perform at extremely high levels within some restricted area of intellectual functioning. For example, Howe and Smith (1988) studied a mentally handicapped 14-year-old boy who had an outstanding ability at calendar calculating. When asked to indicate the day of the week on which a past or future date fell, he could typically supply the correct answer in a matter of seconds—something that the rest of us cannot do!

In spite of the great feats of idiots savants, their abilities are often very restricted. In the case of the boy just discussed, he was very good at subtraction problems expressed in terms of calendar dates (e.g., "If a man was born in 1908, how old would he have been in 1934?"). However, when essentially the *same* subtraction problem was expressed as "What is 34 minus 8?" he took much longer to produce an answer and the answer was often wrong!

One of the most systematic attempts to study the relationship between IQ and performance was reported by Hulin, Henry, and Noon (1990). They carried out various meta-analyses combining data from many studies to investigate the relationship between IQ and performance. There were two key findings:

1. The correlation or association between IQ and performance *decreased* steadily over time as expertise developed.
2. The correlation between IQ and performance was only very slightly positive among individuals with over 5 years of professional experience.

Not surprisingly, Hulin et al. concluded that innate ability (intelligence as assessed by IQ) is of little importance at high levels of expertise. However, many of the studies they included in their meta-analyses were concerned with fairly narrow types of learning. As a result, their conclusions may not apply to more general forms of learning.

The role of natural ability in the development of expertise was considered by Frank and d'Hondt (1979). They randomly assigned teenagers to a compulsory chess group or to a control group. Measures of spatial aptitude, numerical aptitude, and numerical ability all predicted chess-playing expertise 1 year later.

One of the few studies to consider *both* the amount of deliberate practice and innate ability was reported by Horgan and Morgan (1990). They found that improvement in chess-playing performance was determined mainly by deliberate practice, motivation, and the degree of parental support. However, individual differences in non-verbal intelligence were also of importance, accounting for 12% of the variation in chess-playing performance.

Gobet et al. (2004) discussed the evidence on the role of innate ability in the development of chess-playing expertise. They came to the following conclusion: "The fact that chess players tend to have higher IQ scores offers some support to the first explanation [importance of natural ability], but the absence of better visuo-spatial abilities must be seen as negative evidence" (Gobet et al., 2004, p. 178).

EVALUATION AND CHAPTER SUMMARY

Chess playing expertise

- There is reasonably strong evidence that outstanding chess players possess much more template-based knowledge of chess positions than non-experts.
- This knowledge allows them to assess chess positions very rapidly, and thus gives them a substantial advantage when playing chess.
- Template theory makes it understandable that expert chess players can identify key pieces in a board position in under one second (Charness et al., 2001) and can perform effectively when playing blitz chess in which there is very little time for slow search processes (Burns, 2004).
- It also allows us to understand why memory for chess positions is little affected by tasks interfering between seeing a chess position and recalling it.

Deliberate practice

- It is indisputable that extensive practice is absolutely essential for the development of expertise.
- It is also generally agreed that the most effective form of practice is deliberate practice, in which the task is not too easy or too hard, and the situation is set up so that the learner's errors can be corrected.
- There has been much controversy on the issue of whether deliberate practice is both necessary and sufficient for the development of expertise, or whether it is necessary but *not* sufficient.

- The available evidence suggests that innate ability or high IQ is needed as well as deliberate practice for the development of broad and complex skills, but is less crucial when the skills acquired are narrow and less complex.

FURTHER READING

- Gobet, F., Voogt, A. de, & Retschitzki, J. (2004). *Moves in mind: The psychology of board games*. Hove, UK: Psychology Press. This book gives a comprehensive account of the development of expertise in several board games, but focuses mainly on chess expertise.
- Howe, M.J.A. (1998). *Principles of abilities and human learning*. Hove, UK: Psychology Press. This book by a leading authority in the field provides a very accessible account of learning, including the development of expertise.
- Robertson, S.I. (2001). *Problem solving*. Hove, UK: Psychology Press. Chapters 8 and 9 provide a very useful introduction to the topic of expertise.

CHAPTER 26

CONTENTS

Introduction 387

Reasoning problems 389

Theoretical approaches 392

What about individual differences? 397

How rational are we? 399

Evaluation and chapter summary 401

Further reading 403

Reasoning

INTRODUCTION

As Manktelow (2001, p. 4) pointed out, "People have been congratulating themselves for over two thousand years at being the 'rational animal'. Reason, we all agree, is what distinguishes us from other species." If that is the case, we would expect people to perform extremely well when presented with apparently straightforward reasoning problems. We will consider such problems shortly, but for now let's note there are various kinds of reasoning. The emphasis in this chapter is almost exclusively on deductive reasoning. **Deductive reasoning** allows us to draw conclusions that are definitely valid (or invalid) provided that other statements (known as **premises**) are assumed to be true. For example, suppose we are given the premises "Tom is taller than Dick" and "Dick is taller than Harry" and told to assume both premises are true. The conclusion, "Tom is taller than Harry," is necessarily true or valid.

Bear in mind that processes over and above reasoning are used by participants given reasoning problems to solve. Why is this? As Sternberg (2004, p. 444) pointed out, "Reasoning is not encapsulated [enclosed or isolated]. It is part and parcel of a wide array of cognitive functions … many cognitive processes, including visual perception, contain elements of reasoning in them."

One of the most common ways of studying reasoning is by using **syllogisms**, which consist of two premises or statements followed by a conclusion. See how good your reasoning powers are by deciding which of the conclusions below are valid (these syllogisms are taken from Manktelow, 1999, p. 64). Remember that the task involves deciding whether the conclusions follow *logically* from the premises and NOT deciding how sensible the conclusions appear to be in the real world.

1. *Premises*
    All the athletes are healthy.
    Some healthy people are wealthy.
    Conclusion
    Some of the athletes are wealthy.
2. *Premises*
    All the students are poor.
    No students are stupid.
    Conclusion
    Some poor people are not stupid.

KEY TERMS
Deductive reasoning: a form of reasoning in which necessarily valid (or invalid) conclusions can be drawn assuming the truth of certain statements or premises.
Premises: statements that are assumed to be true for the purposes of deductive reasoning.
Syllogism: a logical argument consisting of two premises (e.g., "All X are Y") and a conclusion; syllogisms formed the basis for the first logical system attributed to Aristotle.

3. *Premises*
    All the men are healthy.
    Some healthy people are women.
    Conclusion
    Some of the men are women.
4. *Premises*
    All the monks are men.
    No monks are women.
    Conclusion
    Some men are not women.

Did you decide that the conclusions to syllogisms 1 and 2 are valid, whereas those to syllogisms 3 and 4 are invalid? Hopefully, you didn't! In fact, the conclusions to syllogisms 2 and 4 are valid, whereas those to syllogisms 1 and 3 are invalid. Syllogisms 1 and 3 have the same structure, but it is harder to decide that the conclusion of syllogism 1 is invalid because it is believable. In similar fashion, syllogisms 2 and 4 have the same structure, but it is harder to decide that the conclusion to syllogism 4 is valid because it is unbelievable.

If people really were as proficient at reasoning and rational thought as we tend to imagine, then they would deal with syllogisms in an entirely logical fashion and would pay no attention to the believability or unbelievability of the conclusions. In fact, most people are influenced by the believability of syllogism conclusions. The term **belief bias** refers to the tendency to accept believable conclusions and to reject unbelievable ones, irrespective of their logical validity or invalidity. We can see how strong belief bias can be by considering a study by Evans, Barston, and Pollard (1983). They used syllogisms with four types of conclusions: valid + believable; valid + unbelievable; invalid + believable; and invalid + unbelievable.

The key findings of Evans et al. (1983) are shown in Figure 26.1. The mistaken tendency to accept invalid conclusions as valid was dramatically greater when the conclusions were believable than when they were unbelievable (66% vs. 13%, respectively). This is very strong evidence for belief bias, and

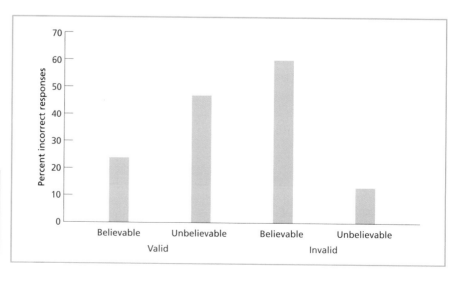

Figure 26.1 Percent incorrect responses to syllogism conclusions as a function of conclusion validity (valid vs. invalid) and believability (believable vs. unbelievable). Data from Evans et al. (1983).

KEY TERM
Belief bias: the tendency to decide whether the conclusion of a syllogism is valid on the basis of whether or not it is believable.

there is additional evidence for belief bias in the tendency to reject as invalid conclusions that are actually valid. When the conclusion was unbelievable, valid conclusions were rejected much more often than when they were believable (38% vs. 14%, respectively). The take-home message (and one confirmed by many other studies such as Klauer, Musch, and Naumer, 2000), is that our ability to reason effectively may (sadly) be much less than we like to imagine.

You may be thinking by now that reasoning research seems limited in that its focus is on forms of thinking of little relevance to everyday life. Aristotle (who may well be the greatest thinker of all time) drew a distinction between pure and practical reasoning that is pertinent at this point. Most laboratory research focuses on pure reasoning; that is, reasoning designed to work out what is true or valid and what is false or invalid. In the real world, in contrast, we spend much of our time working out what to do to achieve the goals we have set ourselves. There are far more studies on pure reasoning than on practical reasoning. However, you may be reassured to discover that there has been a large increase in research on practical reasoning in the past 10 years or so. Such research involves **deontic reasoning**, and its central focus is on making decisions about what we should or shouldn't do. For example, it concerns issues relating to obligations and to social contracts. Research on deontic reasoning will be discussed later in the chapter.

REASONING PROBLEMS

There are various major categories of reasoning problems. Reference has already been made to syllogistic reasoning, which is considered further in this section. We will also consider conditional reasoning, which is basically reasoning with "If." Within conditional reasoning, the most studied problem is Wason's selection task, and we will discuss findings from it in some detail.

What are the main forms of reasoning? What kinds of factors influence each of these forms?

SYLLOGISTIC REASONING

We start by providing a more detailed account of what is involved in syllogistic reasoning than has been provided so far. Here is an example of a syllogism:

> *Premises*
> All A are B.
> All B are C.
> *Conclusion*
> Therefore, all A are C.

A syllogism contains three terms (A, B, and C), with one of them (B) occurring in both premises. The premises and the conclusion each contain one of the following quantifiers: *all*; *some*; *no*; or *some . . . not*. When you are presented with a syllogism, you have to decide whether the conclusion is valid provided the truth of the premises is accepted. Thus, the truth or falsity of the conclusion in the real world is irrelevant.

KEY TERM
Deontic reasoning: a form of reasoning concerned with what we should or should not do; concerned with obligations, rights, and social contracts.

CONDITIONAL REASONING

Conditional reasoning is a form of deductive reasoning involving deciding on the validity of "If . . . then" statements. It had its origins in propositional logic, in which logical operators such as not; as . . . if; if and only if are included in sentences or propositions. A proposition is the meaning conveyed by a sentence asserting or denying something, and as such it can be true or false. In propositional logic, symbols stand for sentences, and logical operators are applied to them to reach conclusions. Thus, in propositional logic, we might use P to stand for the proposition "It is raining," and Q to stand for "Juliet gets wet," and then use the logical operator "*if . . . then*" to relate these two propositions: *If P then Q*.

It is *very* important to note that the meanings of words and propositions in propositional logic differ from their meanings in natural language. For example, propositions in this logic can only have one of two truth-values: they are either true or false. If P stands for "It is raining," then P is either true (in which case it is raining) or P is false (it is not raining). Propositional logic doesn't admit any uncertainty about the truth of P (e.g., where it is not really raining, but is so misty you could almost call it raining).

Differences of meaning between propositional logic and ordinary language are particularly great with respect to "if . . . then." Consider the following, which involves *affirmation of the consequent*:

Premises
If Susan is angry, then I am upset.
I am upset.
Conclusion
Therefore, Susan is angry.

Do you accept the above conclusion as valid? Many people would, but it is *not* valid according to propositional logic. The explanation is as follows: I may be upset for some other reasons (e.g., I have lost my job).

Two of the most important rules of inference in conditional reasoning are *modus ponens* and *modus tollens*, both of which are associated with valid conclusions. Here is an example of modus ponens:

Premises
If it is raining, then Alicia gets wet.
It is raining.
Conclusion
Alicia gets wet.

Here is an example of modus tollens:

KEY TERM
Conditional reasoning: a form of deductive reasoning based on "IF . . . THEN" statements.

Premises
If it is raining, then Alicia gets wet.
Alicia does not get wet.
Conclusion
It is not raining.

People consistently perform much better with modus ponens than with modus tollens.

WASON SELECTION TASK

The most studied reasoning task is Wason's selection task, named after the late British psychologist Peter Wason who devised it. It is not purely a deductive reasoning task, but rather it concerns hypothesis testing using a conditional rule. Here is the original version of the task (Wason, 1968):

> Below is depicted a set of four cards, of which you can see only the exposed face but not the hidden back. On each card, there is a number on one of its sides and a letter on the other.
>
> Also below there is a rule which applies only to the four cards. Your task is to decide which if any of these four cards you *must* turn over in order to decide if the rule is true.
>
> Don't turn over unnecessary cards. Tick the cards you want to turn.
>
> **Rule**: *If there is a vowel on one side, then there is an even number on the other side.*

If you are not familiar with Wason's selection task, think what your answer would be.

The most common answer by far is to select the A and 4 cards. Alas, if you did the same, you got the answer wrong! In fact, what you need to do is to see whether any of the cards *fail* to obey the rule. From this perspective, the 4 card is irrelevant—if there is a vowel on the other side of it, this only tells us the rule *might* be correct. If there is a consonant, we have also discovered nothing about the validity of the rule.

What is the right answer? It involves selecting the A and 7 cards, an answer given by only about 5%–10% of university students (Wason, 1968). The 7 is necessary, because it would definitely disprove the rule if it had a vowel on the other side.

One plausible reason why Wason (1968) obtained such poor levels of performance is because the task was rather abstract—perhaps people would perform better if the task were made more concrete. Wason and Shapiro (1971) used four cards (Manchester, Leeds, car, and train) and the rule, "Every time I go to Manchester I travel by car." The task was to select only those cards needing to be turned over to prove or disprove the rule. The correct answer (i.e., "Manchester" and "train") was given by 62% of the participants, against only 12% given the standard abstract version of the task. However, other studies comparing concrete and abstract versions of the selection task have produced rather inconsistent findings (see Evans, 2002, for a review).

Why do even highly intelligent people struggle so much with Wason's selection task? There are several answers to that question, most of which relate to difficulties that participants have

Figure 26.2 Rule: If there is a vowel on one side of the card, then there is an even number on the other side.

with *interpreting* exactly what the problem is all about. These difficulties were discussed by Stenning and van Lambalgen (2004), and we will consider two here. First, the rule is proposed by an authoritative experimenter, and so the participants may be biased in favor of assuming that the rule is very likely to be correct. Second, participants may not fully realize that they have to make all their choices *before* receiving any feedback.

Stenning and van Lambalgen (2004) carried out a study to see whether the above possible misinterpretations are important by adding clarifications to the instructions. So far as the first misinterpretation is concerned, some participants were instructed, "Also below there appears a rule put forward by an unreliable source. Your task is to decide which cards (if any) you *must* turn in order to decide if the unreliable source is lying." So far as the second misinterpretation is concerned, some participants were instructed: "Assume that you have to decide whether to turn each card before you get any information from any of the turns you make."

Is failing to solve a strict conditional reasoning problem always a bad thing in real life?

The findings indicated that these misinterpretations influenced performance. Only 3.7% of participants given the standard instructions produced the correct answer. In contrast, 13% of those alerted to the possible falsity of the rule got the answer right, as did 18% of those explicitly warned they wouldn't receive any feedback before making all their choices. Of course, performance was still very poor even when attempts were made to correct common misinterpretations of the task.

The standard form of Wason's selection task involves an indicative rule ("If there is a p then there is a q"), and as we have seen performance is generally poor. Other versions of the selection task involve a deontic rule ("If you do p then you *must* do q"). Deontic rules are concerned with detection of rule violation, and are typically much easier for participants to understand because the underlying structure of the problem is more explicit. For example, Griggs and Cox (1982) used the deontic rule, "If a person is drinking beer then that person must be over 19 years of age," with students in Florida, and found that performance was much better than on the standard version of the selection task.

Some of the most dramatic findings based on a deontic rule were reported by Sperber and Girotto (2002). They asked participants to indicate which of the following cards needed to be turned over to decide whether Paolo has bought any non-Italian food items through the internet: "food item"; "non-food item"; "Italian item"; and "non-Italian item." With this deontic rule, 91% of the participants correctly selected the food item and non-Italian item cards.

THEORETICAL APPROACHES

The key question that has to be addressed by theorists is the following: Why is reasoning performance prone to certain kinds of errors? Various answers have been proposed to that question. We will focus mainly on the extremely influential theoretical approach based on mental models (Johnson-Laird, 1983). However, we will start with the abstract-rule theory originally put forward by Braine (1978), and later developed by various theorists (e.g., Braine, 1994, 1998; O'Brien, 2004; Rips, 1994).

ABSTRACT-RULE THEORIES

One of the central assumptions of abstract-rule theories is that people use mental logic when confronted by a reasoning task, and use of this mental logic will often lead to valid reasoning. According to O'Brien (2004, p. 209), "Mental-logic theory was developed from the expectation that there are inference-making procedures that draw short, immediate, and direct inferences." We will explore mental logic in more detail shortly, but it is important for now to note that mental logic is *not* the same as formal logic. As O'Brien (2004, p. 207) pointed out, "We have no reason to assume that a mental logic should be identical to a standard logic of the sort found in a typical textbook than we have reason to assume that basic human intuitions about quantities should correspond to some particular formal mathematical calculus."

If we use mental logic when reasoning, how come we make so many errors? According to Braine, Reiser, and Rumain (1984), there are *three* main reasons why people make reasoning errors:

1. *Comprehension errors*: The premises of a reasoning problem (or the conclusion) are interpreted incorrectly. For example, there is the **conversion error** (e.g., "All As are Bs" is interpreted as meaning "All Bs are As"). We can see this is an error if we take a concrete example: "All cats are animals" clearly doesn't mean that "All animals are cats"! In spite of that, conversion errors are common (Chapman & Chapman, 1959).
2. *Heuristic inadequacy*: The individual's reasoning process fails to locate the correct line of reasoning.
3. *Processing errors*: The participant fails to attend fully to the task in hand or suffers from memory overload.

In a nutshell, the central assumption is that people use mental logic to apply logically valid rules, but they make errors when the *input* to the rules is wrong. For example, people often make errors with affirmation of the consequent because they use the conversational assumptions of everyday life to reinterpret the premises.

Findings

Evidence consistent with abstract-rule theory was reported by Braine et al. (1984). In one experiment, participants were given a simple reasoning task about the presence or absence of letters on an imaginary blackboard. Here is a sample problem:

> If there is a T, there is an L.
> There is a T.
> ?There is an L?

Participants had to decide whether the provided conclusion was true. These problems were designed to be solved in a single step by one of the 16 rules proposed by the theory. As predicted, reasoning on these problems was essentially error-free.

How could you potentially lower the rate of errors made in reasoning problems?

KEY TERM
Conversion error: a mistake in syllogistic reasoning occurring because a statement is invalidly converted from one form into another.

Evidence that people's reasoning is impaired by comprehension errors was reported by Ceraso and Provitera (1971). They tried to reduce conversion errors by spelling out the meaning of the premises more unambiguously (e.g., "All As are Bs" was stated as "All As are Bs, but some Bs are not As"). This produced a substantial improvement in performance, as is predicted by abstract-rule theory.

According to Braine et al. (1984), people have a mental rule corresponding to modus ponens, which is why syllogisms based on modus ponens are easy and pose no comprehension problems. In contrast, modus tollens is a hard inference to make because no single rule can be applied to it. However, evidence that modus ponens is *NOT* always easy was provided by Byrne (1989). She compared reasoning performance on modus ponens under standard conditions or including an additional argument (shown in brackets) providing context:

If she has an essay to write, then she will study late in the library.
(If the library stays open, then she will study late in the library.)
She has an essay to write.
Therefore, ?

The percentage of participants making the valid inference, "She will study late in the library") was about 95% in the standard condition compared to only 40% when an additional argument was provided. This latter finding is hard to interpret within the framework of abstract-rule theories.

MENTAL MODELS

Do we have cognitive processes that are specialized with logical reasoning?

In my opinion, Johnson-Laird's (e.g., 1983, 1999) mental model theory is the most successful theoretical approach to reasoning. His basic starting point is as follows: "Reasoning is just the continuation of comprehension by other means" (Johnson-Laird, 1999, p. 130). You may think that sounds obvious and uninteresting (be honest!). In fact, it is an assumption having profound implications. First, it implies that when we are confronted by a reasoning problem we don't immediately switch on cognitive processes specialized for logical thinking. Instead we use processes closely resembling those you are using to understand this paragraph.

Second, when we read some text, we typically focus on what the writer is trying to tell us. In other words, we concentrate on what *is* the case rather than on what is *not* the case. For example, consider the following sentence: "Rio Ferdinand was the only England soccer player to attend the press conference." It follows that it is false that any other England player attended the press conference, but most of us wouldn't bother to focus on that.

Since Johnson-Laird's entire approach revolves around mental models, it is time to consider what he means by a mental model. In essence, a **mental model** represents a possible state of affairs in the world. In the words of Johnson-Laird (2004, p. 170), "Each mental model represents a possibility, capturing what is common to the different ways in which possibility could occur." For example, a tossed coin has an infinite number of trajectories, but there are only two mental models: heads, tails.

Here is a more complex example of a mental model:

Premises
The lamp is on the right of the pad.
The book is on the left of the pad.
The clock is in front of the book.
The vase is in front of the lamp.

Conclusion
The clock is to the left of the vase.

According to Johnson-Laird (1983), people use the information con-tained in the premises (statements assumed to be true) to construct a mental model of the following state-of-affairs:

book	pad	lamp
clock		vase

The conclusion that the clock is to the left of the vase clearly follows from the mental model. The fact that we cannot construct a mental model consistent with the premises but inconsistent with the conclusion indicates that it is valid.

We have just considered a very simple situation in which only *one* mental model is possible. However, often two or more mental models are all consis-tent with the information provided. For example, Johnson-Laird, Legrenzi, and Girotto (2004) considered the following sentence:

There is either a circle on the board or a triangle, or both.

According to them, people are likely to construct three mental models:

1.   circle
2.   triangle
3.   circle + triangle.

Note that here is another example in which what is false is omitted. Strictly speaking, the first mental model should include the information that it is false that there is a triangle.

Let's summarize some of the main assumptions of the mental model approach:

1.   One or more mental models are constructed, and the conclusions follow-ing from the model(s) are generated.
2.   We try to construct alternative mental models that will falsify the conclu-sion; if we cannot do this, we assume the conclusion is valid.
3.   The construction of mental models involves the limited processing resources of working memory (a system combining attentional processes and temporary storage; see Chapter 12). It follows that we find it harder to solve reasoning problems requiring the construction of several mental models than those requiring only one model.

4.   We typically operate according to the **principle of truth**: "Individuals minimize the load on working memory by tending to construct mental models that represent explicitly only what is true, and not what is false" (Johnson-Laird, 1999, p. 116).

FINDINGS

One of the key assumptions (number 3 above) of the mental model approach is that people's ability to construct mental models is constrained by the limited capacity of working memory. This assumption was tested by Copeland and Radvansky (2004). Participants indicated what conclusions followed validly from sets of premises, and the demands on working memory were varied by manipulating the number of mental models consistent with the premises. Eighty-six percent of participants drew the valid conclusion when the premises only allowed the generation of one mental model. This figure dropped to 39% when two mental models were possible, and to 31% with three mental models.

Copeland and Radvansky (2004) tested the hypothesis that reasoning performance depends on the limitations of working memory in a second way. They assessed participants' working memory capacity (based on the ability to temporarily hold some information in memory while at the same time processing other information). It was predicted that individuals with high working memory capacity would perform better than those with low working memory capacity. That was precisely what was found: the correlation between working memory span and syllogistic reasoning was +.42.

It is often fairly demanding to construct a mental model. As a result, it would be predicted from mental model theory that reasoning problems necessitating the construction of several mental models would take longer than those requiring the construction of only one model. Evidence supporting that prediction was reported by Copeland and Radvansky (2004). The mean response time with one-model syllogisms was 25 seconds, and this increased to 29 seconds with two-model syllogisms and to 33 seconds with three-model ones.

We turn now to the principle of truth, according to which mental models represent what is true but not what is false. There is much support for this principle (e.g., Johnson-Laird, Legrenzi, & Girotto, 2004; Legrenzi, Girotto, & Johnson-Laird, 2003). For example, consider an experiment discussed by Legrenzi et al. (2003). Participants had to decide whether descriptions of everyday objects were consistent or inconsistent, with consistent descriptions being those in which all the statements could be true. Some of the descriptions were cunningly constructed so that participants would be lured into error (illusory inferences) if they followed the principle of truth. Here is an example of an inference that was typically interpreted as consistent (valid) when it is actually inconsistent (invalid):

> Only one of the following assertions is true:
>   The tray is heavy or elegant, or both.
>   The tray is elegant and portable.
> The following assertion is definitely true:
>   The tray is elegant and portable.

You may be puzzled as to why the above problem is inconsistent. Suppose the final assertion is true. It follows, of course, that the second assertion is also true, since the two assertions are identical. If the final assertion is true, it also follows that the first assertion is true—the fact that the tray is elegant is enough to make that assertion true. However, note that the problem starts by stating, "Only one of the following assertions is true . . ." If the final assertion is true, both the first two assertions are also true, but only *one* is allowed to be true (sorry this is so complicated!). Therefore, the problem is inconsistent.

According to Johnson-Laird's theory, people search for counter-examples after having constructed their initial mental model and generated a conclusion. As a result, they will often consider several conclusions and may construct several mental models. Newstead, Handley, and Buck (1999) compared performance on syllogisms permitting either one or multiple mental models. According to mental model theory, more conclusions should have been considered with the multiple-model than with the single-model syllogisms. In fact, there was no difference—1.12 and 1.05 conclusions were considered on average with multiple- and single-model syllogisms, respectively. In a further experiment, Newstead et al. asked participants to draw diagrams of the mental models they were forming while working on syllogisms. The participants consistently failed to produce more mental models on multiple-model problems than on single-model ones.

Other researchers have obtained findings apparently inconsistent with those of Newstead et al. (1999). Bucciarelli and Johnson-Laird (1999) in a study discussed in the next paragraph found that people did search for counter-examples. Copeland and Radvansky (2004) found that individuals with high working memory capacity were more likely than those with low working memory capacity to construct multiple mental models.

Mental model theory focuses on the *general* approach taken by people faced with reasoning problems, and cannot readily account for the wide range of *specific* strategies adopted. For example, Bucciarelli and Johnson-Laird (1999) identified the initial strategies used by people given reasoning problems by videotaping them as they used cut-out shapes to evaluate valid and invalid syllogisms. Some participants started by forming a mental model of the first premise, to which they then added information based on the second premise. Other participants proceeded in the opposite direction, and still others constructed an initial mental model satisfying the conclusion and then tried to show that it was wrong.

WHAT ABOUT INDIVIDUAL DIFFERENCES?

In most theory and research on reasoning, it seems to be assumed there are no individual differences worth taking into account. However, psychologists (even if somewhat late in the day) are starting to give serious attention to the issue of individual differences. There are good reasons for doing this. Stanovich and West (1998b) reported a correlation of +.50 between intelligence and syllogistic reasoning and one of +.36 between intelligence and performance on the Wason selection task. These are moderately high correlations and indicate that individual differences in intelligence make a real difference to reasoning performance.

Why do individual differences have an effect on reasoning? What are the implications of this for cognitive theories?

As we have seen, reasoning performance is related to individual differences in working memory capacity (e.g., Copeland & Radvansky, 2004). That finding is relevant to the evidence showing that intelligence predicts reasoning performance, because working memory capacity and intelligence correlate fairly highly with each other. There has been a fierce controversy about the precise magnitude of that correlation (see Chapter 12). Ackerman, Beier, and Boyle (2005) carried out a meta-analysis (combining numerous findings) from 86 studies and obtained a mean correlation of +.48 between working memory capacity and intelligence. However, Oberauer, Schulze, Wilhelm, and Süß (2005) reported a correlation of +.85 between the same two variables. The figure of +.48 is more in line with previous research (see Ackerman et al., 2005), but in either case there is clearly a substantial overlap between working memory capacity and intelligence.

Of course, it doesn't come as any great surprise that highly intelligent individuals generally perform better than less intelligent ones on reasoning problems. What we really need to do is to identify *how* reasoning processes differ as a result of individual differences in intelligence and working memory capacity.

SYSTEM 1 AND SYSTEM 2

The issue of how individual differences in intelligence influence reasoning processes was addressed by Stanovich and West (2000) and by Evans (2003), who started by distinguishing between System 1 and System 2. According to Evans (2003, p. 454), "System 1 processes are rapid, parallel and automatic in nature; only their final product is posted in consciousness . . . System 2 thinking is slow and sequential in nature and makes uses of the central working memory system . . . Despite its limited capacity and slower speed of operation, System 2 permits abstract hypothetical thinking that cannot be achieved by System 1."

For present purposes, what is of most relevance is that Stanovich and West (2000) and Evans (2003) agreed that individual differences in intelligence are much more associated with the functioning of System 2 than of System 1. One way in which this assumption can be tested is by studying belief bias, which was discussed earlier in the chapter. In essence, belief bias occurs when a conclusion that is logically valid but not believable is rejected as invalid, or a conclusion that is logically invalid but believable is accepted as valid. There is a conflict between belief-based processes in System 1 and logic-based processes in System 2. If more intelligent individuals make more use of System 2 logic-based processes than do less intelligent ones, then they should show less belief bias. This prediction has been confirmed (Stanovich & West, 1998a).

Further evidence that intelligence is more related to System 2 processing than to System 1 processing was reported by Stanovich and West (1998b) in a study using two versions of the Wason selection task. There was a realistic deontic version (dealing with what we should or should not do) and there was also the original abstract version. It was assumed that performance on the deontic version of the task depends on relevant prior knowledge and so reflects System 1 processes. In contrast, performance on the abstract version requires System 2 abstract logical reasoning. As predicted, performance on the abstract version of the task was predicted better by individual differences in intelligence than was performance on the realistic deontic version.

HOW RATIONAL ARE WE?

We have seen that human performance on reasoning tasks often appears unimpressive. For example, we are very prone to belief bias, making several times more errors when valid conclusions are unbelievable and invalid ones believable than when valid conclusions are believable and invalid ones unbelievable (Evans et al., 1983). Another example is performance on the abstract version of the Wason selection task, with only about 5% to 10% of intelligent participants producing the correct solution.

The pessimistic conclusion that most humans are irrational and illogical has been challenged by many psychologists. For example, Evans (1993, 2002) produced three reasons to support his argument that we can reason more effectively than appears from most laboratory studies. First, there is what he called the normative system problem—the system of logic (e.g., propositional logic) used by the experimenter may differ from that used by participants. This is especially likely when participants are simply unfamiliar with the system being used by the experimenter.

Second, there is the interpretation problem—the participants' understanding of a reasoning problem may differ from that of the experimenter. Indeed, some participants who produce the "wrong" answer may actually be reasoning logically based on their interpretation of the problem! We can see the interpretation problem clearly in conditional reasoning problems. In propositional logic, "If a, then b," is valid except in the case of "a" and "not b." However, the word "if" is ambiguous in natural language, with "If a, then b" meaning "If and only if a, then b." Here is an example. If someone says to you, "If you mow the lawn, I will give you five dollars," then you are likely to interpret it to imply, "If you don't mow the lawn, I won't give your five dollars" (Geis & Zwicky, 1971).

Third, there is the external validity problem. The tasks used in psychology experiments on reasoning are artificial, and so may tell us rather little about reasoning in the real world. In other words, failure in the laboratory doesn't necessarily translate into failure in everyday life.

Evans (2002, p. 991) summarized very neatly some reasons why people may mistakenly appear illogical and error-prone when performing reasoning tasks in the laboratory:

> To pass muster, participants are required not only to disregard the problem content but also any prior beliefs they may have relevant to it. They must also translate the problem into a logical representation using the interpretation of key terms that accords with a textbook (not supplied) of standard logic (but not contemporary philosophical logic), while disregarding the meaning of the same terms in everyday natural discourse.

Evans (1993, 2003) has made a strong case for the argument that performance on many reasoning problems *underestimates* people's ability to think logically or rationally. However, we must resist the temptation to go further and start claiming that *all* our reasoning difficulties stem from inadequacies in the problems themselves. Convincing evidence that other factors are also involved comes from the research of Stanovich and West (1998a,

2000) discussed above. Their central finding that highly intelligent individuals perform better than less intelligent ones on several reasoning problems suggests that poor performance on such problems is due in part to processing limitations.

RATIONALITY₁ AND RATIONALITY₂

It has often been argued that it seems paradoxical that most people seem to cope reasonably with everyday problems but often perform very poorly on reasoning problems in the laboratory. In my opinion, this is less paradoxical than often supposed, since we often don't handle life's problems very well and we often perform reasonably well when engaged in reasoning under laboratory conditions.

Evans and Over (1996, 1997) made a useful contribution to the debate about human rationality by distinguishing between two types of rationality: rationality₁ and rationality₂. People have rationality₁, "when they are generally successful in achieving their basic goals, keeping themselves alive, finding their way in the world, and communicating with each other" (Evans & Over, 1997, p. 4). This form of rationality depends on an implicit cognitive system operating at an unconscious level, and permits us to cope with everyday life. There are clear overlaps between rationality1 and Stanovich and West's (1998a) System 1.

In contrast, people display rationality₂ when, "they act with good reasons sanctioned by a normative theory such as formal logic or probability theory" (Evans & Over, 1997, p. 4). Rationality₂ depends on an explicit cognitive system operating at a conscious level. It can only be used effectively by those of moderately high intelligence and it is very useful when confronting reasoning problems under laboratory conditions. Rationality₂ is rather similar to Stanovich and West's (1998a) System 2.

The above approach sheds some light on the paradox with which we started. We mainly rely on rationality₁ to cope with the demands of everyday life, whereas rationality₂ is often needed to succeed on laboratory-based reasoning tasks. We often seem to import rationality₁ into the laboratory, and this can lead to difficulties. For example, Johnson-Lairds's mental model theory is based on the assumption that processes used in everyday life are applied to laboratory reasoning problems. More specifically, he assumes that the processes typically involved in language comprehension are used on reasoning problems, and that these processes often fail to provide a complete representation of such problems.

The distinction between rationality₁ and rationality₂ is interesting and important. However, it is unlikely that all the cognitive processes used in reasoning divide neatly into these two forms of rationality. In fact, there is probably more diversity in cognitive processing than is implied by the approach of Evans and Over. Another criticism is that Evans and Over (1997) have described two forms of rationality, but have failed to provide an explanatory account of human rationality.

EVALUATION AND CHAPTER SUMMARY

Wason selection task

- It has proved surprisingly hard to understand exactly what is happening on Wason's selection task.
- However, performance tends to be better when the task is presented in concrete rather than abstract form.
- In addition, various misinterpretations play a part in producing the low levels of performance typically observed on this task (Stenning & van Lambalgen, 2004).
- When the rule is deontic rather than descriptive, performance is generally greatly improved (e.g., Sperber & Girotto, 2002), because the underlying structure of the problem is much easier to grasp.

Abstract-rule theories

- Abstract-rule theories account for many experimental findings (e.g., the greater accuracy of reasoning with modus ponens than modus tollens).
- Such theories are correct in assuming that inadequate comprehension (e.g., conversion errors) and misunderstandings cause many problems in reasoning.
- There are various limitations with the abstract-rule approach.
- First, the comprehension component is underspecified, with the result that it isn't always clear *what* theoretical predictions should be made.
- Second, the theory doesn't provide an adequate account of context effects (e.g., Byrne, 1989).
- Third, belief bias (conclusions are regarded as valid or invalid on the basis of previous knowledge) is hard to explain within an approach that emphasizes the importance of mental logic.
- Fourth, the approach fails to account for individual differences. For example, Ford (1995) found with syllogisms that some people used mainly spatial processes whereas others used mainly verbal processes. It is unclear how such findings could be explained within abstract-rule theory.
- Fifth, and most important, much of the evidence indicating that people use mental logic when presented with deductive reasoning problems is *indirect* and somewhat unconvincing.

Mental models

- One of the most impressive aspects of mental model theory is that it accounts for reasoning performance across a wide range of reasoning problems.
- The central assumption that reasoning involves very similar processes to normal comprehension is a powerful one, and provides a convincing alternative to the view that we possess a mental logic.
- Most of the evidence supports the notion that we form mental models on reasoning tasks.

- As predicted by the theory, many reasoning errors occur because we typically use the principle of truth and ignore what is false.
- More generally our reasoning ability is limited by the constraints of working memory.
- On the negative side, there are various limitations with the theory.
- First, the processes involved in forming mental models are under-specified. For example, Johnson-Laird and Byrne (1991) argued that people use their background knowledge when forming mental models, but the theory doesn't indicate how we decide *which* pieces of information to include. As a result, "It [mental model theory] offers only relatively coarse predictions about the difficulties of different sorts of inference" (Johnson-Laird, 2004, p. 200).
- Second, it is assumed that people will try to produce mental models to falsify conclusions generated from their initial mental model. However, people (especially those with low working memory capacity) sometimes construct only a single mental model and so make no systematic attempts at falsification (Copeland & Radvansky, 2004; Newstead et al., 1999).
- Third, the theory provides a partial account of individual differences in reasoning performance via its emphasis on working memory capacity. However, it cannot readily explain other kinds of individual differences. For example, Ford (1995) asked people solving syllogisms to say aloud what they were thinking while working on each problem. About 40% used spatial reasoning and a further 35% used verbal reasoning, and in neither case did the representations formed correspond closely to mental models as described by Johnson-Laird.

What about individual differences?
- The evidence supports a distinction between relatively automatic, knowledge- or belief-based processes on the one hand and more abstract, logic-based processes on the other hand.
- In addition, intelligence is related to superior reasoning perform-ance because of individual differences in System 2 processes rather than in System 1 processes.
- However, dual-system theories tend to be rather vague, and we lack detailed information about the kinds of *interactions* occur-ring between the two systems.
- Another limitation is that it seems improbable that we can capture all the richness of human reasoning simply by assuming the existence of two cognitive systems.

FURTHER READING

- Evans, J.St.B.T. (2002). Logic and human reasoning: An assessment of the deduction paradigm. *Psychological Bulletin, 128*, 978–996. This article provides an excellent overview of theory and research on deductive reasoning.
- Leighton, J.P., & Sternberg, R.J. (2004). *The nature of reasoning*. Cambridge: Cambridge University Press. This edited book has impressive chapters by several of the world's leading authorities on deductive reasoning.
- Manktelow, K. (1999). *Reasoning and thinking*. Hove, UK: Psychology Press. Chapters 1–5 of this readable textbook provide a good introduction to theory and research on deductive reasoning.
- Markman, A.B., & Gentner, D. (2001). Thinking. *Annual Review of Psychology, 52*, 223–247. This chapter focuses on the relationship between deductive reasoning and other higher-level cognitive processes.
- Stanovich, K.E., Sà, W.C., & West, R.F. (2004). Individual differences in thinking, reasoning, and decision making. In J.P. Leighton & R.J. Sternberg (Eds.), *The nature of reasoning*. Cambridge: Cambridge University Press. This chapter provides a good overview of recent research focusing on individual differences.

PART V

CONTENTS

27 Cognition and emotion   406

28 What is consciousness?   422

Broader issues

In the course of this book, we have considered numerous topics within cognitive psychology. We have moved at some speed through the areas of perception, attention, learning, memory, language, thinking, and reasoning. This may have created the false impression that each of these topics (and areas) is separate from all the other topics and areas. Nothing could be further from the truth. For most purposes, the human information-processing system works in a coordinated fashion to allow us to cope successfully with diverse cognitive tasks.

In this final section, we consider two broader issues spanning several of the topics discussed earlier in the book. In Chapter 27, we focus on the relationship between cognition and emotion. There used to be surprisingly little interest in this area, but recently there has been a rapid increase in research. An important part of the reason for this increase is the recognition that emotional factors often influence cognition in everyday life. Emotion probably influences virtually every topic discussed in this book. However, that is not yet reflected in the research carried out. Of the topics in this book, emotional factors have been investigated most often in connection with perception without awareness (Chapter 4), forgetting (Chapter 14), autobiographical memory (Chapter 15), and eyewitness testimony (Chapter 16).

Chapter 27 considers the role of emotional factors in relation to various basic cognitive processes. These processes include attention, learning, memory, and interpretation of language. What is striking is that significant effects of emotion have been found with respect to every single one of these processes. The implication is that cognitive psychologists should really devote more of their research to understanding the numerous effects of emotion on cognitive processes.

Last (but certainly not least), we conclude the book with the important topic of consciousness (Chapter 28). The distinction between processes that are conscious and those below the level of conscious awareness has been discussed in connection with several topics. For example, Chapter 4 addressed the issue of whether perception is possible in the absence of conscious awareness. Chapter 11 dealt among other issues with evidence that there can be memory in the absence of conscious recollection. The controversy concerning the existence of implicit learning (learning without conscious awareness of what has been learned) is discussed in Chapter 13.

The emphasis in Chapter 28 is on key questions concerning human consciousness. What are the functions of consciousness? Is it possible for someone to have *two* consciousnesses? What forms of brain activity are associated with consciousness? Preliminary answers to these questions are provided. It is fitting that a chapter on consciousness should conclude this book because it is a topic likely to be of consuming interest to future researchers. Here's to the future!

CHAPTER 27

CONTENTS

Introduction	407
Does affect require cognition?	407
Emotion, learning, and memory	411
Emotion, attention, and perception	418
Evaluation and chapter summary	420
Further reading	421

Cognition and emotion

INTRODUCTION

It has often been argued that laboratory research is artificial. Imagine you agree to take part in a laboratory experiment. You may well find yourself in a windowless cubicle carrying out the instructions of the experimenter while peering at the screen of a computer. You might think the artificiality of most laboratory research doesn't matter much when you are studying human cognition. After all, you can use all your cognitive processes and structures (e.g., attention, perception, learning, language, memory, problem solving) under laboratory conditions.

However, one important aspect of the artificiality of laboratory research really does matter. Most experimenters have chosen to ignore the issue of the effects of emotion on cognition by trying to keep participants in a calm and unemotional state. Why do they take this evasive action? According to Gardner (1985, p. 6), emotion is a factor, "which may be important but whose inclusion at this point would unnecessarily complicate the cognitive-scientific enterprise."

In spite of this negative attitude (admittedly expressed over 20 years ago), there is a growing volume of research on cognition and emotion. Some of this research is discussed in other chapters. For example, Chapters 15 and 16 dealt with the role of emotional states in autobiographical memory and eyewitness testimony, respectively.

In my opinion, there are almost constant interactions between cognition and emotion in everyday life. As a result, any attempt to provide an adequate theory of cognition that ignores emotion is likely to be inadequate.

Before proceeding, it is worth considering some definitions. The term "affect" is very broad. It has been used to cover a wide variety of experiences such as emotions, moods, and preferences. In contrast, the term "emotion" is generally used to refer to fairly brief but intense experiences, but is also sometimes used in a broader sense. Finally, "mood" describes a low-level but more prolonged experience.

DOES AFFECT REQUIRE COGNITION?

Suppose that a stimulus (e.g., a spider) is presented to someone, as a result of which his or her affective response to it changes. Is it essential for the stimulus to be processed cognitively for the changed affective response to occur? This issue is of theoretical importance. If affective responses to all stimuli depend on cognitive processing, theories of emotion should have a distinctly cognitive flavor. In contrast, if cognitive processing is *not* necessary in the development of affective responses to stimuli, then a specifically cognitive approach to emotion may be less necessary.

AFFECT DOESN'T REQUIRE COGNITION!

How may cognitive appraisal affect our affective reaction? What are the implications of this?

Zajonc (1984, p. 117) argued that the affective evaluation of stimuli can occur independently of cognitive processes: "Affect and cognition are separate and partially independent systems and ... although they ordinarily function conjointly, affect could be generated without a prior cognitive process." In contrast, Lazarus claimed that some cognitive processing is essential in order for an affective reaction to a stimulus to occur. According to him, "Cognitive appraisal (of meaning or significance) underlies and is an integral feature of all emotional states" (Lazarus, 1982, p. 1021).

Zajonc (1980) claimed in his affective primacy hypothesis that we often make affective judgments about people and objects even though we have processed very little information about them. He discussed studies in which stimuli such as melodies or pictures were presented either very briefly below the level of conscious awareness or while the participant was involved in a task. Even though these stimuli couldn't subsequently be recognized, participants chose previously presented stimuli more than new ones when selecting the ones they preferred. Thus, there was a positive affective reaction to the previously presented stimuli (as assessed by participants' preference judgments). However, there was no evidence of cognitive processing (as assessed by recognition-memory performance). This phenomenon is the **mere exposure effect**.

As you may be thinking, the mere exposure effect has little relevance to ordinary emotional states. Participants make superficial preference judgments about fairly meaningless stimuli unrelated to their lives, and so only minimal affect is involved. Another major limitation is that the conclusion that the stimuli aren't processed cognitively is based on failures of recognition memory. In fact, it is entirely possible that there is extensive preconscious processing of stimuli not subsequently recognized.

According to the affective primacy hypothesis, simple affective qualities of stimuli can be processed much faster than more cognitive ones. Murphy and Zajonc (1993) provided some support for this hypothesis in a series of priming studies. A priming stimulus was presented for 4 milliseconds or 1 second, and was followed by a second stimulus. In one study, the priming stimuli consisted of happy and angry faces, and there was a no-priming control condition. The priming stimuli were followed by Chinese ideographs [symbols representing ideas], which were given liking ratings. The liking ratings were influenced by the affective primes when presented for only 4 ms, but not when presented for 1 second (see Figure 27.1). Presumably participants in the latter condition realized that their affective reaction was produced by the priming stimulus. As a result, that reaction didn't influence their rating of the second stimulus.

In another study, Murphy and Zajonc (1993) asked participants to make a cognitive judgment. Male or female priming faces were followed by Chinese

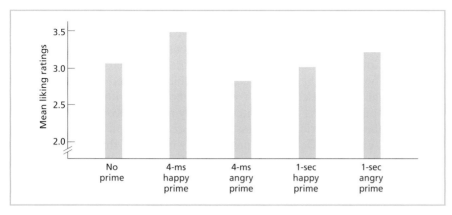

Figure 27.1 Liking ratings for Chinese ideographs following the presentation of a happy or angry priming stimulus for 4 ms or 1 second. Based on data in Murphy and Zajonc (1993).

ideographs that were rated for femininity. These ratings were influenced by the priming faces when presented for 1 second but not when presented for 4 ms. The various findings obtained by Murphy and Zajonc suggest the following conclusions:

1. Affective processing can sometimes occur faster than cognitive processing.
2. The initial affective processing of a stimulus is very different from the later cognitive processing.

Evaluation

The evidence indicates that affective responses can occur in the absence of any conscious awareness of cognitive processing However, the discovery that affective responses can occur independently of conscious cognitive processes doesn't rule out the possibility that preconscious processes always precede affective responses. Many of the findings apparently supporting Zajonc's theoretical position involve little or no affective experience or emotion.

AFFECT DOES REQUIRE COGNITION!

Lazarus (1982, 1991) disagreed with Zajonc, claiming that cognitive appraisal plays a crucial role in determining emotional experience. According to him, **cognitive appraisal** can be subdivided into *three* more specific forms of appraisal:

1. *Primary appraisal*: The environmental situation is regarded as being positive, stressful, or irrelevant to well-being.
2. *Secondary appraisal*: Account is taken of the resources the individual has available to cope with the situation.
3. *Re-appraisal*: The stimulus situation and coping strategies are monitored, with the primary and secondary appraisals being modified if necessary.

Findings

The importance of cognitive appraisal in determining emotional experience has been shown in several studies by Lazarus and his associates. For example,

KEY TERM
Cognitive appraisal: interpreting the current situation to decide whether it is threatening or not, and deciding whether one can cope with it.

Speisman, Lazarus, Mordkoff, and Davison (1964) presented anxiety-evoking films under various conditions. One film showed a Stone Age ritual in which adolescent boys had their penises deeply cut (ouch!), and another film showed various workshop accidents. The most dramatic of these accidents involved a board caught in a circular saw, which rammed with tremendous force through the midsection of a worker who died writhing on the floor. Cognitive appraisal was manipulated by varying the accompanying sound-track, and then comparing the stress experienced against a control condition without a soundtrack. Denial was produced by indicating that the subincision film didn't show a painful operation, or that those involved in the safety film were actors. Intellectualization was produced in the subincision film by con-sidering matters from the perspective of an anthropologist viewing strange native customs. It was produced in the workshop film by telling the viewer to consider the situation objectively. Various psychophysiological measures of arousal or stress (e.g., heart rate, galvanic skin response) were taken continu-ously during the viewing of the film.

Denial and intellectualization both produced substantial reductions in stress as indexed by the psychophysiological measures. Thus, manipulating an individual's cognitive appraisal when confronted by a stressful event can have a significant impact on physiological stress reactions.

Smith and Lazarus (1993) adopted a different approach. They identified *six* appraisal components, two involving primary appraisal and four involving secondary appraisal:

- Primary: Motivational relevance (i.e., related to personal commitments?)
- Primary: Motivational congruence (i.e., consistent with the individual's goals?)
- Secondary: Accountability (i.e., who deserves the credit or blame?)
- Secondary: Problem-focused coping potential (i.e., can the situation be resolved?)
- Secondary: Emotion-focused coping potential (i.e., can the situation be handled psychologically?)
- Secondary: Future expectancy (i.e., how likely is it that the situation will change?)

According to Smith and Lazarus (1993), different emotional states can be distinguished on the basis of which appraisal components are involved. Anger, guilt, anxiety, and sadness all possess the primary appraisal com-ponents of motivational relevance and motivational incongruence (they only occur when goals are blocked). However, they differ in terms of secondary appraisal components. Guilt involves self-accountability, anger involves other-accountability, anxiety involves low emotion-focused coping potential, and sadness involves low future expectancy for future change.

Smith and Lazarus (1993) used scenarios in which participants were asked to identify with the central character. In one scenario, the central char-acter has performed poorly in an important course, and he appraises the situ-ation. Other-accountability was produced by having him put the blame on the unhelpful teaching assistants, and self-accountability was produced by having him accept he made many mistakes (e.g., doing work at the last minute). Low emotion-focused coping potential was produced by thinking there was a great danger he would finish with a poor academic record; and low future expectancy for change was produced by having him think it was impossible to succeed with his chosen academic path. The appraisal manipulations generally had the predicted effects on the emotional states reported by the participants. This indicates that there are close links between appraisal on the one hand and experienced emotion on the other hand.

One of the limitations of Smith and Lazarus' (1993) approach is that they focused on the *structure* of appraisal rather than on the *processes* involved in appraisal. In other words, they emphasized the content of any given appraisal but largely ignored the underlying mechanisms involved in producing appraisals. This issue has been addressed by Smith and Kirby (2001). According to their theory, appraisal involves various processes. First, there is associative processing, which involves priming and activation of memories. This form of processing occurs rapidly and automatically and lacks flexibility. Second, there is reasoning. This process involves deliberate thinking and is slower and more flexible than associative processing. Associative processing and reasoning occur at the same time. Third, there are appraisal detectors that continuously monitor appraisal information coming from the associative and reasoning processes. The emotional state an individual experiences at any given moment in time is determined by the total information registered by the appraisal detectors.

There is much support for the notion that appraisal can involve very rapid associative processes occurring below the level of conscious awareness. For example, Chartrand, van Baaren, and Bargh (2006) found that automatic appraisal processes could influence emotional state. Positive (e.g., music; friends), negative (e.g., war; cancer), or neutral (e.g., building; plant) words were presented repeatedly but so briefly they could not be identified at the conscious level. Participants receiving the negative words reported a more negative mood state than those receiving the positive words.

Evaluation

Appraisal processes are important in determining our emotional reactions to stimuli. Individual differences in cognitive appraisal of a given situation help to explain why individuals differ in their emotional reactions. However, the notion of appraisal is broad and vague, making it hard to assess a given individual's appraisals with precision. In addition, Lazarus's approach is rather limited. As Parkinson and Manstead (1992, p. 146) pointed out, "Appraisal theory has taken the paradigm [model] of emotional experience as an individual passive subject confronting a survival-threatening stimulus." In other words, Lazarus has tended to de-emphasize the social context in which emotion is typically experienced.

EMOTION, LEARNING, AND MEMORY

Bower and his associates (e.g., Bower, 1981; Gilligan & Bower, 1984) put forward a network theory designed to explain several effects of mood on cognitive processes (see Figure 27.2). This theory consists of six main assumptions:

Figure 27.2 Bower's semantic network theory. The ovals represent nodes or units within the network. Adapted from Bower (1981).

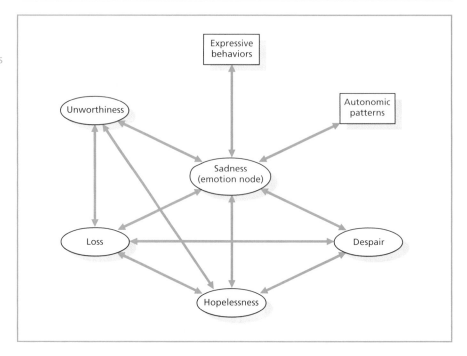

1. Emotions are units or nodes in a semantic network, with numerous connections to related ideas, to physiological systems, to events, and to muscular and expressive patterns.
2. Emotional material is stored in the semantic network in the form of propositions or assertions.
3. Thought occurs via the activation of nodes within the semantic network.
4. Nodes can be activated by external or by internal stimuli.
5. Activation from an activated node spreads to related nodes. This assumption is crucial. It means that activation of an emotional node (e.g., sadness) leads to activation of emotion-related nodes or concepts (e.g., loss, despair) in the semantic network.
6. "Consciousness" consists of a network of nodes activated above some threshold value.

Various predictions follow from these assumptions, and we will focus on three of them. First, there is **mood congruity**: emotionally toned information is learned best when there is similarity between its affective value and the learner's current mood state. For example, someone who is feeling sad should learn sad material better than material that is more positive. According to Gilligan and Bower (1984), mood congruity depends on the fact that emotionally loaded information tends to be associated more strongly with its congruent emotion node than with any other emotion node. For example, those nodes containing information about sadness-provoking events and experiences are associatively linked to the emotion node for sadness (see Figure 27.2). To-be-remembered material congruent with the current mood state links up with this associative network of similar information. This leads to extensive or elaborative encoding of the to-be-remembered material. Such elaborative encoding is generally associated with superior long-term memory.

KEY TERMS
Mood congruity: the finding that learning is often best when the material learned has the same affective value as the learner's mood state.

Second, there is **mood-state-dependent recall**: recall is best when the mood at recall matches that at the time of learning (also discussed in Chapter 14). According to network theory, at the time of learning associations are formed between the activated nodes representing the to-be-remembered items and the emotion node or nodes activated because of the participant's mood state. At the time of recall, the mood state at that time leads to activation of the appropriate emotion node. Activation then spreads from that emotion node to the various nodes associated with it. If there is a *match* between the mood state at learning and at recall, this increases activation of the nodes of to-be-remembered items and leads to enhanced recall. However, the associative links between the to-be-remembered stimulus material and the relevant emotion nodes are likely to be relatively weak. Thus, mood-state-dependent effects will be greater when the memory test is a difficult one offering few retrieval cues (e.g., free recall) than when it provides strong retrieval cues (e.g., recognition memory).

Third, there is **thought congruity**—this means that an individual's free associations, interpretations, thoughts, and judgments are thematically congruent with his or her mood state. Thought congruity occurs for two reasons. First, the current mood state leads to activation of the corresponding emotion node. Second, activation spreads from that emotion node to other, associated nodes. These nodes will generally contain information emotionally congruent with the activated emotion node.

Before turning to a discussion of the evidence, we need to consider the issue of how to ensure that participants are in the appropriate mood state (e.g., happy or sad). One method is to induce the required mood state under laboratory conditions. A popular mood-induction approach is based on the procedure introduced by Velten (1968). Participants read a set of sentences designed to induce increasingly intense feelings of elation or depression. They typically report that their mood has altered as expected. However, they may in part simply be responding in the way they think the experimenter wants them to. Another problem is that this mood-induction procedure typically produces a blend of several mood states rather than just the desired one (Polivy, 1981).

A second method is to make use of naturally occurring mood states (e.g., patients with mood disorders; people just before doing a parachute jump). A third method involves hypnosis combined with self-generated imagery (e.g., Bower, Gilligan, & Monteiro, 1981). Participants are put into a hypnotic state and think of images of a past happy or sad emotional experience, using these images to produce the appropriate mood state. A limitation with this approach is that it is necessary to use participants scoring highly on tests of hypnotic susceptibility.

FINDINGS

The usual procedure in studies on mood congruity is to start by inducing the required mood. After that, participants learn a list or read a story containing emotionally toned material. There is then a memory test for the list or the story after the participants' mood has returned to normal. Mood congruity is shown by recall being greatest when the affective value of the to-be-learned material is the same as the participant's mood state at the time of learning.

How can your current mood affect the way you learn emotional information? Will it affect your memory for the information?

Bower et al. (1981) studied mood congruity. Participants who had been hypnotized to feel happy or sad read a story about two college men, Jack and André. Jack is very depressed and glum, because he is having problems with his academic work, with his girlfriend, and with his tennis. In contrast, André is very happy, because things are going very well for him in all three areas. Participants identified more with the story character whose mood resembled their own while reading the story, and recalled more information about him.

Kwiatkowski and Parkinson (1994) compared memory performance in naturally depressed participants and in those *not* naturally depressed who received a depressed mood induction. Mood congruity was found *only* in the naturally depressed group. These findings probably occurred because naturally occurring depression is much stronger than the depression artificially created in the laboratory.

Mood states produce changes in physiological arousal as well as in cognitive activity (e.g., anxiety or anger produce increased heart rate). Bower (1981) assumed that the cognitive changes were responsible for mood congruity. However, it is possible that mood congruity actually depends on the arousal changes. Varner and Ellis (1998) compared these possibilities in two experiments in which participants were presented with a list of words. Some words were associated with being depressed and the others were related to the organization of skills when writing an essay. There were four conditions:

1. depressed mood induction
2. arousal induction (stepping up and down on a wooden platform)
3. neutral mood induction
4. schema induction (reading statements relevant to writing an essay).

After the list had been presented, there was a test of free recall.

What did Varner and Ellis (1998) find? There was mood congruity in the depressed mood condition but not in the arousal induction condition (see Figure 27.3). Evidence that cognitive processes in the absence of physiological arousal can produce selective recall was found in the schema induction condition. Varner and Ellis obtained similar findings in a second experiment, in which the various induction procedures were used after learning but before

Figure 27.3 Free recall of depression-related and essay-writing-related words in four conditions: depressed mood induction; arousal induction; neutral mood induction; and schema induction. Adapted from Varner and Ellis (1998).

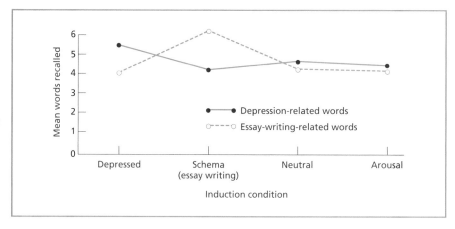

recall. Thus, mood congruity can affect retrieval as well as learning. Varner and Ellis (1998, p. 947) concluded as followed: "The findings indicate that cognitive activity is of central import to the occurrence of mood-congruent processing and that arousal has little or no impact on the selective processing of mood-related information."

There is more evidence of mood congruity with positive affect than with negative affect (see Eysenck & Keane, 2005, for a review). Why is this? Rusting and DeHart (2000) argued plausibly that individuals in a negative mood are much more likely to be motivated to change their mood. They may, for example, try to reduce their negative mood state by retrieving pleasant thoughts and memories, and this may lead to a weakening of any mood-state-dependent effects. Rusting and DeHart tested these ideas. Participants were presented with 20 positive words, 20 negative words, and 20 neutral words, and wrote 60 sentences each containing one of the words. Then there was a negative mood induction in which participants imagined themselves experiencing distressing events. After that, some participants were told to continue to focus on negative thoughts, whereas others were instructed to engage in positive re-appraisal of the distressing events ("List some good things that could occur as a result of any of the negative events in the stories"). Finally, both groups were given an unexpected test of free recall for the 60 words.

What did Rusting and DeHart (2000) find? The usual mood congruity effect was found in the group who continued to focus on negative thoughts. However, individuals in the positive re-appraisal condition failed to show any evidence of mood congruity. This probably happened because these individuals were motivated to improve their mood.

Experimental studies testing for mood-state-dependent memory typically require participants to learn one or two word lists. Learning occurs in one mood state (e.g., happy or sad), and recall occurs in the same mood state or in a different one (see Figure 27.4). When two lists are learned, one list is learned in one mood and the other list is learned in a different mood. Subsequently, participants are put back into one of these two moods and told to recall only the list learned first. The prediction is that recall should be higher when the mood state at the time of recall is the same as that at learning.

Schare, Lisman, and Spear (1984) and Bower, Monteiro, and Gilligan (1978) obtained mood-state-dependent recall with the two-list design but not with the one-list design. Perhaps participants recalling the first list with the mood appropriate to the second list thought of some words from the second list, and this interfered with the task of recalling first-list words.

Eich, Macaulay, and Lam (1997) studied patients suffering from bipolar disorder. Such patients have great mood swings ranging from mania (very excitable) to depression. These patients initially thought of autobiographical

Mood state at learning	Mood state at recall	Predicted level of recall
Happy	Happy	High
Happy	Sad	Low
Sad	Happy	Low
Sad	Sad	High

Figure 27.4 Design for a study of mood-state-dependent memory together with the predicted results on Bower's (1981) theory.

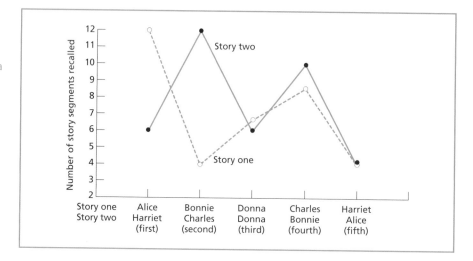

Figure 27.5 Memory performance in a woman suffering from dissociative identity disorder. Based on data in Nissen et al. (1988).

events to cues when in a depressed state. A few days later, they recalled as many of these events as possible. When the patients' mood was the same on both occasions, they recalled 33% of the autobiographical events. This compared to only 23% when there had been a mood change between testing sessions. This is evidence for mood-state-dependent memory.

Macaulay, Ryan, and Eich (1993) found that mood-state-dependent effects can be seen in tests of implicit memory, where conscious recollection is not required. Nissen, Ross, Willingham, Mackenzie, and Schacter (1988) provided relevant evidence for this when they reported an interesting study on a 45-year-old woman suffering from dissociative identity disorder (popularly known as multiple personality disorder). She had 22 different personalities ranging in age from 5 to 45, and each of these personalities could be regarded as corresponding to a different mood state. One of her personalities was Alice, who was 39 years old and working as a nursing assistant. Another personality was Charles, who was 45 years old and an aggressive heavy drinker. A third personality was Bonnie, 36, who was very social and was interested in the theater. The same story was read to five of the personalities in turn, with each personality providing almost immediate recall. There was no systematic improvement in recall across personalities (see Figure 27.5). Thus, large differences in mood and beliefs across personalities made the information learned by one personality inaccessible to the others.

Ucros (1989) reviewed 40 studies on mood-state-dependent memory. There was general support for the phenomenon. However, the effects tended to be weaker when participants were in a negative mood rather than when they were in a positive one. In addition, they were smaller when the learning material lacked personal relevance.

Finally, we turn to thought congruity. One way in which that has been studied involves presenting participants with a list of pleasant and unpleasant words prior to mood induction. Recall is then tested after mood induction. The prediction is that pleasant words will be recalled better after pleasant mood induction than after unpleasant mood induction, with the opposite being the case for unpleasant words. A second method involves asking participants to recall autobiographical memories following mood induction.

Pleasant moods should increase the number of pleasant memories recalled, and unpleasant moods should do the same for unpleasant memories.

Thought congruity has been shown using both of the methods just described (see Blaney, 1986, for a review). For example, Clark and Teasdale (1982) tested depressed patients on two occasions, with the depth of depression being more severe on one occasion than on the other. More depressing or unhappy memories and fewer happy ones were recalled on the more depressed occasion. These findings are consistent with the notion of a vicious circle in depressed patients: depressed mood state leads to recall of depressing memories, and the recall of depressing memories increases the depressed mood state.

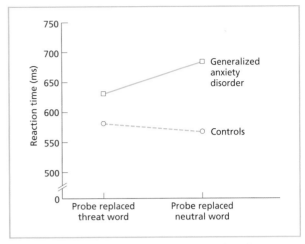

Figure 27.6 Mean reaction times to probes that replaced threat or neutral words in generalized anxiety disorder patients and controls. Data from Macleod, Mathews, and Tata (1986).

EVALUATION

The network approach to emotion and cognition pioneered by Bower (19981) is still regarded as providing the most general explanation of findings in this area (Forgas, 1999). This approach has been developed and extended in recent years (see Forgas, 1999). In spite of some inconsistencies in the findings, there is reasonably convincing evidence for mood congruity, mood-state-dependent memory, and thought congruity. However, it is not clear on network theory why mood-state-dependent memory is stronger when people learn and remember personal events. Bower (1992) argued that memory is only affected by mood state when people believe their emotional state at learning was *caused* by the to-be-learned material. Causal attribution leads to an effective association between the material and the emotional state. This is much more likely to happen with personal events (e.g., feeling delighted after passing a psychology exam) than when an emotional state is induced before presenting the learning task.

There are two major problems with Bower's theory. First, it is difficult to falsify. As Forgas (1999, p. 597) pointed out, "The problem of falsifiability mainly arises because . . . it is difficult to provide a complete *a priori* [ahead of time] specification of the kind of cognitive contents likely to be activated in any particular cognitive task."

Second, Bower's network theory is oversimplified. Emotions or moods and cognitive concepts are both represented as nodes within a semantic network. In reality, however, moods and cognitions are very different from each other. For example, moods tend to change slowly in intensity, whereas cognitions tend to be all-or-none and to change rapidly. As Power and Dalgleish (1997, p. 74) aptly remarked, "A theory that gives emotion the same status as individual words or concepts is theoretically confused." At a basic level, suppose someone thinks or says, "Thank goodness I'm not feeling sad!" According to the theory, it appears that the concept "sad" would be activated leading to a state of sadness! In other words, the factors responsible for creating and maintaining mood states are much more complex than is assumed within network theory.

EMOTION, ATTENTION, AND PERCEPTION

As mentioned in Chapter 1, one way in which cognitive psychology has had a beneficial effect on society is via the development of cognitive therapy. Cognitive therapists claim that patients suffering from anxiety or depression have systematic distortions or biases in their processing of information about themselves and the world around them. Successful therapy involves reducing or eliminating those biases.

Our focus will be on two main cognitive biases found in anxious patients (and non-patients who score high on the personality dimension of trait anxiety). First, there is **attentional bias**, which is selective attention to threat-related rather than neutral stimuli. Second, there is **interpretive bias**, which is the tendency to interpret ambiguous stimuli and situations n a threatening rather than a non-threatening way. For example, Newmark, Frerking, Cook, and Newmark (1973) found that 65% of anxious patients (but only 2% of non-patients) agreed with the statement, "It is essential that one be loved or approved of by virtually everyone in his [sic!] community." The statement, "One must be perfectly competent, adequate, and achieving to consider oneself worthwhile," was agreed to by 80% of anxious patients compared with 25% of non-patients.

FINDINGS

How can cognitive therapy be employed in order to alter affective states?

The existence of attentional bias in anxious patients has been shown in numerous studies (see Eysenck, 1997), many of which used the dot-probe task. In this task, two words are presented at the same time, one to an upper and the other to a lower location on a computer screen. On critical trials, one word is threat-related (e.g., stupid, inept) and the other is neutral. The allocation of attention is measured by recording the speed of detection of a dot that can replace either word. It is assumed that detection latencies are shorter in attended areas.

MacLeod, Mathews, and Tata (1986) made use of the dot-probe task with patients suffering from **generalized anxiety disorder** (a condition involving excessive worry and anxiety about several aspects of life) and with healthy controls. As can be seen in Figure 27.6, the patients selectively allocated attention towards threat-related words, whereas the controls did not. Thus, patients with generalized anxiety disorder have an attentional bias.

So far we have considered attentional bias only in situations in which the stimuli are clearly visible to the participants. Suppose we used the dot-probe task, but presented the stimuli so briefly that the participants had no conscious awareness of them? This has been done in several studies with generalized anxiety disorder patients. Perhaps surprisingly, there is still good evidence that these patients have an attentional bias for threat-related stimuli of which they have no conscious awareness.

Attentional bias is *not* limited to anxious patients, but is also found in non-patients high in trait anxiety (a personality dimension concerned with

KEY TERMS
Attentional bias: selective attention to threat-related stimuli presented at the same time as neutral ones.
Interpretive bias: a tendency to interpret ambiguous stimuli and situations in a threatening way.
Generalized anxiety disorder: a mental disorder characterized by excessive worry and anxiety about many of life's issues.

individual differences in susceptibility to anxiety). MacLeod and Mathews (1988) used the dot-probe task with students 12 weeks and 1 week before an important exam. In the week before the examination, high trait-anxious students showed attentional bias to threat-related stimuli whereas low trait-anxious students did not. However, neither group showed attentional bias 12 weeks before the exam. These findings mean that individuals high in trait anxiety only show an attentional bias when they are stressed (e.g., close to an important exam).

Interpretive bias in anxious patients and in non-patients high in trait anxiety has been reported numerous times. In an early study, Eysenck, MacLeod, and Mathews (1987) used the homonym task. In this task (the only task I have ever invented!), participants write down the spellings of auditorily presented words. Some of these words are homonyms having both a threat-related and a neutral interpretation (e.g., die, dye; pain, pane). Individuals high in trait anxiety wrote down significantly more threat-related words than did those low in trait anxiety, indicating the existence of an interpretive bias.

Eysenck, Mogg, May, Richards, and Mathews (1991) presented generalized anxiety disorder patients and non-patient controls with ambiguous sentences (e.g., "The doctor examined little Emily's growth"). Patients with generalized anxiety disorder were more likely than non-patients to interpret such sentences in a threatening way, showing that these patients had an interpretive bias.

How important are these attentional and interpretive biases? It seems reasonable to assume that attentional and interpretive biases help to maintain or increase anxious individuals' levels of experienced anxiety, and this assumption has been confirmed experimentally. MacLeod, Rutherford, Campbell, Ebsworthy, and Holker (2002) gave non-patient controls a training program with the dot-probe task designed to produce an attentional bias (the dot always replaced the threat word). Those receiving the training program subsequently reported a more negative mood state when performing a stressful anagram task than control participants not receiving the program.

Mathews and MacLeod (2002) used only participants high in trait anxiety. They exposed some of them to a lengthy training program to induce an opposite attentional bias; that is, systematic avoidance of threat-related stimuli (the dot never replaced the threat word). Impressively, those exposed to the training program showed a highly significant reduction in trait anxiety. Mathews and Mackintosh (2000) used a training program to produce an interpretive bias. Those exposed to the training program showed a significant increase in anxious mood afterwards.

MacLeod and Hagan (1992) argued that individuals having an attentional bias are more vulnerable to distress when encountering a serious life event. To test this notion, they initially assessed attentional bias in two conditions, using stimuli that were either below (subliminal condition) or above (supraliminal condition) the threshold of conscious awareness. The participants were females awaiting a colposcopy investigation to test whether they had cervical pathology. The level of emotional distress reported by those participants told they had cervical pathology was greater if they had a strong attentional bias in the subliminal condition than if they had a weak bias. However, emotional distress was *not* related to the extent of attentional bias in the supraliminal condition. Thus, processing of subliminal threat-related stimuli is more directly related to vulnerability to distress than is processing of supraliminal stimuli.

Some research has focused on interpretive bias in patients with panic disorder, a condition characterized by frequent panic attacks. As was discussed in Chapter 1, such patients have an interpretive bias for their physiological symptoms when stressed. They often interpret these symptoms as indicating that they are just about to have a heart attack or to die. In order to find effective forms of treatment for patients with panic disorder, it is valuable to understand the nature of this interpretive bias in more detail. Precisely this was done by Sanderson, Rapee, and Barlow (1989). Panic disorder patients were administered carbon dioxide, which creates many of the symptoms associated with panic attacks. Some of the patients were given potential control over the concentration of carbon dioxide, whereas others were not. In spite of the fact that none of the patients used the control they had been given, those with control had less subjective anxiety and fewer panic symptoms than those without control. They were also far less likely to experience a panic attack, 20% versus 80%, respectively. Thus, the interpretive bias that panic disorder patients have for their bodily symptoms when stressed depends in large measure on the perceived uncontrollability of those symptoms. As a consequence, cognitive therapists focus on trying to persuade patients that their symptoms are *not* uncontrollable.

EVALUATION AND CHAPTER SUMMARY

- There is substantial evidence that patients with anxiety disorders and non-patients high in trait anxiety have attentional and interpretive biases.
- There is evidence that these biases play some role in the development and maintenance of anxiety, which makes them important for therapists treating anxious patients.
- It could be argued that it is fairly obvious that anxious individuals pay particular attention to threatening stimuli and regard the world as more threatening than it actually is.
- However, the detailed patterns of findings are by no means obvious. For example, most people wouldn't have predicted that vulnerability to distress is more related to attentional bias for subliminal stimuli than for supraliminal ones. They would also not have predicted that the crucial ingredient in panic disorder patients' interpretive bias for their own symptoms is perceived uncontrollability of those symptoms.
- The main limitation of research on attentional and interpretive biases is that it has proved difficult to devise experimental conditions that reliably produce large biases.
- Many of the effects that are reported are small in size, and non-significant findings have been obtained in several studies.
- In spite of these problems, however, the cognitive approach to understanding anxiety in general and the anxiety disorders in particular has amply proved its value in recent years.

FURTHER READING

- Dalgleish, T., & Power, M.J. (1999). *Handbook of cognition and emotion*. Chichester, UK: Wiley. Part II of this handbook (devoted to cognitive processes in emotion) is of particular relevance to the topics discussed in this chapter.
- Lewis, M., & Haviland-Jones, J.M. (2000). *Handbook of emotions* (2nd ed.). New York: Guilford Press. Part 5 of this handbook is devoted to cognitive factors associated with emotion.
- Yiend, J. (2004). *Cognition, emotion and psychopathology: Theoretical, empirical and clinical directions*. Cambridge: Cambridge University Press. Several chapters in this book (especially Chapters 2, 3, 4, and 6) are relevant to the contents of this chapter.

CHAPTER 28

CONTENTS

Introduction	423
In two minds?	427
Global workspace theories	430
Evaluation and chapter summary	433
Further reading	435

What is consciousness?

INTRODUCTION

The topic of consciousness is one of the most challenging in the whole of cognitive psychology. However, Sutherland (1989) was clearly exaggerating when he claimed that, "Nothing worth reading has ever been written on it [consciousness]." The good news (as I hope to prove to your satisfaction) is that recently research on consciousness has become much more interesting and informative as researchers have started to grapple successfully with important issues.

Let's make a start on this truly fascinating topic by considering what we mean by the term "consciousness." According to the *Dictionary of psychology* (Colman, 2001), consciousness is, "the normal mental condition of the waking state of humans, characterized by the experience of perceptions, thoughts, feelings, awareness of the external world, and often in humans ... self-awareness."

What needs to be explained by psychologists studying consciousness? It may seem to non-psychologists as if the crucial goal is to explain our experience of consciousness. That is undeniably important, but has proved a difficult goal to achieve. In practice, many psychologists focus on the somewhat different issue of explaining why the firing of neurons in the brain is often accompanied by consciousness. Thus, an important question for psychologists is as follows: What is it about certain kinds of brain activity that permits us to have conscious experience?

FUNCTIONS OF CONSCIOUSNESS

There has been much controversy about the functions of consciousness. An influential suggestion was made by Humphrey (1983), who argued that the main function of consciousness is social. Humans have lived in social groups for tens of thousands of years, and so they have needed to predict, understand, and manipulate the behavior of other people. It is much easier to do this if you possess the ability to imagine yourself in someone else's position. Humans developed conscious awareness of themselves, and this helped them to understand others. In the words of Humphrey (2002, p. 75), "Imagine that a new form of sense organ evolves, an 'inner eye', whose field of view is not the outside world but the brain itself."

Conscious intentions

Why are we conscious? How important is conscious awareness to humans?

Many psychologists have emphasized the notion that a major function of consciousness is to control our actions. Every single day of our lives we find ourselves thinking numerous times of doing something and then doing it (e.g., "I think I'll go to the pub" is followed by us finding ourselves in the familiar surroundings of our local pub). As Wegner (2003, p. 65) pointed out, "It certainly doesn't take a rocket scientist to draw the obvious conclusion ... consciousness is an active force, an engine of will."

I imagine you agree with what was said in the previous paragraph, because it seems to fit so well with our everyday experience. Indeed, it would be extremely unsettling not to do so. In the words of the German psychologist Wilhelm Wundt (quoted in Jaensch, 1920), "Nothing seems to us to belong so closely to our personality, to be so completely our property as our will." However, there has been a systematic onslaught on that position by two teams of researchers led by Daniel Wegner and Benjamin Libet, respectively.

According to Wegner (2002), what we have is only the *illusion* of conscious or free will. Our actions are actually determined by unconscious processes. However, we typically use the evidence available to us to draw the inference that our thought causes our action. The most obvious prediction from this theoretical perspective is that we will often make *mistakes* (e.g., assuming we didn't cause something to happen even though we did). Support for this prediction comes from the unlikely source of the spiritualist movement that swept through nineteenth-century Europe. Advocates of spiritualism believed that spirits of the dead could convey messages and even move tables. For example, several people would sit around a table with their hands resting on the top and pressing down on it. After a while the table would start to vibrate and eventually it would move. The sitters firmly believed that they had not caused movements of the table and that spirits were responsible.

Unfortunately for the spiritualists, the scientist Michael Faraday carried out a careful study of the table-moving phenomenon. He constructed a table with two tops divided by ball bearings, but the sitters thought it was just an ordinary table. Faraday stuck pieces of card onto the upper table-top, and asked the sitters to put their hands on the piece of card in front of them. The key finding was that the *upper* table-top moved *before* the *lower* table-top. Thus, the sitters' fingers were moving the table, rather than the table (possibly via spirits) moving their fingers. That means that sitters' conscious experience that their actions didn't cause the table to move were mistaken. When the sitters realized what Faraday had done, there were no subsequent movements of the table!

Another favorite pastime of the spiritualists was the ouija board (the odd name comes from the French and German words for "yes"). Several people sit around a table with their forefingers on an upturned glass in the center of a ring of letters. Eventually the glass moves and spells out words. Everyone sitting around the table denies they moved the glass, and so it is assumed that spirits of the dead are trying to communicate with the living. In fact, of course, the movements of the glass are caused by their actions even though they experience no conscious intention.

Wegner and Wheatley (1999) decided to carry out a study using an updated version of the ouija board. They used a 20 cm square board mounted onto a computer mouse. There were two participants at a time, both of whom placed their fingers on the same board. When they moved the board, this caused a cursor to move in any direction over a screen showing numerous pictures of small objects. Every 30 seconds or so, the participants were told to stop the cursor, and to indicate the extent to which they had consciously intended the cursor to stop where it did.

Both participants wore headphones. One participant was genuine, but the other was a confederate working for the experimenter. The genuine participant thought they were both hearing different words through the headphones. In fact, however, the confederate was actually receiving instructions to make certain movements. On certain trials, the confederate was told to stop on a given object (e.g., cat), and the genuine participant heard the word "cat" 30 seconds before, 5 seconds before, 1 second before, or 1 second after the confederate stopped the cursor. Genuine participants wrongly believed they had caused the cursor to stop where it did when they heard the name of the object on which it stopped 1 or 5 seconds before the stop (see Figure 28.1). Thus, the participants mistakenly believed their conscious intention had caused the action when it hadn't.

How can we explain such findings? According to Wegner (2003, p. 67), we infer that our conscious thoughts have caused our actions based on the principles of priority, consistency, and exclusivity: "When a thought appears in consciousness just before an action (priority), is consistent with the action (consistency), and is not accompanied by conspicuous alternative causes of the action (exclusivity), we experience conscious will and ascribe authorship to ourselves for the action."

There are two reasons for doubting whether Wegner and Wheatley's (1999) findings are the kiss of death for the notion that conscious intentions play an important role in determining our actions. First, they used a very elaborate and artificial set-up to show that we are sometimes mistaken when we decide we did cause an action. By analogy, no one would say that visual perception is hopelessly fallible simply because we make mistakes when identifying objects in a thick fog!

Second, it is more difficult than it may appear to decide exactly *what* someone is consciously aware of. Schooler (2002) drew a distinction between having an experience (basic consciousness) and explicitly knowing one is having that experience (meta-consciousness). That may sound like a very subtle distinction (or even like mumbo-jumbo!), but can be seen clearly in a study by Schooler, Reichle, and Halpern (in press). Participants read texts and indicated every time they found their minds wandering from the text ("zoning out"). From time to time, they were given a signal and indicated if they had been zoning out when the signal went. Participants often admitted they had been zoning out when the signal went but had failed to report this spontaneously because they

Is conscious intention an illusion?

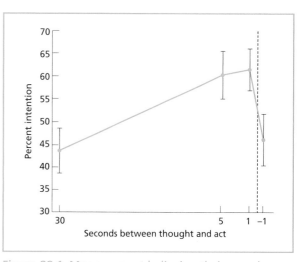

Figure 28.1 Mean percent believing their conscious intention caused the cursor to stop where it did as a function of time between thought and action. From Wegner and Wheatley (1999). Copyright © American Psychological Association. Reprinted with permission.

lacked meta-consciousness that they had been daydreaming. Thus, it is possible to have conscious experience of daydreaming without being explicitly aware that that is the case. With reference to the study by Wegner and Wheatley (1999), it is possible the participants' problems stemmed from deficient meta-consciousness rather than deficient basic consciousness.

Libet's research

Very different findings casting doubt on the importance of conscious intentions in causing action were reported by Libet, Gleason, Wright, and Pearl (1983). They carried out a study in which participants were asked to bend their wrist and fingers at a time of their choosing. The time at which they were consciously aware of the intention to perform the movement and the moment at which the hand muscles were activated were recorded. In addition, they recorded the readiness potential in the brain—this is thought to reflect pre-planning of a bodily movement. The key finding was that the readiness potential occurred 350 ms *before* participants had conscious awareness of the intention to bend the wrist and fingers (conscious awareness preceded the actual hand movement by about 200 ms). According to Libet (1996, p. 112), "Initiation of the voluntary process is developed unconsciously [as indexed by the readiness potential], well before there is any awareness of the intention to act."

One limitation with the findings of Libet et al. (1983) is that the readiness potential doesn't only reflect preparation for bodily movement—it also reflects more general anticipatory processes. What we really need is a measure of brain activity more *directly* reflecting movement preparation. This was done by Trevena and Miller (2002). They measured lateralized readiness potential, which differs depending on whether it is the right or the left hand that is going to be moved. The lateralized readiness potential generally occurred before participants were consciously aware of the decision to move their hand (see Figure 28.2). These findings confirm Libet et al.'s (1983) findings that voluntary initiation of a hand movement (as reflected in brain activity) generally precedes conscious awareness that the decision has been made.

It is useful to apply Schooler's (2002) distinction between basic consciousness and meta-consciousness to findings such as those of Libet et al. (1983) and Trevena and Miller (2002). Explicitly knowing that one has had a conscious intention (meta-consciousness) must occur *after* the intention itself (basic consciousness). It is probably the time taken for meta-consciousness to occur that is being measured in these experiments. As a consequence, it is perfectly possible

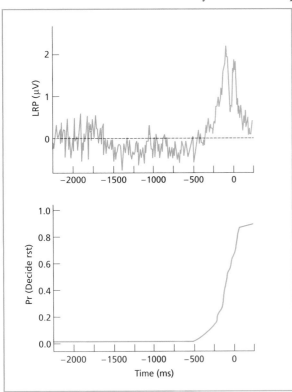

Figure 28.2 Lateralized readiness potential (top panel), and probability of a conscious decision to move the hand (bottom panel) as a function of time in ms before a voluntary hand movement. From Trevena and Miller (2002) with permission from Elsevier.

that the actual conscious intention itself occurs *before* the readiness potential or lateralized readiness potential, in which case there is no mystery to be explained.

KEY ISSUES

If psychologists and other scientists are ever going to understand what consciousness is all about, they need to address several issues. Pinker (1997) argued that there are three main issues:

1.   *Sentience*: This is our subjective experience or phenomenal experience, and is *only* available to the person having the experience. This is what Schooler (2002) called basic consciousness.
2.   *Access to information*: This relates to our ability to report the *content* of our subjective experience, but without the ability to report on the *processes* producing that experience.
3.   *Self-knowledge*: This is the ability to have conscious experience of ourselves, and most people regard this aspect of consciousness as of central importance to them. As Pinker (1997) expressed it, "I cannot only feel pain and see red, but think to myself, 'Hey, here I am, Steve Pinker, feeling pain and seeing red!'" This is what Schooler (2002) called meta-consciousness.

Sad to say, cognitive psychologists and neuroscientists have shed little light on the issue of sentience. This is what Chalmers (1995b, p. 63) famously called the "hard problem," which is "the question of how physical processes in the brain give rise to subjective experience." Chalmers (1995a, pp. 201–203) spelled out in more detail the essence of the hard problem: "If any problem qualifies as *the* problem of consciousness, it is this one ... even when we have explained the performance of all the cognitive and behavioral functions in the vicinity of experience—perceptual discriminations, categorizations, internal access, verbal report—there may still remain a further unanswered question: Why is the performance of these functions accompanied by experience? ... Why doesn't all this information processing go on 'in the dark', free of any feel?"

Chalmers (1995a, 1995b) also identified some "easy problems." These problems (which are only relatively easy!) relate to Pinker's (1997) access-to-information issues. They involve understanding the processes involved in discriminating and categorizing stimuli, integrating information, focal attention, control of behavior, and so on. Theoretical approaches relevant to these easy problems are discussed shortly.

IN TWO MINDS?

One of the few issues relating to consciousness on which there is general agreement is that everyone possesses a single, unitary consciousness. Suppose, however, we were to consider individuals in whom the connections have been severed between the two hemispheres of the brain. (We have a left hemisphere and a right hemisphere and language processing is typically based in the left hemisphere). In these **split-brain patients**, the corpus callosum (the major connection between the two hemispheres) has been cut surgically to contain severe epileptic seizures within one hemisphere. Do split-brain patients have two minds, each with its own consciousness?

Contrasting answers to the above question have been offered by experts in the field. On one side of the argument is Roger Sperry (1913–1994), who won the Nobel Prize for his influential research on split-brain patients. He was firmly of the opinion that these patients *do* have two consciousnesses: "Each hemisphere seemed to have its own separate and private sensations . . . the minor hemisphere [the right one] constitutes a second conscious entity that is characteristically human and runs along in parallel with the more dominant stream of consciousness in the major hemisphere [the left hemisphere]" (Sperry, 1968, p. 723).

If you split the brain, do you also split consciousness?

On the other side of the argument are Gazzaniga, Ivry, and Mangun (2002). According to them, split-brain patients have only a *single* conscious system, based in the left hemisphere, that tries to make sense of the information available to it. They called this system the **interpreter**, and defined it as, "A left-brain system that seeks explanation for internal and external events in order to produce appropriate response behavior" (Gazzaniga et al., 2002, p. G-5). Cooney and Gazzaniga (2003) developed this theoretical position in an interesting way. They argued that brain-damaged patients continue to use the interpreter to produce an understanding of what is going on, even when they have access to only very limited information. As a result, brain-damaged patients' understanding is often incorrect.

FINDINGS

The first patient studied by Sperry and his colleagues was WJ, a charming and socially dominant World War Two veteran. The demonstration that he had a separate processing system in each hemisphere was of great scientific importance. However, according to Gazzaniga (one of the scientists who studied him), "W.J. lives happily in Downey, California, with no sense of the enormity of the findings or for that matter any awareness that he had changed."

If you have read about split-brain patients before, you may have formed the impression that they spend most of their time struggling to cope effectively with the world around them. This is *not* the case—for example, the IQs of split-brain patients are very much the same as they were before the operation. What split-brain patients generally do is move their eyes around to make sure that all the important information from the environment reaches both hemispheres. It was only when Sperry started carrying out experiments in which visual stimuli were presented very *briefly* (thus preventing eye movements) that split-brain patients showed impaired task performance.

Sperry and his colleagues compared the abilities of the two hemispheres by presenting tasks to only *one* hemisphere. The right hemisphere outperformed the left hemisphere on some tasks: "All of these right-brain tasks involved visual or touch perception of difficult configurations, judgments involving exploration of shapes by hand, or manipulative construction of geometric assembles or patterns. It appeared that the right hemisphere was able to note the shape of things more completely than the left" (Trevarthen, 2004, p. 875).

The greatest advantage of the left hemisphere over the right hemisphere was in terms of speech. Patients typically responded fluently when tasks were presented to the left hemisphere. In contrast, when they were presented to the right hemisphere, "The subjects often gave no response. If urged to reply, they said that there might have been some weak and ill-defined event, or else they confabulated [invented] experiences, as if unable to apply a test of truth or falsity to spontaneously imagined answers to questions" (Trevarthen, 2004, p. 875). Note, however, that the right hemisphere had a limited ability to understand simple language.

As you can imagine, the fact that the right hemisphere of most split-brain patients lacks speech makes it hard to know whether it possesses its own consciousness. However, Gazzaniga and LeDoux (1978) found a split-brain patient, Paul S, who had reasonably good right-hemisphere language abilities. The left hand is connected to the right hemisphere, and Paul S showed limited evidence of consciousness in his right hemisphere by responding appropriately to questions using his left hand. For example, he could spell out his own name, that of his girlfriend, his hobbies, and his current mood.

Paul S showed some interesting differences between his hemispheres. His right hemisphere said he wanted to be a racing driver, whereas his left hemisphere wanted him to be a draughtsman. When asked his reactions to President Nixon, who was involved in a scandal that forced him to resign, Paul's right hemisphere indicated "dislike," whereas his left hemisphere indicated "like."

In a further study (Gazzaniga, 1992), Paul S was presented with a chicken claw to his left hemisphere and a snow scene to his right hemisphere. When asked to select relevant pictures from an array, he chose a picture of a chicken with his right hand (connected to the left hemisphere) and he chose a shovel with his left hand (connected to the right hemisphere). These findings may seem to suggest that Paul S had a separate consciousness in each hemisphere. However, here is how he explained his choices: "Oh, that's simple. The chicken claw goes with the chicken, and you need a shovel to clean out the chicken shed" (Gazzaniga, 1992, p. 124). As Gazzaniga pointed out, Paul S's left hemisphere was interpreting behavior initiated by the right hemisphere, and there was no clear evidence that the right hemisphere was contributing much to the interpretation.

Findings indicating that Paul S's left hemisphere often overruled his right hemisphere led Gazzaniga et al. (2002) to argue that Paul S (and other split-brain patients) have very limited right-hemisphere consciousness. For example, the right hemispheres of split-brain patients can understand words such as "pin" and "finger," but they find it very hard to decide which of six words best describes the causal relationship between them ("bleed"). According to Gazzaniga et al. (2002, p. 680), "[The right hemisphere] deals mainly with raw experience in an unembellished [unadorned] way. The left hemisphere, though, is constantly . . . labeling experiences, making inferences as to cause, and carrying out a host of other cognitive activities. The right hemisphere is simply monitoring the world." This is consistent with the notion that the left hemisphere contains an interpreter.

Recent research has produced more promising findings. Baynes and Gazzaniga (2000) discussed the case of VJ, whose writing is controlled by the right hemisphere, whereas her speech is controlled by the left hemisphere.

According to Baynes and Gazzaniga (2000, p. 1362), "She [VJ] is the first split … who is frequently dismayed by the independent performance of her right and left hands. She is discomfited by the fluent writing of her left hand [controlled by the right hemisphere] to unseen stimuli and distressed by the inability of her right hand to write out words she can read out loud and spell." Speculatively, we could interpret the evidence from VJ as suggesting limited dual consciousness.

Finally, we turn to Cooney and Gazzaniga's (2003) hypothesis that the left-hemisphere interpretive system often continues to interpret what is going on even in brain-damaged patients lacking access to important information. As a consequence, its interpretations are sometimes very inaccurate. For example, consider patients with **reduplicative paramnesia**, which involves a belief that there are multiple copies of places and people. Gazzaniga (2000) studied a female patient with this condition. She was being studied at New York Hospital, but was convinced she was at home in Freeport, Maine. When asked to explain why there were several lifts outside the door, she replied, "Do you know how much it cost me to have those put in?"

GLOBAL WORKSPACE THEORIES

It is now time to consider theories of consciousness. Several theorists (e.g., Baars, 1988, 1997a; Baars & Franklin, 2003; Dehaene & Naccache, 2001) have argued that conscious experience occurs "in the theatre of consciousness" (Baars, 1988, p. 31), which is the global workspace. It is very important to note that consciousness is typically associated with activation in large areas of the brain connected to this global workspace. In the words of Baars and Franklin (2003, p. 166), "Consciousness is associated with a global workspace in the brain—a fleeting memory capacity whose focal contents are widely distributed … to many unconscious specialized networks … a global workspace can serve to integrate many competing and co-operating input networks" (Baars & Franklin, 2003, p. 166). Thus, consciousness serves to *integrate* and *combine* information from many specific, non-conscious processes distributed within the brain.

It is assumed by global workspace theorists that conscious awareness depends very much on focal attention. For example, Baars (1997b) invited us to consider sentences such as, "We look in order to see" or "We listen in order to hear." According to Baars (1997b, p. 364), "The distinction is between selecting an experience and being conscious of the selected event. In everyday language, the first word of each pair ['look'; 'listen'] involves attention; the second word ['see'; 'hear'] involves consciousness." Thus, attention resembles choosing a television channel and consciousness resembles the picture on the screen.

DEHAENE AND NACCACHE'S WORKSPACE THEORY

The workspace model of Dehaene and Naccache (2001) and developed by Dehaene and Changeux (2005) uses several of Baars' ideas, but goes further in that the main brain areas associated with conscious awareness are identified. We will first consider some of the main aspects of Dehaene and Naccache's theory, followed by a discussion of relevant research.

Three key assumptions influenced the development of the theory. First, it was assumed that most information processing occurs without conscious awareness. For example, evidence that perceptual and semantic processing can occur below the conscious level has been found in brain-damaged patients with blindsight (Chapter 4), with prosopagnosia or face blindness (Chapter 6), with neglect and extinction (Chapter 9), and with amnesia (Chapter 14).

What aspects of conscious experience does global workspace theory explain? What remains unexplained?

Second, Dehaene and Naccache (2001) assumed that attention is a necessary precondition for consciousness. Evidence comes from extinction, a condition in which brain-damaged patients presented with two visual stimuli at the same time report seeing only the one on the right. In fact, they seem not to attend to the stimulus on the left, which is why they don't perceive it consciously even though it is processed to some extent (see Driver & Vuilleumier, 2001). In similar fashion, Hollingworth and Henderson (2002; see Chapter 8) investigated observers' conscious awareness that there had been a change to a visual scene. Performance was considerably better when the changed object had been attended to previously than when it had not.

Third, Dehaene and Naccache (2001, p. 11) assumed that conscious awareness is essential for several mental operations: "The strategic operations which are associated with planning a novel strategy, evaluating it, controlling its execution, and correcting possible errors cannot be accomplished unconsciously." Various areas of the brain are or can be involved in these processes, but typically they include the prefrontal cortex and the anterior cingulate—the prefrontal cortex is entirely in the frontal lobe, as is much of the anterior cingulate (see Figure 1.4).

Finally, we present a sketch-map of the theory. When a stimulus is presented, this triggers the use of various specific bottom-up processes, most of which are relatively specific and occur in small areas of the brain. These processes operate below the level of consciousness. When top-down processes (essentially attention) integrate and enhance these bottom-up processes, there is conscious perception. In the words of Dehaene and Naccache (2001, p. 14), "Top-down attentional amplification is the mechanism by which modular [specific] processes can be temporarily mobilized and made available to the global workspace, and therefore to consciousness." It follows that the specific brain areas associated with consciousness depend in part on the content of the conscious experience *and* the specific processes involved. However, Dehaene and Naccache (2001) assumed that the prefrontal cortex and the anterior cingulate are typically activated during conscious experience.

Findings

The most general prediction from the global workspace approach is that conscious processing typically involves activation of far more brain areas than processing occurring below the conscious level. There is increasing support for this prediction from studies focusing on various cognitive processes. One general approach involves presenting all participants with the same stimuli and the same task. Brain-imaging data are then analyzed separately for participants who were consciously aware of some aspect of the experimental situation and for those who were not.

An example of the above approach is a study by McIntosh, Rajah, and Lobaugh (1999). They gave participants the task of responding to one visual stimulus (the target) but not to the other (distractor). There were also two tones, one predicting that a visual stimulus would be presented and the other predicting its absence. Participants were divided into those consciously detecting the association between the auditory and visual stimuli (the aware group) and those who did not (the unaware group). The largest difference between the two groups in brain activity produced by the tones was in the left prefrontal cortex, suggesting that this area was associated with conscious awareness of the tones' significance. Of crucial importance, they found that the left prefrontal cortex forms part of a much larger neural system associated with conscious awareness—this system includes the right prefrontal cortex (in the frontal lobe), medial cerebellum (at the back of the brain below the occipital lobe), and occipital cortex (an area at the back of the brain; see Figure 1.4).

Similar findings were reported by Rodriguez et al. (1999). Participants saw pictures that were easily perceived as faces when presented upright (face-perception condition) but which were seen as meaningless black-and-white shapes when presented upside-down (control condition). Event-related potentials (ERPs; see Chapter 1) were calculated based on data obtained from 30 electrodes. The key findings related to brain activity at the time after picture presentation (180–360 ms) at which faces were perceived in the upright condition. There was considerably more coordinated or synchronized activity across the brain in the face-perception condition than in the control condition (see Figure 28.3). As Rodriguez et al. (1999, p. 431) concluded, "Only face perception induces a long-distance pattern of synchronization, correlating to the moment of [conscious] perception itself."

An alternative experimental approach involves presenting the same stimuli so that they can (or can't) be perceived consciously. One way of preventing a stimulus being perceived consciously is to follow it almost immediately with a second stimulus that acts as a mask and inhibits processing of the first stimulus. Dehaene et al. (2001) presented words either masked or unmasked. When the words were masked (and so not consciously perceived), brain activation was mostly restricted to the visual cortex. When the same words were unmasked, there was a much larger increase in activation in the visual cortex, and there was also widespread parietal and prefrontal activation. Baars (2002, p. 47) reviewed 13 studies in which conscious and non-conscious conditions were compared: "Conscious perception ... enables access to widespread brain sources, whereas unconscious input processing is limited to sensory regions."

According to the global workspace model (and the evidence we have just discussed), there are major differences in brain activity between conscious processes and non-conscious ones. Accordingly, there are qualitative differences between conscious and non-conscious processes, and there should be a sudden trans-

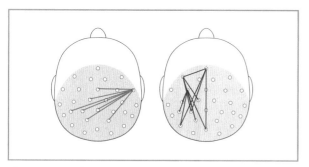

Figure 28.3 Phase synchrony (black lines) and phase desynchrony (blue lines) in EEG 180–360 ms. After stimulus presentation in the no-face-perception and face-perception conditions. From Rodriguez et al. (1999). Copyright © 1999 by the Nature Publishing Group. Reproduced with permission.

ition from non-conscious processing to conscious processing. In contrast, some theorists (e.g., Farah, 2001) have argued that there is a gradual transition from non-conscious to conscious processing.

Sergent and Dehaene (2004) compared the above predictions in an experiment on the **attentional blink**, in which the ability to detect a target presented in a stream of stimuli is inhibited by detection of a preceding target when the interval between targets is about 200–500 ms. The key measure obtained was the rated visibility of the second target. As predicted by global workspace theory, the second target was mostly rated as either entirely invisible or visible. In other words, there was a sudden rather than a gradual transition from non-conscious to conscious perception.

Finally, we consider the assumption that the prefrontal cortex and the anterior cingulate form part of the top-down attentional system involved in conscious awareness. There is much support for this assumption, but we will discuss only two studies. As was mentioned earlier, McIntosh et al. (1999) found that the left prefrontal cortex was at the center of a large brain system associated with conscious awareness. Lumer, Friston, and Rees (1998) carried out a study on **binocular rivalry**: two visual stimuli are presented (one to each eye) and the observer consciously perceives only one of them. However, the stimulus consciously perceived often changes backwards and forwards between the two stimuli over time. Binocular rivalry provides a useful way of assessing brain activity associated with consciousness. The reason is that there are changes in conscious awareness (i.e., shift in stimulus perceived) with no change in the stimuli presented. Lumer et al. presented a red drifting grating to one eye and a green face to the other, and participants indicated which stimulus they were consciously perceiving. Lumer et al. used fMRI to identify the brain areas especially active immediately prior to a switch in conscious perception from one stimulus to the other. As predicted, the anterior cingulate and the prefrontal cortex were among several areas showing increased activation during shifts in conscious perception.

EVALUATION AND CHAPTER SUMMARY

In two minds?
- Research on split-brain patients is fascinating, but has as yet not fully resolved the issue of whether they have two separate consciousnesses.
- The most popular view is that the left hemisphere in split-brain patients plays the dominant role in consciousness, and is the location of an interpreter or self-supervisory system.
- In contrast, the right hemisphere can engage in various relatively low-level processing activities (e.g., identifying shapes) but probably lacks its own consciousness.
- This view is supported by findings showing the left hemisphere overruling the right hemisphere. It is also supported by the persistent failure to observe anything approaching a genuine dialogue between the two hemispheres. However, we still lack definitive evidence.

- There is reasonable evidence that many brain-damaged patients are unaware of their cognitive impairments, leading the left-hemisphere interpreter to provide coherent (but inaccurate) interpretations of events.
- However, many brain-damaged patients are very aware of their cognitive impairments, and so don't produce misleading interpretations of events.
- The processes determining whether there is conscious awareness of the adverse effects of brain damage remain unclear.

Global workspace theories
- The theoretical assumptions of Dehaene and Naccache (2001) have received experimental support.
- For example, most information processing occurs below the level of conscious awareness, and attentional processes seem to be important in determining which fraction of the information being processed at any given moment enters consciousness.
- Several brain areas are associated with conscious experience, and the prefrontal cortex and anterior cingulate are typically involved.
- Of particular importance, integrated, large-scale brain activity underlies much conscious awareness (e.g., Baars, 2002; Dehaene & Changeux, 2005; McIntosh et al., 1999; Rodriguez et al., 1999). Thus, the theory (which builds on several previous theories) provides us with a good overview of many aspects of consciousness.
- In spite of its many successes, global workspace theory provides only a limited account of human consciousness.
- What is missing from Dehaene and Naccache's (2001) theory (but is also missing from most other theories) is an answer to Chalmers' (1995b) hard problem discussed earlier: *why* do physical processes in the brain give rise to conscious experience?
- In the terminology used by Velmans (2000), we can distinguish between first-person and third-person accounts.
- First-person accounts involve a detailed analysis of individuals' own conscious experience, whereas third-person accounts involve an analysis of various brain (and other) processes of relevance to consciousness.
- Global workspace theory provides a third-person account but doesn't provide a first-person account.

FURTHER READING

- Baars, B.J., Banks, W.P. & Newman, J.B. (2003). *Essential sources in the scientific study of consciousness*. Cambridge, MA: MIT Press. This edited book addresses several key scientific issues in the study of consciousness.
- Blackmore, S. (2003). *Consciousness: An introduction*. London: Hodder & Stoughton. If you want an accessible and well-informed introduction to the topic of consciousness, you will find it in this interesting book.
- Koch, C. (2003). *The quest for consciousness: A neurobiological approach*. New York: Roberts & Co. The author of this book emphasizes the progress made in understanding consciousness from a biological perspective.
- Wegner, D.M. (2002). *The illusion of conscious will*. Cambridge, MA: MIT Press. This intriguing book focuses on the controversial view that we are mistaken when we believe that our actions are determined by our conscious intentions.

References

Ackerman, P.L., Beier, M.E., & Boyle, M.O. (2005). Working memory and intelligence: The same or different constructs? *Psychological Bulletin*, *131*, 30–60.

Aggleton, J.P., & Brown, M.W. (1999). Episodic memory, amnesia, and the hippocampal–anterior thalamic axis. *Behavioral and Brain Sciences*, *22*, 425–489.

Ahn, W., Kim, N.S., Lassaline, M.E., & Denis, M. (2000). Causal status as a determinant of feature centrality. *Cognitive Psychology*, *41*, 361–416.

Aizenstein, H.J., Stenger, V.A., Cochran, J., Clark, K., Johnson, M., Nebes, R.D., & Carter, C.S. (2004). Regional brain activation during concurrent implicit and explicit sequence learning. *Cerebral Cortex*, *14*, 199–208.

Allopenna, P.D., Magnuson, J.S., & Tanenhaus, M.K. (1998). Tracking the time course of spoken word recognition using eye movements: Evidence for continuous mapping models. *Journal of Memory and Language*, *38*, 419–439.

Altenberg, B. (1990). Speech as linear composition. In G. Caie, K. Haastrup, A.L. Jakobsen, J.E. Nielsen, J. Sevaldsen, H. Sprecht, & A. Zetterstein (Eds.), *Proceedings from the Fourth Nordic Conference for English Studies*. Copenhagen, Denmark: Copenhagen University Press.

Altmann, G.T.M. (1997). *The ascent of Babel: An exploration of language, mind, and understanding*. Oxford: Oxford University Press.

Anderson, J.R. (1993). *Rules of the mind*. Hillsdale, NJ: Lawrence Erlbaum Associates Inc.

Anderson, J.R., & Lebiere, C. (2003). The Newell Test for a theory of cognition. *Behavioral and Brain Sciences*, *26*, 587–640.

Anderson, R.C., & Pichert, J.W. (1978). Recall of previously unrecallable information following a shift in perspective. *Journal of Verbal Learning and Verbal Behavior*, *17*, 1–12.

Anderson, S.A., & Conway, M.A. (1993). Investigating the structure of autobiographical memories. *Journal of Experimental Psychology: Learning, Memory, & Cognition*, 19, 1178–1196.

Andrade, J. (2001). *Working memory in perspective*. Hove, UK: Psychology Press.

Andres, P., & Van der Linden, M. (2002). Are central executive functions working in patients with focal frontal lesions? *Neuropsychologia*, *40*, 835–845.

Andrews, B., Brewin, C.R., Ochera, J., Morton, J., Bekerian, D.A., Davies, G.M. et al. (1999). The timing, triggers and quality of recovered memories in therapy. *British Journal of Psychiatry*, *175*, 141–146.

Arkes, H.R., & Ayton, P. (1999). The sunk cost and Concorde effects: Are humans less rational than lower animals? *Psychological Bulletin*, *125*, 591–600.

Arkes, H.R., & Blumer, C. (1985). The psychology of sunk cost. *Organizational Behavior and Human Decision Processes*, *35*, 124–140.

Aronson, E., & Carlsmith, J.M. (1968). Experimentation in social psychology. In G. Lindzey & E. Aronson (Eds.). *The handbook of social psychology* (2nd ed., Vol. 2, pp. 1–79). Reading, MA: Addison-Wesley.

Ashby, F.G., & Ell, S.W. (2001). The neurobiology of human category learning. *Trends in Cognitive Sciences*, 5, 204–210.

Ashby, F.G., Ell, S.W., & Waldron, E.M. (2003). Procedural learning in perceptual categorization. *Memory & Cognition*, *31*, 1114–1125.

Ashby, F.G., & Maddox, W.T. (2005). Human category learning. *Annual Review of Psychology*, *56*, 149–178.

Atkinson, R.C., & Shiffrin, R.M. (1968). Human memory: A proposed system and its control processes. In K.W. Spence & J.T. Spence (Eds.), *The psychology of learning and motivation, Vol. 2*. London: Academic Press.

Atkinson, R.C., & Shiffrin, R.M. (1971). The control of short-term memory. *Scientific American, 225*, 82–90.

Atkinson, R.L., Atkinson, R.C., Smith, E.E., & Bem, D.J. (1993). *Introduction to psychology* (11th ed.). New York: Harcourt Brace.

Awh, E., & Pashler, H. (2000). Evidence for split attentional foci. *Journal of Experimental Psychology: Human Perception and Performance, 26*, 834–846.

Baars, B.J. (1988). *A cognitive theory of consciousness*. Cambridge: Cambridge University Press.

Baars, B.J. (1997a). *In the theatre of consciousness: The workspace of the mind*. New York: Oxford University Press.

Baars, B.J. (1997b). Consciousness versus attention, perception, and working memory. *Consciousness and Cognition, 6*, 363–371.

Baars, B.J. (2002). The conscious access hypothesis: Origins and recent evidence. *Trends in Cognitive Sciences, 6*, 47–52.

Baars, B.J., Banks, W.P., & Newman, J.B. (2003). *Essential sources in the scientific study of consciousness*. Cambridge, MA: MIT Press.

Baars, B.J., & Franklin, S. (2003). How conscious experience and working memory interact. *Trends in Cognitive Sciences, 7*, 166–172.

Baddeley, A.D. (1986). *Working memory*. Oxford: Clarendon Press.

Baddeley, A.D. (1990). *Human memory: Theory and practice* (Rev. ed.). Hove, UK: Psychology Press.

Baddeley, A.D. (1996). Exploring the central executive. *Quarterly Journal of Experimental Psychology, 49A*, 5–28.

Baddeley, A.D. (1997). *Human memory: Theory and practice* (Rev. ed.). Hove, UK: Psychology Press.

Baddeley, A.D. (2000). The episodic buffer: A new component of working memory? *Trends in Cognitive Sciences, 4*, 417–423.

Baddeley, A.D. (2001). Is working memory still working? *American Psychologist, 56*, 851–864.

Baddeley, A.D. (2003). New data: Old pitfalls. *Behavioral and Brain Sciences, 26*, 729.

Baddeley, A.D., & Andrade, J. (2000). Working memory and the vividness of imagery. *Journal of Experimental Psychology: General, 129*, 126–145.

Baddeley, A.D., Gathercole, S., & Papagno, C. (1998). The phonological loop as a language learning device. *Psychological Review, 105*, 158–173.

Baddeley, A.D., & Hitch, G.J. (1974). Working memory. In G.H. Bower (Ed.), *The psychology of learning and motivation, Vol. 8*. London: Academic Press.

Baddeley, A.D., & Hitch, G.J. (2000). Development of working memory: Should the Pascual-Leone and the Baddeley and Hitch models be merged? *Journal of Experimental Child Psychology, 77*, 128–137.

Baddeley, A.D., & Logie R.H. (1999). Working memory: The multiple-component model. In A. Miyake & P. Shah (Eds.), *Models of working memory: Mechanisms of active maintenance and executive control*. Cambridge: Cambridge University Press.

Baddeley, A.D., Thomson, N., & Buchanan, M. (1975). Word length and the structure of short-term memory. *Journal of Verbal Learning and Verbal Behavior, 14*, 575–589.

Baddeley, A.D., & Wilson, B. (2002). Prose recall and amnesia: Implications for the structure of working memory. *Neuropsychologia, 40*, 1737–1743.

Bahrick, H.P., Bahrick, P.O., & Wittlinger, R.P. (1975). Fifty years of memory for names and faces: A cross-sectional approach. *Journal of Experimental Psychology: General, 104*, 54–75.

Banich, M.T. (1997). *Neuropsychology: The neural bases of mental function*. New York: Houghton Mifflin.

Banks, S.M., Salovey, P., Greener, S., Rothman, A.J., Moyer, A., Beauvais, J., & Epel, E. (1995). The effects of message framing on mammography utilization. *Health Psychology, 14*, 178–184.

Barnett, S.M., & Ceci, S.J. (2002). When and where do we apply what we learn? A taxonomy for far transfer. *Psychological Bulletin, 128*, 612–637.

Barr, D.J., & Keysar, B. (2002). Anchoring comprehension in linguistic precedents. *Journal of Memory and Language, 46*, 391–418.

Barrett, L.F., Tugade, M.M., & Engle, R.W. (2004). Individual differences in working memory capacity and dual-process theories of the mind. *Psychological Bulletin*, *130*, 553–573.

Barsalou, L.W. (1985). Ideals, central tendency, and frequency of instantiation as determinants of graded structure in categories. *Journal of Experimental Psychology: Learning, Memory, and Cognition*, *11*, 629–654.

Barsalou, L.W. (1987). The instability of graded structure: Implications for the nature of concepts. In U. Neisser (Ed.), *Concepts and conceptual development: Ecological and intellectual factors in categorization*. Cambridge: Cambridge University Press.

Barsalou, L.W. (1988). The content and organization of autobiographical memories. In U. Neisser (Ed.), *Concepts and conceptual development: Ecological and intellectual approaches to the study of memory*. New York: Cambridge University Press.

Barsalou, L.W. (1989). Intra-concept similarity and its implications for inter-concept similarity. In S. Vosniadou & A. Ortony (Eds.), *Similarity and analogical reasoning*. Cambridge: Cambridge University Press.

Barsalou, L.W. (2003). Situated simulation in the human conceptual system. *Language and Cognitive Processes*, *18*, 513–562.

Bartlett, F.C. (1932). *Remembering*. Cambridge: Cambridge University Press.

Bartolomeo, P. (2002). The relationship between visual perception and visual mental imagery: A re-appraisal of the neuropsychological evidence. *Cortex*, *38*, 357–378.

Bartolomeo, P., Bachoud-Levi, A.C., de Gelder, B., Denes, G., Dalla Barba, G., Brugieres, P. et al. (1998). Multiple-domain dissociation between impaired visual perception and preserved mental imagery in a patient with bilateral extrastriate lesions. *Neuropsychologia*, *36*, 239–249.

Bartolomeo, P., & Chokron, S. (2002). Orienting of attention in left unilateral neglect. *Neuroscience and Biobehavioral Reviews*, *26*, 217–234.

Baynes, K., & Gazzaniga, M. (2000). Consciousness, introspection, and the split- brain: The two minds/one body problem. In M.S. Gazzaniga (Ed.), *The new cognitive neurosciences*. Cambridge, MA: MIT Press.

Beauvois, M.-F., & Dérouesné, J. (1979). Phonological alexia: Three dissociations. *Journal of Neurology, Neurosurgery & Psychiatry*, *42*, 1115–1124.

Beauvois, M.-F., Dérouesné, J., & Bastard, V. (1980). *Auditory parallel to phonological alexia*. Paper presented at the Third European Conference of the International Neuropsychological Society, Chianciano, Italy, June.

Ben-Zeev, T. (2002). If "ignorance makes us smart," then does reading books make us less smart? *Contemporary Psychology APA Review of Books*, *47*, 653–656.

Berndt, R.S., Mitchum, C.C., & Haendiges, A.N. (1996). Comprehension of reversible sentences in "agrammatism": A meta-analysis. *Cognition*, *58*, 289–308.

Berntsen, D. (1998). Voluntary and involuntary access to autobiographical memory. *Memory*, *6*, 113–141.

Berntsen, D., & Hall, N.M. (2004). The episodic nature of involuntary autobiographical memories. *Memory & Cognition*, *32*, 789–803.

Biederman, I. (1987). Recognition-by-components: A theory of human image understanding. *Psychological Review*, *94*, 115–147.

Biederman, I., & Gerhardstein, P.C. (1993). Recognizing depth-rotated objects: Evidence for 3–D viewpoint invariance. *Journal of Experimental Psychology: Human Perception and Performance*, *19*, 1162–1182.

Birch, H.G. (1945). The relationship of previous experience to insightful problem solving. *Journal of Comparative Psychology*, *38*, 267–283.

Blackmore, S. (2003). *Consciousness: An introduction*. London: Hodder & Stoughton.

Blaney, P.H. (1986). Affect and memory: A review. *Psychological Bulletin*, *99*, 229–246.

Blasko, D., & Connine, C. (1993). Effects of familiarity and aptness on metaphor processing. *Journal of Experimental Psychology: Learning, Memory, and Cognition*, *19*, 295–308.

Bögels, S.M., & Mansell, W. (2004). Attention processes in the maintenance and treatment of social phobia: Hypervigilance, avoidance and self-focused attention. *Clinical Psychology Review*, *24*, 827–856.

Boland, J.E., & Blodgett, A. (2001). Understanding the constraints on syntactic generation:

Lexical bias and discourse congruency effects on eye movements. *Journal of Memory and Language*, *45*, 391–411.

Borges, J.-L. (1964). *Labyrinths*. London: Penguin.

Bourke, P.A., Duncan, J., & Nimmo-Smith, I. (1996). A general factor involved in dual- task performance decrement. *Quarterly Journal of Experimental Psychology*, *49A*, 525– 545.

Bowden, E.M., & Beeman, M.J. (1998). Getting the right idea: Semantic activation in the right hemisphere may help solve insight problems. *Psychological Science*, *9*, 435–440.

Bowden, E.M., Jung-Beeman, M., Fleck, J., & Kounios, J. (2005). New approaches to demystifying insight. *Trends in Cognitive Sciences*, *9*, 322–328.

Bower, G.H. (1981). Mood and memory. *American Psychologist*, *36*, 129–148.

Bower, G.H. (1992). How might emotions affect learning? In S.-A. Christianson (Ed.), *The handbook of emotion and memory: Research and theory*. Hillsdale, NJ: Lawrence Erlbaum Associates Inc.

Bower, G.H., Black, J.B., & Turner, T.S. (1979). Scripts in memory for text. *Cognitive Psychology*, *11*, 177–220.

Bower, G.H., Gilligan, S.G., & Monteiro, K.P. (1981). Selectivity of learning caused by affective states. *Journal of Experimental Psychology: General*, *110*, 451–473.

Bower, G.H., Montero, K.P., & Gilligan, S.G. (1978). Emotional mood as a context for learning and recall. *Journal of Verbal Learning and Verbal Behavior*, *17*, 573–585.

Braine, M.D.S. (1978). On the relationship between the natural logic of reasoning and standard logic. *Psychological Review*, *85*, 1–21.

Braine, M.D.S. (1994). Mental logic and how to discover it. In J. MacNamara & G.E. Reyes (Eds.), *The logical foundations of cognition*. Oxford: Oxford University Press.

Braine, M.D.S. (1998). Steps towards a mental predicate logic. In M.D.S. Braine & D.P. O'Brien (Eds.), *Mental logic*. Mahwah, NJ: Lawrence Erlbaum Associates Inc.

Braine, M.D.S., Reiser, B.J., & Rumain, B. (1984). Some empirical justification for a theory of natural propositional logic. In G.H. Bower (Ed.), *The psychology of learning and motivation, Vol. 18*. New York: Academic Press.

Bransford, J.D., Barclay, J.R., & Franks, J.J. (1972). Sentence memory: A constructive versus interpretive approach. *Cognitive Psychology*, *3*, 193–209.

Bransford, J.D., & Johnson, M.K. (1972). Contextual prerequisites for understanding. *Journal of Verbal Learning and Verbal Behavior*, *11*, 717–726.

Bridgeman, B., Gemmer, A., Forsman, T., & Huemer, V. (2000). Processing spatial information in the sensorimotor branch of the visual system. *Vision Research*, *40*, 3539–3552.

Brown, A.S., Bracken, E., Zoccoli, S., & Douglas, K. (2004). Generating and remembering passwords. *Applied Cognitive Psychology*, *18*, 641–651.

Brown, R., & Kulik, J. (1977). Flashbulb memories. *Cognition*, *5*, 73–99.

Brown, R., & McNeill, D. (1966). The "tip of the tongue" phenomenon. *Journal of Verbal Learning and Verbal Behavior*, *5*, 325–337.

Bruce, V., Green, P.R., & Georgeson, M.A. (2003). *Visual perception: Physiology, psychology and ecology* (4th ed.). Hove, UK: Psychology Press.

Bruce, V., Henderson, Z., Greenwood, K., Hancock, P., Burton, A.M., & Miller, P. (1999). Verification of face identities from images captured on video. *Journal of Experimental Psychology: Applied*, *5*, 339–360.

Bruce, V., & Young, A.W. (1986). Understanding face recognition. *British Journal of Psychology*, *77*, 305–327.

Bruce, V., & Young, A. (1998). *In the eye of the beholder: The science of face perception*. Oxford: Oxford University Press.

Bruner, J.S., Postman, L., & Rodrigues, J. (1951). Expectations and the perception of color. *American Journal of Psychology*, *64*, 216–227.

Bruno, N., & Cutting, J.E. (1988). Mini-modularity and the perception of layout. *Journal of Experimental Psychology: General*, *117*, 161–170.

Bucciarelli, M., & Johnson-Laird, P.N. (1999). Strategies in syllogistic reasoning. *Cognitive Science*, *23*, 247–303.

Buckhout, R., Eugenio, P., & Grosso, T. (1981). *Is there life after hypnosis? Attempts to revive the memory of eyewitnesses*. Paper presented at the meeting of the American Psychological Association, Los Angeles.

Bunge, S.A., Klingberg, T., Jacobsen, R.B., & Gabrieli, J.D.E. (2000). A resource model of the neural basis of executive working memory. *Proceedings of the National Academy of Science USA, 97*, 3573–3578.

Burman, C. (2004). What are face-blind people like? www.prosopagnosia.com/main/likewhat

Burns, B.D. (2004). The effects of speed on skilled chess performance. *Psychological Science, 15*, 442–447.

Burns, B.D., & Wieth, M. (2004). The collider principle in causal reasoning: Why the Monty Hall dilemma is so hard. *Journal of Experimental Psychology: General, 133*, 434–449.

Burt, J.S., Kemp, S., & Conway, M.A. (2003). Themes, events, and episodes in autobiographical memory. *Memory & Cognition, 31*, 317–325.

Burton, A.M., & Bruce, V. (1993). Naming faces and naming names: Exploring an interactive activation model of person recognition. *Memory, 1*, 457–480.

Burton, A.M., Bruce, V., & Hancock, P.J.B. (1999). From pixels to people: A model of familiar face recognition. *Cognitive Science, 23*, 1–31.

Butcher, K.R., & Kintsch, W. (2003). Text comprehension and discourse processing. In A.F. Healy & R.W. Proctor (Eds.), *Handbook of psychology: Experimental psychology, Vol. 4.* New York: Wiley & Sons.

Butterworth, B. (1985). Jargon aphasia: Processes and strategies. In S. Newman & R. Epstein (Eds.), *Current perspectives in dysphasia.* Edinburgh: Churchill Livingstone.

Byrne, R.M.J. (1989). Suppressing valid inferences with conditionals. *Cognition, 31*, 61–83.

Caccappolo-van Vliet, E., Miozzo, M., & Stern, Y. (2004). Phonological dyslexia: A test case for reading models. *Psychological Science, 15*, 583–590.

Calder, A.J., Young, A.W., Keane, J., & Dean, M. (2000). Configural information in facial expression perception. *Journal of Experimental Psychology: Human Perception and Performance, 26*, 527–551.

Camerer, C., Babcock, L., Loewenstein, G., & Thaler, R. (1997). Labor supply of New York City cabdrivers: One day at a time? *Quarterly Journal of Economics, CXII*, 407–441.

Campion, J., Latto, R., & Smith, Y.M. (1983) Is blindsight an effect of scattered light, spared cortex, and near-threshold vision? *Behavioral and Brain Sciences, 6*, 423–86

Campion, N. (2004). Predictive inferences are represented as hypothetical facts. *Journal of Memory and Language, 50*, 149–164.

Carlson, K.A., & Russo, J.E. (2001). Biased interpretation of evidence by mock jurors. *Journal of Experimental Psychology: Applied, 7*, 91–103.

Carmel, D., & Bentin, S. (2002). Domain specificity versus expertise: Factors influencing distinct processing of faces. *Cognition, 83*, 1–29.

Carreiras, M., & Clifton, C. (1993). Relative clause interpretation preferences in Spanish and English. *Language & Speech, 36*, 353–372.

Casscells, W., Schoenberger, A., & Graboys, T.B. (1978). Interpretation by physicians of clinical laboratory results. *New England Journal of Medicine, 299*, 999–1001.

Ceci, S.J., & Liker, J.K. (1986). A day at the races: A study of IQ, expertise, and cognitive complexity. *Journal of Experimental Psychology: General, 115*, 255–266.

Ceraso, J., & Provitera, A. (1971). Sources of error in syllogistic reasoning. *Cognitive Psychology, 2*, 400–410.

Cermak, L.S., Lewis, R., Butters, N., & Goodglass, H. (1973). Role of verbal mediation in performance of motor tasks by Korsakoff patients. *Perceptual & Motor Skills, 37*, 259–262.

Chabris, C.F., & Hearst, E.S. (2003). Visualization, pattern recognition, and forward search: Effects of playing speed and sight of the position on grandmaster chess errors. *Cognitive Science, 27*, 637–648.

Chalmers, D.J. (1995a). Facing up to the problem of consciousness. *Journal of Consciousness Studies, 3*, 200–219.

Chalmers, D.J. (1995b). The puzzle of conscious experience. *Scientific American* (December), 62–68.

Channon, S., Shanks, D., Johnstone, T., Vakili, K., Chin, J., & Sinclair, E. (2002). Is implicit learning spared in amnesia? Rule abstraction and item familiarity in artificial grammar learning. *Neuropsychologia, 40*, 2185–2197.

Chapman, G.B. (2004). The psychology of medical decision making. In D.J. Koehler &

N. Harvey (2004). *Blackwell handbook of judgment and decision making*. Oxford: Blackwell.

Chapman, L.J., & Chapman, J.P. (1959). Atmosphere effects re-examined. *Journal of Experimental Psychology*, *58*, 220–226.

Charness, N. (1976). Memory for chess positions: Resistance to interference. *Journal of Experimental Psychology: Human Learning and Memory*, *2*, 641–653.

Charness, N. (1981). Search in chess: Age and skill differences. *Journal of Experimental Psychology: Human Perception and Performance*, *7*, 467–476.

Charness, N., & Gerchack, Y. (1996). Participation rates and maximal performance: A log-linear explanation for group differences, such as Russian and male dominance in chess. *Psychological Science*, *7*, 46–51.

Charness, N., Krampe, R.Th., & Mayr, U. (1996). The role of practice and coaching in entrepreneurial skill domains: An international comparison of life-span chess skill acquisition. In K.A. Ericsson (Ed.), *The road to excellence: The acquisition of expert performance in the arts and sciences, sports, and games*. Mahwah, NJ: Lawrence Erlbaum Associates Inc.

Charness, N., Reingold, E.M., Pomplun, M., & Stampe, D.M. (2001). The perceptual aspect of skilled performance in chess: Evidence from eye movements. *Memory & Cognition*, *29*, 1146–1152.

Chartrand, T.L., van Baaren, R.B. & Bargh, J.A. (2006). Linking automatic evaluation to mood and information-processing style: Consequences for experienced affect, impression formation, and sterotyping. *Journal of Experimental Psychology: General*, *135*, 7–77.

Chase, W.G., & Simon, H.A. (1973). Perception in chess. *Cognitive Psychology*, *4*, 55–81.

Chen, Z. (2002). Analogical problem solving: A hierarchical analysis of procedural similarity. *Journal of Experimental Psychology: Learning, Memory, and Cognition*, *28*, 81–98.

Chen, Z., & Klahr, D. (1999). All other things being equal: Children's acquisition of the control of variables strategy. *Child Development*, *70*, 1098–1120.

Chen, Z., Mo, L., & Honomichl, R. (2004). Having the memory of an elephant: Long-term retrieval and the use of analogues in problem solving. *Journal of Experimental Psychology: General*, *133*, 415–433.

Choi. I., Choi, J., & Norenzayan, A. (2004). Culture and decisions. In D.J. Koehler & N. Harvey (Eds.), *Blackwell handbook of judgment and decision making*. Oxford: Blackwell.

Chu, S., & Downes, J.J. (2000). Odor-evoked autobiographical memories: Psychological investigations of Proustian phenomena. *Chemical Senses*, *25*, 111–116.

Chu, S., & Downes, J.J. (2004). Proust re-interpreted: Can Proust's account of odour-cued autobiographical memory recall really be investigated? A reply to Jellinek. *Chemical Senses*, *29*, 459–461.

Churchland, P.S., & Sejnowski, T.J. (1991). Perspectives on cognitive neuroscience. In R.G. Lister & H.J. Weingartner (Eds.), *Perspectives on cognitive neuroscience*. Oxford: Oxford University Press.

Churchland, P.S., & Sejnowski, T. (1994). *The computational brain*. Cambridge, MA: MIT Press.

Cipolotti, L., & Warrington, E.K. (1995). Towards a unitary account of access dysphasia: A single case study. *Memory*, *3*, 309–332.

Clancy, S.A., Schacter, D.L., McNally, R.J., & Pitman, R.K. (2000). False recognition in women reporting recovered memories of sexual abuse. *Psychological Science*, *11*, 26–31.

Claparède, E. (1911). Recognition et moiité. *Archives de Psychologie*, *11*, 75–90.

Clark, D.M. (1986). A cognitive approach to panic. *Behaviour Research and Therapy*, *24*, 461–470.

Clark, D.M. (1999). Anxiety disorders: Why they persist and how to treat them. *Behaviour Research and Therapy*, *37*, S5–S27 Suppl. 1.

Clark, D.M., & Teasdale, J.D. (1982). Diurnal variation in clinical depression and accessibility of memories of positive and negative experiences. *Journal of Abnormal Psychology*, *91*, 87–95.

Clark, D.M., & Wells, A. (1995). A cognitive model of social phobia. In R.G. Heimberg, M.R. Liebowitz, D.A. Hope, & F.R. Schneier (Eds.), *Social phobia: Diagnosis, assessment and treatment*. New York: Guilford Press.

Clark, H.H., & Carlson, T.B. (1981). Context for

comprehension. In J. Long & A. Baddeley (Eds.), *Attention and performance, Vol. IX.* Hillsdale, NJ: Lawrence Erlbaum Associates Inc.

Clark, H.H., & Krych, M.A. (2004). Speaking while monitoring addressees for understanding. *Journal of Memory and Language, 50,* 62–81.

Cleeremans, A., & Jiménez, L. (2002). Implicit learning and consciousness: A graded, dynamic perspective. In R.M. French & A. Cleeremans (Eds.), *Implicit learning and consciousness: An empirical, philosophical and computational consensus in the making.* Hove, UK: Psychology Press.

Clifton, C., Traxler, M.J., Mohamed, M.T., Williams, R.S., Morris, R.K., & Rayner, K. (2003). The use of thematic role information in parsing: Syntactic processing autonomy revisited. *Journal of Memory and Language, 49,* 317–334.

Cohen, N.J., & Squire, L.R. (1980). Preserved learning and retention of pattern- analyzing skill in amnesia using perceptual learning. *Cortex, 17,* 273–278.

Collette, F., & Van der Linden, M. (2002). Brain imaging of the central executive component of working memory. *Neuroscience & Biobehavioral Reviews, 26,* 105– 125.

Colman, A.M. (2001). *A dictionary of psychology.* Oxford: Oxford University Press.

Colom, R., Rebollo, I., Palacios, A., Juan-Espinosa, M., & Kyllonen, P.C. (2004). Working memory is (almost) perfectly predicted by *g. Intelligence, 32,* 277–296.

Coltheart, M. (2001). Assumptions and methods in cognitive neuropsychology. In B. Rapp, (Ed.), *Handbook of cognitive neuropsychology.* Philadelphia, PA: Psychology Press.

Coltheart, M., Curtis, B., Atkins, P., & Haller, M. (1993). Models of reading aloud: Dual-route and parallel-distributed-processing approaches. *Psychological Review, 100,* 589–608.

Coltheart, M., Rastle, K., Perry, C., Langdon, R., & Ziegler, J. (2001). The DRC model: A model of visual word recognition and reading aloud. *Psychological Review, 108,* 204–258.

Connine, C.M. (1990). Effects of sentence context and lexical knowledge in speech processing. In G.T.M. Altmann (Ed.), *Cognitive models of speech processing.* Cambridge, MA: MIT Press.

Connolly, T., & Reb, J. (2003). Omission bias in vaccination decisions: Where's the "omission"? Where's the "bias"? *Organizational Behavior and Human Decision Processes, 91,* 186–202.

Conway, A.R.A., Cowan, N., & Bunting, M.F. (2001). The cocktail party phenomenon revisited: The importance of working memory capacity. *Psychonomic Bulletin and Review, 8,* 331–335.

Conway, A.R.A., Kane, M.J., & Engle, R.W. (2003). Working memory capacity and its relation to general intelligence. *Trends in Cognitive Sciences, 7,* 547–552.

Conway, M.A. (1996). Autobiographical knowledge and autobiographical memories. In D.C. Rubin (Ed.), Remembering our past: Studies in autobiographical memory. *Memory, 11,* 217–224.

Conway, M.A., Anderson, S.J., Larsen, S.F., Donnelly, C.M., McDaniel, M.A., McClelland, A.G.R., & Rawles, R.E. (1994). The formation of flashbulb memories. *Memory & Cognition, 22,* 326–343.

Conway, M.A., & Pleydell-Pearce, C.W. (2000). The construction of autobiographical memories in the self-memory system. *Psychological Review, 107,* 261–288.

Conway, M.A., Pleydell-Pearce, C.W., & Whitecross, S.E. (2001). The neuroanatomy of autobiographical memory: A slow cortical potential study of autobiographical memory retrieval. *Journal of Memory and Language, 45,* 493–524.

Conway, M.A., Pleydell-Pearce, C.W., Whitecross, S.E., & Sharpe, H. (2003). Neuropsychological correlates of memory for experienced and imagined events. *Neuropsychologia, 41,* 334–340.

Conway, M.A., & Rubin, D.C. (1993). The structure of autobiographical memory. In A.F. Collins, S.E. Gathercole, M.A. Conway, & P.E. Morris (Eds.), *Theories of memory.* Hove, UK: Psychology Press.

Cook, A.E., & Myers, J.L. (2004). Processing discourse roles in scripted narratives: The influences of context and world knowledge. *Journal of Memory and Language, 50,* 268–288.

Cooney, J.W., & Gazzaniga, M.S. (2003). Neurological disorders and the structure of human consciousness. *Trends in Cognitive Sciences, 7,* 161–165.

Cooper, L.A., & Shepherd, R.N. (1973). Chronometric studies of the rotation of mental images. In W.G. Chase (Ed.), *Visual information processing*. New York: Academic Press.

Cooper, R., & Shallice, T. (1995). SOAR and the case for unified theories of cognition. *Cognition, 55,* 115–149.

Copeland, D.E., & Radvansky, G.A. (2004). Working memory and syllogistic reasoning. *Quarterly Journal of Experimental Psychology, 57A,* 1437–1457.

Corbetta, M., & Shulman, G.L. (2002). Control of goal-directed and stimulus-driven attention in the brain. *Nature Reviews Neuroscience, 3,* 201–215.

Coren, S., & Girgus, J.S. (1972). Visual spatial illusions: Many explanations. *Science, 179,* 503–504.

Corkin, S. (1968). Acquisition of motor skill after bilateral medial temporal-lobe excision. *Neuropsychologia, 6,* 255–265.

Cosmides, L., & Tooby, J. (1996). Are humans good intuitive statisticians after all? Rethinking some conclusions from the literature on judgment under uncertainty. *Cognition, 58,* 1–73.

Cowan, N. (2000). The magical number 4 in short-term memory: A reconsideration of mental storage capacity. *Behavioral and Brain Sciences, 24,* 87–185.

Cowey, A. (2004). Fact, artefact, and myth about blindsight. *Quarterly Journal of Experimental Psychology, 57A,* 577–609.

Cowley, J.J., Johnson, A.L., & Brooksbank, B.W.L. (1977). The effect of two odorous compounds on performance in an assessment-of-people test. *Psychoneuroendocrinology, 2,* 159–172.

Creem, S.H., & Proffitt, D.R. (2001). Grasping objects by their handles: A necessary interaction between cognition and action. *Journal of Experimental Psychology: Human Perception and Performance, 27,* 218–228.

Crystal, D. (1997). *A dictionary of linguistics and phonetics* (4th ed.). Cambridge, MA: Blackwell.

Cutler, A., & Butterfield, S. (1992). Rhythmic cues to speech segmentation: Evidence from juncture misperception. *Journal of Memory and Language, 31,* 218–236.

Cutler, A., & Clifton, C. (1999). Comprehending spoken language: A blueprint of the listener. In C.M. Brown & P. Hagoort (Eds.), *The neurocognition of language.* Oxford: Oxford University Press.

Cutler, A., Mehler, J., Norris, D., & Segui, J. (1987). Phoneme identification and the lexicon. *Cognitive Psychology, 24,* 381–410.

Dalgleish, T., & Power, M.J. (1999). *Handbook of cognition and emotion.* Chichester, UK: Wiley.

Daneman, M., & Carpenter, P.A. (1980). Individual differences in working memory and reading. *Journal of Verbal Learning and Verbal Behavior, 19,* 450–466.

Darrah, C., English-Lueck, J.A., & Freeman, J. (2001). Multitasking creates health problems. From http://www.applesforhealth.com/Healthy-Business/multihealth3.html

Davidson, D. (1994). Recognition and recall of irrelevant and interruptive atypical actions in script-based stories. *Journal of Memory and Language, 33,* 757–775.

Davis, M.H., Marslen-Wilson, W.D., & Gaskell, M.G. (2002). Leading up the lexical garden path: Segmentation and ambiguity in spoken word recognition. *Journal of Experimental Psychology: Perception and Performance, 28,* 218–244.

De Bleser, R. (1988). Localization of aphasia: Science or fiction? In G. Denese, C. Semenza, & P. Bisiacchi (Eds.), *Perspectives on cognitive neuropsychology.* Hove, UK: Psychology Press.

De Corte, E. (2003). Transfer as the productive use of acquired knowledge, skills, and motivation. *Current Directions in Psychological Science, 12,* 142–146.

de Gelder, B., Vroemen, J., & Pourtois, G. (2001). Covert affective cognition and affective blindsight. In B. de Gelder, E. de Haan, & C.A. Heywood (Eds.), *Out of mind.* Oxford: Oxford University Press.

De Groot, A.D. (1965). *Thought and choice in chess.* The Hague: Mouton.

Debner, J.A., & Jacoby, L.L. (1994). Unconscious perception: Attention, awareness and control. *Journal of Experimental Psychology: Learning, Memory, and Cognition, 20,* 304–317.

Dehaene, S., & Changeux, J.-P. (2005). Ongoing spontaneous activity controls access to consciousness: A neural model for inattentional blindness. *Plos Biol., 3,* e141.

Dehaene, S., & Naccache, L. (2001). Towards a

cognitive neuroscience of consciousness: Basic evidence and a workspace framework. *Cognition*, *79*, 1–37.

Dehaene, S., Naccache, L., Cohen, L., Le Bihan, D., Mangin, J., Poline, J. et al. (2001). Cerebral mechanisms of word masking and unconscious repetition priming. *Nature Neuroscience*, *4*, 752–758.

Dehaene, S., Naccache, L., Le Cle'H, G., Koechlin, E., Mueller, M., Dehaene-Lambertz, G., van de Moortele, P.-F., & Le Bihan, D. (1998). Imaging unconscious semantic priming. *Nature*, *395*, 597–600.

Delaney, P.F., Ericsson, K.A., & Knowles, M.E. (2004). Immediate and sustained effects of planning in a problem-solving task. *Journal of Experimental Psychology: Learning, Memory, and Cognition*, *30*, 1219–1234.

Dell, G.S. (1986). A spreading-activation theory of retrieval in sentence production. *Psychological Review*, *93*, 283–321.

Dell, G.S., & O'Seaghdha, P.G. (1991). Mediated and convergent lexical priming in language production: A comment on Levelt et al. (1991). *Psychological Review*, *98*, 604–614.

DeLucia, P.R., & Hochberg, J. (1991). Geometrical illusions in solid objects under ordinary viewing conditions. *Perception & Psychophysics*, *50*, 547–554.

D'Esposito, M., Detre, J.A., Alsop, D.C., Shin, R.K., Atlas, S., & Grossman, M. (1995). The neural basis of the central executive of working memory. *Nature*, *378*, 279–281.

Dick, F., Bates, E., Wulfeck, B., Utman, J.A., Dronkers, N., & Gernsbacher, M.A. (2001). Language deficits, localization, and grammar: Evidence for a distributive model of language breakdown in aphasic patients and neurologically intact individuals. *Psychological Review*, *108*, 759–788.

Diehl, R.L., Lotto, A.J., & Holt, L.L. (2004). Speech perception. *Annual Review of Psychology*, *55*, 149–179.

Dijkerman, H.C., Milner, A.D., & Carey, D.F. (1998). Grasping spatial relationships: Failure to demonstrate allocentric visual coding in a patient with visual form agnosia. *Consciousness and Cognition*, *7*, 424–437.

Dixon, N.F. (1981). *Preconscious processing*. New York: Wiley.

Dixon, N.F. (2004). Subliminal perception. In R.L. Gregory (Ed.), *The Oxford companion to the mind*. Oxford: Oxford University Press.

Dodds, R.A., Ward, T.B., & Smith, S.M. (2004). A review of the experimental literature on incubation in problem solving and creativity. In M.A. Runco (Ed.), *Creativity research handbook, Vol. 3*. Cresskill, NJ: Hampton Press.

Dosher, B.A., & Corbett, A.T. (1982). Instrument inferences and verb schemata. *Memory & Cognition*, *10*, 531–539.

Driver, J. (2001). A selective review of selective attention research from the past century. *British Journal of Psychology*, *92*, 53–78.

Driver, J., & Spence, C. (1998). Attention and the cross-modal construction of space. *Trends in Cognitive Sciences*, *2*, 254–262.

Driver, J., & Vuilleumier, P. (2001). Perceptual awareness and its loss in unilateral neglect and extinction. *Cognition*, *79*, 39–88.

Duff, S.C., & Logie, R.H. (2001). Processing and storage in working memory span. *Quarterly Journal of Experimental Psychology*, *54A*, 31–48.

Duncan, J., Bundesen, C., Olson, A., Humphreys, G., Chavda, S., & Shibuya, H. (1999). Systematic analysis of deficits in visual attention. *Journal of Experimental Psychology: General*, *128*, 450–478.

Duncker, K. (1945). On problem solving. *Psychological Monographs*, *58* (Whole No. 270).

Eakin, D.K., Schreiber, T.A., & Sergent-Marshall, S. (2003). Misinformation effects in eyewitness memory: The presence and absence of memory impairment as a function of warning and misinformation accessibility. *Journal of Experimental Psychology: Learning, Memory, and Cognition*, *29*, 813–825.

Ebbinghaus, H. (1885/1913). *Über das Gedächtnis*. Leipzig: Dunker (H. Ruyer & C.E. Bussenius, Trans. New York: Teacher College, Columbus University).

Eich, E., Macaulay, D., & Lam, R.W. (1997). Mania, depression, and mood-dependent memory. *Cognition and Emotion*, *11*, 607–618.

Eichenbaum, H. (2001). The hippocampus and declarative memory: Cognitive mechanisms and neural codes. *Behavioural Brain Research*, *127*, 199–207.

Eimer, M., & Schröger, E. (1998). ERP effects of intermodal attention and cross-modal links in spatial attention. *Psychophysiology*, *35*, 317–328.

Elder, J.H., & Goldberg, R.M. (2002). Ecological statistics of Gestalt laws for the perceptual organisation of contours. *Journal of Vision*, *2*, 324–353.

Ellis, A.W., Miller, D., & Sin, G. (1983). Wernicke's aphasia and normal language processing: A case study in cognitive neuropsychology. *Cognition*, *15*, 111–144.

Ellis, A.W., & Young, A.W. (1988). *Human cognitive neuropsychology*. Hove, UK: Psychology Press.

Emilien, G., Durlach, C., Antoniadis, E., van der Linden, M., & Maloteaux, J.-M. (2004). *Memory: Neuropsychological, imaging, and psychopharmacological perspectives*. Hove, UK: Psychology Press.

Engle, R.W., Tuholski, S.W., Laughlin, J.E., & Conway, A.R.A. (1999). Working memory, short-term memory, and general fluid intelligence: A latent-variable approach. *Journal of Experimental Psychology: General*, *128*, 309–331.

Erdelyi, M.H. (1974). A new look at the New Look: Perceptual defense and vigilance. *Psychological Review*, *81*, 1–25.

Erdelyi, M.H. (2001). Defense processes can be conscious or unconscious. *American Psychologist*, *56*, 761–762.

Erickson, T.A., & Mattson, M.E. (1981). From words to meaning: A semantic illusion. *Journal of Verbal Learning and Verbal Behavior*, *20*, 540–552.

Ericsson, K.A., & Chase, W.G. (1982). Exceptional memory. *American Scientist*, *70*, 607–615.

Ericsson, K.A., & Kintsch, W. (1995). Long-term working memory. *Psychological Review*, *102*, 211–245.

Ericsson, K.A., Krampe, R.T., & Tesch-Römer, C. (1993). The role of deliberate practice in the acquisition of expert performance. *Psychological Review*, *100*, 363–406.

Ericsson, K.A., & Lehmann, A.C. (1996). Expert and exceptional performance: Evidence on maximal adaptations to task constraints. *Annual Review of Psychology*, *47*, 273–305.

Eriksen, C.W., & St. James, J.D. (1986). Visual attention within and around the field of focal attention: A zoom lens model. *Perception & Psychophysics*, *40*, 225–240.

Evans, J.St.B.T. (1993). Bias and rationality. In K.I. Manktelow & D.E. Over (Eds.), *Rationality: Psychological and philosophical perspectives*. London: Routledge.

Evans, J.St.B.T. (2002). Logic and human reasoning: An assessment of the deduction paradigm. *Psychological Bulletin*, *128*, 978–996.

Evans, J.St.B.T. (2003). In two minds: Dual-process accounts of reasoning. *Trends in Cognitive Sciences*, *7*, 454–459.

Evans, J.St.B.T., Barston, J.L., & Pollard, P. (1983). On the conflict between logic and belief in syllogistic reasoning. *Memory and Cognition*, *11*, 295–306.

Evans, J.St.B.T., & Over, D.E. (1996). Rationality in the selection task: Epistemic utility versus uncertainty reduction. *Psychological Review*, *103*, 356–363.

Evans, J.St.B.T., & Over, D.E. (1997). Rationality in reasoning: The problem of deductive competence. *Current Psychology of Cognition*, *16*, 3–38.

Eysenck, M.W. (1979). Depth, elaboration, and distinctiveness. In L.S. Cermak & F.I.M. Craik (Eds.), *Levels of processing in human memory*. Hillsdale, NJ: Lawrence Erlbaum Associates Inc.

Eysenck, M.W. (1982). *Attention and arousal: Cognition and performance*. Berlin: Springer.

Eysenck, M.W. (1984). *A handbook of cognitive psychology*. London: Lawrence Erlbaum Associates Ltd.

Eysenck, M.W. (1997). *Anxiety and cognition: A unified theory*. Hove, UK: Psychology Press.

Eysenck, M.W. (2004). *Psychology: An international perspective*. Hove, UK: Psychology Press.

Eysenck, M.W., & Keane, M.T. (2005). *Cognitive psychology: A student's handbook*. Hove, UK: Psychology Press.

Eysenck, M.W., Macleod, C., & Mathews, A. (1987). Cognitive functioning and anxiety. *Psychological Research*, *49*, 189–195.

Eysenck, M.W., Mogg, K., May, J., Richards, A., & Mathews, A. (1991). Bias in interpretation of ambiguous sentences related to threat in anxiety. *Journal of Abnormal Psychology*, *100*, 144–150.

Farah, M.J. (1990). *Visual agnosia: Disorders of*

object recognition and what they tell us about normal vision. Cambridge, MA: MIT Press.

Farah, M.J. (1994). Specialization within visual object recognition: Clues from prosopagnosia and alexia. In M.J. Farah & G. Ratcliff (Eds.), *The neuropsychology of high-level vision: Collected tutorial essays.* Hillsdale, NJ: Lawrence Erlbaum Associates Inc.

Farah, M.J. (1999). Relations among the agnosias. In G.W. Humphreys (Ed.), *Case studies in the neuropsychology of vision.* Hove, UK: Psychology Press.

Farah, M.J. (2001). Consciousness. In B. Rapp (Ed.), *The handbook of cognitive neuropsychology.* Hove, UK: Psychology Press.

Farah, M.J., & Aguirre, G.K. (1999). Imaging visual recognition: PET and fMRI studies of the functional anatomy of human visual recognition. *Trends in Cognitive Sciences, 3,* 179–186.

Feldman, J. (2003). The simplicity principle in human concept learning. *Current Directions in Psychological Science, 12,* 227–232.

Fernández-Duque, D., & Thornton, I.M. (2000). Change detection without awareness: Do explicit reports underestimate the representation of change in the visual system? *Visual Cognition, 7,* 323–344.

Ferreira, F. (2003). The misinterpretation of non-canonical sentences. *Cognitive Psychology, 47,* 164–203.

Ferreira, F., & Clifton, C. (1986). The independence of syntactic processing. *Journal of Memory and Language, 25,* 348–368.

Ferreira, F., & Swets, B. (2002). How incremental is language production? Evidence from the production of utterances requiring the computation of arithmetic sums. *Journal of Memory and Language, 46,* 57–84.

Fery, P., & Morais, J. (2003). A case study of visual agnosia without perceptual processing or structural descriptions impairment. *Cognitive Neuropsychology, 20,* 595–618.

ffytche, D.H., Howard, R.J., Brammer, M.J., David, A., Woodruff, P., & Williams, S. (1998). The anatomy of conscious vision: An fMRI study of visual hallucinations. *Nature Neuroscience, 1,* 738–742.

Fiedler, K. (1988). The dependence of the conjunction fallacy on subtle linguistic factors. *Psychological Research, 50,* 123–129.

Fiedler, K., Brinkmann, B., Betsch, T., & Wild, B. (2000). A sampling approach to biases in conditional probability judgements: Beyond base-rate neglect and statistical format. *Journal of Experimental Psychology: General, 129,* 1–20.

Fink, B., & Penton-Voak, I. (2002). Evolutionary psychology of facial attractiveness. *Current Directions in Psychological Science, 11,* 154–158.

Finke, R.A. (1980). Levels of equivalence in imagery and perception. *Psychological Review, 87,* 113–132.

Finke, R.A., & Kosslyn, S.M. (1980). Mental imagery acuity in the peripheral visual field. *Journal of Experimental Psychology: Human Perception and Performance, 6,* 126–139.

Fisher, R.P. (1999). Probing knowledge structures. In D. Gopher & A. Koriat (Eds.), *Attention and performance XVII: Cognitive regulation of performance: Interaction of theory and application.* Cambridge, MA: MIT Press.

Fisher, R.P., & Geiselman, R.E. (1992). *Memory-enhancing techniques for investigative interviewing: The cognitive interview.* Springfield, IL: C.C. Thomas.

Fisher, R.P., Geiselman, R.E., & Amador, M. (1990). A field test of the cognitive interview: Enhancing the recollections of actual victims and witnesses of crime. *Journal of Applied Psychology, 74,* 722–727.

Fisher, R.P., Geiselman, R.E., Raymond, D.S., Jurkevich, L.M., & Warhaftig, M.L. (1987). Enhancing enhanced eyewitness memory: Refining the cognitive interview. *Journal of Police Science and Administration, 15,* 291–297.

Fitzgerald, J.M. (1988). Vivid memories and the reminiscence phenomenon: The role of a self narrative. *Human Development, 31,* 261–273.

Fivush, R., & Buckner, J.P. (2003). Constructing gender and identity through autobiographical narratives. In R. Fivush & C.A. Haden (Eds.), *Autobiographical memory and the construction of a narrative self: Developmental and cultural perspectives.* Mahwah, NJ: Lawrence Erlbaum Associates Inc.

Fivush, R., & Nelson, K. (2004). Culture and language in the emergence of autobiographical memory. *Psychological Science, 15,* 573–577.

Floro, M.S. (1999). Whose work and whose

leisure? Time use and overlapping activities of men and women. *The Gender Newsletter, 5,* 1–2.

Flowerdew, J., & Tauroza, S. (1995). The effect of discourse markers on second language lecture comprehension. *Studies in Second Language Acquisition, 17,* 455–458.

Fodor, J. (2000). *The mind doesn't work that way: The scope and limits of computational psychology.* Cambridge, MA: MIT Press.

Ford, M. (1995). Two modes of mental representation and problem solution in syllogistic reasoning. *Cognition, 54,* 1–71.

Forgas, J.P. (1999). Network theories and beyond. In T. Dalgleish & M. Power (Eds.), *The handbook of cognition and emotion.* Chichester, UK: Wiley.

Foster, D.H., & Gilson, S.J. (2002). Recognizing novel three-dimensional objects by summing signals from parts and views. *Proceedings of the Royal Society of London B, 269,* 1939–1947.

Fox Tree, J.E. (2000). Co-ordinating spontaneous talk. In L. Wheeldon (Ed.), *Aspects of language production.* Hove, UK: Psychology Press.

Frank, A., & d'Hondt, W. (1979). Aptitudes et apprentissage du jeu d'échecs au Zaire. *Psychopathologie Africaine, 15,* 81–98.

Franklin, S., Turner, J., Ralph, M.A.L., Morris, J., & Bailey, P.J. (1996). A distinctive case of word meaning deafness? *Cognitive Neuropsychology, 13,* 1139–1162.

Frauenfelder, U.H., Segui, J., & Dijkstra, T. (1990). Lexical effects in phonemic processing: Facilitatory or inhibitory? *Journal of Experimental Psychology: Human Perception and Performance, 16,* 77–91.

Frazier, L., & Rayner, K. (1982). Making and correcting errors in the analysis of structurally ambiguous sentences. *Cognitive Psychology, 14,* 178–210.

French, L. (2005). The death of yesterday. *The Observer Magazine,* January 23, 2005.

French, R.M., & Cleeremans, A. (2002). Introduction. In R.M. French & A. Cleeremans (Eds.), *Implicit learning and consciousness: An empirical, philosophical and computational consensus in the making.* Hove, UK: Psychology Press.

Frensch, P.A., & Rünger, D. (2003). Implicit learning. *Current Directions in Psychological Science, 12,* 13–18.

Freud, S. (1901/1975). *The psychopathology of everyday life* (A. Tyson, Trans). Harmondsworth, UK: Penguin. (Original work published 1901).

Freud, S. (1915/1963). Repression. In J. Strachey (Ed.), *Standard edition of the collected works of Sigmund Freud, Vol. 14.* London: Hogarth Press. (Original work published 1915).

Freud, S. (1925/1961). A note upon the "mystic writing pad." In J. Strachey (Ed.), *Standard edition of the collected works of Sigmund Freud, Vol. 19.* London: Hogarth Press. (Original work published 1925).

Frisch, D., & Jones, S.K. (1993). Assessing the accuracy of decisions. *Theory and Psychology, 3,* 115–135.

Frith, C.D., Perry, R., & Lumer, E. (1999). The neural correlates of conscious experience: An experimental framework. *Trends in Cognitive Science, 3,* 105–114.

Frost, R. (1998). Toward a strong phonological theory of visual word recognition: True issues and false trails. *Psychological Bulletin, 123,* 71–99.

Funnell, E. (1983). Phonological processes in reading: New evidence from acquired dyslexia. *British Journal of Psychology, 74,* 159–180.

Gabrieli, J.D.E., Cohen, N.J., & Corkin, S. (1988). The impaired learning of semantic knowledge following bilateral medial temporal-lobe resection. *Brain, 7,* 157–177.

Galton, F. (1880). Statistics of mental imagery. *Mind, 5,* 301–318.

Ganong, W.F. (1980). Phonetic categorisation in auditory word perception. *Journal of Experimental Psychology: Human Perception and Performance, 6,* 110–125.

Gardner, H. (1977). *The shattered mind.* Hove, UK: Psychology Press.

Gardner, H. (1985). *The mind's new science.* New York: Basic Books.

Garnham, A. (2004). Language comprehension. In K. Lamberts & R. Goldstone (Eds.), *Handbook of cognition.* London: Sage.

Garnham, A., Oakhill, J., & Johnson-Laird, P.N. (1982). Referential continuity and the coherence of discourse. *Cognition, 11,* 29–46.

Garrett, M.F. (1980). Levels of processing in sentence production. In B. Butterworth (Ed.),

Language production: Vol. 1. Speech and talk. San Diego, CA: Academic Press.

Gauld, A., & Stephenson, G.M. (1967). Some experiments relating to Bartlett's theory of remembering. *British Journal of Psychology*, *58*, 39–50.

Gauthier, I., Behrmann, M., & Tarr, M.J. (1999). Can face recognition really be dissociated from object recognition? *Journal of Cognitive Neuroscience*, *11*, 349–370.

Gauthier, I., Curran, T., Curby, K.M., & Collins, D. (2003). Perceptual interference supports a non-modular account of face processing. *Nature Neuroscience*, *6*, 428–432.

Gauthier, I., Skudlarski, P., Gore, J.C., & Anderson, A.W. (2000). Expertise for cars and birds recruits brain areas involved in face recognition. *Nature Neuroscience*, *3*, 191–197.

Gauthier, I., & Tarr, M.J. (2002). Unraveling mechanisms for expert object recognition: Bridging brain activity and behavior. *Journal of Experimental Psychology: Human Perception and Performance*, *28*, 431–446.

Gauthier, I., Tarr, M.J., Anderson, A.W., Skudlarski, P., & Gore, J.C. (1999). Activation of the fusiform "face area" increases with expertise in recognizing novel objects. *Nature Neuroscience*, *2*, 568–573.

Gazzaniga, M.S. (1992). *Nature's mind*. London: Basic Books.

Gazzaniga, M.S. (2000). Cerebral specialization and interhemispheric communication: Does the corpus callosum enable the human condition? *Brain*, *123*, 1293–1328.

Gazzaniga, M.S., Ivry, R.B, & Mangun, G.R. (1998). *Cognitive neuroscience: The biology of the mind*. New York: Norton.

Gazzaniga, M.S., Ivry, R.B., & Mangun, G.R. (2002). *Cognitive neuroscience: The biology of the mind* (2nd ed.). New York: Norton.

Gazzaniga, M.S., & LeDoux, J.E. (1978). *The integrated mind*. New York: Plenum Press.

Geis, M., & Zwicky, A.M. (1971). On invited inferences. *Linguistic Inquiry*, *2*, 561– 566.

Geiselman, R.E., & Fisher, R.P. (1997). Ten years of cognitive interviewing. In D.G. Payne & F.G. Conrad (Eds.), *Intersections in basic and applied memory research*. Mahwah, NJ: Lawrence Erlbaum Associates Inc.

Geiselman, R.E., Fisher, R.P., MacKinnon, D.P., & Holland, H.L. (1985). Eyewitness memory enhancement in police interview: Cognitive retrieval mnemonics versus hypnosis. *Journal of Applied Psychology*, *70*, 401–412.

Geisler, W.S., Perry, J.S., Super, B.J., & Gallogly, D.P. (2001). Edge co-occurrence in natural images predicts contour grouping performance. *Vision Research*, *41*, 711–724.

Georgopoulos, A.P. (1997). Voluntary movement: Computational principles and neural mechanisms. In M.D. Rugg (Ed.), *Cognitive neuroscience*. Hove, UK: Psychology Press.

Gibson, J.J. (1950). *The perception of the visual world*. Boston, MA: Houghton Mifflin.

Gibson, J.J. (1979). *The ecological approach to visual perception*. Boston, MA: Houghton Mifflin.

Gick, M.L., & Holyoak, K.J. (1980). Analogical problem solving. *Cognitive Psychology*, *12*, 306–355.

Giersch, A., Humphreys, G., Boucart, M., & Kovacs, I. (2000). The computation of contours in visual agnosia: Evidence for early computation prior to shape binding and figure–ground coding. *Cognitive Neuropsychology*, *17*, 731–759.

Gigerenzer, G. (1996). On narrow norms and vague heuristics: A reply to Kahneman and Tversky (1996). *Psychological Review*, *103*, 592–596.

Gigerenzer, G., & Hoffrage, U. (1999). Overcoming difficulties in Bayesian reasoning: A reply to Lewis and Keren (1999) and Mellers and McGraw (1999). *Psychological Review*, *106*, 425–430.

Gigerenzer, G., & Selten, R. (2001). *Bounded rationality: The adaptive toolbox*. Cambridge, MA: MIT Press.

Gigerenzer, G., Todd, P.N., & the ABC Research Group (1999). *Simple heuristics that make us smart*. Oxford: Oxford University Press.

Gilboa, A. (2004). Autobiographical and episodic memory – one and the same? Evidence from prefrontal activation in neuroimaging studies. *Neuropsychologia*, *42*, 1336–1349.

Gilligan, S.G., & Bower, G.H. (1984). Cognitive consequences of emotional arousal. In C. Izard, J. Kagen, & R. Zajonc (Eds.), *Emotions, cognition, and behavior*. New York: Cambridge University Press.

Gilovich, T., Griffin, D., & Kahneman, D. (2002). *Heuristics and biases: The psychology of intuitive judgment*. Cambridge: Cambridge University Press.

Giora, R. (1997). Understanding figurative and literal language: The graded salience hypothesis. *Cognitive Linguistics, 7*, 183–206.

Giora, R. (2002). Literal vs. figurative language: Different or equal? *Journal of Pragmatics, 34*, 487–506.

Giora, R. (2003). *On our mind: Salience, context and figurative language*. New York: Oxford University Press.

Giora, R., & Fein, O. (1999). On understanding familiar and less-familiar figurative language. *Journal of Pragmatics, 31*, 1601–1618.

Glaser, W.R. (1992). Picture naming. *Cognition, 42*, 61–105.

Glover, S. (2003). Optic ataxia as a deficit specific to the on-line control of action. *Neuroscience and Biobehavioral Reviews, 27*, 447–456.

Glover, S. (2004). Separate visual representations in the planning and control of action. *Behavioral and Brain Sciences, 27*, 3–78.

Glover, S., & Dixon, P. (2001). Dynamic illusion effects in a reaching task: Evidence for separate visual representations in the planning and control of action. *Behavioral and Brain Sciences, 27*, 3–78.

Glover, S., & Dixon, P. (2002). Dynamic effects of the Ebbinghaus illusion in grasping: Support for a planning–control model of action. *Perception and Psychophysics, 64*, 266–278.

Glucksberg, S. (2003). The psycholinguistics of metaphor. *Trends in Cognitive Sciences, 7*, 92–96.

Glushko, R.J. (1979). The organization and activation of orthographic knowledge in reading aloud. *Journal of Experimental Psychology: Human Perception and Performance, 5*, 674–691.

Gobet, F., & Clarkson, G. (2004). Chunks in expert memory: Evidence for the magical number four . . . or is it two? *Memory, 12*, 732–747.

Gobet, F., & Simon, H.A. (1996a). Templates in chess memory: A mechanism for recalling several boards. *Cognitive Psychology, 31*, 1–40.

Gobet, F., & Simon, H.A. (1999b). Recall of rapidly presented random chess positions is a function of skill. *Psychonomic Bulletin & Review, 3*, 159–163.

Gobet, F., Voogt, A. de, & Retschitzki, J. (2004). *Moves in mind: The psychology of board games*. Hove, UK: Psychology Press.

Gobet, F., & Waters, A.J. (2003). The role of constraints in expert memory. *Journal of Experimental Psychology: Learning, Memory, and Cognition, 29*, 1082–1094.

Godden, D.R., & Baddeley, A.D. (1975). Context-dependent memory in two natural environments: On land and under water. *British Journal of Psychology, 66*, 325–331.

Godden, D.R., & Baddeley, A.D. (1980). When does context influence recognition memory? *British Journal of Psychology, 71*, 99–104.

Goldenburg, G., Müllbacher, W., & Nowak, A. (1995). Imagery without perception: A case study of anosognosia for cortical blindness. *Neuropsychologia, 33*, 1373–1382.

Goldinger, S.D., & Azuma, T. (2003). Puzzle-solving science: The quixotic quest for units in speech perception. *Journal of Phonetics, 31*, 305–320.

Goldstein, D.G., & Gigerenzer, G. (1999). The recognition heuristic: How ignorance makes us smart. In G. Gigerenzer, P.M. Todd, & the ABC Research Group. *Simple heuristics that make us smart*. Oxfofd: Oxford University Press.

Goldstein, D.G., & Gigerenzer, G. (2002). Models of ecological rationality: The recognition heuristic. *Psychological Review, 109*, 75–90.

Goldstein, E.B. (1996). *Sensation and perception* (4th ed.). New York: Brooks/Cole.

Gooding, P.A., Mayes, A.R., & van Eijk, R. (2000). A meta-analysis of indirect memory tests for novel material in organic amnesia. *Neuropsychologia, 38*, 666–676.

Gottfredson, L.S. (1997). Why g matters? The complexities of everyday life. *Intelligence, 24*, 79–132.

Graesser, A.C., Millis, K.K., & Zwaan, R.A. (1997). Discourse comprehension. *Annual Review of Psychology, 48*, 163–189.

Graesser, A.C., Singer, M., & Trabasso, T. (1994). Constructing inferences during narrative text comprehension. *Psychological Review, 101*, 371–395.

Graf, P., & Schacter, D.L. (1985). Implicit and explicit memory for new associations in normal and amnesic subjects. *Journal of Experimental*

Psychology: Learning, Memory, & Cognition, 11, 501–518.

Graf, P., Squire, L.R., & Mandler, G. (1984). The information that amnesic patients do not forget. *Journal of Experimental Psychology: Learning, Memory, & Cognition, 10*, 164–178.

Grafton, S., Hazeltine, E., & Ivry, R. (1995). Functional mapping of sequence learning in normal humans. *Journal of Cognitive Neuroscience, 7*, 497–510.

Grammer, K., & Thornhill, R. (1994). Human (homo sapiens) facial attractiveness and sexual selection: The role of symmetry and averageness. *Journal of Comparative Psychology, 108*, 233–242.

Greeno, J.G. (1974). Hobbits and orcs: Acquisition of a sequential concept. *Cognitive Psychology, 6*, 270–292.

Greenwald, A.G. (2003). On doing two things at once: III. Confirmation of perfect timesharing when simultaneous tasks are ideomotor compatible. *Journal of Experimental Psychology: Human Perception and Performance, 29*, 859–868.

Greenwald, A.G. (2004). On doing two things at once: IV. Necessary and sufficient conditions: Rejoinder to Lien, Proctor, and Ruthruff (2003). *Journal of Experimental Psychology: Human Perception and Performance, 30*, 632–636.

Gregory, R.L. (1970). *The intelligent eye*. New York: McGraw-Hill.

Gregory, R.L. (1973). The confounded eye. In R.L. Gregory & E.H. Gombrich (Eds.), *Illusion in nature and art*. London: Duckworth.

Gregory, R.L. (2004). *Oxford companion to the mind*. Oxford: Oxford University Press.

Griffin, D., & Buehler, R. (1999). Frequency, probability, and prediction: Easy solutions to cognitive illusions? *Cognitive Psychology, 38*, 48–78.

Griffin, Z.M. (2001). Gaze durations during speech reflect word selection and phonological encoding. *Cognition, 82*, B1–B14.

Griggs, R.A., & Cox, J.R. (1982). The elusive thematic-materials effect in Wason's selection task. *British Journal of Psychology, 73*, 407–420.

Groeger, J.A. (1984). Evidence of unconscious semantic processing from a forced-error situation. *British Journal of Psychology, 75*, 305–314.

Groeger, J.A. (1997). *Memory and remembering*. Harlow, UK: Addison Wesley Longman.

Guasti, M.T., & Luzzatti, C. (2002). Syntactic breakdown and recovery of clausal structure in agrammatism. *Brain and Cognition, 48*, 385–391.

Haart, E.G.O.-de, Carey, D.P., & Milne, A.B. (1999). More thoughts on perceiving and grasping the Müller-Lyer illusion. *Neuropsychologia, 37*, 1437–1444.

Haber, R.N., & Levin, C.A. (2001). The independence of size perception and distance perception. *Perception & Psychophysics, 63*, 1140–1152.

Haist, F., Gore, J.B., & Mao, H. (2001). Consolidation of human memory over decades revealed by functional magnetic resonance imaging. *Nature Neuroscience, 4*, 1139–1145.

Hamann, S.B., & Squire, L.R. (1997). Intact perceptual memory in the absence of conscious memory. *Behavioral Neuroscience, 111*, 850–854.

Hamilton, E. (1961). *The collected dialogues*. New York: Bollingen Foundation.

Hampton, J.A. (1981). An investigation of the nature of abstract concepts. *Memory & Cognition, 9*, 149–156.

Han, J.J., Leichtman, M.D., & Wang, Q. (1998). Autobiographical memory in Korean, Chinese, and American children. *Developmental Psychology, 34*, 701–713.

Hanley, J.R., & McDonnell, V. (1997). Are reading and spelling phonologically mediated? Evidence from a patient with a speech production impairment. *Cognitive Neuropsychology, 14*, 3–33.

Hanna, J.E., Tanenhaus, M.K., & Trueswell, J.C. (2003). The effects of common ground and perspective on domains of referential interpretation. *Journal of Memory and Language, 49*, 43–61.

Hardman, D., & Harries, C. (2002). How rational are we? *The Psychologist, 15*, 76–79.

Hardman, D., & Macchi, L. (2003). *Thinking: Psychological perspectives on reasoning, judgment and decision making*. Chichester, UK: Wiley.

Hardy, G.R., & Legge, D. (1968). Cross-modal

induction of changes in sensory thresholds. *Quarterly Journal of Experimental Psychology, 20,* 20–29.

Harley, K., & Reese, E. (1999). Origins of autobiographical memory. *Developmental Psychology, 35,* 1338–1348.

Harley, T.A. (2001). *The psychology of language: From data to theory* (2nd. ed.). Hove, UK: Psychology Press.

Harley, T.A. (2004). Does cognitive neuropsychology have a future? *Cognitive Neuropsychology, 21,* 3–16.

Harvey, L.O. (1986). Visual memory: What is remembered? In F. Klix & H. Hagendorf (Eds.), *Human memory and cognitive capabilities.* The Hague: Elsevier.

Hastie, R. (2001). Problems for judgment and decision making. *Annual Review of Psychology, 52,* 653–683.

Hatano, G., & Inagaki, K. (1986). Two courses of expertise. In H. Stevenson, H. Azuma, & K. Hatuka (Eds.), *Child development in Japan.* San Francisco, CA: Freeman.

Hayward, W.G. (2003). After the viewpoint debate: Where next in object recognition? *Trends in Cognitive Sciences, 7,* 425–427.

Hayward, W.G., & Tarr, M.J. (2005). Visual perception II: High-level vision. In K. Lamberts & R.L. Goldstone (Eds.), *The handbook of cognition.* London: Sage.

Healy, A.F., & Proctor, R.W. (2003). *Handbook of psychology: Experimental psychology, Vol. 4.* New York: Wiley & Sons.

Heath, W.P., & Erickson, J.R. (1998). Memory for central and peripheral actions and props after varied post-event presentation. *Legal and Criminal Psychology, 3,* 321–346.

Hegarty, M., Shah, P., & Miyake, A. (2000). Constraints on using the dual-task methodology to specify the degree of central executive involvement in cognitive tasks. *Memory & Cognition, 28,* 376–385.

Henderson, J.J.A., & Anglin, J.M. (2003). Facial attractiveness predicts longevity. *Evolution and Human Behavior, 24,* 351–356.

Henderson, J.M., & Hollingworth, A. (2003). Global transsaccadic change blindness during scene perception. *Psychological Science, 14,* 493–497.

Henke, K., Schweinberger, S.R., Grigo, A., Klos, T.,

& Sommer, W. (1998). Specificity of face recognition: Recognition of exemplars of non-face objects in prosopagnosia. *Cortex, 34,* 289–296.

Hertwig, R., Barron, G., Weber, E.U., & Erev, I. (2004). Decisions from experience and the effect of rare events in risky choice. *Psychological Science, 15,* 534–539.

Hertwig, R., & Todd, P.M. (2003). More is not always better: The benefits of cognitive limits. In D. Hardman & L. Macchi (Eds.), *Thinking: Psychological perspectives on reasoning, judgment and decision making.* Chichester, UK: Wiley.

Heuer, H., & Schmidtke, V. (1996). Secondary-task effects on sequence learning. *Psychological Research, 59,* 119–133.

Hewstone, M., Benn, W., & Wilson, A. (1988). Bias in the use of base rates: Racial prejudice in decision making. *European Journal of Psychology, 18,* 161–176.

Hill, H., & Bruce, V. (1993). Independent effects of lighting, orientation and stereopsis on the hollow face illusion. *Perception, 22,* 887–897.

Holender, D., & Duscherer, K. (2004). Unconscious perception: The need for a paradigm shift. *Perception & Psychophysics, 66,* 872–881.

Hollingworth, A. (2004). Constructing visual representations of natural scenes: The roles of short- and long-term visual memory. *Journal of Experimental Psychology: Human Perception and Performance, 30,* 519–537.

Hollingworth, A., & Henderson, J.M. (2002). Accurate visual memory for previously attended objects in natural scenes. *Journal of Experimental Psychology: Human Perception and Performance, 28,* 113–136.

Hollingworth, A., Williams, C.C., & Henderson, J.M. (2001). To see and remember: Visually specific information is retained in memory from previously attended objects in natural scenes. *Psychonomic Bulletin & Review, 8,* 761–768.

Holmes, V.M. (1988). Hesitations and sentence planning. *Language and Cognitive Processes, 3,* 323–361.

Holtgraves, T.M. (2002). *Language as social action: Social psychology and language use.* Mahwah, NJ: Lawrence Erlbaum Associates.

Horgan, D.D., & Morgan, D. (1990). Chess expertise in children. *Applied Cognitive Psychology, 4,* 109–128.

Horton, W.S., & Keysar, B. (1996). When do speakers take into account common ground? *Cognition*, *59*, 91–117.

Hotopf, W.H.N. (1980). Slips of the pen. In U. Frith (Ed.), *Cognitive processes in spelling*. London: Academic Press.

Howard, D.V., & Howard, J.H. (1992). Adult age differences in the rate of learning serial patterns: Evidence from direct and indirect tests. *Psychology & Aging*, *7*, 232–241.

Howe, M.J.A. (1998). *Principles of abilities and human learning*. Hove, UK: Psychology Press.

Howe, M.J.A., & Smith, J. (1988). Calendar calculating in idiots savants: How do they do it? *British Journal of Psychology*, *79*, 371–386.

Howie, D. (1952). Perceptual defense. *Psychological Review*, *59*, 308–315.

Huey, E.B. (1908). *The psychology and pedagogy of reading*. New York: Macmillan.

Hulin, C.L., Henry, R.A., & Noon, S.L. (1990). Adding a dimension: Time as a factor in the generalizability of predictive relationships. *Psychological Bulletin*, *107*, 328–340.

Humphrey, N. (1983). *Consciousness regained: Chapters in the development of mind*. Oxford: Oxford University Press.

Humphrey, N. (2002*). The mind made flesh: Frontiers of psychology and evolution*. Oxford: Oxford University Press.

Humphreys, G.W. (1999). *Case studies in the neuropsychology of vision*. Hove, UK: Psychology Press.

Humphreys, G.W., & Riddoch, M.J. (1987). *To see but not to see: A case study of visual agnosia*. Hove, UK: Psychology Press.

Indefrey, P., & Levelt, W.J.M. (2004). The spatial and temporal signatures of word production components. *Cognition*, *92*, 101–144.

Intons-Peterson, M.J., & Best, D.L. (1998). *Memory distortions and their prevention*. Mahwah, NJ: Lawrence Erlbaum Associates Inc.

Isurin, L., & McDonald, J.L. (2001). Retroactive interference from translation equivalents: Implications for first language forgetting. *Memory & Cognition*, *29*, 312–319.

Ittelson, W.H. (1951). Size as a cue to distance: Static localization. *American Journal of Psychology*, *64*, 54–67.

Iyengar, S.S., & Lepper, M.R. (2000). When choice is demotivating: Can one desire too much of a good thing? *Journal of Personality and Social Psychology*, *79*, 995–1006.

Jacoby, L.L., Debner, J.A., & Hay, J.F. (2001). Proactive interference, accessibility bias, and process dissociations: Valid subjective reports of memory. *Journal of Experimental Psychology: Learning, Memory, & Cognition*, *27*, 686–700.

Jaensch, E.R. (1920). Zur Methodik experimenteller Untersuchungen und optischen Anschauungsbildern. *Zeitschrift für Psychologie*, *85*, 37–82.

Jakobsen, P. (2004). Quick beginners' guide to magic: Discover the secrets you need to know to become a successful magician. www.themagicschool.com

Jakobson, L.S., Archibald, Y.M., Carey, D.P., & Goodale, M.A. (1991). A kinematic analysis of reaching and grasping movements in a patient recovering from optic ataxia. *Neuropsychologia*, *29*, 803–809.

James, T.W., Culham, J., Humphrey, G.K., Milner, A.D., & Goodale, M.A. (2003). Ventral occipital lesions impair object recognition but not object-directed grasping: An fMRI study. *Brain*, *126*, 2463–2475.

James, W. (1890). *Principles of psychology*. New York: Holt.

Jared, D., Levy, B.A., & Rayner, K. (1999). The role of phonology in the activation of word meanings during reading: evidence from proofreading and eye movements. *Journal of Experimental Psychology: General*, *128*, 219–264.

Jay, T.B. (2003). *The psychology of language*. Upper Saddle River, NJ: Prentice Hall.

Job, R., Peressotti, F., & Cusinato, A. (1998). Lexical effects in naming pseudowords in shallow orthographies: Further empirical data. *Journal of Experimental Psychology: Human Perception and Performance*, *24*, 622–630.

Johnson, E.J., Hershey, J., Meszaros, J., & Kunreuther, H. (1993). Framing, probability distortions, and insurance decisions. *Journal of Risk & Uncertainty*, *7*, 5–51.

Johnson-Laird, P.N. (1983). *Mental models*. Cambridge: Cambridge University Press.

Johnson-Laird, P.N. (1999). Deductive reasoning. *Annual Review of Psychology*, *50*, 109–135.

Johnson-Laird, P.N. (2004). Mental models and

reasoning. In J.P. Leighton & R.J. Sternberg (Eds.), *The nature of reasoning*. Cambridge: Cambridge University Press.

Johnson-Laird, P.N., & Byrne, R.M.J. (1991). *Deduction*. London: Psychology Press.

Johnson-Laird, P.N., Legrenzi, P., & Girotto, V. (2004). How we detect logical inconsistencies. *Current Directions in Psychological Science, 13*, 41–45.

Johnston, V.S., Hagel, R., Franklin, M., Fink, B., & Grammer, K. (2001). Male facial attractiveness: Evidence for hormone-mediated adaptive design. *Evolution and Human Behavior, 22*, 251–267.

Josephs, R.A., Larrick, R.P., Steele, C.M., & Nisbett, R.E. (1992). Protecting the self from the negative consequences of risky decisions. *Journal of Personality and Social Psychology, 62*, 26–37.

Joyce, J. (1922/1960). *Ulysses*. London: Bodley Head.

Juhasz, B.J., & Rayner, K. (2003). Investigating the effects of a set of intercorrelated variables on eye fixation durations in reading. *Journal of Experimental Psychology: Learning, Memory and Cognition, 29*, 1312–1318.

Just, M.A., Carpenter, P.A., Keller, T.A., Emery, L., Zajac, H., & Thulborn, K.R. (2001). Interdependence of non-overlapping cortical systems in dual cognitive tasks. *NeuroImage, 14*, 417–426.

Just, M.A., Carpenter, P.A., & Masson, M.E.J. (1982). *What eye fixations tells us about speed-reading, skimming and normal reading*. Unpublished manuscript, Carnegie Mellon University, Pittsburgh, PA.

Kahneman, D. (1973). *Attention and effort*. Englewood Cliffs, NJ: Prentice Hall.

Kahneman, D. (2003). A perspective on judgment and choice: Mapping bounded rationality. *American Psychologist, 58*, 697–720.

Kahneman, D., & Fredrick, S. (2002). Representativeness revisited: Attribute substitution in intuitive judgements. In T. Gilovich, T.D. Griffin, & D. Kahneman (Eds.), *Heuristics and biases: The psychology of intuitive judgement*. Cambridge: Cambridge University Press.

Kahneman, D., & Henik, A. (1979). Perceptual organization and attention. In M. Kubovy & J.R. Pomerantz (Eds.), *Perceptual organization*. Hillsdale, NJ: Lawrence Erlbaum Associates Inc.

Kahneman, D., & Tversky, A. (1973). On the psychology of prediction. *Psychological Review, 80*, 237–251.

Kahneman, D., & Tversky, A. (1984). Choices, values and frames. *American Psychologist, 39*, 341–350.

Kane, M.J., Bleckley, M.K., Conway, A.R.A., & Engle, R.W. (2001). A controlled-attention view of working-memory capacity. *Journal of Experimental Psychology: General, 130*, 169–183.

Kane, M.J., & Engle, R.W. (2000). Working-memory capacity, proactive interference, divided attention: Limits on long-term memory retrieval. *Journal of Experimental Psychology: Learning, Memory, and Cognition, 26*, 336–358.

Kanizsa, G. (1976). Subjective contours. *Scientific American, 234*, 48–52.

Kanwisher, N., McDermott, J., & Chun, M.M. (1997). The fusiform face area: A module in human extrastriate cortex specialized for face perception. *Journal of Neuroscience, 9*, 605–610.

Kaplan, G.A., & Simon, H.A. (1990). In search of insight. *Cognitive Psychology, 22*, 374–419.

Karnath, H.O., Himmelbach, M., & Küker, W. (2003). The cortical substrate of visual extinction. *NeuroReport, 14*, 437–442.

Karney, B.R., & Frye, N.E. (2002). But we've been getting better lately: Comparing prospective and retrospective views of relationship development. *Journal of Personality and Social Psychology, 82*, 222–238.

Kassin, S.M., Tubb, V.A., Hosch, H.M., & Memon, A. (2001). On the "general acceptance" of eyewitness testimony research. *American Psychologist, 56*, 405–416.

Kaup, B., & Zwaan, R.A. (2003). Effects of negation and situational presence on the accessibility of text information. *Journal of Experimental Psychology: Learning, Memory, and Cognition, 29*, 439–446.

Kazmerski, V.A., Blasko, D.G., & Dessalegn, B.G. (2003). ERP and behavioral evidence of individual differences in metaphor comprehension. *Memory & Cognition, 31*, 673–689.

Keane, M. (1987). Modeling "insight" in practical construction problems. *Irish Journal of Psychology, 11*, 201–215.

Keil, F.C. (2003). Categorization, causation, and

the limits of understanding. *Language and Cognitive Processes*, *18*, 663–692.

Kellogg, R.T. (1995). *Cognitive psychology*. Thousand Oaks, CA: Sage.

Kelly, S.W. (2003). A consensus in implicit learning? *Quarterly Journal of Experimental Psychology*, *56A*, 1389–1391.

Kenealy, P.M. (1997). Mood-state-dependent retrieval: The effects of induced mood on memory reconsidered. *Quarterly Journal of Experimental Psychology*, *50A*, 290–317.

Kentridge, R.W., Heywood, C.A., & Weiskrantz, L. (1999). Effects of temporal cueing on residual visual discrimination in blindsight. *Neuropsychologia*, *37*, 479–483.

Keren, G., & Teigen, K.H. (2004). Yet another look at the heuristics and biases approach. In D. Koehler & N. Harvey (Eds.), *Blackwell handbook of judgment and decision making*. Oxford: Blackwell.

Kersten, D., Mamassian, P., & Knill, D.C. (1997). Moving cast shadows induce apparent motion in depth. *Perception*, *26*, 171–192.

Keysar, B., Barr, D.J., Balin, J.A., & Brauner, J.S. (2000). Taking perspective in conversation: The role of mutual knowledge in comprehension. *Psychological Science*, *11*, 32–38.

Kilpatrick, F.P., & Ittelson, W.H. (1953). The size–distance invariance hypothesis. *Psychological Review*, *60*, 223–231.

Kinder, A., & Shanks, D.R. (2001). Amnesia and the declarative/nondeclarative distinction: A recurrent network model of classification, recognition, and repetition priming. *Journal of Cognitive Neuroscience*, *13*, 648–669.

Kintsch, W. (1988). The role of knowledge in discourse comprehension: A construction–integration model. *Psychological Review*, *95*, 163–182.

Kintsch, W. (1992). A cognitive architecture for comprehension. In H.L. Pick, P. van den Broek, & D.C. Knill (Eds.), *Cognition: Conceptual and methodological issues*. Washington, DC: American Psychological Association.

Kintsch, W. (1998). *Comprehension: A paradigm for cognition*. New York: Cambridge University Press.

Kintsch, W., Welsch, D., Schmalhofer, F., & Zimony, S. (1990). Sentence memory: A theoretical analysis. *Journal of Memory and Language*, *29*, 133–159.

Klauer, K.C., Musch, J., & Naumer, B. (2000). On belief bias in syllogistic reasoning. *Psychological Review*, *107*, 852–884.

Klauer, K.C., & Zhao, Z. (2004). Double dissociations in visual and spatial short-term memory. *Journal of Experimental Psychology: General*, *133*, 355–381.

Klein, G. (2001). The fiction of optimization. In G. Gigerenzer & R. Selten (Eds.), *Bounded rationality: The adaptive toolbox*. Cambridge, MA: MIT Press.

Klein, I., Dubois, J., Mangin, J.-F., Kherif, F., Flandin, G., Poline, J.-B., Denis, M., Kosslyn, S.M., & Lebihan, D. (2004). Retinotopic organization of visual mental images as revealed by functional magnetic resonance imaging. *Cognitive Brain Research*, *22*, 26–31.

Knoblich, G., Ohlsson, S., Haider, H., & Rhenius, D. (1999). Constraint relaxation and chunk decomposition in insight. *Journal of Experimental Psychology: Learning, Memory, & Cognition*, *25*, 1534–1555.

Knowlton, B.J., Ramus, S.J., & Squire, L.R. (1992). Intact artificial grammar learning in amnesia: Dissociations of category-level knowledge and explicit memory for specific instances. *Psychological Science*, *3*, 172–179.

Koch, C. (2003). *The quest for consciousness: A neurobiological approach*. New York: Roberts & Co.

Koehler, D.J., & Harvey, N. (2004). *Blackwell handbook of judgment and decision making*. Oxford: Blackwell.

Koffka, K. (1935). *Principles of Gestalt psychology*. New York: Harcourt Brace.

Köhler, S., & Moscovitch, M. (1997). Unconscious visual processing in neuropsychological syndromes: A survey of the literature and evaluation of models of consciousness. In M.D. Rugg (Ed.), *Cognitive neuroscience*. Hove, UK: Psychology Press.

Köhler, W. (1925). *The mentality of apes*. New York: Harcourt Brace & World.

Kohnken, G., Milne, R., Memon, A., & Bull, R. (1999). The cognitive interview: A meta-analysis. *Psychology of Crime Law*, *5*, 3–27.

Koriat, A., & Goldsmith, M. (1996). Memory metaphors and the real-life/laboratory controversy: Correspondence versus storehouse conceptions of memory. *Behavioral & Brain Sciences*, *19*, 167–188.

Kosslyn, S.M. (1980). *Image and mind.* Cambridge, MA: Harvard University Press.

Kosslyn, S.M. (1994). *Image and brain: The resolution of the imagery debate.* Cambridge, MA: MIT Press.

Kosslyn, S.M., Pascual-Leone, A., Felician, O., Camposano, S., Keenan, J.P., Thompson, W.L., Ganis, G., Sukel, K.E., & Alpert, N.M. (1999). The role of Area 17 in visual imagery: Convergent evidence from PET and rTMS. *Science, 284,* 167–170.

Kosslyn, S.M., & Thompson, W.L. (2003). When is early visual cortex activated during visual mental imagery? *Psychological Bulletin, 129,* 723–746.

Krauss, S., & Wang, X.T. (2003). The psychology of the Monty Hall problem: Discovering psychological mechanisms for solving a tenacious brain teaser. *Journal of Experimental Psychology: General, 132,* 3–22.

Kruschke, J. (1992). ALCOVE: An exemplar-based connectionist model of category learning. *Psychological Review, 99,* 22–44.

Kuiper, K. (1996). *Smooth talkers.* Mahwah, NJ: Lawrence Erlbaum Associates Inc.

Künnapas, T.M. (1968). Distance perception as a function of available visual cues. *Journal of Experimental Psychology, 77,* 523–529.

Kvavilashvili, L., Mirani, J., Schlagman, S., & Kornbrot, D.E. (2003). Comparing flashbulb memories of September 11 and the death of Princess Diana: Effects of time delays and nationality. *Applied Cognitive Psychology, 17,* 1017–1031.

Kwiatkowski, S.J., & Parkinson, S.R. (1994). Depression, elaboration, and mood congruence: Differences between natural and induced mood. *Memory & Cognition, 22,* 225–233.

Kyllonen, P.C., & Christal, R.E. (1990). Reasoning ability is (little more than) working-memory capacity. *Intelligence, 14,* 389–433.

LaBerge, D. (1983). The spatial extent of attention to letters and words. *Journal of Experimental Psychology: Human Perception & Performance, 9,* 371–379.

Laird, D.A. (1935). What can you do with your nose? *Scientific Monthly, 41,* 126–130.

Lamberts, K., & Goldstone, R. (2004). *Handbook of cognition.* London: Sage.

Langlois, J.H., Kalakanis, L., Rubenstein, A.J., Larson, A., Hallam, M., & Smoot, M. (2000). Maxims or myths of beauty? A meta-analytic and theoretical review. *Psychological Review, 126,* 390–423.

Langlois, J.H., Roggman, L.A., & Musselman, L. (1994). What is average and what is not average about attractive faces. *Psychological Science, 5,* 214–220.

Larsen, J.D., Baddeley, A., & Andrade, J. (2000). Phonological similarity and the irrelevant speech effect: Implications for models of short-term memory. *Memory, 8,* 145–157.

Lassiter, G.D. (2000). The relative contributions of recognition and search-evaluation processes to high-level chess performance: Comment on Gobet and Simon. *Psychological Science, 11,* 172–173.

Lazarus, R.S. (1982). Thoughts on the relation between emotion and cognition. *American Psychologist, 37,* 1019–1024.

Lazarus, R.S. (1991). *Emotion and adaptation.* Oxford: Oxford University Press.

Leake, J. (1999). Scientists teach chimpanzees to speak English. *Sunday Times.*

Leask, J., Haber, R.N., & Haber, R.B. (1969). Eidetic imagery in children: II. Longitudinal and experimental results. *Psychonomic Monograph Supplements, 3* (Whole No. 35), 25–48.

Lee, H.W., Hong, S.B., Seo, D.W., Tae, W.S., & Hong, S.C. (2000). Mapping of functional organization in human visual cortex: Electrical cortical stimulation. *Neurology, 54,* 849–854.

Legrenzi, P., Girotto, V., & Johnson-Laird, P.N. (2003). Models of consistency. *Psychological Science, 14,* 131–137.

Leichtman, M.D., Wang, Q., & Pillemer, D.B. (2003). Cultural variations in interdependence and autobiographical memory: Lessons from Korea, China, India and the United States. In R. Fivush & C. Haden (Eds.), *Connecting culture and memory: The social construction of the autobiographical self.* Mahwah, NJ: Lawrence Erlbaum Associates.

Leighton, J.P., & Sternberg, R.J. (2004). *The nature of reasoning.* Cambridge: Cambridge University Press.

Lesch, M.F., & Hancock, P.A. (2004). Driving performance during concurrent cell-phone use: Are drivers aware of their performance decrements? *Accident Analysis and Prevention, 36,* 471–480.

Levelt, W.J.M., Roelofs, A., & Meyer, A.S. (1999).

A theory of lexical access in speech production. *Behavioral and Brain Sciences*, 22, 1–38.

Levin, D.T., Drivdahl, S.B., Momen, N., & Beck, M.R. (2002). False predictions about the detectability of visual changes: The role of beliefs about attention, memory, and the continuity of attended objects in causing change blindness blindness. *Consciousness and Cognition*, 11, 507–527.

Levin, D.T., & Simons, D.J. (1997). Failure to detect changes to attended objects in motion pictures. *Psychonomic Bulletin and Review*, 4, 501–506.

Levin, D.T., & Simons, D.J. (2000). Perceiving stability in a changing world: Combining shots and integrating views in motion pictures and the real world. *Media Psychology*, 2, 357–380.

Levine, M. (1971). Hypothesis theory and non-learning despite ideal S-R reinforcement contingencies. *Psychological Review*, 78, 130–140.

Lewis, M., & Haviland-Jones, J.M. (2000). *Handbook of emotions* (2nd ed.). New York: Guilford Press.

Libet, B. (1996). Neural processes in the production of conscious experience. In M. Velmans (Ed.), *The science of consciousness: Psychological, neuropsychological and clinical reviews*. London: Routledge.

Libet, B., Gleason, C.A., Wright, E.W., & Pearl, D.K. (1983). Time of conscious intention to act in relation to onset of cerebral activity (readiness potential): The unconscious initiation of a freely voluntary act. *Brain*, 106, 623–642.

Lichtenstein, S., Slovic, P., Fischhoff, B., Layman, M., & Combs, J. (1978). Judged frequency of lethal events. *Journal of Experimental Psychology: Human Learning and Memory*, 4, 551–578.

Lief, H., & Fetkewicz, J. (1995). Retractors of false memories: The evolution of pseudo-memories. *The Journal of Psychiatry & Law*, 23, 411–436.

Lin, E.L., & Murphy, G.L. (1997). Effects of background knowledge on object categorization and part detection. *Journal of Experimental Psychology: Human Perception and Performance*, 23, 1153–1169.

Lindsay, D.S., Allen, B.P., Chan, J.C.K., & Dahl, L.C. (2004a). Eyewitness suggestibility and source similarity: Intrusions of details from one event into memory reports of another event. *Journal of Memory and Language*, 50, 96–111.

Lindsay, D.S., Hagen, L., Read, J.D., Wade, K.A., & Garry, M. (2004b). True photographs and false memories. *Psychological Science*, 15, 149–154.

Loftus, E.F. (1979). *Eyewitness testimony*. Cambridge, MA: Harvard University Press.

Loftus, E.F. (1992). When a lie becomes memory's truth: Memory distortion after exposure to misinformation. *Current Directions in Psychology*, 1, 121–123.

Loftus, E.F. (2004). Memories of things unseen, *Current Directions in Psychological Science*, 13, 145–147,

Loftus, E.F., Loftus, G.R., & Messo, J. (1987). Some facts about weapon focus. *Law and Human Behavior*, 11, 55–62.

Loftus, E.F., & Palmer, J.C. (1974). Reconstruction of automobile destruction: An example of the interaction between language and memory. *Journal of Verbal Learning and Verbal Behavior*, 13, 585–589.

Logie, R.H. (1995). *Visuo-spatial working memory*. Hove, UK: Psychology Press.

Logie, R.H. (1999). State of the art: Working memory. *The Psychologist*, 12, 174–178.

Logie, R.H., Baddeley, A.D., Mane, A., Donchin, E., & Sheptak, R. (1989). Working memory and the analysis of a complex skill by secondary task methodology. *Acta Psychologica*, 71, 53–87.

Logie, R.H., & Della Sala, S. (2003). Working memory as a mental workspace: Why activated long-term memory is not enough. *Behavioral and Brain Sciences*, 26, 745.

Luchins, A.S. (1942). Mechanization in problem solving: The effect of Einstellung. *Psychological Monographs*, 54 (Whole No. 248).

Luchins, A.S., & Luchins, E.H. (1959). *Rigidity of behavior*. Eugene, OR: University of Oregon Press.

Lumer, E.D., Friston, K.J., & Rees, G. (1998). Neural correlates of perceptual rivalry in the human brain. *Science*, 280, 1930–1934.

Macaulay, D., Ryan, L., & Eich, E. (1993). Mood dependence in implicit and explicit Memory. In P. Graf & M.E.J. Masson (Eds.), *Implicit memory: New directions in cognition, development, and neuropsychology*. Hillsdale, NJ: Lawrence Erlbuam Associates Inc.

MacDonald, M.C., Pearlmutter, N.J., & Seidenberg, M.S. (1994). Lexical nature of syntactic ambiguity resolution. *Psychological Review*, *101*, 676–703.

MacGregor, J.N., Ormerod, T.C., & Chronicle, E.P. (2001). Information processing and insight: A process model of performance on the nine-dot and related problems. *Journal of Experimental Psychology: Learning, Memory, and Cognition*, *27*, 176–201.

Mack, A., & Rock, I. (1998). *Inattentional blindness*. Cambridge, MA: MIT Press.

Mackintosh, N.J. (1998). *IQ and human intelligence*. Oxford: Oxford University Press.

Mackintosh, N.J., & Bennett, E.S. (2003). The fractionation of working memory maps onto different components of intelligence. *Intelligence*, *31*, 519–531.

MacLeod, C., & Hagan, R. (1992). Individual differences in the selective processing of threatening information, and emotional responses to a stressful life event. *Behaviour Research and Therapy*, *30*, 151–161.

MacLeod, C., & Mathews, A. (1988). Anxiety and the allocation of attention to threat. *Quarterly Journal of Experimental Psychology*, *38A*, 659–670.

MacLeod, C., Mathews, A., & Tata, P. (1986). Attentional bias in emotional disorders. *Journal of Abnormal Psychology*, *95*, 15–20.

MacLeod, C., Rutherford, E., Campbell, L., Ebsworthy, G., & Holker, L. (2002). Selective attention and emotional vulnerability: Assessing the causal basis of their association through the experimental manipulation of attentional bias. *Journal of Abnormal Psychology*, *111*, 107–123.

Maddox, W.T., & Ashby, F.G. (2004). Dissociating explicit and procedural-learning based systems of perceptual category learning. *Behavioural Processes*, *66*, 309–332.

Maddox, W.T., Ashby, F.G., Ing, A.D., & Pickering, A.D. (2004). Disrupting feedback processing interferes with rule-based but not information-integration category learning. *Memory & Cognition*, *32*, 582–591.

Madison, P. (1956). Freud's repression concept: A survey and attempted clarification. *International Journal of Psychoanalysis*, *37*, 75–81.

Malone, D.R., Morris, H.H., Kay, M.C., & Levin, H.S. (1982). Prosopagnosia: A double dissociation between the recognition of familiar and unfamiliar faces. *Journal of Neurology, Neurosurgery, & Psychiatry*, *45*, 820–822.

Manktelow, K. (1999). *Reasoning and thinking*. Hove, UK: Psychology Press.

Manktelow, K. (2001). Reasoning: The pure and the practical. In L. Webber (Ed.), Recent developments in the psychology of thinking. *Special Bulletin Student Members Group BPS*, *2*, 1–6.

Manns, J.R., Hopkins, R.O., & Squire, L.R. (2003). Semantic memory and the human hippocampus. *Neuron*, *38*, 127–133.

Marcel, A.J. (1998). Blindsight and shape perception: Deficit of visual consciousness or of visual function? *Brain*, *121*, 1565–1588.

Markman, A.B., & Gentner, D. (2001). Thinking. *Annual Review of Psychology*, *52*, 223–247.

Marsh, E.J., & Tversky, B. (2004). Spinning the stories of our lives. *Applied Cognitive Psychology*, *18*, 491–503.

Marshall, J., Robson, J., Pring, T., & Chiat, S. (1998). Why does monitoring fail in jargon aphasia? *Brain and Language*, *63*, 79–107.

Marshall, J.C., & Halligan, P.W. (1994). The yin and yang of visuo-spatial neglect: A case study. *Neuropsychologia*, *32*, 1037–1057.

Marslen-Wilson, W.D. (1990). Activation, competition, and frequency in lexical access. In G.T.M. Altmann (Ed.), *Cognitive models of speech processing: Psycholinguistics and computational perspectives*. Cambridge, MA: MIT Press.

Marslen-Wilson, W.D., & Tyler, L.K. (1980). The temporal structure of spoken language comprehension. *Cognition*, *6*, 1–71.

Martin, A., & Caramazza, A. (2003). Neuropsychological and neuroimaging perspectives on conceptual knowledge: An introduction. *Cognitive Neuropsychology*, *20*, 195–221.

Martin, R.C., Miller, M., & Vu, H. (2004). Lexical-semantic retention and speech production: Further evidence from normal and brain-damaged participants for a phrasal scope of planning. *Cognitive Neuropsychology*, *21*, 625–644.

Martinez, A., Anllo-Vento, L., Sereno, M.I., Frank. L.R., Buxton, R.B., Dubowitz, D.J., et al. (1999). Involvement of striate and extrastriate visual cortical areas in spatial attention. *Nature Neuroscience*, *4*, 364–369.

Martone, M., Butters, N., Payne, M., Becker, J.T., & Sax, D.S. (1984). Dissociations between skill learning and verbal recognition in amnesia and dementia. *Archives of Neurology, 41,* 965–970.

Marzi, C.A., Girelli, M., Natale, E., & Miniussi, C. (2001). What exactly is extinguished in unilateral visual extinction? *Neuropsychologia, 39,* 1354–1366.

Massaro, D.W. (1985). Attention and perception: An information-integration perspective. *Acta Psychologica, 60,* 211–243.

Mather, G. (1997). The use of image blur as a depth cue. *Perception, 26,* 1147–1158.

Mathews, A., & Mackintosh, B. (2000). Induced emotional interpretation bias and anxiety. *Journal of Abnormal Psychology, 109,* 602–615.

Mathews, A., & MacLeod, C. (2002). Induced processing biases have causal effects on anxiety. *Cognition and Emotion, 16,* 331–354.

Matlin, M.W., & Foley, H.J. (1997). *Sensation and perception* (4th ed.). Boston, MA: Allyn & Bacon.

Mattys, S.L. (2004). Stress versus coarticulation: Toward an integrated approach to explicit speech segmentation. *Journal of Experimental Psychology: Human Perception and Performance, 30,* 397–408.

Maule, A.J., & Hodgkinson, G.P. (2002). Heuristics, biases and strategic decision making. *The Psychologist,* 15, 69–71.

McCarthy, R., & Warrington, E.K. (1984). A two-route model of speech production. *Brain, 107,* 463–485.

McCarthy, R.A., & Warrington, E.K. (1986). Visual associative agnosia: A clinico-anatomical study of a single case. *Journal of Neurology, Neurosurgery and Psychiatry, 49,* 1233–1240.

McClelland, J.L., & Elman, J.L. (1986). The TRACE model of speech perception. *Cognitive Psychology, 18,* 1–86.

McClelland, J.L., Rumelhart, D.E., & the PDP Research Group (1986). *Parallel distributed processing: Vol. 2. Psychological and biological models.* Cambridge, MA: MIT Press.

McCloskey, M. (2001). The future of cognitive neuropsychology. In B. Rapp (Ed.), *The handbook of cognitive neuropsychology: What deficits reveal about the human mind.* Philadelphia: Psychology Press.

McCloskey, M.E., & Glucksberg, S. (1978).

Natural categories: Well defined or fuzzy sets? *Memory & Cognition,* 6, 462–472.

McDermott, K.B., & Roediger, H.L. (1994). Effects of imagery on perceptual implicit memory tests. *Journal of Experimental Psychology: Learning, Memory, and Cognition, 20,* 1379–1390.

McDonald, S.A., & Shillcock, R.C. (2003). Eye movements reveal the on-line computation of lexical probabilities during reading. *Psychological Science, 14,* 648–652.

McGlinchey-Berroth, R., Milber, W.P., Verfaellie, M., Alexander, M., & Kilduff, P.T. (1993). Semantic processing in the neglected visual field: Evidence from a lexical decision task. *Cognitive Neuropsychology, 10,* 79–108.

McGlone, M.S., & Manfredi, D. (2001). Topic–vehicle interaction in metaphor comprehension. *Memory & Cognition,* 29, 1209–1219.

McGurk, H., & MacDonald, J. (1976). Hearing lips and seeing voices. *Nature, 264,* 746–748.

McIntosh, A.R., Rajah, M.N., & Lobaugh, N.J. (1999). Interactions of prefrontal cortex in relation to awareness in sensory learning. *Science, 284,* 1531–1533.

McKelvie, S.J. (1995). The VIQ as a psychometric test of individual differences in visual imagery vividness: A critical quantitative review and plea for direction. *Journal of Mental Imagery, 19,* 1–106.

McKone, E. (2004). Isolating the special component of face recognition: Peripheral identification and a Mooney face. *Journal of Experimental Psychology: Learning, Memory and Cognition, 30,* 181–197.

McKone, E., Martini, P., & Nakayama, K. (2001). Categorical perception of face identity in noise isolates configural processing. *Journal of Experimental Psychology: Human Perception and Performance, 27,* 573–599.

McKoon, G., & Ratcliff, R. (1992). Inference during reading. *Psychological Review,* 99, 440–466.

McLeod, P. (1977). A dual-task response modality effect: Support for multiprocessor models of attention. *Quarterly Journal of Experimental Psychology, 29,* 651–667.

McNeil, B.J., Pauker, S.G., Sox, H.C., & Tversky, A. (1982). On the elicitation of preferences for alternative therapies. *New England Journal of Medicine, 306,* 1259– 1262.

McNeil, J., & Warrington, E.K. (1993). Prosopagnosia: A face-specific disorder? *Quarterly Journal of Experimental Psychology, 46A,* 1–10.

McQueen, J.M. (1991). The influence of the lexicon on phonetic categorization: Stimulus quality in word-final ambiguity. *Journal of Experimental Psychology: Human Perception and Performance, 17,* 433–443.

McQueen, J.M. (2004). Speech perception. In K. Lamberts & R. Goldstone (Eds.), *The handbook of cognition.* London: Sage.

Mealey, L., Bridgstock, R., & Townsend, G.C. (1999). Symmetry and perceived facial attractiveness: A monozygotic co-twin comparison. *Journal of Personality and Social Psychology, 76,* 151–158.

Merikle, P.M., & Daneman, M. (1996). Memory for unconsciously perceived events: Evidence from anesthetized patients. *Consciousness and Cognition, 5,* 525–541.

Merikle, P.M., Smilek, D., & Eastwood, J.D. (2001). Perception without awareness: Perspectives from cognitive psychology. *Cognition, 79,* 115–134.

Merritt, J.O. (1979). None in a million: Results of mass screening for eidetic ability. *Behavioral and Brain Sciences, 2,* 612.

Mervis, C.B., & Pani, J.R. (1980). Acquisition of basic object categories. *Cognitive Psychology, 12,* 496–522.

Metcalfe, J., & Weibe, D. (1987). Intuition in insight and noninsight problem solving. *Memory & Cognition, 15,* 238–246.

Meulemans, T., & Van der Linden, M. (2003). Implicit learning of complex information in amnesia. *Brain and Cognition, 52,* 250–257.

Miceli, G., Silveri, M.C., Romani, C., & Caramazza, A. (1989). Variation in the pattern of omissions and substitutions of grammatical morphemes in the spontaneous speech of so-called agrammatic patients. *Brain & Language, 36,* 447–492.

Miller, G.A. (1956). The magic number seven, plus or minus two: Some limits on our capacity for processing information. *Psychological Review, 63,* 81–93.

Milner, A.D., & Goodale, M.A. (1995). *The visual brain in action.* Oxford: Oxford University Press.

Milner, A.D., & Goodale, M.A. (1998). The visual brain in action. *Psyche, 4,* 1–14.

Milner, A.D., Perrett, D.I., Johnston, R.S., Benson, P.J., Jordan, T.R., Heeley, D.W., & Bettuci, D. (1991). Perception and action in "visual form agnosia." *Brain, 114,* 405–428.

Miyake, A., Friedman, N.P., Emerson, M.J., Witzki, A.H., Howerter, A., & Wager, T. (2000). The unity and diversity of executive functions and their contributions to complex "frontal lobe" tasks: A latent variable analysis. *Cognitive Psychology, 41,* 49–100.

Miyake, A., & Shah, P. (1999). *Models of working memory: Mechanisms of active maintenance and executive control.* New York: Cambridge University Press.

Morgan, M. (2003). *The space between our ears: How the brain represents visual space.* London: Weidenfeld & Nicolson.

Morrison, D.J., Bruce, V., & Burton, A.M. (2003). Understanding provoked overt recognition in prosopagnosia. *Visual Cognition, 8,* 47–65.

Morsella, E., & Miozzo, M. (2002). Evidence for a cascade model of lexical access in speech production. *Journal of Experimental Psychology: Learning, Memory, and Cognition, 28,* 555–563.

Moss, H., & Hampton, J. (2003). *Conceptual representations.* Hove, UK: Psychology Press.

Most, S.B., Simons, D.J., Scholl, B.J., Jimenez, R., Clifford, E., & Chabris, C.F. (2001). How not to be seen: The contribution of similarity and selective ignoring to sustained inattentional blindness. *Psychological Science, 12,* 9–17.

Motley, M.T. (1980). Verification of "Freudian slips" and semantic prearticulatory editing via laboratory-induced spoonerisms. In V.A. Fromkin (Ed.), *Errors in linguistic performance: Slips of the tongue, ear, pen, and hand.* New York: Academic Press.

Motley, M.T., Baars, B.J., & Camden, C.T. (1983). Experimental verbal slip studies: A review and an editing model of language encoding. *Communication Monographs, 50,* 79–101.

Mueser, P.R., Cowan, N., & Mueser, K.T. (1999). A generalized signal detection model to predict rational variation in base rate use. *Cognition, 69,* 267–312.

Müller, M.M., Malinowski, P., Gruber, T., & Hillyard, S.A. (2003a). Sustained division of the attentional spotlight. *Nature*, *424*, 309–312.

Müller, N.G., Bartelt, O.A., Donner, T.H., Villringer, A., & Brandt, S.A. (2003b). A physiological correlate of the "zoom lens" of visual attention. *Journal of Neuroscience*, *23*, 3561–3565.

Murphy, G.L. (2002). *The big book of concepts*. Cambridge, MA: MIT.

Murphy, G.L., & Medin, D.L. (1985). The role of theories in conceptual coherence. *Psychological Review*, *92*, 289–316.

Murphy, S.T., & Zajonc, R.B. (1993). Affect, cognition, and awareness: Affective priming with optimal and suboptimal stimulus exposures. *Journal of Personality and Social Psychology*, *64*, 723–739.

Murray, J.D., & Burke, K.A. (2003). Activation and encoding of predictive inferences. The role of reading skill. *Discourse Processes*, *35*, 81–102.

Muter, P. (1978). Recognition failure of recallable words in semantic memory. *Memory & Cognition*, *6*, 9–12.

Nairne, J.S. (2002). Remembering over the short-term: The case against the standard model. *Annual Review of Psychology*, *53*, 53–81.

Nairne, J.S., Whiteman, H.L., & Kelley, M.R. (1999). Short-term forgetting of order under conditions of reduced interference. *Quarterly Journal of Experimental Psychology*, *52A*, 241–251.

Neisser, U. (1978). Memory: What are the important questions? In M.M. Gruneberg, P.E. Morris, & R.N. Sykes (Eds.), *Practical aspects of memory*. London: Academic Press.

Neisser, U. (1996) Remembering as doing. *Behavioral & Brain Sciences*, *19*, 203–204.

Newell, A., & Simon, H.A. (1972). *Human problem solving*. Englewood Cliffs, NJ: Prentice Hall.

Newell, B.R., Weston, N.J., & Shanks, D.R. (2003). Empirical tests of a fast and frugal heuristic: Not everyone "takes-the-best." *Organizational Behavior and Human Decision Processes*, *91*, 82–96.

Newmark, C.S., Frerking, R.A., Cook, L., & Newmark, L. (1973). Endorsement of Ellis irrational beliefs as a function of psychpathology. *Journal of Clinical Psychology*, *29*, 300–302.

Newstead, S.E., Handley, S.J., & Buck, E. (1999). Falsifying mental models: Testing the predictions of theories of syllogistic reasoning. *Memory & Cognition*, *27*, 344–354.

Nisbett, R.E., & Wilson, T.D. (1977). Telling more than we can know: Verbal reports on mental processes. *Psychological Review*, *84*, 231–259.

Nissen, M.J., & Bullemer, P. (1987). Attentional requirements of learning: Evidence from performance measures. *Cognitive Psychology*, *19*, 1–32.

Nissen, M.J., Ross, J., Willingham, D., Mackenzie, T., & Schacter, D. (1988). Memory and amnesia in a patient with multiple personality disorder. *Brain & Cognition*, *8*, 117–134.

Nissen, M.J., Willingham, D., & Hartman, M. (1989). Explicit and implicit remembering: When is learning preserved in amnesia? *Neuropsychologia*, *27*, 341–352.

Norman, J. (2002). Two visual systems and two theories of perception: An attempt to reconcile the constructivist and ecological approaches. *Behavioral and Brain Sciences*, *23*, 299–370.

Norris, D., McQueen, J.M., & Cutler, A. (2000). Merging information in speech recognition: Feedback is never necessary. *Behavioral and Brain Sciences*, *25*, 73–144.

Norris, D., McQueen, J.M., & Cutler, A. (2003). Perceptual learning in speech. *Cognitive Psychology*, *47*, 204–238.

Norris, D., McQueen, J.M., Cutler, A., & Butterfield, S. (1997). The possible-word constraint in the segmentation of continuous speech. *Cognitive Psychology*, *34*, 191–243.

Nosofsky, R.M. (1991). Tests of an exemplar model for relating perceptual classification and recognition memory. *Journal of Experimental Psychology: Human Perception and Performance*, *17*, 3–27.

Novick, L.R., & Sherman, S.J. (2003). On the nature of insight solutions: Evidence from skill differences in anagram solution. *Quarterly Journal of Experimental Psychology*, *56A*, 351–382.

Oberauer, K., Schulze, R., Wilhelm, O., & Süß, H.-M. (2005). Working memory and intelligence – Their correlation and their relation: Comment on Ackerman, Beier, and Boyle (2005). *Psychological Bulletin*, *131*, 61–65.

O'Brien, D.P. (2004). Mental-logic theory: What it proposes, and reasons to take this proposal seriously. In J.P. Leighton & R.J. Sternberg (Eds.), *The nature of reasoning*. Cambridge: Cambridge University Press.

O'Craven, K., Downing, P., & Kanwisher, N. (1999). FMRI evidence for objects as the units of attentional selection. *Nature, 401,* 584–587.

Ogden, J.A., & Corkin, S. (1991). Memories of H.M. In W.C. Abraham, M.C. Corballis, & K.G. White (Eds.), *Memory mechanisms: A tribute to G.V. Goddard*. Hillsdale, NJ: Lawrence Erlbaum Asociates Inc.

Ohlsson, S. (1992). Information processing explanations of insight and related phenomena. In M.T. Keane & K.J. Gilhooly (Eds.), *Advances in the psychology of thinking*. London: Harvester Wheatsheaf.

O'Kane, G., Kensinger, E.A., & Corkin, S. (2004). Evidence for semantic learning in profound amnesia: An investigation with patient H.M. *Hippocampus, 14,* 417–425.

Oppenheimer, D.M. (2003). Not so fast! (and not so frugal!): Re-thinking the recognition heuristic. *Cognition, 90,* B1–B9.

Oppenheimer, D.M. (2004). Spontaneous discounting of availability in frequency judgment tasks. *Psychological Science, 15,* 100–105.

O'Rourke, T.B., & Holcomb, P.J. (2002). Electrophysiological evidence for the efficiency of spoken word processing. *Biological Psychology, 60,* 121–150.

O'Shea, R.P., Blackburn, S.G., & Ono, H. (1994). Contrast as a depth cue. *Vision Research, 34,* 1595–1604.

Ost, J., & Costall, A. (2002). Misremembering Bartlett: A study in serial reproduction. *British Journal of Psychology, 93,* 243–255.

Ost, J., Vrij, A., Costall, A., & Bull, R. (2002). Crashing memories and reality monitoring: Distinguishing between perceptions, imaginations and 'false memories.' *Applied Cognitive Psychology, 16,* 125–134.

Papagno, C., Valentine, T., & Baddeley, A.D. (1991). Phonological short-term memory and foreign-language learning. *Journal of Memory & Language, 30,* 331–347.

Parkin, A.J. (1996). *Explorations in cognitive neuropsychology*. Oxford: Blackwell.

Parkin, A.J. (2001). The structure and mechan-

isms of memory. In B. Rapp (Ed.), *The handbook of cognitive neuropsychology: What deficits reveal about the human mind*. Hove, UK: Psychology Press.

Parkinson, B., & Manstead, A.S.R. (1992). Appraisal as a cause of emotion. In M.S. Clark (Ed.), *Review of personality and social psychology, Vol. 13*. New York: Sage.

Parks, A.M. (1991). Drivers' business decision making ability whilst using carphones. In E. Lovessey (Ed.), *Contemporary ergonomics: Proceedings of the Ergonomic Society annual conference*. London: Taylor & Francis.

Pashler, H. (1993). Dual-task interference and elementary mental mechanisms. In D.E. Meyer & S. Kornblum (Eds.), *Attention and performance, Vol. XIV*. London: MIT Press.

Pashler, H., Johnston, J.C., & Ruthruff, E. (2001). Attention and performance. *Annual Review of Psychology, 52,* 629–651.

Payne, J. (1976). Task complexity and contingent processing in decision making: An information search and protocol analysis. *Organizational Behavior and Human Performance, 16,* 366–387.

Payne, J.W., Bettman, J.R., & Johnson, E.J. (1988). Adaptive strategy selection in decision making. *Journal of Experimental Psychology: Learning, Memory and Cognition, 14,* 534–552.

Pelphrey, K.A., Mack, P.B., Song, A., Guzeldere, G., & McCarthy, G. (2003). Faces evoke spatially differentiated patterns of BOLD activation and deactivation. *NeuroReport, 14,* 955–959.

Perenin, M.-T., & Vighetto, A. (1988). Optic ataxia: A specific disruption in visuomotor mechanisms: 1. Different aspects of the deficit in reaching for objects. *Brain, 111,* 643–674.

Perfect, T.J., & Hollins, T.S. (1996). Predictive feeling of knowing judgments and postdictive confidence judgments in eyewitness memory and general knowledge. *Applied Cognitive Psychology, 10,* 371–382.

Perrett, D.I., Penton-Voak, I.S., Little, A.C., Tiddeman, B.P., Burt, D.M., Schmidt, N., Oxley, R., Kinloch, N., & Barrett, L. (2002). Facial attractiveness judgments reflect learning of parental age characteristics. *Proceedings of the Royal Society of London B, 269,* 873–880.

Perruchet, P., Chambaron, S., & Ferrel-Chapus,

C. (2003). Learning from implicit learning literature: Comment on Shea, Wulf, Whitacre, and Park (2001). *Quarterly Journal of Experimental Psychology, 56A*, 769–778.

Peterson, L.R., & Peterson, M.J. (1959). Short-term retention of individual verbal items. *Journal of Experimental Psychology, 58*, 193–198.

Peterson, R.R., & Savoy, P. (1998). Lexical selection and phonological encoding during language production: Evidence for cascaded processing. *Journal of Experimental Psychology: Learning, Memory, and Cognition, 24*, 539–557.

Pexman, P.M., Lupker, S.J., & Reggin, L.D. (2002). Phonological effects in visual word recognition: Investigating the impact of feedback activation. *Journal of Experimental Psychology: Learning, Memory, and Cognition, 28*, 572–584.

Pezdek, K. (2003). Event memory and autobiographical memory for the events of September 11, 2001. *Applied Cognitive Psychology, 17*, 1033–1045.

Pickering, M.J. (1999). Sentence comprehension. In S. Garrod & M.J. Pickering (Eds.), *Language processing*. Hove, UK: Psychology Press.

Pickering, M.J., & Garrod, S. (2004). Toward a mechanistic psychology of dialogue. *Behavioral and Brain Sciences, 27*, 169–226.

Pillemer, D.B. (1998). What is remembered about early childhood events? *Clinical Psychology Review, 18*, 895–913.

Pillemer, D.B., Goldsmith, L.R., Panter, A.T., & White, S.H. (1988). Very long-term memories of the first year in college. *Journal of Experimental Psychology: Learning, Memory, & Cognition, 14*, 709–715.

Pinard, M., Chertkow, H., Black, S., & Peretz, I. (2002). A case study of pure word deafness: Modularity in auditory processing? *Neurocase, 8*, 40–55.

Pinker, S. (1997). *How the mind works*. New York: W.W. Norton.

Pinker, S. (1999). *How the mind works*. Harmondsworth, UK: Penguin Books.

Pitt, M.A. (1995). The locus of the lexical shift in phoneme identification. *Journal of Experimental Psychology: Learning, Memory, and Cognition, 21*, 1037–1052.

Plaut, D.C., McClelland, J.L., Seidenberg, M.S., & Patterson, K. (1996). Understanding normal and impaired word reading: Computational principles in quasi-regular domains. *Psychological Review, 103*, 56–115.

Poeppel, D. (2001). Pure word deafness and the bilateral processing of the speech code. *Cognitive Science, 21*, 679–693.

Poldrack, R.A., & Gabrieli, J.D.E. (2001). Characterizing the neural mechanisms of skill learning and repetition priming: Evidence from mirror reading. *Brain, 124*, 67–82.

Poldrack, R.A., Selco, S.L., Field, J.E., & Cohen, N.J. (1999). The relationship between skill learning and repetition priming: Experimental and computational analyses. *Journal of Experimental Psychology: Learning, Memory, and Cognition, 25*, 208–235.

Polivy, J. (1981). On the induction of emotion in the laboratory: Discrete moods or multiple affect states? *Journal of Personality and Social Psychology, 41*, 803–817.

Posner, M.I. (1980). Orienting of attention: The VIIth Sir Frederic Bartlett lecture. *Quarterly Journal of Experimental Psychology, 32A*, 3–25.

Power, M., & Dalgleish, T. (1997). *Cognition and emotion: From order to disorder*. Hove, UK: Psychology Press.

Proust, M. (1922/1960). *Swann's way*. London: Chatto & Windus.

Putnam, B. (1979). Hypnosis and distortion in eyewitness memory. *International Journal of Clinical and Experimental Hypnosis, 27*, 437–448.

Pylyshyn, Z. (2002). Mental imagery: In search of a theory. *Behavioral and Brain Sciences, 25*, 157–238.

Pylyshyn, Z. (2003). Seeing and visualizing: It's not what you think. Cambridge, MA: MIT Press.

Quinlan, P.T., & Wilton, R.N. (1998). Grouping by proximity or similarity? Competition between the Gestalt principles in vision. *Perception, 27*, 417–430.

Rafal, R., Smith, J., Krantz, A., Cohen, A., & Brennan, C. (1990). Extrageniculate vision in hemianopic humans: Saccade inhibition by signals in the blind field. *Science, 250*, 118–121.

Rahman, R.A., Sommer, W., & Olada, E. (2004). I recognise your face, but I can't remember your name: A question of expertise? *Quarterly*

Journal of Experimental Psychology, 57A, 819–834.

Rapee, R.M., & Lim, L. (1992). Discrepancy between self and observer ratings of performance in social phobics. *Journal of Abnormal Psychology, 101,* 728–731.

Rayner, K., & Pollatsek, A. (1989). *The psychology of reading.* Englewood Cliffs, NJ: Prentice Hall.

Rayner, K., Warren, T., Juhasz, B.J., & Liversedge, S.P. (2004). The effect of plausibility on eye movements in reading. *Journal of Experimental Psychology: Learning, Memory, and Cognition, 30,* 1290–1301.

Reber, A.S. (1967). Implicit learning of artificial grammars. *Journal of Verbal Learning and Verbal Behavior, 6,* 855–863.

Reber, A.S. (1993). *Implicit learning and tacit knowledge: An essay on the cognitive unconscious.* Oxford: Oxford University Press.

Reber, P.J., & Squire, L.R. (1994). Parallel brain systems for learning with and without awareness. *Learning & Memory, 1,* 217–229.

Redelmeier, D., Koehler, D.J., Liberman, V., & Tversky, A. (1995). Probability judgement in medicine: Discounting unspecified alternatives. *Medical Decision Making, 15,* 227–230.

Redelmeier, D.A., & Tibshirani, R.J. (1997). Association between cellular-telephone calls and motor vehicle collisions. *The New England Journal of Medicine, 336,* 453– 458.

Rees, G., Wojciulik, E., Clarke, K., Husain, M., Frith, C., & Driver, J. (2000). Unconscious activation of visual cortex in the damaged right hemisphere of a parietal patient with extinction. *Brain, 123,* 82–92.

Reichle, E.D., Pollatsek, A., Fisher, D.L., & Rayner, K. (1998). Toward a model of eye movement control in reading. *Psychological Review, 105,* 125–157.

Reichle, E.D., Rayner, K., & Pollatsek, A. (2003). The E-Z Reader model of eye- movement control in reading: Comparisons to other models. *Behavioral and Brain Sciences, 26,* 445–526.

Reingold, E.M. (2004). Unconscious perception and the classic dissociation paradigm: A new angle? *Perception & Psychophysics, 66,* 882–887.

Rensink, R.A. (2002). Change detection. *Annual Review of Psychology, 53,* 245– 277.

Riddoch, G. (1917). Dissociations of visual perceptions due to occipital injuries, with especial reference to appreciation of movement. *Brain, 40,* 15–57.

Riddoch, M.J., & Humphreys, G.W. (2001). Object recognition. In B. Rapp (Ed.), *The handbook of cognitive neuropsychology: What deficits reveal about the human mind.* Hove, UK: Psychology Press.

Rips, L.J. (1994). *The psychology of proof: Deductive reasoning in human thinking.* Cambridge, MA: MIT Press.

Rips, L.J., & Collins, A. (1993). Categories and resemblance. *Journal of Experimental Psychology: General, 122,* 468–486.

Ritov, I., & Baron, J. (1990). Reluctance to vaccinate: Omission bias and ambiguity. *Journal of Behavioral Decision Making, 3,* 263–277.

Robbins, T.W., Anderson, E.J., Barker, D.R., Bradley, A.C., Fearnyhough, C., Henson, R., Hudson, S.R., & Baddeley, A. (1996). Working memory in chess. *Memory & Cognition, 24,* 83–93.

Robertson, S.I. (2001). *Problem solving.* Hove, UK: Psychology Press.

Robson, J., Pring, T., Marshall, J., & Chiat, S. (2003). Phoneme frequency effects in jargon aphasia: A phonological investigation of nonword errors. *Brain and Language, 85,* 109–124.

Rock, I., & Palmer, S. (1990). The legacy of Gestalt psychology. *Scientific American* (December), 48–61.

Rodriguez, E., George, N., Lachaux, J., Martinerie, J., Renault, B., & Varela, F.J. (1999). Perception's shadow: Long-distance synchronization of human brain activity. *Nature, 397,* 430–433.

Roediger, H.L. (1980). Memory metaphors in cognitive psychology. *Memory & Cognition, 8,* 231–246.

Rogers, B.J., & Collett, T.S. (1989). The appearance of surfaces specified by motion parallax and binocular disparity. *Quarterly Journal of Experimental Psychology, 41A,* 697–717.

Rogers, B.J., & Graham, M.E. (1979). Motion parallax as an independent cue for depth perception. *Perception, 8,* 125–134.

Rosch, E., & Mervis, C.B. (1975). Family resemblances: Studies in the internal structure of categories. *Cognitive Psychology, 7,* 573–605.

Rosch, E., Mervis, C.B., Gray, W.D., Johnson, D.M., & Boyes-Braem, P. (1976). Basic objects in natural categories. *Cognitive Psychology*, *8*, 382–439.

Ross, M., & Wilson, A.E. (2002). It feels like yesterday: Self-esteem, valence of personal past experiences, and judgments of subjective distance. *Journal of Personality and Social Psychology*, *82*, 792–803.

Rossion, B., Caldara, R., Seghier, M., Schuller, A.M., Lazayras, F., & Mayer, E. (2003). A network of occipito-temporal face-sensitive areas besides the right middle fusiform gyrus is necessary for normal face processing. *Brain*, *126*, 2381–2395.

Roy, D.F. (1991). Improving recall by eyewitnesses through the cognitive interview: Practical applications and implications for the police service. *The Psychologist*, *4*, 398–400.

Rozenblit, L.R., & Keil, F.C. (2002). The misunderstood limits of folk science: An illusion of explanatory depth. *Cognitive Science*, *26*, 521–562.

Rubin, D.C. (2000). The distribution of early childhood memories. *Memory*, *8*, 265–269.

Rubin, D.C., Rahhal, T.A., & Poon, L.W. (1998). Things learned in early adulthood are remembered best. *Memory & Cognition*, *26*, 3–19.

Rubin, D.C., & Schulkind, M.D. (1997). The distribution of autobiographical memories across the lifespan. *Memory & Cognition*, *25*, 859–866.

Rubin, D.C., & Wenzel, A.E. (1996). One hundred years of forgetting: A quantitative description of retention. *Psychological Bulletin*, *103*, 734–760.

Rubinstein, J., Meyer, D., Evans, J. (2001). Executive control of cognitive processes in task switching. *Journal of Experimental Psychology: Human Perception and Performance*, *27*, 763–797.

Ruchkin, D.S., Berndt, R.S., Johnson, R., Grafman, J., Ritter, W., & Canoune, H.L. (1999). Lexical contributions to retention of verbal information in working memory: Event-related brain potential evidence. *Journal of Memory and Language*, *41*, 345–364.

Ruchkin, D.S., Grafman, J., Cameron, K., & Berndt, R.S. (2003). Working memory retention systems: A state of activated long-term memory. *Behavioral and Brain Sciences*, *26*, 709–777.

Rumelhart, D.E., McClelland, J.L., & the PDP Research Group (1986). *Parallel distributed processing, Vol. 1: Foundations*. Cambridge, MA: MIT Press.

Rumelhart, D.E., & Ortony, A. (1977). The representation of knowledge in memory. In R.C. Anderson, R.J. Spiro, & W.E. Montague (Eds.), *Schooling and the acquisition of knowledge*. Hillsdale, NJ: Lawrence Erlbaum Associates Inc.

Rusting, C.L. & DeHart, T. (2000) Retrieving positive memories to regulate negative mood: Consequences for mood-congruent memory. *Journal of Personality and Social Psychology*, *78*, 737–752.

Ryan, J.D., Althoff, R.R., Whitlow, S., & Cohen, N.J. (2000). Amnesia is a deficit in relational memory. *Psychological Science*, *11*, 454–461.

Sala, J.B., Rämä, P., & Courtney, S.M. (2003). Functional topography of a distributed neural system for spatial and nonspatial information maintenance in working memory. *Neuropsychologia*, *41*, 341–356.

Samuel, A.G. (1981). Phonemic restoration: Insights from a new methodology. *Journal of Experimental Psychology: General*, *110*, 474–494.

Samuel, A.G. (1987). The effects of lexical uniqueness on phonemic restoration. *Journal of Memory and Language*, *26*, 36–56.

Samuel, A.G. (1997). Lexical activation produces potent phonemic percepts. *Cognitive Psychology*, *32*, 97–127.

Sanderson, W.C., Rapee, R.M., & Barlow, D.H. (1989). The influence of an illusion of control on panic attacks induced via inhalation of 5.5% carbon-dioxide enriched air. *Archives of General Psychiatry*, *46*, 157–162.

Santhouse, A.M., Howard, R.J., & ffytche, D.H. (2000). Visual hallucinatory syndromes and the anatomy of the visual brain. *Brain*, *123*, 2055–2064.

Savoy, R.L. (2001). History and future directions of human brain mapping and functional neuroimaging. *Acta Psychologica*, *107*, 9–42.

Schacter, D.L., Wagner, A.D., & Buckner, R.L. (2000). Memory systems of 1999. In E. Tulving & F.I.M. Craik (Eds.), *The Oxford handbook of memory*. New York: Oxford University Press.

Schare, M.L., Lisman, S.A., & Spear, N.F. (1984). The effects of mood variation on state-dependent retention. *Cognitive Therapy & Research, 8,* 387–408.

Schendan, H.E., Searl, M.M., Melrose, R.J., & Stern, C.E. (2003). An fMRI study of the role of the medial temporal lobe in implicit and explicit sequence learning. *Neuron, 37,* 1013–1025.

Schieb, J.E., Gangestad, S.W., & Thornhill, R. (1999). Facial attractiveness, symmetry and cues of good genes. *Proceedings of the Royal Society of London Series B: Biological Sciences, 266,* 1913–1917.

Schmitt, B.M., Münte, T.F., & Kutas, M. (2000). Electrophysiological estimates of the time course of semantic and phonological encoding during implicit picture naming. *Psychophysiology, 37,* 473–484.

Schneider, W., & Shiffrin, R.M. (1977). Controlled and automatic human information processing: 1. Detection, search, and attention. *Psychological Review, 84,* 1–66.

Schooler, J.W. (2002). Re-representing consciousness: Dissociations between experience and meta-consciousness. *Trends in Cognitive Sciences, 6,* 339–344.

Schooler, J.W., Ohlsson, S., & Brooks, K. (1993). Thoughts beyond words: When language overshadows insight. *Journal of Experimental Psychology: General, 122,* 166–183.

Schooler, J.W., Reichle, E.D., & Halpern, P.V. (in press). Zoning-out during reading: Evidence for dissociations between experience and meta-consciousness. In D. Levin (Ed.), *Visual meta-consciousness: Thinking about seeing.* Westport, CT: Praeger.

Schumacher, E.H., Seymour, T.L., Glass, J.M., Fencsik, D.E., Lauber, E.J., Kieras, D.E., & Meyer, D.E. (2001). Virtually perfect time sharing in dual-task performance: Uncorking the central cognitive bottleneck. *Psychological Science, 12,* 101–108.

Schwartz, B. (2004). *The paradox of choice: Why more is less.* New York: HarperCollins.

Schwartz, B., Ward, A., Monterosso, J., Lyubomirsky, S., White, K., & Lehman, D.R. (2002). Maximizing versus satisficing: Happiness is a matter of choice. *Journal of Personality and Social Psychology, 83,* 1178–1197.

Schwartz, B.L., & Hashtroudi, S. (1991). Priming is independent of skill learning. *Journal of Experimental Psychology: Learning, Memory, and Cognition, 17,* 1177–1187.

Schwartz, J.A., Chapman, G.B., Brewer, N.T., & Bergus, G.B. (2004). The effects of accountability on bias in physician decision making: Going from bad to worse. *Psychonomic Bulletin & Review, 11,* 173–178.

Schwartz, M.F., Saffran, E.M., & Marin, O.S.M. (1980). Fractionating the reading process in dementia: Evidence for word-specific print-to-sound associations. In M. Coltheart, K.E. Patterson, & J.C. Marshall (Eds.), *Deep dyslexia.* London: Routledge & Kegan Paul.

Schweinberger, S.R., & Burton, A.M. (2003). Covert recognition and the neural system for face processing. *Cortex, 39,* 9–30.

Schwitzgebel, E. (2002). How well do we know our own conscious experience? The case of visual imagery. *Journal of Consciousness Studies, 9,* 35–53.

Scoville, W.B., & Milner, B. (1957). Loss of recent memory after bilateral hippocampal lesions. *Journal of Neurology, Neurosurgery, & Psychiatry, 20,* 11–21.

Searle, J. (1979). Metaphor. In A. Ortony (Ed.), *Metaphor and thought.* Cambridge: Cambridge University Press.

Sedlmeier, P., Hertwig, R., & Gigerenzer, G. (1998). Are judgments of the positional frequencies of letters systematically biased due to availability? *Journal of Experimental Psychology: Learning, Memory, and Cognition, 24,* 754–770.

Sejnowski, T.J., & Rosenberg, C.R. (1987). Parallel networks that learn to pronounce English text. *Complex Systems, 1,* 145–168.

Sekuler, R., & Blake, R. (2002). *Perception* (4th ed.). New York: McGraw-Hill.

Sergent, C., & Dehaene, S. (2004). Is consciousness a gradual phenomenon? *Psychological Science, 15,* 720–728.

Shah, P., & Miyake, A. (1996). The separability of working memory resources for spatial thinking and language processing: An individual differences approach. *Journal of Experimental Psychology: General, 125,* 4–27.

Shallice, T. (1991). From neuropsychology to mental structure. *Behavioral & Brain Sciences, 14,* 429–439.

Shallice, T., & Butterworth, B. (1977). Short-term memory impairment and spontaneous speech. *Neuropsychologia, 15*, 729–735.

Shallice, T., & Warrington, E.K. (1970). Independent functioning of verbal memory stores: A neuropsychological study. *Quarterly Journal of Experimental Psychology, 22*, 261–273.

Shallice, T., & Warrington, E.K. (1974). The dissociation between long-term retention of meaningful sounds and verbal material. *Neuropsychologia, 12*, 553–555.

Shanks, D.R. (2004). Implicit learning. In K. Lamberts and R. Goldstone (Eds.), *Handbook of cognition*. London: Sage.

Shanks, D.R., & St. John, M.F. (1994). Characteristics of dissociable human learning systems. *Behavioral and Brain Sciences, 17*, 367–394.

Shea, C.H., Wulf, G., Whitacre, C.A., & Park, J.-H. (2001). Surfing the implicit wave. *Quarterly Journal of Experimental Psychology, 54A*, 841–862.

Shiffrin, R.M., & Schneider, W. (1977). Controlled and automatic human information processing: 2. Perceptual learning, automatic attending, and a general theory. *Psychological Review, 84*, 127–190.

Sides, A., Osheron, D., Bonini, N., & Vitale, R. (2002). On the reality of the conjunction fallacy. *Memory & Cognition, 30*, 191–198.

Simcock, G., & Hayne, H. (2002). Breaking the barrier? Children fail to translate their preverbal memories into language. *Psychological Science, 13*, 225–231.

Simon, D., Krawczyk, D.C., & Holyoak, K.J. (2004). Construction of preferences by constraint satisfaction. *Psychological Science, 15*, 331–336.

Simon, H.A. (1957). *Models of man: Social and rational*. New York: Wiley.

Simon, H.A. (1966). Scientific discovery and the psychology of problem solving. In H.A. Simon (Ed.), *Mind and cosmos: Essays in contemporary science and philosophy*. Pittsburgh, PA: University of Pittsburgh.

Simon, H.A. (1974). How big is a chunk? *Science, 183*, 482–488.

Simon, H.A. (1978). Rationality as process and product of thought. *American Economic Association, 68*, 1–16.

Simon, H.A. (1990). Invariants of human behavior. *Annual Review of Psychology, 41*, 1–19.

Simon, H.A., & Reed, S.K. (1976). Modeling strategy shifts on a problem solving task. *Cognitive Psychology, 8*, 86–97.

Simons, D.J. (2000). Current approaches to change blindness. *Visual Cognition, 7*, 1–15.

Simons, D.J., & Chabris, F. (1999). Gorillas in our midst: Sustained inattentional blindness for dynamic events. *Perception, 28*, 1059–1074.

Simons, D.J., & Levin, D.T. (1998). Failure to detect changes to people during a real-world interaction. *Psychonomic Bulletin and Review, 5*, 644–649.

Simonson, I., & Staw, B.M. (1992). De-escalation strategies: A comparison of techniques for reducing commitment to losing courses of action. *Journal of Applied Psychology, 77*, 419–426.

Sinai, M.J., Ooi, T.L., & He, Z.H. (1998). Terrain influences the accurate judgment of distance. *Nature, 395*, 497–500.

Singer, M. (1994). Discourse inference processes. In M.A. Gernsbacher (Ed.), *Handbook of psycholinguistics*. San Diego, CA: Academic Press.

Sirigu, A., & Duhamel, J.R. (2001). Motor and visual imagery as two complementary but neurally dissociable mental processes. *Journal of Cognitive Neuroscience, 13*, 910–919.

Sloboda, J.A., Davidson, J.W., Howe, M.J.A., & Moore, D.G. (1996). The role of practice in the development of performing musicians. *British Journal of Psychology, 87*, 287–309.

Sloman, S.A., & Over, D.E. (2003). Probability judgment: From the inside and out. In D.E. Over (Ed.), *Evolution and the psychology of thinking*. Hove, UK: Psychology Press.

Smarnia, N., Martini, M.C., Gambina, G., Tomelleri, G., Palamara, A., Natale, E. et al. (1998). The spatial distribution of spatial attention in hemineglect and extinction patients. *Brain, 121*, 1759–1770.

Smith, C.A. & Kirby, L.D. (2001). Toward delivery on the promise of appraisal theory. In K.R. Scherer, A. Schoor, & T. Johnstone (Eds.) *Appraisal processes in emotion: Theory, methods, research*. Oxford: Oxford University Press.

Smith, C.A., & Lazarus, R.S. (1993). Appraisal components, core relational themes, and the emotions. *Cognition and Emotion, 7*, 233–269.

Smith, E.E., & Jonides, J. (1997). Working

memory: A view from neuroimaging. *Cognitive Psychology, 33,* 5–42.

Smith, E.E., & Jonides, J. (1999). Storage and executive processes in the frontal lobes. *Science, 283,* 1657–1661.

Smith, J.D., & Minda, J.P. (2000). Thirty categorization results in search of a model. *Journal of Experimental Psychology: Learning, Memory, and Cognition, 26,* 3–27.

Smith, M. (2000). Conceptual structures in language production. In L. Wheeldon (Ed.), *Aspects of language production.* Hove, UK: Psychology Press.

Smith, S., & Blankenship, S. (1991). Incubation and the persistence of fixation in problem solving. *American Journal of Psychology, 104,* 61–87.

Smyth, M.M., Morris, P.E., Levy, P., & Ellis, A.W. (1987). *Cognition in action.* Hove, UK: Psychology Press.

Snedeker, J., & Trueswell, J. (2003). Using prosody to avoid ambiguity: Effects of speaker awareness and referential context. *Journal of Memory and Language, 48,* 103–130.

Snodgrass, M., Bernat, E., & Shevrin, H. (2004). Unconscious perception at the objective detection threshold exists. *Perception & Psychophysics, 66,* 888–895.

Soler, C., Núñez, M., Gutiérrez, R., Núñez, J., Medina, P., Sancho, M., Alvarez, J., & Núñez, A. (2003). Facial attractiveness in men provides clues to semen quality. *Evolution and Human Behavior, 24,* 199–207.

Solso, R.L. (1994). *Cognition and the visual arts.* Cambridge, MA: MIT Press.

Spearman, C.E. (1927). *The abilities of man: Their nature and measurement.* London: Macmillan.

Speisman, J.C., Lazarus, R.S., Mordkoff, A.M., & Davison, L.A. (1964). Experimental reduction of stress based on ego-defense theory. *Journal of Abnormal Psychology, 68,* 367–380.

Spelke, E.S., Hirst, W.C., & Neisser, U. (1976). Skills of divided attention. *Cognition, 4,* 215–230.

Spence, C., & Driver, J. (1996). Audio-visual links in endogenous covert spatial attention. *Journal of Experimental Psychology: Human Perception and Performance, 22,* 1005–1030.

Sperber, D., & Girotto, V. (2002). Use or misuse of the selection task? Rejoinder to Fiddick, Cosmides, and Tooby. *Cognition, 85,* 277–290.

Sperry, R.W. (1968). Hemisphere deconnection and unity in conscious awareness. *American Psychologist, 23,* 723–733.

Spiers, H.J., Maguire, E.A., & Burgess, N. (2001). Hippocampal amnesia. *Neurocase, 7,* 357–382.

Spivey, M.J., Tanenhaus, M.K., Eberhard, K.M., & Sedivy, J.C. (2002). Eye movements and spoken language comprehension: Effects of visual context on syntactic ambiguity resolution. *Cognitive Psychology, 45,* 447–481.

Sporer, S.L., Penrod, S., Read, D., & Cutler, B. (1995). Choosing, confidence, and accuracy: A meta-analysis of the confidence–accuracy relation in eyewitness identification studies. *Psychological Bulletin, 118,* 315–327.

Standing, L.G., Conezio, J., & Haber, N. (1970). Perception and memory for pictures: Single-trial learning of 2,500 visual stimuli. *Psychonomic Science, 19,* 73–74..

Stanovich, K.E., Sà, W.C., & West, R.F. (2004). Individual differences in thinking, reasoning, and decision making. In J.P. Leighton & R.J. Sternberg (Eds.), *The nature of reasoning.* Cambridge: Cambridge University Press.

Stanovich, K.E., & West, R.F. (1998a). Evaluating principles of rational indifference: Individual differences in framing and conjunction effects. *Thinking & Reasoning, 4,* 289–317.

Stanovich, K.E., & West, R.F. (1998b). Individual differences in rational thought. *Journal of Experimental Psychology: General, 127,* 161–188.

Stanovich, K.E., & West, R.F. (2000). Individual differences in reasoning: Implications for the rationality debate? *Behavioral and Brain Sciences, 23,* 645–665.

Steblay, N.M. (1997). Social influence in eyewitness recall: A meta-analytic review of line-up instruction effects. *Law and Human Behavior, 21,* 283–298.

Steblay, N.M., Dysart, J., Fulero, S., & Lindsay, R.C.L. (2001). Eyewitness accuracy rates in sequential and simultaneous line-up presentations: A meta-analytic comparison. *Law and Human Behavior, 25,* 459–474.

Stein, B.E., & Meredith, M.A. (1993). *The merging of the senses.* Cambridge, MA: MIT Press.

Stemberger, J.P. (1982). The nature of segments in the lexicon: Evidence from speech errors. *Lingua, 56,* 235–259.

Stenning, K., & van Lambalgen, M. (2004). A little logic goes a long way: Basing experiment on semantic theory in the cognitive science of conditional reasoning. *Cognitive Science, 28*, 481–529.

Sternberg, R.J. (2004). What do we know about the nature of reasoning? In J.P. Leighton & R.J. Sternberg (Eds.), *The nature of reasoning.* Cambridge: Cambridge University Press.

Sternberg, R.J., & Ben-Zeev, T. (2001). *Complex cognition: The psychology of human thought.* Oxford: Oxford University Press.

Stoerig, P., & Cowey, A. (1997). Blindsight in man and monkey. *Brain, 120,* 535–559.

Stopa, L., & Clark, D.M. (1993). Cognitive processes in social phobia. *Behaviour Research and Therapy, 31,* 255–267.

Storms, G., De Boeck, P., & Ruts, W. (2000). Prototype and exemplar-based information in natural language categories. *Journal of Memory and Language, 42,* 51–73.

Strayer, D.L., & Johnston, W.A. (2001). Driven to distraction: Dual-task studies of simulated driving and conversing on a cellular telephone. *Psychological Science, 12,* 462–466.

Stromeyer, C.F., & Psotka, J. (1970). The detailed texture of eidetic images. *Nature, 225,* 346–349.

Suh, S., & Trabasso, T. (1993). Inferences during reading: Converging evidence from discourse analysis, talk-aloud protocols, and recognition priming. *Journal of Memory and Language, 32,* 279–300.

Sulin, R.A., & Dooling, D.J. (1974). Intrusion of a thematic idea in retention of prose. *Journal of Experimental Psychology, 103,* 255–262.

Sullivan, L. (1976). Selective attention and secondary message analysis: A reconsideration of Broadbent's filter model of selective attention. *Quarterly Journal of Experimental Psychology, 28,* 167–178.

Sun, R., Slusarz, P., & Terry, C. (2005). The interaction of the explicit and the implicit in skill learning: A dual-process approach. *Psychological Review, 112,* 159–192.

Süß, H., Oberauer, K., Wittman, W., Wilhelm, O., & Schulze, R. (2002). Working memory capacity explains reasoning ability – And a little bit more. *Intelligence, 30,* 261–288.

Sussman, H.M., Hoemeke, K.A., & Ahmed, F.S. (1993). A cross-linguistic investigation of locus equations as a phonemic descriptor for place of articulation. *Journal of the Acoustical Society of America, 94,* 1256–1268.

Sutherland, N.S. (Ed.) (1989). *Macmillan dictionary of psychology.* London: Macmillan.

Svartik, J., & Quirk, R. (1980). *A corpus of English conversation.* Lund, Sweden: CWK Gleerup.

Sweller, J., & Levine, M. (1982). Effects of goal specificity on means–ends analysis and learning. *Journal of Experimental Psychology: Learning, Memory, and Cognition, 8,* 463–474.

Talarico, J.M., & Rubin, D.C. (2003). Confidence, not consistency, characterizes flashbulb memories. *Psychological Science, 14,* 455–461.

Tanaka, J.W., & Taylor, M.E. (1991). Categorization and expertise: Is the basic level in the eye of the beholder? *Cognitive Psychology, 23,* 457–482.

Tanenhaus, M.K., Spivey-Knowlton, M.J., Eberhard, K.M., & Sedivy, J.C. (1995). Integration of visual and linguistic information in spoken language comprehension. *Science, 268,* 1632–1634.

Tarr, M.J., & Bülthoff, H.H. (1995). Is human object recognition better described by geon structural descriptions or by multiple views? Comment on Biederman and Gerhardstein (1993). *Journal of Experimental Psychology: Human Perception and Performance, 21,* 1494–1505.

Tarr, M.J., & Bülthoff, H.H. (1998). Image-based object recognition in man, monkey and machine. *Cognition, 67,* 1–20.

Tetlock, P.E. (1991). An alternative metaphor in the study of judgment and choice: People as politicians. *Theory and Psychology, 1,* 451–475.

Tetlock, P.E. (2002). Social functionalist frameworks for judgment and choice: Intuitive politicians, theologians, and prosecutors. *Psychological Review, 109,* 451–471.

Tetlock, P.E., & Mellers, B.A. (2002). The great rationality debate. *Psychological Science, 13,* 94–99.

Todd, P.N., & Gigerenzer, G. (2000). Precise of simple heuristics that make us smart. *Behavioral and Brain Sciences, 23,* 727–780.

Trappery, C. (1996), A meta-analysis of consumer choice and subliminal advertising. *Psychology & Marketing, 13,* 517–30.

Treisman, A.M., & Davies, A. (1973). Divided

attention to ear and eye. In S. Kornblum (Ed.), *Attention and performance, Vol. IV*. London: Academic Press.

Trevarthen, C. (2004). Split-brain and the mind. In R. Gregory (Ed.), *The Oxford companion to the mind* (2nd ed.). Oxford: Oxford University Press.

Trevena, J.A., & Miller, J. (2002). Cortical movement preparation before and after a conscious decision to move. *Consciousness and Cognition, 11*, 162–190.

Trueswell, J.C., Tanenhaus, M.K., & Garnsey, S.M. (1994). Semantic influences on parsing: Use of thematic role information in syntactic disambiguation. *Journal of Memory and Language, 33*, 285–318.

Tuckey, M.R., & Brewer, N. (2003a). How schemas affect eyewitness memory over repeated retrieval attempts. *Applied Cognitive Psychology, 7*, 785–800.

Tuckey, M.R., & Brewer, N. (2003b). The influence of schemas, stimulus ambiguity, and interview schedule on eyewitness memory over time. *Journal of Experimental Psychology: Applied, 9*, 101–118.

Tulving, E. (1972). Episodic and semantic memory. In E. Tulving & W. Donaldson (Eds.), *Organization of memory*. London: Academic Press.

Tulving, E. (1979). Relation between encoding specificity and levels of processing. In L.S. Cermak & F.I.M. Craik (Eds.), *Levels of processing in human memory*. Hillsdale, NJ: Lawrence Erlbaum Associates Inc.

Tulving, E. (2002). Episodic memory: From mind to brain. *Annual Review of Psychology, 53*, 1–25.

Tulving, E., & Pearlstone, Z. (1966). Availability versus accessibility of information in memory for words. *Journal of Verbal Learning and Verbal Behavior, 5*, 381–391.

Turner, M.L., & Engle, R.W. (1989). Is working-memory capacity task dependent? *Journal of Memory and Language, 28*, 127–154.

Tversky, A. (1972). Elimination by aspects: A theory of choice. *Psychological Review, 79*, 281–299.

Tversky, A., & Kahneman, D. (1974). Judgment under uncertainty: Heuristics and biases. *Science, 185*, 1124–1131.

Tversky, A., & Kahneman, D. (1983). Extensional versus intuitive reasoning: The conjunction fallacy in probability judgment. *Psychological Review, 91*, 293–315.

Tversky, A., & Kahneman, D. (1987). Rational choice and the framing of decisions. In R. Hogarth & M. Reder (Eds.), *Rational choice: The contrast between economics and psychology*. Chicago: University of Chicago Press.

Tversky, A., & Koehler, D.J. (1994). Support theory: A non-extensional representation of subjective probability. *Psychological Review, 101*, 547–567.

Tversky, A., & Shafir, E. (1992). The disjunction effect in choice under uncertainty. *Psychological Science, 3*, 305–309.

Tyler, C.W., & Clarke, M.B. (1990). The autostereogram. *SPIE Proceedings, 1256*.

Ucros, C.G. (1989). Mood state-dependent memory: A meta-analysis. *Cognition and Emotion, 3*, 139–167.

Umiltà, C. (2001). Mechanisms of attention. In B. Rapp (Ed.), *The handbook of cognitive neuropsychology*. Philadelphia, PA: Psychology Press.

Underwood, B.J., & Postman, L. (1960). Extra-experimental sources of interference in forgetting. *Psychological Review, 67*, 73–95.

Valentine, T., Bredart, S., Lawson, R., & Ward, G. (1991). What's in a name? Access to information from people's names. *European Journal of Cognitive Psychology, 3*, 147–176.

Valentine, T., Pickering, A., & Darling, S. (2003). Characteristics of eyewitness identification that predict the outcome of real line-ups. *Applied Cognitive Psychology, 17*, 969–993.

Vallar, G., & Baddeley, A.D. (1984). Phonological short-term store, phonological processing and sentence comprehension: A neuropsychological case study. *Cognitive Neuropsychology, 1*, 121–141.

Vallar, G., Di Betta, A.M., & Silveri, M.C. (1997). The phonological short-term store- rehearsal system: Patterns of impairment and neural correlates. *Neuropsychologia, 35*, 795–812.

Vallar, G., & Perani, D. (1987). The anatomy of spatial neglect in humans. In M. Jeannerod (Ed.), *Neurophysiological and neuropsychological aspects of spatial neglect*. Amsterdam: Elsevier.

Van Gompel, R.P.G., Pickering, M.J., & Traxler, M.J. (2001). Re-analysis in sentence processing: Evidence against current constraint-based and two-stage models. *Journal of Memory and Language, 45,* 225–258.

Van Petten, C., Coulson, S., Rubin, S., Plante, E., & Parks, M. (1999). Time course of word identification and semantic integration in spoken language. *Journal of Experimental Psychology: Learning, Memory, and Cognition, 25,* 394–417.

Van Selst, M.V., Ruthruff, E., & Johnston, J.C. (1999). Can practice eliminate the Psychological Refractory Period effect? *Journal of Experimental Psychology: Human Perception and Performance, 25,* 1268–1283.

van Turrennout, M., Hagoort, P., & Brown, C.M. (1998). Brain activity during speaking: From syntax to phonology in 40 milliseconds. *Science, 280,* 572–574.

Vanrie, J., Béatse, E., Wagemans, J., Sunaert, S., & van Hecke, P. (2002). Mental rotation versus invariant features in object perception from different viewpoints: An fMRI study. *Neuropsychologia, 40,* 917–930.

Vargha-Khadem, F., Gadian, D.G., & Mishkin, M. (2002). Dissociations in cognitive memory: The syndrome of developmental amnesia. In *Episodic memory: New directions in research 2002.* New York: Oxford University Press.

Vargha-Khadem, F., Gadian, D.G., Watkins, K.E., Connelly, A., Van Paesschen, W., & Mishkin, M. (1997). Differential effects of early hippocampal pathology on episodic and semantic memory. *Science, 277,* 376–380.

Varner, L.J., & Ellis, H.C. (1998). Cognitive activity and physiological arousal: Processes that mediate mood-congruent memory. *Memory & Cognition, 26,* 939–950.

Velmans, M. (2000). *Understanding consciousness.* London: Routledge.

Velten, E. (1968). A laboratory task for induction of mood states. *Behaviour Research & Therapy, 6,* 473–482.

Vigliocco, G., Antonini, T., & Garrett, M.F. (1997). Grammatical gender is on the top of Italian tongues. *Psychological Science, 8,* 314–317.

Vigliocco, G., & Hartsuiker, R.J. (2002). The interplay of meaning, sound, and syntax in sentence production. *Psychological Bulletin, 128,* 442–472.

Vinette, C., Gosselin, F., & Schyns, P.G. (2004). Spatio-temporal dynamics of face recognition in a flash: It's in the eyes. *Cognitive Science, 28,* 289–301.

von Neumann, J., & Morgenstern, O. (1947). *Theory of games and economic behavior.* Princeton, NJ: Princeton University Press.

Wachtel, P. (1973). Psychodynamics, behavior therapy and the implacable experimenter: An inquiry into the consistency of personality. *Journal of Abnormal Psychology, 82,* 324–334.

Wagenaar, W.A. (1986). My memory: A study of autobiographical memory over six years. *Cognitive Psychology, 18,* 225–252.

Wagenaar, W.A. (1994). Is memory self-serving? In U. Neisser & R. Rivush (Eds.), *The remembering self: Construction and accuracy in the self-narrative.* Cambridge: Cambridge University Press.

Wagner, U., Gais, S., Haider, H., Verleger, R., & Born, J. (2004). Sleep inspires insight. *Nature, 427,* 352–355.

Wallas, G. (1926). *The art of thought.* London: Cape.

Walsh, V., & Rushworth, M. (1999). A primer of magnetic stimulation as a tool for neuropsychology. *Neuropsychologia, 37,* 125–135.

Wang, X.T. (1996). Domain-specific rationality in human choices: Violations of utility axioms and social contexts. *Cognition, 60,* 31–63.

Warren, R.M., & Warren, R.P. (1970). Auditory illusions and confusions. *Scientific American, 223,* 30–36.

Warrington, E.K., & Shallice, T. (1972). Neuropsychological evidence of visual storage in short memory tasks. *Quarterly Journal of Experimental Psychology, 24,* 30–40.

Warrington, E.K., & Taylor, A.M. (1978). Two categorical stages of object recognition. *Perception, 7,* 695–705.

Wason, P.C. (1968). Reasoning about a rule. *Quarterly Journal of Experimental Psychology, 23,* 63–71.

Wason, P.C., & Reich, S.S. (1979). A verbal illusion. *Quarterly Journal of Experimental Psychology, 31,* 591–597.

Wason, P.C., & Shapiro, D. (1971). Natural and contrived experience in reasoning problems. *Quarterly Journal of Experimental Psychology, 23,* 63–71.

Wearing, D. (2005). *Forever today – A memoir of love and amnesia*. New York: Doubleday.

Weber, E.U., & Hsee, C.K. (2000). Culture and individual judgment and decision making. *Applied Psychology: An International Review, 49*, 32–61.

Webopedia (2004). Multitasking. www.webopedia.com/TERM/multitasking.html

Wegner, D.M. (2002). *The illusion of conscious will*. Cambridge, MA: MIT Press.

Wegner, D.M. (2003). The mind's best trick: How we experience conscious will. *Trends in Cognitive Sciences, 7*, 65–69.

Wegner, D.M., & Wheatley, T. (1999). Apparent mental causation: Sources of the experience of the will. *American Psychologist, 54*, 480–492.

Weisberg, R.W., & Suls, J. (1973). An information-processing model of Duncker's candle problem. *Cognitive Psychology, 4*, 255–276.

Weiskrantz, L. (1980). Varieties of residual experience. *Quarterly Journal of Experimental Psychology, 32*, 365–386.

Weiskrantz, L. (1997). *Consciousness lost and found*. Oxford: Oxford University Press.

Weiskrantz. L. (2004). Blindsight. In R.L. Gregory (Ed.), *Oxford companion to the mind*. Oxford: Oxford University Press.

Weiskrantz, L., Warrington, E.K., Sanders, M.D., & Marshall, J. (1974). Visual capacity in the hemianopic field following a restricted occipital ablation. *Brain, 97*, 709–728.

Weisstein, N., & Wong, E. (1986). Figure–ground organization and the spatial and temporal responses of the visual system. In E.C. Schwab & H.C. Nusbaum (Eds.), *Pattern recognition by humans and machines, Vol. 2*. New York: Academic Press.

Welford, A.T. (1952). The psychological refractory period and the timing of high speed performance. *British Journal of Psychology, 43*, 2–19.

Wells, A., & Clark, D.M. (1997). Social phobia: A cognitive approach. In G. Davey (Ed.), *Phobias: A handbook of theory, research and treatment*. Chichester, UK: Wiley.

Wells, A., Clark, D.M., Salkovskis, P., Ludgate, J., Hackmann, A., & Gelder, M. (1995). Social phobia – The role of in-situation safety behaviors in maintaining anxiety and negative beliefs. *Behavior Therapy, 26*, 153–161.

Wells, A., & Papageorgiou, C. (1998). Social phobia: Effects of external attention on anxiety, negative beliefs, and perspective taking. *Behavior Therapy, 29*, 357–370.

Wells, G.L., Malpass, R.S., Lindsay, R.C.L., Fisher, R.P., Turtle, J.W., & Fulero, S.M. (2000). From the lab to the police station: A successful application of eyewitness research. *American Psychologist, 55*, 581–598.

Wells, G.L., & Olson, E.A. (2003). Eyewitness testimony. *Annual Review of Psychology, 54*, 277–295.

Wessinger, C.M., Fendrich, R., & Gazzaniga, M.S. (1997). Islands of residual vision in hemianopic patients. *Journal of Cognitive Neuroscience, 9*, 203–221.

Westen, D. (1996). *Psychology: Mind, brain, and culture*. New York: Wiley.

Wheatstone, C. (1838). Contributions to the physiology of vision. Part 1: On some remarkable and hitherto unobserved phenomena of binocular vision. *Philosophical Transactions of the Royal Society of London, 128*, 371–394.

Wheeldon, L.R (2000). *Aspects of language production*. Hove, UK: Psychology Press.

Wheeler, M.A., Stuss, D.T., & Tulving, E. (1997). Toward a theory of episodic memory: The frontal lobes and autonoetic consciousness. *Psychological Bulletin, 121*, 331–354.

Wickens, C.D. (1984). Processing resources in attention. In R. Parasuraman & D.R. Davies (Eds.), *Varieties of attention*. London: Academic Press.

Wilkinson, L., & Shanks, D.R. (2004). Intentional control and implicit sequence learning. *Journal of Experimental Psychology: Learning, Memory, and Cognition, 30*, 354–369.

Willmes, K., & Poeck, K. (1993). To what extent can aphasic syndromes be localized? *Brain, 116*, 1527–1540.

Wilson, A.E., & Ross, M. (2003). The identity function of autobiographical memory: Time is on our side. *Memory, 11*, 137–149.

Winningham, R.G., Hyman, I.E., & Dinnel, D.L. (2000). Flashbulb memories? The effects of when the initial memory report was obtained. *Memory, 8*, 209–216.

Wise, R.A., & Safer, M.A. (2004). What US judges know and believe about eyewitness testimony. *Applied Cognitive Psychology, 18*, 427–443.

Wixted, J.T. (2004). The psychology and neuroscience of forgetting. *Annual Review of Psychology*, *55*, 235–269.

Woike, B., Gershkovich, I., Piorkowski, R., & Polo, M. (1999). The role of motives in the content and structure of autobiographical memory. *Journal of Personality and Social Psychology*, *76*, 600–612.

Wojciulik, E., Kanwisher, N., & Driver, J. (1998). Modulation of activity in the fusiform face area by covert attention: An fMRI study. *Journal of Neurophysiology*, *79*, 1574–1579.

Wright, G. (1984). *Behavioral decision theory*. Harmondsworth, UK: Penguin.

Wynn, V.E., & Logie, R.H. (1998). The veracity of long-term memories – Did Bartlett get it right? *Applied Cognitive Psychology*, *12*, 1–20.

Yasuda, K., Watanabe, O., & Ono, Y. (1997). Dissociation between semantic and autobiographic memory: A case report. *Cortex*, *33*, 623–638.

Yates, F.A. (1966). *The art of memory*. London: Routledge & Kegan Paul.

Yates, J.F., Lee, J., Shinotsuka, H., Patalano, A.L., & Sieck, W.R. (1998). Cross- cultural variations in probability accuracy: Beyond general knowledge overconfidence? *Organizational Behavior and Human Decision Processes*, *74*, 89–117.

Yiend, J. (2004). *Cognition, emotion and psychopathology: Theoretical, empirical and clinical directions*. Cambridge: Cambridge University Press.

Young, A.W., Hay, D.C., & Ellis, A.W. (1985). The faces that launched a thousand slips: Everyday difficulties and errors in recognizing people. *British Journal of Psychology*, *76*, 495–523.

Young, A.W., Hellawell, D., & de Haan, E. (1988). Cross-domain semantic priming in normal subjects and a prosopagnosic patient. *Quarterly Journal of Experimental Psychology*, *40*, 561–580.

Young, A.W., McWeeny, K.H., Hay, D.C., & Ellis, A.W. (1986a). Naming and categorization latencies for faces and written names. *Quarterly Journal of Experimental Psychology*, *38A*, 297–318.

Young, A.W., McWeeny, K.H., Hay, D.C., & Ellis, A.W. (1986b). Matching familiar and unfamiliar faces on identity and expression. *Psychological Research*, *48*, 63–68.

Young, A.W., Newcombe, F., de Haan, E.H.F., Small, M., & Hay, D.C. (1993). Face perception after brain injury: Selective impairments affecting identity and expression. *Brain*, *116*, 941–959.

Zajonc, R.B. (1980). Feeling and thinking: Preferences need no inferences. *American Psychologist*, *35*, 151–175.

Zajonc, R.B. (1984). On the primacy of affect. *American Psychologist*, *39*, 117–123.

Zwaan, R.A., & van Oostendop, U. (1993). Do readers construct spatial representations in naturalistic story comprehension? *Discourse Processes*, *16*, 125–143.

Glossary

Accommodation: adjustment in the shape of the eye's lens when focusing on objects; a cue used in depth perception.

Adaptive expertise: using acquired knowledge to solve familiar problems efficiently; see routine expertise.

Algorithms: computational procedures providing specified sets of steps to a solution.

Agrammatism: a condition in brain-damaged patients in which speech lacks grammatical structure and many function words and word endings are omitted.

Amnesia: a condition caused by brain damage in which there is substantial impairment of long-term memory; the condition includes both anterograde amnesia and retrograde amnesia.

Anterograde amnesia: a reduced ability to remember information acquired *after* the onset of amnesia.

Anton's syndrome: a condition found in some blind people in which their visual imagery is misinterpreted as visual perception.

Aphasia: impairment in the comprehension or production of language due to brain damage.

Apperceptive agnosia: this is a form of visual agnosia in which there is impaired perceptual analysis of familiar objects.

Artificial intelligence: this involves developing computer programs producing intelligent outcomes in ways different from human functioning; see computational modeling.

Associative agnosia: this is a form of visual agnosia in which perceptual processing is fairly normal but there is an impaired ability to derive the meaning of objects.

Attentional bias: selective attention to threat-related stimuli presented at the same time as neutral ones.

Attentional blink: reduced ability to identify a target presented in a rapid sequence of stimuli when it is preceded shortly beforehand with another target requiring identification.

Auditory phonological agnosia: a condition in which there is poor perception of unfamiliar words and non-words, but not familiar words.

Autostereogram: a complex two-dimensional image that is perceived as three-dimensional when it is *not* focused on for a period of time.

Availability heuristic: the assumption that the frequencies of events can be estimated accurately by their accessibility in memory.

Back-propagation: a learning mechanism in which the responses produced by a computer network are compared against the correct responses.

Base-rate information: the relative frequency with which an event occurs in a population.

Belief bias: the tendency to decide whether the conclusion of a syllogism is valid on the basis of whether or not it is believable.

Binocular cues: cues to depth requiring both eyes to be used together.

Binocular disparity: the slight difference in optical images on the retina of each eye when an object is observed.

Binocular rivalry: this occurs when an observer perceives only one visual stimulus when two are presented, one to each eye.

Blindsight: the ability of some brain-damaged patients to respond appropriately to visual stimuli in the absence of conscious visual perception.

Bottom-up processing: processing that is directly influenced by environmental stimuli.

Bounded rationality: the notion that people are as rational as their processing limitations permit.

Bridging inferences: inferences that are drawn to increase the coherence between the current and preceding parts of a text.

Broca's aphasia: a form of language disorder in brain-damaged patients involving non-fluent speech and grammatical errors.

Category-specific deficits: problems in identifying members of certain semantic categories as a consequence of brain damage.

Central executive: a modality-free, limited capacity, component of working memory.

Change blindness: failure to detect changes in the visual environment.

Change blindness blindness: people's mistaken belief that they would notice visual changes that are in fact very rarely detected.

Charles Bonnet syndrome: a condition associated with eye disease involving recurrent and detailed hallucinations.

Chunks: stored units formed from integrating smaller pieces of information.

Clause: part of a sentence that contains a subject and a verb.

Co-articulation: the finding that the production of a phoneme in speech is influenced (and distorted) by the production of the previous sound and preparations for the next sound.

Cognitive appraisal: interpreting the current situation to decide whether it is threatening or not, and deciding whether one can cope with it.

Common ground: the mutual knowledge and beliefs shared by a speaker and a listener.

Computational modeling: constructing computer programs that simulate or mimic some aspects of human cognitive functioning; see artificial intelligence.

Concepts: mental representations of categories of objects or items.

Conditional reasoning: a form of deductive reasoning based on "IF . . . THEN" statements.

Conjunction fallacy: the mistaken belief that the probability of a conjunction of two events (A and B) is greater than the probability of one of them (A or B).

Connectionist networks: these consist of elementary units or nodes connected together; each network has various structures or layers.

Consolidation: a process that is mostly completed within several hours, but can last for years, and that fixes information in long-term memory.

Convergence: a cue to depth based on the eye turning inwards more when focusing on very close objects.

Conversion error: a mistake in syllogistic reasoning occurring because a statement is invalidly converted from one form into another.

Cross-modal attention: the coordination of attention across two or more modalities (e.g., vision and hearing).

Cued recall: recall in which relevant cues are presented to assist retrieval; see free recall.

Deductive reasoning: a form of reasoning in which necessarily valid (or invalid) conclusions can be drawn assuming the truth of certain statements or premises.

Defining attributes: those semantic features that are both necessary and sufficient for something to be an instance of a given concept.

Deliberate practice: systematic practice in which the learner is given informative feedback about his or her performance and has the opportunity to correct his or her errors.

Deontic reasoning: a form of reasoning concerned with what we should or should not do; concerned with obligations, rights, and social contracts.

Depictive representations: representations (e.g., visual images) resembling pictures in that objects within them are organized spatially.

Digit span: the number of random digits that can be repeated back correctly in order after hearing them once; it is used as a measure of short-term memory capacity.

Direct retrieval: involuntary recall of autobiographical memories triggered by a specific retrieval cue (e.g., being in the same place as the original event); see generative retrieval.

Discourse markers: spoken words and phrases that don't contribute directly to the content of what is being said but still serve various functions (e.g., clarification of the speaker's intentions).

Dissociation: the finding that a brain-damaged patient performs one task at a normal level but performs very poorly on a second task.

Double dissociation: the finding that some individuals (often brain-damaged) do well on task A and poorly on task B, whereas others show the opposite pattern.

Ecological validity: the extent to which the findings of laboratory studies are applicable to everyday settings.

Egocentric heuristic: a comprehension strategy in which listeners interpret what they hear based on their own knowledge rather than on knowledge they share with the speaker.

Eidetic imagery: visual imagery resembling visual perception of the same scene or object.

Elaborative inferences: inferences that add details to a text that is being read.

Encoding specificity principle: the notion that retrieval depends on the overlap between the information available at retrieval and the information within the memory trace.

Endogenous spatial attention: attention to a given spatial location determined by voluntary or goal-directed mechanisms; see exogenous spatial attention.

Episodic buffer: a component of working memory that can hold information from the phonological loop, the visuospatial sketchpad and long-term memory.

Episodic memory: a form of long-term memory concerned with personal experiences or episodes that happened in a given place at a specific times; see semantic memory.

Estimator variables: factors influencing the accuracy of eyewitness testimony over which the criminal justice system has no control; see system variables.

Event-related potentials (ERPs): the pattern of electroencephalograph (EEG) activity obtained by averaging the brain responses to the same stimulus presented repeatedly.

Exogenous spatial attention: attention to a given spatial locations determined by "involuntary" mechanisms triggered by external stimuli (e.g., loud noise); see endogenous spatial attention.

Expertise: the specific knowledge an expert has about a given domain (e.g., that an engineer may have about bridges).

Explicit learning: learning that involves conscious awareness of what has been learned; see implicit learning.

Explicit memory: retrieval of information from long-term memory based on the use of conscious recollection; see implicit memory.

Exposure therapy: a form of therapy used with some anxiety disorders in which the patient is confronted by the feared stimuli or situations.

Extinction: a disorder of visual attention in which a stimulus presented to the side opposite the brain damage is not detected when another stimulus is presented at the same time.

Family resemblances: the notion that members of a category share some (but not all) features or attributes with other category members.

Far transfer: beneficial effects of previous learning on current learning in a dissimilar context; a form of positive transfer.

Figurative language: forms of language (e.g., metaphor) that are not intended to be taken literally.

Figure–ground segregation: the perceptual organization of the visual field into a figure (object of central interest) and a ground (less important background).

Flashbulb memories: vivid and detailed memories of dramatic events (e.g., September 11, 2001).

Framing effect: the influence of irrelevant aspects of a situation (e.g., wording of the problem) on decision making.

Free recall: a memory test in which the to-be-remembered items are recall in any order; see cued recall.

Freudian slip: an error in speech (or action) that is motivated and reveals the speaker's underlying desires or thoughts.

Functional fixedness: the inflexible use of the usual function of an object in problem solving.

Functional magnetic resonance imaging (fMRI): a technique providing information about brain activity based on the detection of magnetic changes; it has reasonable temporal and spatial resolution.

Fuzzy logic: used to combine information from cues in perception when the available information is imprecise.

Generalized anxiety disorder: a mental disorder characterized by excessive worry and anxiety about many of life's issues.

Generative retrieval: deliberate or voluntary construction of autobiographical memories based on an individual's current goals; see direct retrieval.

Goal-derived categories: categories in which all the members of the category satisfy some goal (e.g., increasing human happiness).

Graphemes: basic units of written language.

Hallucinations: visual experiences similar to visual perception occurring in the absence of the relevant environmental stimulus.

Heuristics: rules of thumb that often (but not invariably) solve any given problem.

Hill climbing: a heuristic involving changing the present state on a problem into one apparently closer to the goal.

Homonyms: words having one pronunciation but two spellings (e.g., "pain"; "pane").

Idiots savants: individuals who have limited outstanding expertise in spite of being mentally retarded.

Ill-defined problems: problems in which the definition of the problem statement is imprecisely specified; the initial state, goal state, and methods to be used to solve the problem may be unclear; see well-defined problems.

Implicit learning: learning information without conscious awareness of having learned; see explicit learning.

Implicit memory: retrieval of information from long-term memory that doesn't depend on conscious recollection; see explicit memory.

Inattentional blindness: failure to detect an unexpected object appearing in a visual display; see change blindness.

Incubation: the finding that a problem is solved more easily when it is put aside for some time; sometimes claimed to depend on unconscious processes.

Infantile amnesia: the inability of adults to recall autobiographical memories from early childhood (also known as childhood amnesia).

Inflecting language: a language in which grammatical relationships are shown by altering word endings (e.g., -s to indicate plural nouns).

Inner scribe: the component of the visuospatial sketchpad that deals with spatial and movement information.

Insight: the experience of suddenly realizing how to solve a problem.

Integrative agnosia: impaired object recognition due to problems in integrating or combining elements of objects.

Interpreter: the notion proposed by Gazzaniga et al. (2002) that only the left side of the brain is involved in seeking explanations for events occurring externally and internally.

Interpretive bias: a tendency to interpret ambiguous stimuli and situations in a threatening way.

Jargon aphasia: a brain-damaged condition in which speech is reasonably correct grammatically, but there are great problems in finding the right words.

Knowledge-lean problems: problems that can be solved without the use of much prior knowledge, with most of the necessary information being provided by the problem statement; see knowledge-rich problems.

Knowledge-rich problems: problems that can only be solved through the use of considerable amounts of prior knowledge; see knowledge-lean problems.

Korsakoff's syndrome: a condition caused by chronic alcoholism in which there are severe problems with long-term memory.

Lemmas: abstract words possessing semantic and syntactic features but not phonological ones.

Lexical decision task: a task in which participants decide rapidly whether a letter string forms a word.

Lexical identification shift: the finding that an ambiguous sound tends to be perceived to form a word rather than a non-word.

Lexicon: mental dictionary in which the words we know are stored.

Logical inferences: inferences depending solely on the meaning of words.

Long-term working memory: this is used by experts to store relevant information in long-term memory and to access it through retrieval cues in working memory.

Loss aversion: the notion that individuals are more sensitive to potential losses than they are to potential gains.

Magneto-encephalography (MEG): a brain-scanning technique based on recording the magnetic fields generated by brain activity; it possesses very good temporal resolution and reasonable spatial resolution.

McGurk effect: the phoneme perceived in speech is influenced by visual and acoustic information when the two are in conflict.

Means–ends analysis: a commonly used heuristic based on noting the difference between the current and goal states, and creating a sub-goal to reduce this difference.

Mental model: a representation of a possible state of affairs in the world.

Mere exposure effect: an effect in which stimuli previously presented (even if not perceived consciously) are preferred to new ones.

Meta-analysis: statistical analyses based on combining data from numerous studies on a given issue.

Metacognition: an individual's beliefs and knowledge about his or her own cognitive processes and strategies.

Metaphor: a figure of speech in which a word is said to mean something that it only resembles; for example, a timid person is described as a sheep.

Misdirection: the various techniques used by magicians to make spectators focus on some irrelevant aspect of the situation while they perform the crucial part of a trick.

Mixed error effect: speech errors that are semantically and phonologically related to the intended word.

Modularity: the assumption that the cognitive system consists of several fairly independent processors or modules.

Monocular cues: cues to depth that can be used with only one eye, but can also be used with both eyes.

Mood congruity: the finding that learning is often best when the material learned has the same affective value as the learner's mood state.

Mood-state-dependent memory (or recall): the finding that memory is better when the mood state at retrieval is the same as that at learning than when the two mood states differ.

Morphemes: the smallest units of meaning within words.

Motion parallax: a cue to depth based on the tendency of images of closer objects to move faster across the retina than images of more distant objects.

Multitasking: performing two or more tasks at the same time by switching rapidly between tasks.

Near transfer: beneficial effects of previous learning on current learning in a similar context; a form of positive transfer.

Negative transfer: past experience in solving one problem disrupts the ability to solve a similar current problem.

Neglect: a disorder of visual attention in which stimuli or parts of stimuli presented to the side opposite the brain damage are undetected and not responded to; the condition resembles extinction, but is more severe.

Neologisms: made-up words produced by patients with jargon aphasia.

Normative theories: as applied to decision making, theories focusing on how people should make decisions.

Oculomotor cues: cues to depth based on sensations produced by contractions of the muscles around the eye.

Omission bias: the tendency to prefer inaction over action when engaged in decision making.

Operation span: the maximum number of items (arithmetical questions + words) from which an individual can recall all the last words; used to assess working memory capacity.

Optic ataxia: a condition in which there are problems with making visually guided movements.

Optic flow: the structured pattern of light falling on the retina.

Optimization: the selection of the best choice in decision making.

Overconfidence bias: overestimating the probability that an answer to a general-knowledge or other question is correct.

Panic disorder: an anxiety disorder characterized by frequent panic attacks.

Parallel processing: two or more cognitive processes occurring at the same time; see serial processing.

Parsing: an analysis of the syntactical or grammatical structure of sentences.

Perceptual defense: greater difficulty in perceiving threatening or taboo stimuli than neutral ones.

Perceptual priming: enhanced processing (identification) of a specific degraded stimulus when it has previously been presented in a non-degraded form; see priming.

Perceptual representation system: a long-term memory system that underlies perceptual priming.

Pheromones: chemical substances produced by individuals that influence the behavior of others.

Phonemes: basic speech sounds conveying meaning.

Phonemic restoration effect: the finding that listeners are unaware that a phoneme has been deleted from an auditorily presented sentence.

Phonological dyslexia: a condition in which familiar words can be read, but there are problems with reading unfamiliar words and non-words.

Phonological loop: a component of working memory in which speech-based information is held and subvocal articulation occurs.

Phonological similarity effect: the finding that immediate recall of word lists in the correct order is impaired when the words sound similar to each other.

Phonology: information about the sounds of words and parts of words.

Phrase: a group of words expressing a single idea; it is smaller in scope than a clause.

Planning fallacy: the tendency to underestimate the time it will take to complete a task resembling similar tasks completed in the past.

Positive transfer: past experience of solving one problem makes it easier to solve a similar current problem.

Positron emission tomography (PET): a brain-scanning technique based on the detection of positrons; it has reasonable spatial resolution but poor temporal resolution.

Pragmatics: the study of the ways in which language is used and understood in the real world, including a consideration of its intended meaning.

Predictive inferences: making assumptions about what will happen next on the basis of what is currently happening.

Preformulation: this is used in speech production to reduce processing costs by using phrases often used previously.

Premises: statements that are assumed to be true for the purposes of deductive reasoning.

Prepositions: grammatical words indicating a relation; examples are "with" and "to."

Priming: facilitated processing of a repeated stimulus when presented for the second or subsequent time; see perceptual priming.

Principle of truth: the notion that we represent assertions by constructing mental models containing what is true but not what is false.

Proactive interference: disruption of memory by previous learning (often of similar material); see retroactive interference.

Problem representation: the way in which the problem solver represents a problem based on what seem to be its crucial features.

Problem space: an abstract description of all the possible states of affairs that can occur in a problem situation.

Procedural memory: a long-term memory system concerned with motor and cognitive skills; it may also be involved in priming.

Production systems: these consist of numerous "IF . . . THEN" production rules in which the action is carried out whenever the appropriate condition is present.

Progress monitoring: this is a heuristic used in problem solving in which insufficiently rapid progress towards solution produces criterion failure and the adoption of a different strategy.

Proposition: a statement that makes an assertion or denial and which can be true or false.

Prosodic cues: features of spoken language such as stress and intonation.

Prosopagnosia: a condition caused by brain damage in which patients cannot recognize familiar faces but can recognize familiar objects.

Prototype: a central description or abstraction that represents a category.

Proust phenomenon: the tendency for odors to be especially strong cues for recalling very old vivid and emotional personal memories.

Psychological refractory period (PRP) effect: the slowing of response to the second of two stimuli when they are presented close together in time.

Pure word deafness: a condition involving severely impaired speech perception combined with good speech production, reading, writing, and perception of non-speech sounds.

Rationalization: in Bartlett's theory, the tendency in recall of stories to produce errors that conform to the cultural expectations of the rememberer.

Reading span: the largest number of sentences read for comprehension from which an individual can recall all the final words more than 50% of the time, it is used as a measure of working memory capacity.

Recognition heuristic: using the knowledge that only one out of two objects is recognized to make a judgment.

Reduplicative paramnesia: a memory disorder in which the person believes multiple copies of people and places exist.

Reminiscence bump: the tendency of older people to recall a disproportionate number of autobiographical memories from the years of adolescence and early adulthood.

Representativeness heuristic: the assumption that representative or typical members of a category are encountered most frequently.

Repression: motivated forgetting of traumatic or other very threatening events.

Retroactive interference: disruption of memory by learning of other material during the retention interval; see proactive interference.

Retrograde amnesia: impaired memory for events occurring before the onset of amnesia.

Routine expertise: using acquired knowledge to develop strategies for dealing with novel problems; see adaptive expertise.

Saccade: a fast eye movement or jump that cannot be altered after being initiated.

Satisficing: selection of the first choice that meets certain minimum requirements; the word is formed from the two words "satisfactory" and "sufficing."

Schemas: organized packets of information about the world, events, or people that are stored in long-term memory.

Scripts: organized information or schemas that represent typical events (e.g., going to a restaurant).

Segmentation problem: the listener's problem of dividing the almost continuous sounds of speech into separate phonemes and words.

Semantic memory: a form of long-term memory consisting of general knowledge about the world, language, and so on; see episodic memory.

Serial processing: processing in which one process is completed before the next process starts; see parallel processing.

Single-unit recording: an invasive technique permitting the study of activity in single neurons

Size constancy: objects are perceived to have a given size regardless of the size of the retinal image.

Social phobia: an anxiety disorder characterized by extreme fear (and avoidance) of social situations.

Speedreading: a technique for reading that is about seven times faster than normal reading but allegedly results in no loss of understanding.

Spillover effect: any given word is fixated longer during reading when it is preceded by a rare word rather than a common word.

Split attention: allocation of attention to two non-adjacent regions of visual space.

Split-brain patients: these are patients in whom most of the direct links between the two hemispheres have been severed; as a result, they can experience problems in coordinating their processing and behavior.

Spoonerism: a speech error where the initial letter or letters of two words are switched.

Spreading activation: the notion that activation or energy spreads from an activated node (e.g., word) to other nodes related nodes.

Stereopsis: a cue to depth based on binocular disparity.

Stroop effect: the finding that naming the colors in which words are printed is slower when the words are conflicting color words (e.g., the word RED printed in green).

Subliminal perception: perception occurring below the level of conscious awareness.

Subordinate clause: a minor clause differing from a main clause in that it cannot form a sentence on its own; it generally starts with a word such as "that," "which," or "who."

Subtractivity: the notion that brain damage can subtract or remove aspects of brain functioning but cannot lead to the development of new ones.

Sunk-cost effect: expending additional resources to justify some previous commitment (e.g., throwing good money after bad).

Surface dyslexia: a condition in which brain-damaged patients cannot read irregular words but can read regular ones.

Syllable: a unit of speech consisting of a vowel sound with or without one or more consonants.

Syllogism: a logical argument consisting of two

premises (e.g., ("All X are Y")) and a conclusion; syllogisms formed the basis for the first logical system attributed to Aristotle.

System variables: factors influencing the accuracy of eyewitness testimony over which the criminal justice system does have control; see estimator variables.

Template: as applied to chess - an abstract, schematic structure consisting of a mixture of fixed and variable information about chess pieces.

Texture gradient: the rate of change of texture density from front to back of a slanting object.

Thought congruity: the finding that an individual's free associations and thoughts are often congruent with his or her mood state.

Tip-of-the-tongue phenomenon: the experience of having a specific concept in mind but being unable to access the correct word to describe it.

Top-down processing: stimulus processing that is affected by internal factors such as the individual's past experience and expectations.

Typicality gradient: the ordering of the members of a category in terms of how typical of that category they seem to be.

Unconscious perception: perceptual processes occurring below the level of conscious awareness.

Underspecification: a strategy used to reduce processing costs in speech production by producing simplified expressions.

Utility: the subjective desirability of a given outcome in decision making.

Ventriloquist illusion: the mistaken perception that sounds are coming from their apparent visual source, as in ventriloquism.

Viewpoint-dependent theories: theories of object recognition based on the assumption that objects can be recognized more easily from some angles than from others; see viewpoint-invariant theories.

Viewpoint-invariant theories: theories of object recognition based on the assumption that objects can be recognized equally easily from all angles; see viewpoint-dependent theories.

Visual agnosia: a condition in which there are great problems in recognizing objects presented visually even though visual information reaches the visual cortex.

Visual buffer: within Kosslyn's theory, the part of the brain involved in producing depictive representations in visual imagery and visual perception.

Visual cache: the component of the visuospatial sketchpad that stores information about visual form and color.

Visuospatial sketchpad: a component of working memory that is involved in visual and spatial processing of information.

Wallpaper illusion: a visual illusion in which staring at patterned wallpaper makes it seem as if parts of the pattern are floating in front of the wall.

Weapon focus: the finding that eyewitnesses pay so much attention to the weapon that they tend to ignore other details.

Well-defined problems: problems in which the initial state, goal, and methods available for solving them are clearly laid out; see ill-defined problems.

Wernicke's aphasia: a form of language disorder in brain-damaged patients involving impaired comprehension and fluent speech with many content words missing.

Word-length effect: fewer long words than short words can be recalled immediately after presentation in the correct order.

Word meaning deafness: a condition involving impairment of the ability to understand spoken (but not written) language.

Working memory: a system having the functions of cognitive processing and the temporary storage of information.

Working memory capacity: individual differences in the ability to process and store information at the same time; assessed in various ways including by reading span.

Author index

ABC Research Group 332, 337
Ackerman, P. L. 175, 398
Aggleton, J. P. 153
Aguirre, G. K. 80
Ahmed, F. S. 254
Ahn, W. 318, 320
Aizenstein, H. J. 186, 187
Alexander, M. 119
Allen, B. P. , 204, 223
Allopenna, P. D. 260, 266
Alpert, N. M. 97
Alsop, D. C. 136, 171
Altenberg, B. 289
Althoff, R. R. 148, 149
Altman, G. T. M. 243
Amador, M. 229
Anderson, A. W. 82
Anderson, E. J. 167
Anderson, J. R. 10, 20
Anderson, R. C. 278
Anderson, S. A. 217
Anderson, S. J. 192, 193
Andrade, J. 94, 152, 169, 177
Andres, P. 172
Andrews, B. 196, 203
Anglin, J. M. 77
Anllo-Vento, L. 121
Antoniadis, E. 163
Antonini, T. 297
Archibald, Y. M. 33
Aristotle, 49, 279, 308, 389
Arkes, H. R. 344, 345
Aronson, E. 144
Ashby, F. G. 315, 316, 317, 320, 321
Atkins, P. 249
Atkinson, R. C. 9, 151, 152, 160, 161, 162, 165, 176, 234
Atkinson, R. L. 234
Atlas, S. 136, 171
Awh, E. 117
Ayton, P. 344, 345
Azuma, T. 254

Baars, B. J. 294, 430, 432, 434, 435
Babcock, L. 349, 350
Bachoud-Levi, A. C. 98
Baddeley, A. D. 94, 136, 138, 143, 144, 150, 152, 161, 165, 166, 167, 168, 169, 171, 173, 174, 176, 177, 205
Bahrick, H. P. 192
Bahrick, P. O. 192
Bailey, P. J. 262

Balin, J. A. 264, 265, 267
Banich, M. T. 8
Banks, S. M. 345
Banks, W. P. 435
Barclay, J. R. 274, 284
Barker, D. R. 167
Barnett, S. M. 373
Baron, J. 346, 354
Barr, D. J. 264, 265, 267
Barrett, L. 77
Barron, G. 347
Barsalou, L. W. 210, 309, 312, 313, 319
Barston, J. L. 388, 399
Bartelt, O. A. 116, 117
Bartlett, F. C. 225, 275, 276, 277, 279
Bartolomeo, P. 95, 97, 98, 100, 120
Bastard, P. 262
Bates, E. 301, 302
Baynes, K. 429, 430
Béatse, E. 67
Beauvais, J. 345
Beauvois, M.-F. 240, 262
Beck, M. R. 103, 104
Becker, J. T. 160
Beeman, M. J. 362
Behrmann, M. 82
Beier, M. E. 175, 398
Bekerian, D. A. 196, 203
Bem, D. J. 234
Ben-Zeev, T. 338, 373, 375, 376
Benn, W. 339
Bennett, E. S. 173
Benson, P. J. 34, 70
Bentin, S. 78
Bergus, G. B. 350
Bernat, E. 51, 57, 59
Berndt, R. S. 152, 153, 302
Bernsten, D. 217
Best, D. L. 205
Betsch, T. 331
Bettman, J. R. 353
Bettuci, D. 34, 70
Biederman, I. 64, 65
Birch, H. G. 361
Black, J. B. 275, 285
Black, S. 262
Blackburn, S. G. 40
Blackmore, S. 435
Blake, R. 23
Blaney, P. H. 415

Blankenship, S. 364
Blasko, D. 280
Bleckley, M. K. 175
Blodgett, A. 245, 246
Blumer, C. 344
Bögels, S. M. 17
Boland, J. E. 245, 246
Bonini, N. 338
Borges, J.-L. 307
Born, J. 364
Boucart, M. 70
Bourke, P.A. 136, 137
Bowden, E. M. 361, 362
Bower, G. H. 275, 285, 411, 412, 413, 414, 416
Boyes-Braem, P. 308
Boyle, M. O. 175, 398
Bracken, E. 191
Bradley, A. C. 167
Braine, M. D. S. 392, 393, 394
Brammer, M. J. 92
Brandt, S. A. 116
Bransford, J. D. 274, 277, 284
Brauener, J. S. 264, 265, 267
Bredart, S. 86
Brennan, C. 55, 56
Brewer, N. T. 225, 350
Brewin, C. R. 196, 203
Bridgeman, B. 10, 31, 34
Bridgstock, R. 76
Brinkmann, B. 331
Brooks, K. 361
Brooksbank, B. W. L. 53
Brown, A. S. 191
Brown, C. M. 297, 298
Brown, M. W. 153
Brown, R. 192
Bruce, V. 10, 31, 34, 37, 42, 43, 44, 47, 73, 79, 83, 84, 86, 87, 226
Brugieres, P. 98
Bruner, J. S. 4
Bruno, N. 43
Brysbaert, M. 152
Bucciarelli, M. 397
Buchanan, N. 168
Buck, E. 397, 402
Bucker, R. L. 158, 162
Buckhout, R. 228
Buckner, J. P. 213
Buehler, R. 331, 334
Bull, R. 193, 229
Bullemer, P. 182
Bülthoff, H. H. 64, 65, 66
Bundesen, C. 121
Bunge, S. A. 139, 172
Bunting, M. F. 175
Burgess, N. 151, 156, 159
Burke, K. A. 275, 284
Burns, B. D. 358, 359, 380, 384
Burt, D. M. 77
Burton, A. M. 79, 86, 226
Butcher, K. R. 286
Butterfield, S. 253
Butters, N. 160
Butterworth, B. 169, 302
Buxton, R. B. 121
Byrne, R. M. J. 394, 401, 402

Caccapoppolo-van Vliet, E. 242, 249
Caldara, R. 78, 80
Calder, A. J. 84
Camden, C. T. 294
Camerer, C. 349, 350
Cameron, K. 152
Campbell, L. 418
Campion, J. 56
Campion, N. 275
Camposano, S. 97
Caramazza, A. 71, 302
Carey, D. P. 31, 32, 33, 34
Carlsmith, J. M. 144
Carlson, K. A. 342
Carlson, T. B. 290
Carmel, D. 78
Carpenter, P. A. 138, 140, 174, 272
Carreiras, M. 244, 245
Carter, C. S. 186, 187
Casscells, W. 327, 330
Ceci, S. J. 373, 375, 376, 382, 383
Ceraso, J. 394
Cermak, L. S. 160
Chabris, C. F. 380
Chabris, F. 103, 104, 106, 107
Chalmers, D. J. 427, 434
Chambaron, S. 183
Chan, J. C. K. 204, 223
Changeaux, J.-P. 430, 434
Channon, S. 182, 184, 185, 187
Chapman, G. B. 347, 350, 393
Chapman, J. P. 393
Charness, N. 377, 380, 381, 382, 383, 384
Chase, W. G. 376, 378, 379, 382
Chavda, S. 121
Chen, Z. 366, 367, 368
Chertkow, H. 262
Chiat, S. 302, 303
Chin, J. 182, 185, 187
Choi, I. 339, 347, 354
Choi, J. 339, 347, 354
Chokron, S. 120
Chomsky, N. 234
Christal, R. E. 174, 175
Chronicle, E. P. 371, 373
Chu, S. 211
Chun, M. M. 80
Churchland, P. S. 11, 13
Cipolotti, L. 242
Clancy, S. A. 197
Claparède, E. 147, 148, 152
Clark, D. M. 16, 17, 18, 415
Clark, H. H. 290, 291
Clark, K. 120, 186, 187
Clarke, M. B. 43
Clarkson, G. 379, 380
Cleeremans, A. 179, 180, 181, 188
Clifford. E. 106
Clifton, C. 244, 245, 268
Cochran, J. 186, 187
Cohen, A. 55, 56
Cohen, L. 51, 432
Cohen, N. J. 55, 56, 148, 149, 156, 157, 160
Collett, T. S. 43
Collette, F. 172
Collins, A. 313

Collins, D. 82
Colman, A. M. 90, 423
Colom, R. 175
Coltheart, M, 7, 239, 240, 241, 242, 249
Combs, J. 335
Conezio, J. 192
Connelly, A. 156, 157
Connine, C. M. 255, 260, 280
Connolly, T. 347
Conway, A. R. A. 128, 175, 199, 204
Conway, M. A. 192, 193, 207, 209, 214, 215, 217, 218, 219
Cook, A. E. 283, 286
Cook, L. 417
Cooney, J. W. 428, 430
Cooper, R, 12
Copeland, D. E. 396, 397, 398, 402
Corbett, A. T. 274
Corbetta, M. 120
Coren, S. 29
Corkin, S. 156, 160
Cosmides, L. 330, 331
Costall, A7. 193, 276
Coulson, S. 260
Courtney, S. M. 171, 176
Cowan, N. 149, 150, 175, 334
Cowey, A. 54, 56, 59
Cowley, J. J. 53
Cox, J. R. 392
Creem, S. H. 35
Crystal, D. 233
Culham, T. 34
Curby, K. M. 82
Curran, T. 82
Curtis, B. 249
Cusinato, A. 242
Cutler, A. 253, 257, 268
Cutler, B. 224
Cutting, J. E. 43

Dahl, L. C. 204, 223
Dalgleish, T. 416, 420
Dalla Barba, G. 98
Daneman, M. 53, 174
Darling, S. 224, 225
Darrah, C. 127
David, A. 92
Davidson, D. 278, 279, 284
Davidson, J. W. 383
Davies, A. 135, 139, 140
Davies, D. R. 139
Davies, G. M. 196, 203
Davis, M. H. 258
Davison, L. A. 410
De Bleser, R. 301
De Broeck, P. 314, 319
De Corte, E. 368
de Gelder, B. 98
De Groot, A. D. 378
de Haan, E. 79, 84
Dean, M. 84
Debner, J. A. 52, 199, 204
Dehaene, S. 51, 185, 430, 431, 432, 433, 434
Delaney, P. F. 370, 371
Dell, G. S. 293, 295, 296, 297, 298, 299, 301, 303, 304
Della Sala, S. 161
DeLucia, P.R. 28, 29

Denis, M. 97, 99, 318, 320
Dérouesné, J. 240, 262
D'Esposito, M. 136, 139, 171
Dessalegn, B. G. 280
Detre, J. A. 136, 171
d'Hondt, W. 384
Di Betta, A. M. 169
Dick, F. 301, 302
Diehl, R. L. 268
Dijkerman, H. C. 34
Dijkstra, T. 257, 266
Dinnel, D. L. 193
Dixon, N. F. 49, 53, 58
Dixon, P. 32
Dodds, R. A. 363
Donchin, E. 169
Donnelly, C. M. 192, 193
Donner, T. H. 116, 117
Dooling, D. J. 277
Dosher, B. A. 274
Douglas, K. 191
Downes, J. J. 211
Downing, P. 118
Drivdahl, S. B. 103, 104
Driver, J. 119, 120, 121, 123, 125, 431
Dronkers, N. 301, 302
Dubois, J. 97, 99
Dubowitz, D. J. 121
Duff, S. C. 174
Duhamel, J. R. 97
Duncan, J. 121, 136, 137
Duncker, K. 364, 365, 366
Durlach, C. 163
Duscherer, K. 57
Dysart, J. 227

Eakin, D. K. 223
Eastwood, J. D. 50, 59
Eberhard, K. M. 246, 261, 264
Ebbinghaus, H. 195, 196
Ebsworthy, G. 418
Eich, E. 414, 415
Eichenbaum, H. 202
Eimer, M. 122, 123
Elder, J. H. 63
Ell, S. W. 316
Ellis, A. W. 85, 259, 295, 302
Ellis, H. C. 413, 414
Elman, J. L. 256
Emerson, M. J. 172
Emery, L. 138, 140
Emilien, G. 163
Engle, R. W. 128, 174, 175, 199, 204
English-Lueck, J. A. 127
Epel, E. 345
Erdelyi, M. H. 57, 58, 196
Erev, I. 347
Ericsson, K. A. 370, 371, 376, 382, 383
Erickson, J. R. 224
Erickson, T. A. 272
Eriksen, C. W. 115
Eugenio, P. 228
Evans, J. E. 127, 129, 141
Evans, J. St. B. T. 388, 391, 398, 399, 400, 403
Eysenck, M.W. 10, 13, 16, 20, 123, 134, 203, 227, 417, 418

Farah, M. J. 54, 68, 79, 80, 82, 433
Faraday, M. 424
Fearnyhough, C. 167
Fein, O. 281, 285
Feldman, J. 315, 319
Feldman Barrett, L. F. 175
Felician, O. 97
Fencsik, D. E. 131, 132, 135
Fendrich, R. 56
Fernández-Duque, D. 109
Ferreira, F. 244, 272, 292, 293
Ferrel-Chapus, C. 183
Fery, P. 71
Fetkewicz, J. 197
fftyche, D. H. 92
Fiedler, K. 330, 331
Field, J. E. 157
Fink, B.. 77, 87
Finke, R. A. 92, 93
Fischhoff, B. 335
Fisher, D. L. 247, 248, 250
Fisher, R. P. 222, 227, 228, 229, 230, 231
Fitzgerald, J. M. 214
Fivush, R. 212, 213
Flandin, G. 97, 99
Fleck, J. 361, 362
Floro, M. S. 127
Flowerdew, J. 290
Fodor, J, 11
Foley, H. J. 29
Ford, M. 401, 402
Forgas, J. P. 416
Forsman, T. 31, 34
Foster, D. H. 67
Fox Tree, J. E. 290
Frank, A. 384
Frank, L. R. 121
Franklin, M. 77
Franklin, S. 262, 430
Franks, J. J. 274, 284
Frauenfelder, U. H. 257, 266
Frazier, L. 243, 263
Fredrick, S. 336, 337, 338
Freeman, J. 127
French, L. 154
French, R. M. 179, 188
Frensch, P. A. 188
Frerking, R. A. 417
Freud, S. 52, 58, 149, 196, 212, 294
Friedman, N. P. 172
Frisch, D. 354
Friston, K. J. 433
Frith, C. D. 57, 120
Frye, N. E. 210
Fulero, S. 222, 227
Funnell, E. 240

Gabrieli, J. D. E. 139, 156, 158, 172
Gadian, D. G. 156, 157
Gais, S. 364
Gallogly, D. P. 63
Galton, F. 90
Gambina, G. 121
Gangestad, S. W. 76
Ganis, G. 97
Ganong, W. F. 256, 257

Gardner, H. 300, 407
Garnham, A. 286, 294
Garnsey, S. M. 244, 245, 246
Garrett, M. F. 291, 293, 297
Garrod, S. 289, 290
Garry, M. 198
Gaskell, M. G. 258
Gathercole, S. 169
Gauld, A. 276
Gauthier, I. 65, 66, 72, 82
Gazzaniga, M. S. 13, 20, 56, 428, 429, 430
Geis, M. 399
Geiselman, R. E. 228, 229, 230
Geisler, W. S. 63
Gelder, M. 18, 55
Gemmer, A. 31, 34
Gentner, D. 403
George, N. 432, 434
Georgeson, M. A. 37, 42, 43, 44, 47, 73
Gerchak, Y. 377
Gerhardstein, P.C. 65
Gernsbacher, M. A. 301, 302
Gershkovich, I. 214, 215, 216, 217
Gibson, J. J. 39, 40, 41
Gick, M. L. 366
Giersch, A. 70
Gigerenzer, G. 329, 331, 332, 333, 335, 337, 338, 355
Gilboa, A. 207, 208
Gilligan, S. G. 411, 412, 413, 414
Gilovich, T. 339
Gilson, S. J. 67
Giora, R. 279, 281, 285, 286
Girelli, M. 119
Girgus, J. S. 29
Girotto, V. 392, 395, 396, 401
Glaser, W. R. 299
Glass, J. M. 131, 132, 135
Gleason, C. A. 426
Glover, S. 31, 32, 33
Glucksberg, S. 280, 309
Glushko, R. J. 241
Gobet, F. 377, 379, 380, 381, 384, 385
Godden, D. R. 205
Goldberg, R. M. 63
Goldenberg, G. 98
Goldinger, S. D. 254
Goldsmith, L. R. 214
Goldsmith, M. 144
Goldstein, D. G. 30
Goldstein, E. B. 332, 333
Goldstone, R. 250
Goodale, M. A. 27, 29, 30, 31, 33, 34, 37
Goodglass, H. 160
Gooding, P. A. 187
Gordon, I. 90
Gore, J. C. 82, 202
Gosselin, F. 77
Gottfredson, L. S. 377
Graboys, T. B. 327, 330
Graesser, A. C. 274, 284, 286
Graf, P. 148, 159
Grafman, J. 152, 153
Grafton, S. 185, 187
Graham, M. E. 39
Grammer, K. 76, 77
Gray, W. D. 308

Green, P. R. 37, 42, 43, 44, 47, 73
Greener, S. 345
Greeno, J. G. 372
Greenwald, A. G. 132, 135, 136
Greenwood, K. 226
Gregory, R.L. 28, 29, 44
Griffin, D. 292, 293, 339
Griffin, Z. M. 331, 334
Griggs, R. A. 392
Grigo, A. 82
Groeger, J. A. 52, 209
Grossman, M. 136, 171
Grosso, T. 228
Gruber, T. 118
Guasti, M. T. 302
Guzeldere, G. 80

Haart, E. G. O.-de. 31, 32
Haber, N. 192
Haber, R. B. 90
Haber, R. N. 45, 46, 90
Hackmann, A. 18
Haendiges, A. N. 302
Hagel, R. 77
Hagen, L. 198
Hagoort, P. 297
Haider, H. 363, 364
Haist, F. 202
Hall, M. N. 217
Hallam, M. 76, 77
Haller, M. 249
Halligan, P. W. 118
Halpern, P. V. 425
Hamann, S. B. 160
Hamilton, E. 147
Hampton, J. A. 312, 319, 321
Han, J. J. 213
Hancock, P. A. 130
Hancock, P. J. B. 86, 226
Handley, S. J. 397, 402
Hanley, J. R. 238
Hanna, J. E. 265, 268
Hardman, D. 339, 354, 355
Hardy, G. R. 53
Harley, K. 243, 244, 246
Harley, T. A. 21, 250, 268, 285, 286, 305
Harries, C. 354
Hartman, M. 185
Hartsuiker, R. J. 305
Harvey, N. 92, 98, 339, 355
Hashtroudi, S. 158
Hastie, R. 329, 339
Hatano, G. 381
Haviland-Jones, J. M. 420
Hay, D. C. 84, 85
Hay, J. F. 199, 204
Hayne, H. 213
Hayward, W. G. 65, 67, 73
Hazeltine, E. 185, 187
He, Z. H. 41
Healy, A. F. 163, 177, 219
Hearst, E. S. 380
Heath, W.P. 224
Heeley, D. W. 34, 70
Hegarty, M. 137, 138
Hellawell, D. 79

Henderson, J. J. A. 77
Henderson, J. M. 107, 108, 109, 110, 111, 112, 113, 431
Henderson, Z. 226
Henik, A. 132
Henke, K. 82
Henry, R. A. 383, 384
Henson, R. 167
Hershey, J. 329
Hertwig, R. 335, 336, 347
Heuer, H. 183
Hewstone, M. 339
Heywood, C. A. 55
Hill, H. 44
Hillyard, S. A. 118
Himmelbach, M. 119
Hirst, W. C. 128, 129, 132
Hitch, G. J. 143, 144, 165, 176
Hochberg, J. 28, 29
Hodgkinson, G. P. 336
Hoemeke, K. A. 254
Hoffrage, U. 329, 331
Holcomb, P. J. 259
Holender, D. 57
Holker, L. 418
Holland, H. L. 228, 229
Hollins, T. S. 224, 225
Hollingworth, A. 107, 108, 109, 110, 111, 112, 113, 431
Holmes, V. M. 291, 293
Holt, l. L. 268
Holtgraves, T. M. 291, 305
Holyoak, K. J. 353, 366
Hong, S. B. 98
Hong, S. C. 98
Honomichl, R. 368
Hopkins, R. O. 202
Horgan, T. T. 384
Horton, W. S. 291
Hosch, H. M. 224
Hotopf, W. H. N. 295
Howard, D. V. 182, 185
Howard, R. J. 92, 182, 185
Howe, M. J. A. 376, 383, 385
Howerter, A. 172
Howie, D. 49
Hsee, C. K. 341, 342, 347
Hudson, S. R. 167
Huemer, V. 31, 34
Hulin, C. L. 383, 384
Hull, C. 143
Humphrey, G. K. 34
Humphrey, N. 423
Humphreys, G. W. 68, 69, 70, 72, 121
Hussain, M. 120
Hyman, I. E. 193

Inagaki, K. 381
Indefrey, P. 298
Ing, A. D. 317
Intons-Peterson, M. J. 205
Isurin, L. 199, 203
Ittelson, W. H. 42, 44
Ivry, R. B. 13, 20, 185, 187, 428
Iyengar, S. S. 341

Jacobsen, R. B. 139, 172
Jacoby, L. L. 52, 199, 204

Jaensch, E. R. 424
Jakobsen, P. 104
Jakobson, L. S. 33
James, T. W. 34
James, W. 115
Jared, D. 238
Jay, T. B. 268, 305
Jiménez, J. 179, 180, 181
Jimenez, R. 106
Job, R. 242
Johnson, A. L. 53
Johnson, D. M. 308
Johnson, E. J. 329, 353
Johnson, M. K. 277
Johnson, M. 186, 187
Johnson, R. 153
Johnson-Laird, P. N. 294, 392, 394, 395, 396, 397, 400, 402
Johnston, V. S. 77
Johnston, W. A. 130
Johnston, J. C. 131, 135, 139, 141
Johnston, R. S. 34, 70
Johnstone, T. 182, 185, 187
Jones, S. K. 354
Jonides, J. 170, 171
Jordan, T. R. 34, 70
Josephs, R. A. 347, 354
Joyce, J. 323
Juan-Espinosa, M. 175
Juhasz, B. J. 248
Jung-Beeman, M. 361, 362
Jurkevich, L. M. 228, 229
Just, M. A. 138, 140, 272

Kahneman, D. 132, 136, 328, 333, 334, 335, 336, 337, 338, 339, 343, 345, 355
Kalakanis, L. 76, 77
Kane, M. J. 175, 199, 204
Kanizsa, G. 41
Kanwisher, N. 80, 118, 121
Kaplan, G. A. 360
Karnath, H. O. 119
Karney, B. R. 210
Kassin, S. M. 224
Kaup, B. 283, 285
Kazmerski, V. A. 280
Kay, M. C. 84
Keane, J. 84
Keane, M. T. 10, 13, 20, 123, 366
Keenan, J. P. 97
Keil, F. C. 318
Keller, T. A. 138, 140
Kelley, M. R. 150, 151
Kellogg, R. T. 334
Kelly, S. W. 186
Kemp, S. 209
Kenealy, P. M. 200, 201
Kensinger, E. A. 156
Kentridge, R. W. 55
Keren, G. 329, 338
Kersten, D. 41
Keysar, B. 264, 265, 267, 291
Kherif, F. 97, 99
Kieras, D. E. 131, 132, 135
Kilduff, P. T. 119
Kilpatrick, F. P. 44
Kim, N. S. 318, 320

Kinder, A. 187
Kinloch, N. 77
Kintsch, W. 281, 282, 286, 382
Klahr, D. 367
Klauer, K. C. 170, 176, 389
Klein, G. 352
Klein, I. 97, 99
Klingberg, T. 139, 172
Klos, T. 82
Knill, D. C. 41
Knoblich, G. 363
Knowles, M. E. 370, 371
Knowlton, B. J. 184, 187
Koch, C. 435
Koehler, D. J. 328, 339, 355
Koffka, K. 62
Köhler, S. 62, 360, 361
Köhler, W. 54
Kohnken, G. 229
Koriat, A. 144
Kornbrot, D. E. 193
Kosslyn, S. M. 15, 92, 94, 95, 96, 97, 98, 99, 100
Kounios, J. 361, 362
Kovacs, I. 70
Krampe, R. Th. 382, 383
Krantz, A. 55, 56
Krauss, S. 358
Krawczyk, D. C. 353
Kruschke, J. 313
Krych, M. A. 290, 291
Kuiper, K. 289
Küker, W. 119
Kulik, J. 192
Künnapas, T. M. 42
Kunreuther, H. 329
Kutas, M. 298
Kvavilashvili, L. 193
Kwiatkowski, S. J. 413
Kyllonen, P. C. 174, 175

LaBerge, D. 115, 116
Lachaux, J. 432, 434
Laird, D. A. 211
Lam, R. W. 414
Lamberts, K. 250
Langdon, R. 239, 240, 241, 242, 249
Langlois, J. H. 76, 77
Larrick, R. P. 347, 354
Larsen, J. D. 152, 169
Larsen, S. F. 192, 193
Larson, A. 76, 77
Lasseline, M. E. 318, 320
Lassiter, G. D. 382
Latto, R. 56
Lauber, E. J. 131, 132, 135
Laughlin, J. E. 128
Lawson, R. 86
Layman, M. 335
Lazarus, R. S. 408, 409, 410, 411
Lazayras, F. 78, 80
Le Bihan, D. 51, 432
Leake, J. 233
Leask, J. 90
Lebiere, C. 10, 20
Lebihan, D. 97, 99
LeDoux, J. E. 430

Lee, H. W. 98
Lee, J. 339
Legge, D. 53
Legrenzi, P. 395, 396
Lehman, D. R. 352, 354
Lehmann, A. C. 382
Leichtman, M. D. 212, 213
Leighton, J. P. 403
Lepper, M. R. 341
Lesch, M. F. 130
Levelt, W. J. M. 296, 297, 298, 299
Levin, C. A. 45, 46
Levin, D. T. 103, 104, 105, 106
Levin, H. S. 84
Levine, M. 365, 370
Levy, B. A. 238
Levy, P. 295
Lewis, M. 420
Lewis, R. 160
Liberman, V. 328
Libet, B. 424, 426
Lichtenstein, S. 335
Lief, H. 197
Liker, J. K. 375, 376, 382, 383
Lim, L. 16
Lin, E. L. 317, 318
Lindsay, D. S. 198, 204, 223
Lindsy, R. C. L. 222, 227
Lisman, S. A. 414
Little, A. C. 77
Liversedge, S. P. 248
Lobaugh, N. J. 432, 433, 434
Loewenstein, G. 349, 350
Loftus, E. F. 198, 204, 205, 222, 223, 224, 231
Loftus, G. R. 224
Logie, R. H. 152, 161, 169, 170, 174, 176, 177, 277
Lotto, A. J. 268
Luchins, A. S. 365
Luchins, E. H. 365
Ludgate, J. 18
Lumer, E. 57
Lumer, E. D. 433
Lupker, S. J. 238
Luzzati, C. 302
Lyubomirsky, S. 352, 354

Macaulay, D. 414, 415
McCarthy, G. 80
McCarthy, R. 240, 262
Macchi, L. 339, 355
McClelland, A. G. R. 10, 192, 193
McClelland, J. L. 240, 241, 242, 249, 256
McCloskey, M. 6, 309
McDaniel, M. A. 192, 193
McDermott, J. 80
McDermott, K. B. 93
McDonald, J. L. 199, 203, 254
MacDonald, M. C. 243, 245, 246, 263
McDonald, S. A. 248
McDonnell, V. 238
McGlinchey-Berroth, R. 119
McGlone, M. S. 281, 285
McGreggor, J. N. 371, 373
McGurk, H. 254
McIntosh, A. R. 432, 433, 434
Mack, A. 106, 113

Mack, P. B. 80
McKelvie, S. J. 90
Mackenzie, T. 415
MacKinnon, D. P. 228, 229
Mackintosh, B. 418
Mackintosh, N. J. 173, 377
McKone, E. 80
McKoon, G. 274
MacLeod, C. 417, 418
McLeod, P. 135
McNally, R. J. 197
McNeil, B. J. 345
McNeill, D. 297
McNeill, J. 80
McQueen, J. M. 253, 257, 266, 268
McWeeny, K. H. 85
Madison, P. 196
Maddox, W. T. 315, 316, 317, 320, 321
Magnuson, J. S. 260, 266
Maguire, E. A. 151, 156, 159
Malinowski, P. 118
Malone, D. R. 84
Maloteaux, J.-M. 163
Malpass, R. S. 222, 227
Mamassian, P. 41
Mandler, G. 159
Mane, A. 169
Manfredi, D. 281, 285
Mangin, J.-F. 97, 99
Mangun, G. R. 13, 20, 428
Manktelow, K. 387, 403
Manns, J. R. 202
Mansell, W. 17
Manstead, A. S. R. 411
Mao, H. 202
Marcel, A. J. 55
Marin, O. S. M. 242
Markman, A. B. 403
Marshall, J. 55, 302, 303
Marshall, J. C. 118
Marslen-Wilson, W. D. 258, 259, 260
Martin, A. 71
Martin, R. C. 292, 293
Martinerie, J. 432, 434
Martinez, A. 121
Martini, M. C. 121
Martone, M. 160
Marzi, C. A. 119
Massaro, D. W. 44
Masson, M. E. J. 272
Mather, G. 42
Mathews, A. 417, 418
Matlin, M. W. 29
Mattson, M. E. 272
Mattys, S. L. 254
Maule, A. J. 336
May, J. 418
Mayer, E. 78, 80
Mayes, A. R. 187
Mayr, U. 382, 383
Mealy, L. 76
Medin, D. L. 312, 317, 319
Mehler, J. 257
Mellers, B. A. 350
Melrose, R. J. 186
Memon, A. 224, 229

Meredith, M. A. 123
Merikle, P. M. 50, 53, 59
Merritt, J. O. 91
Mervis, C. B. 308, 310, 311, 312
Messo, J. 224
Meszaros, J. 329
Metcalfe, J. 361
Meulemans, T. 185
Meyer, A. S. 296, 297, 299
Meyer, D. E. 127, 129, 131, 132, 135, 141
Miceli, G. 302
Milber, W. P. 119
Miller, D. 149, 150
Miller, G. A. 226
Miller, J. 426
Miller, M. 292, 293, 302
Millis, K. K. 284, 286
Milne, A. B. 31, 32
Milne, R. 229
Milner, A. D. 27, 29, 30, 31, 33, 34, 37, 70
Minda, J. P. 314, 319
Miniussi, C. 119
Miozzo, M. 242, 249, 299, 304
Mirani, J. 193
Mishkin, M. 156, 157
Mitchum, C. C. 302
Miyake, A. 137, 138, 166, 171, 172, 173
Mo, L. 368
Mogg, K. 418
Mohamed, M. T. 245
Momen, N. 103, 104
Monteiro, K. P. 413, 414
Monterosso, J. 352, 354
Moore, D. G. 383
Morais, J. 71
Mordkoff, A. M. 410
Morgan, D. 384
Morgan, M. 37, 47, 73, 87
Morgenstern, O. 344
Morris, H. H. 84
Morris, J. 262
Morris, P. E. 295
Morris, R. K. 245
Morrison, D. J. 79
Morsella, E. 299, 304
Morton, J. 196, 203
Moscovitch, M. 54
Moss, H. 321
Most, S. B. 106
Motley, M. T. 294
Moyer, A. 345
Mueser, K. T. 334
Mueser, P. R. 334
Müllbacher, W. 98
Müller, M. M. 118
Müller, N. G. 116, 117
Münsterberg, H. 198
Münte, T. F. 298
Murphy, G. L. 307, 312, 317, 318, 319, 321
Murphy, S. T. 408, 409
Murray, J. D. 275, 284
Musch, J. 389
Musselman, L. 76
Muter, P. 201
Myers, J. L. 283, 286

Naccache, L. 51, 185, 430, 431, 532, 434
Nairne, J. S. 150, 151
Natale, E. 119, 121
Naumer, B. 389
Nebes, R. D. 186, 187
Neisser, U. 128, 129, 132, 144
Nelson, K. 212
Newcombe, F. 84
Newell, A. 368, 369, 370, 371, 372, 373
Newell, B. R. 333, 337
Newman, J. B. 435
Newmark, C. S. 417
Newmark, L. 417
Newstead, S. E. 397, 402
Nimmo-Smith, I. 136, 137
Nisbett, R. E. 180, 347, 354
Nissen, M. J. 182, 185, 415
Noon, S. L. 383, 384
Norenzayan, A. 339, 347, 354
Norman, J. 34
Norris, D. 253, 257
Nosofsky, R. M. 313
Novick, L. R. 362
Nowak, A. 98

Oakhill, J. 294
Oberauer, K. 175, 398
O'Brien, D. P. 392, 393
Ochera, J. 196, 203
O'Craven, K. 118
Ohlsson, S. 361, 363
O'Kane, G. 156
Olada, E. 85, 86, 87
Olson, A. 121
Olson, E. A. 225, 230, 231
Ono, H. 40
Ono, Y. 157
Ooi, T. L. 41
Oppenheimer, D. M. 333, 336, 337
Ormerod, T. C. 371, 373
O'Rourke, T. B. 259
Ortony, A. 273
O'Seaghdha, P.G. 295, 296
O'Shea, R. P. 40
Osherson, D. 338
Ost, J. 193, 276
Over, D. E. 331, 400
Oxley, R. 77

Palacios, A. 175
Palarama, A. 121
Palmer, J. C, 204, 222, 223
Palmer, S. 63
Pani, J. R. 312
Panter, A. T. 214
Papageorgiou, C. 17
Papagno, C. 169
Parasuraman, R. 139
Park, J.-H. 183
Parkin, A. J. 148, 154
Parkinson, B. 411, 413
Parks, A. M. 140
Parks, M. 260
Pascual-Leone, A. 97
Pashler, H. 117, 131, 138, 141
Patalano, A. L. 339

Patterson, K. 240, 241, 242, 249
Pauker, S. G. 345
Pavlov, I. P. 10
Payne, M. 160
Payne, J. 353
PDP Research Group 10
Pearl, D. K. 426
Pearlmutter, N. J. 243, 245, 246
Pearlstone, Z. 195
Pelphrey, K. A. 80
Penrod, S. 224
Penton-Voak, I. 77, 87
Perani, D. 120
Perenin, M.-T. 33
Peressotti, F. 242
Peretz, I. 262
Perfect, T. J. 224, 225
Perrett, D. I. 34, 70, 77
Perruchet, P. 183
Perry, C. 239, 240, 241, 242, 249
Perry, J. S. 63
Perry, R. 57
Peterson, L. R. 150
Peterson, M. J. 150
Peterson, R. R. 299, 304
Pexman, P. M. 238
Pezdek, K. 193
Pichert, J. W. 278
Pickering, A. D. 224, 225, 317
Pickering, M. J. 251, 267, 289, 290
Pillemer, D. B. 213, 214
Pinard, M. 262
Pinker, S. 11, 427
Piorkowski, R. 214, 215, 216, 217
Pitman, R. K. 197
Pitt, M. A. 256
Plante, E. 260
Plaut, D. C. 240, 241, 242, 249
Pleydell-Pearce, C. W. 207, 214, 215, 218, 219
Poeck, K. 300
Poeppel, D. 262
Poldrack, R. A. 157, 158
Poline, J. 51, 97, 99, 432
Polivy, J. 413
Pollard, P. 388, 399
Pollatsek, A. 247, 248, 250, 271
Polo, M. 214, 215, 216, 217
Pomplun, M. 380, 384
Poon, L. W. 213, 214
Posner, M. I. 115
Postman, L. 4, 198
Pourtois, G. 55
Power, M. J. 420
Pring, T. 302, 303
Proctor, R. W. 163, 177, 219
Proffitt, D. R. 35
Provitera, A. 394
Psotka, J. 91
Putnam, B. 228
Pylyshyn, Z. W. 15, 91, 95, 96, 99, 100

Quinlan, P. T. 64
Quirk, R. 289

Radvansky, G. A. 396, 397, 398, 402
Rafal, R. 55, 56

Rahhal, T. A. 213, 214
Rahman, R. A. 85, 86, 87
Rajah, M. N. 432, 433, 434
Ralph, M. A. L. 262
Rämä, P. 171, 176
Ramus, S. J. 184, 187
Rapee, R. M. 16, 419
Rastle, K. 239, 240, 241, 242, 249
Ratcliffe, R. 274
Rawles, R. E. 192, 193
Raymond, D. S. 228, 229
Rayner, K. 238, 243, 245, 247, 248, 250, 263, 271
Read, D. 224
Read, J. D. 198
Reb, J. 347
Reber, A. S. 180, 185
Rebolo, I. 175
Redelmeier, D. A. 130, 328
Reed, S. K. 370
Rees, G. 433
Reese, E. 120
Reggin, L. D. 238
Reich, S. S. 272
Reichle, E. D. 247, 248, 250, 425
Reingold, E. M. 51
Reiser, B. J. 393, 394
Renault, B. 432, 434
Rensink, R. A. 106, 110, 111, 113
Retschitzki, J. 377, 384, 385
Rheingold, E. M. 380, 384
Rhenius, D. 363
Richards, A. 418
Riddoch, G. 54, 68, 69/**69**, 70, 72
Rips, L. J. 313, 392
Ritov, I. 346, 354
Ritter, W. 153
Robbins, T. W. 167
Robertson, S. I. 369, 373, 385
Robson, J. 302, 303
Rock, I. 63, 106, 113
Rodrigues, J. 4
Rodriguez, E. 432, 434
Roediger, H. L. 93, 147
Roelofs, A. 296, 297, 299
Rogers, B. J. 39, 43
Roggman, L. A. 76
Romani, C. 302
Rosch, E. 308, 310, 311, 312
Rosenberg, C. R, 11
Ross, J. 415
Ross, M. 210
Rossion, B. 78, 80
Rothman, A. J. 345
Roy, D.F. 228
Rozenblit, L. R. 318
Rubenstein, A. J. 76, 77
Rubin, D. C. 193, 194, 195, 212, 213, 214, 217
Rubin, S. 260
Rubinstein, J. S. 127, 129, 141
Ruchkin, D. S. 152, 153
Rumain, B. 393, 394
Rumelhart, D. E. 10, 273
Rünger, D. 188
Rushworth, M. 14
Russo, J. E. 342
Rutherford, E. 418

Ruthruff, E. 131, 135, 139, 141
Ruts, W. 314, 319
Ryan, J. D. 148, 149
Ryan, L. 415

Sà. W. C. 403
Safer, M. A. 221
Saffran, E. M. 242
St. James, J. D. 115
St. John, M. F. 181, 182
Sala, J. B. 171, 176
Salkovskis, P. 18
Salovey, P. 345
Samuel, A. G. 255, 260
Sanders, M. D. 55
Sanderson, W. C. 419
Santhouse, A. M. 92
Savage-Rumbaugh, S. 233
Savoy, P, 14
Savoy, R. L. 299, 304
Sax, D. S. 160
Schacter, D. L. 148, 158, 162, 163, 197, 415
Schare, M. L. 414
Scheib, J. E. 76
Schendan, H. E. 186
Schlagman, S. 193
Schmalhofer, F. 282
Schmidt, N. 77
Schmidtke, V. 183
Schmitt, B. M. 298
Schneider, W. 133, 134, 140
Schoenberger, A. 327, 330
Scholl, B. J. 106
Schooler, J. W. 361, 426, 425, 427
Schreiber, T. A. 223
Schröger, E. 122, 123
Schulkind, M. D. 213
Schuller, A. M. 78, 80
Schulze, R. 175, 398
Schumacher, E. H. 131, 132, 135
Schwartz, B. 158, 242
Schwartz, J. A. 350, 352, 354
Schwartz, M. F. 242
Schweinberger, S.R. 79, 82
Schwitzgebel, E. 89
Schyns, P. G. 77
Searl, M. M. 186
Searle, J. 279
Sedelmeier, P. 335
Sedivy, J. C. 246, 261, 264
Seghier, M. 78, 80
Segui, J. 257, 266
Seidenberg, M. S. 240, 241, 242, 243, 245, 246, 249
Sejnowski, T. J. 11, 13
Sekuler, R. 23, 37
Selco, S. L. 157
Selten, R. 355
Seo, D. W. 98
Sereno, M. I. 121
Sergent, C. 433
Sergent-Marshall, S. 223
Seymour, T. L. 131, 132, 135
Shafir, E. 343, 348, 349
Shah, P. 137, 138, 166, 171, 172, 173
Shallice, T, 8, 12, 151, 169
Shanks, D. R. 181, 182, 183, 184, 185, 186, 187, 188, 333, 337

Shapiro, D. 391
Sharpe, H. 218
Shea, C. H. 183
Sheptak, R. 169
Sherman, S. J. 362
Shevrin, H. 51, 57, 59
Shibuya, H. 121
Shiffrin, R. M. 9, 133, 134, 140, 151, 152, 160, 161, 162, 165, 176
Shillcock, R. C. 248
Shin, R. K. 136, 171
Shinotsuka, H. 339
Shulman, G. L. 120
Sides, A. 338
Sieck, W. R. 339
Silveri, M. C. 169, 302
Simcock, G. 213
Simon, D. 353
Simon, H. A. 149, 352, 360, 364, 368, 369, 370, 371, 372, 373, 376, 378, 379, 381, 382
Simons, D. J. 103, 104, 105, 106, 107, 113
Simonson, I. 350, 351
Sin, G. 302
Sinai, M. J. 41
Sinclair, E. 182, 185, 187
Singer, M. 274
Sirigu, A. 97
Skinner, Fred, 143
Skudlarski, P. 82
Sloboda, J. A. 383
Sloman, S. A. 331
Slovic, P. 335
Slusarz, P. 184, 187
Small, M. 84
Smarnia, N. 121
Smilek, D. 50, 59
Smith, C. A. 410
Smith, E. E. 170, 171, 234
Smith, M. 289
Smith, J. 55, 56, 383
Smith, J. D. 314, 319
Smith, S. M. 363, 364
Smith, Y. M. 55, 56
Smoot, M. 76, 77
Smyth, M. M. 295
Snedeker, J. 263, 290
Snodgrass, M. 51, 57, 59
Socrates, 49, 147
Solso, R. L. 377
Sommer, W. 82, 85, 86, 87
Song, A. 80
Sox, H. C. 345
Spear, N. F. 414
Spearman, C. E. 372
Spelke, E. S. 128, 129, 132
Spence, C. 123, 125
Sperber, D. 392, 401
Sperry, R. W. 428
Spiers, H. J. 151, 156, 159
Spiesman, J. C. 410
Spivey-Knowton, M. J. 246, 263, 264
Spivey, M. J. 246, 261, 264
Sporer, S. L. 224
Squire, L. R. 159, 160, 184, 185, 187, 202
Stampe, D. M. 380, 384
Standing, L. G. 192
Stanovich, K. E. 397, 398, 399, 400, 403

Staw, B. M. 350, 351
Steblay, N. M. 227
Steele, C. M. 347, 354
Stein, B. E. 123
Stemberger, J. P. 294
Stenger, V. A. 186, 187
Stenning, K. 392, 401
Stephenson, G. M. 276
Stern, C. E. 186
Stern, Y. 242, 249
Sternberg, R. J. 373, 375, 376, 387, 403
Stoerig, P. 54
Stopa, L. 17
Storms, G. 314, 319
Strayer, D. 130
Stromeyer, C. F. 91
Stuss, D. T. 156, 162
Suh, S. 274
Sukel, K. E. 97
Sulin, R. A. 277
Sullivan, L. 135
Sun, R. 184, 187
Sunaert, S. 67
Super, B. J. 63
Süß, H.-M. 175, 398
Sussman, H. M. 254
Sutherland, N. S. 423
Svartvik, J. 289
Sweller, J. 370
Swets, B. 292, 293

Tae, W. S. 98
Talarico, J. M. 193, 194
Tanaka, J. W. 308
Tanenhaus, M. K. 244, 245, 246, 260, 261, 263, 264, 265, 266, 268
Tarr, M. J. 64, 65, 66, 72, 73, 82
Tata, P. 417
Tauroza, S. 290
Taylor, A. M. , 70
Taylor, M. E. 308
Teasedale, J. D. 415
Teigen, K. H. 329, 338
Terry, C. 184, 187
Tesch-Römer, C. 383
Tetlock, P. E. 348, 349, 350, 355
Thaler, R. 349, 350
Thompson, W. L. 15, 94, 95, 96, 97, 99, 100
Thomson, N. 168
Thornhill, R. 76
Thornton, I. M. 109
Thulborn, K. R. 138, 140
Tibshirani, R. J. 130
Tideman, B. P. 77
Todd, P. N. 332, 336, 337
Tomeleri, G. 121
Tooby, J. 330, 331
Townsend, G. C. 76
Trabasso, T. 274
Trappery, C. 50
Traxler, M. J. 245, 251
Treisman, A. M. 135, 139, 140
Trevena, J. A. 426
Trevarthen, C. 428, 429
Trueswell, J. C. 244, 245, 246, 263, 265, 268, 290
Tubb, V. A. 224

Tuckey, M. R. 225
Tugade, M. M. 175
Tuholski, S. W. 128
Tulving, E. 156, 157, 162, 195, 200, 201, 204
Turner, J. 262
Turner, M. L. 174
Turner, T. S. 275, 285
Turtle, J. W. 222, 227
Tversky, A. 328, 333, 334, 335, 338, 343, 345, 348, 349, 352
Tyler, C. W. 43
Tyler, L. K. 258, 259

Ucros, C. G. 201, 415
Umiltà, C. 121, 125
Underwood, B. J. 198
Utman, J. A. 301, 302

Vakili, K. 182, 185, 187
Valentine, T. 86, 169, 224, 225
Vallar, G. 120, 169
Van der Linden, M. 163, 172, 185
van Eijk, R. 187
Van Gompel, R. P. G. 251
van Hecke, P. 67
van Lambalgen, M. 392, 401
van Oostendop, U. 283, 285
Van Paesschen, W. 156, 157
Van Petten, C. 260
Van Selst, M. V. 131, 135, 139
van Turennout, M. 297
Vanrie, J. 67, 72
Varella, F. J. 432, 434
Vargha-Khadem, F. 156, 157
Varner, J. L. 413, 414
Velmans, M. 434
Velten, E. 412
Verfaellie, M. 119
Verleger, R. 364
Vicary, J. 49
Vighetto, A. 33
Vigliocco, G. 297, 305
Villringer, A. 116, 117
Vinette, C. 77
Vitale, R. 338
von Neumann, J. 344
Voogt, A. 377, 384, 385
Vrij, A. 193
Vroemen, J. 55
Vu, H. 292, 293
Vuilleumier, P. 119, 431

Wachtel, P, 6
Wade, K. A. 198
Wagenaar, W. A. 209
Wager, T. 172
Wagermans, J. 67
Wagner, A. D. 158, 162, 163
Wagner, U. 364
Waldron, E. M. 316
Wallas, G. 363
Walsh, V. 14
Wang, Q. 212, 213
Wang, X. T. 345, 346, 354, 358
Ward, A. 352, 354
Ward, G. 86
Ward, T. B. 363

Warhaftig, M. L. 228, 229
Warren, R. M.. 255
Warren, R. P. 255
Warren, T. 248, 255
Warrington, E. K. 55, 70, 80, 151, 240, 242, 262
Wason, P. 272, 391
Watanabe, O. 157
Waters, A. J. 379, 381
Watkins, K. E. 156, 157
Watson, John, 143
Wearing, D. 1634
Weber, E. U. 341, 342, 347
Wegner, D. M. 424, 425, 426, 435
Weibe, D. 361
Weiskrantz, L. 55, 56, 59
Weisstein, N. 63
Welford, A. T. 131
Wells, A. 16, 17, 18
Wells, G. 75
Wells, G. L. 225, 222, 227, 230, 231
Welsh, D. 282
Wenzel, A. E. 195
Wertheimer, A. 62
Wessinger, C. M. 56
West, R. F. 397, 398, 399, 400, 403
Westen, D. 228
Weston, N. J. 333, 337
Wheatley, T. 424, 425, 426
Wheatstone, C. 42
Wheeldon, L. R. 305
Wheeler, M. A. 156, 162
Whitacre, C. A. 183
White, K. 352, 354
White, S. H. 214
Whitecross, S. E. 207, 218
Whiteman, H. L. 150, 151
Whitlow, S. 148, 149
Wickens, C. D. 139, 140
Wieth, M. 358, 359
Wild, B. 331
Wilhelm, O. 175, 398

Wilkinson, L. 182, 183, 184, 186
Williams, C. C. 109
Williams, R. S. 245
Williams, S. 92
Willingham, D. 185, 415
Willmes, K. 300
Wilson, A. E. 173, 210, 339
Wilson, T. D. 180
Wilton, R. N. 64
Winningham, R. G. 193
Wise, R. A. 221
Wittlinger, R. P. 192
Wittman, W. 175
Witzki, A. H. 172
Wixsted, J. T. 202, 204, 205
Woike, B. 214, 215, 216, 217
Wojciulik, E. 120, 121
Wong, E. 63
Woodruff, P. 92
Wright, E. W. 426
Wright, G. 351
Wulf, G. 183
Wulfeck, B. 301, 302
Wynn, V. E. 277

Yasuda, K. 157
Yates, F. A. 89
Yates, J. F. 339
Yiend, J. 420
Young, A. W. 79, 83, 84, 85, 86, 87, 259

Zajac, H. 138, 140
Zajonc, R. B. 408, 409
Zhao, Z. 170, 176
Ziegler, J. 239, 240, 241, 242
Zimony, S. 282
Zoccoli, S. 191
Zwaan, R. A. 283, 284, 285, 286
Zwicky, A. M. 399

Subject index

Page references to figures and diagrams appear in **bold**.
Page references to tables appear in *italic*.

Abstract-rule theory, 392, 393–394, 401
   comprehension error, 393, 394, 401
   conversion error, 393, 401
   mental-logic theory, 393, 401
Accommodation, 42
Adaptive Control of Thought (ACT-R) model, 11, 12
Adaptive expertise, 381
Advertising, use of subliminal stimuli, 49–50
Aerial perspective, 40, 42
Affect, 407; *see also* Emotion
Affective primacy hypothesis, 408–409, **409**
Agnosia, **70**
   apperceptive, 68–70
   associative, 68–70
   auditory phonological, 262
Agrammatism, 301–302, 304
Alcohol abuse, and amnesia, 148, 153
Algorithms, 368–369, 372
Alzheimer's disease, 143
Ames room, 45/**45**
Amnesia, 147, 148
   anterograde, 153, 162
   brain systems, 153, **154**, 157
   case studies, 154–155, 160
   and disease, 155, 160
   explicit/implicit memory study, 148, **149**, 153
   and head injury/stroke, 153
   and implicit learning, 181, 184–185, 187
   infantile/childhood *see* Infantile/childhood amnesia
   Korsakoff's syndrome, 148, 153
   and long-term memory, 153, 156–157, 159, 160, 162
   retrograde, 153, 157, 162, 202, 217–218
   see also Remembering/forgetting
Animals
   decision making, 344–345
   insight, 361
   language learning, chimpanzee study, 233–234
   thinking/reasoning, 323
Anterograde amnesia, 153, 162
Anton's syndrome, 98
Anxiety *see* Generalized anxiety disorder
Aphasia
   Broca's, 300–301, 304
   Jargon, 302–303, **303**, 304, 305
   Wernicke's, 300–301, 304
   see also Speech disorders
Apperceptive agnosia, 68–70

Appraisal theory *see* Cognitive appraisal
Artificial intelligence, 9
Aspects of language production, 305
Associative agnosia, 68–70
Attention
   bias *see* Attentional bias
   focal, consciousness as, 430, 431
   role of emotion in, 416–419
   visual *see* below
Attention and performance, 231
Attention, visual, 24, 115–125
   cross-modal attention, 122–123, 124–125
   endogenous/voluntary spatial attention, 122–123
   exogenous/involuntary spatial attention, 122, 123
   extinction, 119–120, 124
   further reading, 125
   object or location, 118–119, 124
   split attention, 116–118, **117**
   unattended stimuli, 119–122, 124; *see also* Change blindness; Neglect
   ventriloquist illusion, 122
   zoom lens metaphor, 24, 115–116, **116**, **117**/117, 118
Attentional bias, 416, 417, 418–419
   cognitive approaches to treating, 17–18
   generalized anxiety disorder studies, **415**, 416, 417–420, **417**
   homonym task, 418
Attentional blink, 433
Attentional capacity, 199, **200**
Attentional control, 175
Attentional systems, 120, 121
   goal-directed/top-down, 120, 121
   stimulus-driven/bottom-up, 120
Auditory phonological agnosia, 262
Autobiographical memory, 144, 207–219
   accuracy, 210
   autobiographical knowledge base, 215
   beliefs, 210–211
   brain activation patterns, 218
   brain imaging studies, 207–209, **208**
   diary studies, 209–210, **209**
   direct retrieval, 217, 219
   elderly people, 211, **212**
   emotional personal memories, 214–215, **216**, 217
   and episodic memory, 207
   further reading, 219
   generative retrieval, 216–217, 218, 219
   infantile/childhood amnesia, 211, 212–213
   model, 215–218
   personality types study, agentic/communal, 214–215, **216**

Autobiographical memory *continued*
  Proust phenomenon, 210–211
  reminiscence bump, 211, 213–214
  retention function, 211
  retrograde amnesia studies, 217–218
  working self, 216, 219
Automaticity, and multitasking, 132–135, 140
  direct/indirect stimulus-response relationships, 132, 136, 141
  inflexibility of automatic processes, 134, 141
  mapping, consistent/varied, 133–134, **134**
   Stroop effect, 132–133
Autostereograms, 43
Availability heuristic, 335–336

Back propagation, 241
Base-rate information, 328, 339
Bayes' rule, **335**
Belief bias, 388–389, **388**, 398, 399, 401
The big book of concepts, 321
Binocular cues, 40, 44–43
Binocular rivalry, 433
Bipolar disorder study, 414–415
Blackwell handbook of judgment and decision making, 339, 355
Blindness
  change *see* Change blindness
  denial, (Anton's syndrome), 98
  inattentional, 103, 104, 106, 113
  face-blindness, *see* Prosopagnosia
Blindsight, 7, 54–56, 58
  case studies, 55–56/**56**
  types, 56
  validity, 56
Bottom-up processing, 3
  attentional systems, 120
  speech perception, 256, 257, 273
Bounded rationality, 352–354
Bounded rationality: The adaptive toolbox, 355
Brain function/activation patterns
  amnesia, 153, **154**, 157
  autobiographical memory, 207–209, **208**, 218
  blindsight, 54
  concepts, 316, 320
  consciousness, 431–433, **432**, 434
  consolidation, 202
  episodic memory, 207, **208**
  eye movements, 248
  face recognition, 79, 80, 82, 86
  implicit learning, 181, 185–186, 187
  insight/problem-solving, 362
  long-term memory, 153, **154**, 157, 158, 159, 162
  memory systems, brain damage study, 150–151, 160
  multitasking, 138–139, 141
  neglect/unilateral neglect, 120–121, **120**, **121**
  rule-based vs. information-integration category-learning systems, 316, 320
  serial processing 297–298, **298**, 304
  speech disorders, 300, **301**
  speech perception, 261/**261**, 262
  unconscious perception, 51
  visual imagery, 94–98, **95**, 99
  visual perception, 30/**30**, 34, 35
  working memory, 150–151, 160, 169, 171–172
  see also Cognitive neuroscience
Brain imaging techniques, 3, 5; *see also* Brain function/activation patterns; Cognitive neuroscience

Brain structure *see* Cerebral cortex
Bridging inferences, 273
Broca's aphasia, 300–301, 304

Cab driver example, decision making, 349–350
Category-specific deficits, 71
Central executive, 166, 171–173
  brain areas involved, 171–172
  verbal/spatial separation, 172, 173
Central sulcus, 14
Cerebral cortex, structure, **13**, 14
  fusiform face area/fusiform gyrus, 79, 80, 82, 86
  occipital face area, 80
  terms, definition, 14
Change blindness, 24, 103–113, **104**
  attention, 107–109, **108**, **109**
  causes, 109–112
  coherence theory, 110–111, **112**, 113
  further reading, 113
  incidental approach, 106
  intentional approach, 106
  long-term memory studies, 110–111, **111**, 113
  method of assessment, 108–109, 113
  misdirection, 104–105, **105**
  movies/continuity perception, 105–106
  similarity function, 106–107, **107**
Change blindness blindness, 104
Charles Bonnet syndrome, 92, 99
Chess-playing, 377–382, 384
  adaptive expertise, 381
  chunking theory, 378–379, 380
  and gender, 377
  memory, 377, 378, 379
  practice, 377
  routine expertise, 381
  template theory, 379–382
  working memory study, 167/**167**
Chess program, Deep Blue, 9
Childhood amnesia *see* Infantile/childhood amnesia
Choice, having too much, 341; *see also* Decision making
Chunking theory, 378–379, 380
Chunks, memory, 149
Clause, 291–292
Closure, law of, 62/**62**
Co-articulation, 254
Cognition, emotion and psychopathology, 420
Cognitive appraisal/appraisal theory, 409–411; *see also* Emotion
Cognitive interview, 228–229, **229**, 230
Cognitive neuropsychology, 5, 6–7, 19–20
  dissociations, 7–8
  individual vs. group-based approach, 8
  language example, 8
  modularity, 7
  prosopagnosia, 7; *see also* Face recognition
  subtractivity, 7
  strengths/limitations, 8–9
  transcranial magnetic stimulation (TMS), 9, *12*, 15
  see also Blindsight
Cognitive neuroscience, 5, 12–15, 20
  cerebral cortex, structure, **13**, 14
  major techniques, *12*, 13
  spatial/temporal ranges, **13**
  strengths/limitations, 14–15
  threshold levels, 14, 412
  unconscious perception, 51

visual imagery/visual perception example, 15
see also Brain function/activation patterns; Brain imaging
Cognitive neuroscience: The biology of the mind, 20
Cognitive psychology, 3–21
   computational, 5, 9–12, 20
   experimental, 5–6, 19
   further reading, 20–21
   information processing approach, 3, **4**
   usefulness of discipline, 15–18, 20
   see also Cognitive neuropsychology; Cognitive neuroscience;
      Cognitive therapy
Cognitive psychology: A student's handbook, 20
Cognitive therapy
   anxiety, 15, 20
   attentional bias, 17–18
   depression, 15, 20
   interpretive bias, 16, 17, 18
   panic disorder, 16
   safety-seeking behaviours, 16, 17, 18
   social phobia, 16–18, **17**
Coherence theory, 110–111, **112**, 113
Cohort model, speech perception, 258–260, **259**, 266–267
Common ground, 264, 265, **265**, 268, 291, 303
Complex cognition: The psychology of human thought, 373
Comprehension of language *see* Inference drawing;
      Understanding/comprehension
Computational cognitive science, 5, 9–12, 20
   artificial intelligence, 9
   see also Computational modeling
Computational modeling, 9–10
   Adaptive Control of Thought (ACT-R) model, 11, 12
   connectionist networks, 10–11, 12
   memory model example, 9–10
   production systems, 10
   strengths/limitations, 11–12
Concepts, 307–321
   brain areas involved, 316, 320
   causal explanations, 318
   common regularities, 315
   concept instability, 309–310
   defining attributes, 308–309
   exemplar approach, 313–315, **314**, 319–320
   family resemblances, 310, 312/**312**
   further reading, 321
   goal-derived categories, 312/**312**
   illusion of explanatory depth, 318
   knowledge-based views, 317–318, **317**, 320
   learning, 315–318
   one vs. several mechanisms, 315–317, 320
   rule-based vs. information-integration category-learning
      systems, 315–317, **317**, 320
   typicality gradients, 309, **312**
   prototype theory, 310–312, *311*, 314/**314**, 318–319
   types, 308
Conceptual representations, 321
Conjunction fallacy, 328, 330
Connectionist networks, 10–11
   important features/assumptions, 11
   NETtalk language learning example, 11
Consciousness, 405, 423–435
   access to information, 427
   attentional blink, 433
   basic and meta-consciousness, 425–426, 427
   binocular rivalry, 433
   brain areas involved in, 431–433, **432**, 434
   definitions, 412, 423

focal attention, 430, 431
first/third-person accounts, 434
functions, 423–427
further reading, 435
global workspace theories, 430–433, 434
illusion of free will, 424
information processing below conscious awareness, 431,
      434
intentions/actions, control of, 424–427
interpreter, 428, 429, 430, 434
readiness potential studies, 426–427, **426**
reduplicative paramnesia, 430
sentience/hard problem of consciousness, 427, 434
social function, 423
speech/writing, 429–430
spiritualist/ouija boards experiments, 424–425, **425**
split-brain patient research, 427–430, 433–434
workspace model, 430–431
Consciousness: An introduction, 435
Consciousness lost and found, 59
Consolidation, 201–202, 203, 205
   brain areas involved, 202
   retrograde amnesia studies, 202
Construction-integration model, 281–284, **281**, **282**, 285
   levels of text representation, 282–283, **282**, 285–286
Continuity perception, 105–106
Convergence, 42
Conversion error, 393, 401
Cross-modal attention, 122–123, 124–125
Cued recall, 195, 200
Cultural differences *see* Individual/cultural differences
Cushion hypothesis, 341–342

Decision making, 341–355
   accountability/justifying decisions, 349–351, **351**, 355
   animal decisions, 344–345
   Asian disease problem, 345–346
   based on experience vs. descriptions, 347, 355
   bounded rationality, 352–354
   cab driver example, 349–350
   changing one's mind, 353
   choice, having too much, 341
   complex decisions, 351–354, 355
   cultural differences, 341–342, 347, 354
   cushion hypothesis, 341–342
   deterministic vs. probabilistic choices, 346/**346**
   doctor example, 350–351
   elimination-by-aspects theory, 352–353
   framing effect, 345–346, 354
   further reading, 355
   individual differences, 354
   intuitive politicians, 349
   jurors, 342
   loss aversion, 343, 344
   losses and gains, 342–347, 354
   normative theories, 344, 354
   omission bias, 346–347
   optimization, 352
   over-generalization, 345
   prospect theory, 343–347, **343**, 354, 355
   rational man, 344
   real life study, 353–354
   satisficing, 352
   and self-esteem, 347, 355
   social context, 348–351, **348**
   social functionalist approach, 349–351, 354–355

Decision making *continued*
    sunk-cost effect, 344–345, 350, **351**, 354
    time pressure, 353
    utility theory, 344, 351, 354
    vaccination studies, 346–347
Deductive reasoning, 387
Deep Blue chess program 9
Defining attributes, concepts, 308–309
Deliberate practise, 376, 377, 382–383, 384, 385; *see also*
        Expertise
Denial, 410
Deontic reasoning, 389, 392, 398
Depictive representations, 94–95
Depression
    cognitive approaches to treating, 15, 20
    vicious circles, 415–416
    see also Bipolar disorder
Depth perception, 39–47
    accommodation, 42
    additivity and selectivity strategies, 43–44
    Ames room, 45/**45**
    autostereograms, 43
    binocular/oculomotor cues, 40, 42–43
    convergence, 42
    familiarity, 42
    further reading, 47
    fuzzy logic, 44
    hollow face illusion, 44
    image blur, 42
    integrating cue information, 43–44
    interposition, 41
    monocular cues, 40–42
    motion parallax, 39
    optic flow, 39, **40**
    perspective, 40, 42
    pictorial cues, 40
    pseudoscopic viewing, 44
    role of memory, 45–46
    shadows, 41
    size-distance invariance hypothesis, 44
    and size perception, 44–46
    stereopsis, 42–43
    texture gradients, 41
    wallpaper illusion, 43
Differences, individual/cultural *see* Individual/cultural
        differences
Digit span, 149
Dimensionality, perceiving *see* Depth perception
Direct retrieval, 217, 219
Discourse markers, 290, 303
Dissociations, 7–8
Distance perception *see* Depth perception
Distributed connectionism, 240–242, 249
Double dissociations, 8
Driving study/mobile phone use study, 130–131, 140
    and gender, 130–131
Dual-process models
    judgments, 336–337, 338
    visual perception, 34–35/35
Dual-route cascaded model, 239–240, **239**, 241, 242, 249
    phonological dyslexia, 240
    surface dyslexia, 240 b
Dyslexia, 240

Ebbinghaus illusion, 27, **28**, 29, 30, 32
Ecological validity, 6, 144

Egocentric heuristic, 264, 265, **265**, 267, 268
Eidetic imagery, 90–91, 98
Elaborative inferences, 273, 274
Emotion, 405, 406–420
    affective primacy hypothesis, 408–409, **409**
    attentional bias, 416, 417, 418–419
    bipolar disorder study, 414–415
    cognition, role, 407–411
    cognitive appraisal/appraisal theory, 409–411
    and consciousness, 412
    definitions, 407
    denial, 410
    further reading, 420
    generalized anxiety disorder studies, **415**, 416, 417–420,
        417
    intellectualization, 410
    homonym task, 418
    interpretive bias, 416–418, 419
    laboratory experiments, limitations, 407
    learning and memory/semantic network theory, 411–416,
        411
    mere exposure effect, 408
    mood congruity, 412–414, 416
    mood induction, 412–413
    mood-state-dependent memory, 412, 413–415, **414**, 416
    multiple personality disorder study, **414**, 415
    panic disorder study, 419
    primary/secondary appraisal, 410
    thought congruity, 412, 415–416
    vicious circles in anxious/depressed patients, 415–416, 418,
        419
Encephalitis, 155, 160
Encoding specificity principle, 200–201, 203, 204–205
Endogenous/voluntary spatial attention, 122–123
Episodic buffer, 173
Episodic memory, 156–157, 161, 162, 207, **208**
Essential sources in the scientific study of consciousness, 435
Estimator variables, 222
Event-related potentials (ERPs), *12*, 51
Exogenous/involuntary spatial attention, 122, 123
Experience, and problem solving, 364–368, 372
    far transfer, 367–368, **367**, 372
    functional fixedness, 364–366, **365**
    metacognition, 368
    near transfer, 372
    positive/negative transfer, 366
    similarity between problems, 366–367
    see also Expertise
Experimental cognitive psychology, 5–6, 19
Expertise, 375–385
    deliberate practise, 376, 377, 382–383, 384, 385
    digit-span study, 376
    face recognition, 81, 82, 82, 86
    further reading, 385
    idiot savants, 376, 383
    and IQ/innate ability, 375–376, 383–384, 385
    long-term working memory, 382
    performance over time and IQ, 383
    task complexity and IQ, 377, 384, 385
    memory, 377, 378, 379, 382
    see also Chess-playing; Experience
Explicit learning, 179, 180, 184, 185, 186
Explicit memory, 148, 149, 155, 160, 161
    study of amnesia, 148, **149**, 153
Exposure therapy, 17–18
Extinction, 119–120, 124

Eye movements, 246–247
  brain areas associated, 248
  E–Z reader model, 247–248, 250
  saccades, 247
  spillover effect, 247
Eyewitness testimony, 144, 204, 221–231
  car accident study, 222–223, **223**
  CCTV study, 226/**226**
  cognitive interview, 228–229, **229**, 230
  distortion/accuracy, 145
  estimator variables, 222
  eyewitness confidence, 224–225
  further reading, 231
  hypnosis, 227–228
  identification line-ups, 225–227, **226**, 230
  influences on accuracy, 222–225
  misinformation acceptance, 223
  mistaken identification, 75, 222
  post-event information, 222–224
  proactive interference, 223
  retroactive interference, 223
  schema theory, 225
  system variables, 222
  weapon focus, 224
E–Z reader model, 247–248, 250

Face-blindness *see* Prosopagnosia
Face recognition, 24, 75–87
  brain processing areas, 79, 80, 82, 86
  expertise, 81, 82, 82, 86
  facial identity vs. facial expression, 84–85, **84**, **85**, 87
  familiar vs. unfamiliar faces, 84, 86
  familiarity, identity, name, 85–86, 87
  further reading, 87
  holistic processing, 79, 80, 81, 82, 86
  individual differences in ability, 76
  inverted faces, 80–81/**81**
  and object recognition, 78, 79, 80, 81–82, 86
  other face effect, 81–82
  as specialized function, 79–81, 86
  speed, 77–78, 83, 85
  Thatcher illusion, 80
  theoretical model, 83–87, **83**
  see also Eyewitness testimony; Facial attractiveness;
      Prosopagnosia; Visual perception
Faces-goblet figure, 63/**63**
Facial attractiveness, 75–76
  computer-generated averaged faces, 76–77
  masculine faces, 77
  meta-analysis of findings, 76
  relation to health, 77
  symmetry, 76–77
False memories, 197–198, **197**
Family resemblances, 310, 312/**312**
Far transfer, 367–368, **367**, 372
Figurative language, 279, 285
Figure-ground segregation, 62–63
Flashbulb memories, 191, 192–195, **193**
  accuracy/consistency, 193–195, **194**
  as special, 192–193
Forever today – A memoir of love and amnesia, 163
Forgetting *see* Remembering/forgetting
Framing effect, 345–346, 354
Free recall, 195, 200
Free will, illusion of, 424
French drop trick, 104–105, **105**

Freudian slip, 294
Frontal lobe, 14
Functional fixedness, 364–366, **365**
Functional magnetic resonance imaging (fMRI), *12*, 51
Fundamentals of cognition, structure of book, 18–19
Fusiform face area/fusiform gyrus, 79, 80, 82, 86
Fuzzy logic, 44

Garden-path model, 243–245, 246, 263, 264
  principle of late closure, 244, 245
  principle of minimal attachment, 244, 245
Gender
  and chess playing, 377
  and infantile amnesia, 212, 213
  and multitasking, 127, 130–131, 140
General Problem Solver, 368–371, 372–373
  algorithms, 368–369, 372
  balancing strategies, 370
  heuristics, 368–372, **371**
  maze problem, 370/**370**
  planning, 370–371, 372
  problem space, 369
  strategy changes, 371, 373
  Tower of hanoi problem, 369/**369**
  see also Problem-solving
Generalized anxiety disorder, **415**, 416, 417–420, **417**
  attentional bias, 416, 417, 418–419
  cognitive approaches to treating, 15, 20
  homonym task, 418
  interpretive bias, 416–418, 419
  vicious circles in anxious patients, 418, 419
Generative retrieval, 216–217, 218, 219
Gestaltism, 62–64
  conflicting laws, 64/**64**
  faces-goblet figure, 63/**63**
  figure-ground segregation, 62–63
  law of closure, 62/**62**
  law of good continuation, 62/**62**, 63
  law of Prägnanz, 62/**62**
  law of proximity, 62/**62**, 63
  law of similarity, 62/**62**
Goal-derived categories, 312/**312**
Good continuation, law of, 62/**62**, 63
Graded salience hypothesis, 279–281, 285

Hallucinations, 92, 99
Handbook of cognition, 188, 250, 268, 286
Handbook of cognition and emotion, 420
The handbook of cognitive neuropsychology, 125
Handbook of emotions, 420
Handbook of psychology: Experimental psychology, 47, 163,
    177, 219, 286
Hard problem of consciousness, 427, 434
Heuristics, 332–336, 337–339, 368
  anti-looping, 370
  availability, 335–336
  Bayes' rule, **335**
  dual-process model, 336–337, 338
  egocentric, 264, 265, **265**, 267, 268
  hill climbing, 369, 372
  means-ends analysis, 369, 370, 372
  nine-dot problem, 371/**371**
  overconfidence bias, 338–339
  progress monitoring, 371, 373
  recognition, 332–333
  representativeness, 333–335, **335**

Heuristics *continued*
  satisficing, 352
  see also Judgments; Problem solving
Heuristics and biases: The psychology of intuitive judgment, 339
Hill climbing heuristic, 369, 372
Hollow face illusion, 44
Homonyms, 238
  task, 418
Houdini, Harry, 105
Human memory: theory and practice, 205
Human problem solving, 368
Hypnosis, 227–228

Identification line-ups, 225–227, 230
  CCTV study, 226/**226**
  sequential line-ups, 226–227, 230
  see also Eyewitness testimony
Idiot savants, 376, 383
Ill-defined problems, 357
The illusion of conscious will, 435
Illusions, 23, 27–33
  Ebbinghaus, 27, **28**, 29, 30, 32
  faces-goblet figure, 63/**63**
  hollow face, 44
  illusory square, 41
  incorrect comparison theory, 29
  Müller-Lyer, 27–28/**28**, **29**, **31**/31–32
  paradox of, 27–29
  perception-action/two visual systems model, 29–33, 36
  planning-control model, **32**/32–33
  Ponzo, 27–28, **28**
  size constancy principal, 28, 29/**29**
  Thatcher, 80
  ventriloquist, 122
  vertical-horizontal illusion, 28, **29**
  wallpaper, 43
  see also Magic tricks
Imagery, visual *see* Visual imagery
Implicit learning, 144, 179–188
  amnesics, learning, 181, 184–185, 187
  artificial grammar learning studies, 179–180, 182, 184, 185, 186, 187
  brain-imaging research, 181, 185–186, 187
  Commander Data theory, 180–181
  complex normal learning, 181–184, 186–187
  and explicit learning, 180, 184, 185, 186
  further reading, 188
  future directions, 186
  and implicit memory, 184
  information/sensitivity criteria, 181, 182
  role of consciousness, 180–181
  serial reaction time studies, 182, 183/**183**, 184, 185, 186
  zombie theory, 181
Implicit learning and consciousness, 188
Implicit memory, 148, 149, 152, 155, 160, 161
  and implicit learning, 184
  and object recognition, 79
  study of amnesia, 148, **149**, 153
In the eye of the beholder: The science of face perception, 87
Inattentional blindness, 103, 104, 106, 113; *see also* Change blindness
Inattentional blindness, 113
Incubation, 363–364
Individual/cultural differences, 6
  autobiographical memory, 214–215, **216**
  cognitive neuropsychology, 8

decision making, 341–342, 347, 354
  face recognition, 76
  heuristics, 339
  infantile/childhood amnesia, 212, 213
  reasoning, 397–398, 401, 402
  visual imagery, 90–91, 98
Infantile/childhood amnesia, 211, 212–213
  individual/cultural differences, 212, 213
  repression, 212
  role of language, 212, 213
  social-cultural-developmental theory, 212–213
Inference drawing, 273–275
  bridging inferences, 273
  constructionist/search-after-meaning theory, 274, 284
  elaborative inferences, 273, 274
  and IQ, 275, 284
  instrumental inferences, 274
  logical inferences, 273
  minimalist hypothesis, 274–275, 284
  predictive inferences, 275, 284
  top-down/bottom-up processes, 273
Inflecting languages, 301
Information-integration vs. rule-based category-learning systems, 315–317, **317**, 320
Innate ability *see* IQ/innate ability
Inner scribe, 170
Insight, 360–364
  ape example, 361
  brain areas involved, 362
  incubation, 363–364
  mutilated checkerboard problem, 360/**360**, 363
  parallel vs. serial processing, 363
  pop-out solutions, 362–363
  problem-representation, 360–361
  Remote Associates Test, 361–362, 364
  representational change theory, 363
  verbalization, 361
  warmth, 361
  see also Problem solving
Integrative agnosia, 70/**70**
Intellectualization, 410
Intelligence *see* IQ/innate ability
Interference theory, 198–200, 203–204
  and attentional capacity, 199, **200**
  proactive interference, 198–200, **199**, 203, 204
  retroactive interference, 198–199, **199**, 202, 203, 204, 205
Interpreter, 428, 429, 430, 434
Interpretive bias, anxious patients, 416–418, 419
  cognitive approaches to treating, 16, 17, 18
Interviewing techniques with eyewitnesses, 227, 228–229, **229**, 230
Intuitive politicians, 349
IQ/innate ability
  and expertise, 375–376, 383–384, 385
  and inference drawing, 275, 284
  and multitasking, 128, 140
  and understanding/comprehension of language, 280
  and working memory, 174–175, 396, 397, 398, 402

Jargon aphasia, 302–303, **303**, 304, 305
Judgments, 327–339
  base-rate information, 328, 339
  conjunction fallacy, 328, 330
  further reading, 339
  Linda problem, 328, 330/**330**, 338
  natural frequencies, 329–331

planning fallacy, 331
  support theory, 328–329
  see also Heuristics
Juries, pre-decisional distortion, 342

Knowledge-lean problems, 358
Knowledge-rich problems, 357–358
Korsakoff's syndrome, 148, 153

Laboratory studies
  learning/memory, 144
  limitations, 6, 407
Language, 233–234
  chimpanzee study, 233–234
  Dictionary of Psychology definition, 233
  functions, 233
  split brain research, 429–430
  see also Concepts; Inference drawing; Reading; Speech
    perception; Speech production;
    Understanding/comprehension
Language as social action, 305
Laws, object recognition
  closure, 62/**62**
  good continuation, 62/**62**, 63
  Prägnanz, 62/**62**
  proximity, 62/**62**, 63
  similarity, 62/**62**
Learning/memory, 143–145
  implicit *see* Implicit learning
  role of emotion, *see* Semantic network theory
  systems, 315–317, **317**, 320
  see also Amnesia; Autobiographical memory; Eyewitness
    testimony Long-term memory; Memory systems;
    Remembering/forgetting; Semantic network theory;
    Working memory
Lemmas, 297
Lexical decision task, 238
Lexical identification shift, 256, 257
Linear perspective, 40
Lip-reading, 254
Logical inferences, 273
Long-term memory
  and amnesia, 153, 156–157, 159, 160, 162
  brain regions/systems, 153, **154**, 157, 158, 159, 162
  episodic, 156–157, 161, 162, 207, **208**
  explicit memory, 148, 149, 155, 160, 161
  implicit memory, 148, 149, 152, 155, 160, 161
  perceptual priming, 157–158, 159, 160, 162
  perceptual representation, 155, 157, 159, 162
  priming, 157, 158, 159/**159**
  procedural, 155, 158, 159, 160, 162
  rehearsal, 150, 152, 161, 165
  semantic memory, 155, 156–157, 161, 162
  systems, 155
  see also Memory systems
Long-term working memory, 382
Loss aversion, 343, 344

McGurk effect, 254
Magic Eye books, 43
Magic tricks, 104
  French drop trick, 104–105, **105**
  Houdini, Harry, 105
  see also Illusions
Magneto-encephalography (MEG) , *12*
Maze problem, 370/**370**

Meaning, understanding, *see* Inference drawing;
    Understanding/comprehension
Means-ends analysis, 369, 370, 372
Memory distortions and their prevention, 205
Memory/learning, 143–145
  constraints on reasoning, 396, 397, 398, 400, 402
  and expertise, 377, 378, 379
  false/recovered memories, 196–198, **197**
  long-term working, 382
  poor memory, 192
  repression of traumatic memories, 196, 203
  role in chess playing, 377, 378, 379
  role in depth/size perception, 45–46
  role of emotion, *see* Semantic network theory
  and schemas, 276, 278/**278**, 279
  see also Amnesia; Autobiographical memory; Eyewitness
    testimony; Implicit learning; Long-term memory;
    Memory systems; Recall; Remembering/forgetting;
    Semantic network theory; Working memory
*Memory: Neuropsychological imaging, and
    psychopharmacological perspectives*, 163
Memory systems, 147–163
  activated long-term, short-term memory as, 152–153,
    161
  analogies of memory, 147, 149
  brain damage study, 150–151, 160
  capacity, 150, 160
  chunks, 149
  conscious/unconscious processes in, 148
  digit span, 149
  further reading, 163
  multi-store model, 151–152, **151**, 160–161, 176
  retention/decay, 150/**150**, **151**
  short-term/long-term, distinctions, 8, 143, 149–153, 160
  see also Amnesia; Long-term memory;
    Remembering/forgetting; Working memory model
Mental-logic theory, 393, 401
Mental models of reasoning, 394–397, 400, 401–402
  principle of truth, 396, 402
  working memory constraints, 396, 397, 398, 402
Mental set (functional fixedness), 364–366, **365**
Mere exposure effect, 408
Meta-analysis of findings, facial attractiveness, 76
Metacognition, 368
Meta-consciousness, 425–426, 427
Metaphor, 279–280
Mind's eye *see* Visual imagery
Misdirection, 104–105, **105**
Mixed error effect, 296, 304
Mobile phone/driving study, 130–131, 140
  and gender, 130–131
*Models of working memory: Mechanisms of active maintenance
    and executive control*, 177
Modularity, 7, 8
Modus ponens, 390, 391, 394
Modus tollens, 390, 391, 394
Monocular cues, 40–42
Monty Hall problem, 358–360, **359**
Mood, 407
  congruity, 412–414, 416
  induction, 412–413
  see also Emotion
Mood-state-dependent memory, 200–201, **201**, 204, 412–416,
    414
Morphemes, 293
Motion parallax, 39

Moves in mind: The psychology of board games, 385
Müller-Lyer illusion, 27–28/**28**, **29**, **31**/31–32
Multi-store model of memory, 151–152, **151**, 160–161, 176
Multiple personality disorder study of emotion, **414**, 415
Multitasking, 24, 127–41
    automaticity, 132–135, 140, 141
    central capacity/central executive theories, 136–139, **137**, 141
    direct/indirect stimulus-response relationships, 132, 136, 141
    driving/mobile phone use study, 130–131, 140
    dual-task interference, 131–132, **131**, 135, 140
    fMRI study, 138–139, 141
    and gender, 127, 130–131, 140
    and intelligence, 128, 140
    mapping, consistent/varied, 133–134, **134**
    modern day trend towards, 127
    multiple resource model, 139–140, **139**
    paper folding/card rotation/identical pictures experiment,
        137–138, **138**
    performance costs, 128–130, **129**, 140
    performance determinants, 131–136
    and practice, 128, 129–130, 140
    psychological refractory period (PRP) effect, 131
    similarity of stimulus modality, 135
     Stroop effect, 132–133
    task difficulty, 135–136
    theoretical perspectives, 136–140, **137**, **138**, **139**, 141
Mundane realism, 144
Mutilated checkerboard problem, 360/**360**, 363

The nature of reasoning, 403
Near transfer, 372
Negative transfer, 366
Neglect/unilateral neglect, 119, 124
    brain networks, 120–121, **120**, **121**
    goal-directed/top-down attentional system, 120, 121
    stimulus-driven/bottom-up attentional system, 120
Neo-connectionist networks, 10
Neologisms, 303
NETtalk language learning, 11
The neurocognition of language, 268
Neuropsychology, *see* Cognitive neuropsychology
Neuroscience, *see* Brain function/activation patterns; Brain
        imaging techniques; Cognitive neuroscience
Normative theories, decision-making, 344, 354

Object recognition, 24, 61–73
    agnosia, 68–70, **70**
    category-specific deficits, 71
    disorders of, 68–71, 72
    edge grouping, 69, 70
    faces-goblet figure, 63/**63**
    feature binding, 69, 70
    figure-ground segregation, 62–63
    further reading, 73
    Gestaltism, 62–64, **62**, **63**, **64**
    hierarchical model of object recognition, 69–71, **69**
    law of closure, 62/**62**
    law of good continuation, 62/**62**, 63
    law of Prägnanz, 62/**62**
    law of proximity, 62/**62**, 63
    law of similarity, 62/**62**
    and prosopagnosia, 78, 79, 80, 81, 82, 86
    perceptual organization, 62–64
    recognition-by-components theory, 64–65
    semantic system, 70, 71
    structural description, 70, 71/**71**

view normalization, 69, 70–71
    viewpoint-dependence/invariance, 64–68, **66**, **67**, 72
Occipital face area, 80
Occipital lobe, 14
Oculomotor cues, 40, 42–43
Omission bias, 346–347
On our mind: Salience, context and figurative language, 286
Operation span, 174
Optic ataxia, 33
Optic flow, 39, **40**
Optimization, 352
Ouija boards experiments, 424–425, **425**
Overconfidence bias, 338–339
The Oxford handbook of memory, 163

Panic disorder
    cognitive approaches to treating, 16
    study, 419
The paradox of choice: Why more is less, 341
Parallel distributed processing (PDP) models, 10
Parallel processing, 4
Parietal lobe, 14
Parieto-occipital sulcus, 14
Parsing, 243–246, 263–264, **264**, 267
    constraint-based theory, 245–246, 263, 264
    garden-path model, 243–245, 246, 263, 264
Passwords, remembering, 191
Perception, 37, 47
Perception
    unconscious *see* Unconscious perception
    visual *see* Visual perception
Perception-action/two visual systems model, 33–34, 35, 36
Perceptual anticipation theory, 94–95, 97, 99
Perceptual defense, 49, 52–53, 58; *see also* Unconscious
        perception
Perceptual priming, 157–158, 159, 160, 162
Perceptual representation, 155, 157, 159, 162
    perceptual priming, 157–158, 159, 160, 162
    priming, 157, 158, 159/**159**
Perspective
    aerial, 40, 42
    linear, 40
Pheromones, 53
Phonemes, 253, 254
Phonemic restoration effect, 255
Phonological dyslexia, 240
Phonological loop, 166, 167–169, **168**
    articulatory control process, 168–169
    phonological/speech-based store, 168, 169
    word-length effect, 168, 169
Phonological similarity effect, 168
Phonology/phonological model, 237–238
Photographic memory (eidetic imagery), 90–91, 98
Phrase, 292
Planning fallacy, 331
Ponzo illusion, 27–28, **28**
Pop-out solutions, 362–363; *see also* Insight
Positive transfer, 366
Positron emission tomography (PET), *12*
Practical reasoning, 389
Practice
    and expertise *see* Deliberate practise
    and mult-tasking, 128, 129–130, 140; *see also* Automaticity
Pragmatics, 279–281, **280**, 285
    figurative language, 279, 285
    graded salience hypothesis, 279–281, 285

and IQ, 280
  metaphor, 279–280
Prägnanz, law of, 62/**62**
Predictive inferences, 275, 284
Preformulation, 289, 303
Pre-occipital notch, 14
Premises, 387
Prepositions, 302
Priming, 157, 158, 159/**159**
Princess Diana, death of *see* Flashbulb memories
Principle/s
  of late closure, 244, 245
  of minimal attachment, 244, 245
  of truth, 396, 402
Principles of abilities and human learning, 385
Proactive interference, 198–200, **199**, 203, 204
Problem-representation, 360–361
  representational change theory, 363
Problem solving, 373, 385
Problem solving, 357–373
  further reading, 373
  ill-defined problems, 357
  knowledge-lean problems, 358
  knowledge-rich problems, 357–358
  Monty Hall problem, 358–360, **359**
  well-defined problems, 357
  see also Experience; General Problem Solver; Heuristics;
    Insight
Procedural memory, 155, 158, 159, 160, 162
Production systems, 10
Progress monitoring, 371, 373
Problem space, 369
Propositions/propositional theory, 95
Prosodic cues, 290, 303
Prosopagnosia, 7, 78–79, 86
  and object recognition, 78, 79, 80, 81, 82, 86
  overt/covert recognition, 79
  semantic priming, 79
Prospect theory, 343–347, **343**, 354, 355
Prototype theory, 310–312, *311*, 314/**314**, 318–319
  family resemblances, 310, 312/**312**
  goal-derived categories, 312/**312**
Proust phenomenon, 210–211
Proximity, law of, 62/**62**, 63
Prozac, 16, 18
Psychological refractory period (PRP) effect, 131]
The psychology of language, 250, 268, 286, 305
Pure reasoning, 389
Pure word deafness, 262

The quest for consciousness: A neurobiological approach, 435

Rational man, 344
Rational model, 11
Rationality, 399–400
  external validity problem, 399
  interpretation problem, 399
  normative system problem, 399
  rationality$_1$/rationality$_2$, 400
  see also Reasoning
Rationalization, 276
Reading, 8, 237–251
  back propagation, 241
  brain areas associated, 248
  constraint-based theory, 245–246
  distributed connectionist approach, 240–242, 249

dual-route cascaded model, 239–240, **239**, 241, 242, 249
  eye movements, 246–247
  E–Z reader model, 247–248, 250
  further reading, 250–251
  garden-path model, 243–245, 246
  homonyms, 238
  lexical decision task, 238
  parsing, 243–246
  phonological dyslexia, 240
  phonology/phonological model, 237–238
  principle of late closure, 244, 245
  principle of minimal attachment, 244, 245
  reading aloud, 238–239
  saccades, 247
  speedreading, 271–272
  spillover effect, 247
  surface dyslexia, 240
Reading Efficiency Index, 271
Reading span, 174
Reasoning, 387–403
  abstract-rule theory, 392, 393–394, 401
  belief bias, 388–389, **388**, 398, 399, 401
  comprehension error, 393, 394, 401
  conditional, 390–391
  conversion error, 393, 401
  deductive, 387
  deontic, 389, 392, 398
  further reading, 403
  individual differences, 397–398, 401, 402
  memory constraints, 396, 397, 398, 400, 402
  mental-logic theory, 393, 401
  mental models, 394–397, 400, 401–402
  modus ponens, 390, 391, 394
  modus tollens, 390, 391, 394
  premises, 387
  principle of truth, 396, 402
  pure/practical, 389
  rationality, 399–400
  system 1/system 2 thinking, 398, 402
  syllogisms/syllogistic reasoning, 387–388, 389, 397
  Wason selection task, 391–392, 398, 399, 401
  working memory and IQ, 398, 402
Reasoning and thinking, 403
Recall, memory, 144
  cued, 195, 200
  free, 195, 200
  see also Memory/learning; Remembering/forgetting
Recognition-by-components theory, 64–65
Recognition heuristic, 332–333
Recognition memory, 144
Recovered memories, 196–198, **197**
Reduplicative paramnesia, 430
Remembering/forgetting, 191–205
  and attentional capacity, 199, **200**
  brain areas involved, 202
  consolidation, 201–202, 203, 205
  context, 204
  cued recall, 195, 200
  encoding specificity principle, 200–201, 203, 204–205
  eyewitness testimony, 204
  flashbulb memories, 191, 192–195, **193**, **194**
  forgetting rates over time/forgetting curve, 195, **196**, 202
  free recall, 195, 200
  further reading, 205
  future directions, 202–203
  interference theory, 198–200, 203–204

Remembering/forgetting *continued*
   passwords, 191
   poor memory, 192
   proactive interference, 198–200, **199**, 203, 204
   recovered memories, 196–198, **197**
   repression of traumatic memories, 196, 203
   retrieval failure, 195
   retroactive interference, 198–199, **199**, 202, 203, 204, 205
   retrograde amnesia studies, 202
   see also Amnesia; Mood-state-dependent memory; Recall
Reminiscence bump, 211, 213–214
Remote Associates Test, 361–362, 364
Representational change theory, 363
Representativeness heuristic, 333–335, **335**
Repression, 212
   of traumatic memories, 196, 203
Retroactive interference, 198–199, **199**, 202–205
Retrograde amnesia, 153, 157, 162, 202, 217–218
Routine expertise, 381
Rule-based vs. information-integration category-learning
   systems, 315–317, **317**, 320

Saccades, 247
Safety-seeking behaviours, cognitive approaches to treating,
   16, 17, 18
Satisficing, 352
Savants, idiot, 376, 383
Schema theory, 225
Schemas, 275–279, **277**, 284, 285
   naturalistic studies, 277
   rationalization, 276
   and recall, 276, 278/**278**, 279
   schema-inconsistent information, 278–279, 284
   scripts, 275, 285
Scripts, 275, 285
Segmentation problem 253
Self-esteem, and decision making, 347, 355
Self, working *see* Working self
Semantic memory, 155, 156–157, 161, 162
Semantic network theory, 411–416, **411**
   bipolar disorder study, 414–415
   consciousness, 412
   generalized anxiety disorder study, **415**
   mood congruity, 412–414, 416
   mood induction, 412–413
   mood-state-dependent memory, 412, 413–415, **414**, 416
   multiple personality disorder study, **414**, 415
   thought congruity, 412, 415–416
   vicious circles in depressed patients, 415–416
Sentience/hard problem of consciousness, 427, 434
Serial processing, 3, 297–298, 299
   brain imaging studies, 297–298, **298**, 304
   lemmas, 297
   tip-of-the-tongue phenomenon, 297, 304
Short-term memory *see* Working memory
Similarity, law of, 62/**62**
Single-unit recording, *12*
Size constancy theory, 28, 29/**29**
Size-distance invariance hypothesis, 44
Size perception, 44–46
   Ames room, 45/**45**
   role of memory, 45–46
   see also Depth perception
Sleeping on problems, 363–364
Social functionalist approach to decision making, 349–351,
   354–355

accountability/justifying decisions, 349–351, **351**, 355
   cab driver example, 349–350
   doctor example, 350–351
   intuitive politicians, 349
Social phobia, 16–18, **17**
   cognitive approaches to treating, 16–18, **17**
The space between our ears, 37, 47, 73, 87
Speech disorders, 299–303, 304–305
   agrammatism, 301–302, 304
   brain areas affected, 300, **301**
   Broca's aphasia, 300–301, 304
   historical perspective, 300–301
   jargon aphasia, 302–303, **303**, 304, 305
   neologisms, 303
   of perception, 260–262, 267
   Wernicke's aphasia, 300–301, 304
   see also Speech errors; Speech production
Speech errors, 293–296, 303–304
   categorical rules, 295, 296
   Freudian slip, 294
   insertion rules, 295
   interpreting, 295–296
   mixed error effect, 296, 304
   morpheme-exchange errors, 294–295, 296
   semantic substitution errors, 295, 296
   sound-exchange errors, 294, 296
   spoonerisms, 294, 296
   spreading activation theory, **293**, 295–296, 297, 299, 300,
     303–304
   types of error, 294–295, 303
   word-exchange errors, 293, 296
   see also Speech disorders; Speech production
Speech perception, 253–268
   auditory phonological agnosia, 262
   co-articulation, 254
   cognitive routes for processing speech, 261/**261**, 262
   cohort model, 258–260, **259**, 266–267
   common ground, 264, 265, **265**, 268
   context, 255–256, 264, 266]
   disorders, 260–262, 267
   egocentric heuristic, 264, 265, **265**, 267, 268
   further reading, 268
   lexical identification shift, 256, 257
   lip-reading, 254
   McGurk effect, 254
   parsing, 263–264, **264**, 267
   phonemes, 253, 254
   phonemic restoration effect, 255
   pure word deafness, 262
   and rate of speech production, 253
   segmentation problem 253
   stress, 253
   syllables, 253, 254
   TRACE model, 256–258, **258**, 266
   word meaning deafness, 262
   see also Understanding/comprehension
Speech production, 289–305
   clause, 291–292
   common ground, 291, 303
   dialogue/monologue, 289–290
   discourse markers, 290, 303
   facilitating communication, 290–291
   flexibility, 292–293, 298, 303
   further reading, 305
   inflecting languages, 301
   levels of processing, 293/**293**, 295–298, 303, 304

morphemes, 293
phrase, 292
preformulation, 289, 303
prepositions, 302
prosodic cues, 290, 303
rates, 253
subordinate clauses, 302
speech planning, 291–293
underspecification, 289, 303
see also Serial processing; Speech disorders; Speech errors;
    Word processing
Speedreading, 271–272
Spillover effect, 247
Spiritualist/ouija boards experiments, 424–425, **425**
Split attention, 116–118, **117**
donut-shaped nature, 118
Split-brain patient research on consciousness, 427–430,
    433–434
interpreter, 428, 429, 430, 434
reduplicative paramnesia, 430
speech/writing, 429–430
Spoonerisms, 294, 296
Spreading activation theory, **293**, 295–296, 297, 299, 300,
    303–304
Stereopsis, 42–43
Stroop effect, 132–133
Subliminal stimuli, advertising/consumer effects, 49–50; *see
    also* Unconscious perception
Subordinate clauses, 302
Subtractivity, 7
Sunk-cost effect, 344–345, 350, **351**, 354
Surface dyslexia, 240
Syllables, 253, 254
Syllogisms/syllogistic reasoning, 387–388, 389, 397
System 1/system 2 thinking, 398, 402
System variables, 222

Talking *see* Speech production
Template theory, 379–382
adaptive expertise, 381
limitations, 381–382
routine expertise, 381
Temporal lobe, 14
Testimony, eyewitness *see* Eyewitness testimony
Texture gradients, 41
Thatcher illusion, 80
Therapy, cognitive *see* Cognitive therapy
*Thinking: Psychological perspectives on reasoning, judgment
    and decision making*, 339, 355
Thinking, 323–324; *see also* Decision-making; Experience;
    Expertise; General Problem Solver; Heuristics; Insight;
    Judgments; Problem solving; Reasoning
Thought congruity, 412, 415–416
Tip-of-the-tongue phenomenon, 297, 304
Top-down processing, 4/**4**
attentional systems, 120, 121
consciousness, 431
speech perception, 256, 257, 273
Tower of hanoi problem, 369/**369**
TRACE model, speech perception, 256–258, 266
bottom-up/top-down processing, 256, 257
study challenging, 258/**258**
Transcranial magnetic stimulation (TMS), 9, *12*, 15
Traumatic memories, repression, 196, 203
Typicality gradients, 309, **312**

Unconscious perception, 49–59
advertising/consumer effects, 49–50
auditory, 53
blindsight, 54–56, 58
further reading, 59
multiple stage nature of perception, 57, **58**
neuroscientific studies, 51
perceptual defense, 49, 52–53, 58
repetition suppression, 51
response bias, 53
smell/pheromones, 53
studies investigating, 51–53, **52**
subjective/objective thresholds, 50–51
theoretical basis, 57
visual, 23–24
Underspecification, 289, 303
Understanding/comprehension, 264–265, **265**, 267–268,
    271–286
common ground, 264, 265, **265**, 268
construction-integration model, 281–284, **281**, **282**, 285
egocentric heuristic, 264, 265, **265**, 267, 268
figurative language, 279, 285
further reading, 286
graded salience hypothesis, 279–281, 285
and IQ, 280
levels of text representation, 282–283, **282**, 285–286
limited, 272
metaphor, 279–280
pragmatics, 279–281, **280**, 285
Reading Efficiency Index, 271
speedreading, 271–272
see also Inference drawing; Schemas
Utility theory, 344, 351, 354

Vaccination studies, 346–347
Ventriloquist illusion, 122
Vertical-horizontal illusion, 28, **29**
Vicious circles
in anxious patients, 418, 419
depressed patients, 415–416
Viewpoint-dependence/invariance, 64–68, **66**, **67**, 72
recognition-by-components theory, 64–65
Visual agnosia, 33–34
Visual attention *see* Attention, visual
The visual brain in action, 37
Visual buffer, 95
Visual cache, 170
Visual illusions *see* Illusions
Visual imagery, 89–100
Anton's syndrome, 98
brain damage studies, 96, 97–98, 99
brain imaging data, 95, 96–97, 99
brain systems, 94–98, **95**, 99
Charles Bonnet syndrome, 92, 99
depictive representations, 94–95
eidetic imagery, 90–91, 98
facilitation effect, 93, 99
field of resolution study, 92–93, **93**, 99
further reading, 100
generation, 98
hallucinations, 92, 99
interference effect, 93, 94/**94**, 99
perceptual anticipation theory, 94–95, 97, 99
propositions/propositional theory, 95
stereogram study, 91/**91**
tasks/exercizes, 89–90, **90**

Visual imagery *continued*
  and visual perception, 15, 24, 91–94, 95, 99
  Vividness of Visual Imagery Questionnaire (VVIQ), 90, 98
Visual perception, 23
  brain areas/neural pathways, 30/**30**, 34, 35
  cognitive representation, 34
  conscious/unconscious, 23–24
  dual-process model, 34–35/*35*
  functions of vision, 27
  further reading, 37
  importance of accuracy, 23, 27
  optic ataxia, 33
  perception-action/two visual systems model, 33–34, 35, 36
  sensori-motor representation, 34
  visual agnosia, 33–34
  and visual imagery, 15, 24, 91–94, 95, 99
  see also Attention; Change blindness; Depth perception;
      Face recognition; Illusions; Multitasking;
        Object recognition; Unconscious perception; Visual
        imagery
Visual perception: Physiology, psychology and ecology, 37, 47,
    73
Visuospatial sketchpad, 166, 169–171, 176
  components, 169–170, **170**
  experimental study of, 170–171, **170**
  inner scribe, 170
  visual cache, 170
Vividness of Visual Imagery Questionnaire (VVIQ), 90, 98

Wallpaper illusion, 43
Wason selection task, 391–392, 398, 399, 401
Weapon focus, 224
WEAVER++ model, 296–297, 298, 299, 300, 304
Well-defined problems, 357
Wernicke's aphasia, 300–301, 304
Witness testimony *see* Eyewitness testimony
Word-length effect, 168, 169
Word meaning deafness, 262
Word processing, ordered/disordered, 296–299, 304
  brain imaging studies, 297–298, **298**, 304
  lemmas, 297
  parallel processing, 298–299

serial processing, 297–298, 299
tip-of-the-tongue phenomenon, 297, 304
WEAVER ++ model, 296–297, 298, 299, 300, 304
Working memory, 165–177
  activated long-term, short-term memory as, 152–153, 161
  attentional control, 175
  brain damage studies, 150–151, 160, 169
  capacity, 150, 160
  chunks, 149
  digit span, 149
  further reading, 177
  and intelligence, 174–175, 396, 397, 398, 402
  vs. long-term, 8, 143, 149–153, 160
  model of, *see below*
  operation span, 174
  processing speed, 175
  reading span, 174
  retention/decay, 150/**150**, **151**
  verbal rehearsal, 150, 152, 161, 165, 168
Working memory model, 166–167, **166**, 176
  articulatory control process, 168–169
  central executive, 166, 171–173
  chess playing study, 167/**167**
  episodic buffer, 173
  further reading, 177
  inner scribe, 170
  phonological loop, 166, 167–169, **168**
  phonological similarity effect, 168
  phonological/speech-based store, 168, 169
  visual cache, 170
  visuospatial sketchpad, 166, 169–171, **170**, 176
  word-length effect, 168, 169
  see also Memory systems
Working memory in perspective, 177
Working self, 216, 219
  direct retrieval, 217, 219
  generative retrieval, 216–217, 218, 219
Workspace model of consciousness, 430–431
World Trade Center bombing *see* Flashbulb memories

Zoom lens metaphor, 24, 115–116, **116**, **117**/117, 118